A DICTIONARY OF PHILOSOPHY

IN THE WORDS OF PHILOSOPHERS.

EDITED,

With an Introduction,

BY

J. RADFORD THOMSON, M.A

PROFESSOR OF PHILOSOPHY IN NEW COLLEGE, LONDON,
AND IN HACKNEY COLLEGE.

LONDON:
REEVES AND TURNER, 196 STRAND.
R. D. DICKINSON, FARRINGDON STREET
1887

PREFACE.

THE collection of passages from philosophical writers which has formed the basis of this Dictionary was made by a collator of experience. When, at the request of the Publisher, I examined the manuscript, it appeared to me that, whilst some authors were too fully represented, there was an inadequate representation of several important schools, and that some topics of moment were scarcely touched upon. I felt it necessary, in editing the volume and preparing it for the press, to deal somewhat freely with the material placed in my hands.

Passages of undue length have in many instances been cut down. On the other hand, very many new quotations have been introduced from writers of recognised merit and influence. More particularly, a fair representation has been secured of the teaching of (1) the physiological and evolutional psychologists of our own time, and (2) the 'rational idealists' who have of late years taken so prominent a position in British Philosophy. The material has also been completely re-arranged

In carrying out this work I have been efficiently assisted by the Rev. Alfred Goodall, who has, under my guidance, made extracts comprising a large portion of the passages contained in this volume. He has also aided me in verifying quotations, and in reading the proofs; and the Indexes are entirely his work. To him accordingly my appreciative acknowledgments are due

The revived and extended interest in philosophical studies leads to the hope that a Dictionary upon the plan of this work may be acceptable and useful. The leading topics of psychological, metaphysical, and ethical interest will be found elucidated in this volume by passages from authors of acknowledged position, but belonging to very various schools of thought. The quotations are, for the most part, taken from the works of *modern* writers, and from books in the *English* language. At the same time, many passages are inserted which have been taken from translations into English of classical works, and of works by modern French and

German authors. That learned readers who may consult this volume will find many books and even authors omitted that it would have been desirable to include, may be expected. Yet in this modest attempt, the endeavour has been, consistently with the limits of space, to give a fair, impartial, and comprehensive representation of different schools and tendencies of thought.

In a comparatively small number of cases the full references have not been given. Usually the references are, in the case of standard works, to book and chapter, or to lecture or essay. But in the case of works where one edition may be expected to be commonly consulted, the references are to volume and page. In this matter many difficulties have been encountered. A few quotations have been allowed to stand which have a literary rather than a strictly philosophical bearing and interest. And in some cases it has been thought more useful to present the opinions of a writer in the summary of an historian than in the language of the writer himself.

It is hoped that the copious Indexes appended to this book will render it useful to students. The Alphabetical arrangement would have been altogether impracticable; but by referring to the Indexes the reader may gain all the advantages of consulting a Dictionary arranged upon the ordinary plan.

The Introduction has been written for the sake of beginners in philosophical studies, with the view of affording to such readers a general survey of the field of thought before them.

It is hoped that no apology is needed for the copious use here made of the works of several living authors, both British and American. Some readers may, I trust, be led, by consulting this Dictionary, to undertake the study of writers the quality of whose mind they have tasted in these pages.

J. R. T.

LONDON, *March* 1887

INTRODUCTION.

I. THE DEFINITION OF PHILOSOPHY.

Few words are more ambiguous than the word 'Philosophy.' It comes to us from the Greeks, by whom it was at first used in its etymological sense as signifying the love of wisdom. The general designation 'Philosophy' was deemed by the Stoics to include the three sciences: Logic, the science of Thought; Physics, the science of Nature; and Ethics, the science of Conduct.

In modern times the term 'Philosophy' has been and is employed in several different significations. It is popularly used to denote practical wisdom and self-command, as when a man is said to bear misfortune with 'philosophic calmness,' or 'like a philosopher.' It is also applied in cases where science would be more suitable; as when persons speak of 'the philosophy of growth,' or 'the philosophy of the tides.' Usage sanctions a similar employment of the term in the phrase 'natural philosophy,' which designates a certain department of physical science. Such applications as these may be dismissed as altogether loose and unimportant.

Bacon divided all human knowledge into revealed theology and philosophy, including under the latter natural theology and natural philosophy,—the latter comprising both physics and metaphysics. A very extensive application of 'philosophy' is still common, as may be seen in the classification of books in libraries.

But the tendency has long been to employ this term in a more restricted sense. The most usual definition of Philosophy is 'the study and knowledge of first principles.' First principles may be taken as equivalent to unity amidst diversity,—to the causes or origins of all things,—to the universal, the necessary, the ultimate.

In the apprehension of some thinkers, this definition is too vague. Thus Mr. Herbert Spencer endeavours to define philosophy more exactly as 'knowledge of the highest degree of generality;' 'Science is partially unified knowledge;' 'Philosophy is completely unified knowledge.'

The Comtists or Positivists reject Philosophy, except as Anthropology or the science of man, and for them this science is twofold, including Biology and

Sociology. If man is to be studied otherwise than as a bodily organism, he must, according to this doctrine, be studied as he exists in society.

At the other extreme from the Comtists are the Hegelians, in whose view the history of Philosophy is Philosophy. According to this school, the successive stages of systematised human thought form a philosophical unity; an organic whole has been, and is, developing and revealing itself in the long history of the philosophical evolution of intellectual humanity.

There is a disposition among many contemporary writers to limit the term Philosophy to what is ordinarily called Metaphysics, to set the philosophical in antithesis to the scientific. Some Psychologists are very anxious to avoid,—at all events to appear to avoid,—all philosophical controversy; with what success every reader can judge It does not appear practicable altogether to separate between the observations and generalisations of Psychology and the wider and higher truths or speculations of Philosophy in the sense of Metaphysics.

It seems well in defining Philosophy to avoid the two extremes: on the one hand, to avoid including in this study the sum of human knowledge; on the other hand, to avoid limiting Philosophy to Metaphysics. If we were to define it to be the study of the principles of human knowledge and conduct, it might seem that we were limiting Philosophy to Psychology and Ethics; but such a definition, liberally interpreted, would surely include far more than these studies.

Since, in order to understand what is known, we must to some extent understand the nature that knows, Philosophy investigates the laws of the human intellect, with whatever is subordinate to, or connected with it. Since we cannot be satisfied with knowing facts, but are constrained to ascend to generalisations and explanations, to bring what we know into relation of harmony, mutual dependence, and unity, Philosophy aims at discovering in the intelligible universe those mental bonds of system and causation, which give meaning and consistency to what would otherwise be incomprehensible Since human life is in our view even more important than science, Philosophy investigates its hidden springs in the very structure of our nature, in our intuitions of right and of duty, in the constitution and relations of society It has been well said: 'The business of Philosophy, in the true sense of the word, is to answer three questions—(1.) What can I know? (2.) What ought I to do? (3.) What may I hope for? These are the highest questions which can interest human beings.'

It may be objected that such a description of Philosophy makes it almost conterminous with science and with practice. This may be admitted, with the important qualification that there is a philosophical side to every intellectual pursuit, and even to all practical systems; and that it is open for the student to determine how far he will concern himself with the scientific, how far with the philosophical aspect of the study which he cultivates. It is certain that our intellectual and practical life suggests at every point questions which Science—in the more limited sense of the term—does not profess or attempt to answer, which yet possess an interest for many minds, and a fascination for some. It cannot be overlooked, further, that knowledge and action alike prompt the mind to inquiry and to speculation, with regard to the Wisdom which is infinite, and the Righteousness which is unchanging and eternal.

II. *THE DIVISIONS OF PHILOSOPHY.*

Premising that no system of terminology will meet with universal approval, we will endeavour to distribute the topics of philosophical study into several departments, designating them by terms more or less generally accepted.

PSYCHOLOGY is the study of the natural history of mental phenomena, and of the generalisations which they yield. This designation has of late been much in favour. It is said that if studies of the class under consideration are to be prosecuted, this must be done upon a scientific and not upon a scholastic method. There are those who object to all metaphysics, who yet are ready to admit that anthropology, in order to be complete, must comprise more than a scientific description of man's bodily organs and functions. Anatomy and Physiology are only a part of the science of man; a true Biology must comprise the mental and moral life of humanity. Even those who regard man as only the most highly organised of animals, and thought as a function of the brain, will grant as much as this. It is then agreed that the special functions by which men are differentiated from brutes shall be studied, shall where possible be traced downwards to their roots in the cruder forms of animal life and sentience, and upwards to their highest developments in civilised and cultivated society. The knowledge thus reached may fairly be regarded as scientific, and its scientific character is not invalidated because it is enriched by observations upon man's social life in its varying phases. Psychology thus understood skirts the province of physiology; for, in explaining the raw material of feeling and of knowledge, and the mechanism of human activity, it is necessary to study the structure and function of nerve, both at the centres in spinal cord and encephalon, and at the periphery, especially as differentiated into the special senses.

Whilst speculative or metaphysical philosophy has in many quarters been disparaged, the physical sciences have, during the present century, developed their stringent methods of inquiry and of verification, and have surprised the world by their results. There has been, at the same time, a growing disposition to study the phenomena known as psychical, and to apply to this study the methods which have been so successful elsewhere. In France, Auguste Comte, who scornfully repudiated metaphysics, nevertheless, by his great treatises, gave an impulse to the study of sociology, *i.e.*, of human nature as traceable by its manifestations in the common life of humanity. In Germany, the most careful and delicate observations have been made, especially in elucidation of the phenomena of sensation and of movement. The modern German text-books on Psychology abound in generalisations thus attained, which, in some instances, are expressed in the form of mathematical laws. In our own country several manuals of Psychology have appeared, embodying the results of German research, and adding the fruits of independent observation. Similar manifestations of intellectual activity have not been wanting in the United States, in our Colonies, and in our Indian possessions.

It is maintained by some writers on Psychology that it is possible to treat their theme without making metaphysical assumptions, or yielding to metaphysical predilections. Their treatises, however, furnish conspicuous examples of the unreasonableness of their professions, for they constantly involve metaphysical doctrine. Divided as is opinion upon questions of vital importance, it is natural that many Psychologists should desire to prosecute their observations, and to formulate their doctrines, without taking a side in controversy. The same principle actuates university examiners, who are anxious to test the knowledge of candidates, whilst steering clear of questions and difficulties which some regard as insoluble, and which others profess to solve by opposed methods and with conflicting results. The consequence necessarily is that stress is laid upon matters of minor interest, and that matters of deep and permanent concern are kept in abeyance. Both writers and examiners sometimes lose sight of the fact that to ignore controversy is in some cases equivalent to taking a side. It is observable, however, that Mr. Ward, in his article in the *Encyclopædia Britannica*, and Mr. Sully, in his *Outlines*, proceed upon the assumption of the mind's existence.

At the same time that the prevalent tendency is to restrict the scope of Psychology, there appears to be a disposition in some quarters to enlarge its scope, and to make it a most comprehensive study. Thus Hamilton considered that Ontology or Metaphysics proper might be designated Inferential Psychology, and Mansel supposed a Rational Psychology which should frame definitions exhibiting the essential nature of the soul, &c. If such expansions be admitted, it is questionable whether any real advantage will attend the use of the term 'Psychology,' whether it will not be equally ambiguous with the familiar terms 'Metaphysics' and 'Philosophy.'

LOGIC is, by general consent, reckoned among the philosophical sciences. Its aim is to lay down the laws of the ratiocinative or discursive intellect. The processes of reasoning engaged the attention of the Greek thinkers; and the main features of deductive Logic, as known and taught to-day, were traced, with something like completeness, by the master-hand of Aristotle. As a valuable discipline of the mind, testing closeness of attention and keenness of intellectual discrimination, Logic has continued to hold its place in the academic curriculum. Its territory lies, as it were, within a ring fence, and its compactness and succinctness have made it especially useful for the purpose of education.

There was no doubt a time when Dialectic was over-rated. Logic has often been treated as an Art of disputation, and victory over an antagonist in argument, whether in law, religion, or opinion, is sure to be highly prized by minds of a certain order. But in the ratio in which truth is valued above victory, will dialectical skill be depreciated, and methods of discovery be cultivated in its place. If, however, Logic be regarded, as it should be, as an analysis of the mental processes involved in passing from judgment to judgment, its value is seen to be, not adventitious, but real. Certainly, the intellectual processes which Logic reveals in their formal simplicity, must ever be an interesting and valuable theme of study.

But as knowledge is gained, not only by proceeding downwards from principles to facts, but by proceeding upwards from facts to principles, it is evident that deductive Logic needs to be supplemented by a Logic which can deal with the processes of scientific discovery. Since the ancient and haphazard methods of investigating nature have been discarded, in favour of the strict methods of observation and experiment, of hypothesis and verification, discontent with the Aristotelian syllogism has been very common; and the mistake has frequently been made of blaming that form of reasoning for not sufficing to ends which it does not contemplate. It has been said that the Logic of consistency is one thing, and the Logic of truth, of discovery, another and a different thing. Whether any kind of reasoning can dispense with the syllogistic principle, may be questioned. But it is certain that, in the formation of general laws and in the construction of major premises, there is need of a system specially adapted to this purpose,—a purpose which, to many scientific investigators, is all-important.

From the time of Bacon, a Logic has been desiderated which should serve the purpose of the Inductive student. In our own time, much has been done towards supplying this deficiency. Hitherto, scientific men have gone their own way, often trusting to the spontaneous guidance of acquired experience, and often scarcely able to explain the reasons of their successes and failures; whilst logicians have gone their own way, heedless of the altered requirements of modern science, and incurring as a consequence the neglect of those who ought to be fellow-labourers in the same cause,—the establishment of sound and scientific knowledge.

This reproach has now been rolled away, and that very largely through the genius and the patient diligence of English philosophers. The science of Inductive

Logic is the creation of our own age. If there is apparent incongruity in the combination of Deductive and Inductive methods of reasoning in the same treatise, there is satisfaction in knowing that by this combination much has been done to harmonise human knowledge, and to bring the various processes of the human intellect under the sway of acknowledged laws. Probably great advances have yet to be made in this direction. The incongruity referred to may disappear when a completer theory of the mutual relations of nature and intelligence is attained, when all knowledge is more clearly apprehended as the transcription by the human mind of the thoughts of the universal and Divine Intellect. Certain it is. if we may judge by the large number of able works on Logic which have been produced in recent years, that the study of Logic, as amended and amplified, as applied to the several realms of knowledge, is regarded with far more interest and respect than was the case a generation or two ago.

METAPHYSICS is a term almost as ambiguous as is 'Philosophy' itself. Originally used to designate the subjects treated by Aristotle 'after Physics' (τὰ μετὰ τὰ φυσικά), *i e.*, the Science of Being as Being, it has been employed in a variety of acceptations. Usage has sometimes sanctioned the extension of the term to include all studies distinct from those that are physical,—*i e.*, all that have to do with the mental and the moral; whilst sometimes it has been employed to designate the facts and laws of the intellect alone, what is often termed 'Intellectual Philosophy.'

But the modern tendency is decidedly towards restricting the application of the term 'Metaphysics' to the ultimate and necessary principles of intelligence, and perhaps of morals (as in Kant's 'Metaphysic of Ethics'), and further, to existence, as it is in itself, and as distinguished from the phenomenal.

Such being the common application of the term, it is not surprising that, in the view of empirical and agnostic Psychologists, all that is Metaphysical should be dismissed into the limbo appointed by modern Science for effete superstitions. But even amongst upholders of man's spiritual nature and students of Theology, there obtains great difference of opinion with regard to metaphysical inquiries. There are those who would treat all metaphysical ideas as inferences from the positive data of the understanding. The immortal soul, the eternal God, the realm of Being, are by them regarded as provable by evidence furnished by Psychology. On the other hand, there are Transcendental Philosophers who regard experience of all kinds as incapable of yielding such results, and who hold that mind is gifted with a power of Intuition, which assures of realities altogether above the grasp of experiential faculties. These several tendencies are exemplified in schools of philosophic thought which have taken prominent positions, both in England and upon the Continent of Europe, during the present century.

The term EPISTEMOLOGY is sometimes used for the study of knowledge as such. According to the bent of the student's mind, such a study must partake more or less of a metaphysical character.

By ONTOLOGY is understood (if the word is allowable in such a connection) the Science of Being,—the most abstract of all studies which have engaged the human intelligence. It has been common for English Psychologists altogether to ignore ontological speculation; and although there has been during the last few years a marked change in this matter, still it is observable that those who cultivate this abstruse department of study are usually under the influence of German theories and systems. It should not be overlooked that one of the most brilliant thinkers and fascinating writers whom Scotland has produced in this century, Professor Ferrier, designated his chief work, 'The Institutes of Metaphysic, or the Theory of Knowing and of Being.' Since Ferrier's time, the British Hegelian school have familiarised the reader of philosophical literature with their doctrine of the relation between knowledge and existence. There seems no likelihood that speculation upon the ultimate mystery of knowledge and of existence will ever cease. The agnosticism favoured by many men of science seems of necessity to evoke a reaction in the direction of what has been called Gnosticism, or the doctrine that these ultimate problems are by no means insoluble, but that their solution is the perfect satisfaction of the mind, and the master-key to all human knowledge.

ETHICS or MORAL PHILOSOPHY is the name given to the science which theorises upon human conduct and life. Such a study has a definitely practical bearing, which imparts to it an interest more general and profound than attaches to those previously mentioned. It is sometimes represented that morals are concerned, not with what is, but with what ought to be; not with the actual, but with the ideal. On the other hand it is objected that, if this representation be just, the claims of Ethics to be regarded as a science are so far invalidated; inasmuch as it is presumed that science is actual knowledge, which must be of fact. However this may be, it is certain that, by general consent of the educated and thoughtful, not to say the virtuous, no study has an interest so deep as that which centres in the moral character, conditions, and actions of mankind.

To take the lowest view of the subject, it is undeniable that the happiness of individuals, and the prosperity of communities, are bound up with the moral principles and rules generally accepted and acted upon. Moral goodness and moral evil cannot be regarded with indifference, even by those who care little for theories of perception and for categories of thought. Accordingly, the questions, What is virtue? What are vice and crime? What is the authority of conscience? What are the foundations of Moral Law? are questions of perennial interest, which will never be heard with indifference or studied with apathy. And these questions, to all who take a just and exalted view of man's being and capacities, who believe in his Divine origin and immortal prospects, do and must possess an importance far above any that can be conferred by their connection with material and earthly interests.

Even with regard to matters of practical concern, as to what men ought to do and what they ought to refrain from doing, there is often room for difference of opinion But when the reasons for right conduct come to be considered, there at once arises controversy of a kind philosophically vital. Since men are bound to act, not merely upon habit, but upon reason, it is evident that Philosophy must be engaged upon the foundations of human virtue, upon the ultimate ideals towards which human nature should aspire. As a matter of fact, from the times of Greek speculation, debate has prevailed upon these great questions. Nor did the introduction of Christianity by any means put an end to ethical controversy. As the ancients had their Stoics and their Epicureans, so we have our Intuitionists and our Utilitarians, our Transcendentalists and our Naturalists; we have among us those who trace all moral authority to the physical constitution of man, those who derive all obligation from political law and physical punishment, and those who base all human duty upon our relations to the paramount law, the eternal reason and righteousness of the Deity.

The science of Ethics has always taken something of its tone from the changing conditions of human society. The city in ancient Hellas, the empire of Rome, the polity and comity of modern European states, could none of them be without influence upon the form in which moral questions have been apprehended and treated, whilst it is well known how powerfully the Church and its organisations affected mediæval morals. Deeper than political and ecclesiastical distinctions are those religious differences which have, often insensibly, but always mightily, affected the moral life and consequently the moral theories of men There have been states of society in which religion and morals have been all but disconnected, and there have been periods in which religion has penetrated and saturated, for good and for evil, the individual and social life Christianity itself has been at some times predominatingly an institution, at other times predominatingly a spirit How the moral life and habits of Christendom have been affected by the priesthood and the confessional, how casuistry became the most prominent development of Ethics —this is known, not only to the student of Church history, but to the student of morals. It is instructive to see how the modern attempt to construct society upon the basis, not of religious loyalty, but of common pleasures, and of mutual services to this end, has coloured the ethical doctrine and the moral standards of recent generations.

The student will find in this department the utmost variety of treatment; and he will do well to be upon his guard against the arrogant assumptions, too common in all schools of thought, which would deter him from a comprehensive and catholic survey. It may be questioned whether he will find any department of literature which has, more than this study of morals, evinced and illustrated the intellectual powers of the human race. Our own nation has, in the province of Ethics, abundantly sustained its reputation, not only for literary ability but for originality in speculation and in constructive thought.

Whilst some philosophers would make Morals a development from Psychology, others, especially in recent times, have tended to deduce ethical laws from the relations of human society.

SOCIOLOGY is the name now applied to designate the study of mankind in their social conditions and relations. Much attention has of late been given to the institutions and usages of men in less advanced states of society, and even to those of savage tribes. Some have expected that research into the habits and customs of so-called primitive man will cast light upon the genesis of moral ideas and sentiments. But apart from such expectations, it is important that human conduct should be studied under all possible conditions. And probably those who have favoured the use of the term 'sociology' have for the most part done so in the belief that Ethics must prove to be a science based upon observation, and yielding 'laws' which partake of the character of empirical generalisations rather than of authoritative counsels and precepts.

POLITICAL PHILOSOPHY studies men as federated into communities, whether tribal or more especially national, and describes the relations involved in, and the mutual duties springing from such federations. The State is, among all civilised communities, regarded with interest, and with a measure of veneration, both as a development of social human nature, and also as a power immensely affecting the general well-being. Still, whilst there are those who esteem the political life of a nation as among the most august and sacred realities, and who conceive national authority as possessing organic character and force all its own, there are others in whose view government is little more than police.

It has always been common for the treatment of Ethics and Politics to be conjoined. In Plato's 'Republic' no attempt was made to separate the two; whilst Aristotle regarded his 'Ethics' as introductory to his 'Politics.' The reader of modern English literature upon morals may be reminded that Paley includes in the same treatise Moral and Political Philosophy, and that Bentham's best known work is denominated 'Principles of Morals and Legislation.' Those who hold that Morals have their very foundation in political life and organisation, naturally treat the two as almost inseparably allied in exposition. On the whole, however, the tendency is to separate the two studies in treatment, however they may be conceived as radically united.

NATURAL THEOLOGY or RELIGION, termed by the French Théodicée, is properly a province of Philosophy Its aim is to rise to that knowledge of God which is possible apart from Revelation, and which is the complement and the crown of human knowledge However Theists may differ in their estimate of the comparative validity of the several lines of argument by which we establish the existence, the attributes, and the rule of God, they are agreed in referring the conception of Deity to a mental power, and in completing that conception by the consideration of moral convictions and sentiments To Agnostics such processes may seem to have little actual importance; but all believers in God hold natural as distinct from revealed Theology to be based upon the very constitution and natural activity of the mind Monotheists and Pantheists of varying shades agree that the Deity underlies and explains both human knowledge and cosmic order, and that the denial of God is the subversion of Philosophy. The justice is obvious of assigning all belief in the Infinite Power,—which is Wisdom, Righteousness, and Love,—to metaphysical rather than to physical data In this the adherent of Scottish philosophy is at one with the Hegelian, who would identify our higher nature with the spiritual principle that pervades the universe, and makes it intelligible. It may be remarked that speculation has lately been very active in studying the nature and character of the ultimate Power in the universe Whilst there is among the educated very little bare atheism, there are to be met with doctrines, or rather theories, regarding the supreme Power and Cause, of every degree of divergence from the orthodox Christian faith.

III *THE ORIGIN OF PHILOSOPHY.*

In a fairly peaceful and settled state of society, when urgent bodily wants are supplied, the opening intelligence of men directs itself to inquiries which their condition and their nature alike suggest Solitary meditation, and the contact and friction of mind with mind, awaken thought, and thought occupies itself with those themes which experience assures us possess a perennial interest.

In the first instance the thinker exercises his powers upon the vast universe, of which every movement reveals to him some fragment, some aspect; which, by the avenue of every sense, addresses itself to his observation; and which, by its ever-varying surprises, arouses his curiosity. Nature, in all its manifold and mysterious aspects, appeals to the understanding To become acquainted with the multitudinous phenomena of the universe, is the ambition of the alert and inquisitive mind But such knowledge in itself does not satisfy; there is an intellectual impulse urging to comprehend, to explain, to harmonise what is known. Hence the speculations, partaking more or less of the nature of science, which characterise the dawn of Philosophy. With the advance of human knowledge the province of physical science is more clearly mapped out, and the rigidly scientific mind endeavours to confine its interest within the boundaries of fact and law, of uniformities in coexistence and sequence. Still, ever and anon, there arises in the ranks of the cultivators of physical science, an ardent investigator who is at the same time a bold speculator, who cannot content himself within the limits generally accepted. Mystical and pantheistic theorists study Nature as the garb, the language of Spirit; for them this view of Nature is the only enriching and satisfying view. The critic must be very short-sighted who believes that the world has seen the last of theorists such as these.

The thinker, however, comes, perhaps gradually, to distinguish himself from the universe, of which, in a sense, he forms a part. By an almost irresistible impulse he is thrown back upon his own intellectual and moral being and character,—as surpassing in interest, even the dazzling splendours, the half-comprehended order, the baffling perplexities of the material world. The distinction between human conduct and all cosmical processes, thrusts itself upon the attention of the reflective. Self-consciousness bears a witness which can neither be silenced nor perverted. Every man feels and knows himself to be a mirror of nature and a centre of force. The mystery of his own being urges him to the study of that self which remains the same amidst the utmost diversity of experience. It is in vain that the man is assured that he is but a speck, a mere breath, in the vast encompassing universe, that as such he is unworthy even of attention, in comparison with the wonders of the world, its illimitable forces, its revolving cycles,—that he is only the creature of a day, whilst the universe has neither bounds, beginning, nor end. They who so reason are themselves unconvinced by such sophisms. The majesty of man is superior to such attacks. There is doubtless a sense in which man is a microcosm corresponding with the macrocosm of the universe. Yet it remains unquestionable that mind masters matter; it can do more than control, direct, and constrain it; it can perceive and apprehend it. It is the glory of intellect that it gives to all things material their meaning, and indeed their very reality. All attempts to construe mind as material have failed; but matter is unknown and non-existent save in terms of mind. Whether or not reflection can cast any light upon the origin, the substance, of mind, it is certain that men will not cease to study its working, its processes, and powers. As Socrates is commonly said to have brought Philosophy down to man, so in every age of thought and culture, man proves his sense of his own nobility, by making his inner nature and life the topic of meditation and inquiry. Let men be psychologists, or social philosophers, or moralists; in any case it may be taken for granted that, as surely as they think at all, they must think of what is distinctively and pre-eminently human.

But the movements now described do not exhaust the philosophic impulse It has been proved, by the long experience of humanity, that the mind is not satisfied to reflect only upon the material universe and upon its own powers and operations, its own capacities and prospects There is a deep desire to reach a higher unity, an all-comprehending cause,—in a word, to know God It must be acknowledged that there are many, even amongst thoughtful students, to whom this tendency of intellectual man seems to be the offspring of illusion, which can never issue in any solid, satisfactory result. There are those who say that the spontaneous invention of deities,—so common among men in certain stages of development,—is merely the projection of their own personality into the realm of nature, and is accounted for by well-known psychological laws There are those who argue that, as we have no method of verifying our supposed knowledge of the supernatural, we must relegate the Divine to the province of imagination and of emotion, for there can be no place found for it in the province of understanding,—which comprises only the human and the physical, and whatsoever is amenable to observation and experiment. These objections have, in our own time, been systematised and presented in a scientific guise, and are the foundations of so-called Agnosticism This doctrine confines our knowledge to the sensible and the phenomenal, and dismisses all else to the category of the unscientific and imaginative

There is an obvious explanation of the favour with which agnostic doctrines have been received by a large school of scientific thinkers in our own days But it is enough here to note the fact, and to repeat that, as a matter of history, it has ever been a sign of the philosophic impulse deep-seated in human nature that men have sought a super-sensible Power, the explanation and source, the unity and the illumination of all existence

---

IV *A BRIEF SKETCH OF THE HISTORY OF PHILOSOPHY.*

It has been usual to refer the origin of Philosophy to the genius of the Hellenic race Owing to the modern tendency to enlarge the scope of inductive inquiry, and to pursue the scientific method of comparison, there has recently been a disposition to include Oriental speculation among the sources of philosophical life and activity. There can be no doubt that the Hindu mind has always evinced peculiar aptitude for the subtleties of metaphysical thought Indian religion and Indian philosophy have been, broadly speaking, identical The Vedas and Vedantas, which constitute the literary treasure of Brahman priests and philosophers, contain in abundance speculation and reflection upon the mystery of Being. In fact, it is the problem of existence rather than that of cognition which has the strongest attraction for the Hindu intellect. And for the Hindu mind the intellectual and moral elements of philosophy are less discriminated than for ourselves. The great rival systems of the East, Brahmanism and Buddhism, profoundly as they differ, are alike in this: they aim at offering a speculative and practical solution of the perplexities of human thought and the difficulties of human life.

The Hellenic tribes were, intellectually and æsthetically, the most gifted people of antiquity. They produced the most perfect forms of architecture and of sculpture; by swift steps they brought the drama to its highest point; they wrought with master-hand in every form of literature, both historical and imaginative. It is not surprising, then, that in pure thought they should not merely have excelled all nations, but should have fashioned the very moulds into which the intellect of all other nations should be compelled to run and to take shape. It has been pointed out by Zeller that the Greek religion was of a peculiarly idealistic character, and was distinguished by the absence both of a professional hierarchy and of theological dogmatism; and that these characteristics largely contributed to the freedom of Greek thinking. The rich and varied aspects of national life among the Greeks are so many manifestations of a spirit—bold, energetic, and original—which could scarcely fail to attempt the task of explaining and unifying all the phenomena which address the observation and excite the curiosity and speculation of mankind.

Cosmology was anticipated in a mythologic form by the early poets, especially by Hesiod; practical morality was embodied in sayings attributed to the sages of Greece; and reflections upon human nature abounded in Homer. But the earliest development of what is strictly called Philosophy is to be looked for among the Ionians of Asia Minor. Our knowledge of their speculations is but vague. Yet we can see that their great theme of study was Nature,—this universe, which awakens in all observing and reflecting minds questionings which even the wisest in our own day can but partially satisfy, and which these Ionian sages, six centuries before Christ, sought each in his own way to resolve Thus Thales of Miletus regarded water as the principle or ground of all existing things; Anaximander deemed the undefined—perhaps unformed, chaotic matter—as the ultimate principle of Nature; whilst Anaximenes assigned this all-important position and power to air. These thinkers were evidently working upon the same lines, all of them in a way we should regard as utterly unscientific. It is not their conclusions which interest us, but their aim,—which was to find unity in diversity, to employ the mind in unravelling the mysterious secret of Being

This first movement of Greek Philosophy was like the opening of a wondering childhood to that which impresses the senses, but which has not yet power to unfold the imagination or to inspire the reason. Nature to these thinkers was the all. They cannot strictly be called materialists, for the distinction between the spiritual and the material had not yet consciously emerged. But succeeding stages of speculation reveal a more developed mode of thinking.

The Ionians were followed by the Pythagoreans. So far as they were cosmologists, their tenets may be summed up in the statement that for them number was the essence and substance of all things. The marvellous properties of number, and the marvellous results which arithmetic achieves, may well lead mathematicians to attribute to it a virtue and importance of the highest order. But Pythagoras seems to have regarded number as the explanation of all things, as the very substance of the Universe. This exaggerated view led him into many fanciful absurdities, which are so remote from reason that it is difficult to feel great interest in them.

In the view of many students the Pythagorean school is still more important in the history of Philosophy because of its ethical and religious tendencies. The adherents of this school practised not only virtue but asceticism. They probably knew little of religion in our acceptation of the word, but they believed in the transmigration of souls,—a tenet which seemed to them an incitement to a virtuous life.

There were, however, among the early Greek thinkers those who, in contrast to the materialism of the Ionians and the mysticism of the Pythagoreans, took a more purely intellectual view of the universe. The Eleatics were the true Idealists of Greece. Of this school the leading representatives were Xenophanes, who is called the theologian of the Eleatics, and Parmenides, who is deemed their metaphysician. According to the latter, Thought and the object of Thought—thinking and being—are one and the same. The school was continued by Zeno and Melissus.

At the other extreme from the Eleatics was Heracleitus; for, whilst those held a doctrine of Unity which led them to deny plurality, a doctrine of Being which led them to deny becoming, this philosopher held that the one substance is in perpetual movement and change. All things are in flux, and the perpetual becoming is the law of Nature. Of this incessant change Fire is the apt symbol; from this element all things arise, to this all things return; pure fire is even the substance of the soul. In much of this teaching we see an affinity between Heracleitus and his Ionian predecessors. Yet he had points of sympathy with the Eleatics: he believed in one substance, and in an all-pervading reason,—in the government of a rational law. Heracleitus would seem to have been a philosopher of a remarkably comprehensive mind: the fragments of his sayings which remain give us a high idea of his wisdom. He is popularly remembered as the 'weeping philosopher.'

Another great figure in these early days is the Sicilian philosopher Empedocles. In him we see the effect of both the tendencies above described. He treats of the four elements, but always as penetrated and governed by two principles, Love and Hate. This curious combination gave rise to many fantastic speculations of little interest As a man he was impressive and imposing, and the end which is assigned by tradition to his life—he is said to have leapt into the crater of Ætna—harmonises poetically with his claim to Deity

The Atomists were a school of great importance, and their general principles were an anticipation of the atheistical materialism which sprang up in France towards the close of the last century, and revived again in Germany in more recent times. Leucippus is deemed the founder of the sect, and Democritus, the 'laughing philosopher,' its chief expositor They asked for no other first principles than atoms and the void, and they endeavoured with no other assumptions than these to account for the existing universe. Material and mechanical principles were held sufficient to explain all things that are:—a curious parallelism with fashionable doctrines of our own times.

At the same time that the materialists were endeavouring to show that matter has within itself the formative power which issues in the universal order, and which brings the mental—the spiritual—into existence, Anaxagoras arose to teach a sounder and more reasonable faith. According to him, Mind is the power which fashions and moulds all things, the true cause of motion and of order.

It may be noted that Zeller regards these last mentioned philosophers—Heracleitus, Anaxagoras, Leucippus, and Democritus—as a second development of Ionian speculation.

It thus appears that the early Greek philosophers occupied themselves with the endeavour to understand the universe as a whole; that they were students of cosmology, trying to look behind physical facts, and to discover explanations, whether materialistic or spiritual. There was a very inadequate basis of knowledge for their speculations, and the results of their philosophy were far from certain. The time came when the most vigorous thinkers turned their attention away from cosmical inquiries towards matters of *human* interest. The first indication that this change was taking place appeared when the Sophists began to attract the attention especially of the Athenian public. These were a class of well-informed, clever, eloquent, and ambitious men, who seem to have thought chiefly of their own advancement,—to be secured by a profession and public practice of what they deemed philosophy. Very different estimates have been formed of their merits. But there can be no question that they provoked inquiry and spread knowledge, and that they advanced politics to a very prominent position, training the wealthy and aspiring youth of Athens in the arts of disputation 'The Sophists rendered general culture universal. Thus Protagoras was celebrated as a teacher of morals, Gorgias as a rhetorician and politician, Prodicus as a grammarian and etymologist, and Hippias as a polymath.' There is no doubt that the influence of the Sophists was in the direction of scepticism, they undermined established beliefs, and in no way replaced them.

In the fifth century B.C occurred the great crisis in Greek Philosophy. This came with the public life and 'ministry' of Socrates, concerning whose habits and teaching we learn much from the pens of his disciples, Xenophon and Plato. Socrates was the ideal wise man; yet he wrote no books, delivered no set lectures, but went about the city of Athens, conversing with all who were disposed to listen to him and to answer his questions. Whether his companions were plain citizens, young politicians, or famous sophists, they were all subjected to his acute, ironical, and yet earnest questioning. His aim was to sift real knowledge from pretence, to bring to birth the thoughts of those who had any power of thinking, though little articulate.

Socrates brought philosophy down to earth, to man. He seems to have interested himself very little in the problems which had engaged the attention of his predecessors: to him human nature, human life, human virtues and vices, human thought and knowledge were the 'chief concern.' It was not merely the thing known that attracted him, it was the power of knowing. And with his inquiry into knowledge was connected the inquiry into morals. He sought, by examining the notions he found in himself and in his fellow-men, to discover the reality of things, to penetrate through conventionality to truth. Ethics were to Socrates of supreme importance, and the outcome of his investigations was the identifying of virtue with knowledge. He was a true philosopher, a lover of wisdom; and a true moralist, who rose, in moral character, above the standard of his day, who both exemplified and taught human virtue. He was not, in the common sense of the term, a politician; but he cherished a loyal affection for the State. And with regard to religion, it is unquestionable that his notions of the Supreme Being were exalted, and that the charge of atheism brought against him was only just in so far as he was confessedly above the popular polytheism, whilst yet he did not yield to the irreligious influences to which so many of his contemporaries succumbed. If the life of Socrates was a true philosopher's life, his death was worthy of the career it closed, and has ever been regarded as a noble martyrdom submitted to in the cause of Truth and Loyalty. And it is from Socrates, as from a fountain-head, that the living streams of psychology and of ethics have flowed down through the centuries of human history.

Leaving aside the Megaric school, we observe that two schools, known as the 'one-sided Socraticists,' sprang from the teaching of the great sage. One of these, the Cynic school, advocated and exemplified Asceticism. The Cynics—Antisthenes, Diogenes, and their followers—despised, not only luxury, but conventionality, and extolled the dignity of a severely virtuous and independent life. Opposed to these were the Cyrenaics, of whom Aristippus was the leader, who regarded pleasure as the chief good. The tendencies of mind and habits of life, observable in these schools, have reappeared again and again in both ancient and modern society. Intellectual speculation always leads to ethical systems, or, at all events, to ethical maxims and practices, and these are usually found to incline to one or other of the systems just described.

But, whilst the 'one-sided' schools based their practical teaching on certain characteristics of Socrates's teaching, the real continuators, especially of his intellectual influence, were Plato and Aristotle. These are the two greatest names among ancient philosophers, if not among the philosophers of the whole world, of all ages.

Plato is the great Idealist. Not content to limit our knowledge to the sensible and changing world, he held that Reason contemplates eternal truth. His theory of ideas, of reminiscence, of the metaphysical good, are characteristic in a special manner of Plato, and can only be understood by patient study of the 'Dialogues.' In Morality, it is observable that for Plato the State is of supreme interest; the individual is subordinate to the community, and the State presents the sphere in which the several virtues are embodied and displayed.

If Plato was the sublimest, Aristotle was the most comprehensive intellect of antiquity. As Plato was scholar to Socrates, so Aristotle was pupil of Plato, of whom (even when dissenting from him) he speaks with deep respect, and of whose influence his writings bear manifold tokens. The great Stagirite seems to have acquired all knowledge at that time in the possession of men; he wrote on Physics and Metaphysics, on Logic and Rhetoric, on Ethics and Politics; and indeed was the founder of some of these realms of human knowledge. The distinctive characteristic of Aristotle's method is his habit of relying upon experience; and it is in method rather than in result that the unity of Aristotle's philosophy is to be found. It may be mentioned that, in the view of many students, the Ethics of Aristotle are the most intrinsically valuable among the works which have come down to us from classical antiquity. Aristotle was no Hedonist; the end of human action, according to him, is happiness, or rather welfare, and this consists in the exercise of the distinctively human faculty, which is Reason. The ideal is rational, even philosophical, activity, yet in circumstances not sordid, not cramping to the exercise of an honourable and liberal nature.

In passing from the noble systems of Plato and Aristotle to the subsequent philosophies of Greece, we are conscious of a narrowing of horizon, of interest, and sympathy. With the earlier philosophers the chief aim had been the explanation of the universe. Socrates and his great successors had dealt first and chiefly with the nature and validity of knowledge. But the later schools turned away from these vaster and profounder studies, and directed their attention to the individual life. Hence they were more predominatingly moral than their predecessors.

About 300 B.C. Zeno was lecturing in Athens, in the painted porch from which his sect took their designation 'Stoics.' He and his successors, Cleanthes and Chrysippus, wrought out a philosophy which for centuries exercised a vast influence over men of a select type—both Greeks and Romans. The Stoics, like the earlier thinkers, had their system of physics; it has been called a 'pantheistic materialism:' 'the world is God's body, God the world's soul.' Their system of morals harmonised with their belief that reason, order, and law are present throughout the universe. The Stoics held that the moral life is that which accords with nature, that, as reason governs all material things, it should govern the soul, the life of man. They extolled virtue; and, though they did not go so far as the Cynics in despising all pleasure, yet they also conceived that man should be independent of circumstances, and should find his well-being in following nature and reason. It should be remarked that the Stoics were celebrated for their cultivation of Logic.

The rival sect of the Epicureans arose about the same time with the Stoics. There is no doubt that Epicurus and his followers have been greatly maligned, and that the founder of the school was a man of simple habits and reputable life. Still, the Epicurean doctrine has been on the whole debasing. Physics were studied in the school, but chiefly for the purpose of guarding against the superstitious terrors often inspired by natural calamities or portents. It was, however, in morals that the influence of Epicurus was mainly felt; he taught his followers to seek the *summum bonum* in pleasure, to which he regarded virtue as the means. The similarity is obvious between this doctrine and that of the modern Hedonist and Utilitarian. Many virtuous and benevolent characters have been formed under both systems. Yet the result of undermining the independent basis of morality, and especially of doing this by substituting personal feeling for a law of righteousness, cannot be other than corrupting.

The four schools described:—The Academy, or Platonists; the Lyceum, or Peripatetics, followers of Aristotle; the Stoics of the Porch; and the Epicureans of the Garden—continued to hold their position at Athens for several centuries. There were, indeed, other sects, especially the Sceptics, of whom Pyrrho had been the founder, and who at a later time were represented by Ænesidemus, Agrippa, and Sextus Empiricus.

These Grecian Philosophies exercised great influence over the educated classes among the Romans. But, whilst the Romans were great in arms, in laws, and in good faith and piety, they did not share the Greek gift of speculation and dialectic. They were content to receive lessons from their subjects. Carneades the Academic, Critolaus the Peripatetic, and Diogenes the Stoic, are mentioned as having introduced Grecian philosophy among the Romans. One great philosopher was formed in the Epicurean school, Lucretius the poet, whose verse is steeped in the doctrines of Democritus and Epicurus. At least three great names among the Romans were associated with Stoicism, those of Seneca, and, at a later period, Marcus Aurelius and Epictetus. In the writings of these Roman Stoics, the non-Christian morality may be said to have reached its highest pitch of dignity and elevation. Yet the community at large was probably quite unaffected by the beliefs and writings of these select philosophers.

Cicero, the most important of Latin writers on Philosophy, professed himself a disciple of the New Academy, but had much sympathy with the Stoics. In his writings we meet with much information regarding the philosophers of the age preceding his own.

Christianity, which made all things new, could not but exert a transforming influence upon the highest exercises of the human intellect. The religion of Jesus was a morality, laying anew and deeper the foundations of ethical life, both individual and social. But it is a very superficial view of Christianity to regard it wholly as a moral power. It professes to be a revelation; and the Incarnation and Atonement are a Divine provision for bridging over the gulf between the created and the Creator Spirit. God is declared to man, and man is harmonised with God. Light of the most precious kind is cast upon Theology and Pneumatology (as a complete Psychology has sometimes been termed). And if Cosmology is less illuminated, still our Religion represents the world as the work and the garb of God, and as the means appointed for the spiritual education of humanity.

Many of the great Christian Divines and Apologists of the early Christian centuries came from the schools of Philosophy, brought with them philosophical ideas, and learned to solve philosophical problems by the aid of Revelation. Justin Martyr professes to have found in Christ what he had sought elsewhere in vain, and Clemens Alexandrinus, in a well-known passage, taught that, as the Law had been a schoolmaster to the Jews, so Philosophy had been the schoolmaster providentially appointed for the Gentiles, to bring them to Christ. Among the Latin Fathers, Augustine is pre-eminent for his knowledge of Philosophy, and for his penetration with the philosophic spirit. With him, and with many other Christian theologians, Plato held a paramount position of authority among the ancient masters of human philosophy.

The last effort of the philosophical spirit of antiquity was made by the Neo-Platonists, who, from the third to the sixth centuries, sought to resuscitate at Alexandria, Rome, and Athens, a purely intellectual and spiritual power, which might contend with the growing energy of the Christian Religion. The names of Plotinus and Porphyry are the most famous in the earlier development, those of Iamblichus and Proclus in the later. Against the prevalent scepticism the Neo-Platonists strove with the weapons of mysticism. The intuition of absolute truth, the vision of God by the purified and illumined soul, was to replace all the halting processes of psychology. If such is their 'epistemology,' or doctrine of knowledge, their 'cosmology' is no less abstract and transcendental From the One,—the Divine Being,—there emanate successively, reason, the world-soul, and then the material world. Individual souls, partaking of both reasonable and sensible nature, may, by mortification and asceticism, attain to communion and union with the eternal, uncreated Deity.

The fall of the Roman Empire and the spread of Christianity throughout Europe, were events which filled centuries of human history. During this epoch it cannot be said that Philosophy flourished; in fact, it scarcely existed. With the exceptions of Boethius, in the sixth century, who may be regarded as the after-glow of the classic day, and of John Erigena, in the ninth century, who may be considered the morning star heralding the twilight of scholasticism, no great names occur to light up the ages which, philosophically, were 'dark' indeed.

The period of Scholastic Philosophy lasted from Anselm in the eleventh century to Wyclif in the fourteenth. During these three centuries Philosophy was 'the handmaid of Theology,' being cultivated entirely by churchmen, and being employed in the elucidation and defence of the orthodox faith. That great minds in this epoch dealt with great questions, is not to be questioned. An acuter logician than Abelard, a profounder mystic than Hugh of St. Victor, a keener theologian than Peter of Lombardy, the Master of Sentences, a more universal encyclopædist than Albertus Magnus, a more dogmatic controversialist than Thomas Aquinas, a subtler doctor than Duns Scotus,—the history of Christendom does not tell of. Yet there is among Protestants a general notion that the abilities and learning of the great Scholastics were largely wasted. The critical and historical methods of modern theology are very remote from the mediæval definitions, deductions, and demonstrations. During the latter part of the period in question, Aristotle's authority may be said to have been supreme; though at an earlier time many of Aristotle's writings were known only indirectly through the labours of the Arabian scholars. At the same time, it is to be observed that of the great Scholastics some were undoubtedly under Platonic influence.

The controversy between Realists and Nominalists raged now and again among these mediæval philosophers. Realism was the orthodox doctrine; but it was vigorously attacked. Roscellin, at the end of the eleventh century, was the first to profess Nominalism; and Occam, in the fourteenth century, did more than any other to undermine the foundations of Realism. The doctrine of Abelard upon this debated question was that Conceptualism which is intermediate between the two extreme theories.

Reason gradually asserted itself against authority. Philosophy had, during the Middle Ages, taken for granted the authority of the Church, and of the Scriptures and the works of the Fathers which the Church guaranteed The time came when the conditions of thinking were altered, and its long-endured restrictions were outgrown. The revival of learning was accompanied by the revival of independent thought, and was followed by the Reformation of Religion. The middle of the fifteenth century, when the learned Greeks came into Western Europe, and when the art of printing was invented, was the commencement of this great movement. The shackles of mediævalism were cast off, and the era of liberty began. The study of Plato was, of literary influences, the strongest to help in overturning the long dominant Aristotelianism. The investigation of nature led to many fanciful interpretations, but also to revolutionary, and in some cases well-founded conclusions upon astronomical and cosmical science. A general activity of intellect insured attention and independent thought to the most difficult and the most interesting of all themes. Thus it was that Modern Philosophy came to be born.

In England the first sign that a new era was beginning was the publication by Lord Bacon of new methods of studying nature. Immature as these were, they were nevertheless revolutionary, for they were a sign that the reign of authority was passing away. But it was Descartes who was 'the father of the experimental philosophy of the human mind.' He was, however, far more than this. His doubt and his faith, his idealistic starting-point and his dualistic system, account for the directions taken by many succeeding thinkers. Doubting all things but his own existence (which he perceived so clearly that he could not doubt it), he reasoned from this one fact to the belief in God, and thence to the belief in the world; and laid down the doctrine, which has been so widely accepted, that matter, as distinguished by extension, stands over against mind characterised by thought, in an eternal antithesis. It was thus from Descartes that the philosophy of Continental Europe received its bias. To bridge over the chasm between mind and matter, Geulinx perfected the theory of 'occasional causes,' and Malebranche elaborated his virtually idealistic doctrine that we see all things in God. And it was the difficulty of the Cartesian dualism which ultimately led to the monism, the pantheism of the great Spinoza. The simplicity and profundity of Spinozism, its postulation of the one Substance, of which matter and mind are conceived as modes, its assertion of absolute necessity in Morals, have led to its revived study and adoption by many scientific thinkers of our own century.

The course of Philosophy in Britain was different; the studies of British thinkers were more psychological and less ontological. *Individualism* was their keynote. Locke's 'Essay,' notwithstanding its diffuseness and its flagrant inconsistencies, took and long retained a leading position in not only English, but European controversy. How far Locke was opposing Descartes, and how far Lord Herbert of Cherbury, it would be hard to decide. But his appeal to plain men's understanding and observation, his 'new way of ideas,' his reference of all ideas to sensation and reflection (the two modes of experience), as their source and origin, his explanation of the several kinds of knowledge: however these may to us seem superficial and unsatisfactory, fell in with the temper of Locke's countrymen in his own and in the succeeding age. Still, Locke prepared the way for the scepticism which followed, and for which he would certainly have felt no sympathy. Berkeley simply abandoned belief in material 'substance,' in which Locke believed, though he had abandoned all ground for his belief, and 'knew not' what it was that he believed. And Hume simply took the last step upon the same road, and abandoned belief in spiritual as well as material substance. As a philosopher, Hume was a pure phenomenist, and consequently a sceptic, for whom the voice of Reason contradicted the voice of Nature. When Personality and Causation had gone, it was difficult to see that anything worth contending for was left.

A movement, to some extent parallel with that above described, had taken place in Ethical thought and theory. Hobbes had revolted from the old religious basis and sanctions of morals, and had founded them upon personal interest and upon the supreme power of the State, which he held sufficient to constitute right and wrong. Locke, who traced knowledge to the feeling of the individual, assigned a similar origin to morality. For him pleasure was the test of the ethically good: taking this position he became the forerunner of the modern Hedonists and Utilitarians.

Against the derivative morality of Hobbes and Locke, very powerful protests were raised. It was taught that the right, the morally good, has an independent foundation. Cumberland and More regarded Benevolence as a divinely-appointed law and principle. Cudworth and Clarke asserted the eternity and immutability of the moral law. Butler's great endeavour was to establish the supremacy of conscience, its right to govern in preference to inferior principles. As an intermediate theory, there was advanced in the eighteenth century the famous system of the Moral Sense, connected with the names of Shaftesbury and Hutcheson; and, in close connection with this system, Adam Smith's doctrine that Sympathy is the all-sufficient explanation of morality. The ethics of Feeling are considered to have reached their last development in Hume, who thus occupies a position in morals very similar to that which he takes in Intellectual Philosophy. Hume's great office in speculative thought seems to have been to carry to the extremest limit the doctrines of the eighteenth century, and thus to prepare the way for subsequent reaction.

In Germany the prevalent philosophy during the eighteenth century was that of Leibnitz, as modified by Wolff. Leibnitz, dissatisfied with Occasional Causes, as an explanation of the communion between mind and matter, invented his famous doctrine of Pre-established Harmony, and of Monads, substituting, as

Professor E. Caird has observed, 'one all-embracing miracle' for the continuing miracle. The same author designates the system of Wolff the 'unconscious revival of Scholasticism.'

It was in Germany that the new movement commenced. Kant commenced to teach upon the lines of the current dogmatism and optimism. But Hume roused him from what he afterwards acknowledged was his 'slumber;' and he could neither acquiesce in the routine scholasticism to which he had been accustomed, nor accept the alternative of scepticism and intellectual nakedness. Thus he was led to inaugurate a new era, in which his influence has been predominant, though this influence has by no means been proved by a general acceptance of his conclusions.

Kant's philosophy is known as Criticism, on account of his having undertaken a criticism, both of the pure (or speculative) and the practical reason. His aim was to establish the validity of human knowledge, and especially to show that experience alone cannot account for knowledge, inasmuch as there are mental conditions, forms, categories, &c., which are necessary in order that experience itself may be possible. At the same time it must be borne in mind that Kant consistently taught that all knowledge is relative, and that 'things in themselves' are unknown to us. Thus he held that, on grounds of pure reason, we can have no knowledge of God and of immortality. It was, however, his aim to show that our moral nature leads us in these directions further than we could otherwise attain. Freedom, Duty, God, were to him the most sacred of all realities. The command of conscience Kant held to be unconditionally binding and authoritative. No one more resolutely opposed the Ethics of consequences.

A reaction against Hume's Scepticism took place in Scotland with a similar intent as in Germany. Reid's philosophy of Common-sense has been very variously estimated; but there is no doubt that he aimed at basing the ordinary beliefs of men upon primitive intuitions and axioms and upon general consent. In this aim he was seconded by Stewart. Hamilton endeavoured to give a more philosophical complexion to the teaching of the Scottish school, and to combine (somewhat inconsistently) a doctrine of Natural Realism or Dualism with a doctrine of relativity of knowledge.

Turning again to France, it is curious to observe that the philosophical movement most distinctive of that country in the eighteenth century, received its impulse from England. The Sensationalism of Condillac does not historically derive from Gassendi but from Locke. The second source of experience was dropped out of sight, and it was sought to account by sense alone for all mental possessions, whilst the very faculties or functions of the mind were represented as nothing more than 'transformed sensations.' Of this extravagant doctrine yet more extravagant developments were to follow, in the scepticism of the encyclopædists, in the gross materialism of De la Mettrie, d'Holbach, and Destutt de Tracy, and in the selfish morality of Helvetius.

The reaction against Materialism and Sensationalism in France took place in the earlier part of this century. Maine de Biran worked his way out of the slough of 'ideology,' until he found rest upon the rock of spiritualism. Cousin was intellectually influenced by the Scottish Reid and the German Kant; and his philosophy was justly named Eclectic. Jouffroy and Royer Collard were among the best known of this high-minded but somewhat rhetorical school.

The most distinguished French thinker of the middle of our century reverted, in a measure, to the earlier type. Comte was the incarnation of the modern scientific spirit. The Positive Philosophy (considered apart from the 'Religion of Humanity') professes to found itself upon observation scientifically verified. It is, in fact, a classification of human knowledge, whilst its Psychology is Biology combined with Sociology.

The English tendency during the present century has been to follow upon the lines of Berkeley, and of Hartley and Hume; although, for the most part, our English psychologists have ignored the theological side of Berkeley's philosophy, whilst they have offered no substitute for the explanation the great Idealist gave of the order of the universe. And it may be added that, generally speaking, they have not put forward the sceptical nihilism which gave in the writings of Hume offence so serious to the British public. The peculiarities of this school have been its attention to Empirical Psychology, and the stress laid by it upon the principle of Association. This principle, received from Hartley and Hume, has been applied by the two Mills and Bain to the solution of all the problems of Psychology, and is supposed by them to render unnecessary the assumption of any innate faculty of mind.

The application of Evolution to mind and morals is the work of our own time, and is touched upon in the following section of this Introduction.

The course of philosophy in Germany since the time of Kant has been very remarkable, but is very difficult thoroughly to trace. The following are, however, the chief developments:—(1.) German Idealism advanced with very rapid strides. It is common to say that Fichte's subjective Idealism was followed by the objective Idealism of Schelling, and that by the absolute Idealism of Hegel. But such a description can convey no meaning to the ordinary reader. (2.) In reaction from this tendency was the modern German materialism, expounded by Moleschott, Vogt, and Buchner,—a modification of the ancient atomism, according to conceptions of modern science. (3.) A development of one side of Kant's philosophy was the Pessimism of Schopenhauer and Von Hartmann. According to the former of these the absolute existence which Kant held to be unknown is Will, whilst the latter lays the greatest stress upon the Unconscious. These thinkers are, however, better known for their theory of human life, of which both take a gloomy and despondent view (4) Herbart by no means accompanied the progress of the post-Kantian Idealists; he is characterised by Schwegler as 'extending the monadology of Leibnitz' (5.) Ulrici and Lotze may be taken as examples of German philosophers who hold by the spiritual interpretation of human nature.

V. *REVIEW OF THE PRESENT STATE OF BRITISH PHILOSOPHY.*

There has, during the last half century, been a marked revival of interest in philosophy, both in the national seats of learning and among the educated and reading public. Several causes have concurred to bring about this intellectual movement. Its commencement may be traced to Sir William Hamilton, whose lectures in the University of Edinburgh and whose contributions to the *Edinburgh Review* certainly excited a widespread interest both in the history of philosophy and in the investigation of metaphysical and logical problems. The amazing and brilliant progress made in many of the physical sciences acted in two ways It no doubt led to the concentration of many able minds upon strictly scientific study. Yet, on the other hand, it aroused a new interest in those deeper questions which no processes of observation and experiment have ever been able to solve or even to touch, and prompted speculation upon the foundations of our deepest and most permanent beliefs,—in our personal and spiritual existence, in the objective universe, in the being and providence of God. Another cause may be found in the 'Oxford revival,' which proved stimulative of historical research, but even more of independent thought upon themes of vital interest and of momentous and many-sided importance. Increased intercourse with the great literary nations of the Continent of Europe has, during the present century, established a fellowship of thought which has affected philosophy fully as much as other departments of mental activity German works, representing every school of thought—transcendental and empirical, pessimist, materialistic, and Christian,—have been translated into English, evidently in response to a not inconsiderable demand. America, too, sends us the writings of philosophical professors who are carrying on the movement which originated in Scotland, upon the principles of 'common sense,' and masterly and original treatises in exposition, expansion, and criticism of the distinctively English doctrine of Evolution elaborated by Wallace, Darwin, and Spencer. And our Indian and Colonial Empire asserts fellowship with the mother-country, not only in political and commercial relations, but in the less interested relations of philosophy. English students have cordially welcomed the handbooks of Professors Clark Murray and Jardine as evidence that the vigorous and independent thought characteristic of our countrymen bears transplanting to other and distant climes.

An unmistakable sign of increased interest in Philosophy is afforded by the space occupied in our periodical literature of the highest grade by the discussion of metaphysical and ethical as well as psychological questions. We have indeed no pretension to vie in this respect with France and Germany. And for many years the only philosophical review in our language was published in a Western city of the United States of America. Since, however, the appearance of *Mind* under the able editorship of Professor G. Croom Robertson, of University College, London, this reproach has been removed. And the quarterly, and more especially some of the monthly reviews, have freely admitted articles upon Philosophy, and articles of this class have often been the most prominent and attractive items in their contents.

There is among English students at the present time a tendency—which has, no doubt, been fostered over a large area by the Examinations of the University of London—to substitute Psychology for the broader study of Philosophy. The motive of this tendency is to be found in the agnosticism of the day, in a disposition to regard all ontology as futile, and all metaphysical problems as insoluble, and accordingly unworthy of human attention and energy. It is endeavoured to treat what was formerly called 'mental philosophy' as a branch of natural history—of anthropology—by the methods of observation and experiment, bringing to light and then classifying the phenomena which are expressive of the distinctively human nature and character. At the same time, the attempt is made to leave the existence of the mind an open question. This and other metaphysical data are relegated to another study, Philosophy proper, of which it is represented that Psychology is perfectly independent. Whilst it is impossible to treat Psychology without either asserting or presuming philosophical doctrines, it is quite possible to give attention mainly to those mental co-existences and sequences which are regarded as peculiarly scientific knowledge. And it is admitted that conclusions of interest and value have been reached by the method in question. The observations of Wundt (*Physiologische Psychologie*), of Waitz (*Lehrbuch der Psychologie*), of Volkmann (*Lehrbuch der Psychologie*) have been a rich mine to our English students of the natural history of perceptive and intellectual man. E. H. Weber's experiments upon the power of discriminating points by means of touch, and Fechner's law of the relation between stimulus and the corresponding sensation, have long been familiar to readers of our text-books. M. Taine's work on 'Intelligence' has been translated from the French, and as a manual of psychological facts, and of theories recommended by their originality as well as by the style in which they are expressed, has made for itself no ordinary position in literature of this class. And Mr. Sully has made a position as a psychologist by his works on 'Sensation and Intuition,' and on 'Illusions,' quite as much as by his more recent 'Outlines of Psychology.'

The advance which has in our time been made in the sciences of anatomy, physiology, and pathology, has naturally led to a closer study of the connection between mental processes upon the one hand, and changes in nerve and brain upon the other. No student of the human mind can do other than rejoice in the establishment of connections of this kind, however he may resent some of the conclusions which he may conceive to be unwarrantably deduced from the premises. Dr. W. B. Carpenter's 'Mental Physiology' is perhaps the most popular treatise on the subject which has appeared amongst us; but Dr. H. Maudsley's 'Physiology of Mind' also abounds with interesting facts. Dr. Ferrier's work, 'The Functions of the Brain,' in its successive editions, has rather offered material for theorisers than propounded particular doctrines. Dr. Calderwood, in his 'Relations of Mind and Brain,' has handled the facts with a view of exhibiting them in a light friendly to spiritual philosophy. Dr. Bastian's able work, 'The Brain as the Organ of Mind,' proceeds upon a purely physiological method, and regards mind, under which unconscious nervous action is included, as a function of the brain and nervous system. This may be fairly called materialism. The work in question contains a succinct, excellent, and classified account of those phenomena of lost memory of words popularly known under the designation, 'Aphasia.'

Perhaps the form of Philosophy just now most prevalent among general readers, as distinct from students, is evolutional agnosticism. Whilst the Psychologists simply profess to record and classify facts, and to abstain from all deliverances upon strictly philosophical questions, the Agnostics declare that we are incapable of knowing anything which lies outside of the realm of experience. The Positivists, or followers of Auguste Comte,—at all events those who follow him in his former, but not in his later steps,—reject all theology and metaphysics. Mr. Herbert Spencer, on the other hand, maintains that we are constrained to believe in the existence and action of the 'Unknowable,' as accounting for all things that are: subject and object, and God Himself, exist, but are unknown. He speaks of the unknown 'plexus' which unites together the qualities of body or matter known in experience, and the unknown 'plexus,' which conjoins our sensations, conceptions, &c., in the unity commonly designated mind. The facts of which we are conscious are in this philosophy represented as manifestations of the Unknowable. How anything knowable is to be known otherwise than by its manifestations we are not told, and probably most persons will be found content with such knowledge as manifestations afford, and will believe that of anything not manifested it is allowable to doubt its existence. In fact, however, the philosophy of Mr. Spencer is more interesting as evolutional than as agnostic; the positive element is more important than the negative. So far as it is philosophy, it consists in the higher generalisation of the conclusions of science. A law, of which no explanation is given, and which is not attributed to the wisdom of a Divine Intelligence, is represented as the ultimate principle or reason of all the processes of nature and of mind. No attempt is made to bridge the chasm between the material and the mental; Mr. Spencer is an ardent defender of realism, though he seems to misapprehend the rival theory of idealism. The dualism is postulated as the twofold manifestation of the Unknowable. But matter and mind alike are subject to the supreme law of evolution and dissolution. And in the comprehension beneath this rhythmic law of all the movements of bodies, animate as well as lifeless, of all the activities of mind, of all the forms and changes of society, the evolutionists find philosophy, which thus becomes the science of sciences, the *summum genus* of all knowledge.

Mr. G. H. Lewes, who wrote the 'Biographical History of Philosophy' in order to prove the vanity of philosophical studies, wrote five volumes, dealing with 'Problems of Life and Mind,' with a view to prove that psychology is simply a development of biology, and to exhibit what he termed the 'physical basis' of mind. This accomplished writer was under two chief influences, that of Comte in his earlier and scientific stage, and that of Darwin and Spencer,—the promulgators of the Evolution theory.

The chief American expositor of the philosophy of evolution is Mr. Fiske, who, however, is by no means, like his English master, an agnostic. The 'Cosmic Philosophy' may be regarded as the ablest illustration which has reached us from beyond the Atlantic of the hold which Evolution has taken upon scientific men.

It is in conformity with that rhythmic principle which appears so characteristic of the movements of the human intellect, that the extremes of physiological psychology and of evolutional agnosticism on the one hand, should evoke an opposite and contrary tendency on the other. As Professor Fraser has put it, we have Agnosticism and Gnosticism side by side, competing for the suffrages of the studious. Provoked by the complacent professions of human ignorance, some of the noblest and acutest minds in our generation have asserted our possession of absolute truth. The Rational Idealism of the English and Scottish post-Kantians or Hegelians is something utterly different from the subjective, yet theological, idealism of Berkeley, and still more so from the sensational idealism of Messrs. Mill and Bain, which, although lineally descended from Berkleianism, repudiates its theological implications, and attaches itself rather to the scepticism of David Hume. It may be traced, no doubt, to the absolute idealism of Hegel; yet it is a distinct type of philosophy, having special reference to English rather than to German antecedents, especially in its polemical aspects. The doctrines of Hume have been accepted by many of those English students of science who have interested themselves in the theory of knowledge. If Professor Huxley's work on Hume, and occasional utterances on philosophical questions, may be taken as a fair specimen, such students are quite unaffected by the revulsion from Hume's phenomenism and empiricism, which has been very general both in this country and upon the Continent of Europe It seems still to be supposed by some that knowledge consists of sensations unrelated except by a power of habit or association, that experience, in the most limited sense of that term, *i.e.*, impressions and their copies or images, constitute the whole of our intellectual possessions, and that belief in personality, human or Divine, is an effete superstition Our modern rational or idealist school set themselves to show the utter fallacy of this belief. The late Professor Green, in his Introduction to Hume's philosophical works, and in his posthumous 'Prolegomena to Ethics,' has shown, it may be said conclusively, that experience cannot account for that which alone makes experience possible,—the native and constitutive energy of mind itself; that intellectual relations, and not sense-impressions, are the constituents of reality. At the same time, he and others of the same school of thought have exhibited with great force the complete dependence of matter upon mind Their idealism is subversive not only of sensationalism, but also of that materialism which in varying aspects of inconsistency has exerted in our time so great an influence over the popular mind. This modern idealism has been cultivated, not only in the University of Oxford, where Professors Wallace and Green have familiarised the minds of the younger generation of philosophical students with Hegelianism in an English garb, but in the University of Glasgow, where Principal Caird and Professor Edward Caird have done much to counteract the popular sensationalism and empiricism. Before the time of these distinguished thinkers, much had been done to check sensationalism by the bold speculations and confident teaching of Professor Ferrier of St. Andrews Dr. Hutchison Stirling has the credit not only of being among the first to introduce the 'Secret of Hegel' to the British reader, but also of offering a conclusive reply to the somewhat flimsy materialism of the day. Professor Herbart's 'Realistic Assumptions of Men of Science Examined' contains closely reasoned and powerful argument, and has done good service in exposing some very prevalent and mischievous fallacies.

The extreme opinions above described are not, however, allowed to divide between them the field of philosophical thought. The Scottish school is not extinct,—the school which boasts that it proceeds upon the sober method of observation, and distrusts the *à priori* method of absolute idealism, whilst, at the same time, it contests the sensationalist empiricism which finds favour with not a few Englishmen of science Professor Fraser, of Edinburgh, the editor of 'Berkeley,' has, in his writings, rather criticised the work of others than propounded original doctrines of his own But he has given abundant evidence that his position is that of an advocate of spiritual philosophy. Good service has been rendered to intuitional morality and to non-materialistic psychology by Professor Calderwood. And Professor Seth has very ably vindicated the Scottish claim on behalf of Reid,—as having furnished a reply to Hume in some respects equal, if not superior, to the more scholastic criticism of the great sage of Königsberg.

Although Dr M'Cosh long ago transferred his services from Belfast to Princeton, he cannot be regarded as either Irish or American; he is, in his literary, religious, and philosophical affinities, a thorough Scot. His work on 'The Scottish Philosophy' is a proof of his wide and careful reading in the metaphysical literature of North Britain; he has explored even untrodden paths. In the course of his lengthened career, Dr. M'Cosh has not only vindicated the truths of natural religion, and assailed with vigour several forms of error which have met with a partial and temporary popularity; he has attempted, in his 'Intuitions of the Mind,' a work of philosophical constructiveness. Both by his polemical writings and by his text-books on 'Psychology' and 'The Emotions,' he has honourably maintained the reputation of the school in which he was trained, and which he has never deserted. Dr. Noah Porter, President of Yale College, occupies a somewhat similar philosophical position; his work has been less controversial, and in his 'Human Intellect' he has furnished a valuable contribution to the stores of psychological knowledge.

The position of Dr. Martineau is peculiar. Trained in the school of Hartley, Priestley, and Bentham, he came to break the fetters in which he had been early bound. Finding for himself the means of spiritual liberty, he led others into the joys of the same freedom. After his philosophical conversion, he ceased to carry into philosophy the inapplicable assumptions of physical science; and, abandoning the principle of determinism as inconsistent with the deliverances of the moral consciousness, he found the inappropriateness of physical law to the cognitive and æsthetic as well as to the moral side of life. 'The metaphysic of the world,' he says, 'had come home to me, and never again could I say that phenomena, in their clusters and chains, were all, or find myself in a universe with no categories but the like and unlike, the synchronous and successive. The possible also *is*, whether it happens or not; and its categories of the right, the beautiful, the necessarily true, may have their contents defined and held ready for realisation, whatever centuries lapse ere they appear. To do this is the work, not of objective science, but of self-reflection.' *

If Logic be regarded in the old and Aristotelian light, little need be said in explanation of its present position. Old text-books have been republished, and new text-books have been written, very much upon the old lines. Dean Mansel

* 'Types of Ethical Theory,' preface.

ably investigated the foundations of all reasoning in his 'Prolegomena Logica.' The most noticeable addition which has in recent times been made to the theory of Deductive Logic, is the doctrine of the Quantification of the predicate, discovered by Hamilton, and expounded by his pupil, Mr. T. Spencer Baynes, in his 'New Analytic of Logical Forms.' Professor De Morgan was also a discoverer of this doctrine. It was presented in the guise of new formulæ by Archbishop Thomson in his 'Laws of Thought.' This doctrine is not, however, generally regarded as anything more than a logical curiosity. The late Professor Stanley Jevons elucidated the regular and formal nature of the ordinary logic by his teaching, in the 'Substitution of Similars,' that all reasoning consists in the equivalence and interchangeability of terms; and even more strikingly by the mechanical contrivances, the logical abacus and the logical machine, by which conclusions are drawn from given premises with the same precision which distinguishes the operations of the calculating machines as applied to numbers.

In the Science of Inductive Logic great progress has been made through the learned labours of Whewell, Mill, and Jevons. Many definite laws have been established for the guidance of observers and investigators; and Induction is no longer guess-work,—is no longer at the mercy of empirics.

The present state of Moral Philosophy in Great Britain is, equally with that of Intellectual Philosophy, one of controversy between schools of thinkers divided upon fundamental questions. The questions raised by Ethics are many, and are mutually complicated:—What is the chief good? What the law of life? What the standard of right conduct? Does goodness lie in dispositions, or in actions? Do we judge of moral quality by reason, or do we pronounce upon it according to our feelings? Is the moral faculty or conscience a simple or a compound faculty? Is it capable of education, or not? Is it innate or acquired? Is it anything more than a reflection of external, *i.e.*, social or political authority? Is morality possible apart from religious belief, religious sanctions? Is pleasure the supreme test of the right? Is an excess of pleasure over pain within the general reach of human beings, or hopelessly beyond it? If pleasure cannot be enjoyed in a measure to compensate pain, is life worth living? Is morality to proceed upon the assumption that man is merely a sensitive organism, or upon the belief that he is the child of the Eternal Father? Is Christianity necessary to the full development of morals? Shall we accept the ethics of evolution, of naturalism; or shall we regard moral beings and moral law as above nature?

All these are vital questions, debated among our own countrymen and in our own day. It is an encouraging sign of the times that questions so profoundly affecting the highest life of man should be studied with eagerness and discussed with earnestness. There is a general conviction among students of Ethics that the connection is very close between moral philosophy and the foundations of religion. No doubt there are those who have no suspicion of the danger to religious convictions and a religious life which lurks in what have been called 'the ethics of naturalism.' But it is becoming growingly evident that there are two alternative theories of human nature and human life, which diverge from each other, and, proceeding in different directions, can never meet in reconciliation. Either man is a mere animal, with a higher organisation than other inhabitants of this earth, an animal whose larger range of susceptibility to pleasure and pain renders him more amenable to remoter impulses, in which case morality is merely a factor in evolution; or he has the prerogative of reason and conscience, and is responsible to a Divine Lawgiver in virtue of his voluntary constitution, in which case the phenomena of feeling are altogether subordinate, and his true life is interpreted by righteousness, by duty, and by love.

That modern variety of Hedonism, which is known as Utilitarianism, is largely maintained by the adherents of the empirical philosophy of our day. The bare, bald Hedonism of Bentham has been outgrown, but various qualifications and modifications of the doctrine have taken its place. Mr. Mill's Utilitarianism has met with much acceptance, as on the one hand based upon what seems to many the common sense doctrine of 'the greatest happiness of the greatest number,' and as on the other hand disclaiming Bentham's paradoxical doctrine that pleasures are to be estimated, not by their character, but only by their volume. Yet this last mentioned position of Mill is evidently inconsistent with pure Hedonism, whilst the test of 'greatest happiness' is evidently one difficult, if not utterly impossible, to apply. Various modifications of this universalistic Hedonism have been advocated by Mr. Sidgwick, by Mr. Leslie Stephen, and others. But the most interesting and scientific development of the principle is that of Mr. Herbert Spencer, termed by its author *Rational* Utilitarianism. Whereas Bentham and Mill propose to calculate the results of actions, and in this way to determine their rightness or wrongness, it is maintained by Mr. Spencer that such a method of proceeding is empirical rather than scientific, and that moral science must proceed upon a method which recognises the universality of causation. Accordingly, dealing with the question in his usual manner, upon the several planes—physical, biological, psychological, and sociological—Mr. Spencer seeks to establish the principle that evolution is the true test of morality, and that conduct is right so far as it promotes the 'complete living' of all in a perfectly developed condition of human society. His discussion of the relative importance of the two principles of 'egoism' and 'altruism' is of great interest; it is shown that neither can be dispensed with, except at the peril of dissolving society; yet on the whole Spencer depicts the future victory of 'altruism.' Among the paradoxes which it is endeavoured to establish in 'The Data of Ethics,' none is more remarkable than the prediction that evolution will be destructive of obligation; it is, however, only just to remember that, like Professor Bain, Mr. Spencer regards obligation as the product of that fear of punishment, from either earthly or heavenly authority, which seems so unreasonably exaggerated in importance by most of those who advocate the morality of consequences.

The 'Positivist' school have their ethical doctrine, and, generally speaking, may be said to have accepted the principle of their master, and to have applied that principle to individual and to national life. 'Live for others' is the moral motto, and 'Altruism' is the designation of the doctrine. It is evident that such a rule cannot be taken as absolute, although it is valuable as tempering human selfishness. It is obviously inferior to the Christian law of social life, 'Thou shalt love thy neighbour *as thyself*' A protest against selfishness is valuable; but the Positivist habit of representing Christianity as a religion of selfishness is so evidently uncandid, that the Positivists are perhaps not credited with such merit as really belongs to them. Their English leaders are known for many a brave protest against the rapacity and love of aggrandisement which are too characteristic of enterprising and vigorous nations.

Utilitarians are, however, by no means keeping the field of Moral Philosophy to themselves. Among the most vigorous opponents of the system may be mentioned the late Professor F D. Maurice, who, in his work on 'Conscience,' singled out Professor Bain's theory of moral obligation as peculiarly deserving of reprobation. According to Bain, Conscience is merely the effect of education and habit, consolidating the repeated fears awakened by threats and experiences of punishment into a principle of action and restraint; in a word, the mirror within of authority without, and authority inflicting punishment and arousing dread. The baseness of this view of man's moral nature is admirably and effectively exhibited by Maurice; and, so far as criticism and controversy are concerned, he carries the judgment of his readers with him. Who can help sympathising with a protest against a system which, if consistently carried out, resolves the highest impulses to virtue and heroism into the fear of punishment and suffering, and which utterly breaks down the distinction between Might and Right?

The more fundamental doctrine of Hedonism, its assertion that pleasure is the standard of morality, has been assailed with great force from various quarters. Not to mention such incidental assaults as that of Mr. Lecky in his 'History of European Morals,' we may refer to the learned and powerful refutation of Utilitarianism by the late Professor Grote, who has also elaborated a constructive system in his work on 'Moral Ideals.' He is opposed to the habit, necessary to the Hedonist position, of looking at morality in the view of results, as though something to be attained and enjoyed (*acquirendum*) were the matter of chief importance; he lays more stress upon the exercise of the powers (*faciendum*), and upon the ideal aim which is truly to consecrate and govern their use.

From the more modern standpoint of what is sometimes called 'Oxford Hegelianism,' Professors Green and Bradley have in their works shown a more excellent way than that adopted by Hedonistic schools. The radical difference between Mr Green and Mr Mill is that, according to the former, man is not a part of nature, but is a subject in whom the eternal consciousness reproduces itself, and as a knowing substance is a free cause. The will is neither intellect nor desire, nor both combined, but is the man himself, carrying his own self to realise the idea of its good. Green agrees with Kant in laying all stress upon a good will. The morally good, which for the Utilitarian is pleasure, is for the Idealist something at once less definite and more satisfactory. Individual perfection and social progress are represented as ideals present to a divine consciousness, reproduced more or less completely in the mind of the individual man. Moral goodness is devotion to the moral end or ideal. Green, like Martineau, lays more stress upon the motive than upon the result of an action as determining its moral quality; he denies that the effect can constitute moral goodness, but holds that, so far as the effect is considered, it is not pleasure so much as perfection that is to absorb our regard.

The whole question between the ethics of the ideal and the ethics of consequence is treated with great ability and knowledge by Mr Sorley in his 'Ethics of Naturalism,' in which are exhibited the unreasonableness and untenableness of the philosophy which regards man as a product of natural forces amenable to natural laws.

Dr. Martineau, as a moralist, stands very much apart. The theory which he sketched in his 'Essays' has been carefully wrought out in his later work, 'Types of Ethical Theory.' He is opposed to those who deem morality to lie in those results of actions which are of the nature of pleasure and pain. But instead of regarding man as endowed with a faculty of intuitively perceiving this action to be right, and that to be wrong, he regards man as deciding among motives in their various grades, and places virtue in the rejection of lower and the adoption of higher motives. On this account the system is known as the 'Preferential' theory of Ethics. The author has drawn up a scale of motives in regular ascending degree of dignity; and actions are estimated according as they are prompted by this desire or principle or by that. Justice consists in the preference and adoption of the higher rather than the lower motive.

The intuitional theory of morals has in our own time been defended by men of great learning and ability. Dr Whewell was a champion of the native powers of mind in both the cognitive and the ethical realms. In Scotland, Professor Calderwood has written a 'Handbook of Moral Philosophy,' which, though not altogether a model of lucid method, contains sound thinking and able discussion. It is an exposition of rational morality, *i.e.*, of the doctrine that the foundations of moral law are laid in the nature of things, in eternal and unchangeable relations, which must be discerned by the reason alone. This doctrine is opposed, not only to all forms of Hedonism, but also to the ethics of feeling or sentiment. The method of this philosophy is intuitional, the intellect being deemed capable of discerning immediately the relations and distinctions which obtain amongst moral actions, and between such actions and the laws to which they conform or which they violate. The Duke of Argyll, in his 'Unity of Nature,' has also vigorously upheld the independence of morality, and especially the 'idea, conception, or sentiment of obligation,' in which he discerns 'a meaning which is incapable of reduction.'

From the above review it appears that, at the present time, there are amongst us two distinct and opposed schools of ethics. On the one hand, we have the doctrine that man is a part of nature, that he is governed in his actions by motives which when analysed are simply modes of sensitiveness, *i.e.*, by pleasure and pain, that he is accordingly what he is, and does what he does, of necessity. On the other hand, we have the doctrine that man is a spiritual and rational being, capable of apprehending and reverencing Divine law, of accepting or rejecting motives, of realising his own independent personality, and consciously and voluntarily aiming at a moral ideal. This latter doctrine is no doubt differently represented, the difference being of a metaphysical order; the strictly Scottish school laying stress upon individuality, and the 'Hegelian' school somewhat merging that individuality in the universal and eternal consciousness. But from one quarter as much as from the other, a protest is raised against the so-called scientific doctrine that man is merely natural, and governed, like material objects, by mechanical and irresistible 'law.'

LIST OF PRINCIPAL WORKS QUOTED,

WITH THE EDITIONS REFERRED TO

(*Works quoted only once or twice are not, as a rule, inserted here*)

ADAMSON, ROBERT On the Philosophy of Kant. Edinburgh. 1879.
——— Fichte ('Blackwood's Philosophical Classics'). Edinburgh. 1881.
ALLEN, GRANT. Physiological Æsthetics. London. 1877.
ANCILLON. Essais Philosophiques.
ARTHUR, WILLIAM. On the Difference between Physical and Moral Law. London. 1884.
AUSTIN, JOHN. Lectures on Jurisprudence. London. 1869.

BACON, Lord. Works (Bohn's Library).
BAIN, A. Logic, Deductive and Inductive. London. 1870.
——— The Senses and the Intellect. London.
——— The Emotions and the Will. London. 1865.
——— Mental and Moral Science. London. 1884.
——— Mind and Body. London. 1874.
BARRY, ALFRED. The Manifold Witness for Christ. London. 1880.
BASTIAN, H. C. The Brain as an Organ of Mind. London. 1884.
BENTHAM, JEREMY. Introduction to the Principles of Morals and Legislation. Clarendon Press. 1879.
BERKELEY, Works of. Edited by A. C. Fraser. 4 vols. London. 1871.
BERNSTEIN, J. The Five Senses of Man. London. 1876.
BIRKS, T. R. First Principles of Moral Science. London. 1873.
BOWEN, F. Modern Philosophy. London. 1877.
BRADLEY, F. H. Ethical Studies. London. 1876.
BROWN, T. Lectures on Ethics. Edinburgh. 1846.
BÜCHNER, L. Force and Matter (translated by J. F. Collingwood). London. 1870.
BUNSEN, Baron. God in History (translated by S. Winkworth). 3 vols. London. 1868–1870.
BUTLER, JOSEPH. The Analogy of Religion and Sermons (Bohn's Standard Library). London.
———, SAMUEL. Reflections on Reason.

CAIRD, E. The Philosophy of Kant. Glasgow. 1877
——— Hegel. Edinburgh. 1883
CALDERWOOD, H. Philosophy of the Infinite. 1861.
——— Handbook of Moral Philosophy. London. 1881.
——— Relations of Mind and Brain. London. 1879.
CAPES, W. W. Stoicism. London. 1880.
CARPENTER, W. B. Principles of Mental Physiology. Fourth edition. London. 1876.
CHALLIS, JAMES. The Scriptural Doctrine of Immortality. London. 1880.
CHRISTLIEB, TH. Modern Doubt and Christian Belief. Fourth edition. Edinburgh. 1879.
COLERIDGE, S. T. The Friend. 3 vols. London. 1837.
——— Aids to Reflection. Sixth edition. London. 1848.
COMTE, AUG. Traité de la Législation. Paris.
——— Positive Philosophy (translated by Harriet Martineau). 2 vols. London. 1875.
——— System of Positive Polity (translated). 4 vols. London. 1875–7.
CONDER, E. R. The Basis of Faith. London.
COURTNEY, W. L. Studies in Philosophy. London. 1882.
COUSIN, V. History of Modern Philosophy (translated by Wright). 2 vols. New York. 1852.
——— Lectures on the True, the Beautiful, and the Good (translated). Edinburgh. 1854.
CRAWFORD, T. J. The Scripture Doctrine of the Atonement. Second edition. Edinburgh. 1874.
CROOKS and HURST. Theological Encyclopædia and Methodology. New York. 1884.

DALE, R. W. Lectures on Preaching. London. 1877.
DARWIN, C. The Expression of the Emotions in Man and Animals. London. 1872.
——— The Descent of Man. London. 1883.
DELITZSCH, F. System of Biblical Psychology. Second edition. Edinburgh. 1875.
DESCARTES. Method, Meditations, &c. (translated by Veitch). Edinburgh. 1881.
DICTIONARY of Christian Antiquities (Cheetham & Smith). 2 vols. London. 1875.

EDWARDS, JONATHAN. An Inquiry into the Prevailing Notions of the Freedom of the Will. London. 1855.
ELLICOTT, C. J. The Destiny of the Creature. Second edition. London. 1862.
ELY, R. T. French and German Socialism. New York. 1883.
ENCYCLOPÆDIA BRITANNICA. Ninth edition. Edinburgh.
EPICTETUS. Translated by George Long, Bohn's Classical Library. London. 1877.

FAIRBAIRN, A. M. The City of God. London. 1883.
FERRIER, DAVID. The Functions of the Brain. London. 1876.
———, JAMES F. Institutes of Metaphysics. Edinburgh. 1834.
FISKE, J. Outlines of Cosmic Philosophy. 2 vols. London. 1874.
FLEMING, W. The Vocabulary of Philosophy. Second edition. London. 1858.
FLINT, R. Anti-Theistic Theories. Edinburgh. 1879.
FOWLER, T. John Locke (English Men of Letters). London. 1880.

FOWLER, T. Shaftesbury and Hutcheson. London. 1882.
FRASER, A. C. Selections from Berkeley. Clarendon Press. 1874.

GALTON, F. Inquiries into Human Faculty. London. 1883.
GEORGE, H. Social Problems. London. 1884.
——— Progress and Poverty. London. 1884.
GODWIN, J. H. Active Principles. London. 1885.
GRANT, Sir A. The Ethics of Aristotle. London. 1885.
GREEN, T. H. Philosophical Works. 2 vols. London. 1885.
——— Prolegomena to Ethics. Oxford. 1883.
GROTE, GEORGE. Aristotle. London. 1880.
——— History of Greece. 12 vols. London. 1869.
———, JOHN. Examination of Utilitarian Philosophy. Cambridge. 1870.
——— Moral Ideals. Cambridge. 1876.

HALL, JOSEPH. Works. 10 vols. Pratt's edition. London. 1808.
HAMILTON, Sir W. Lectures on Metaphysics. 2 vols. Edinburgh. 1859.
——— Lectures on Logic. 2 vols. Edinburgh. 1860.
——— Discussions on Philosophy and Literature. London. 1852.
HARDY, R. S. Eastern Monachism. London. 1850.
HARTLEY, D. Observations on Man. Bath. 1810.
HARTMANN, E. VON. Philosophy of the Unconscious (English and Foreign Philosophical Library). 3 vols. London. 1884.
HAY, D. R. The Science of Beauty. London. 1856.
HEARD, J. B. The Tripartite Nature of Man. Fifth edition. Edinburgh. 1882.
HODGSON, SHADWORTH H. Time and Space. London. 1865.
HUME, D. Philosophical Works. Edited by T. H. Green and T. H. Grose. 4 vols. London. 1875.
HUTCHESON, F. System of Moral Philosophy. London. 1755.
HUXLEY, T. H. Hume (English Men of Letters). London. 1879.

IRONS, W. J. On the Whole Doctrine of Final Causes. London. 1836.
IVERACH, J. Is God Knowable? London. 1884.

JANET, P. Final Causes (translated). Edinburgh. 1883.
——— Theory of Morals (translated). Edinburgh. 1884.
JARDINE, R. Psychology of Cognition. London. 1884.
JEVONS, W. S. Lessons in Logic. Fourth edition. London. 1874.
——— The Principles of Science. Third edition. London. 1879.
JOUFFROY, T. S. Introduction to Ethics (translated). 1838.

KAMES, Lord HENRY H. Elements of Criticism. 2 vols. 1788.
KANT, EM. The Critique of Pure Reason (translated by Professor Max Müller, with Historical Introduction by Ludwig Noiré). London. 1881.
——— The Metaphysic of Ethics (edited by Dr. H. Calderwood). Edinburgh. 1871.
——— Theory of Ethics (translated by J. K. Abbott). London. 1883.
KILLICK, A. H. Student's Handbook to Mill's Logic. London. 1880.

LANGE. History of Materialism 3 vols (translated) London 1877–1881.
LAVELEYE, E DE. Socialism of To-day London. 1884.
LECKY, W. E H History of European Morals. 2 vols. Second edition London 1869
LEWES, G. H. History of Philosophy 2 vols London 1880
——— Comte's Philosophy of the Science (Bohn's Philosophical Library). London
——— Problems of Life and Mind London 1874–1879.
LIGHTFOOT, J B Epistle to the Philippians Second edition London 1869.
LOCKE, JOHN. Philosophical Works. 2 vols Bohn's edition 1877
LOTZE, R. H Microcosmus. 2 vols. (translated). Edinburgh. 1885.
LUTHARDT, C E The Fundamental Truths of Christianity. Edinburgh. 1873
——— The Moral Truths of Christianity Edinburgh 1873.

MACKINTOSH, JAMES Dissertation on the Progress of Ethical Philosophy. Edinburgh 1833
MAINE, Sir H S Ancient Law. London 1861
MAITLAND, BROWNLOW. Theism, or Apostiocism. London. 1878
MALEBRANCHE Traité de Morale
MANSEL, H. L. The Limits of Religious Thought Examined Second edition. London 1858.
——— Prolegomena Logica Second edition Oxford. 1860.
——— Metaphysics Second edition Edinburgh 1866
MARTENSEN, H Christian Ethics 3 vols Edinburgh. 1873–1882.
MARTINEAU, JAMES Types of Ethical Theory 2 vols. London. 1866.
——— A Study of Spinoza London 1883
——— Modern Materialism London 1876
MASSON, D Recent British Philosophy. London. 1877.
MAUDSLEY, H Physiology of Mind London
MAURICE, F D. Moral and Metaphysical Philosophy 2 vols London. 1873
——— The Conscience London. 1868
——— Life. By his son London. 1884
M'COSH, J The Intuitions of the Mind Third edition London 1882
——— The Method of Divine Government. Edinburgh 1850
——— The Emotions London 1880.
——— An Examination of Mr. J S Mill's Philosophy London 1866
MILL, JAMES Analysis of the Human Mind. Second edition. 1871
MILL, J. S. A System of Logic 2 vols Sixth edition London 1865
——— Utilitarianism Seventh edition London 1879.
——— An Examination of Sir W. Hamilton's Philosophy Third edition London 1867.
MONCK, W H S Sir W Hamilton (English Philosophers) London 1881.
MORELL, J. D. An Historical and Critical View of the Speculative Philosophy of Europe in the Nineteenth Century Second edition London. 1847
——— An Introduction to Mental Philosophy on the Inductive Method. London. 1862
MÜLLER, J. The Christian Doctrine of Sin Edinburgh. 1877.
MURPHY, J G The Human Mind Belfast 1882
MURRAY, J CLARK. Handbook of Psychology. London. 1885.

PICTON, J. A The Mystery of Matter London 1873

POLLOCK, F Spinoza. London 1880.
POPE, W. B. Compendium of Christian Theology. 3 vols. Second edition. London 1877.
PORTER, NOAH. The Human Intellect. London. 1872.
——— Agnosticism. London 1882
PUSEY, E B. The Minor Prophets. Oxford. 1869.

RAE, J. Contemporary Socialism. London 1884.
RAMSAY, G. Analysis and Theory of Emotions. Edinburgh. 1848.
REID, T. Words edited by Sir W. Hamilton. Edinburgh 1863.
RIBOT, TH Contemporary English Psychology. London 1873.
——— Diseases of Memory. London 1882.
RUSKIN, J Modern Painters. 5 vols. 1851–1860
——— The Seven Lamps of Architecture. 1849
RYLAND, J. Students' Handbook of Psychology and Ethics. London 1882.

SANDERSON, R. Lectures on Conscience and Human Law. Wordsworth's edition. London 1877
SCHOPENHAUER, A. The World as Will and Idea (English and Foreign Philosophical Library). 3 vols London 1883–1886.
SCHWEGLER, ALBERT History of Philosophy. Translated by Stirling. Edinburgh 1868.
SIDGWICK, H The Methods of Ethics Second edition. London. 1877
——— Outlines of the History of Ethics. London. 1886
SMITH, ADAM. Theory of Moral Sentiments Bohn's edition London.
SMITH, SYDNEY. Sketches of Moral Philosophy. London. 1866.
SPENCER, HERBERT First Principles London 1884
——— The Principles of Psychology 2 vols Third edition. London. 1881.
——— The Data of Ethics Second edition. London. 1879.
——— Sociology. Third edition. London. 1885
STEPHEN, LESLIE. The Science of Ethics. London 1882.
STEWART, D. Works. Sir W Hamilton's edition. Edinburgh. 1855.
STIRLING, J H. The Secret of Hegel 1885.
——— As Regards Protoplasm Edinburgh and London 1869.
SULLY, J. Outlines of Psychology. Second edition. London. 1885.
——— Pessimism London. 1877.
——— Illusions (International Scientific Series) London. 1881.

TAINE, H. On Intelligence (translated by T. D Haye). London 1871.
TAYLOR, ISAAC Elements of Thought. 1833
TAYLOR, JEREMY. Works 10 vols. Eden's edition. London. 1864.
TENNEMANN. Manual of the History of Philosophy (Bohn's Philosophical Library) London 1852
THOMSON, WM. An Outline of the Necessary Laws of Thought London. 1864.

UEBERWEG, F. History of Philosophy 2 vols. London 1880
——— System of Logic and History of Logical Doctrine London 1871

VAUGHAN, R. A. Hours with the Mystics. Third edition London.
VÉRON, EUGÈNE. Æsthetics (Armstrong's translation). London. 1879.

WACE, H. Christianity and Morality. Fourth edition. London. 1878.
WALLACE, W. Logic of Hegel. 1874.
——— Epicureanism. London. 1880.
WARD, W. G. On Nature and Grace. London 1860.
WESTCOTT, B. F. The Gospel of the Resurrection. London. 1879.
WHATELY, R. Elements of Logic. Ninth edition. London. 1865.
——— Elements of Rhetoric. Seventh edition. London 1865.
WHEWELL, WM. The Elements of Morality. Fourth edition Cambridge. 1864.
——— The Philosophy of Discovery. 1860.
——— The Philosophy of the Inductive Sciences 2 vols. 1840.
WILBERFORCE, R. J. The Doctrine of the Holy Eucharist. London. 1853.
WYLD, R. S. The Physics and Philosophy of the Senses. London 1875.

ZELLER, E. History of the Greek Philosophy from the Earliest Period to the Time of Socrates (translated). London. 1881.

DICTIONARY OF PHILOSOPHY.

I.

DESIGNATIONS, DEFINITIONS, AND DIVISIONS.

I. PHILOSOPHY

Etymological Definition.

Philosophy is a term of Greek origin—a compound of φίλος, a *lover* or *friend*, and σοφια, *wisdom*—speculative wisdom. Philosophy is thus, literally, *a love of wisdom.*—*Hamilton*, '*Metaphysics*,' i. 45.

General Definitions.

Ancient.

In Greek antiquity there were in all six definitions of philosophy which obtained celebrity.

The first of these definitions of philosophy is, 'the knowledge of things existent, as existent.'

The second is, 'the knowledge of things divine and human.' These are both from the object matter; and both were referred to Pythagoras.

The third and fourth, the two definitions of philosophy from its end, are, again, both taken from Plato. Of these the third is, 'philosophy is a meditation of death;' the fourth, 'philosophy is a resembling of the Deity in so far as that is competent to man.'

The fifth, that from its pre-eminence, was borrowed from Aristotle, and defined philosophy, 'the art of arts, and science of sciences.'

Finally, the sixth, that from the etymology, was, like the first and second, carried up to Pythagoras;—it defined philosophy 'the love of wisdom.'—*Hamilton*, '*Metaphysics*,' i. 51, 52.

Modern.

Philosophy is the science of principles.—*Ueberweg*, '*Hist. of Phil.*,' i. 1.

The knowledge of effects as dependent on their causes.—*Hamilton*, '*Metaphysics*,' i. 58.

Philosophy is reflection, the thinking consideration of things.—*Schwegler*, '*Hist. of Phil.*,' p. 1.

Philosophy is the attainment of truth *by the way of reason.*—*Ferrier*, '*Institutes of Metaphysics*,' p. 2.

It is *the systematisation of the conceptions furnished by science.* It is ἐπιστήμη ἐπιστημῶν. As science is the systematisation of the various generalities reached through particulars, so philosophy is the systematisation of the generalities of generalities. In other words, Science furnishes the Knowledge, and Philosophy the Doctrine.—*Lewes*, '*Hist of Phil.*,' Proleg. xviii.

Philosophy is the explanation of the phenomena of the universe.—*Comte*, '*Philosophy of the Sciences*,' p. 18.

Philosophy is *completely unified* knowledge.—*Spencer*, '*First Principles*,' p. 134.

Theoretical and Moral Philosophy Distinguished.

The object of one is to answer the question, What conditions on the part of consciousness are implied in the fact that there is such a thing as knowledge, or that a 'cosmos' arises in consciousness? Of the other to answer the question, What are the conditions on the part of consciousness implied in the fact that there is such a thing as morality?—*Green, 'Philosophical Works,'* ii 84.

Objects and Divisions of Philosophy.

Science does not include its own end, but is pure knowledge, whose end is something external to itself, while philosophy is carried on for the sake of the learning and knowing alone which it involves —*Hodgson, 'Time and Space,'* p. 13

Philosophy has three objects, viz, God, nature, and man; as also three kinds of rays—for nature strikes the human intellect with a direct ray, God with a refracted ray, from the inequality of the medium betwixt the Creator and the creatures, and man, as exhibited to himself, with a reflected ray, whence it is proper to divide philosophy into the doctrine of the Deity, the doctrine of nature, and the doctrine of man —*Bacon, 'Adv. of Learn,'* bk iii ch i.

The whole of philosophy is the answer to these three questions: 1. What are the facts or phenomena to be observed? 2 What are the laws which regulate these facts, or under which these phenomena appear? 3 What are the real results, not immediately manifested, which these facts or phenomena warrant us in drawing?—*Hamilton, 'Metaphysics,'* i. 121.

II PSYCHOLOGY.

Nature of the Science.

Definition and Explication.

Psychology, strictly so denominated, is the science conversant about the phenomena, or modifications, or states of the mind. The term is of Greek compound, signifying discourse or doctrine treating of the human mind —*Hamilton, 'Metaphysics,'* i. 129, 130

Psychology is the analysis and classification of the *sentient functions and faculties*, revealed to observation and induction, completed by the reduction of them to their *conditions of existence*, biological or sociological —*Lewes, 'Problems of Life and Mind,'* third series, i 6.

Psychology is the science of the human soul. The appellation is of comparatively recent use by English writers, but has been familiar in its Latin and German equivalents—*Psychologia* and *Psychologie*—to writers on the Continent for more than two centuries It is now generally accepted and approved among us as the most appropriate term to denote the scientific knowledge of the whole soul, as distinguished from a single class of its endowments or functions The terms in frequent use—*mental philosophy, the philosophy of the mind, intellectual philosophy,* &c.—can be properly applied only to the power of the soul to know, and should never be used for its capacity to feel and to will, or for all its endowments collectively.—*Porter, 'Human Intellect,'* p 5

An Old Study.

The name may be new, but the study is old It is recommended in the saying ascribed to Socrates—"Know thyself." The recommendation is renewed in the *Cogito ergo sum* of Descartes; and in the writings of Malebranche, Arnauld, Leibnitz, Locke, Berkeley, Hume, psychological inquiries held a prominent place Still further prominence was given to them by the followers of Kant and Reid, and psychology, instead of being treated as an introduction to logic, to ethics, and to metaphysics, which all rest upon it, is now treated as a separate department of science.—*Fleming, 'Vocab. of Phil.,'* p 411.

Materials of it.

The facts or materials with which psychology has to do are derived from two sources — consciousness and sense-perception. Consciousness is the source from which these materials are directly derived, and it is the facts of consciousness which psychology primarily and almost exclusively seeks to arrange in a scientific method and to explain by scientific principles But, indirectly, sense-perception comes to the aid and support of consciousness, as physiology furnishes that knowledge of the functions and states of the body which prepare the objects of the sense-perceptions, and are the essential conditions of the development and the activity of the soul. The facts of this class are attested by the senses and interpreted by induction, and are in all respects subject to the laws and methods of the other sciences of matter. Both these classes of facts must be considered in conjunction, must be observed with attention, must be analysed into their ultimate elements, must be compared, classed, and interpreted according to the methods which are common to it and the other inductive sciences.—*Porter*, '*Human Intellect*,' p. 51, 52.

Method of Psychological Study.

As there is an anatomy of the body, so there is an anatomy of the mind. The psychologist dissects mental phenomena into elementary states of consciousness, as the anatomist resolves limbs into tissues, and tissues into cells. The one traces the development of complex organs from simple rudiments, the other follows the building up of complex conceptions out of simpler constituents of thought. As the physiologist inquires into the way in which the so-called 'functions' of the body are performed, so the psychologist studies the so-called 'faculties' of the mind. Even a cursory attention to the ways and works of the lower animals suggests a comparative anatomy and physiology of the mind; and the doctrine of evolution presses for application as much in the one field as in the other.—*Huxley*, '*Hume*,' p. 50.

Division into two Parts.

The psychology of the human mind consists of two parts, which have not been sufficiently distinguished. There is first of all what may be called Abstract Psychology, which establishes the final classification of mental phenomena, and formulates the general laws of their sequence and combination as observable in the course of individual mental development, and with the assistance of direct subjective reflection. Secondly, subordinate to this first, there is the department of Concrete Psychology, which discusses the growth of specific and individual varieties of idea and emotion, applying the general laws of mental change to certain orders of elementary facts and their combinations. Under this branch there should fall the discussion of all such subjects as the origin of the belief in the external world, and the processes by which the moral sentiments and other emotions reach their present forms.—*Sully*, '*Sensation*,' &c., pp. 11, 12.

Psychology has been divided into two parts—1. The *empirical*, having for its object the phenomena of consciousness and the faculties by which they are produced. 2. The *rational*, having for its object the nature or substance of the soul, its spirituality, immutability, &c.—*Fleming*, '*Vocab. of Phil.*,' p. 413.

Its Province.

There are three things to which the psychologist may successively attend—1. To the phenomena of consciousness. 2. To the faculties to which they may be referred. 3. To the Ego, that is, the soul or mind in its unity, individuality, and personality. These three things are inseparable; and the consideration of them belongs to psychology.—*Fleming*, '*Vocab. of Phil.*,' p. 413.

Psychology inquires into the operations of the mind of man, with the view of discovering its laws and its faculties. The founder of this science is undoubtedly Aristotle in ancient times. Locke may be described as its second founder in modern times. It is a science throughout of facts and the co-ordination of facts. As a whole, it has made a gradual progress since its origin in Greece, and its second rise in the seventeenth century.—*M'Cosh*, '*Intuitions of the Mind*,' p. 356.

Relation of Psychology to

PHYSIOLOGY.

Psychology is the science of mind. This science may seek—and I follow those who think it *ought* to seek—important means of investigation in the laws of physiology; just as physiology itself must seek important aids in chemistry and physics. But as an independent branch of inquiry, its results cannot be amenable to physiological canons; their validity cannot be decided by agreement or disagreement with physiological laws. To cite an example: Psychology announces that the mind has different faculties. That fact seems established on ample evidence, and is valid in psychology, although hitherto no *corresponding* fact in physiology has been discovered.—*Lewes*, '*Physiology of Common Life*,' i 2, 3

There is a close and intimate connection between psychology and physiology No one doubts that, at any rate, some mental states are dependent for their existence on the performance of the functions of particular bodily organs There is no seeing without eyes, no hearing without ears. If the origin of the contents of the mind is truly a philosophical problem, then the philosopher who attempts to deal with that problem, without acquainting himself with the physiology of sensation, has no more intelligent conception of his business than the physiologist who thinks he can discuss locomotion without acquaintance with the principles of mechanics, or respiration without some tincture of chemistry—*Huxley*, '*Hume*,' p. 50.

The fields of inquiry belonging to physiology and psychology are so related, that neither science can adequately interpret its own facts without reference to the other Those phenomena of consciousness known as sensation and perception expressly require physiological aid for their explanation. And the physiology of nerve and brain needs no less the testimony of consciousness in order to interpret ascertained facts In one respect the pathology of nerve and brain comes even more closely into contact with psychology, as all diseased or disordered action of physical organism throws in upon consciousness forms of experience otherwise unknown. This holds true in the widest and most important sense of the brain, which is distinctively the organ of mind or self. All the facts connected with a disordered brain are thus fitted to cast important light on the action of mind as related to the action of brain Hence the peculiar value to mental philosophy of all scientific investigation as to the experience of the insane.—*Calderwood*, '*Moral Philosophy*,' p. 10, 11.

Life and the functions of our organised body belong to physiology; and, although there is a close connection between soul and body, and mutual action and reaction between them, that is no reason why the two departments of inquiry should be confounded, unless to those who think the soul to be the product or result of bodily organisation. Broussais said he could not understand those philosophers who shut their eyes and ears in order to hear themselves think But if the capacity of thinking be anterior to, and independent of, sense and bodily organs, then the soul which thinks, and its faculties or powers of thinking, deserve a separate consideration.—*Fleming*, '*Vocab of Phil.*,' p. 412.

LOGIC.

Logic throws us back on psychology, and on an inductive psychology, not indeed to justify the laws of thought, but to discover them Not that psychology and logic are identical, or that they should be mixed up with one another. Psychology, in treating of the operations of the mind generally, will meet with thought, and will seek by classification to discover the faculties of thought, and these are specially the comparative or correlative powers. It will seek even to discover in a general way the laws involved in thought. But when it has gone so far in this direction, it will stop. It does not make a very minute analysis of these laws, it does not seek to present them in all possible forms, it does not make an application of them to discursive investigation. It leaves this to logic as its special province.—*M'Cosh*, '*Intuitions of the Mind*,' p. 358.

METAPHYSICS.

Does psychology tend to separate itself from metaphysics? Instead of deciding this question, I prefer to place certain facts before the reader. In the seventeenth century the science of the soul was called metaphysics. There is no other word in Descartes, Malebranche, and Leibnitz. Locke and Condillac employ the same language. Nevertheless, the word psychology, invented by the obscure Goclenius, was used by Wolf as the title of a work. The Encyclopædists, while continuing to use the term metaphysics, limited its sense. The Scotch employ it with reserve, and prefer the expression 'philosophy of the human mind.' In short, the word psychology is coming into current use, and is common in France, Germany, and England. It may be further observed, that in the two last-named countries psychology is cultivated as an independent science, and expurgated of metaphysics.—*Ribot*, '*English Psychology*,' p. 23.

Psychology must have metaphysical assumptions.—Psychology, like every science, like physics, chemistry, physiology, contains ultimate, transcendental questions,—questions of principles, of causes, of substances. What is the soul? Whence does it come? Whither is it going? These are purely philosophical discussions.—*Ribot*, '*English Psychology*,' p. 15.

ETHICS.

In the intellectual department of mental science, psychology deals with the facts of our experience belonging to morals, as with all the facts of consciousness, but simply to determine their nature as mental facts. In the ethical department of mental science, psychology ascertains the nature of mental facts only as a preliminary step for determining their moral significance.

The psychology of ethics is completed only by constructing a philosophy of all that belongs to our personality as moral beings. Each characteristic must be looked at, not only apart, but also in relation to other features of our moral nature. 'The value of every ethical system must ultimately be tested on psychological grounds,' Mansel's *Prolegomena*, Pref.—*Calderwood*, '*Moral Philosophy*,' p. 16.

THE PRACTICAL SCIENCES.

All the practical sciences which aim at guiding or influencing our thoughts, feelings, or actions, have their footing in psychology. Thus the principles of oratory, of legislation, and so on, are based on a knowledge of the properties and laws of the human mind. These relations may be roughly set forth as follows:—

(A.) Psychology, as a whole, supplies the basis of education, or the practical science which aims at cultivating the mind on the side of Knowing, Feeling, and Willing alike.

(B.) In its special branches, psychology supplies a basis to the following practical sciences:—

Psychology of Knowing.—Logic, or the regulation of reasoning processes; together with the allied arts, rhetoric, or the art of persuasion, and that of forming opinion.

Psychology of Feeling.—Æsthetics, or the regulation of feeling according to certain rules or principles—to wit, the admirable or beautiful.

Psychology of Willing.—Ethics, or the determination of the ends of action and the regulation of conduct by principles of right and wrong, together with the allied arts of politics and legislation.—*Sully*, '*Outlines of Psychology*,' pp. 15, 16.

How Psychology may be affected by the Evolution Theory.

First of all, it leads one to view all successive manifestations of individual mind as one continuous phenomenon, and to seek for the antecedent of any habit or emotion just as easily in the psychical life of some remote parental race, as in the experiences and impressions of the same individual development. And, secondly, the evolutionist, instead of carrying on *pari passu* the process of subjective observation, and that of objective inquiry into the visible actions of other minds and the nervous conditions of their intelligence, has to confine his researches through a large part of his field to the objective side of the phenomena, the appeal to subjective knowledge being clearly precluded in dealing with the ideas and feelings of the lower animals.—*Sully*, '*Sensation*,' &c., p. 1

III. LOGIC.

Various names which have been given to it.

(*a.*) It has been called the Architectonic Art, by which is meant that it occupies the same position with regard to the sciences and arts in general that architecture does to the labours of the carpenter, the mason, the pavior, the plumber, and the glazier. (*b.*) By the followers of Aristotle it was called the Instrument (or Organon) and the Instrument of Instruments. Other names which establish the pre-eminence of Logic over the real sciences are (*c.*) the Art of Arts, (*d.*) the System of Systems, (*e.*) the Key of Wisdom, (*f.*) the Head and Crown of Philosophy. As it offers rules for seeking after truth, it has been called (*g.*) Zetetic, or the Art of Seeking; as these rules are not given in vain, we may regard it also as (*h.*) Heuristic, or the Art of Discovering Truth. As it cures the mind of prejudice and errors, it is called (*i.*) *Medicina mentis*, and (*k.*) the Cathartic of the Mind. As teaching the right use of the faculties in the discussion of any question, it is called (*l.*) Dialectic.—*From Thomson's* '*Laws of Thought*,' pp. 54–57.

Definitions of Logic.

The Art of Reasoning.—*Aldrich.*

The Science and Art of Reasoning.—*Whately.*

The Science of the Laws of Thought as Thought.—*Hamilton.*

The Science which expounds the operations of the Intellect in its pursuit of Truth. —*Mill.*

The Science of the Laws of Thought.—*Thomson*, following *Kant.*

The Science of the regulative Laws of human knowledge.—*Ueberweg.*

The Science of Reasoning.—*Jevons.*

1. Inference.

Defined.

Inference in the widest sense is the derivation of a judgment from any given elements.—*Ueberweg*, '*Logic*,' p. 225.

We are said to infer whenever we draw one truth from another, or pass from one proposition to another.—*Jevons*, '*Logic*,' p. 81.

To infer is nothing but by virtue of one proposition laid down as true, to draw in another as true, *i.e.*, to see or suppose such a connexion of the two ideas of the inferred proposition. Tell a country gentlewoman that the wind is south-west, and the weather lowering and like to rain, and she will easily understand it is not safe for her to go abroad thin clad in such a day, after a fever; she clearly sees the probable connexion of all these, viz., south-west wind, and clouds, rain, wetting, taking cold, relapse, and danger of death.—*Locke*, '*Human Understanding*,' bk. iv. ch. xvii. § 4.

Various Views.

Inference indicates the carrying out into the last proposition what was virtually contained in the antecedent judgments.—*Hamilton*, '*Logic*,' i. 279.

The question, What is Inference? is involved, even to the present day, in as much uncertainty as that ancient question, What is Truth? Inference never does more than explicate, unfold, or develop the information contained in certain premises or facts. Neither in deductive nor inductive reasoning can we add a tittle to our implicit knowledge, which is like that contained in an unread book or a sealed letter.—*Jevons*, '*Principles of Science*,' p. 118.

Most of the propositions, whether affirmative or negative, universal, particular, or singular, which we believe, are not believed on their own evidence, but on the ground of something previously assented to, from which they are said to be *inferred*. To infer a proposition from a previous proposition or propositions; to give credence to it, or claim credence for it, as a conclusion from something else; is to *reason*, in the most extensive sense of the term. There is a narrower sense, in which the same reasoning is confined to the form of inference which is termed ratiocination, and of which the syllogism is the general type.

In some cases the inference is apparent, not real. This occurs when the proposition ostensibly inferred from another appears on analysis to be merely a repetition of the same, or part of the same, assertion which was contained in the first.—*Mill*, '*Logic*,' i. 178 *sq*.

An inference is a proposition which is perceived to be true, because of its connection with some known fact. There are many things and events which are always found together, or which constantly follow each other, therefore, when we observe one of these things or events we *infer* that the other also exists, or has existed, or will soon take place. If we see the prints of human feet on the sands of an unknown coast, we infer that the country is inhabited; if these prints appear to be fresh and also below the level of high water, we infer that the inhabitants are at no great distance; if the prints are those of naked feet, we infer that these inhabitants are savages; or if they are the prints of shoes, we infer that they are in some degree civilised.—*Taylor*, '*Elements of Thought*.'

Forms of Inference

Mediate and Immediate

Derivation from a single notion or from a single judgment is Immediate Inference, or immediate consequence. Derivation from at least two judgments is Mediate Inference, or inference in the stricter sense. —*Ueberweg*, '*Logic*,' p. 225.

In some cases we are unable to decide that the terms of the question agree with or differ from one another, without finding a third, called the middle term, with which each of the others may be compared in turn. This is Mediate Inference. If one suspects that 'this liquid is poison,' it may be impossible to convert the suspicion into certainty, until one has found that 'it contains arsenic;' 'containing arsenic' will then be the middle term, which will be compared in a judgment with each of the others in turn, and the whole argument will run, 'This liquid contains arsenic, and everything that contains arsenic is poisonous; consequently this liquid is.'

But sometimes, instead of a third term, differing entirely from the other two, the premise only need contain the two terms of the conclusion, or some modification of them. Thus, from 'All good rulers are just,' we infer that 'No unjust rulers can be good,' a judgment introducing, indeed, no new *matter*, *i.e.*, making us acquainted with no new facts, but still distinct from that from which we drew it. This is Immediate Inference.—*Thomson*, '*Laws of Thought*,' p. 145 *sq*.

Inductive and Deductive

Inference, according to Aristotle, has two forms, the syllogism, which descends from the universal to the particular, and induction, which rises to the universal from a comparison of the single and particular.—*Ueberweg*, '*Hist. of Phil.*,' i. 152.

The Great Rule of Inference.

The fundamental action of our reasoning faculties consists in inferring or carrying to a new instance of a phenomenon whatever we have previously known of its like, analogue, equivalent, or equal. Sameness or identity presents itself in all degrees, and is known under various names, but the great rule of inference embraces all degrees, and affirms that so far as there exists sameness, identity, or likeness, what is true of one thing will be true of the other—*Jevons*, '*Principles of Science*,' p. 9.

Distinguished from Proof.

He who infers proves, and he who proves infers; but the word 'infer' fixes the mind *first* on the premiss and then on the conclusion; the word 'prove,' on the contrary, leads the mind *from* the conclusion to the premiss. Inferring and proving are not two different things, but the same thing regarded in two different points of view; like the road from London to York, and the road from York to London. One might, therefore, define Proving, 'the assigning of a reason or argument for the support of a *given* proposition,' and Inferring, 'the deduction of a Conclusion from *given* Premises.'—*Whately*, '*Logic*,' p. 173.

2. DEDUCTION.

The Process. (See INDUCTION.)

Deduction is the process of deriving facts from laws, and effects from their causes, *e.g.*, if from the general principle that all bodies tend to fall towards the earth, we argue that the stone we throw from our hands will show the same tendency, we deduce.—*Thomson*, '*Laws of Thought*,' p. 216.

Deduction is reasoning from the whole to its parts.—*Hamilton*, '*Metaphysics*,' ii 338.

In deduction we are engaged in developing the consequences of a law. We learn the meaning, contents, results, or inferences which attach to any given proposition.—*Jevons*, '*Principles of Science*,' p. 11.

In Deduction there is the application of a general proposition to a particular case coming under it. The following is a deduction:—'All arsenic is poison; now this substance is arsenic, therefore this substance is poison.' In other words, Deduction is the application or extension of Induction to *new cases*. By the help of the inductive methods we are satisfied that 'iron is a magnetic substance,' and we apply the proposition, as occasion requires, to individual specimens of iron. It is the deductive process that has been developed into the forms of the syllogism.—*Bain*, '*Logic, Deduction*,' pp. 17, 40.

The General Problem of Deduction.

This may be stated as follows:—From one or more propositions called premises to draw such other propositions as will necessarily be true when the premises are true. By deduction we investigate and unfold the information contained in the premises.—*Jevons*, '*Principles of Science*,' p. 49.

The Axiom of Deduction.

The Axiom or First Principle at the basis of Deduction is expressed in a variety of forms, which are reducible substantially to two:—

(1.) Whatever is true of a whole class is true of what can be brought under the class.

(2.) Things co-existing with the same thing co-exist with one another.

The first form is the one suitable to the exposition of the syllogism. The second form can be shown to be equivalent to the first.—*Bain*, '*Logic, Deduction*,' p. 18.

The Deductive Method.

The full scope of the Deductive Method comprises three operations:—

1. There must be certain pre-established Inductions. [See INDUCTION, last section.]

2. Deduction proper, which involves two stages of complexity, (*a*.) The simple extension of an inductive law to a new case, and (*b*.) The combination of several laws in a conjoint result, involving processes of computation. Supposing that the inductive proposition, 'all matter gravitates,' has been formed upon solids and liquids, shall we apply it to gases? This depends upon whether gases are matter. If they possess the properties of matter the proposition is extended to them. The more difficult em-

ployment of Deduction is in the concurrence of different agents to a combined result, as when we deduce the path of a projectile from gravity, the force of projection, and the resistance of the air, or the tides from the united action of the sun and the moon.

3. The Deductive process is completed by verification. This is done by actual observation of cases. In Astronomy, verification has been most thoroughly worked. Upwards of fifty observatories are incessantly engaged in watching celestial phenomena. —*Bain*, '*Logic, Induction*,' pp 95–101.

The Results of Deduction.

We must by no means suppose that, when a scientific truth is in our possession, all its consequences will be foreseen. Deduction is certain and infallible, in the sense that each step in deductive reasoning will lead us to some result, as certain as the law itself. But it does not follow that deduction will lead the reasoner to every result of a law, or combination of laws. Whatever road a traveller takes he is sure to arrive somewhere, but unless he proceeds in a systematic manner it is unlikely that he will reach every place to which a network of roads will conduct him. Many phenomena were never discovered until accident or systematic empirical observation disclosed their existence —*Jevons*, '*Principles of Science*,' p. 534.

3. INDUCTION.

What it is and is not.

Defined.

Induction is the inference from the individual or special to the universal.—*Ueberweg*, '*Logic*,' p 476.

Induction is the arriving at general propositions by means of observation or fact. In an induction, there are three essentials :—(1) The result must be a *proposition*—an affirmation of concurrence or non-concurrence—as opposed to a notion (2) The proposition must be *general*, or applicable to all cases of a given kind (3.) The method must be an appeal to *observation* or fact.—*Bain*, '*Logic, Induction*,' p. 1.

Induction may be defined as the operation of discovering and proving general propositions. Induction, therefore, is that operation of the mind by which we infer that what we know to be true in a particular case or cases, will be true in all cases which resemble the former in certain assignable respects. In other words, induction is the process by which we conclude that what is true of certain individuals of a class is true of the whole class, or that what is true at certain times will be true in similar circumstances at all times.—*Mill*, '*Logic*,' i. 316, 321.

Induction is the mental operation by which, from a number of individual instances, we arrive at a general law.—*Monck*, '*Sir W. Hamilton*,' p. 181.

It is a synthetic process.

Having discovered by observation and comparison that certain objects agree in certain respects, we generalise the qualities in which they coincide,—that is, from a certain number of individual instances we infer a general law; we perform an act of induction. This induction is erroneously viewed as analytic; it is purely a synthetic process —*Hamilton*, '*Metaphysics*,' i. 101.

'Inductions improperly so called.'

Induction, as above defined, is a process of inference. it proceeds from the known to the unknown; and any operation involving no inference, any process in which what seems the conclusion is no wider than the premises from which it is drawn, does not fall within the meaning of the term. Yet in the common books of logic we find this laid down as the most perfect, indeed the only quite perfect, form of induction. If we were to say, All the planets shine by the sun's light, from observation of each separate planet, or All the Apostles were Jews, because this is true of Peter, Paul, John, and every other apostle,—these, and such as these, would, in the phraseology in question, be called perfect, and the only perfect, induction This, however, is a totally different kind of induction from ours, it is not an inference from facts known to facts unknown, but a mere short-hand registration of facts known —*Mill*, '*Logic*,' i 321

On this point there is great difference of opinion Sir W Hamilton held that 'the process of induction is only logically valid when all the instances included in the law are enumerated' See below on 'perfect and imperfect induction'

The Doctrine of Induction as held by various Philosophers

First introduced by Socrates

We read in the *Metaphysics* of Aristotle (xiii. 4) that Socrates introduced the method of induction and definition (which sets out from the individual and ends in the definition of the general notion) The field of investigation in which Socrates employed this method is designated by Aristotle as the ethical These statements are fully confirmed by Plato and Xenophon —*Ueberweg*, '*Hist of Phil*,' i. 85

Inductive Method of Socrates

Proceeding from some concrete case, the philosopher contrived, ever comparing particular with particular, and so gradually separating and casting out what was contingent and accidental, to bring to consciousness a universal truth, a universal discernment, that is, to *form notions* (universals) To find, for example, the notion of justice, of fortitude, departure was taken from several particular examples of justice, of fortitude, and from them the universal *nature*, the notion of these virtues, was abstracted [This is induction only in a very limited sense, *i.e*, the generalisation of notions]—*Schuegler*, '*Hist of Phil*,' p 50

Aristotle

In induction we conclude from the observation that a more general concept includes (several or) all of the individuals included under another concept of inferior extension, that the former concept is a predicate of the latter Induction leads from the particular to the universal The Greek term for induction suggests the ranging of particular cases together in files, like troops. The complete induction is the only strictly scientific induction.—*Ueberweg*, '*Hist of Phil*,' i. 156.

Bacon.

That induction which Aristotle and the scholastics taught, Bacon describes as *inductio per enumerationem simplicem*; and adds that it lacks the methodical character (which Bacon himself rather seeks than really attains). Together with the positive instances, the negative instances must be considered, and differences of degree should be marked and defined; cases of decisive importance are as prerogative instances to receive special attention; from the particular we should not at once hurry on, as if on wings, to the most general, but should advance first to the intermediate propositions, those of inferior generality, which are the most fruitful of all. The theory of induction was materially advanced by Bacon, although not completely and purely developed —*Ueberweg*, '*Hist of Phil*,' ii 38

The essential part of the service rendered by Bacon to science was his protest in favour of basing generalities on a patient collection and accurate comparison of facts —*Bain*, '*Logic, Induction*,' p. 403.

Whewell

Induction is not the same thing as experience and observation. Induction is experience or observation *consciously* looked at in a *general* form This consciousness and generality are necessary parts of that knowledge which is science —'*Philosophy of Discovery*,' p. 245

According to Whewell, the business of the discoverer, after familiarising himself with facts, is to compare them with conception after conception, in the view of finding out, after a longer or shorter process of trial and rejection, what conception is exactly 'appropriate' to the facts under his consideration When the investigator has at length, by a happy guess, hit upon the appropriate conception, he is said to 'colligate' the facts, to 'bind them into a unity.'—*Bain*, '*Logic Induction*,' p. 411.

John Stuart Mill. (See p 9, '*Inductions improperly so called.*')

Stanley Jevons.

Induction is the inverse operation of deduction, and cannot be conceived to exist without the corresponding operation The truths to be ascertained are more general than the data from which they are drawn. Given events obeying certain unknown laws, we have to discover the laws obeyed Induction is the deciphering of the hidden meaning of natural phenomena. Any laws being supposed, we can, with ease and certainty, decide whether the phenomena obey those laws. But the laws which may exist are infinite in variety, so that the chances are immensely against mere random guessing The only modes of discovery consist either in exhaustively trying a great number of supposed laws, a process which is exhaustive in more senses than one, or else in carefully contemplating the effects, endeavouring to remember cases in which like effects followed from known laws In whatever manner we accomplish the discovery, it must be done by the more or less conscious application of the direct process of deduction —'*Principles of Science*,' pp. 121, 125.

The Ground of Induction.

The statement of this varies as one or other doctrine of induction is held. According to—

Mill.

There is an assumption involved in every case of induction This is an assumption with regard to the course of nature and the order of the universe, namely, that there are such things in nature as parallel cases; that what happens once, will, under a sufficient degree of similarity of circumstances, happen again, and not only again, but as often as the same circumstances recur. If we consult the actual course of nature, we find that the assumption is warranted.—'*Logic*,' i. 343

Fleming

This principle is involved in the words of the wise man, 'the thing that hath been, it is that which shall be; and that which is done, is that which shall be done' (Eccles. i 9). In nature there is nothing insulated The same effects produce the same causes. —'*Vocab. of Phil.*,' p 254.

Bain.

Hence the sole evidence for inductive truths is universal agreement. What is found true wherever we have been able to carry our observations, is to be accepted as universally true, until exceptions are discovered —'*Logic, Induction*,' p. 7.

The great foundation of all possible inference is stated in many forms of language. 'Nature repeats itself,' 'the future will resemble the past,' 'the universe is governed by laws,' 'the uniformity of nature is the ultimate major premise of every inductive inference'—'*Logic, Induction*,' p. 8.

Stanley Jevons.

I hold that in all cases of inductive inference we must invent hypotheses, until we fall upon some hypothesis which yields deductive results in accordance with experience We can only argue from the past to the future, on the general principle that what is true of a thing will be true of the like. So far then as one object or event differs from another, all inference is impossible; particulars as particulars can no more make an inference than grains of sand can make a rope We must always rise to something which is general or same in the cases.—'*Principles of Science*,' p. 228.

Some writers have asserted that there is a principle called the uniformity of nature, which enables us to affirm that what has often been found to be true of anything will continue to be found true of the same sort of thing. If there be such a principle it is liable to exceptions. Thus there was a wide and unbroken induction tending to show that all the satellites in the planetary system went in one uniform direction round their planets. Nevertheless, the satellites of Uranus when discovered were found to move in a *retrograde* direction, or in an opposite direction to all satellites previously known, and the same peculiarity attaches to the satellite of Neptune more lately discovered.—'*Logic*,' p. 217.

The Conditions of Legitimate Induction.

Two at least are requisite.

1. In the first place, it is necessary, That the particular judgments out of which the total or general judgment is inferred be all of the same quality. For if one even of the particular judgments had an opposite quality, the whole induction would be subverted. For example, the general assertion, All dogs bark, is refuted by the instance of the dogs of Labrador or California (I forget which),—these do not bark.

2. The second condition required is, That a competent number of the individual objects from which the induction departs should have been observed, for otherwise the comprehension of other objects under the total judgment would be rash. What is the number of such objects which amounts to a competent induction, it is not possible to say in general. In some cases the observation of a very few particular or individual examples is sufficient to warrant an assertion in regard to the whole class; in others, the total judgment is hardly competent until our observation has gone through each of its constituent parts.—*Hamilton*, '*Logic*,' ii. 168 *sq.*

J. S. Mill's Canons of Inductive Method.

The Method of Agreement.

1. If two or more instances of the phenomenon under investigation have only one circumstance in common, the circumstance in which alone all the instances agree, is the cause (or effect) of the given phenomenon.

The Method of Difference.

2. If an instance in which the phenomenon under investigation occurs, and an instance in which it does not occur, have every circumstance in common save one, that one occurring only in the former; the circumstance in which alone the two instances differ, is the effect, or the cause, or an indispensable part of the cause, of the phenomenon.

The Indirect Method of Difference or the Joint Method of Agreement and Difference.

3. If two or more instances in which the phenomenon occurs have only one circumstance in common, while two or more instances in which it does not occur have nothing in common save the absence of that circumstance; the circumstance in which alone the two sets of instances differ, is the effect, or the cause, or an indispensable part of the cause, of the phenomenon.

The Method of Residues.

4. Subduct from any phenomenon such part as is known by previous inductions to be the effect of certain antecedents, and the residue of the phenomenon is the effect of the remaining antecedents.

The Method of Concomitant Variations.

5. Whatever phenomenon varies in any manner whenever another phenomenon varies in some particular manner, is either a cause or an effect of that phenomenon, or is connected with it through some fact of causation.—'*Logic*,' bk. iii. ch. viii.

The Use of Induction.

It is engaged in detecting the general laws or uniformities, the relations of cause and effect, or in short all the general truths that may be asserted concerning the numberless and very diverse events that take place in the natural world around us. The greater part, if not, as some philosophers think, the whole of our knowledge, is ultimately due to inductive reasoning.—*Jevons, 'Logic,'* p. 212.

In a certain sense all knowledge is inductive. We can only learn the laws and relations of things in nature by observing those things. But the knowledge gained from the senses is knowledge only of particular facts, and we require some process of reasoning by which we may collect out of the facts the laws obeyed by them. Experience gives us the materials of knowledge; induction digests those materials, and yields us general knowledge.—*Jevons, 'Principles of Science,'* p. 11.

"Perfect" and "Imperfect" Induction.

An induction is called *perfect* when all the possible cases or instances, to which the conclusion can refer, have been examined and enumerated in the premises. If, as usually happens, it is impossible to examine all cases, since they may occur at future times or in distant parts of the earth or other regions of the universe, the induction is called *imperfect*. The assertion that all the months of the year are of less length than thirty-two days is derived from perfect induction, and is a certain conclusion because the calendar is a human institution, so that we know beyond doubt how many months there are, and can readily ascertain that each of them is less than thirty-two days in length. But the assertion that all the planets move in one direction round the sun, from west to east, is derived from imperfect induction; for it is possible that there exists planets more distant than the most distant-known planet, Neptune, and to such a planet of course the assertion would apply.—*Jevons, 'Logic,'* p. 212, 213.

The Problem of Inductive Logic.

Why is a single instance, in some cases, sufficient for a complete induction, while in others, myriads of concurring instances, without a single exception known or presumed, go such a very little way towards establishing a universal proposition? Whoever can answer this question knows more of the philosophy of logic than the wisest of the ancients, and has solved the problem of induction.—*Mill, 'Logic,'* i. 352.

How the Certainty of an Imperfect Induction may be Estimated.

Four Rules.

Induction is more certain (1) in proportion to the number and diversity of the objects observed; (2) in proportion to the accuracy with which the observation and comparison have been conducted; (3) in proportion as the agreement of the objects is clear and precise; (4) in proportion as it has been thoroughly explored, whether there exist exceptions or not.—*Esser, 'Logik,'* § 152.

By a Calculation of Probabilities.

Our inferences always retain more or less of a hypothetical character, and are so far open to doubt. Only in proportion as our induction approximates to the character of perfect induction, does it approximate to certainty. The amount of uncertainty corresponds to the probability that other objects than those examined may exist and falsify our inferences; the amount of probability corresponds to the amount of information yielded by our examination; and the theory of probability will be needed to prevent us from over-estimating or under-estimating the knowledge we possess.—*Jevons, 'Principles of Science,'* p. 229.

Induction and Deduction Compared.

Induction is the process of discovering laws from facts, and causes from effects; and deduction that of deriving facts from laws, and effects from their causes.—*Thomson, 'Laws of Thought,'* p. 215.

Deduction consists in passing from more general to less general truths; induction is the contrary process from less to more general truths. In deduction we are engaged in developing the consequences of a law Induction is the exactly inverse process. Given certain results or consequences, we are required to discover the general law from which they flow.—*Jevons*, '*Principles of Science*,' p 11

Note.—The limits of this work do not admit of a detailed treatment of logic.

IV METAPHYSICS—ONTOLOGY.

The name metaphysics is a creation of the Aristotelian commentators. Plato's word for it was dialectics, and Aristotle uses instead of it the phrase 'first (fundamental) philosophy.' The relation of this first philosophy to the other sciences is defined by Aristotle as follows. Every science, he says, selects for investigation a special sphere, a particular species of being, but none of them applies itself to the notion of being as such. There is a science necessary, therefore, which shall make an object of inquiry on its own account, of that which the other sciences accept from experience, and, as it were, hypothetically. This is the office of the first philosophy, which occupies itself, therefore, with being as being, whereas the other sciences have to do with special concrete being. Metaphysics constituting, then, as this science of being and its elementary grounds, a presupposition for the other disciplines, are, naturally, *first* philosophy.—*Schwegler*, '*Hist. of Phil.*,' p. 98.

Changes in Meaning

Among the various changes which the language of philosophy has undergone in the gradual progress of human knowledge, there is none more remarkable than the different significations which, in ancient and modern times, have been assigned to the term metaphysics,—a term at first sight almost equally indefinite in its etymological signification and in its actual use. As given to the writings on first philosophy, by Aristotle, it signifies nothing more than the fact of something else having preceded. The title, thus indefinite in its etymological signification, does not at first sight appear to admit of more precision with reference to its actual application. Dugald Stewart notices 'the extraordinary change which has gradually and insensibly taken place, since the publication of Locke's *Essay*, in the meaning of the word *metaphysics*,—a word formerly appropriated to the ontology and pneumatology of the schools, but now understood as equally applicable to all those inquiries which have for their object to trace the various branches of human knowledge to their first principles in the constitution of our nature.'—*Mansel*, '*Metaphysics*,' pp 1–3 (abridged).

Nature of the Science

Definition and Division.

Metaphysics is the science which inquires into the original or intuitive convictions of the mind, with the view of generalising and expressing them, and also of determining what are the objects revealed by them.—*M'Cosh*, '*Intuitions of the Mind*,' p. 320

The term metaphysics has been at different times used in two principal senses: (1.) As synonymous with ontology, to denote that branch of philosophy which investigates the nature and properties of *Being* or *Reality*, as distinguished from *phenomenon* or *appearance*. (2.) As synonymous with psychology, to denote that branch of philosophy which investigates the *faculties, operations, and laws of the human mind.* These two sciences may be regarded as investigations of the same problem from opposite points of view. Metaphysics will thus naturally divide itself into two branches,—*Psychology*, or the science of the facts of consciousness as such; and *Ontology*, or the science of the same facts considered in their relation to realities existing without the mind.—*Mansel*, '*Metaphysics*,' pp. 23, 26.

Pure metaphysics or ontology is the knowledge of being in its universal principles.—*Fraser*, '*Selections*,' &c., p. 7.

The science which considers what is universal in the objects of all the sciences.—*Trendelenburg*

The humorous yet profound definition of Professor De Morgan may be added: 'The science to which ignorance goes to learn its knowledge, and knowledge to learn its ignorance. On which all men agree that it is the key, but no two upon how it is to be put into the lock.'—'*Memoirs of Augustus De Morgan*.'

The division of Wolff and Kant

Wolff divides metaphysics into ontology, which treats of the existent in general; rational psychology, which treats of the soul as a simple, non-extended substance; cosmology, which treats of the world as a whole, and rational theology, which treats of the existence and attributes of God.—*Ueberweg*, '*Hist. of Phil.*,' ii. 116

The whole system of metaphysic consists of four principal parts:—(1) Ontology; (2) Rational Physiology; (3) Rational Cosmology; (4) Rational Theology.—*Kant*, '*Critique of Reason*,' ii. 727.

In the Wolfian school, which proposed to systematise the scattered philosophy of Leibnitz, metaphysics was asked to deal with three grand topics,—God, the world, and the soul,—and should aim to construct a rational theology, a rational physics, and a rational psychology. Kant takes up this view of metaphysics, but labours to show that the speculative reason cannot construct any one of these three sciences. The only available metaphysics, according to him, is a criticism of the reason, unfolding its *à priori* elements. He arrives at the conclusion that all the operations of the speculative reason are mere subjective exercises, which imply no objective reality, and admit of no application to things; and he saves himself from scepticism by a criticism of the practical reason which guarantees the existence of God, freedom, and immortality.

In the schools which ramified from Kant, metaphysics is represented as being a systematic search after the absolute,—after absolute being, its nature, and its method of development.—*M'Cosh*, '*Intuitions of the Mind*,' p. 317, 318.

The Problem of Metaphysics

The problem of metaphysics, as conceived by Plato and Aristotle, may be perhaps clearly stated in modern language as follows: 'To determine the relation that exists between the subjective necessities of thought and the objective necessities of things.' In mathematical demonstration, for example, we start from certain axiomatic principles, of which, as mathematicians, we can give no other account than that they are *self-evident*; that is to say, we are compelled by the constitution of our minds to admit them. But this opens a further question. What is the relation of self-evidence to reality? Is the necessity, of which I am conscious, of thinking in a certain manner, any sure guarantee of a corresponding relation in the objects about which I think? In other words, are the laws of thought also laws of things; or, at least, do they furnish evidence by which the laws of things can be ascertained? Is thought *identical* with being, so that every mode of the one is at the same time a mode of the other? Is thought an exact *copy* of being, so that every mode of the one is an adequate representative of some corresponding mode of the other? Or, finally, is thought altogether *distinct* from being, so that we cannot issue from the circle of our ideas, to seize the realities which those ideas are supposed to represent? Does anything exist beyond the phenomena of our own consciousness? and if it does exist, what is the path by which it is to be reached?—*Mansel*, '*Metaphysics*,' p. 12, 13.

The Province of Metaphysics

Metaphysics is a collection of truths outside and above all demonstration, because they are the foundation of all demonstration; it is negatively determined by the collective action of all the sciences, which eliminate everything that outruns them.—*Ribot*, '*English Psychology*,' p. 12.

The province allotted to metaphysics is quite a defined one. It is not the science of all truth, but it is the science of an important department,—it is the science of fundamental truth It should not venture to ascertain the nature of all knowledge, divine and human; it should be satisfied if it can find what are the original knowing powers of man. It should not pretend to settle the nature of all being, or the whole nature of any one being, but it would try to find what we can know of certain kinds of being by intuition It should not presume to discover all causes,—which are to be discovered only partially by all the sciences,—but it should expound the nature of our original conviction regarding causation. It should not start with the absolute, and thence derive all dependent existence; but it is competent to prove that our convictions, aided by obvious facts, lead us to believe in an Infinite Being. It has a field in which it is perfectly competent to discover truth The body of truth thus reached constitutes, in a special sense, philosophy; and 'philosophical' is an epithet which may be applied to every inquiry which reaches it in the last resort, or which begins with it and uses it.—*M'Cosh*, '*Intuitions*,' p. 321.

Metaphysics is the substitution of true ideas—that is, of necessary truths of reason —in the place of the oversights of popular opinion and the errors of psychological science.—*Ferrier*, '*Institutes*,' p. 34.

Relation to Psychology.

Metaphysics evolves the original conceptions which appear in all science, and the ultimate relations which are assumed in the language and inquiries of all the special philosophies But what are these original conceptions, these prime relations, these categories, of which every particular assertion and every actual belief is only a special exemplification? Psychology only can answer, as, by her analysis, she shows that man performs processes and achieves results in which he necessarily originates and applies these conceptions and relations By studying the mind we discover the laws by which both mind and matter can be studied aright. By studying the mind we unveil and evolve the necessary conceptions and primary beliefs by which the mind itself interprets, or under which it views the universe of matter and spirit It is then through psychology that we reach the very sciences to which psychology itself is subject and amenable. Psychology is the starting-point from which we proceed. Psychology is also the goal to which we must return, if we retrace the path along which science has led us. In synthesis we begin, in analysis we end, with this mother of all the sciences.—*Porter*, '*Human Intellect*,' p. 15.

Doctrine of Being.—Ontology.

Every man is cognisant of absolute existence when he knows—himself and the objects by which he is surrounded, or the thoughts or feelings by which he is visited; every man is ignorant (in the strict sense of having no experience) of all absolute existence except this—his own individual case. But a man is not ignorant of all absolute existences except himself and his own presentations, in the sense of having no conception of them He can conceive them as conceivable, that is to say, as non-contradictory. He has given to him, in his own case, the type or pattern by means of which he can conceive other cases of absolute existence. Hence he can affirm, with the fullest assurance, that he is surrounded by absolute existences constituted like himself, although it is impossible that he can ever know them as they know themselves, or as he knows himself.—*Ferrier*, '*Institutes*,' pp. 508, 509

Absolute existence is the synthesis of the subject and object—the union of the universal and the particular—the concretion of the ego and non-ego; in other words, the only true, and real, and independent existences are minds together with that which they apprehend.—*Ferrier*, '*Institutes*,' p. 500.

Ontological Proof of the Existence of God.

All absolute existences are contingent *except one*, in other words, there is One, but only one, Absolute Existence which is strictly *necessary*; and that existence is a supreme, and infinite, and eternal Mind in synthesis with all things

In the judgment of reason there never can have been a time when the universe was without God *That* is unintelligible to reason; because time is not time, but is nonsense, without a mind; space is not space, but is nonsense, without a mind; all objects are not objects, but are nonsense, without a mind, in short, the whole universe is neither anything nor nothing, but is the sheer contradictory, without a mind. And, therefore, inasmuch as we cannot help thinking that there was a time before man existed, and that there was space before man existed, and that the universe was something or other before man existed; so neither can we not help thinking that, before man existed, a supreme and eternal intelligence existed, in synthesis with all things.—*Ferrier*, '*Institutes*,' pp. 511, 512.

Value of the Study of Metaphysics

In regard to other departments of knowledge.

The difficulties of metaphysics lie at the root of all science; those difficulties can only be quieted by being resolved, and until they are resolved, positively whenever possible, but at any rate negatively, we are never assured that any human knowledge, even physical, stands on solid foundations. —*Mill*, '*Examination of Hamilton*,' p 2

When people in general regard metaphysics as a curious puzzle, in which arguers give reasons for things which have nothing to do with nature or common sense, but entirely belong to an artificial speciality created by an understanding among themselves, they should be reminded sometimes of the fact that everybody is a metaphysician, and cannot help being one. Metaphysics could not possibly have had any existence except there had been some great leading ideas in man's mind upon the foundation of which they had arisen Thus, take the first idea of this class that occurs to one—the idea of infinity. This is a metaphysical idea; it arises out of our own minds, it is not a copy from nature, as many images in our minds are We never saw any object or extent that was infinite; it would be a contradiction to say that we had Is this metaphysical idea an idea without reality, without interest? On the contrary, it is an idea which appeals vividly to our imagination; it is an actual attribute of this material world. Everybody then is a metaphysician, just as everybody is a poet. —*Mozley, in* '*Faith and Free Thought*,' pp. 2–4

In Theology.

Metaphysics, without entering theology, may lend it some aid

1. It may show that the difficulties and mysteries which meet us in theology are the same as those which come up in metaphysics, being those which arise from the limitation of our faculties and the imperfection of our knowledge 'No difficulty,' says Sir W. Hamilton, 'emerges in theology, which has not previously emerged in philosophy.' The difficulties of revealed religion chiefly congregate round the doctrines of the Trinity, of the decrees of God, and original sin Metaphysics are competent to demonstrate that no man can deliver himself from these difficulties by fleeing from Christianity to what may be represented as a rational theism.

2. Metaphysics may furnish not a few evidences in favour of Christianity. Thus it supplies the main elements in the proof of those great doctrines which the Word of God presupposes, such as the existence of

the infinity and unity of God, and the immortality of the soul, and a judgment-day—truths very much lost sight of in heathenism, and the prominence given to which in the Jewish Scriptures is a proof of their being divinely inspired. All works of natural theology, properly constructed, have a tendency to strengthen the foundations of Christianity. In particular, the inductive investigation of the moral faculty in man may yield a number of evidences in favour of the divine origin of our religion.

3. Metaphysics can give a philosophic method and manner to the treatment of theological topics.—*M'Cosh, 'Intuitions of the Mind,'* pp. 467–470.

II.

MIND.

I. MIND.

The Noblest Object of Study.

Considered in itself, a knowledge of the human mind, whether we regard its speculative or its practical importance, is confessedly of all studies the highest and the most interesting. 'On earth,' says an ancient philosopher, 'there is nothing great but man; in man there is nothing great but mind.' No other study fills and satisfies the soul like the study of itself. No other science presents an object to be compared in dignity, in absolute or in relative value, to that which human consciousness furnishes to its own contemplation. What is of all things the best, asked Chilon of the Oracle. 'To know thyself,' was the response. This is, in fact, the only science in which all are always interested, for while each individual may have his favourite occupation, it still remains true of the species that

'The proper study of mankind is man.'

—*Hamilton, 'Metaphysics,'* i. 24.

Various Definitions of Mind.

The Scottish School.

Mind can be defined only from its manifestations. What it is in itself, that is, apart from its manifestations,—we philosophically know nothing, and, accordingly, what we mean by mind is simply that which perceives, thinks, feels, wills, desires, &c.—*Hamilton, 'Metaphysics,'* i. 157.

By the mind of a man, we understand that in him which thinks, remembers, reasons, wills. The essence both of body and of mind is unknown to us.—*Reid, 'Works,'* p. 220.

The Idealists.

Besides all the endless variety of ideas or objects of knowledge, there is likewise something which knows or perceives them and exercises divers operations, as willing, imagining, remembering, about them. This perceiving, active being is what I call *mind, spirit, soul* or *myself*. By which words I do not denote any one of my ideas, but a thing entirely distinct from them, wherein they exist, or, which is the same thing, whereby they are perceived—for the existence of an idea consists in being perceived. —*Berkeley, 'Principles of Human Knowledge,'* Part I. 2.

The Empirical and Associational School.

What we call a mind is nothing but a heap or collection of different perceptions, united together by certain relations, and supposed, though falsely, to be endowed with a perfect simplicity and identity.—*Hume, 'Works,'* i. 495.

My mind is but a series of feelings, or, as it has been called, a thread of consciousness, however supplemented by believed possibilities of consciousness which are not, though they might be, realised.—*Mill, 'Examination of Hamilton,'* p. 236

If mind, as commonly happens, is put for the sum total of subject-experiences, we may define it negatively by a single fact—the absence of extension. But as object-experience is also in a sense mental, the only account of mind strictly admissible in scientific psychology consists in specifying three properties or functions—feeling, will or volition, and thought or intellect—through which all our experience, as well objective as subjective, is built up. This positive enumeration is what must stand for a definition.—*Bain, 'Mental Science,'* pp. 1, 2.

Classifications of the Mind.

Aristotle.

Soul is to organised body as form to matter, as actualiser to the potential; not similar or homogeneous, but correlative; the two being only separable as distinct logical points of view in regard to one and the same integer or individual. Aristotle recognises many different varieties of soul, or rather many distinct functions of the same soul, from the lowest or most universal to the highest or most peculiar and privileged, but the higher functions presuppose or depend upon the lower as conditions, while the same principle of relativity pervades them all. 'The soul is in a certain way all existent things, for all of them are either perceivables or cogitables, and the cogitant soul is in a certain way the matters cogitated, while the percipient soul is in a certain way the matters perceived.' The percipient and its *percepta*—the cogitant and its *cogitata*—each implies and correlates with the other: the percipient is the highest form of all *percepta*, the cogitant is the form of forms, or the highest of all forms, cogitable or perceivable. The percipient or cogitant subject is thus conceived only in relation to the objects perceived or cogitated, while these objects again are presented as essentially correlative to the subject. The realities of nature are particulars, exhibiting form and matter in one, though for purposes of scientific study—of assimilation and distinction—it is necessary to consider each of the two abstractedly from the other.—*Grote's 'Aristotle,'* pp. 493, 494.

Thomas Aquinas.

I. Powers preceding the Intellect.
   1. Vegetative: (*a*) Nutrition; (*b*) Growth; (*c*) Generation. 2. External senses—five. 3. Internal senses: (*a*) Common sense; (*b*) Imagination; (*c*) Memory (including Reminiscence).

II. The Intellect.
   1. Memory (the retention or conservation of *species*). 2. Reason. 3. Intelligentia. 4. Practical and speculative reason. 5. Conscience.

Gassendi.

I. Sense.
II. Phantasy.
III. Intellect. 1. Apprehension. 2. Reflection. 3. Reasoning.

Thomas Reid.

I. Intellectual Powers.
   1. External senses. 2. Memory. 3. Conception. 4. Abstraction. 5. Judgment. 6. Reasoning. 7. Taste.

II. Active Powers.
   1. Mechanical principles of action: (*a*) Instinct; (*b*) Habit. 2. Animal principles: (*a*) Appetites; (*b*) Desires; (*c*) Affections. 3. Rational principles: (*a*) Self-love; (*b*) Duty.

Dugald Stewart.

I. Intellectual Powers.
   1. Consciousness. 2. External perception. 3. Attention. 4. Conception. 5. Abstraction. 6. Association of ideas. 7. Memory. 8. Imagination. 9. Reasoning.

II. Active Powers.
1. Instinctive principles of action: (a.) Appetites; (b.) Desires; (c.) Affections. 2. Rational and governing principles of action: (a.) Prudence; (b.) Moral Faculty; (c.) Decency; (d.) Sympathy; (e.) The ridiculous; (f) Taste.

Thomas Brown.

I. External Affections.
1. Sensation. 2. Organic states.

II. Internal Affections.
1. Intellectual states. 2. Emotions.

Sir W. Hamilton.

I. Phenomena of our cognitive faculties, or faculties of knowledge.

II. Phenomena of our feelings, or of pleasure and pain.

III. Phenomena of our conative powers, or of will and desire.

Alexander Bain.

I. The Senses.
1. Muscular feelings. 2. Sensation. 3. Appetites. 4. Instincts.

II. The Intellect.
Primary attributes are—1. Difference. 2. Agreement. 3. Retentiveness.

III. The Emotions.
1. Novelty, surprise, wonder. 2. Terror. 3. Love, admiration, reverence, esteem. 4. Self-complacency. 5. Power. 6. Anger. 7. Plot-interest. 8. Sympathy.

IV. The Will.
1. Voluntary power. 2. Self control. 3. Motives. 4. Deliberation, resolution, effort. 5. Desire. 6. Belief. 7. Moral habits. 8. Prudence, duty. 9. Liberty and necessity.

These divisions are formal for purposes of study.

Although we divide the soul into several powers and faculties there is no such division in the soul itself, since it is the *whole soul* that remembers, understands, wills, or imagines. Our manner of considering the memory, understanding, will, imagination, and the like faculties, is for the better enabling us to express ourselves in such abstracted subjects of speculation, not that there is any such division in the soul itself. —*Addison*, '*Spectator*,' No. 600.

Connection of Mind and Body. (See also 'MATERIALISM,' Sec. xiii. 8.)

Mutual dependence.

Mind and body constitute a unity in the life of a single person. They are not independent of each other, yet each can perform a different part, for which the other is incompetent. They are inter-dependent, if I may use the term, as the only one which adequately conveys the mutual dependence which subsists, along with the power of acting independently. But the inter-dependence varies in the course of personal history, the dependence of mind upon body being greatest at the early stages of life; the dependence of body upon mind being greatest at the advanced stages. . . .

Professor Bain has said that 'one substance with two sets of properties, two sides, the physical and the mental—a *double-faced unity*—would appear to comply with all the exigencies of the case.' A substance with two sets of properties, and these directly antagonistic, as represented by voluntary and involuntary actions, seems an unwarrantable hypothesis. Man represents more than sensori-motor apparatus, working an elaborate muscular system by means of stores of nerve energy. That which is highest in him is not nerve force, and the further his 'higher nature' is developed the more obvious does this become.—*Calderwood*, '*Relation of Mind and Brain*,' pp. 314, 315.

There is an intimate connection between mind and body, as is shown by the physical expression of emotion.

The feelings possess a natural language

or expression The smile of joy, the puckered features in pain, the stare of astonishment, the quivering of fear, the tones and glance of tenderness, the frown of anger—are united in seemingly inseparable association with the states of feeling that they indicate Not merely are the grosser forms of feeling thus linked with material adjuncts; in the artist's view, the loftiest, the noblest, the holiest of the human emotions have their marked and inseparable attitude and deportment. In the artistic conceptions of the Middle Ages more especially, the most divine attributes of the immaterial soul had their counterpart in the material body, the martyr, the saint, the Blessed Virgin, the Saviour Himself, manifested their glorious nature by the sympathetic movements of the mortal framework So far as concerns the entire compass of our feelings or emotions, it is the universal testimony of mankind that these have no independent spiritual subsistence, but are in every case embodied in our fleshly form —*Bain*, '*Mind and Body*,' pp 6–8

The effects produced on mental states by bodily changes, and vice versâ

As to the influence of bodily changes on mental states, we have such facts as the dependence of our feelings and moods upon hunger, repletion, the state of the stomach, fatigue and rest, pure and impure air, cold and warmth, stimulants and drugs, bodily injuries, disease, sleep, advancing years These influences extend not merely to the grosser modes of feeling, and to such familiar exhibitions as after-dinner oratory, but also to the highest emotions of the mind—love, anger, æsthetic feeling and moral sensibility Intellectual faculties have no exemption from the general rule The memory rises and falls with the bodily condition, being vigorous in our fresh moments, and feeble when we are fatigued or exhausted

The influence of mental changes upon the body is supported by an equal force of testimony Sudden outbursts of emotion derange the bodily functions Fear paralyses the digestion Great mental depression enfeebles all the organs —*Bain*, '*Mind and Body*,' pp 9–11

The hindrance to mental progress by sense

The human mind is so much clogged and borne downward by the strong and early impressions of sense, that it is wonderful how the ancients should have made even such a progress, and seen so far into intellectual matters, without some glimmering of a divine tradition Whoever considers a parcel of rude savages left to themselves, how they are sunk and swallowed up in sense and prejudice, and how unqualified by their natural force to emerge from this state, will be apt to think that the first spark of philosophy was derived from heaven.—*Berkeley*, '*Siris*,' '*Works*,' ii p. 481.

Theories as to the Nature of the Connection.

Theory of occasional causes or divine assistance.

The following theory was held by the older followers of Descartes, especially Geulinx, and by the older adherents of the Scottish philosophical school:—

The mind and the body are two entirely different substances possessing entirely different qualities. The mind has been brought into connection with the body, inhabits the body, and uses the body as its instrument of carrying out its purposes and communicating with the external world; but they are in nature so entirely different, that there is, and can be, no truly causal connection between the phenomena of the one and those of the other An impression upon an organ is only *an occasion* on which, by some mysterious power, a sensation is produced in the mind So the occurrence of a volition or determination in the mind is only an occasion on which, *by divine interference*, a movement is excited in some of the muscles of the body The connection between the mind and body is only accidental, and might have been otherwise. The one is now inhabiting and employing the other, but has an existence really independent of the other; and our knowledge of the one cannot be increased to any material extent by a study of the other.—*Jardine, 'Psychology of Cognition,'* p. 10.

The brain does not act immediately and really upon the soul; the soul has no direct cognisance of any modification of the brain; this is impossible. It is God Himself who, by a law which He has established, when movements are determined in the brain, produces analogous modifications in the conscious mind. In like manner, suppose the mind has a volition to move the arm; this volition is, of itself, inefficacious, but God, in virtue of the same law, causes the answering motion in our limb. The body is not, therefore, the real cause of the mental modifications; nor the mind the real cause of the bodily movements. God is the necessary cause of every modification of body, and of every modification of mind. The organic changes, and the mental determinations, are nothing but simple conditions, and not real causes; in short, they are occasions or occasional causes. This doctrine is involved in the Cartesian theory, but it was fully evolved by De la Forge and Malebranche. Dr. Reid inclines to it, and it is expressly maintained by Mr Stewart. —*Hamilton, 'Metaphysics,'* i 301, 302.

Theory of pre-established harmony.

Leibnitz reproaches the Cartesians with converting the universe into a perpetual miracle and degrading the Divinity by making Him act like a watchmaker, who having constructed a timepiece would still be obliged himself to turn the hands, to make it mark the hours. He denies all real connection, not only between spiritual and material substances, but between substances in general; and explains their apparent communion from a previously decreed co-arrangement of the Supreme Being, in the following manner:—'In the infinite variety of possible souls and bodies, it was necessary that there should be souls whose series of perceptions and determinations would correspond to the series of movements which some of these possible bodies would execute; for in an infinite number of souls, and in an infinite number of bodies, there would be found all possible combinations. Now, suppose that, out of a soul whose series of modifications correspond exactly to the series of modifications which a certain body was destined to perform, and of this body whose successive movements were correspondent to the successive modifications of this soul, God should make a man,—it is evident, that between the two substances which constitute this man, there would exist the most perfect harmony. The soul and the body are thus like two clocks accurately regulated, which point to the same hour and minute, although the spring which gives motion to the one is not the spring which gives motion to the other. This harmony was established before the creation of man; and hence it is called the pre-established harmony.'—*Hamilton, 'Metaphysics,'* i. 303. (See also Sec. xiii. 3.)

Theory of Materialism.

It is held by Comte, G. H. Lewes, and others, that the mind is a function of the brain. In order to understand this, we must bear in mind the relation between function and organ in the vegetable and animal kingdoms. An organ is a constituent part of an organised body which has some definite duty or function to perform. The function of the leg of an animal is to walk or run, that of the wing of a bird is to beat the air so as to enable the bird to fly. The stomach is a large internal organ of the body, whose function it is to contain the food which we swallow, until it has been prepared for being taken into the blood. The liver is another organ, whose function it is to secrete bile, which is poured into the stomach to assist in the digestion of our food. Every organ has got some special work or function to perform in the body to which it belongs. In the same way, it is argued, the brain has a function to perform in the animal system, and that is to produce the various mental phenomena of which we are conscious.—*Jardine*, '*Psychology of Cognition*,' p. 8.

We know ourselves as body-mind; we do not know ourselves as body *and* mind, if by that be meant two co-existent independent existents; the illusion by which the two aspects appear as two reals may be made intelligible by the analysis of any ordinary proposition. For example, when we say 'this fruit is sweet,' we express facts of feeling—actual or anticipated—in abstract terms. The concrete facts are these: a coloured feeling, a solid feeling, a sweet feeling, &c, have been associated together, and the coloured, solid, sweet group is symbolised in the abstract term 'fruit.' But the colour, solidity, and sweetness are also abstract terms, representing feelings associated in other groups, so that we find 'fruit' which has no 'sweetness,' and 'sweetness' in other things besides 'fruits' Having thus separated ideally the 'sweetness' from the 'fruit'—which in the concrete sweet-fruit is not permissible—we easily come to imagine a real distinction. This is the case with the concrete living organism when we cease to consider it in its concrete reality, and fix our attention on its abstract terms—Body and Mind.—*Lewes*, '*Problems of Life and Mind*,' 2d series, p. 350.

The Truth is, the Exact Nature of the Conditions is Unknown.

The sum of our knowledge of the connection of mind and body is this,—that the mental modifications are dependent on certain corporeal conditions; but of the nature of these conditions we know nothing For example, we know, by experience, that the mind perceives only through certain organs of sense, and that, through these different organs, it perceives in a different manner. But whether the senses be instruments, whether they be media, or whether they be only partial outlets to the mind incarcerated in the body,—on all this we can only theorise and conjecture.—*Hamilton*, '*Metaphysics*,' ii. 128.

How the immaterial can be united with matter, how the unextended can apprehend extension, how the indivisible can measure the divided,—this is the mystery of mysteries to man.—*Hamilton*, '*Reid's Works*,' p. 880.

Man is to himself the mightiest prodigy of nature. For he is unable to conceive what is Body, still less what is Mind, and, least of all, how there can be united a body and a mind.—*Pascal*.

The Action of Body and Mind is Reciprocal.

That the two have been so constituted as that the bodily organism acts on mind, while mind is also capable of operating on the organism, this seems to me to be the most satisfactory as it is certainly the simplest account which can be given of the connection. But let us properly understand what, on such a supposition, is the precise cause. It is a complex one in every case; it is the mind and the body in a particular relation to each other. The co-existence of the two is necessary to any effect being produced, and the effect is the result of the two operating and co-operating. Thus in all perception through the senses there is a cerebral power and there is mental power, and without both there will be no result, no object perceived. There seems also to be a duality in the effect; there is certainly a mental effect, for the mind now perceives; and the cerebral mass, in the very act of producing mental action, may undergo a change; thus there seems to be a fatigue and exhaustion produced in the organism by the very act of perceiving an immense number of objects within a brief time, as when we travel a great distance by railway, and this can be accounted for by supposing that the organism is affected by the action which has taken place.—*M'Cosh*, '*Intuitions*,' p. 191.

Mind is the Originating Power.

Matter cannot originate anything, while mind may. Matter, being the seat of force, acts according to necessity in the circumstances in which it is placed; and its different species, being brought into juxtaposition, will go through a definite series of combinations, resolutions, and alterations, corresponding with the accidents in which their properties come into contact, and calculable by a mind competent to discern their several natures and conditions. Hence it merely develops its fixed potencies and capacities, without originating anything new. Mind, on the other hand, being a seat of power—that is, of potency governed by intelligence and choice—may call into existence new circumstances, laws, necessities, and forces, to the utmost extent of its inherent ability.—*Murphy*, '*Human Mind*,' p. 18.

II. THE INTELLECT.

Definition of Intellect, as a Primary Division of Mind.

Thought, Intellect, Intelligence, or Cognition, includes the powers known as Perception, Memory, Conception, Abstraction, Reason, Judgment, and Imagination.—*Bain*, '*Mental Science*,' p. 2.

The term *Intellect* is derived from a verb (*intelligo*), which signifies to understand: but the term itself is usually so applied as to imply a Faculty which recognises Principles explicitly as well as implicitly; and abstract as well as applied; and therefore agrees with the Reason rather than the Understanding; and the same extent of signification belongs to the adjective *intellectual*.—*Whewell*, '*Elements of Morality*,' p. 25.

The Primary Attributes of Intellect, as stated by

Bain.

The primary attributes of Intellect are—(1.) Consciousness of *Difference*. This is an essential of intelligence. If we were not distinctively affected by different things, as by heat and cold, red and blue, we should not be affected at all. The beginning of knowledge, or ideas, is the discrimination of one thing from another. Where we are most discriminative we are most intellectual. (2.) Consciousness of *Agreement*. Supposing us to experience for the first time a certain sensation, as redness; and, after being engaged with other sensations, to encounter redness again; we are struck with the feeling of identity or recognition; the old state is recalled at the instance of the new, by the fact of agreement, and we have the consciousness of agreement in diversity. All knowledge finally resolves itself into Differences and Agreements. (3.) *Retentiveness*. This attribute has two aspects or degrees. (*a*) The persistence or continuance of the mental agitation, after the agent is withdrawn. When the ear is struck by the sound of a bell there is a mental awakening, termed the sensation of sound; and the silencing of the bell does not silence the mental excitement; there is a continuing, though feebler consciousness, which is the memory or idea of the sound. (*b*.) There is a further and higher power,—the recovering under the form of ideas, past and dormant impressions, without the originals and by mere mental agencies. It is possible, at an after time, to be put in mind of sounds formerly heard, without a repetition of the sensible effect. Every properly intellectual function involves one or more of these attributes and nothing else.—'*Mental Science*,' pp. 82–84 (abridged).

Jevons.

The mental powers employed in the acquisition of knowledge are probably three in number. They are substantially as Professor Bain has stated them: The Power of Discrimination, the Power of Detecting Identity, the Power of Retention. We exert the first power in every act of perception. Consciousness would almost seem to consist in the break between one state of mind and the next, just as an induced current of electricity arises from the beginning or the ending of the primary current. Yet had we the power of discrimination only, science could not be created. To know that one feeling differs from another gives purely negative information. It cannot teach us what will happen. In such a state of intellect each sensation would stand out distinct from every other; there would be no tie, no bridge of affinity between them. We want a unifying power by which the present and the future may be linked to the past; and this seems to be accomplished by a different power of mind — the power of identification. This rare property of mind consists in penetrating the disguise of variety and seizing the common elements of sameness; and it is this property which furnishes the true measure of intellect. Plato said of this unifying power, that if he met the man who could detect *the one in the many*, he would follow him as a god. —'*Principles of Science*,' pp. 4, 5.

Noah Porter.

The leading faculties of the intellect are three: *The presentative, or observing faculty, the representative, or creative faculty, the thinking, or the generalising faculty.* More briefly, the *faculty of experience*, the *faculty of representation*, and the *faculty of intelligence.* Each of these has its place in the order of intellectual growth and development. Each has its appropriate products or objects. Each acts under certain conditions or laws.—'*Human Intellect*,' p. 77.

J. Sully

The essential operation in all varieties of knowing is the detecting of relations between things. The most comprehensive relations are difference or unlikeness and agreement or likeness. All knowing means discriminating one impression, object, or idea from another (or others), and assimilating it to yet another (or others). Hence Discrimination and Assimilation have been called properties or functions of intellect.

Another property of intellect, according to Professor Bain, is Retentiveness. All knowledge clearly implies the capability of retaining, recalling, or reproducing past impressions. But retentiveness occupies a different place in knowing from that of discrimination, &c. It is rather the condition of knowing, of coming to know, and continuing to know than a part of the active knowing process itself.—'*Outlines of Psychology*,' p. 26.

The several Powers of the Intellect co-operate.

The several powers of the intellect act together in the earlier stages of its growth, and in both the earlier and later periods of its history both aid and direct one another. The action of a single power of the intellect does not exclude the co-action of the other powers. Yet, on the other hand, it is to be remembered, that as the energy of the whole soul is so far limited that one psychical state is pre-eminently a state of feeling, another intellectual, and another voluntary, so, in the intellectual activities, one is likely to be predominantly an act of sense rather than an act of memory.—*Porter*, '*Human Intellect*,' p. 76.

The Work of the Intellect.

Besides our feelings, a careful analysis shows us in our consciousness a second element—that of *relation*. It is indefinable and exists only in the terms which it unites. Take away the like things, and the relation of likeness disappears also. Relations are the product of the mind's activity; they are due to the mind, imposed by it on the sensations. This *relationing* is the work of the Intellect, it is what we mean by Intellect. All operations of Thought are nothing else than the becoming conscious of relations, the imposing of relations on things previously (for us) out of relation. As Mr. Spencer puts it, Reasoning is the classification of relation, just as 'classification,' in the ordinary use of the word, is classification of things. The process of thought is everywhere the same. But at each step relations, before only implicit, are rendered explicit. The simple relations give rise to the higher—from Difference and Agreement, Sequence, and Co-existence, we proceed to such complex bonds as Cause and Effect, Reciprocal Action, Life, Consciousness.—*Rylands*, '*Handbook of Psychology*,' pp. 55, 56.

The Uses of Intellect.

It is by those powers and faculties which compose that part of his nature commonly called his intellect or understanding that man acquires his knowledge of external objects; that he investigates truth in the sciences; that he combines means in order to attain the ends he has in view; and that he imparts to his fellow-creatures the acquisitions he has made.—*Stewart*, '*Active and Moral Powers*,' introd.

Intellect is not merely the tool which you will presently use for the business of life. Intellect is the eye which may be tutored accurately and truly to see truth; it is the faculty which, quickened by adoring love and sanctified by grace, is for an eternity to have as its object the eternal and infinite God.—*Liddon*, '*University Sermons*,' p. 45.

It is Perfected by Activity rather than Knowledge.

'The intellect,' says Aristotle, 'is perfected not by knowledge but by activity;' and in another passage, 'The arts and sciences are powers, but every power exists only for the sake of action; the end of philosophy, therefore, is not knowledge, but the energy conversant about knowledge.' Scotus declares that a man's knowledge is measured by the amount of his mental activity.—*Hamilton*, '*Metaphysics*,' i. 12.

III. THE FACULTIES OF THE INTELLECT.

Their Nature.

Defined and explained.

Faculty (*facultas*) is derived from the obsolete Latin *facul*, the more ancient form of *facilis*, from which again *facilitas* is formed. It is properly limited to active power, and therefore is abusively applied to the mere passive affections of mind, to which latter *capacity* is more properly limited.—*Hamilton*, '*Metaphysics*,' i. 177.

A faculty, according to Hamilton, is not anything *in* the mind, or any separable portion *of* the mind, but is a general name for the mind when acting in a particular way. Similar mental acts are referred to the same faculty; dissimilar acts to different faculties.—*Monck*, '*Sir W. Hamilton*,' p. 177.

Faculty is the ability of the mind to behave in a certain way, either within itself or towards anything else. It displays itself in voluntary, and therefore conscious acts. Hence it is obvious that the faculties are as numerous as the forms of activity we discover in the mind.—*Murphy*, '*Human Mind*,' p. 20.

I am capable of feeling, of perceiving external objects, of recollecting, of imagining, of desiring, of willing, of contracting my muscles, and in this respect Peter, Paul, and other men are similar to myself. These qualities are capacities and faculties. Moreover, in addition to these capacities common to all men, I have others special to myself; for instance, I am able to understand a Latin book; this porter can carry a weight of three hundred pounds. Thus, faculty and capacity are wholly relative terms; they are equivalent to *power*; and, whatever be the power, that of a dog which can run, that of a mathematician who can solve an equation, that of an absolute king who can cause heads to be cut off, the word never does more than state that the conditions of an event, or of a class of events, are present. A power is nothing in itself, except an aspect, an extract, a particularity of certain events, the particularity they have of being possible because their conditions are given.—*Taine*, '*Intelligence*,' pp. 358–360.

They are not separate organs.

We do not find that the soul is divided into separate parts or organs, of which one may be active while the others are at rest. The plant and the animal have distinct and separate organs, of which each performs its appropriate and peculiar function, which none of the others can fulfil. The root, the bark, the leaf, the flower, in the one, and the stomach, the heart, the skin, and the eye, in the other, each performs an office which is peculiar to itself, and which it shares with no other organ. While one of these organs is active, the others may be as yet undeveloped or in a state of comparative repose. There is no evidence of such a division of the soul into organs. The whole soul, so far as we are conscious of its operations, acts in each of its functions. The identical and undivided *ego* is present, and wholly present, in every one of its conscious acts and states. We can find no part, we can infer no part, which is not called into activity whenever the soul acts at all. We can discover and conjecture no organs, of which some are at rest while others are in activity.—*Porter*, '*Human Intellect*,' p. 41.

If it be reasonable to suppose and talk of faculties as distinct beings, that can act, it is fit that we should make a speaking faculty, and a walking faculty, and a dancing faculty, by which those actions are produced, which are but several modes of motion.—*Locke*, '*Human Understanding*,' II. xxi. 17.

The words *faculty*, *capacity*, *power*, which have played so great a part in psychology, are only convenient names by means of which we put together, in distinct compartments, all facts of a distinct kind; these names indicate a character common to all the facts under a distinct heading; they do not indicate a mysterious and profound essence, remaining constant and hidden under the flow of transient facts.—*Taine*, '*Intelligence*,' p. ix.

I feel that there is no more reason for believing my mind to be made up of distinct entities, or attributes, or *faculties*, than that my foot is made up of walking and running. My mind, I firmly believe, thinks and wills, and remembers, just as simply as my body walks, and runs, and rests.—*Irons*, '*Final Causes*,' p. 93.

Their Classification.

Sir W. Hamilton.

The best classification of the Intellectual operations by Faculties is that of Sir W. Hamilton ('*Metaphysics*,' ii. 17), who divides them thus:—

1. Presentative	a. External	=	Perception (not mere Sensation alone).
	b. Internal	=	Self-consciousness.
2. Conservative	= Memory	=	Retentiveness.
3. Reproductive	a. Without Will	=	Suggestion.
	b. With Will	=	Reminiscence.
4. Representative	= Imagination.		
5. Elaborative	= Comparison	=	Reasoning, Judgment, &c.
6. Regulative	= Source of necessary or *à priori* truths.		

He is very careful to tell us that they are mere classes of mental phenomena; and that between them there is only a formal or logical distinction.—*Rylands*, '*Handbook*, *&c.*,' p. 59.

These [Hamilton's], however, are properly the Cognitive faculties, and do not include the Emotions and the Will. Consciousness is not a Faculty, but includes all the Faculties.—*Monck*, '*Sir W. Hamilton*,' p. 177.

Kant.

All the faculties of the soul, says Kant, may be reduced to three, which three admit not of being reduced to any other. They are cognition, emotion, and will. For all the three the first contains the principles, the regulating laws.—*Schwegler*, '*Hist. of Phil.*' p. 217.

Their Relations to Intuitions.

The relation between the innate principles, or the fundamental laws of the mind, on the one hand, and the faculties of the mind, on the other, has seldom been properly understood. The former seem to me to be the rules of the operation of the latter.—*M'Cosh, 'Intuitions, &c.,'* p. 245.

Their Limitation of the Higher Faculties is rather of Scope than of Power.

Nothing certainly in the human mind is more wonderful than this: that it is conscious of its own limitations. Such consciousness would be impossible, if these limitations were in their nature absolute. The bars which we feel so much, and against which we so often beat in vain, are bars which could not be felt at all, unless there were something in us, which seeks a wider scope. It is as if these bars were a limit of opportunity, rather than a boundary of power. No absolute limitation of mental faculty ever is, or ever could be, felt by the creatures whom it affects. Of this we have abundant evidence in the lower animals, and in those lower faculties of our own nature which are of like kind to theirs. All their powers, and many of our own, are exerted without any sense of limitation, and this because of the very fact that the limitation of them is absolute and complete. In their own nature, they admit of no larger use. The field of effort and attainable enjoyment is, as regards them, co-extensive with the whole field of view. Nothing is seen or felt by them which may not be possessed. In such possession all exertion ends, and all desire is satisfied. This is the law of every faculty subject to a limit which is absolute.—*Duke of Argyll, 'Contemporary Review,'* December 1880, p. 868.

IV. PERSONALITY—THE EGO.

Personality is Indefinable.

What is personality, is a question which the wisest have tried to answer, and have tried in vain. Man, as a person, is one, yet composed of many elements;—not identical with any one of them, nor yet with the aggregate of them all; and yet not separable from them by any effort of abstraction. Man is one in his thoughts, in his actions, in his feelings, and in the responsibilities which these involve. It is *I* who think, *I* who act, *I* who feel; yet I am not thought, nor action, nor feeling, nor a combination of thoughts, and actions, and feelings heaped together.—*Mansel, 'Limits of Religious Thought,'* p. 96.

This self personality, like all other simple and immediate presentations, is indefinable; but it is so because it is superior to definition. It can be analysed into no simpler elements, for it is itself the simplest of all; it can be made no clearer by description or comparison, for it is revealed to us in all the clearness of an original intuition, of which description and comparison can furnish only faint and partial resemblances.—*Mansel, 'Prolegomena Logica,'* p. 138.

The Ego or Self is Revealed in Consciousness, and depends upon this.

Of the *ego* itself we are directly conscious. Not only are we conscious of the varying states and conditions, but we know them to be *our own states; i.e.*, each individual observer knows his changing individual states to belong to his individual self, or to himself, the individual. The states we know as varying and transitory. The self we know as unchanged and permanent. It is of the very nature and essence of a psychical state to be the act or experience of an individual *ego*. We are not first conscious of the state or operation, and then forced to look around for a something to which it is to be referred, or to which it may belong; but what we know, and as we know it, is the state of an individual person. A mental state which is not produced or felt by an individual self, is as inconceivable as a triangle without three angles, or a square without four sides. This relation of the act or state to the self is not inferred, but is directly known.—*Porter, 'Human Intellect,'* p. 95.

The Self, the I, is recognised in every act

of intelligence, as the subject to which that act belongs. It is I that perceive, I that imagine, I that remember, I that attend, I that compare, I that feel, I that desire, I that will, I that am conscious. The I, indeed, is only manifested in one or other of these special modes; but it is manifested in them all; they are all only the phenomena of the I.—*Hamilton*, '*Metaphysics*,' i. 166.

Self is that conscious thinking thing, whatever substance made up of (whether spiritual or material, simple or compounded, it matters not), which is sensible or conscious of pleasure and pain, capable of happiness or misery, and so is concerned for itself, as far as that consciousness extends. Thus every one finds, that whilst comprehended under that consciousness, the little finger is as much a part of himself as what is most so Upon separation of this little finger, should this consciousness go along with the little finger, and leave the rest of the body, it is evident the little finger would be the person, the same person, and self then would have nothing to do with the rest of the body. As in this case it is the consciousness that goes along with the substance, when one part is separate from another, which makes the same person, and constitutes this inseparable self; so it is in reference to substances remote in time. That with which the consciousness of this present thinking thing can join itself, makes the same person, and is one self with it, and with nothing else, and so attributes to itself, and owns all the actions of that thing as its own, as far as that consciousness reaches, and no farther. Personal identity consists, not in the identity of substance, but in the identity of consciousness.—*Locke*, '*Human Understanding*,' II. xxvii. 17.

The idea of ourselves is comprised in all our recollections, in almost all our previsions, in all our pure conceptions or imaginations. Moreover, it is called up by all our sensations in any way strange or vivid, especially those of pleasure or pain, and we often forget the external world almost completely and for a considerable length of time, to recall some agreeable or interesting passage of our life, to imagine or desire some great good fortune, to observe in the distance, either past or future, some series of our emotions. But this *ourselves*, to which, by a perpetual recurrence, we attach each of our successive events, is far more extensive than any one of them. It is drawn out before our eyes with certainty like a continuous thread, backwards, over twenty, thirty, forty years, up to the most distant of our recollections, and further still up to the beginning of our life, and it is drawn out too, by conjecture, forwards into other indeterminate and obscure distances.—*Taine*, '*On Intelligence*,' pp. 356–7.

Dawning of the Consciousness of the Ego.

The first step which the child makes toward the cognition of self, is to distinguish its body from other bodies and other persons. When it knows its name it applies it first to its body, and usually speaks of this self in the third person. It is a great step forward when it can use the pronoun I, a step not taken till the child has developed decided wishes, and some exhibition of character, in the form of emotion, passion, or purpose. Jean Paul Richter records of himself: 'Never shall I forget the phenomenon in myself, never till now recited, when I stood by the birth of my own self-consciousness, the place and time of which are distinct in my memory. On a certain forenoon I stood, a very young child, within the house-door, and was looking out toward the wood-pile, as, in an instant, the inner revelation, 'I am I,' like lightning from heaven, flashed and stood brightly before me; in that moment h d I seen myself as I, for the first time and forever!'—*Porter*, '*Human Intellect*,' p. 101.

"The baby, new to earth and sky,
What time his tender palm is pressed
Against the circle of the breast,
Has never thought that 'this is I.'

> But as he grows, he gathers much,
> And learns the use of 'I' and 'me,'
> And finds 'I am not what I see,
> And other than the things I touch;'
>
> So rounds he to a separate mind,
> From whence clear memory may begin,
> As thro' the frame that binds him in,
> His isolation grows defined"

—*Tennyson*, '*In Memoriam*,' xliv.

Our Perception of Personality

(1.) *We know self as having being, existence.* The knowledge we have in self-consciousness, which is associated with every intelligent act, is not of an impression, as Hume would say, nor of a mere quality or attribute, as certain of the Scottish metaphysicians affirm, nor of a phenomenon, in the sense of appearance, as Kant supposes, but of a thing or reality.

(2.) *We know self as not depending for its existence on our observation of it.* Of course we can know self only when we know self; our knowledge of self exists not till we have the knowledge, and it exists only so long as we have the knowledge. But when we come to know self, we know it as already existing, and we do not look on its continued existence as depending on our recognition of it.

(3.) *We know self as being in itself an abiding existence.* Not that we are to stretch this conviction so far as to believe in the self-existence of mind, or in its eternal existence. We believe certainly in the permanence of mind independent of our cognition of it, and amidst all the shiftings and variations of its states. Yet this does not imply that there never was a time when self was non-existing. For aught this conviction says, there may have been a time when self came into existence —another conviction assures us that when it did, it must have had a cause. It must be added that this conviction does not go the length of assuring us that mind must exist for ever, or that it must exist after the dissolution of the body. Intuition does indeed seem to say that, if it shall cease to exist, it must be in virtue of some cause adequate to destroy it; and it helps to produce and strengthen the feeling which the dying man cherishes when he looks on the soul as likely to abide when the body is dead. But as to whether the dissolution of the bodily frame is a sufficient cause of the decease of the soul,—as to whether it may abide when the bodily frame is disorganised, —this is a question to be settled not altogether by intuition, but by a number of other considerations, and more particularly by the conviction that God will call us into judgment at last, and is most definitely settled, after all, by the inspired declarations of the Word of God.—*M'Cosh*, '*Intuitions of the Mind*,' pp. 149–152.

Characteristics of Personality.

It is indivisible.

All mankind place their personality in something that cannot be divided, or consist of parts. A part of a person is a manifest absurdity. When a man loses his estate, his health, his strength, he is still the same person, and has lost nothing of his personality. If he has a leg or an arm cut off, he is the same person he was before. The amputated member is no part of his person, otherwise it would have a right to a part of his estate, and be liable for a part of his engagements; it would be entitled to a share of his merit and demerit—which is manifestly absurd. A person is something indivisible.—*Reid*, '*Works*,' p. 345.

It supposes intelligence.

If the substance be unintelligent in which the quality exists, we call it a thing or substance, but if it be intelligent we call it a *person*, meaning by the word person to distinguish a thing or substance that is intelligent from a thing or substance that is not intelligent.—*Taylor*, '*Apology of Ben Mordecai*,' Letter i. p. 85.

It implies limitation and relation.

Personality, as we conceive it, is essentially a limitation and a relation. Personality is presented to us as a relation between the conscious self and the various modes of his consciousness. Personality is also a limitation, for the thought and the thinker are distinguished from and limit each other. If I am any one of my own thoughts, I live and die with each successive moment of my consciousness.—*Mansel*, '*Limits of Religious Thought*,' p. 59.

But limitation is the occasion, not the cause, of Personality.

Is it in our own case the limitation of self by the cosmical non-ego which is the *cause* of our consciousness reflecting upon itself, and thus becoming *self*-conscious or personal, so that without the non-ego our personality would cease to exist? No, this limitation is merely the *occasion*; the original cause of the self-reflection consists in the peculiar constitution of the human subject as a spirit, which points to a primal spirit-subject as its Creator.—*Christlieb*, '*Modern Doubt*,' p. 169.

Human personality has two necessary conditions.

There remain two conditions which I conceive as essential to my personal existence in every possible mode, and such as could not be removed without the destruction of myself as a conscious being. These two conditions are *time* and *free agency*. The consciousness of any object, as such, is only possible to human beings under the condition of change, and change is only possible under the condition of succession. Succession in time is thus manifested as a constituent element of my personal existence. Again, consciousness in its human manifestation implies an active as well as a passive element;—a power of attending to the successive states of consciousness. But in attention we remark, obscurely indeed, but certainly, the presence of the power of volition.—*Mansel*, '*Metaphysics*,' p. 360.

Continuance of Personality.

The sense of it is indestructible.

Man thinks, he wills, he loves: therefore he is, and knows that he is. That consciousness is simply indestructible. It matters not that extending knowledge tells him his infinite physical littleness. It matters not that both science and experience show him how greatly his life is affected by circumstances, bodily constitution, human influence. It matters not that, to his infinite wonder, he finds this treasure hidden in a mere earthen vessel, always in decay, liable at any instant to be shattered. In some sense it matters not that consciousness shows him his blindness of thought, his weakness, or sinfulness of will. In spite of all, the simplest child and the wisest philosopher alike know that there is in them a distinct individuality, armed with these three great powers to think, to will, and to love.—*Barry*, '*Manifold Witness*,' p. 215.

All imagination of a daily change of that living agent which each man calls himself for another, or of any such change throughout our whole present life, is entirely borne down by our natural sense of things. Nor is it possible for a person in his wits to alter his conduct with regard to his health or affairs, from a suspicion that though he should live to-morrow he should not, however, be the same person he is to-day.—*Butler*, '*Dissertation*,' i.

Personality survives death.

The body is dissolved in death. How can man still exist in his true nature and personality? The difficulty of answering this question, and of conceiving a true personality in a disembodied soul—the mere 'shade' (as ancient poetry has it) of its former self—threw a gloom of vagueness and darkness over the future world, which prevented its being realised with any vividness of power; and indeed, after an almost grotesque device for putting off the perplexity by a notion of transmigration of souls, often ended in the conception of an absorption of the soul into the *Anima mundi*, perhaps to pass away altogether in respect of individuality, perhaps to be sent forth again into another cycle of earthly existence. Humanity waited for some clear, unwavering light, which might scatter the darkness of doubt. That longed-for light was given by the declaration of the Resurrection in all its full meaning. For, first, it brought the present spirituality of man out of the region of mere speculation Then, as inseparable from this, came the certainty of a future resurrection, brought again out of speculation and hope to the plain light of day. It showed distinctly that the body was a part of our true self; that in the future perfection of man it should have its appointed place.—*Barry*, '*Manifold Witness*,' pp 135-7 (abridged).

Practical Importance of the Fact of Personality.

A ground of belief in God

It is important to observe that it is only through the consciousness of personality that we have any ground of belief in the existence of a God If we admit the arguments by which this personality is annihilated, whether on the side of Materialism or on that of Pantheism, we cannot escape from the consequence to which those arguments inevitably lead,—the annihilation of God Himself —*Mansel*, '*Limits of Religious Thought*,' p. 88.

The first requisite of philosophy.

Personality is the first requisite for philosophising. Where there is not self-consciousness, or knowledge of Self, as possessing power for self-direction, under conditions of intelligence, there cannot be a philosophy either of our own nature or of any other form of being —*Calderwood*, '*Moral Phil.*,' p. 14

The basis of Morals

Personality is the basis of Morality. Where there is not knowledge of Self, as the intelligent source of action, there is no discrimination of motive, act, and end; and where such discrimination does not exist, there is no morality. The knowledge of moral distinctions, and the practice of morality, are in such a case equally impossible —*Calderwood*, '*Moral Phil.*,' p. 14

Its influence in works of art

In works which interest us the authors in a way substitute themselves for nature. However common or vulgar the latter may be, they have some rare and peculiar way of looking at it. It is Chardin himself whom we admire in his representation of a glass of water. We admire the genius of Rembrandt in the profound and individual character which he imparted to every head that posed before him. —*Burger*, 1863

A Belief in our Personality is Irreconcilable with Pantheism.

Pantheism is inconsistent with the consciousness of self, with the belief in our personality. It may seem a doctrine at once simple and sublime to represent the universe as Ἓν καὶ πᾶν, but it is inconsistent with one of the earliest and most ineradicable of our primary convictions. If it can be shown that there are two or more persons it follows that all is not one, that all is not God According to every scheme of pantheism, I, as a part of the universe, am part of God, part of the whole which constitutes God. But in all consciousness of self we know ourselves as persons, in all knowledge of other objects we know them as different from ourselves, and ourselves as different from them. Every man is convinced of this; no man can be made to think otherwise. If there be a God, then, as all His works proclaim, He must be different from at least one part of His works,—He must be different from me. In the construction of his artificial system of *à priori* forms, Kant most unfortunately omitted the knowledge of a personal self, and thus speculation, in the hands of his successors, was allowed to flow out into a dreary waste of pantheism When we restore the conviction of the separate existence of self, and the belief in our continued personality to its proper place, we are rearing an effective barrier in the way of the possible introduction of any system in which man can be identified with God or with anything else.—*M'Cosh*, '*Intuitions of the Mind*,' p. 453.

V. NATURE OF MAN.

1. Is Man's Nature Threefold or Twofold?

Arguments for the Tripartite Nature.

The early Christian Church inherited the ancient philosophical Trichotomy, as expounded by Plato. The soul was regarded as the principle of animal life, common to man and the lower orders, and the spirit as added by the divine inbreathing to be man's special prerogative: whether as a new substance or a new qualification of the soul was never determined. But this distinction, which is adopted for practical purposes by St. Paul, was perverted to heretical ends. Hence the healthier tone of Christian teaching, especially in the West, found it needful to hold fast the Dichotomy of human nature body and soul, flesh and spirit, being interchangeable expressions for the dual nature of man. It will be obvious, however, to those who weigh well the utterances of Scripture, that the whole religious history of man requires a certain distinction between soul and spirit.—*Pope, 'Christian Theology,'* i. 435.

The only trichotomy which will stand the test of our advanced school of physiologists is this, that the bodily organism, the intellectual faculties, and that higher spiritual consciousness by which we know and serve God, are not separable natures, but separate manifestations of the one nature. That relation of the Persons of the Trinity, which is called Sabellianism, is the best expression of that which we hold with regard to the nature of man. However defective such a theory may be to express the relations of the Persons of the Triune Jehovah, it is not objectionable to speak of the three manifestations of one nature in man. The will or personality, the original monad or centre of force, has three forms of consciousness—that of sense, of self, and of God-consciousness. Man has not three lives, but one life; he is not three persons, but one person. The will or the ego is at one moment more present to sense-consciousness, and then again it passes into self-consciousness, or into God-consciousness, passing thus through the outer court of the holy place into the holiest of all; but it is always one and the same will. Our personality is the same, whether the will acts through the body, the soul, or the spirit. This is the difference, therefore, between the Trinity and the trichotomy, that in the one case the person is distinct, as well as the work, in the other case not. The Trinity is three persons in one nature or substance—the trichotomy is three natures in one person.—*Heard, 'Tripartite Nature of Man,'* p. 138.

Body, Soul and Spirit are the three component parts of man's nature. Spirit and soul together make up our incorporeal nature.

(1.) The *spirit* is the higher side of our incorporeal nature,—the *mind*, as it is termed in Scripture, when contemplated under its intellectual aspects,—the *inner man*, as it is also denoted, when viewed in its purely theological relations, in a word, the moving, ruling, and animating principle of our nature. It is also the medium of our communication with, and the very temple of the Holy Ghost. Thus the spirit may be regarded more as the realm of the intellectual forces, and the shrine of the Holy Ghost.

(2.) The *soul* is the lower side of our incorporeal nature, and the subject of the spirit's sway. It may be regarded more as the region of the feelings, affections, and impulses, of all that peculiarly individualises and personifies. But it should be observed that Scripture often represents the soul to us as almost necessarily involving and including the spirit. Thus the Scripture never speaks of the salvation of the spirit, but the salvation of the *soul*.

(3.) The body we know as the outward tabernacle, the corporeal part of our nature.

Lastly, these three parts are intimately associated and united, and form the media of communication, both with each other, and with the higher and lower elements.

As the body is the medium of communication between the soul and the phenomenal world, so the soul is the medium of communication between the body and the spirit, and the spirit the medium between the soul and the Holy Spirit of God.—*Ellicott, 'Destiny of the Creature, &c.'*, pp 120–4 (abridged).

Arguments for Duality of Human Nature.

The phrase, spirit, soul, body, is not a mere rhetorical amplification, nor yet of itself a proof of a trichotomy of human nature, borrowed by Paul from Philo or Plato. The phraseology of Scripture is as exact as it is popular, but it does not favour such a division. Scripture distinguishes between the spirit and the soul, but not necessarily as between *constituent parts*, substances, but as between two *relations*, sides, functions of the same essence, according to its upward or downward direction.—*Auberlen.*

The Scriptures teach that God formed the body of man out of the dust of the earth, and breathed into him the breath of life, and he became a living soul. According to this account, man consists of two distinct principles, a body and a soul: the one material, the other immaterial; the one corporeal, the other spiritual. The Scriptural doctrine of the nature of man is that as a created being he consists of two, and only two, distinct elements or substances, matter and mind. Scriptural doctrine is opposed to Trichotomy, or the doctrine that man consists of three distinct substances, body, soul, and spirit. In opposition to all forms of trichotomy, it may be remarked: (1.) It is opposed to the account of the creation of man as given in Gen. ii. 7. (2.) It is opposed to the uniform usage of Scripture, seeing Soul and Spirit designate one and the same thing, and are constantly interchanged. (3.) We may appeal to the testimony of consciousness. We are conscious of our bodies, and we are conscious of our souls, *i.e.*, of the exercises and states of each; but no man is conscious of the soul as different from the spirit. Consciousness reveals the existence of two substances in the constitution of our nature; but it does not reveal the existence of three substances, and therefore the existence of more than two cannot rationally be assumed.—*Hodge, 'Systematic Theology,'* ii. 42–9 (abridged).

2. Body.

Distinguished from Matter

Monboddo ('Ancient Metaphysics,' bk. ii chap. 1) distinguishes between *matter* and *body*, and calls *body* matter sensible, that is with those qualities which make it perceptible to our senses. This leaves room for understanding what is meant by a spiritual body, of which we read in 1 Cor. xv. 44. He also calls body, 'matter with form,' in contradistinction to 'first matter,' which is matter without form.—*Fleming, 'Vocab. of Phil.,'* p. 67.

An Essential Part of Man's Nature.

The body is an essential part of man's entity—he is a corporeal, spiritual being. Scripture describes *the body* as that which first exists, which is fundamental. And it still is so in the case of every individual human being. With respect to his body, man belongs to the corporeal world, and forms its completion. His body is the recapitulation of material nature, whose various provinces are here repeated in a higher grade, and united in a perfect living organism. It is characteristic of the scriptural view, that while it does not make the body the very essence of man, it yet regards it as an essential component of his entirety. It thus occupies the middle ground between the view which esteems the body as all in all, so that life after death is degraded, as in Homer, into a melancholy and shadow-like existence; and the spiritualistic view of Plato, which regards the body as a prison and a fetter, to be freed from which forms the happiness of man—a doctrine whose proximate consequence is the stoical wisdom of suicide.—*Luthardt, 'Fundamental Truths,'* p. 126.

Its Identity—How Dependent

The identity of the body, even in this life, depends not on the mere material particles, which are being dissolved and renewed at every moment, but on the impress of individuality, which these changes do not impair, and which gives to the body a distinctive character in each one of the countless millions of human kind.—*Barry, 'Manifold Witness, &c.,'* p 139

It is

The organ for attaining knowledge

It is through the bodily organism that the intelligence of man attains its knowledge of all material objects beyond This is true of the infant mind, it is true also of the mature mind We may assert something more than this regarding the organism It is not only the medium through which we know all bodily objects beyond itself, it is itself an object primarily known; nay, I am inclined to think that, along with the objects immediately affecting it, it is the only object originally known Intuitively man seems to know nothing beyond his own organism, and objects immediately affecting it, in all further knowledge there is a process of inference proceeding on a gathered experience This theory seems to me to explain all the facts, and it delivers us from many perplexities —*M'Cosh, 'Intuitions of the Mind,'* p 103

The agent of the spirit

The entire spiritual life is rooted in this corporeal soil, and uses the bodily organism as its instrument The spirit has no independent agency, it acts only through and in the body. It can manifest itself only by means of its necessary instrument, the body Hence every disturbance of the body will produce, by reaction, a corresponding disturbance in the mode in which the mind is accustomed to manifest itself What we call mental disease, because the mind's mode of manifestation seems disturbed, is in fact a bodily disorder It is the disorder of its corporeal instrument which makes the mind appear disordered When the strings of the instrument are out of tune, though the piece of music be correct, and the player perform it with the greatest accuracy, its execution will produce but discord. It is thus that we must understand the intellectual dulness of old age It is the bodily organism which refuses its office, and the mind, thus hindered in its external manifestations, retires into its own secret world, and very little of it can be seen through the veil of the body All that is at fault is the external manifestation and instrumentality of the bodily organism —*Luthardt, 'Fundamental Truths,'* p 125–6

It is adapted to the Soul.

The body is in general and particular adapted to the habits and uses of the species and of the individual soul with which it is connected This adaptation is so manifold and complete as to indicate that the agent that forms and moulds these peculiarities is the same that uses and applies them The human body is unlike the body of every other species of animals, not merely in its external features of form and function, but also in its special capacities to be the servant of the human soul The hand is not merely a more dexterous and finely moulded instrument than the forefoot of the quadruped and the paw of the monkey, but is specially fitted to be used by the inventive and skilful mind Every other part of the human body is also especially harmonious to and congruous with the human soul, as intellect, sensibility, and will Not only is there a general harmony between the body and soul of the species as a whole, but there is in individuals a special harmony between the body and soul The eye that is capable of discerning the nicest shades of colour, or tracing graceful outlines of form, is usually conjoined with a special delight in colour and form, as well as with a capacity of hand to reproduce what delights both soul and eye The ear that is physically refined in its discrimination of sounds and musical tones, is usually attended by a special sensibility of the soul to the delights of elocution and music, and with the physical and psychical capacity to produce the sounds which give it such pleasure Quickness of intellect is attended by organs that are mobile and acute and a temperament that is harmonious with both intellect and organism.—*Porter*, '*Human Intellect*,' p 37.

3. Soul and Spirit.

Soul and Spirit Defined and Distinguished from each other.

Soul and Spirit.

τὸ πνεῦμα is the *spirit*, the highest and distinctive part of man, the immortal and responsible *Soul*, in our common parlance; ἡ ψυχή is the lower or animal *soul*, containing the passions and desires, which we have in common with the brutes, but which in us is ennobled and drawn up by the spirit.—*Alford*, '*Greek Testament*,' iii. 282.

The spirit is the spiritual nature of man as directed upward, and as capable of living intercourse with God The soul is the spiritual nature as the quickening power of the body, as in animals; hence excitable through the senses, with faculties of perception and feeling —*Auberlen.*

Among modern philosophers in Germany a distinction is taken between soul and spirit. According to Professor Schubert, a follower of Schelling, the *soul* is the inferior part of our intellectual nature. The *spirit* is that part of our nature which tends to the purely rational, the lofty, and divine —*Fleming*, '*Vocab of Phil*.,' p. 474

The word *soul* differs from spirit as the species from the genus: soul being limited to a spirit that either is or has been connected with a body or material organisation; while spirit may also be applied to a being that has not at present, or is believed never to have had, such connection.—*Porter*, '*Human Intellect*,' p 6.

The Soul is, indeed, the very counterpart of the spirit. It is of similar nature with the spirit, but not similar to it. The psychical functions which are the types of the spiritual, correspond to the spiritual functions, but are not like to them: they are rather the broken rays of their colours. The soul is no Ego, distinguishing itself from the spirit The self-consciousness which forms the background of its spirit-copied functions, is that of the spirit from which it has its origin.—*Delitzsch*, '*Biblical Psychology*,' p 235.

The Existence of the Soul.

A necessary doctrine of religion

The doctrine of the existence of the soul is a necessary premiss of all religion, of all morality, nay of every exalted and intellectual view of human life If man has no soul, human life is equally without a soul, —without the soul of poetry, the soul of every exalted emotion, the soul of the fellowship of hearts, of moral consciousness and moral effort, and finally of life in and for God. In short, the whole world is but a flower-grown cemetery We have, however, the direct assurance of our feelings that we do possess a soul,—*i.e.*, an independent principle of spiritual life, interwoven, indeed, most intimately with the bodily principle, yet neither identical with it nor its mere manifestation The notion of the soul is a universal one It is found among all nations and in all stages of civilisation It is, therefore, a necessary and not an accidental notion —*Luthardt*, '*Fundamental Truths*,' p. 128

The phenomena of the soul are real.

It is important to remember, whatever views we accept of the nature of the soul, that its phenomena are as real as any other, and that their peculiarities are entitled to a distinct recognition by the true philosopher. Whatever psychical properties or laws can be established on appropriate evidence, they all deserve to be accepted as among the real agencies and laws of the actual universe Perception, memory, and reasoning are processes that are as real as are gravitation and electrical action In one aspect, their reality is more worthy of confidence and respect, as it is by means of perception and reasoning that we know gravitation and electricity. Their peculiar conditions, elements, and laws, so far as they can be ascertained and resolved, are to be judged by their appropriate evidence, and to be accepted on proper testimony. The evidence and testimony which is pertinent to them, may be as pertinent and convincing, though different in its kind, as that which can be furnished for the facts of sense or the laws of matter. If the soul knows itself, its acts and products, by a special activity, then what it knows ought to be confided in, as truly as what it knows of matter by a different process.—*Porter*, '*Human Intellect*,' p. 26.

The Nature of the Soul

Ancient views.

They who thought that the soul is a subtile matter, separable from the body, disputed to which of the four elements it belongs—whether to earth, water, air, or fire. Of the three last, each had its particular advocates. Water had its champion in Hippo; air in Anaximenes and Diogenes; fire in Democritus and Leucippus. But some, like Empedocles, were of opinion that it partakes of all the elements; that it must have something in its composition similar to everything we perceive; and that we perceive earth by the earthly part, water by the watery part, and fire by the fiery part of the soul. The most spiritual and sublime notion concerning the nature of the soul to be met with among the ancient philosophers I conceive to be that of the Platonists, who held that it is made of that celestial and incorruptible matter of which the fixed stars were made, and therefore has a natural tendency to rejoin its proper element.—*Reid*, '*Works*,' p. 203.

Among the ancient philosophers the atomists explained life by the fortuitous mixture of atoms, acting by the mechanical laws which were by them rudely conceived and defined. A very large number, however, accounted for these phenomena by a separate agent, called the soul, which, alike in plants and animals, was thought to be the cause of the organic structure and its organic functions. In the higher forms of being, as in man, this soul or vital principle was supposed to attain to certain emotional and intellectual functions. As the capacity for the highest functions it received another appellation, and in the opinion of Aristotle, as he is generally interpreted, this higher nature, the Νοῦς, was in some way added to the lower forces, and qualified to maintain a separate existence after the destruction of the body.

Plato taught positively, though in mythical language, that the soul is pre-existent to the body, and immortal in its duration; that it is ethereal in its essence, opposite in every respect to the matter to which it is reluctantly subjected, and which soils its purity, obscures its intelligence, and weakens its energy.—*Porter*, '*Human Intellect*,' p. 29.

Modern views.

Discussions and controversies in respect to the nature of the soul began in the seventeenth century and were prosecuted during the greater part of the eighteenth. There was a conspicuous tendency to materialism. This materialism assumed a variety of forms, and its positions were urged in several distinct and almost incompatible lines of argument. The materialists of the school of Hobbes were reinforced in their confidence by the position taken by Locke against the fundamental doctrine of Descartes in regard to the essence of the soul,—Locke asserting that there was no inherent impossibility that matter should be endowed with the power of thinking, as against Descartes' axiom that the essence of spirit is thought. The mechanical philosophy common to Descartes and Newton favoured their reasonings in some degree. Many of the so-called Free Thinkers, or Deists, were avowed Materialists.—*Ueberweg*, '*Hist. of Phil.*,' ii 371.

In modern philosophy, in consequence of Platonic and Christian ideas, and under the influence of the philosophy of Descartes, the soul has been more sharply contrasted with matter and extension in all its forms. As a natural result, the soul, as the principle and agent of the higher functions, was separated from the agent of living, organised matter, or the principle of life. Under the influence of the new philosophy, —the mechanical philosophy of Descartes and of Newton,—the question, what is the living principle, assumed a new interest. With the progress of modern anatomy and physiology, the mechanical structure of the skeleton came to be more perfectly understood, and the adaptation of the form and adjustments of every one of its parts to the communication of force and the direction of motion, familiarised and deepened the conviction that the human frame, in its structure and activities, may be explained by mechanical relations and laws.

This theory is rejected as unsatisfactory by very many eminent physiologists and physiological chemists. They contend with equal earnestness that the phenomena peculiar to living beings cannot be explained without the supposition of some additional property or agent, which is essential to their formation and preservation, as well as to the performance of many of their peculiar functions.—*Porter*, '*Human Intellect*,' p. 30.

The soul is immaterial.

(*a.*) *Arguments for the materiality of the soul.* The materialist urges—1. That we know the soul only as connected with a material organisation. Of a soul which acts or manifests its acts apart from the body, we have no experience. 2. The powers of the soul are developed along with the powers and capacities of this organised structure; they are unfolded as the body is developed. Hence it would seem as though what we call the soul is but a name for the capacity to perform certain higher functions which belong to a finely organised and fully developed material organism. 3. The soul is dependent on the body for much of its knowledge and many of its enjoyments. It is through the eye only that it perceives and enjoys colour, and through the ear only that it apprehends and is delighted with sound. 4. The soul is dependent on the body and on matter for its energy and activity. The capacity to fix the attention so as to perceive clearly, to remember accurately and to comprehend fully, varies with the condition of the stomach and the action of the heart. A change in the structure or in the functions of the brain may induce insanity. When the organisation of the body is destroyed the soul ceases to act, and, for aught we can observe, it ceases to exist. —*Porter*, '*Human Intellect*,' pp. 19–21 (abridged).

(*b.*) *Counter arguments.* The considerations which may be urged in proof that the substance of the soul is not material are the following:—1. The phenomena of the soul are in kind unlike the phenomena which pertain to matter. All material phenomena are discerned by the senses. Certain phenomena of the soul, at least, are known by consciousness, and, as thus known, are directly discerned to be totally unlike all those events and occurrences which the senses apprehend. 2. The soul distinguishes itself from matter. It knows that the agent which sees and hears is not the matter which is seen and heard. It also distinguishes itself and its inner states from the organised matter—*i.e.*, its own bodily organs—by means of which it perceives and is affected by other matter. 3. The soul is self-active. Matter of itself is inert. The soul is impelled to action from within by its own energy. 4. The soul is not dependent on matter in its highest activity. To very many of the states of the soul no changes or affections of the organism can be observed or traced, as their condition or prerequisite. What change or affection of the material organism occurs, when the soul, at the sight of a landscape images another like it, calls up in memory a similar scene, or, by creative acts of its own, constructs picture after picture that are more beautiful than any it ever saw?—*Porter*, '*Human Intellect*,' pp. 22–25 (abridged).

Difference between the human and the brute soul.

The Holy Scriptures themselves attribute to beasts a soul as the vital principle of the corporeal organism. But in the beasts we see the consciousness of a soul unenlightened by any beam of the spirit, obscure and incapable of forming the conception of an Ego; in man, real *self-consciousness*. In the beasts we have mere natural impulses, directed towards the satisfaction of material wants, and serving no other purpose than the maintenance of the *genus*, for which reason the individual beast, as such, has no value; in man, we have the *moral* consciousness of a *person* who possesses in himself the purpose of his existence, and is therefore of infinite value and eternal significance. In short, in one case there is a living but irrational *soul*, in the other, the rational, God-like *spirit*.—*Christlieb*, '*Modern Doubt*,' p. 154.

The human soul differs from the soul of the brute by its spiritual character, which is founded in the higher energy of its elementary faculties.—*Beneke, in Ueberweg's 'Hist. of Phil.'*, ii. 290.

The soul of the beast, which forms its body, is so entirely incorporated with it, that it may in the strictest sense of the term be said, that the body of the wolf or the lamb, for instance, the eagle or the dove, is the creature's visible soul. But the human soul is not one and the same with his bodily frame; the first has an inward infiniteness, an invisible amount of resource, which does not come into view.—*Martensen*, '*Christian Ethics*,' i. 85.

The Relation of the Soul to the Body.

The soul's action on the body limited.

Every one finds in himself that his soul can think, will, and operate on his body in the place where that is, but cannot operate on a body, or in a place an hundred miles distant from it. Nobody can imagine that his soul can think or move a body at Oxford, whilst he is at London; and cannot but know, that, being united to his body, it constantly changes place all the whole journey between Oxford and London, as the coach or horse does that carries him.—*Locke*, '*Human Understanding*,' ii. xxiii. 20.

The soul moulds the body.

It is not by chance that a certain individuality of soul carries along with it a certain bodily form, for it is the soul which fashions the body. This old idea, which was maintained by G. F. Stahl [1660–1734], but afterwards fell into disfavour, is now again recovering its position, and can scarcely be gainsaid if kept within its proper limits, if by the soul we understand not merely the self-conscious soul, but the soul antecedent to consciousness in its indissoluble union with the plastic power, or the power to form its bodily frame. It is the soul which appropriates the bodily to itself and fashions it after its own *schema*.—*Martensen*, '*Christian Ethics*,' i. 82.

The soul is manifested by the body.

The sudden influence of vivid conceptions, or of excited feelings upon the muscular activities, is an example of the power of the soul over the body. The imagination of a scene of cruelty and suffering makes the flesh creep, puts the limbs into attitudes of defence and aversion, and awakens the features to expressions of disgust or horror. Terror induces fainting, convulsions, and death. The capacity of the body in look, gesture, and speech, to express the thoughts and feelings of the soul, and the capacity of the soul to interpret these bodily movements and effects as language, and to look through them into the soul within, by an impulse and an art which could never be either taught or learned if nature itself did not prepare the way—all these phenomena which elevate the body itself almost to a spiritual essence, are more easy of explanation, if we suppose that with the capacity for the psychical activities which are peculiar to every individual, there are also connected in oneness of essence those vital powers which act in such fine and subtle harmony with them.—*Porter*, '*Human Intellect*,' p. 38.

The soul is united to the body not as a man in a tent, or a pilot in a ship, or a spider in its web, or the image in the wax, nor as water in a vessel, nor as one liquor is mingled with another, nor as heat in the fire, nor as a voice through the air:

'But as the fair and cheerful morning light
Doth here and there her silver beams impart,
And in an instant doth herself unite
To the transparent air in all and every part.

. . . .

'So doth the piercing soul the body fill,
Being all in all, and all in part diffused.'

—*Davies, in Ueberweg's* '*Hist. of Phil.*,' ii. 353.

The point in which it is most generally acknowledged that the human frame is an expression of the mental character, is the physiognomy, especially of the face, in which is perceived a visible index, not merely of the intellectual, but also of the moral being, the inherent qualities of the individual, whether considered as character, or only as individual capacity or possibility of development in a certain direction.—*Martensen*, '*Christian Ethics*,' i. 85.

'For of the soul the body form doth take,
For soul is form, and doth the body make'

—*Spenser*, '*Hymn in Honour of Beauty*'

The body reacts on the soul.

What is the relation of the soul, with its transcendent powers and capacities, to that body through which we are linked to the material world? Is the body a part of our true self, or merely an imperfect instrument, a temporary vesture, of the soul? The natural tendency in all who believed in the spirituality and immortality of man was to embrace the latter alternative. Many religions and some of the noblest philosophies held that even in life the body was but an encumbrance or a prison-house, and accordingly, in any conception of the hereafter, rejoiced to think that it had mouldered into nothingness, and left the soul naked and free. But the fuller investigation in modern days of the complex being of man—of the power of physical influence over him, of the need of physical machinery, not only for act and word but even for thought, of the undoubted action and reaction of body and soul on each other—soon dispelled this first conviction. It showed that the body is a part of man's true self. —*Barry*, '*Manifold Witness*,' p. 135.

Certain it is that the body does hinder many actions of the soul: it is an imperfect body, and a diseased brain, or a violent passion, that makes fools; no man hath a foolish soul; and the reasonings of men have infinite difference and degrees, by reason of the body's constitution. From whence it follows, that because the body casts fetters and restraints, hindrances and impediments, upon the soul, that the soul is much freer in the state of separation.—*Taylor*, '*Works*,' viii. 439.

But the soul may not be essentially dependent on the organism.

It seems very easy to conceive the soul to exist in a separate state (*i.e.*, divested from those limits and laws of motion and perception with which she is embarrassed here), and to exercise herself on new ideas, without the intervention of those tangible things we call bodies. It is even very possible to conceive how the soul may have ideas of colour without an eye, or of sounds without an ear.—'*Berkeley, Fraser's Life and Letters of*,' p. 181.

The Soul is Man's Essence and Glory.

There lives in us a spirit which comes immediately from God, and constitutes man's most intimate essence. As this spirit is present to man in his highest, deepest, and most personal consciousness, so the giver of this spirit, God Himself, is present to man through the heart as nature is present to him through the external senses.

No sensible object can so move the spirit, or so demonstrate itself to it as a true object, as do those absolute objects, the true, good, beautiful, and sublime, which can be seen with the eye of the mind. We may even hazard the bold assertion that we believe in God because we see Him, although He cannot be seen with the eyes of this body. It is a jewel in the crown of our race, the distinguishing mark of humanity, that these objects reveal themselves to the rational soul. With holy awe man turns his gaze towards those spheres from which alone light falls in upon the darkness of earth.—*Jacobi, in Ueberweg's 'Hist. of Phil.,'* ii. 200.

VI. CONSCIOUSNESS.

Its Nature.

Is the term definable?

Nothing has contributed more to spread obscurity over a very transparent matter than the attempts of philosophers to define consciousness. Consciousness cannot be defined,—we may be ourselves fully aware what consciousness is, but we cannot, without confusion, convey to others a definition of what we ourselves clearly apprehend. The reason is plain. Consciousness lies at the root of all knowledge. Consciousness is itself the one highest source of all comprehensibility and illustration,—how, then, can we find aught else by which consciousness may be illustrated or comprehended? To accomplish this, it would be necessary to have a second consciousness, through which we might be conscious of the mode in which the first consciousness was possible. Many philosophers have defined consciousness a *feeling*. But how do they define a feeling? They define, and must define it, as something of which we are conscious; for a feeling of which we are not conscious is no feeling at all. Here, therefore, they are guilty of a logical seesaw, or circle. They explain the same by the same, and thus leave us in the end no wiser than we were in the beginning. In short, the notion of consciousness is so elementary that it cannot possibly be resolved into others more simple. It cannot, therefore, be brought under any more general conception, and, consequently, it cannot be defined.—*Hamilton, 'Metaphysics,'* i. 190, 191.

Meaning of the term.

The meaning of a word is sometimes best attained by means of the word opposed to it. *Unconsciousness*, that is, the want or absence of *consciousness*, denotes the suspension of all our faculties. *Consciousness*, then, is the state in which we are when all or any of our faculties are in exercise. It is the condition or accompaniment of every mental operation.—*Fleming, 'Vocab. of Phil.,'* p. 109.

Consciousness is a word used by philosophers to signify that immediate knowledge which we have of our present thoughts and purposes, and, in general, of all the present operations of our minds. Whence we may observe that consciousness is only of things present.—*Reid, 'Works,'* p. 222.

Consciousness is the perception of what passes in a man's own mind.—*Locke, 'Human Understanding,'* ii. 1, 19.

Brown treats consciousness as equivalent 'to the whole series of states of the mind, whatever the individual momentary states may be,' and denies that there is a power by which the mind knows its own states, or that to this power the name of consciousness is applied.—*Ueberweg, 'Hist. of Phil.,'* ii. 411.

The word Consciousness has been ambiguously employed, but we may specify two or three main uses:—

(1.) It sometimes denotes only the recognition by the mind of its own states (Self-consciousness).

(2.) It sometimes is used to include all mental phenomena, with or without explicit reference to the Ego, in so far as those phenomena are not latent. Thus:—'Consciousness is the word which expresses, in the most general way, the various manifestations of psychological life It consists of a continuous current of sensations, ideas, volitions, feelings,' &c. (Professor Ribot)

(3.) It sometimes is used as equivalent to Immediate Knowledge (Intuition)—whether of the Ego or the Non-ego. Thus:—'Consciousness and immediate knowledge are terms universally convertible' (Sir W. Hamilton).

Hamilton uses the word in all three senses; so do many other psychologists. There now seems a tendency to use the word more exactly in the second sense discriminated above Taking the term in this sense we at once see that it would be impossible to explain what it means to any one who had it not.—*Ryland*, '*Handbook of Psych.*,' p. 9.

Metaphorical description of Consciousness.

Consciousness is often figuratively described as the 'witness' of the states of the soul, as though it were an observer separate from the soul itself, inspecting and beholding its processes. It is called the 'inner light,' 'an inner illumination,' as though a sudden flash or steady radiance could be thrown within the spirit, revealing objects that would otherwise be indistinct, or causing those to appear which would otherwise not be seen at all. Appellations like these are so obviously figurative, that it is surprising that any philosopher should use them for scientific purposes, or should reason upon, or use them with scientific rigour. However they are intended, they are liable to this objection, that they often mislead the student by furnishing him a sensuous picture, a pleasing fancy, or an attractive image, when he needs an exact conception or a discriminated definition.—*Porter*, '*Human Intellect*,' p. 84.

'Instead of attempting to conceive consciousness as a distinct mental faculty, . . . we will consider it under the analogy of an inner illumination.' 'The conception is not of a faculty, but of a light; not of an action, but of an illumination; not of a maker of phenomena, but of a revealer of them as already made by the appropriate intellectual operation.'—*Hickok*, '*Empirical Psychology*,' Introduction, chap. iii. 2.

We not only *feel*, but we *know* that we feel; we not only *act*, but we *know* that we act; we not only *think*, but we *know* that we think; to think, without knowing that we think, is as if we should not think; and the peculiar quality, the fundamental attribute of thought, is to have a *consciousness* of itself. Consciousness is this interior light which illuminates everything that takes place in the soul; consciousness is the accompaniment of all our faculties; and is, so to speak, their echo.—*Cousin*, '*Hist. of Mod. Phil.*,' i. 274.

Analysis of Consciousness. By

Sir W. Hamilton.

Consciousness is, on the one hand, the recognition by the mind or ego of its acts and affections; in other words, the self-affirmation, that certain modifications are known by me, and that these modifications are mine. But, on the other hand, consciousness is not to be viewed as anything different from these modifications themselves, but is, in fact, the general condition of their existence within the sphere of intelligence. Consciousness thus expresses a relation subsisting between two terms. These terms are, on the one hand, an I or Self, as the subject of a certain modification,—and on the other, some modification, state, quality, affection, or operation belonging to the subject. Consciousness, thus, in its simplicity, necessarily involves three things,—(1) A recognising or knowing subject; (2) a recognised or known modification; and (3) a recognition or knowledge by the subject of the modification.—'*Metaphysics*,' i. 193.

Bain.

'The word consciousness signifies mental life, with its various energies, in so far as it is distinguished from the purely vital functions, and from the conditions of sleep, torpor, insensibility,' &c. It also indicates that the mind is occupied with itself, instead of being applied to the exterior world The primitive and fundamental attributes of intelligence are :—(1.) *Consciousness of difference* This is the most primitive fact of thought; it consists of seeing that two sensations are different in nature or in intensity. Consciousness is entirely produced by change. If we imagine in any one a single and invariable sensation, there is not yet consciousness If there are two successive sensations, with a difference of nature between them, then we have more or less clear consciousness. (2.) *Consciousness of resemblance.* An impression which constantly remains without variation, ceases to affect us; but if it produces another, and this first impression returns afterwards, then we recognise it, we have consciousness of resemblance.—*Ribot*, '*Contemporary English Psychology*,' p. 214 (abridged).

Herbert Spencer

To be conscious is to think; to think is to put together impressions and ideas; and to do this, is to be the subject of internal changes. It is admitted on all hands that without change consciousness is impossible: consciousness ceases when the changes in consciousness cease To constitute a consciousness, however, incessant change is not the sole thing needed If the changes are altogether at random, no consciousness, properly so called, exists Consciousness is not simply a succession of changes, but an *orderly* succession of changes—a succession of changes *combined and arranged* in special ways. The changes form the raw material of consciousness, and the development of consciousness is the organisation of them.

We have seen that the condition on which alone consciousness can begin to exist, is the occurrence of a change of state; and that this change of state necessarily generates the terms of a relation of unlikeness Consciousness must be for ever passing from one state into a different state. In other words, there must be a *continuous differentiation* of its states. But states of consciousness successively arising can become elements of thought only by being known as like certain before-experienced states. If no note be taken of the different states as they occur—if they pass through consciousness simply as images pass over a mirror; there can be no intelligence, however long the process be continued Intelligence can arise only by the classification of these states with those of the same nature In being known, then, each state must become one with certain previous states — must be integrated with those previous states. That is to say, there must be a *continuous integration* of states of consciousness. Under its most general aspect, therefore, all mental action whatever is definable as the continuous differentiation and integration of states of consciousness—'*Principles of Psychology*,' ii 291–301.

Conditions of Consciousness.

The special conditions of consciousness are :—

(1.) It is an actual and not a potential knowledge. Thus a man is said to know that $7 + 9 = 16$, though that equation be not, at the moment, the object of his thought; but we cannot say that he is conscious of this truth unless while actually present to his mind

(2.) Consciousness is an immediate not a mediate knowledge [Thus my remembrance of St Paul's Cathedral is mediate, my present mental representation of it immediate knowledge]

(3.) It supposes a contrast,—a discrimination. We are conscious only so far as we distinguish the thing from what it is not.

(4.) It involves judgment, for it is impossible to discriminate without judging

(5.) The fifth condition is memory, without which our mental states could not be compared and distinguished from each other. —*Hamilton*, '*Metaphysics*,' i 201–5

A little reflection would appear to show that by actual, as opposed to potential knowledge, Hamilton only means conscious as opposed to unconscious knowledge; and again Discrimination seems to involve Consciousness. The second condition alone remains; and thus we come back to the definition, that Consciousness is equivalent to Immediate Knowledge.—*Rylands, 'Handbook of Philosophy,'* p. 12.

Two Kinds of Consciousness.

Consciousness, in its relation to the subject or person conscious, is of two kinds, or rather is composed of two elements. (1.) Presentative or intuitive consciousness, which is the consciousness of an *individual object*, that is, an object occupying a definite position in space or time. I see a triangle drawn on paper, without knowing that the figure is called a triangle. I simply see a figure. This is presentative consciousness or intuition. (2.) Representative or reflective consciousness, which is the consciousness primarily and directly of a *general notion or concept*. Thus having once seen a triangle I gather a general notion of its figure, and this general notion is representative of any number of possible triangles, and is now actually exhibited in a mental image.—*Mansel, 'Metaphysics,'* pp. 33-5 (abridged).

Consciousness is exercised in two forms or species of activity, viz., the natural or spontaneous, and the artificial or reflective. They are also called by some writers *the primary* and *the secondary consciousness*. The one form is possessed by all men, the other is attained by few. The first is a gift of Nature and product of spontaneous growth; the second is an accomplishment of art and the reward of special discipline. The natural precedes the reflective in the order of time and of actual development. But it does not differ from it in kind, only in an accidental element, which brings its results within our reach, and retains them for our service.—*Porter, 'Human Intellect,'* p. 87.

Province of Consciousness.

Let us endeavour to ascertain its precise province. (1.) In mental science it is the observing agent. We bend back the mental eye and observe what is passing within as it passes. (2.) It is the main agent in examining the origin of ideas, by giving us directly a knowledge of our own mental operations, and indirectly an acquaintance with those of others. It must ascertain not only that certain ideas exist, but also all that is in them.—*M'Cosh, 'Examination of Mill,'* p. 30 *et seq.* (abridged).

Testimony of Consciousness.

To the ego and non-ego.

When I concentrate my attention in the simplest act of perception, I return from my observation with the most irresistible conviction of two facts, or rather two branches of the same fact;—that I am,—and that something different from me exists. In this act, I am conscious of myself as the perceiving subject, and of an external reality as the object perceived. —*Hamilton, 'Metaphysics,'* i. 288.

As intelligent beings, we are conscious of the recognition of two different classes of phenomena, the one belonging to an external world, with which we are connected, the other belonging to the internal world of mind, in which we are conscious of our own personal existence, and where all thoughts, feelings, and desires are regarded as our own. This is the distinction between *self* and *not self*, which is unmistakably the first distinction involved in consciousness. —*Calderwood, 'Philosophy of the Infinite,'* p. 30.

The coexistence of subject and object is a deliverance of consciousness, which, taking precedence of all analytic examination, but subsequently verified by analytic examination, is a truth transcending all others in certainty.—*Spencer, 'Principles of Psychology,'* i. 209.

Its certainty.

According to all philosophers, the evidence of consciousness, if only we can obtain it pure, is conclusive. The verdict of consciousness, or, in other words, our immediate and intuitive conviction, is admitted on all hands to be a decision without appeal What is called the testimony of consciousness to *something beyond itself* may be and is denied, but what is denied has almost always been that consciousness gives the testimony; not that, if given, it must be believed.—*Mill*, '*Examination of Hamilton*,' pp. 151, 166.

Of consciousness I cannot doubt, because such doubt being itself an act of consciousness, would contradict, and consequently annihilate itself.—*Hamilton, in Reid's* '*Works*,' p 129.

The facts of consciousness are the most certain of all facts. The objects which consciousness presents are, if possible, more real and better attested than the objects of sense. We can question whether the eye and the ear do not deceive us; whether the sights which we see and the sounds which we hear are not illusions. We ask, at times, whether this entire sensible world is not a succession of shifting phantasmagoria; but we cannot doubt whether we perform the acts of seeing and hearing We may question whether these objects are what they seem to be, but not whether certain acts are in reality performed. We may doubt whether this or that object be a reality or a phantasm, but we cannot doubt that we doubt Nothing in the universe is so certain, and deserves so well to be trusted, as the psychical phenomena of which each man is conscious.—*Porter*, '*Human Intellect*,' p. 115.

Consciousness is to the philosopher what the Bible is to the theologian.—*Hamilton*, '*Discussions*,' p 84

If our immediate internal experience could possibly deceive us, there could be no longer for us any truth of fact, nay, nor any truth of reason.—*Leibnitz*, '*Nouveaux Essais*,' ii. 27, 13.

Consciousness is the Source of Mental Philosophy.

All theories of the human mind profess to be interpretations of Consciousness: the conclusions of all of them are supposed to rest on that ultimate evidence, either immediately or remotely. What Consciousness directly reveals, together with what can be legitimately inferred from its revelations, composes, by universal admission, all that we know of the mind, or indeed of any other thing When we know what any philosopher considers to be revealed in Consciousness, we have the key to the entire character of his metaphysical system.—*Mill*, '*Examination of Hamilton*,' p. 131.

All philosophy is evolved from consciousness, and no philosophical theory can pretend to truth except that single theory which comprehends and develops the fact of consciousness on which it founds without retrenchment, distortion, or addition.—*Hamilton*, '*Metaphysics*,' i. 285.

The Study of Consciousness.

Difficulties

The difficulties in psychological observation are such as these:—

(1.) The conscious mind is at once the observing subject and the object observed. The mental energy is thus divided in two divergent directions. In all states of strong mental emotion the passion is itself to a certain extent a negation of the tranquillity requisite for observation, so that we are thus impaled on the awkward dilemma,—either we possess the necessary tranquillity for observation, with little or nothing to observe, or there is something to observe, but we have not the necessary tranquillity for observation

(2.) Want of mutual co-operation. He who would study the internal world must isolate himself in the solitude of his own thought.

(3.) No fact of consciousness can be accepted at second hand In the science of mind we can believe nothing upon authority, take nothing upon trust Except we observe and recognise each fact of consciousness ourselves, we cannot comprehend what it means.

(4.) The phenomena of consciousness are not arrested during observation,—they are in a ceaseless and rapid flow, and can only be studied through memory.

(5.) The phenomena naturally blend with each other, and are presented in complexity—*e.g.*, pleasure, pain, desire slide into each other.—*Hamilton*, '*Metaphysics*,' i. 375–9 (abridged).

Facilities.

These are peculiar. There is indeed only one external condition on which the study is dependent, and that is language—a language copious and pliable enough to express its abstractions. The philosopher has no new events to seek, no new combinations to form. If he only effectively pursue the method of observation and analysis, he may even dispense with the study of philosophical systems. This is at best only useful as a mean towards a deeper and more varied study of himself.—*Hamilton*, '*Metaphysics*,' i. 382.

Laws for.

There are three grand laws :—

(1.) That no fact be assumed as a fact of consciousness but what is ultimate and simple.

(2.) That the whole facts of consciousness be taken without reserve or hesitation, whether given as constituent, or as regulative data.

(3.) That nothing but the facts of consciousness be taken, or only such inferences of reasoning as are legitimately deduced from, and in subordination to, the immediate data of consciousness.—*Hamilton*, '*Metaphysics*,' i. 269.

2. *Preconscious mental activity.*

By tracing the evidences there are in man of *unconscious* mental activity; by showing that we have instances of it in the case of habits, secret associations of ideas, mechanical and instinctive actions, &c.; by discovering, in this way, that the intelligent principle within us is independent of consciousness, and can operate by its own laws, whether in the light of consciousness or out of it; we are enabled to carry the analogy up to a *preconscious* era of our existence, and conclude that there are mental activities analogous to these going on even in this early period of our being, out of which activities consciousness itself is at last evolved.—*Morell*, '*Introduction to Mental Philosophy on the Inductive Method*,' pp. 53, 54.

3. *Unconscious mental action.*

Cerebral changes may take place *unconsciously* if the sensorium be either in a state of absolute torpor, or be for a time nonreceptive as regards those changes, its activity being exerted in some other direction; or, to express the same fact psychologically, that mental (?) changes, of whose *results we subsequently* become conscious, may go on *below the plane* of consciousness, either during profound sleep, or while the attention is wholly engrossed by some entirely different train of thought.—*Carpenter*, '*Mental Physiology*,' p. 516.

Example of unconscious action.

When we have been *trying to recollect* some name, place, phrase, occurrence, &c., —and after vainly employing all the expedients we can think of for bringing the desiderated idea to our minds, have abandoned the attempt as useless,—it will often occur *spontaneously* a little while afterwards, suddenly flashing, as it were, into our consciousness, either when we are thinking of something altogether different, or on waking out of profound sleep. Now it is important to note, in the *first* case, that the mind may have been entirely engrossed in the meantime by some entirely different subject of contemplation, and that we cannot detect any link of association whereby the result has been obtained, notwithstanding that the whole 'train of thought' which has passed through the mind in the interval may be most distinctly remembered; and, in the *second*, that the missing idea seems more likely to present itself when the sleep has been profound than when it has been disturbed.—*Carpenter*, '*Mental Physiology*,' p. 519.

If we admit (what physiology is rendering more and more probable) that our mental feelings, as well as our sensations, have for their physical antecedents particular states of the nerves, it may well be believed that the apparently suppressed links in a chain of association really are latent; that they are not even momentarily felt, the chain of causation being continued only physically, by one organic state of the nerves succeeding another so rapidly that the state of mental consciousness appropriate to each is not produced. —*Mill*, '*Examination of Hamilton*,' p 341.

4. *Sub-consciousness.*

Two main questions arise as to the limits of the sub-consciousness region (1.) How far does it extend in relation to the organism and its processes? Do all organic processes modify it in some way? (2.) To what extent is it modified by past psychical activities? Do things long forgotten, yet capable of being revived, somehow affect the whole state of mind in the interval? Without troubling ourselves about this difficult question, we may say that at any time there is a whole aggregate or complex of mental phenomena, sensations, impressions, thought, &c., most of which are obscure, transitory, and not distinguished. With this wide obscure region of the sub-conscious, there stands contrasted the narrow luminous region of the clearly conscious. An impression or thought must be presumed to be already present in the first or sub-conscious region before the mind by an effort of attention can draw it into the second region. To adopt the metaphor of Wundt, the whole mental region (conscious and sub-conscious) answers to the total field of view present to the eye in varying degrees of distinctness at any moment when the organ is fixed in a certain direction, the latter region, that of attention or clear consciousness, correspond to that narrow area of 'perfect vision' on which the glance is fixed.—*Sully*, '*Outlines of Psychology*,' p. 74.

Take the case of a player on the pianoforte while still a learner, and before the succession of volitions has attained the rapidity which practice ultimately gives it. In this stage of progress there is, beyond all doubt, a conscious volition, anterior to the playing of each particular note. Yet has the player, when the piece is finished, the smallest remembrance of each of these volitions as a separate fact? In like manner, have we, when we have finished reading a volume, the smallest memory of our successive volitions to turn the pages? On the contrary, we only know that we must have turned them, because without doing so we could not have read to the end. Yet these volitions were not latent; every time we turned over a leaf we must have formed a conscious purpose of turning; but, the purpose having been instantly fulfilled, the attention was arrested in the process for too short a time to leave a more than momentary remembrance of it.—*Mill*, '*Examination of Hamilton*,' p. 337.

A.—PSYCHOLOGY AND PHILOSOPHY OF COGNITION.

III.

METHODS OF PSYCHOLOGY.

THE method of psychology is double: it studies psychological phenomena, subjectively, by means of consciousness, memory, and reasoning; objectively, by means of the facts, signs, opinions, and actions which interpret them. Psychology does not study the facts of consciousness simply in the adult state, it endeavours to discover and to follow their development. It also has recourse to the comparative method, and does not disdain the humblest manifestations of psychical life.—*Ribot,* '*Contemporary English Psychology,*' p. 323.

I. SUBJECTIVE METHOD—INTROSPECTION.

Description of the Method.

Introspection is the turning of the Mind round on itself so as to view its own states. This power of internal observation we call Self-consciousness, the Internal Sense (Kant), or Reflection (Locke). An Introspective element seems to be present in all mental states, though only implicitly, and this we can develop by a special effort of attention, *e.g.*, I may develop the consciousness that I see a house, into: I *see* a house, where the thing that is chiefly dwelt on is the sensation of sight and not the object seen; or into: *I* see a house, where my own personality is the thing chiefly, though not exclusively, prominent.—*Rylands,* '*Handbook, &c.,*' p. 2.

Its Use.

In the study of the human mind we use self-consciousness or the internal sense just as in the study of the material universe we employ the external sense as the organ or instrument. I certainly do not propose to find out the intuitions of the mind by the bodily eye, aided or unaided by the microscope, nor discover their mode of operation by the blowpipe. They are in their nature spiritual, and so sense cannot see them, or hear them, or handle them, nor can the telescope in its widest range detect them. Still they are *there* in our mental nature; there is an eye of wider sweep than the telescope, and more searching than the microscope, ready to be directed towards them. By introspection we may look on them in operation, by abstraction or analyses we may separate the essential peculiarity from the rough concrete presentations; and by generalisation we may rise to the law which they follow.—*M'Cosh,* '*Intuitions of the Mind,*' p. 3.

Difficulties of the Subjective Method.

We have it not in our power to ascertain, by any direct process, what consciousness told us at the time when its revelations were in their pristine purity. It only offers itself to our inspection as it exists now, when those original revelations are overlaid and buried under a mountainous heap of acquired notions and perceptions.—*Mill,* '*Examination of Hamilton,*' p. 171.

Consciousness, our principal instrument, is not sufficient, in its ordinary state; it is no more sufficient in psychological inquiries than the naked eye in optical inquiries. For its range is not great; its illusions are many and invincible; it is necessary continually to test and correct its evidence, nearly always to assist it, to present objects to it in a brighter light, to magnify them, and construct for its use a kind of microscope and telescope.—*Taine,* '*On Intelligence,*' p. x.

It needs therefore to be Supplemented.

In order to correct the narrowness of our personal observations we must look to external quarters; we must gather what are the convictions of other men from their deeds, ever passing under our notice, and as recorded in history, and from their conversation and their writings, as the expression of human thought and sentiment. —*M'Cosh*, '*Examination of Mill,*' p. 31.

But it is always Essential to Mental Study.

Notwithstanding its drawbacks, Introspection must have an important place in any system of Psychology. It must be remembered that we should not have any notion of Mind at all if it were not for Introspection.—*Rylands*, '*Handbook, &c.,*' p 3.

Objection to the Use of Introspection in Psychology.

To direct consciousness inwardly to the observation of a particular state of mind is to isolate that activity for the time, to cut it off from its relations, and therefore to render it unnatural. In order to observe its own action, it is necessary that the mind pause from activity, and yet it is the train of activity that is to be observed. So long as you cannot effect the pause necessary for self-contemplation, there cannot be a sufficient observation of the current of activity: if the pause is effected, then there can be nothing to observe, there would be no consciousness, for consciousness is awakened by the transition from one physical or mental state to another. This cannot be accounted a vain and theoretical objection, for the results of introspection too surely confirm its validity: what was a question once is a question still, and instead of being resolved by introspective analysis is only 'fixed and fed.'—*Maudsley*, '*Physiology of Mind,*' pp. 16, 17.

The Objection Answered.

If we would know what is within, how shall we be satisfied but by looking within? Impossible, says an acute physiologist, the thing cannot be done;—if you turn attention on the current of thoughts and feelings passing within you disturb the current, nay, even break it, and so lose the thing for which you are seeking. This much Dr Maudsley has borrowed from Comte, and to small advantage. Every man is conscious of his thoughts and feelings, that is, he knows them as elements in his own experience. The physician does not hesitate to ask his patient how he feels. He does not apologise for the question, as if it hazarded a sudden termination of all experience save sudden perplexity. Every one possesses the ability to describe his own experience, and is well aware that it is possible to concentrate attention on a definite class of facts in his experience without seriously disturbing the current of his thoughts and attendant feelings. If there is to be any regard to the facts of personal experience,—and all physiologists admit that attention must be given to them,—it is impossible save by reference to consciousness, and such reference involves introspection.

On the other hand, it is impossible to construct an adequate philosophy of mind by use of introspection alone. Experience does not carry its own explanation. There is very much essentially connected with our experience which nevertheless does not come within experience. We must, therefore, turn observation in other directions. And he who grants the validity of observation, when turned upon the inner sphere, will no less freely grant its value when turned upon the outer.—*Calderwood*, '*Relations of Mind and Brain,*' pp 6, 7.

II. OBJECTIVE METHOD—OBSERVATION. (See also EXPERIENCE.)

In what it Consists.

The objective method consists in studying psychological facts from the outside, not from the inside; in the internal facts which translate them, not in the consciousness which gives them birth. The natural expression of the passions, the variety of languages, and the events of history are so many facts which permit us to trace the mental causes that have produced them. the morbid derangement of the organism which produces intellectual disorders; anomalies, monsters in the psychological order, are to us as experiences prepared by nature, and all the more precious as the experimentation is more rare. Study of the instincts, passions, and habits of the different animals supplies us with facts whose interpretation (often difficult) enables us by induction, deduction, or analogy to reconstruct a mode of psychological existence. In short, the objective method, instead of being personal, like the simple method of reflection, lends to facts an impersonal character; it bends before them; it moulds its thrones upon the reality.—*Ribot, 'English Psychology,'* p. 25

Objective observation embraces not only the mental phenomena of the individuals who are personally known to us, old and young, but those of others of whom we hear or read in biography, &c. Also it includes the study of minds in masses or aggregates, as they present themselves in national sentiments and actions, and in the events of history. It includes, too, a comparative study of mind by observing its agreements and differences among different races, and even among different grades of animal life. The study of the simpler phases of mind in the child, in backward and uncivilised races, and in the lower animals, is especially valuable for understanding the growth of the mature or fully-developed human mind.

Finally, the external or objective method includes the study of mental phenomena in connection with bodily and more particularly nervous processes. All external observation of mental phenomena takes place by noting some of their bodily accompaniments (movements of expression, vocal actions, and so on). In addition to this, psychology considers the actions of the nervous system in so far as they affect and determine mental activity.—*Sully, 'Outlines of Psychology,'* pp. 5, 6.

It is, however, valueless by itself.

M. Comte claims for physiologists alone the scientific knowledge of intellectual and moral phenomena. He totally rejects psychological observations, properly so called, the internal consciousness. He thinks that we have to acquire our knowledge of the human mind by observing others. How we can observe and interpret the mental operations of others without previously knowing our own, he does not tell us. But he considers it evident that the observation of ourselves by ourselves can teach us only very little concerning feelings, and nothing on the subject of understanding. "It is not necessary," says Mr Stuart Mill, "to refute a sophism at length, whose most surprising part is, that it should have imposed on any one."—*Ribot, 'English Psychology,'* p. 84.

Objective Psychology, so far as it relates to inferior forms of life, is merely a field for more or less probable conjecture, in which the basis of certainty diminishes the further we depart from the human type. Knowledge garnered from our own experiences and those of our fellow-creatures affords, as it were, the lamp wherewith we seek to illuminate the dark places of animal Psychology. — *Bastian, 'The Brain, &c.,'* p. 168.

Whatever explanation the brain, nerves, and physical forces may furnish of the rise of certain states of mind, they can render no account of peculiarly mental facts, such as consciousness, intelligence, emotion, the appreciation of beauty, and the sense of moral obligation. These must ever be studied by self-consciousness, and not by any method of sensible observation, or of weighing and measuring, and the results reached by careful self-inspection can never be set aside or superseded by any inquiry into unconscious and unthinking forces. In particular, physiology can never settle for us the nature of intuition as an exercise of mind, nor determine the ultimate laws of thought and belief.—*M'Cosh, 'Intuitions of the Mind,'* p. 8.

The Two Methods must be Combined.

Discussions between those who will admit nothing but interior observation like Jouffroy, and those who recognise nothing but exterior observation like Broussais, resemble indecisive battles, after which both the combatants claim the victory. The former triumphantly produce their analysis and defy their adversaries to divine, without the aid of reflection, what it is to feel, to desire, to wish, to abstract. The latter reply that the dialogue of the *ego* with the *ego* cannot last long, and that they prefer to cultivate the fertile soil of experience. On both sides the question is only half understood. Each of these systems has need of the other. They complete each other reciprocally, the subjective method proceeding by analysis, and the objective method by synthesis; the interior method being the most necessary, since without it we do not even know of what we are talking; the exterior method being the most fruitful, since the field of its investigation is almost unlimited.—*Ribot*, '*English Psychology*,' p. 24.

To try to discover mental phenomena and their laws solely by watching the external signs and effects of others' thoughts, feelings, and volitions, would plainly be absurd. For these external manifestations are in themselves as empty of meaning as words in an unknown tongue, and only receive their meaning by a reference to what we ourselves have thought and felt. On the other hand, an exclusive attention to the contents of our individual mind would never give us a *general* knowledge of mind. In order to eliminate the effects of individuality we must at every step compare our own modes of thinking and feeling with those of other minds. The wider the area included in our comparison the sounder are our generalisations likely to be.—*Sully*, '*Outlines of Psychology*,' pp. 6, 7.

III. THE SOCIOLOGICAL METHOD.

The special resource of sociology is that it participates directly in the elementary composition of the common ground of our intellectual resources. It is plain that this logical co-operation of the new science is as important as that of any of the anterior sciences. Sociology adds to our other means of research that which I have called the *historical method*, and which will hereafter, when we are sufficiently habituated to it, constitute a fourth fundamental means of observation. But, though sociology has given us this resource, it is more or less applicable to all orders of scientific speculation. We have only to regard every discovery, at the moment it is effected, as a true social phenomenon, forming a part of the general series of human development, and on that ground subject to the laws of succession and the methods of investigation which characterise that great evolution.—*Comte*, '*Positive Philos.*,' ii. 102.

Progress in intelligence, associated with progress in language, has to be treated as accompanying social progress; which, while furthering it, is furthered by it. From experiences which accumulate, come comparisons leading to generalisations of simple kinds. Gradually the ideas of uniformity, order, and cause, becoming nascent, gain clearness with each fresh truth established. And while there has to be noted the connection between each phase of science and the concomitant phase of social life, there have also to be noted the stages through which, within the body of science itself, there is an advance from a few, simple, incoherent truths, to a number of specialised sciences forming an agreement of truths that are multitudinous, varied, exact, coherent.—*Spencer*, '*Sociology*,' i. 430.

IV. THE LOGICAL METHOD IN PSYCHOLOGY: ANALYSIS AND SYNTHESIS.

The respective values of these different sources of knowledge (the Subjective and the Objective) respecting psychical facts will appear more plainly if we keep clearly in view the aim of psychology and the logical methods to be followed. Briefly, we may say that psychology has to classify mental phenomena and to determine the laws of their production, to show how simple states combine in complex states Now this can be effected in one of two ways.

(*a.*) We may proceed, first of all, from effects to antecedent conditions, products to factors. This mode of proceeding in psychology is commonly spoken of as the analytical method It may also be called the inductive method, since the general laws respecting the aggregation and production of mental states are in the first instance reached in this way

(*b.*) In the second place, we may set out from elementary facts, and by help of certain laws of composition (reached by the analytical way, supplemented if necessary by hypothesis) reconstruct the successive stages of psychical production This is the synthetical method in psychology It may also be called the genetic method. It is deductive in so far as it reasons down from laws reached by previous inductions or by hypotheses.—*Sully*, '*Outlines of Psychology*,' p 684

Repudiation by Ontology of Psychological Method.

Psychology, or 'the science of the human mind,' instead of attempting to correct, does all in her power to ratify, the inadvertent deliverances of ordinary thought, —to prove them to be right Hence psychology must, of necessity, come in for a share of the castigation which is doled out and directed upon common and natural opinion It would be well if this could be avoided, but it cannot Philosophy must either forego her existence, or carry on her operations corrective of ordinary thinking, and subversive of psychological science. It is, indeed, only by accident that philosophy is inimical to psychology: it is because psychology is the abettor and accomplice of common opinion *after the act*, but in reference to natural thinking, she is essentially controversial Philosophy, however, is bound to deal much more rigorously and sternly with the doctrines of psychology than with the spontaneous judgments of unthinking man, because while these in themselves are mere oversights or inadvertencies, psychology converts them into downright falsities by stamping them with the countersign or *imprimatur* of a specious, though spurious science In the occasional cases, moreover, in which psychology, instead of ratifying, endeavours to rectify the inadvertencies of popular thinking, she only makes matters worse, by complicating the original error with a new contradiction, and sometimes with several new ones, of her own creation.—*Ferrier*, '*Institutes of Metaphysics*,' pp 32, 33

V ATTENTION.

Defined

The same act of knowledge, with similar objective conditions, may be performed with greater or less energy This greater or less energy in the operation of knowing is called *attention*; which word, as its etymology suggests, is another term for tension or effort, and was doubtless first transferred to the spiritual operation from the strained condition of the part or whole of the bodily organism, which accompanies or follows such effort.—*Porter*, '*The Human Intellect*,' p. 69

Attention may be defined as the concentration of consciousness, or the direction of mental energy upon a definite object or objects.—'*Encyclop. Brit.*,' iii 52

Attention may be roughly defined as the active self-direction of the mind to any object which presents itself to it at the moment It is somewhat the same as the mind's 'consciousness' of what is present to it The field of consciousness, however, is wider than that of attention Consciousness admits of many degrees of distinctness I may be very vaguely or indistinctly conscious of some bodily sensation, of some haunting recollection, and so on To attend is to intensify consciousness by concentrating or narrowing it on some definite and restricted area. It is to force the mind or consciousness in a particular direction so as to make the objects as distinct as possible.—*Sully*, '*Outlines of Psychology*,' p. 73.

Nature of Attention

It is usually a voluntary act.

Attention is a voluntary act; it requires an active exertion to begin and to continue it, and it may be continued as long as we will.—*Reid*, '*Works*,' p. 239.

But not always so.

When occupied with other matters, a person may speak to us, or the clock may strike, without our having any consciousness of the sound, but it is wholly impossible for us to remain in this state of unconsciousness intentionally and with will. We cannot determinately refuse to hear by voluntarily withholding our attention; and we can no more open our eyes, and by an act of will, avert our mind from all perception of sight, than we can, by an act of will, cease to live. We may close our ears or shut our eyes, as we may commit suicide; but we cannot with our organs unobstructed, wholly refuse our attention at will.—*Hamilton*, '*Metaphysics*,' i. 247.

It is of three degrees or kinds.

The first, a mere vital and irresistible act; the second, an act determined by desire, which, though involuntary, may be resisted by our will; the third, an act determined by a deliberate volition.—*Hamilton*, '*Metaphysics*,' i. 248.

The beginnings and development of attention.

From the condition of unconscious activity the soul is aroused, when it begins to attend either to its sensational condition, or to the responsive perceptional act. The soul scarcely can be said to have sensations even, till it is conscious of some sharp or positive experience of pain or pleasure. Much less can it be said to perceive, till its attention is aroused, repeated, and fixed upon some single sensible percept. We are not to suppose that the attention is developed at a single bound, or that its energy is attained by one spasm of effort; nor that the soul maintains itself always in the attent condition which it at first occasionally attains. All analogies from the states of our mature experience would lead us to believe that the soul now rises into a moment's fixed attention, and then sinks again to blank inanition. Again it is roused a second time by some earnest and intruding solicitation, attends for an instant, and relapses a second time into the merely instinctive life.—*Porter*, '*The Human Intellect*,' pp. 180, 181.

It is not a special faculty of the mind.

Attention is not a separate faculty, or a faculty of intelligence at all, but merely an act of will or desire, subordinate to a certain law of intelligence. This law is that the greater the number of objects to which our consciousness is simultaneously extended, the smaller is the intensity with which it is able to consider each, and consequently the less vivid and distinct will be the information it obtains of the several objects. Such being the law it follows that, when our interest in any particular object is excited, and when we wish to obtain all the knowledge concerning it in our power, it behoves us to limit our consideration to that object, to the exclusion of others. This is done by an act of volition or desire, which is called *attention*.—*Hamilton*, '*Metaphysics*,' i. 237.

Its relation to consciousness.

Attention is to consciousness, what the contraction of the pupil is to sight; or to the eye of the mind, what the microscope or telescope is to the bodily eye. Attention doubles all the efficiency of the special faculties, and affords them a power of which they would otherwise be destitute.—*Reid*, '*Works*,' p. 941.

To view attention as a special act of intelligence, and to distinguish it from consciousness, is utterly inept. Consciousness may be compared to a telescope, attention to the pulling out or in of the tubes in accommodating the focus to the object. Attention is consciousness, and something more. It is consciousness voluntarily applied to some determinate object, it is consciousness concentrated.—*Hamilton*, '*Metaphysics*,' i. 238.

Circumstances determining attention.

In the first place there are certain mechanical influences only partly subject to the will, such are the force and vividness of the impression, the interest attaching to an object, the trains of associated ideas exciting, or the emotions roused by its contemplation. There is, secondly, an exercise of volition employed in fixing the mind upon some definite object; this is a purely voluntary act, which can be strengthened by habit, is variable in different individuals, and to which, as being its highest stage, the name Attention is sometimes restricted —'*Encyclop. Brit.*,' iii. 52.

Can we Attend to more than a Single Object at once?

Dugald Stewart holds that we cannot.

There is indeed a great variety of cases in which the mind apparently exerts different acts of attention at once; but all this may be explained by the astonishing rapidity of thought, without supposing those acts to be co-existent. For example: in viewing a mathematical figure, say of a thousand sides, we view each side by a separate effort of attentive regard, till we have passed around the outline by successive acts of perception. The eye and the mind do this so rapidly, that when the outline is not very complicated, they seem to grasp and master the whole by a single and instantaneous act. So, in listening to a concert of music, we think we hear—*i.e.*, attentively listen to—all the instruments and separate parts together, whereas in fact we can attend to but one. When we seem to ourselves to listen to all, we, in fact, pass so rapidly from one to another as to think we attend to all together.—'*Works*,' ii. 140–143 (abridged).

Sir W. Hamilton and others say we can.

What are the facts in Stewart's example of a concert? In a musical concert we have a multitude of different instruments and voices emitting at once an infinity of different sounds. These all reach the ear at the same indivisible moment in which they perish, and, consequently, if heard at all, much more if their mutual relation or harmony be perceived, they must be all heard simultaneously. This is evident. For if the mind can attend to each minimum of sound only successively, it consequently requires a minimum of time in which it is exclusively occupied with each minimum of sound. Now in this minimum of time, there coexist with it, and with it perish, many minima of sound, which, *ex hypothesi*, are not perceived,—are not heard, as not attended to. In a concert, therefore, on this doctrine, a small number of sounds only could be perceived, and above this petty maximum all sounds would be to the ear as zero. But what is the fact? No concert, however numerous its instruments, has yet been found to have reached, far less to have surpassed, the capacity of mind and its organ. Either then we can attend to two different objects at once, or all knowledge of relation and harmony is impossible.—*Hamilton*, '*Metaphysics*,' i. 243.

The theory of Stewart labours under the following difficulties:—It excludes the possibility of comparing objects with one another. In order to compare objects so as to discern that they are alike or diverse, they must be considered together—that is, they must be attentively perceived in combination. We cannot see that two surfaces of colour are alike or unlike without perceiving them both in connection, and perceiving them both by a single attentive act. It is obvious that the mind can apprehend more than a single object at once. If it could not, it would be for ever and entirely cut off from the most important part of its knowledge, viz., the knowledge of relations, which knowledge can only be attained by the apprehension of at least two objects together —*Porter*, '*The Human Intellect*,' p. 208

Schleiermacher was able to carry on an intellectual conversation, and at the same time to see and hear all that occurred and was spoken round about him, even at the farthest side of the room.—*Martensen*, '*Christian Ethics*,' ii. 418.

Value of the Power of Attention

The greater capacity of continuous thinking that a man possesses, the longer and more steadily can he follow out the same train of thought,—the stronger is his power of attention; and in proportion to his power of attention will be the success with which his labour is rewarded. When we turn for the first time our view on any given object a hundred other things still retain possession of our thoughts. But if we are vigorous enough to pursue our course in spite of obstacles, every step as we advance will be found easier, the distractions gradually diminish; the attention is more exclusively concentrated upon its object. Thus the difference between an ordinary mind and the mind of a Newton consists principally in this, that the one is capable of the application of a more continuous attention than the other,—that a Newton is able without fatigue to connect inference with inference in one long series towards a determinate end, while the man of inferior capacity is soon obliged to break or let fall the thread which he had begun to spin. This is, in fact, what Sir Isaac, with equal modesty and shrewdness, himself admitted. To one who complimented him on his genius, he replied that if he had made any discoveries it was owing more to patient attention than to any other talent.—*Hamilton*, '*Metaphysics*,' i. 255, 256.

Genius is nothing but a continued attention.—*Helvetius*.

The power of applying an attention, steady and undissipated, to a single object is the sure mark of a superior genius.—*Chesterfield*, '*Letters to his Son*,' lxxxix.

The discovery of truth can only be made by the labour of attention, because it is only the labour of attention which has light for its reward.—*Malebranche*, '*Traité de Morale*,' Pt. I. ch. vi. § 1.

Without the labour of attention we shall never comprehend the grandeur of religion, the sanctity of morals, the littleness of all that is not God, the absurdity of the passions, and of all our internal miseries.—*Malebranche*, '*Traité de Morale*,' Pt. I. ch. v. § 4.

Growth of Attention.

With the general progress of mental development, the direction of the Attention to *ideas* rather than to sense impressions, which was at first difficult, becomes more and more easy; its *continuous* fixation upon one subject becomes so completely habitual that it is often less easy to break the continuity than to sustain it; and the time at last arrives when the *direction* of that attention is given by the individual's *own* will instead of by the will of another.—*Carpenter*, '*Mental Physiol.*,' pp. 136–37.

Non-Voluntary and Voluntary Attention.

When the mind is acted upon by the mere force of the object presented, the act of attention is said to be non-voluntary. It may also be called reflex (or automatic), because it bears a striking analogy to reflex movement, that is to say, movement following sensory stimulation without the intervention of a conscious purpose. On the other hand, when we attend to a thing under the impulse of a desire, such as curiosity, or a wish to know about a thing, we are said to do so by an act of will or voluntarily.—*Sully*, '*Outlines of Psychology*,' p. 80.

The contrast between the *volitional* and the automatic states of Attention is particularly well shown in the effects of *painful* impressions on the nervous system. It is well known that such impressions as would ordinarily produce severe pain, may for a time be *completely unfelt*, though the exclusive direction of the attention elsewhere; and this direction may either depend (*a*) upon the *determination of the ego*, or (*b*) upon the *attractiveness of the object*, or (*c*, *d*, *e*) on the combination of both.—*Carpenter*, '*Mental Physiol.*,' p. 138.

The Nervous Concomitants of Attention

The fact that attention is an act of the mind would suggest that its nervous concomitants are certain processes in those motor centres which we know to be especially concerned in movement or action. This conjecture is borne out by the fact that the act of attention is commonly accompanied by muscular contractions. Among these are the muscular actions which subserve the intellectual operation, such as the fixing of the eye on an object or the turning of the ear in the direction of a sound. In addition to these there are other actions which constitute the characteristic expression of attention. Attention is commonly accompanied by a fixing of the eyes, head, and whole body; and this fixity is maintained by an act of will. In very close attention, as in trying to recall something, there are other bodily accompaniments, such as the compression of the lips, frowning, and so on. Finally, in all close attention there is a feeling of tension or strain which appears to indicate muscular effort. As Fechner says, in looking steadfastly this feeling is referred to the eye, in listening closely, to the ear, in trying to 'think' or recollect, to the head or brain.—*Sully*, '*Outlines of Psychology*,' p. 77.

VI. REFLECTION.

Its Nature.

Definition.

Reflection is properly attention directed to the phenomena of mind.—*Hamilton*, '*Metaphysics*,' i. 236.

It is in our power when we come to the years of understanding, to give attention to our own thoughts and passions, and the various operations of our minds. And, when we make these the objects of our attention, either while they are present or when they are recent and fresh in our memory, this act of the mind is called *reflection*.—*Reid*, '*Works*,' p. 232.

Reflection is not concerned with objects themselves, in order to obtain directly concepts of them, but is a state of the mind in which we set ourselves to discover the subjective conditions under which we may arrive at concepts.—*Kant*, '*Critique*,' vol. ii. 226.

As described by Locke.

By reflection I mean that notice which the mind takes of its own operations, and the manner of them, by reason whereof there come to be ideas of these operations in the understanding. It is the perception of the operations of our own mind within us, as it is employed about the ideas it has got; which operations when the soul comes to reflect on and consider, do furnish the understanding with another set of ideas, which could not be had from things without; and such are perception, thinking, doubting, believing, reasoning, knowing, willing, and all the different actings of our own minds, which we being conscious of and observing in ourselves, do from these receive into our understandings as distinct ideas, as we do from bodies affecting our senses. This source of ideas every man has wholly in himself; and though it be not sense, as having nothing to do with external objects, yet it is very like it, and might properly enough be called internal sense.—*Locke*, '*Human Understanding*,' II. i. 4.

Reflection, in Locke's meaning of the word (and this is the more correct), is only Consciousness, concentrated by an act of Will on the phenomena of Mind—*i.e.*, internal attention.—*Hamilton, in Reid's* '*Works*,' p. 420, note.

Among many English writers reflection is freely used as the exact equivalent of consciousness. It is the great and distinctive merit of Locke to have called attention to it as a separate source of knowledge, and to have claimed for the knowledge which it furnishes equal authority and certainty with that which is received through the senses. —*Porter*, '*Human Intellect*,' p 86.

Dean Mansel, however, says—

The term reflection is unfortunately chosen, as it naturally suggests the notion of a *turning back* of the mind upon an object previously existing; and thus represents the phenomena of consciousness as distinct from the act of reflecting upon them. Understood in this sense, reflection can have no other objects than the phenomena of sensation in some one of its modes; for sensation and reflection are with Locke the only recognised sources of knowledge, and if reflection implies a previously existing operation of mind, that operation can be none other than sensation. Interpreting Locke in this sense, Condillac and his followers were only carrying out the doctrine to its legitimate consequences when they maintained that sensation was the only original source of ideas, and furnished the whole material of our knowledge.—'*Metaphysics*,' pp. 143, 144.

It is a sustained act of the mind.

We can certainly repeat a mental state again and again, allowing no other activity to intervene. As we thus repeat the activity in a series of similar acts, we present to our consciousness substantially the same object, and so secure an opportunity for bestowing upon it that continuous or sustained attention which is essential to exact observation What we fail to notice at one look, we catch by another. What we only faintly apprehend at the first sight, we fix and confirm by the second What we observe incorrectly or partially in one act, we discern truly and completely in the act which follows This retention or repetition of the object becomes the condition of the continuity of the act of consciousness, and hence it is a distinguishing characteristic of the philosophic consciousness It is because the mind does, as it were, turn in upon itself, that this effort of consciousness is termed *reflection*—*i.e.*, the bending back or retortion of the soul on itself. It is because this repetition of the object, or retortion in the act, is found to be practically necessary, in order to any accurate and successful observation of consciousness, that consciousness the act, has been supposed to be a remembrance, a sort of second thought, and the power has been resolved into memory. Second-thinking is, indeed, necessary to reflective consciousness; and not only second-thinking, but a sustained and continued application of the attention to the continuously repeated act. —*Porter*, '*Human Intellect*,' p. 107.

It is the last of the mental powers to be developed.

The power of reflection upon the operations of their own minds does not appear at all in children. Men must be come to some ripeness of understanding before they are capable of it. Of all the powers of the human mind, it seems to be the last that unfolds itself. From infancy, till we come to the years of understanding, we are employed solely about external objects And, although the mind is conscious of its operations, it does not attend to them; its attention is turned solely to the external objects, about which those operations are employed. Thus, when a man is angry, he is conscious of his passion; but his attention is turned to the person who offended him, and the circumstances of the offence, while the passion of anger is not in the least the object of his attention. Most men seem incapable of acquiring the power of reflection in any considerable degree.—*Reid*, '*Works*,' pp. 239, 240.

Power comes by practice.

Like all our other powers, reflection is greatly improved by exercise; and until a man has got the habit of attending to the operations of his own mind, he can never have clear and distinct notions of them, nor form any steady judgment concerning them. To acquire this habit is a work of time and labour, even in those who begin it early, and whose natural talents are tolerably fitted for it; but the difficulty will be daily diminishing, and the advantage of it is great.—*Reid*, '*Works*,' p. 240.

Its Function.

Reflection creates nothing—can create nothing; everything exists previous to reflection in the consciousness, but everything pre-exists there in confusion and obscurity; it is the work of reflection in adding itself to consciousness, to illuminate that which was obscure, to develop that which was enveloped. Reflection is for consciousness what the microscope and the telescope are for the natural sight; neither of these instruments makes or changes the objects; but in examining them on every side, in penetrating to their centre, these instruments illuminate them, and discover to us their characters and their laws.—*Cousin*, '*Hist. of Mod. Phil.*,' i. 275.

Its Relation to Consciousness.

Reflection ought to be distinguished from consciousness. All men are conscious of the operations of their own minds, at all times, while they are awake; but there are few who reflect upon them, or make them objects of thought.—*Reid*, '*Works*,' p. 239.

Locke nowhere in form defines the relation of consciousness to reflection. It never seems to have occurred to him that they are related, or that he ought to explain what their relations are. The questions which, since his time, have assumed so great interest and importance, did not present themselves to his mind. From the use which he makes of these terms, however, we are fully authorised to derive the following as a just statement of the opinions which he would have expressed had his attention been called to the relation of consciousness to reflection. In order to gain ideas or permanent knowledge of the mind, we must use a certain power with reflection and consideration. But the power itself is not created or first exercised by or in such acts or efforts. These are but exercises of this power in a given way and energy. The power itself is the capacity of the mind to know its acts or states. This power is consciousness, which Locke himself has defined to be "the perception of what passes in a man's own mind," and without which man never thinks at all. When this power is used in a peculiar way and with energy or concentration enough to secure a certain effect, it becomes *reflection*. *Reflection* is therefore *consciousness* intensified by attention. Inasmuch, however, as the power is rarely referred to except as giving the results of actual knowledge, *reflection* is the word by which it is usually known.—*Porter*, '*Human Intellect*,' p. 87.

Transcendental Reflection (according to *Kant*).

Transcendental Reflection is the act whereby I confront the comparison of ideas generally, with the cognitive faculty in which the comparison is instituted, and distinguish whether the ideas are compared with each other as belonging to the pure understanding or to sensuous intuition.—*Ueberweg*, '*Hist. of Phil.*,' ii. 173.

VII. INTUITION. (See Intuitions, Innate Ideas.)

Defined and Described.

Intuition is used to denote the apprehension we have of self-evident truths—the immediate consciousness of an object—an *insight*.—*Hamilton*, '*Logic*,' i. 127, ii. 73.

Intuition is opposed to thought and its various products. It is an immediate knowledge or cognition of something in space, in time, or both. Its object is sometimes said to be individual; which is so far true that the object of an intuition can never be general; but, on the one hand, an intuition often consists of many separable parts, and, on the other hand, in order to recognise an individual object as the same that we previously knew, we must have at least two intuitions (a present and a past one) and institute a comparison between them.—*Monck*, '*Sir W Hamilton*,' p 181.

What we know or apprehend as soon as we perceive or attend to it, we are said to know by intuition, things which we know by intuition cannot be made more certain by arguments, than they are at first We know by intuition that all the parts of a thing together are equal to the whole of it. Axioms are propositions known by intuition —*Taylor*, '*Elements of Thought*.'

In intuition we look into the object, we discover something in it, or belonging to it, or we discover a relation between it and some other object Intuitively the mind contemplates a particular body as occupying space and being in space, and it is by a subsequent intellectual process, in which abstraction acts an important part, that the idea of space is formed Intuitively the mind contemplates an event as happening in time, and then by a further process arrives at the notion of time. The mind has not intuitively an idea of cause or causation in the abstract, but, discovering a given effect, it looks for a specific cause It does not form some sort of a vague notion of a general infinite, but, fixing its attention on some individual thing,—such as space, or time, or God,—it is constrained to believe it to be infinite The child has not formed to itself a refined idea of moral good, but, contemplating a given action, it proclaims it to be good or evil The same remark holds good of the intuitive judgments of the mind ; that is, when it compares two or more things, and proclaims them at once to agree or disagree. I do not, without a process of discursive thought, pronounce, or even understand, the general maxim that things which are equal to the same things are equal to one another, but, on discovering that first one bush and then another bush are of the same height as my staff, I decide that the two bushes are equal to one another —*M'Cosh*, '*Intuitions of the Mind*,' p 27

Intuition is the immediate knowledge which we have of any object of consciousness Thus consciousness is coextensive with intuition, and therefore it might appear that the term intuition was useless But it is convenient to have some word to distinguish the knowledge given in consciousness from the knowledge which is the result of inference, and the word we have used appears the best suited for that purpose Moreover, consciousness is more properly applied to our knowledge of *objects* or *phenomena*; whereas we have now to bring into prominence the *relations between* objects The *simple* objects of intuition are identical with the objects of consciousness. A sensation, an idea, an emotion, any phenomenon of the mind, is given to us in an intuition —*Jardine*, '*Psychology*,' p 229.

Sometimes the mind perceives the agreement or disagreement of two ideas immediatly by themselves, without the intervention of any other; and this I think we may call intuitive knowledge For in this the mind is at no pains of proving or examining, but perceives the truth as the eye doth light, only by being directed toward it Thus the mind perceives that white is not black, that a circle is not a triangle, that three are more than two, and equal to one and two Such kind of truths the mind perceives at the first sight of the ideas together, by bare intuition, without the intervention of any other idea; and this kind of knowledge is the clearest and most certain that human frailty is capable of. This part of knowledge is irresistible, and, like bright sunshine, forces itself immediately to be perceived, as soon as ever the mind turns its view that way. It is on this intuition that depends all the certainty and evidence of all our knowledge —*Locke*, '*Human Understanding*,' iv ii. 1.

Some judgments are, in the proper sense of the word, intuitions Such are termed axioms, first principles, principles of common sense, self-evident truths.—'*Reid*, *Summarised by Ueberweg*'

Forms of Intuition according to Kant.

The forms of intuition are space and time Space is the form of external sensibility; time is the form of internal and indirectly of external sensibility. On the *à priori* nature of space depends the possibility of geometrical, and on *à priori* nature of time depends the possibility of geometrical judgments.—*Ueberweg*, '*Hist. of Phil.*,' ii. 157.

The two Principal Modes of Religious Intuition

These are the Feeling of Dependence, and the Conviction of Moral Obligation. To these two facts of the inner consciousness may be traced, as to their sources, the two great outward acts by which religion in various forms has been manifested among men; *Prayer*, by which they seek to win God's blessing upon the future; and *Expiation*, by which they strive to atone for the offences of the past.—*Mansel*, '*Limits of Religious Thought*,' p. 78.

VIII COMMON SENSE.

The phrase is loose and ambiguous.

The phrase 'common sense' is an unfortunate, because a loose and ambiguous one. Common sense (besides its use by Aristotle) has two meanings in ordinary discourse. It may signify, *first*, that unacquired, unbought, untaught sagacity, which certain men have by nature, and which other men never could acquire, even though they were subjected to the process mentioned by Solomon (Prov. xxvii. 22), and brayed in a mortar. Or it might signify the *communis sensus*, or the perceptions and judgments which are common to all men. It is only in this latter sense that the argument from common sense is a philosophic one, that is, only on the condition that the appeal be to convictions which are in all men; and further, that there has been a systematic exposition of them. Reid did make a most legitimate use of the argument from common sense, appealing to convictions in all men, and bringing out to view, and expressing with greater or less accuracy, the principles involved in these convictions. But then he has also taken advantage of the first meaning of the phrase; he represents the strength of these original judgments as *good sense*.—*M'Cosh*, '*Intuitions of the Mind*,' p 93

Its various meanings.

The various meanings in which the term Common Sense is met with, in ancient and modern times, may, I think, be reduced to four; and these fall into two categories, according as it is, or is not, limited to the sphere of sense proper.

1. *As restricted to sense proper.*

(*a*) Under this head Common Sense has only a single meaning It was employed by Aristotle to denote the Central or Common Sensory, that is, the faculty in which the various reports of the several senses are reduced to the unity of a common apperception.

2. As *not limited to the sphere of sense proper*, it comprises three meanings.

(*b*) It denotes the complement of those cognitions or convictions which we receive from nature; which all men therefore possess in common; and by which they test the truth of knowledge and the morality of actions This is the meaning in which the expression is now emphatically employed in philosophy, and which may be, therefore, called its *philosophical* signification. Thus employed, it does not denote a peculiar sense, distinct from intelligence, by which truth is apprehended or revealed.

(*c*) In the third signification, Common Sense may be used with emphasis on the adjective or on the substantive. In the former case, it denotes such an ordinary complement of intelligence, that if a person be deficient therein, he is accounted mad or foolish In the latter case, it expresses native, practical intelligence, natural prudence, mother wit, tact in behaviour, acuteness in the observation of character, &c., in contrast to habits of acquired learning, or of speculation away from the affairs of life.

(*d*) In the fourth and last signification, Common Sense is no longer a natural quality; it denotes an acquired perception or feeling of the common duties and proprieties expected from each member of society—a sense of conventional decorum.—*Hamilton, in Reid's* '*Works*,' Note a, pp. 756–59.

Reid's conception of Common Sense was indefinite and inconsistently conceived Common Sense was at one time appealed to as the power of knowledge in general, as it is possessed and employed by a man of ordinary development and opportunities. At another it was treated as the Faculty of Reason—or the Source of Principles, the *Light of Nature*, &c. &c.—*Ueberweg*, '*Hist. of Phil*,' ii. 396.

The following extracts may serve as illustrations of the varied use of this phrase:—

This phrase embraces the primary, original, or ultimate facts of consciousness, on which all the others depend.—*Monck*, '*Hamilton*,' p. 171.

It is by the help of an innate power of distinction that we recognise the differences of things, as it is by a contrary power of composition that we recognise their identities. These powers, in some degree, are common to all minds; and as they are the basis of our whole knowledge, they may be said to constitute what we call *common sense*.—*Harris*, '*Philosophical Arrange.*,' chap. ix.

The Stoics recognised notions which all men equally receive and understand. These cannot be opposed to one another; they form what is called common sense.—*Bouvier*, '*Hist. de la Phil*,' i. 149.

Dr. Beattie uses the phrase to denote that power by which the mind perceives the truth of any intuitive proposition. It should be restricted to that class of intuitive truths which I have called 'fundamental laws of belief.'—*Stewart*, '*Life of Reid*,' p. 27.

Philosophy of Common Sense.

The Philosophy of Common Sense is that which accepts the testimony of our faculties as trustworthy within their respective spheres, and rests all human knowledge on certain first truths or primitive beliefs, which are the constitutive elements or fundamental forms of our rational nature, and the regulating principles of our conduct.—*Fleming*, '*Vocab. of Phil.*,' p. 95.

To argue from common sense is nothing more than to render available the presumption in favour of the original facts of consciousness,—*that what is by nature necessarily* BELIEVED *to be, truly* is. Aristotle thus enounces the argument: "What *appears to all*, that we affirm *to be*, and he who rejects this *belief*, will assuredly advance nothing better worthy of credit." The argument from common sense postulates and founds on the assumption—that our original beliefs be not proved self-contradictory.—*Hamilton*, '*Discussions*,' p. 88.

Principles of Common Sense (Compare INTUITIONS.)

If there are certain principles, as I think there are, which the constitution of our nature leads us to believe, and which we are under a necessity to take for granted in the common concerns of life, without being able to give a reason for them,—these are what we call the principles of common sense. Such original and natural judgments are a part of that furniture which nature hath given to the human understanding. They serve to direct us in the common affairs of life, where our reasoning faculty would leave us in the dark. They are a part of our constitution; and all the discoveries of our reason are grounded upon them.—*Reid*, '*Works*,' pp. 108, 209.

Province of Common Sense.

Its province is more extensive in refutation than in confirmation. A conclusion drawn by a train of just reasoning from true principles cannot possibly contradict any decision of common sense, because truth will always be consistent with itself. Neither can such a conclusion receive any confirmation from common sense, because it is not within its jurisdiction But it is possible that, by setting out from false principles, or by an error in reasoning, a man may be led to a conclusion that contradicts the decisions of common sense In this case, the conclusion is within the jurisdiction of common sense—*Reid*, '*Works*,' p. 425.

Characteristics and Truths of Common Sense.

Spontaneity, impersonality, and universality are the characteristics of truths of common sense; and hence their truth and certainty. The moral law, human liberty, the existence of God, and immortality of the soul are truths of common sense.—*Jaques.*

The Root of Philosophy

Philosophy has no other root but the principles of Common Sense; it grows out of them, and draws its nourishment from them. Severed from this root, its honours wither, its sap is dried up, it dies and rots —*Reid*, '*Works*,' p. 101.

IX EXPERIENCE

Various Senses of the Term.

The word "experience" is a very uncertain one, and may cover a number of very different mental actions and affections. (1.) Everything that has been within our consciousness, all that we have seen or felt, may be said in a vague general sense to have fallen under experience. In this sense, our intuitions of sense and consciousness, our original beliefs and primitive judgments all come within our experience. But thus understood, experience can explain nothing, can be the cause of nothing The thing experienced may, but not the experience; that is, the mere consciousness or feeling As to the thing experienced, it should not be called experience; and as to what it may produce we must determine this by looking at the nature of the thing, and not at our experience of it (2.) In another sense, experience means an induction of instances to establish a general rule or law. Such a gathered experience can generate a strong conviction, such as the trust we put in testimony, and our belief in the uniformity or rather uniformities of nature—*M'Cosh*, '*Examination of Mill*,' p 41.

Experience, in its strict sense, applies to what has occurred within a person's own knowledge. Experience, in this sense, of course, relates to the *past* alone Thus it is that a man knows by Experience what sufferings he has undergone in some disease; or, what height the tide reached at a certain time and place More frequently the word is used to denote that Judgment which is derived from *Experience in the primary sense*, by reasoning from that, in combination with other data. Thus, a man may assert, on the ground of experience, that he was cured of a disorder by such a medicine—that that medicine is generally beneficial in that disorder; that the tide may always be expected, under such circumstances, to rise to such a height. Strictly speaking, none of these can be known *by* Experience, but are conclusions derived *from* Experience. It is in this sense only that Experience can be applied to the *future*, or, which comes to the same thing, to any *general* fact; as, *e.g.*, when it is said that we know by Experience that water exposed to a certain temperature will freeze.—*Whately*, '*Logic*,' p. 198.

Mr Stuart Mill treats throughout of Experience as though it meant the proceeds and results of individual acquaintance with cosmical facts, Mr. Lewes explains it in a larger sense as the inheritance of the whole race—*Courtney*, '*Studies in Philosophy*,' p 96.

Experience is Claimed by Locke as the Source of all Knowledge.

Whence comes the mind by that vast store which the busy and boundless fancy of man has painted on it with an almost endless variety? Whence has it all the materials of reason and knowledge? To this I answer in one word, From experience; in that all our knowledge is founded, and from that it ultimately derives itself. Our observation employed either about external sensible objects, or about the internal operations of our minds, perceived and reflected on by ourselves, is that which supplies our understandings with all the materials of thinking. These two are the fountains of knowledge from whence all the ideas we have, or can naturally have, do spring.—*Locke*, '*Human Understanding*,' II. i. 2.

What is given in experience—actual fact—that their material (i.e., of the sciences) is the material of philosophy also.—*Schuegler*, '*Hist. of Phil.*,' p. 1.

But this Claim is Contested.

Because it does not account for self-evident truths.

So far from experience being able to account for innate principles, innate principles are required to account for the treasures of experience. For how is it that man is enabled to gather experience? How is he different in this respect from the stock or the stone, from the vegetable or the brute, which can acquire no experience, at least no such experience? Plainly because he is endowed with capacities for this end; and these faculties must have some law or principle on which they proceed. From the known man can discover the unknown, from the past he can anticipate the future; and when he does so he must proceed on some principle which is capable of exposition, and which ought to be expressed. And if man be capable, as I maintain he is, of reaching necessary and universal truth, he must proceed on principles which cannot be derived from experience. Twenty times have we tried, and found that two straight lines do not enclose a space: this does not authorise us to affirm that they never can enclose a space, otherwise we might argue that, because we had seen a judge and his wig twenty times together they must therefore be together through all eternity. A hundred times have I seen a spark kindle gunpowder: this does not entitle me to declare that it will do so the thousandth or the millionth time, or wherever the spark and the gunpowder are found. The gathered knowledge and wisdom of man, and his power of prediction, thus imply more than experience, they presuppose faculties to enable him to gather experience, and in some cases involve necessary principles which enable him, and justify him, as he acts on his ability, to rise from a limited experience to an unlimited and necessary law.—*M'Cosh*, '*Intuitions of the Mind*,' p. 23.

Or Generalisations.

We may have seen one circle and investigated its properties, but why, when our individual *experience* is so circumscribed, do we assume the same relations of all? Simply because the understanding has the conviction intuitively that similar objects will have similar properties; it does not acquire this idea by sensation or custom; the mind develops it by its own intrinsic force—it is a law of our faculties, ultimate and universal, from which all reasoning proceeds.—*Mill*, '*Essays*,' p. 337.

It is contended that man has knowledge *à priori*—knowledge which experience neither does nor can give, and knowledge without which there could be no *experience*—inasmuch as all the generalisations of *experience* proceed and rest upon it.—*Fleming*, '*Vocab. of Phil.*,' p. 178.

There are convictions which are as strong in early youth, and in early stages of society, as in later life and in more advanced communities, and which allow of no limitation or exception. As examples we may give mathematical axioms, as that two straight lines cannot enclose a space, and moral maxims, as that ingratitude for favours deserves reprobation. Our convictions of this description spring up on the bare contemplation of the objects, and need not a wide collection of instances; and their necessity and universality cannot be accounted for by a gathered experience.—*M'Cosh, 'Examination of Mill,'* p. 43.

Or Causation.

I do not see that experience could satisfy us that every change in nature actually has a cause. In the far greatest part of the changes in nature that fall within our observation the causes are unknown; and therefore from experience we cannot know whether they have causes or not.—*Reid, 'Works,'* p. 456.

Or what is necessary.

We may know from experience what is or what was, and from that may probably conclude what shall be in like circumstances; but with regard to what must necessarily be, experience is perfectly silent.—*Reid, 'Works,'* p. 521.

Without Induction it is useless.

Take away the light of the Inductive principle and Experience is as blind as a mole: she may, indeed, feel what is present, and what immediately touches her, but she sees nothing that is either before or behind, upon the right hand or upon the left, future or past.—*Reid, 'Works,'* p. 200.

Prof. Green's Criticism of Experience.

It is evident that the ground on which we make this statement, that mere sensations form the matter of experience, warrants us in making it, if at all, only as a statement in regard to the mental history of the individual. Even in this reference it can scarcely be accepted. There is no positive basis for it but the fact that, so far as memory goes, we always find ourselves manipulating some data of consciousness, themselves independent of any intellectual manipulation which we can remember applying to them. But on the strength of this to assume that there are such data in the history of our experience, consisting in mere sensations, antecedently to any action of the intellect, is not really an intelligible inference from the fact stated. It is an abstraction which we may put into words, but to which no real meaning can be attached. For a sensation can only form an object of experience in being determined by an intelligent subject which distinguishes it from itself, and contemplates it in relation to other sensations, so that to suppose a primary datum or matter of the individual's experience, wholly void of intellectual determination, is to suppose such experience to begin with what could not belong to, or be an object of, experience at all.—*Green, 'Prolegomena to Ethics,'* p. 47.

X.—HEREDITY.

The Doctrine of Hereditary Transmission.

Statement of the law.

The law is that habitual psychical successions entail some hereditary tendency to such successions which, under persistent conditions will become cumulative in generation after generation. To external relations that are often experienced during the life of a single organism, answering internal relations are established that become next to automatic. Such a combination of psychical changes as that which guides a savage in hitting a bird with an arrow, becomes, by constant repetition, so organised as to be performed almost without thought of the processes of adjustment gone through. Skill of this kind is so far transmissible, that particular races of men become characterised by particular aptitudes, which are nothing else than partially organised psychical connections.—*Spencer, 'Principles of Psychology,'* i. 466.

Exposition of the Doctrine.

Hereditary transmission applies to psychical peculiarities as well as to physical peculiarities. While the modified bodily structure produced by new habits of life is bequeathed to future generations, the modified nervous tendencies produced by such new habits of life are also bequeathed; and if the new habits of life become permanent the tendencies become permanent.

Let us glance at the facts. We know that there are warlike, peaceful, nomadic, maritime, hunting, commercial races—races that are independent or slavish, active or slothful; we know that many of these, if not all, have a common origin; and hence it is inferable that these varieties of disposition, which have evident relations to modes of life, have been gradually produced in the course of generations. The tendencies to certain combinations of psychical changes have become organic.—*Spencer, 'Principles of Psychology,'* i. 422.

Each organism does not acquire all its knowledge by 'experience' through the avenues of Sense—each inherits a complex mechanism, already attuned during the lives of a long line of progenitors to be affected in certain ways and to act in certain modes. Possibilities of intellectual affection and action are bequeathed to an organism in the already elaborated nervous system which it inherits. Within this nervous system lie latent the creature's 'forms of Intuition,' or 'forms of Thought,' which need only the coming of appropriate stimuli to rouse them into harmonious action.—*Bastian, 'The Brain, &c.,'* p. 193.

Every new individual possesses at birth not only a certain type of organism but probably also a number of predispositions to certain habits of thought and action. That a mental predisposition can be thus inherited, will at once be allowed by all who have clearly grasped the meaning of the intimate connection of mind and body. In respect to the lower regions of human consciousness, the instincts and appetites, no explanation is possible without a reference to the laws of organic descent. In the higher regions of individual consciousness, modes of feeling present themselves which appear to owe their origin to some congenital peculiarities of the cerebral structure. Thus there appear to lie hidden, in all the more passionate emotions, as love, terror, and anger, ingredients which cannot be traced to any confluence of past sensations of the same individual. It is desirable to mark off this bequeathed part of the infant's mental furniture from its own subsequent acquisitions.—*Sully, 'Sensation, &c.,'* pp. 3, 4.

The human brain is an organised register of infinitely numerous experiences received during the evolution of life. The effects of the most uniform and frequent of these experiences have been successively bequeathed, principal and interest; and have slowly amounted to that high intelligence which lies latent in the brain of the infant—which the infant in after life exercises and perhaps strengthens or further complicates—and which, with minute additions, it bequeaths to future generations. And thus it happens that the European inherits from twenty to thirty cubic inches more brain than the Papuan. Thus it happens that out of savages unable to count up to the number of their fingers, and speaking a language containing only nouns and verbs, arise at length our Newtons and Shakespeares.—*Spencer, 'Principles of Psychology,'* i. 471.

Arguments pro and con.

The opponents of heredity quote facts which appear to them conclusive: the frequent absence of resemblance between parents and children, and the frequent mediocrity of the descendants of men of genius. Pericles produced a Paralus and a Xanthippus. The austere Aristides produced the infamous Lysimachus. The powerful-minded Thucydides was represented by an idiotic Milesias and a stupid Stephanos. Was the great soul of Oliver Cromwell to be found in his son Richard? What were the inheritors of Henry IV, and of Peter the Great? What were the children of Shakespeare and the daughters of Milton? What was the only son of Addison? An idiot.

The supporters of heredity retort upon this argument by saying, What is the meaning of these proverbial phrases, 'the wit of the Montemarts,' 'the wit of the Sheridans,' if one does not believe in transmission? Torquato Tasso was the son of a celebrated father. We have the two Herschels, the two Colmans, the Kemble family, and the Coleridges. Finally, the most striking example is that of Sebastian Bach, whose musical genius was found, in an inferior degree, among three hundred Bachs, the children of very various mothers.

We must take account of the disturbing causes which explain the exceptions. A child may inherit from both parents, or from one only. The aptitudes of the parents may be different, the influence of one of the two parents may destroy that of the other, and, consequently, the apparent exceptions to the law of heredity may on the contrary confirm that law.—*Ribot, 'Eng Psych.,'* p. 313

Applications of the Doctrine

The doctrine of 'Inherited Acquisition' is not only widely applicable in explanation of the genesis of Mind in the animal series, it suffices, moreover, to reconcile the adverse doctrines of the 'Transcendental' and the 'Empirical' schools of Philosophy. It shows that the former were right in a certain sense, in contending for the existence of 'innate ideas;' though, looked at from a larger point of view, it strongly tends to confirm the views of the experiential school of philosophy [See *Innate Ideas.*]—*Bastian, 'The Brain, &c.,'* p. 187.

IV.

EXTERNAL SOURCES OF KNOWLEDGE.

I. SENSATION.

Sensation Described.

What it is.

A sensation is defined as the mental impression, feeling, or conscious state, resulting from the action of external things on some part of the body, called on that account sensitive. Such are the feelings caused by tastes, smells, sounds, or sights. —*Bain, 'Mental Science,'* p. 27.

What we commonly mean, when we use the terms Sensation or phenomena of Sensation, are the feelings which we have by the five senses,—SMELL, TASTE, HEARING, TOUCH, and SIGHT. These are the feelings from which we derive our notions of what we denominate the external world;—the things by which we are surrounded: that is, the antecedents of the most interesting consequents, in the whole series of feelings, which constitute our mental train, our existence.—*Mill, 'Human Mind,'* i. 3.

Sensation proper does not occur alone or apart. Pure sensation is simply an ideal or imaginary experience. Its nature can be determined only by laying out of view certain characteristics which always attend it. Though sensation always occurs with perception, it may be clearly distinguished from it. Sensation, thus considered, is

A subjective experience of the soul, as animating an extended sensorium, usually more or less pleasurable or painful, and always occasioned by some excitement of the organism.—*Porter, 'Human Intellect,'* p. 128.

Is Sensation Resolvable into Simpler Elements?

(*a*) *Many philosophers say, No.*

It is allowed on all hands [?] that sensation cannot be positively defined. This arises from its being a simple quality, and there is nothing simpler into which to resolve it. All we can do in the way of unfolding its nature, is to bid every man consult his consciousness when any bodily object is affecting his senses or sensibility. —*M'Cosh, 'Examination of Mill,'* p. 71.

A sensation is the feeling existing in the

mind itself of *a certain effect of another thing from without*, acting upon it through an organ and nerve of sense. The sensor nerves connect the organs of sense with the brain If the nerve be affected at its extremity, the cause is external to the body. If at any intermediate point, the cause is within the body, but still external to the mind The sensations in these two cases are quite definite and distinct in their character and in their origin. The same applies to the sensations from the different organs, as well as the various sensations coming by the same organ The elements now enumerated—the feeling of a *certain effect* of *another* thing from *without* on the organs of sense—constitute the bare sensation Of the three elements, the effect alone is apprehended by the sense, the otherhood and the externality of its cause by a quite different faculty, to be examined presently—namely intuition From all three we learn that a sensation is a look-out. This makes it the groundwork of a perception, which is a farther look-out.—*Murphy*, '*Human Mind*,' p. 28.

(*b*) *Some, however, maintain it is.*

The resolution of sensations into simpler elements is shown to be possible most clearly with reference to the senses of hearing and sight. In connection with the former, every one is familiar with what we call a musical sound. That this sound is really a complex sensation is shown in several ways, and amongst others by experiments with the wheel of *Savart*. This wheel is a flat circular steel plate, having its circular edge cut to some depth into fine elastic teeth, and made to revolve with great rapidity upon an axle. 'When this wheel is turned at a uniform rate, its teeth, which are at equal distances, strike a bar in passing, and this regular succession of similar concussions excites a regular succession of similar sensations of sound. Now, while the wheel turns sufficiently slowly, the sensations, being discontinuous, are distinct, and each of them being compound is a sound. But when the wheel is set to turn fast enough, *a new sensation arises*, that of a musical note. It distinguishes itself from the remains of the noises which still go on and continue distinct, and stands out as a fact of a different kind; among the different elementary sensations which make up each sound, there is one which the operation has separated; and this now ceases to be distinct from the *similar elementary sensation* following in each of the succeeding sounds. *All these similar sensations now combine in one long continuous sensation*—their mutual limits are effaced, experience, just as in a chemical analysis, has extracted an elementary sensation from the complex group in which it was included, has joined it to an absolutely similar elementary sensation, and formed a new compound—the sensation of musical sound.'[1] Thus it is seen that a particular sensation, that of a musical note, is capable of being resolved into more elementary sensations, each of which is distinctly in consciousness If we now examine a sensation of light, we shall see that it also is resolvable into more elementary sensations. The resolution of the sensation is effected by the resolution of its most important condition, the ray of light The prismatic spectrum comprehends a variety of distinct sensations which, previous to the analysis, must have been contained in the complex sensation of white light A well-known optical toy, consisting of a disc of card-paper with the spectral colours painted upon it, and made to revolve rapidly upon its axis, shows that the separate sensations may, by rapidity of succession, become blended together again and form one complex sensation more or less closely resembling the original one.—*Jardine*, '*Psychology*,' p. 49–51.

Origin of Sensation.

It arises through external stimulation.

How does the Sensation arise? 'Odorous particles which proceed from the object' reach the organ of smell, and, in some way

[1] Taine, 'On Intelligence,' p. 108.

to us unknown, make an impression on the nerve, of which impression the sensation in some way unknown is the consequent. Or, as Hume says (*Treat. on Hum. Nat.* i 1, 2), 'Sensations arise in the soul originally from unknown causes.' That the impression is transmitted to the nerve-centre in the brain is acknowledged. Beyond this Physiology makes no averment. Every one is able to tell from his own consciousness when he has a sensation of smell.—*Calderwood, 'Moral Philosophy,'* p. 100

Where does it exist?

Are our sensations affections of mind, or of body, or of both? On the one hand, Consciousness, in all its modes, seems manifestly to be a state of mind. On the other hand, sensitive consciousness appears with the concomitant condition of extension, which is an attribute of body. The general voice of modern philosophers has pronounced that sensations, as such, belong to mind and not to body.—*Mansel, 'Metaphysics,'* p. 90.

Sensation pertains properly to the soul, as contradistinguished from material things or corporeal agents. The sensation of touch is not in the orange, the sensation of heat is not in the burning flame, but both are experienced by the sentient soul. The sensation of sweetness is not in the sugar, that of sourness is not in the vinegar. There can be no music when orchestra and audience are both stone-deaf. As all sensations pertain to the soul which experiences them, they can properly be said to be subjective. As the most of them are positively agreeable or the opposite, they are nearly akin to those emotions, as hope or terror, or those passions, as anger and envy, which are acknowledged by all to belong exclusively to the spirit, and to involve no relation whatever to matter or the bodily organism. Such feelings are not infrequently styled sensations, though improperly.

Yet the sensations, though subjective in the sense already defined, are experienced by the soul as connected with a corporeal organism, and are directly distinguished in this from emotions proper on the one hand, and from perceptions proper on the other. The soul has a subjective experience of heat, hardness, sweetness, sourness, &c., but it has this experience as an agent which is connected with and animates an extended sensorium.—*Porter, 'Human Intellect,'* p. 128.

Nature of Sensation.

Sensation is usually mingled with experience.

It should be remembered that the mature sensations are the product not only of the present external stimulation, but also of the individual's past experiences. It is impossible to produce, and at the same time to obtain an account of, what may be called a virgin sensation, such as may be conceived to be the impression of an infant mind, if indeed even this may be supposed to exist pure from all accretions of transmitted association. Subtly interwoven with all our familiar sensations are ideas of past experiences, so that it is a matter of extreme difficulty to separate the net amount of sensation from the rest of the momentary impression.—*Sully, 'Sensation, &c.,'* p. 38.

Attention is a necessary factor in sensation.

Some measure of attention is a necessary factor in every distinct sensation. No doubt there are myriads of vague feelings constantly flitting around the outer zones of consciousness, which being unnoticed cannot be recalled by memory. Yet even these are scarcely to be dignified by the name of sensations. They lack those elements of discrimination and comparison, without which no distinct mental state is possible.—*Sully, 'Sensation, &c.,'* p. 64

Perception and Sensation distinguished. (See under PERCEPTION.)

Perception is the knowledge of the object presenting itself to the senses, whether in the organism or beyond it. Sensation is the feeling associated,—the feeling of the organism. These two always co-exist. There is never the knowledge without an organic feeling; never a feeling of the organism without a cognitive apprehension of it These sensations differ widely from each other, as our consciousness testifies; some of them being pleasant, some painful; others indifferent as to pleasure and pain, but still with a feeling Some we call exciting, others dull; some we designate as warm, others as cold, and for most of them we have no name whatever,—indeed they so run into each other that it would be difficult to discriminate them by a specific nomenclature The perceptions again are as numerous and varied as the knowledge we have by all the senses. Now these two ever mix themselves up with each other The sensation of the odour mingles with the apprehension of the nostrils; the flavour of the food is joined with the recognition of the palate; the agreeableness or disagreeableness of the sound comes in with the knowledge of the ear as affected; and the feeling organ which we localise has an associated sensation —*M'Cosh*, '*Intuitions of the Mind*,' p. 118

Sensations may become idealised.

If a clear bright light be kept for a short time before the eye and then removed, the sensation produced will persist for a time, and at intervals perhaps be revived. The same is the case with tastes, smells, and other sensations. But the sensation, as persistent or revived, is not so clear and vivid as it was originally—it has become idealised The appearance before consciousness of idealised sensations is not fortuitous, but takes place in certain regular and connected series.—*Jardine*, '*Psychology*,' p. 58.

Functions of Sensation

As a gateway of knowledge

The sensations, though they are not the only and sufficient gateways of knowledge, are yet chief and indispensable elements, without these it is certain we could have no acquaintance whatever, either with the world, with our vital organism, nor, so far as we can see, even with our existence. It is the law of our being that the mind, though it possesses wonderful powers, and is capable of reaching truths which far transcend mere bodily considerations, is destined to commence its growth by conceptions which have reference merely to these sensations and the objects which excite them. It is first roused into a sense of its existence by impressions made on the physical organism with which it is connected; nor can we easily conceive how it could become conscious of its existence except through these, for even when it has attained maturity it is only conscious of sensations, ideas, actions, passions, memories, reflections, and never of itself. These, and such as these, constitute all the mind knows of its own being.—*Wyld*, '*Physics and Philosophy of the Senses*,' p. 472.

As making us acquainted with the external world.

All knowledge through the senses is accompanied with an organic feeling, that is, a sensation. Our immediate acquaintance with the external world is always through the organism, and is therefore associated and combined with organic affections, pleasing or displeasing. Certain sounds are felt to be harsh or grating, others are relished as being sweet or melodious or harmonious Some colours, in themselves or in their associations, are felt to be glaring or discordant, while others are enjoyed as being agreeable or exciting. In short, every sense perception is accompanied with a sensation, the perception being the knowledge, and the sensation the bodily affection felt by the conscious mind as present in the organism. —*M'Cosh*, '*Intuitions of the Mind*,' p. 321.

II THE BRAIN AND NERVOUS SYSTEM.

The Brain, general description.

Underneath the solid, hard covering of the cranium, and enveloped within three membranes, is the brain proper, or cerebrum. Below this, and to the rear, are grouped three important though smaller and subordinate subdivisions of the great central mass, the cerebellum or little brain, the pons or bridge; the medulla oblongata, or elongated mass, in direct relation with the upper part of the spinal cord. These four taken together constitute the great nerve centre, the brain proper being the most important by far, not only larger but much more complicated in structure. . .

Of the three membranes which cover the brain, the outermost (*dura mater*) is the toughest and strongest. From this tough covering strong bands, as the falx and tentorium, pass between different parts of the encephalon. In this membrane are also situated the channels or blood sinuses which convey the venous blood from the brain. Below this tough covering is the intermediate membrane (*arachnoid mater*), a much more delicate structure, stretching round the whole brain, but without descending into the various inequalities which are presented over its surface. Between the outermost and intermediate covering there is a supply of serum, moistening the inner surface of the tougher covering and the upper surface of the more delicate membrane. Below this second covering is a third membrane (*pia mater*), which not only encompasses the whole, as the others do, but, keeping close to the surface of the brain, descends into the various furrows and conveys blood vessels into its substance. These three coverings enclose the spinal cord, as they enclose the brain.

Within this threefold covering lies the brain, a large soft mass, in two halves or hemispheres, of a reddish-grey tint, arranged in folds or convolutions which have a definite position and direction. By means of these convolutions there is a large exposed surface within the narrow limits which the skull affords, the soft mass being arranged alternately in ridges and in grooves or furrows (*sulci*).—*Calderwood, 'Relation of Mind and Brain,'* pp. 10–12.

The Nervous System.

The brain is brought into relation with the periphery by thirty-one pairs of spinal and twelve cranial nerves. These nerves or cords of communication are separable into two great divisions, according to the nature of the functions they perform. One set carry impressions from the periphery to the cord and brain, and are therefore called *afferent* nerves; while the other set carry impulses from the brain and cord to the periphery, and are therefore called *efferent* nerves. The most prominent functions performed by these nerves being the conveyance of sensory impressions and motor stimuli respectively, the restricted terms *sensory* and *motor* are frequently employed in lieu of the wider terms afferent and efferent.

The spinal nerves are connected to the spinal cord by two roots, one of which, the efferent or motor, arises from the anterior aspect of the cord; the other, the afferent or sensory, is connected with the posterior surface. After a short independent course, and the development of a ganglion on the posterior root, the two unite to form one trunk, which is, therefore, a mixed nerve, containing both afferent and efferent fibres. The nerve distributes itself by minute ramifications in the receptive and active organs at the periphery, each filament remaining distinct in its whole course.

The spinal cord consists of grey matter and white conducting columns or strands. The grey matter has the form of a double crescent, with the convex surfaces joined by commissures, in the centre of which the central canal of the spinal cord is seen, and the horns of the crescents are connected respectively with the anterior and posterior roots of the spinal nerves.—*Ferrier, 'Functions of the Brain,'* pp. 2, 3.

Functions of the Brain.

Functions of the Medulla Oblongata.

The medulla oblongata is a co-ordinating centre of reflex actions essential to the maintenance of life. If all the centres above the medulla be removed, life may continue, the respiratory movements may go on with their accustomed rhythm, the heart may continue to beat, and the circulation be maintained; the animal may swallow if food be introduced into the mouth, may react to impressions made on its sensory nerve, withdrawing its limbs or making an irregular spring if pinched, or even utter a cry as if in pain, and yet will be merely a non-sentient, non-intelligent, reflex mechanism.—*Ferrier, 'Functions of the Brain,'* pp. 31, 32.

Ferrier's Classification of the functions of the Mesencephalon, the Pons Varolii, Corpora Quadrigemina, and Cerebellum.

1. The function of equilibration, or maintenance of the bodily equilibrium.

2. Co-ordination of locomotion.

3. Emotional expression.—*'Functions of the Brain,'* p. 46.

III. SPONTANEOUS MOVEMENT.

Reflex and Automatic Action.

Of the early movements which precede voluntary ones, the first class is that known as spontaneous, unprompted, or random movements. These include all movements which result from the excitation of motor centres. They are not preceded by a conscious element, feeling, or desire, and have no psychical accompaniment at all beyond the muscular experience attending the carrying out of the movement. They appear as altogether wanting in purpose, and so are called 'random' movements. They are described as the spontaneous overflow of energy locked up in the central motor organs, as the result of the disposition of a healthy and vigorous motor organ to fall into a state of activity. Many of the spasmodic and irregular movements of young animals and children soon after birth belong to this class. Such are movements of the arms, legs, eyes, &c., which appear to be due to no impression received from without, and no internal feeling.—*Sully, 'Outlines of Psychology,'* pp. 593-4.

Reflex Action of the Spinal Cord.

The spinal cord of the vertebrate animals . . . may be regarded as composed of thirty-one connected segments, each of which, with its pair of nerves, is a bilateral repetition of the central ganglion with its afferent and efferent fibres. . . . The impression on the sensory surface is conveyed to the cord, and there originates an impulse, which, travelling outwards along the efferent nerve, excites the muscles to contraction.—*Ferrier, 'Functions of the Brain,'* pp. 16-17.

Illustrations of the above.

In the frog.—If the body of a frog be divided transversely, the lower half will still retain its vitality for a considerable period. . . . If the foot be irritated, the muscles of the leg will be thrown into action, and this will occur so long as the grey matter of the cord is intact, and its connections with the periphery are maintained.—*Ferrier, 'Functions of the Brain,'* p. 17.

In man.—When, as the result of injury or disease, there is a solution of the continuity of the cord at any point, all the parts deriving their nervous supply from the cord below the seat of lesion become paralysed, both as regards voluntary motion and sensation. If, however, the soles of the feet be tickled, the legs will be thrown into convulsive action, of which the individual is not conscious, and which it is out out of his power in the slightest degree to control.—*Ferrier, 'Functions of the Brain,'* p. 17.

Automatic Actions.

Some of these are *primarily* or *originally* automatic; whilst others, which were volitional in the first instance, come by frequent repetition to be performed independently of the will, and thus become *secondarily* automatic. Some of the automatic movements, again, can be controlled by the will, whilst others take place in opposition to the strongest volitional effort. There is a large class of secondarily-automatic actions which the will can initiate, and which then go on of themselves in sequences established by previous Habit, but which the Will can stop, or of which it can change the direction, as easily as it set them going; and these it will be convenient to term *voluntary*, as being entirely under the control of the will, although actually maintained automatically.—*Carpenter*, '*Mental Physiology*,' p. 16

Instances of Automatic Action.

Those movements of which the uninterrupted performance is essential to the maintenance of life are *primarily* automatic, and are not only independent of the will, but entirely beyond its control. The 'beating of the heart,' which is a typical example of such movements, though liable to be affected by *emotional* disturbance, cannot be altered either in force or frequency by any *volitional* effort. And only one degree removed from this is the act of Respiration; which, though capable in man of being so *regulated* by the will as to be made subservient to the uses of speech, cannot be *checked* by the strongest exertion of it for more than a few moments. If we try to 'hold our breath' for such a period that the aeration of the blood is seriously interfered with, a feeling of distress is experienced, which every moment increases in intensity until it becomes absolutely unbearable; so that the automatic impulse which prompts its relief can no longer be resisted. So when a crumb of bread or a drop of water passes 'the wrong way,' the presence of an irritation of the windpipe automatically excites a combination of muscular movements, which tends to an expulsion of the offending particle by an explosive cough. The strongest exertion of the will is powerless to prevent this action, which is repeated in spite of every effort to repress it until that result has been obtained.—*Carpenter*, '*Mental Physiology*,' p. 16, 17

IV. INSTINCT.

Origin of Instincts.

Instinct is defined as untaught ability. It is the name given to what can be done prior to experience or education; as sucking in the child, walking on all fours by the newly dropped calf, picking by the bird just emerged from its shell, the maternal attentions of animals generally. —*Bain*, '*Mental Science*,' p. 68.

An instinct is a propensity prior to experience and independent of instruction. —*Paley*, '*Natural Theology*,' ch. xviii.

Instinct is a term which does not admit of rigid definition, because, as ordinarily used, the meaning of the term is not rigidly fixed. The nearest approach we can make is perhaps the following:—Instinct is a generic term comprising all those faculties of mind which lead to the conscious performance of actions that are adaptive in character, but pursued without necessary knowledge of the relation between the means employed and the ends attained.—*Romanes*, '*Encyc. Brit.*,' xiii. 157.

Restricting the word to its proper signification, Instinct may be described as—compound reflex action. I say described rather than defined, since no clear line of demarcation can be drawn between it and simple reflex action. That the propriety of thus marking off Instinct from primitive reflex action may be clearly seen, let us take an example. A chick, immediately it comes out of the egg, not only balances itself and runs about, but picks up fragments of food; thus showing us that it can adjust its muscular movements in a way appropriate for grasping an object in a position that is accurately perceived. This action implies impressions on retinal nerves, impressions on nerves proceeding from muscles which move the eyes, and impressions on nerves proceeding from muscles which adjust their lenses—implies that all these nerves are excited simultaneously in special ways and degrees; and that the complex co-ordination of muscular contractions by which the fly is caught, is the result of this complex co-ordination of stimuli. So that while in the primitive forms of reflex action, a single impression is followed by a single contraction; while in the more developed forms of reflex action a single impression is followed by a combination of contractions; in this which we distinguish as Instinct, a combination of impressions is followed by a combination of contractions; and the higher the Instinct the more complex are both the directive and executive co-ordinations.—*Spencer*, '*Psychology*,' i. 432-4.

Instincts of Animals classified.

The principal instincts of animals have been grouped by naturalists under three heads:—

(1.) Those dependent, immediately or remotely, upon incitations from the alimentary canal (*e.g.*, mode of seeking, capture, seizing, storing, or swallowing of food; and some cases of migration).

(2.) Those dependent upon incitations from the generative organs (*e.g.*, pairing, nidification, oviposition, care of young; and some cases of migration)

(3.) Those dependent upon more general impressions, perhaps partly internal and partly external in origin (hybernation and migration.—*Bastian*, '*The Brain, &c.*,' p. 227.

Origin of Instincts.

Through organised and inherited habit.

All instincts probably arose in one or other of two ways (1.) By the effects of habit in successive generations, mental activities which were originally intelligent become, as it were, stereotyped into permanent instincts. Just as in the lifetime of the individual adaptive actions, which were originally intelligent, may by frequent repetition become automatic, so in the lifetime of the species, actions originally intelligent may, by frequent repetition and heredity, so write their effects on the nervous system that the latter is prepared, even before individual experience, to perform adaptive actions mechanically which in previous generations were performed intelligently.—*Romanes*, '*Encyc. Brit.*,' xiii 157.

Let it be granted that the more frequently psychical states occur in a certain order, the stronger becomes their tendency to cohere in that order, until they at last become inseparable; let it be granted that this tendency is, in however slight a degree, inherited, so that if the experiences remain the same, each successive generation bequeaths a somewhat increased tendency; and it follows that there must eventually result an automatic connection of nervous actions, corresponding to the external relations perpetually experienced. Similarly if, from some change in the environment of any species, its members are frequently brought in contact with a relation having terms a little more involved; if the organisation of the species is so far developed as to be impressible by these terms in close succession, then an inner relation corresponding to this new outer relation will gradually be formed, and will in the end become organic. And so on in subsequent stages of progress.—*Spencer*, '*Psychology*,' i. 439.

Through natural selection.

The other mode of origin consists in natural selection, or survival of the fittest, continuously preserving actions which, although never intelligent, yet happen to have been of benefit to the animals which first chanced to perform them. Thus, for instance, take the instinct of incubation. It is quite impossible that any animal can ever have kept its eggs warm with the intelligent purpose of hatching out their contents, so we can only suppose that the incubating instinct began by warm-blooded animals showing that kind of attention to their eggs which we find to be frequently shown by cold-blooded animals. Thus crabs and spiders carry about their eggs for the purpose of protecting them; and if, as animals gradually became warm-blooded, some species for this or any other purpose adopted a similar habit, the imparting of heat would have become incidental to the carrying about of the eggs. Consequently, as the imparting of heat promoted the process of hatching, those individuals which most constantly cuddled or brooded over their eggs would, other things equal, have been most successful in rearing progeny; and so the incubating instinct would be developed without there having been any intelligence in the matter —*Romanes*, '*Encyc. Brit.*,' xiii. 157.

Variability of Instinct.

As a matter of fact, instincts are eminently variable, and therefore admit of being modified as modifying circumstances may require, their variability gives them plasticity whereby they may be moulded always to fit an environment, however continuously the latter may be subject to gradual change. The view commonly entertained as to the unalterable character of instinct is erroneous —*Romanes*, '*Encyc. Brit.*,' xiii 158.

The most curious instance of a change of instinct is mentioned by Darwin. The bees carried over to Barbadoes and the Western Isles ceased to lay up any honey after the first year; as they found it not useful to them. They found the weather so fine, and materials for making honey so plentiful, that they quitted their grave, prudent, and mercantile character, became exceedingly profligate and debauched, eat up their capital, resolved to work no more, and amused themselves by flying about the sugar-houses and stinging the blacks. The fact is, that by putting animals in different situations you may change and even reverse any of their original propensities —*Sydney Smith*, '*Moral Philosophy*,' p. 246.

Purpose of Instinct.

In animals it serves solely for self-preservation.

All the wonderful instincts of animals are given them only for the combination or preservation of their species. If they had not these instincts, they would be swept off the earth in an instant. This bee, that understands architecture so well, is as stupid as a pebble-stone out of his own particular business of making honey; and, with all his talents, he only exists that boys may eat his labours and poets sing about them. *Ut pueris placeas et declamatio fias.* A peasant girl of ten years old puts the whole republic to death with a little smoke; their palaces are turned into candles, and every clergyman's wife makes mead-wine of the honey; and there is an end of the glory and wisdom of the bees! Whereas, man has talents that have no sort of reference to his existence; and without which his species might remain upon earth in the same safety as if they had them not. The bee works at that particular angle which saves most time and labour; and the boasted edifice he is constructing is only for his egg, but Somerset House, and Blenheim, and the Louvre, have nothing to do with breeding. Epic poems, and Apollo Belvideres, and Venus de Medicis, have nothing to do with living and eating. We might have discovered pig-nuts without the Royal Society, and gathered acorns without reasoning about curves of the ninth order. The immense superfluity of talent given to man, which has no bearing upon animal life, which has nothing to do with the mere preservation of existence, is one very distinguishing circumstance in this comparison. There is no other animal but man to whom mind appears to be given for any *other* purpose than the preservation of body.—*Sydney Smith*, '*Moral Philos.*'

In man it subserves intellectual progress.

Man possesses in his instinct of imitation perhaps the most efficacious of all instruments for the realisation of the progress of which his cerebral construction renders him capable. Every one must have remarked the power of this instinct among children, and those who have had to bring them up know what an important place it occupies among means of education. Without it, the bare communication of language would occupy an indefinite time. —*Véron*, '*Æsthetics*,' pp. 9, 10.

Instinct and Reason

Instinctive actions are very commonly tempered with what Pierre Huber calls 'a little dose of judgment or reason' But, although reason may thus, in varying degrees, be blended with instinct, the distinction between the two is sufficiently precise, for reason, in whatever degree present, only acts upon a definite and often laboriously acquired knowledge of the relation between means and ends Moreover, adjustive actions due to instinct are similarly performed by all individuals of a species under the stimulus supplied by the same appropriate circumstances, whereas adjustive actions due to reason are variously performed by different individuals Lastly, instinctive actions are only performed under particular circumstances, which have been frequently experienced during the life-history of the species, whereas rational actions are performed under varied circumstances, and serve to meet novel exigencies which may never before have occurred even in the life-history of the individual —*Romanes*, '*Encyc Brit.*,' xiii 157.

The most common notion now prevalent with respect to animals, is, that they are guided by *instinct*; that the discriminating circumstance between the minds of animals and of men is, that the former do what they do from instinct, the latter from reason. Now, the question is, is there any meaning to the word *instinct?* what is that meaning? and what is the distinction between instinct and reason? If I desire to do a certain thing, adopt certain means to effect it, and have a clear and precise notion that those means are directly subservient to that end,—there I act from reason; but, if I adopt means subservient to the end, and am uniformly found to do so, and am not in the *least* degree conscious that these means *are* subservient to the end,—there I certainly do act from some principle very different from reason; and to which principle it is *as* convenient to give the name of instinct as any other name Bees, it is well known, construct their combs with small cells on both sides, fit for holding their store of honey, and for receiving their young. There are only three *possible* figures of the cells, which can make them all equal and similar, without any useless interstices; these are the equilateral triangle, the square, and the regular hexagon It is well known to mathematicians that there is not *a fourth* way *possible*, in which a plane may be cut into little spaces, that shall be equal, similar, and regular, without leaving any interstices Of the three, the *hexagon* is the most proper both for conveniency and strength, and, accordingly, bees—as if they were acquainted with these things—make all their cells regular hexagons. As the combs have cells on both sides, the cells may either be exactly opposite, having partition against partition,—or the bottom of a cell may rest upon the partitions, between the cells, on the other side; which will serve as a buttress to strengthen it The last way is the best for strength; accordingly, the bottom of each cell rests against the point where three partitions meet on the other side, which gives it all the strength possible The bottom of a cell may either be one plane perpendicular to the side partitions, or it may be composed of several planes meeting in a solid angle in the middle point It is only in one of these two ways that all the cells can be similar without losing room; and, for the same intention, the planes of which the bottom is composed —if there be more than one—must be exactly three in number, and neither more nor less. It has been demonstrated also, that, by making the bottom to consist of three planes meeting in a point, there is a saving of materials and labour by no means inconsiderable The bees, as if acquainted with the principles of solid geometry, follow them most accurately; the bottom of each cell being composed of three planes, which make obtuse angles with the side partitions, and with one another, and meet in a point in the middle of the bottom; the three angles of this bottom being supported by three partitions on the other side of the comb, and the point of it by the common intersection of those three partitions.

One instance more of the mathematical skill displayed in the structure of a honeycomb deserves to be mentioned. It is a curious mathematical problem at what precise angle the three planes which compose the bottom of a cell ought to meet, in order to make the greatest possible saving, or the least expense of materials and labour. This is one of those problems belonging to the higher parts of mathematics, which are called problems of maxima and minima. It has been resolved by some mathematicians, particularly by Mr. Maclaurin, by a fluxionary calculation, which is to be found in the ninth volume of the *Transactions of the Royal Society of London.* He has determined precisely the angle required; and he found, by the most exact mensuration the subject could admit, that it is the *very* angle in which the three planes in the bottom of the cell of a honeycomb do actually meet. How is all this to be explained? Imitation it certainly is not; for, after every old bee has been killed, you may take the honeycomb and hatch a new swarm of bees that cannot possibly have had any communication with, or instruction from, the parents. The young of every animal, though they have never seen the dam, will do exactly as all their species have done before them. A brood of young ducks, hatched under a hen, take to the water in spite of the remonstrances and terrors of their spurious parents. All the great habitudes of every species of animals have repeatedly been proved to be independent of imitation. — *Sydney Smith,* '*Moral Philosophy,*' pp. 234–36.

V. SENSIBILITY—MUSCULARITY.

Sensibility

The mind's capacity of being acted upon or affected by the medium of the stimulation of a sensory nerve is called sensibility. Sensibility is simply another name for the mind's capability of having sensations.—*Sully,* '*Outlines of Psychology,*' p. 109.

Two Kinds of Sensibility.

All parts of the organism supplied with sensory nerves, and the actions of which are consequently fitted to give rise to sensations, are said to possess sensibility of some kind. But this property appears under one of two very unlike forms. The first of these is common to all sensitive parts of the organism, and involves no special nervous structure at the extremity. The second is peculiar to certain parts of the bodily surface, and implies special structures or organs. To the former is given the name Common or General Sensibility; to the latter, Special Sensibility.—*Sully,* '*Outlines of Psychology,*' pp. 109, 110.

The Muscular Sense

Our ordinary movements are guided by what is termed the *muscular sense;* that is, by a feeling of the condition of the muscles, that comes to us through their own afferent nerves. How necessary this is to the exercise of muscular power may be best judged of from cases in which it has been deficient. Thus a woman who had suffered complete loss of sensation in one arm, but who retained its motor power, found that she could not support her infant upon it without constantly looking at the child; and that if she were to remove her eyes for a moment, the child would fall, in spite of her knowledge that her infant was resting upon her arm, and of her desire to sustain it. Here, the Muscular sense being entirely deficient, the sense of Vision supplied what was required, so long as it was exercised upon the object; but as soon as this guiding influence was withdrawn, the strongest will could not sustain the muscular contraction.—*Carpenter,* '*Mental Physiology,*' pp. 83, 84.

The views expressed at different times in regard to the 'Muscular Sense,' and the means by which we appreciate 'resistance,' have been so various and contradictory as to make it almost impossible to give the student of this question any adequate notion of the real problems requiring solution without bringing together some historical notes illustrative of the various opinions that have been held on the subject. (These Dr Bastian gives in an Appendix, '*The Brain, &c.*,' p. 691.)

We may much more reasonably and conveniently, in the face of all the disagreements concerning the 'muscular sense,' speak of a *Sense of Movement*, as a separate endowment, of a complex kind, whereby we are made acquainted with the position and movements of our limbs, whereby we judge of 'weight' and 'resistance,' and by means of which the brain also derives much unconscious guidance in the performance of movements generally, but especially in those of the automatic type. Impressions of various kinds combine for the perfection of this sense of movement; and in part its cerebral seat or area coincides with that of the sense of Touch. There are included under it, as its several components, cutaneous impressions, impressions from muscles and other deep textures of the limbs (such as fasciæ, tendons, and articular surfaces), all of which yield Conscious Impressions of various degrees of definiteness; and in addition there seems to be a highly important set of 'unfelt' Impressions, which guide the motor activity of the Brain by automatically bringing it into relation with the different degrees of contraction of all muscles that may be in a state of action.

Such impressions, in such groups, differ from those of all other Sense Endowments, inasmuch as they are 'results' rather than 'causes' of Movement, in the first instance; and are subsequently used only as guides for promoting the continuance of movements already begun.—*Bastian*, '*The Brain, &c.*,' pp. 542–544.

VI. THE SENSES.

Classification of the Senses.

The common enumeration is now held to be defective.

The sensations are classified according to their bodily organs; hence the division into Five Senses. But the common enumeration of the Five Senses is defective. When the senses are regarded principally as sources of knowledge, or the basis of intellect, the five commonly given are tolerably comprehensive; but when we advert to sensation in the aspect of pleasure and pain, there are serious omissions. Hunger, thirst, repletion, suffocation, warmth, and the variety of states designated by physical comfort and discomfort, are left out; yet these possess the characteristics of sensation, having a local organ or seat, a definite agency, and a characteristic mode of consciousness. The omission is best supplied by constituting a group of Organic Sensations, or Sensations of Organic Life.—*Bain*, '*Mental Science*,' p. 27, 28.

The feelings, however, which belong to the five external Senses are not a full enumeration of the feelings which it seems proper to rank under the head of Sensations, and which must be considered as bearing an important part in those complicated phenomena which it is our principal business, in this inquiry, to separate into their principal elements and explain. Of these unnamed, and generally unregarded, Sensations, two principal classes may be distinguished,—first, those which accompany the action of the several muscles of the body; and, secondly, those which have their place in the alimentary canal.—*James Mill*, '*Analysis, &c.*,' pp. 3, 6.

These various modes of sensibility seem to be fitly grouped together under the common head of Sensations of Organic Life, their detail being arranged according to the several organs, viz., the Alimentary Canal, Lungs, Circulation, Nervous System, &c. These would make a sixth Sense properly so called, or a department of passive sensibility.—*Bain*, Note on Mill, ibid.

The Sensations are usually classified according to their bodily organs. This classification seems to be immediate and innate, not acquired by experience; we cannot confound a sight with a sound. Psychology merely recognises the old distinctions

Thus we get the Five Senses To them we must, however, add the Sensations of Organic Life, which are very important as feelings (pleasure and pain), though of small intellectual value These last, which are also called Systematic Sensations (the older *Sensus communis, Sensus vagus*, &c.), for the most part originate on the inner surfaces of the body. They are thus distinguishable from Sensations of the Five Senses, which originate on the exterior surface, and from the Emotions, which do not originate on the surface at all.—*Ryland*, '*Handbook, &c.*,' p. 22.

The Organic Sensations

As might be anticipated, the several kinds of [organic] Sensation are not capable of being very sharply distinguished, since the feelings arise from nerves distributed on surfaces placed at all gradations of depth

Professor Bain gives the following classification of the Organic Sensations —

(1.) Organic Sensations of Muscle, Bones, &c., *e.g*, those caused by wounds, cramp, fatigue, &c.

(2.) Organic Sensations of Nervous Tissue, *e.g.*, neuralgia.

(3.) Feelings connected with Circulation and Nutrition, *e.g.*, thirst, starvation, *not* hunger.

(4.) Feelings of the Respiratory Organs, *e.g.*, suffocation.

(5.) Feelings of Heat and Cold, connected chiefly with the skin, though not exclusively

(6.) Organic Sensations of the Alimentary Canal—(not to be confounded with Taste proper)—*e.g.*, relish, hunger, nausea, dyspepsia.

(7.) Feelings connected with the Sexual Organs, mammary and lachrymal glands, &c.—*Ryland*, '*Handbook, &c.*,' p. 23.

Complete Classification

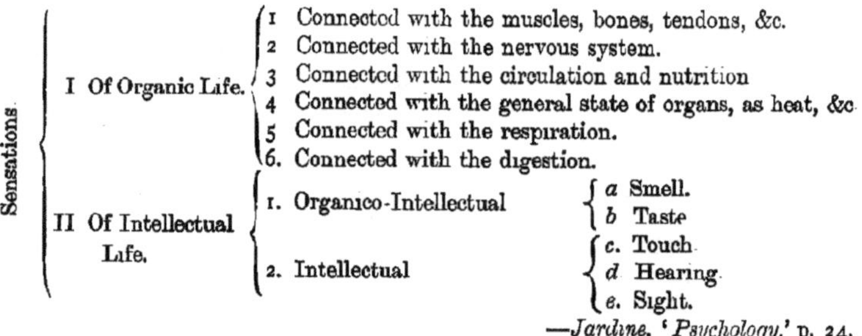

—*Jardine*, '*Psychology*,' p. 24.

General Psychological Characteristics of the Five Senses

In some the sensation so far predominates over the perception that the sense manifests itself as a source of feeling rather than of knowledge, and has often, though erroneously, been regarded as consisting of the former element only. In others the reverse is the case; the perceptive element or cognition of an object, predominating over the sensitive element or consciousness of a personal affection. In this point of view the senses of smell and taste may be distinguished as especially subjective or sensational; those of hearing and sight as objective or perceptional. Touch has no special organ, and is diffused in various degrees over the various parts of the body. In other words, smell and taste are chiefly known as vehicles of the mental emotions of pleasure and pain, hearing and sight as informing us of the nature of the bodily attributes of sound and colour Touch may contribute to the one or the other end, according to the part of the body in which it resides, and the manner in which it is brought into exercise.—*Mansel*, '*Metaphysics*,' p. 70.

Veracity of the Senses.

The Eleatics looked upon the senses as deceiving, and appealed to the reason as discovering the abiding (τὸ ὄν) amid the fleeting. The question arose: Since the senses are delusive, what reason have we for thinking that the reason is trustworthy? Heraclitus the Dark thought that the senses give only the transient, and that man can discover nothing more. Plato mediated between the two schools, and thought that there were two elements in sense-perception, an external and an internal. This theory has ever since been maintained by a succession of thinkers, including the school of Kant. Unfortunately they can give us no rule to enable us to distinguish between what we are to allot to subjective and what to the objective factors. Possibly the following passage, affirming that science is not in sensations, but in our reasoning about them, may have suggested the theory of Aristotle, which has long divided the philosophic world with that of Plato: Ἐν μὲν ἄρα τοῖς παθήμασιν οὐκ ἔνι ἐπιστήμη, ἐν δὲ τῷ περὶ ἐκείνων συλλογισμῷ (107).

Aristotle, with his usual judgment and penetration, started the right explanation (see *De Anima*, Lib. III. Chaps. i. iii. vi.) He says that perception by a sense of things peculiar to that sense is true, or involves the smallest amount of error. But when such objects are perceived in their accidents (that is, as to things not falling peculiarly under that sense), there is room for falsehood, when, for instance, a thing is said to be white there is no falsehood, but when the object is said to be this or that (if the white thing is said to be Cleon, *cf.* III. i. 7), there may be falsehood. Aristotle saw that the difficulties might be cleared up by attending to what each sense testifies, and separating the associated imaginations and opinions or judgments. The full explanation, however, could not be given till Berkeley led men to distinguish between the original and acquired perceptions of the senses, by showing that the knowledge of distance by the eye is an acquisition.

In modern times, metaphysicians have vacillated between the Platonic and Aristotelian theories, some, as Kant and Hamilton, making every perception partly subjective, and others ascribing the supposed deception to wrong deductions from the matter supplied by the senses. The Sensational School of France and T. Brown make all external perception an inference from sensations in the mind, and refer the mistakes to wrong reasoning. The question will be settled when it is determined what are the original perceptions through the senses.

On the supposition that what we intuitively perceive is our organism, and by the muscular sense and sight the objects immediately affecting it, we can explain most of the phenomena of the senses, and give a rational explanation of their apparent deceptions.—*M'Cosh, 'Intuitions, &c.,'* p. 123.

The Five Senses.

TOUCH.

The peculiarity of the skin by which it recognises the form of an object, is called the *sense of touch*, its peculiarity of estimating the force with which the object which it touches presses upon it, is called the *sense of pressure*; the peculiarity of recognising heat or cold, the *sense of temperature*. From the combination of these three sensations is formed our faculty of discovering the properties of an object to a certain extent by touch alone. The tactile sense of the skin is divided into these three qualities, which are generally united in a simultaneous sensation.—*Bernstein, 'Five Senses,'* p. 13.

The course of the nerve between brain and skin along which the excitement passes can be followed anatomically with a certain degree of exactness. A nervous fibre which ends in the skin forms as far as its union with the spinal cord or brain a long, fine, continuous thread. The fibres which terminate in the skin very soon unite in small branches, and finally in thick nerve trunks, before they enter the central organ of the nervous system, but in no case do two nerve fibres coalesce in these nerve branches. We may, therefore, assume that every part of the skin is provided with isolated connections with the centre of the nervous system, which are united there just as telegraph lines unite at a terminus.—*Bernstein*, '*Five Senses*,' pp. 18, 19.

Delicacy of the Sense of Touch—Weber's Experiment.

Two persons are required for this experiment, one of whom tests the sense of touch of the other. For this purpose a pair of compasses are taken, whose points, somewhat blunted, are placed at a certain distance from one another on a part of the skin of the other person. The latter must then say, with closed eyes, whether he feels the contact of two points, or whether both points seem to be merged into one.

The result of this experiment upon the less sensitive parts of the skin is very surprising. If, for instance, the points are placed on the forearm in the direction of the length of the arm, at a distance of about four centimetres (1.58 inch) apart, the sensation is then evidently a double one; but as soon as the distance between the points is less than three centimetres (1.18 inch) the contact is then felt as that of a single point—that is to say, both contacts are united into a single sensation. . . . By this test the tip of the tongue is found to be the most sensitive, for the two points are distinguished when at a distance of only a millimetre apart (.0394 inch).—*Bernstein*, '*Five Senses*,' pp. 25, 26.

SIGHT.

The Organ of Sight.

The eye is a ball nearly spherical in shape, the interior of which forms a dark chamber like the photographer's *camera obscura*. The only aperture, by which light can find admittance into this chamber, is the pupil, which shows like a black spot in consequence of the intense darkness of the interior. This darkness is owing to a black pigment in the internal lining of the eye: otherwise the interior is perfectly pervious to light, being filled with transparent humours. Of these humours the most important is called the *crystalline lens*. It lies directly behind the pupil, so that it refracts every ray of light that enters the eye. Being a convexo convex lens, it brings to a focus the rays of light radiating from objects in front of the pupil, and thus forms an image of these objects on the internal coat of the eye. This coat is called the *retina*, because it is mainly a network of minute fibres from the optic nerve. These nerve fibres are excited by the rays of light converging upon them, and visual sensation is the result.—*J. Clark Murray*, '*Handbook of Psychology*,' p. 54.

The Agent of Sight.

Physics teach us that light is transmitted by the *ether*, a substance of extraordinary tenuity, which extends throughout the universe, penetrates all substances, exists also in empty space, and that it is produced by vibrations of the ether of extraordinary rapidity. As these vibrations reach the interior of the eye through its transparent organs, they produce in us a sensation of light, and by means of the wonderful formation of the eye, we are not only able to perceive the impressions of light emitted by bodies, merely as such, but also to perceive their form, size, and nature.—*Bernstein*, '*Five Senses*,' pp. 48–9.

The rays of light which fall upon the eye penetrate the cornea, the aqueous humour, the crystalline lens, and the vitreous humour, before they reach the retina, and on their way are refracted in such a manner that they unite with a distinct picture upon the background of the eye.—*Bernstein*, '*Five Senses*,' p. 53.

The Perception of Colours

The theory of Thos. Young and Helmholtz.

All the phenomena of the sensation of colour may be explained on the supposition that, in each point of the retina, three kinds of nerve fibres terminate, one of which is sensitive to *red*, another to *green*, and the third to *violet*.

Exactly as white light is produced by the combination of red, green, and violet, all other shades of colours may be formed by the combination of these primary colours. If white light falls upon the retina, then all these kinds of fibres, those sensitive to red, green, and violet, are irritated, and this simultaneous irritation produces the sensation of white. If the retina is illuminated by red light, then the fibre sensitive to red is irritated most strongly. It is, however, very probable that the other two kinds of fibres are irritated at the same time though in a less degree; first, the fibre sensitive to green, because green lies nearer to the red in the spectrum, and then that sensitive to violet.

According to this theory, *yellow* light irritates equally the fibres sensitive to red and to green, and only slightly that sensitive to violet. Yellow therefore is not a primary colour, but, physiologically speaking, a compound colour, because it is due to a combination of the sensations of red and green.

Green light irritates principally the fibres sensitive to green, and very slightly those sensitive to red and violet.

Blue light irritates simultaneously the fibres sensitive to green and violet in an equal degree, and very slightly those sensitive to red. Blue, therefore, physiologically considered, is also a compound colour.

Violet light irritates very strongly the fibres sensitive to violet, and the other two only slightly.—*Bernstein*, '*Five Senses*,' pp. 112, 113.

HEARING.

The Ear, the organ of hearing, is divisible into (1) the External ear; (2) the Tympanum or Middle ear; and (3) the Labyrinth or Internal ear.

The two first divisions are appendages or accessories of the third, which contains the sentient surface.

The Outer ear includes the wing of the ear—augmenting the sound by reflection, and the passage of the ear, which is closed at the inner end by the membrane of the tympanum.

The Middle ear, or Tympanum, is a narrow irregular cavity, extending to the labyrinth, and communicating with the throat, through the Eustachian tube. It contains a chain of small bones, stretching from the inner side of the membrane of the tympanum to an opening in the labyrinth; there are also certain very minute muscles attached to these bones. The inner wall of the tympanum, which is the outer wall of the labyrinth, is an even surface of bone, but chiefly noted for two openings—the oval and the round—both closed with membrane. It is to the oval opening that the inner end of the chain of bones, the stirrup bone, is applied. Of the muscles, the largest is attached to the outer bone of the chain (the malleus), and is called *tensor tympani*, because its action is to draw inwards, and tighten, the tympanum. Two or three other muscles are named, but their action is doubtful.

The Internal ear, or Labyrinth, contained in the petrous or hard portion of the temporal bone, is made up of two structures, the bony and the membranous labyrinth. The bony labyrinth presents externally a spiral shell called the cochlea, and three projecting rings called the semicircular canals. The interior is hollow, and filled with a clear liquid secreted from a thin lining membrane. It contains a membranous structure corresponding in shape to the tortuosities of the bony labyrinth, hence called the membranous labyrinth; this structure encloses a liquid secretion, and supports the ramifications of the auditory nerve.—*Bain*, '*Mental Science*,' pp. 51, 52.

SMELL.

The action of the organ of smell is due to a special nerve, the *olfactory nerve*, which differs from the others, both in origin, position, and extension. It has its origin in the anterior portion of the cranium in a bulbous swelling, the *olfactory ganglion*, which is strongly developed in the lower animals. Its fibres spread themselves out in the base of the skull, and force their way through the *cribriform plate* of the cribriform bone, which lies between the sockets of the eyes, by a great number of small apertures into the upper portion of the nose. This part of the nostril is itself divided into three mussel-shaped passages, which are covered by a mucous membrane.

The inferior and partly the middle passage of the nostril serve principally for inhaling and exhaling the air, and are, therefore, called the *respiratory region* (*regio respiratoria*). Like the other air-passages in the windpipe and lungs it is covered with cylindrical cells (epithelial cells), packed closely together, and at their free extremity provided with fine hairs, which by a sort of waving motion propel outwards all mucous secretion and dust.

The upper and partly the lower passages of the nostril are occupied by the sensory organ for the sensation of smell, and have therefore been called the olfactory region (*regio olfactoria*). It is distinguished from the respiratory region by its yellow colour, caused by pigments, and, unlike the latter, is not covered with hairy epithelial cells, but presents a different organisation upon its surface.—*Bernstein*, '*Five Senses*,' pp. 285, 286.

TASTE.

The entire surface of the tongue is covered with little elevations called *gustative papillæ*, which are visible to the naked eye. Some of them terminate in a bundle of fibres, and others are broad and bushy on their surface. At the root of the tongue a semicircle is formed by larger papillæ, each of which is surrounded by a circular mound. Small depressions have been observed surrounding these circumvallate papillæ. The papillæ stand in the depressions formed by the mounds, and are filled internally with oblong cells, which are connected by prolongations with nerve-fibres. Similar organs have been observed upon the other papillæ of the mucous membrane of the tongue, and it is probable that in them we must look for the true instruments of taste. It is not so easy to decide whether there be a special nerve of taste, as was the case with the other senses. There is certainly a nerve, the *glosso-pharyngeal nerve*, which must without doubt be regarded as the most important nerve of taste, but its gustative fibres are connected with innumerable motor nerves of the lower part of the head, whilst the optic, auditory, and olfactory nerves are entirely free from any foreign admixture. When this nerve has been severed, it has been observed that animals, after this operation, will devour food, even when mixed with the bitterest substances, which an animal in a normal condition would refuse to touch.

Besides the nerve named above, another sensory nerve is found in the tongue, the *lingual nerve*, which provides it with a sense of touch and with sensitiveness. It is still uncertain whether it possesses gustative fibres besides the ordinary sensitive fibres. At any rate, it can certainly be excited by sapid substances, when they are of a sharp caustic nature, such as strong acids, alkali, strong roots, &c.—*Bernstein*, '*Five Senses*,' pp. 296, 297.

Localisation of Sensations.

When we experience a sensation we localise it: we refer such a pain, such a feeling of heat, such a sensation of contact, to the hand, to the leg, to such and such a part of the body, such a sensation of smell to the interior of the nose, such a sensation of taste to the palate, to the tongue, to the back of the mouth. But there is here an ulterior operation engendered by experience; a group of images has combined with the sensation to attribute to it this position: this group gives it a situation which really it has not, and in general places it at the extremity of the nerve whose action excites it. Sometimes again a second operation removes it to a still more distant place; sounds and colours, which are sensations only, at present appear to us situated, not in our organs, but at a distance, in the air, or on the surface of external objects —*Taine*, '*Intelligence*,' p. 100.

VII LAWS OF SENSIBILITY

Every wave-impulse is irradiated and propagated *throughout* the system

Having stated the law, we must add that, like the first Law of Motion, it is an *ideal construction*, and not a transcript of objective observation Just as the uniform rectilinear motion never can be observed in the real world of infinite motions which deflect, accelerate, and retard each other, so there can never be an irradiation throughout the central tissue, because each wave-impulse must be arrested and deflected, as it is compounded with multitudinous impulses from other sources

Hence the second law Every impulse is restricted, and by its restriction a group is formed —*Lewes*, '*Problems of Life and Mind*,' 3d Series, pp 44, 45

Fechner's or Weber's Psycho-Physical Law.

In order that the intensity of a sensation may increase in arithmetical progression, the stimulus must increase in a geometrical progression —*Sully*, '*Outlines of Psychology*,' p 114

The Doctrine of Wundt

Every stimulus must reach a certain intensity before any appreciable sensation results This point is known as the threshold or liminal intensity

When the stimulus is increased up to a certain point, any further increase produces no appreciable increase in the sensation Thus a very powerful sound may be increased without our detecting any difference Similarly in the case of a light stimulus. We do not notice any difference in brightness between the central and peripheral portion of the sun's disc, though the difference of light-intensity is enormous Wundt calls this upper or maximum limit the Height of Sensibility of a Sense The higher this point in the scale the greater, according to him, the Receptivity (*Reiz-Empfänglichkeit*) of the organ

Finally, by taking together the Threshold and Height we have what Wundt calls the Range of Sensibility (*Reiz-Umfang*) The lower the former or minimum limit, and the higher the latter or maximum, the greater the range of sensibility That is to say, the relative range is measured by a fraction of which the numerator is the Height, and the denominator the Threshold It is important to add that these aspects of sensibility to stimulus do not vary together Fechner ascertained that parts of the skin equal in respect of absolute sensibility to pressure differed considerably in discriminative sensibility.—*Sully*, '*Outlines of Psychology*,' p 114

V.

KNOWLEDGE

I. KNOWLEDGE (in General).

There is great difficulty in defining Knowledge

We may suppose the question to be put, What is Knowledge? To this the reply must be that we cannot positively define knowledge, so as to make it intelligible to one who did not know it otherwise. Still we can, by analysis, separate it from other things with which it is associated,—such as sensations, emotions and fancies,—and make it stand out distinctly to the view of those who are already conscious of it The science which thus unfolds the nature of knowledge may be called Gnosiology, or Gnosilogy —*M'Cosh*, '*Intuitions of the Mind*,' p. 284

No definition or description can convey, to him who has never *known*, the conception of what an act of knowledge is. All definitions and descriptions presuppose that the person to whom they are addressed can understand their import and verify their truth by referring to his own conscious acts. But we may not rest in this general assent to the reality, nor in our general impressions of the nature of knowledge. We require a more exact determination of its import and relations.

The nearer and more attentive consideration of knowledge gives us the following propositions:

1. *To know, is an active operation.*—To know, is an operation of the soul acting as the intellect, an operation in which it is pre-eminently active. In knowing, we are not so much recipients as actors.

2. *Exercised under conditions.*—The intellect exercises its capacity to know under certain conditions. Like every other agent in nature, it is limited in respect to the mode, energy, and results of its action, by the occasions and circumstances under which it acts.—*Porter*, '*Human Intellect*,' p. 61.

Attempts at definition by—

The Platonists.

All knowledge is the gathering up into one, and the indivisible apprehension of this unity by the Knowing Mind.

The Stoics.

The Stoics defined Knowledge as the certain and incontestable apprehension, through the concept, of the thing known.—*Ueberweg*, '*Hist. of Phil.*,' i. 192.

John Locke.

Knowledge is nothing but the perception of the connexion and agreement, or disagreement and repugnancy of any of our ideas.—'*Human Understanding*,' bk. iv. ch. i. § 2.

Reid.

Knowledge, I think, sometimes signifies things known; sometimes that act of the mind by which we know them.—'*Works*,' p. 426.

What Knowledge implies.

Knowledge implies three things: 1st, firm *belief*, 2d, of what is *true*, 3d, on sufficient *grounds*. If any one, *e.g.*, is in *doubt* respecting one of Euclid's demonstrations, he cannot be said to *know* the proposition proved by it; if, again, he is fully *convinced* of anything that is not *true*, he is mistaken in supposing himself to know it; lastly, if two persons are each *fully confident*, one that the moon is inhabited, and the other that it is not (though one of these opinions must be *true*), neither of them could properly be said to *know* the truth, since he cannot have sufficient *proof* of it. —*Whately*, '*Logic*, p. 165.

Knowledge supposes three terms: a *being* who knows, an *object* known, and a *relation* determined between the knowing being and the known object. This relation properly constitutes knowledge.—*Fleming*, '*Vocab. of Phil.*,' p. 281.

The ultimate distinction in human knowledge is that between thought and being. This distinction is involved in all knowledge.—*Trendelenburg.*

Knowledge is of relations.

We have no scruple in accepting duly verified knowledge as representing reality, though what is known consists in nothing else than relations. . . . No knowledge can properly be called a phenomenon of consciousness. It may be *of* phenomena. . . . A man's knowledge of a proposition in Euclid means a relation in his consciousness between certain parts of a figure determined by the relation of those parts to other parts. The knowledge is made up of those relations as in consciousness. . . . The system of related facts, which forms the objective world, reproduces itself, partially and gradually, in the soul of the individual who in part knows it. . . . The attainment of the knowledge is only explicable as a reproduction of itself, in the human soul, by the consciousness for which the cosmos of related facts exists,—a reproduction of itself, in which it uses the sentient life of the soul as its organ.—*Green*, '*Prolegomena to Ethics*,' pp. 24, 61, 62.

The Classification of Knowledge according to its Source

As Empirical and Philosophical.

We set up a broad distinction between two kinds of knowledge, calling the one empirical and the other philosophical; the one knowledge by observation, and the other knowledge by principles or reasons. We should remember, when we make this distinction, that in the two there is but one and the same mind which knows; that the same intellect observes and reasons upon the same subject-matter. It follows that the same mind uses two ways or processes of knowing, and that these assist and correct each other. There must, then, be a relation of dependence between the two. The one must be subject to the other, in the mind's own judgment, and according to the ordinances of the mind's own constitution. In other words, the mind that observes, knows that, by thinking, it can correct and aid its own observing, and that the one method of knowing has a certain authority over the other. Not that the one can take place without the other, or that the one can take place so as to dispense with the other. This is contradicted by the facts of the mind's own development. It is refuted by the psychological relation of the two processes. But while one is psychologically necessary to the other, and involved in the other, the one is subordinated to the other in importance and trustworthiness.—*Porter*, '*Human Intellect*,' p. 71.

À priori and à posteriori.

Knowledge *à posteriori* is knowledge acquired from experience. Knowledge *à priori*, called likewise native, pure, or transcendental knowledge, consists of native cognitions, and embraces those principles which, as the conditions of the exercise of its faculties of observation and thought, are consequently not the result of that exercise.—*Hamilton*, '*Metaphysics*,' ii. 26.

Intuitive and Inferential.

Truths are known to us in two ways: some are known directly and of themselves; some through the medium of other truths. The former are the subject of Intuition or Consciousness; the latter of Inference. The truths known by Intuition are the original premises from which all others are inferred. Our assent to the conclusion being grounded on the truth of the premises, we never could arrive at any knowledge by reasoning, unless something could be known antecedently to all reasoning.

Examples of truths known to us by immediate consciousness are our own bodily sensations and mental feelings. Examples of truths which we know only by way of inference are occurrences which took place while we were absent, the events recorded in history, or the theorems of mathematics. —*Mill*, '*Logic*,' introd., sec. 4.

Nature of Knowledge

As Mediate and Immediate, or Presentative and Representative.

A thing is known *immediately* or proximately, when we cognise it in itself; *mediately* or remotely, when we cognise it in or through something numerically different from itself. Immediate cognition, thus the knowledge of a thing in itself, involves the *fact* of its existence; mediate cognition, thus the knowledge of a thing in or through something not itself, involves only the *possibility* of its existence.

An immediate cognition, inasmuch as the thing known is itself presented to observation, may be called a *presentative*, and inasmuch as the thing presented, is, as it were, viewed by the mind face to face, may be called an *intuitive* cognition. A mediate cognition, inasmuch as the thing known is held up or mirrored to the mind in a vicarious representation, may be called a *representative* cognition.—*Hamilton in Reid's* '*Works*,' p. 804.

I call up an image of the Cathedral. In this operation, it is evident that I am conscious or immediately cognisant of the Cathedral, as imaged in my mind; so it is equally manifest, that I am not conscious or immediately cognisant of the Cathedral as existing But still I am said to know it; it is even called the object of my thought. I can, however, only know it mediately,—only through the mental image, which represents it to consciousness. From this example is manifest, what in general is meant by immediate or intuitive,—what by mediate or representative knowledge.—*Hamilton*, '*Metaphysics*,' ii. 68.

Philosophers have drawn the distinction between Presentative and Representative Knowledge. In the former the object is present at the time, we perceive it, we feel it, we are conscious of it as now and here and under our inspection. In Representative Knowledge there is an object now present, representing an absent object. Thus I may have an image or conception of Venice, with its decaying beauty, and this is now present, and under the eye of consciousness; but it represents something absent and distant, of the existence of which I am at the same time convinced. When I was actually in Venice, and gazed on its churches and palaces rising out of the waters, there would be no propriety in saying that I believed in the existence of the city,—the correct phrase is that I knew it to exist.—*M'Cosh*, '*Intuitions of the Mind*,' p. 168.

Application.

Practical and Speculative.

Knowledge is either practical or speculative. In practical knowledge it is evident that truth is not the ultimate end; for in that case, knowledge is for the sake of application. The knowledge of a moral, of a political, of a religious truth, is of value only as it affords the preliminary or condition of its exercise. Speculative knowledge is only pursued, and is only held of value, for the sake of intellectual activity.—*Hamilton*, '*Metaphysics*,' i. 9.

Symbolical and Intuitive.

For the most part we do not view at once the whole characters or attributes of the thing, but in place of these we employ signs, the explication of which into what they signify, we are wont, at the moment of actual thought, for the sake of brevity, to omit. Thus when I think a chiliagon (or polygon of a thousand equal sides), I do not always consider the various attributes, of the side, of the equality, and of the number a thousand, but use these words (whose meaning is obscurely and imperfectly presented to the mind) in lieu of the notions which I have of them:—this kind of thinking I am used to call *blind* or *symbolical*: we employ it in Algebra and in Arithmetic, but in fact universally. But where we can think at once all the ingredient notions, I call the cognition *intuitive*.—*Leibnitz*, '*De Cognitione, Veritate, et Ideis*.'

Subject-Matter.

As Historical, Scientific, Philosophical, &c.

We are endowed by our Creator with certain faculties of observation, which enable us to become aware of certain appearances or phenomena. The information that certain phenomena are, or have been, is called Historical knowledge; it is simply the knowledge that something is. But things do not exist, events do not occur, isolated, apart, by themselves; they exist, they occur, and are by us conceived, only in connection. We therefore set about an inquiry into the causes of phenomena. This knowledge of the cause of a phenomenon is called philosophical, or scientific, or rational knowledge; it is the knowledge why or how a thing is.—*Hamilton*, '*Metaphysics*,' i. 58.

Origin of our Knowledge.

This subject is discussed under the head of Ideas. It may suffice here to note, without controversy,

The Main Sources of our Knowledge.

Man's knowledge is derived from Four Sources:—

First, We obtain knowledge from sensation, or rather sense-perception. Such is the knowledge we have of body, and of body extended and resisting pressure, and of our organism as affecting us, or as being affected with smells, tastes, sounds, and colours.

Secondly, We obtain knowledge from self-consciousness. Such is the knowledge we have of self, and of its modes, actions, affections,—say, as thinking, feeling, resolving.

I am convinced that from these two sources we obtain not all our knowledge, but all the knowledge we have of separately existing objects. We do not know, and we cannot so much as conceive of a distinctly existing thing, excepting in so far as we have become acquainted with it by means of sensation and reflection, or of materials thus derived. Here Locke held by a great truth, though he did not see how to limit it on the one hand, nor what truths required to be added to it on the other. For man has other sources of knowledge.

Thirdly, By a further Cognitive or Faith exercise we discover Qualities and Relations in objects which have become known by the senses external and internal. Of this description are the ideas which the mind forms of such objects as space, time, the infinite, the relation between cause and effect, and moral good. There is a wide difference between this Third Class and the Second, though the two have often been confounded. In self-consciousness we look simply at what is passing within, and as it passes within. But the mind has a capacity of discovering further qualities and relations among the objects which have been revealed to it by sensation and consciousness.

Fourthly, The mind can reach truth necessary and universal, that is, universally true. This may be regarded as knowledge, and it is knowledge which goes far beyond that derived from the other sources. We are certain that gratitude and holy love, which are good here, must be good all through the wide universe.—*M'Cosh*, '*Intuitions of the Mind*,' p. 287.

Acquisition of Knowledge

It is gained by mental activity.

Let us consider how knowledge is gained by the mind. Knowledge is not acquired by a mere passive affection, but through the exertion of spontaneous activity on the part of the knowing subject. This mental activity is an energy of the self-active power of a subject one and indivisible.—*H. Schmid*, '*Versuch einer Metaphysik des inneren Natur*,' p. 231.

The eye by long use comes to see even in the darkest cavern; and there is no subject so obscure but we may discern some glimpse of truth by long poring over it. It is Plato's remark, in his *Theætetus*, that while we sit still we are never the wiser, but going into the river, and moving up and down, is the way to discover its depths and shallows. If we exercise and bestir ourselves we may discover something.—*Berkeley*, '*Siris*,' 367, 368.

And often perfected by communication to others.

Communication of thought is conducive to the perfecting of thought itself. For the mind may be determined to more exalted energy by the sympathy of society, and by the stimulus of opposition; or it may be necessitated to more distinct, accurate, and orderly thinking, as this is the condition of distinct, accurate, and orderly communication. 'It is maintained,' says the subtle Scaliger, 'by Vives, that we profit more by silent meditation than by dispute. This is not true. For as fire is elicited by the collision of stones, so truth is elicited by the collision of minds.' —*Hamilton*, '*Logic*,' iv. 207.

Hindrances to its acquirement.

Some of the chief of these may be referred to the following heads:—

(1) The imperfections of language, both as an instrument of thought and a medium of communication.

(2) A disposition to grasp at general principles, without submitting to the previous study of particular facts.

(3.) The difficulty of ascertaining facts

(4.) The great part of life which is spent in making useless literary acquisitions.

(5.) Prejudices arising from a reverence for great names, and from the influence of local institutions.

(6.) A predilection for singular and paradoxical opinions.

(7.) A disposition to unlimited scepticism.—*Stewart*, '*Works*,' ii 9

The joy of acquisition.

The real animating power of knowledge is only in the moment of its being first received, when it fills us with wonder and joy That man is always happy who is in the presence of something which he cannot know to the full, which he is always going on to know.—*Ruskin*, '*Stones of Venice*,' III ch ii. § 28.

The design of knowledge.

Knowledge is not a couch whereon to rest a searching and reckless spirit, or a terrace for a wandering and variable mind to walk up and down with a fair prospect, or a tower of state for a proud mind to raise itself upon, or a fort or commanding ground for strife and contention, or a shop for profit or sale; but a rich storehouse for the glory of the Creator, and the relief of man's estate.—*Bacon.*

Importance of systematic knowledge.

There may be possessed by a man a great deal of knowledge which can be of no use whatever, in consequence of inability to bring together into one view related facts, to see their significance, and to give them their proper place in the system of knowledge. Thus, the knowledge which many possess, although very extensive, is a perfect chaos, a jumble of confusion, and of no practical use in the guidance of life To reason with a man frequently means nothing more than to point out the relation between different things which he already knows, and thus bring into order what was before confusion. There are to every man hundreds of 'open secrets,' facts related in particular ways which relations he cannot see; and it is the function of what is commonly called reasoning to convert this chaos of confused facts into a cosmos of order and harmony, so that men may see clearly what has always been under their eyes, and understand clearly the relations and significance of what they have blindly perceived.—*Jardine*, '*Elements of Psychology*,' p. 235

The goals of knowledge.

There are two sorts of ignorance: we philosophise to escape ignorance, and the consummation of our philosophy is ignorance; we start from the one, we repose in the other; they are the goals from which and to which we tend; and the pursuit of knowledge is but a course between two ignorances, as human life is itself only a travelling from grave to grave. The highest reach of human science is the scientific recognition of human ignorance The grand result of human wisdom is thus only a consciousness that what we know is as nothing to what we know not.—*Hamilton*, '*Discussions*,' p. 601.

Who knows nothing, and thinks that he knows something, his ignorance is twofold.—*A Rabbi*

The Limits of Knowledge.

What are the limits of man's power of acquiring knowledge? The answer is, that he cannot know, at least in this world, any substance or separate existence other than those revealed by sense and consciousness There may be, very probably there are, in the universe, other substances besides matter and spirit, other existences which are not substances, as well as space and time; but these must ever remain unknown to us in this world. Again, he can never know any qualities or relations among the objects thus revealed to the outward and inward sense, except in so far as we have special faculties of knowledge; and the number and the nature of these are to be ascertained by a process of induction, and by no other process either easier or more difficult.—*M'Cosh*, '*Intuitions of the Mind*,' p. 294

As young men, when they knit and shape perfectly, do seldom grow to a further stature; so knowledge, while it is in aphorisms and observations, it is in growth; but when it once is comprehended in exact methods, it may perchance be further polished and illustrated, and accommodated for use and practice, but it increaseth no more in bulk and substance.—*Bacon*, '*Advancement of Learning*,' bk. 1.

II COGNITION (See Knowledge.)

The Term

Its psychological significance.

Cognition is a general name which we may apply to all those mental states in which there is made known in consciousness either some affection or activity of the mind itself, or some external quality or object. The Psychology of Cognition analyses knowledge into its primary elements, and seeks to ascertain the nature and laws of the processes through which all our knowledge passes in progressing from its simplest to its most elaborate condition.—*Jardine*, '*Elements of Psychology*,' p 1.

Its use in Logic

The impression which any object makes upon the mind may be called a Presentation. Some presentations are admitted into the mind without being noticed. A man stares his friend in the face without recognising him; when his friend awakens his attention, the recognition takes place. But he knows that it is not the impression upon his eye which begins at that point of time, but his attention to the impression. Presentations, then, are divided into Clear and Obscure; and the former, with which alone Logic is concerned, may be called Notions or Cognitions.—*Thomson*, '*Laws of Thought*,' p. 71.

It is often synonymous with knowledge

I frequently employ *cognition* as a synonym of knowledge. It is necessary to have a word of this signification, which we can use in the plural. Now the term *knowledges* has waxed obsolete, though I think it ought to be revived. We must, therefore, have recourse to the term *cognition*, of which the plural is in common usage.—*Hamilton*, '*Metaphysics*,' ii. 19.

When dividing all mental states, however, into Cognitions, Feelings, and Conations, Hamilton uses the word Cognition in its widest sense, to include all the products of intuition and thought—of the senses and the intellect—thus including both knowledge proper and Belief. In fact *belief* is not often opposed to *cognition*, though it frequently is to *knowledge*.—*Monck*, '*Sir W. Hamilton*,' p. 171.

Distinctions among Cognitions.

As empirical and noetic.

The principal distinctions of Empirical and Noetic Cognitions are the following.—1 Empirical cognitions originate exclusively in experience, whereas noetic cognitions are virtually at least before or above all experience,—all experience being only possible through them. 2. Empirical cognitions come piecemeal and successively into existence, and may again gradually fade and disappear, whereas noetic cognitions, like Pallas, armed and immortal from the head of Jupiter, spring at once into existence, complete and indestructible. 3. Empirical cognitions find only an application to those objects from which they were originally abstracted, and, according as things obtain a different form, they also may become differently fashioned; noetic cognitions, on the contrary, bear the character impressed on them of necessity, universality, sameness.—*Esser*, '*Logik*,' § 171.

As Confused and Distinct.

Cognitions or Clear Presentations are subdivided into confused and distinct. Where the marks or attributes which make up the presentation cannot be distinguished, it is confused, where they can be distinguished and enumerated, it is distinct. For example, we have a clear notion of the colour red, but we cannot tell by what marks we identify it; we could not describe it intelligibly to another; and hence our cognition is confused. again we have a clear notion of house, but we can declare its various marks, namely, that it is an enclosed and covered building fit for habitation, and therefore our notion is distinct. —*Thomson*, '*Laws of Thought*,' p. 72.

As à priori and à posteriori

We understand by knowledge *à priori* knowledge which is *absolutely* independent of all experience, and not of this or that experience only. Opposed to this is empirical knowledge, or such as is possible *à posteriori* only, that is, by experience. Knowledge *à priori*, if mixed up with nothing empirical, is called *pure*.—*Kant*, '*Critique*,' vol. i. p. 399.

As drawn by Spinoza

Spinoza distinguishes three kinds of cognitions. By the first, which he calls *opinio* or *imaginatio*, he understands the development of perceptions and of universal notions derived from them, out of the impressions of the senses through unregulated experience, or out of signs, particularly words, which, through the memory, call forth imaginations. The second kind of cognition, called by Spinoza *ratio*, consists in adequate ideas of the peculiarities of things. The third and highest kind of cognition is the intuitive knowledge which the intellect has of God. Cognition of the first kind is the only source of deception; that of the second and third teaches us to distinguish the true from the false.—*Ueberweg*. '*Hist. of Phil.*,' iv. 75.

III. INTUITIONS (See INTUITION, INNATE IDEAS.)

Definitions

Intuitions are perceptions formed by looking in upon objects, they are native convictions of the mind. These convictions seem to be of the nature of perceptions, that is, something is presented to us, and the cognition, belief, or judgment is formed.—*M'Cosh*, '*Intuitions of the Mind*,' p. 25.

We class under the general denomination of *Intuitions*, all those states of consciousness in which the actual presence of an object, within or without the mind, is the primary fact which leads to its recognition as such, by the subject; and from these may be distinguished, under the name of *Thoughts*, all those states of consciousness in which the presence of the object is the result of a representative act on the part of the subject. In the former case, the presence of the object is involuntary, in the latter it is voluntary.—*Mansel*, '*Metaphysics*,' p. 53.

Synonymous Terms

'They have been denominated κοιναὶ προλήψεις, κοιναὶ ἔννοιαι, φυσικαὶ ἔννοιαι, πρῶται ἔννοιαι, πρῶτα νοήματα, *naturæ judicia*, *judicia communibus hominum sensibus infixa*, *notiones* or *notitiæ connatæ* or *innatæ*, *semina scientiæ*, *semina omnium cognitionum*, *semina æternitatis*, *zopyra* (living sparks), *præcognita necessaria*, *anticipationes*, first principles, common anticipations, principles of common sense, self-evident or intuitive truths, primitive notions, native notions, innate cognitions, natural knowledges (cognitions), fundamental reasons, metaphysical or transcendental truths, ultimate or elemental laws of thought, primary or fundamental laws of human belief or primary laws of human reason, pure or transcendental or *à priori* cognitions, categories of thought, natural beliefs, rational instincts, &c. &c. (Hamilton, *Met. Lec.*, 38).—*Porter*, '*Human Intellect*,' p. 500.

Reality of their Existence

There are in the mind such existences and powers as primary perceptions and fundamental laws of belief, but they are very different in their nature from the picture which is frequently given of them, and they are by no means fitted to accomplish the ends to which they have often been turned in metaphysical and theological speculation I would as soon believe that there are no such agents as heat, chemical affinity, and electricity in physical nature, as that there are no immediate perceptions and native-born convictions in this mind of ours. I consider the one kind of agents, like the other, to be among the deepest and most potent at work in this world, mental and material; and yet the one class, like the other, while operating every instant in soul or body, are apt to hide themselves from the view. Indeed they discover themselves only by their effects, and their law can be detected only by a careful observation of its actings; and it should be added, that both are capable of evil as well as good, and are to be carefully watched and guarded in the application which is made of them.—*M'Cosh, 'Intuitions of the Mind,'* p. 1.

That there are intuitive principles operating in the mind may be established by the following propositions:—

1. *The mind has something native or innate.*

Even on the supposition that it is like a surface of wax or a sheet of white paper, ready to receive whatever is impressed or written on it, the soul must have something inborn. If it has but a power of impressibility, it has in this something innate. The very wax and paper, in the inadequate illustration referred to, have capabilities, the capacity of taking something on them, and retaining it. But such comparisons have all a misleading tendency. Surely the mind has something more than a mere receptivity. It is not a mere surface, on which matter may reflect itself as on a mirror: our consciousness testifies that, in comparison with matter, it is active; that it has an original, and an originating potency.

2. *This something has rules, laws, or properties.*

Matter, with all its endowments, inorganic and organic, is regulated by laws which it is the office of physical and physiological science to discover. All the powers or properties of material substance have rules of action; for example, gravitation and chemical affinity have appointed modes of operation which can be expressed in quantitative proportions. That mind also has properties is shown by its action; and surely these properties do not act capriciously or lawlessly. There are rules involved in the very constitution of its active properties, and these are not beyond the possibility of being discovered and expressed. The senses indeed cannot detect them, but they may be found out by internal observation. It is true that this law cannot be discovered immediately by consciousness any more than the law of gravitation can be perceived by the eye. But the operations of the mental properties are under the observation of consciousness just as those of gravitation are under the senses; and by careful observation, analysis, and generalisation, we may from the acts reach the laws of the acts. He who has reached the exact expression of our mental properties is in possession of a law which is native or innate.

3. *The mind has original perceptions, which may be described as intuitive.*

Every one will acknowledge that it has perceptions through the senses, and it may be shown that there are perceptions of the understanding and of the moral faculty. Some of these perceptions are no doubt secondary and derivative, but the secondary imply primary perceptions, and the derivative original ones. Thus perception of distance by the eye may be derivative; but it implies an original perception, by the eye, of a surface. It is by a process of reasoning that I know that the square of the hypothenuse of the right-angled triangle is equal to the square of the other two sides; but this reasoning proceeds on certain axiomatic truths whose certainty is seen at once, as that 'if equals be added to equals the wholes are equal.' Let it be observed that we are now in a region in which are loftier powers than those possessed by inert matter; still these higher have rules as well as the lower or material properties. The original perceptions by sense, or reason, or moral power, all have their laws, which it should be the business of psychology or of metaphysics to discover and determine These perceptions may be represented as intuitions, inasmuch as they look immediately on the object or truth. The rules or laws which they obey may be described as intuitive; and it is the office of mental science to discover them by a process of introspection, abstraction, and comparison.—*M'Cosh*, '*Intuitions of the Mind*,' pp. 20, 21.

How they Arise.

They are not perceived by sense-perception, nor felt by consciousness; they are neither reproduced in memory nor represented or created by the phantasy; they are not generalised by the power to classify and name; they are neither proved by deduction nor inferred by induction. They are developed and brought to view in connection with these processes, and are assumed in them all.

It has been extensively taught and believed that these original ideas and first truths are discerned by direct insight or intuition, independently of their relation to the phenomena of sense and spirit The power to behold them is conceived as a special sense for the true, the original, and the infinite; as a divine Reason which acts by inspiration, and is permitted to gaze directly upon that which is eternally true and divine The less the soul has to do with the objects of sense the better—the more it is withdrawn from these the more penetrating and clear will be its insight into the ideas which alone are permanent and divine. Such are the representations of Plato, Plotinus, &c., among the ancients Similar language has been employed by many in modern times who have called themselves Platonists. Platonising theologians have freely availed themselves of this phraseology, and have seemed to sanction the views which this language signifies. Thus the Platonising and Cartesian divines of the seventeenth century, as Henry More, John Smith of Cambridge, Ralph Cudworth, and multitudes of others freely express themselves. Philosophers who Platonise in thought or language have adopted similar phraseology; some have even pressed these doctrines to the most literal interpretation Malebranche, Schelling, Coleridge, Cousin, and others have allowed themselves to use such language, and have given sanction to such views more or less clearly conceived and expressed Those who combine with philosophic acuteness the power of vivid imagination and of eloquent exposition, not infrequently meet the difficulties which attend the analysis and explanation of the foundations of knowledge, by these half-poetic and half-philosophical representations.

Whatever may be their real meaning, it is manifest that the representations which they give are not true when literally interpreted It cannot be successfully, scarcely soberly maintained, that these ideas and truths are discerned by the mind out of all relation to actual beings and concrete phenomena. It is so far from being true that the mind needs to be delivered from, or to look away from the sensible in order to discern the rational, that it should always be remembered that it is only by means of the sensible that permanent principles and relations can ever be reached. No direct inspection of primitive ideas and principles is conceivable It is not by withdrawing the attention from, but by fixing it upon the facts and phenomena of the actual world that the truths and relations of the world, which is ideal and rational, can be discerned at all.—*Porter*, '*Human Intellect*,' pp. 499, 518.

For further discussion, see IDEAS (Origin of).

Their Tests

But how are we to distinguish a primitive conviction which does not need probation, and which we may not even doubt, from propositions which we are not required to believe till evidence is produced? Are we entitled to appeal, when we please and as we please, to supposed first truths? Have we the privilege, when we wish to adhere to a favourite opinion, to declare that we see it to be true intuitively, and thus at once get rid of all objections, and of the necessity for even instituting an examination? When hard pressed or defeated in argument may we resort, as it suits us, to an original principle which we assume without evidence, and declare to be beyond the reach of refutation? There can be tests propounded sufficient to determine with precision what convictions are and what convictions are not entitled to be regarded as intuitive, and these tests are such that they admit of an easy application, requiring only a moderate degree of careful consideration of the maxim claiming our assent.

1. *The primary mark of intuitive truth is self-evidence*

It must be evident, and it must have its evidence in the object. The mind on the bare contemplation of the object, must see it to be so and so, must see it to be so at once, without requiring any foreign evidence or mediate proof. That the planet Mars is inhabited, or that it is not inhabited, is not a first truth, for it is not evident on the bare contemplation of the object. That the isle of Madagascar is inhabited, even this is not a primary conviction; we believe it because of secondary testimony. Nay, that the three angles of a triangle are together equal to two right angles, is not a primitive judgment, for it needs other truths coming between to carry our conviction. But that there is an extended object before me when I look at a table or a wall, that I who look at these objects exist, and that two marbles added to two marbles here will be equal to two marbles added to two marbles there,—these are truths that are evident on the bare contemplation of the objects, and need no foreign facts or considerations derived from any other quarter to establish them.

2. *Necessity is a second mark of intuitive truth.*

I would not ground the evidence on the necessity of belief, or fix on this as the original or essential characteristic, but I would ascribe the irresistible nature of the conviction to the self-evidence. As the necessity flows from the self-evidence, so it may become a test of it, and a test not difficult of application.

When an object of truth is self-evident, necessity always attaches to our convictions regarding it. And according to the nature of the conviction, so is the necessity attached. We shall see that some of our original convictions are of the nature of knowledge, others of the nature of belief, a third class of the nature of judgments, in which we compare objects known or imagined or believed in. In the first our cognition is necessary, in the second our belief is necessary, in the third our judgment is necessary. I know self as an existing thing: this is a necessary cognition; I must entertain it, and never can be driven from it. That space exceeds my widest imagination of space: this is a necessary belief, I must believe it. That every effect has a cause: this is a necessary judgment; I must decide in this way. Wherever there is such a conviction, it is a sign of an intuitive perception. Necessity, too, may be employed in a negative form, and this is often the most decisive form. If I know immediately that there is an extended object before me in the book which I read, I cannot be made to know that there is not an extended object before me. If I must believe that time has had no beginning, I cannot be made to believe that it has had a beginning. Necessitated as I am to decide that two parallel lines cannot meet, I cannot be made to decide that they can meet. Necessity as a test may thus assume two forms, and we may take the one best suited to our purpose at the time. In the use of a very little care and discernment, this test will settle for us as to any given truth, whether it is or is not self-evident.

3. *Catholicity may be employed as a tertiary test.*

By catholicity is meant that the conviction is entertained by all men, or at least by all men possessed of intelligence, when the objects are presented I am not inclined to use this as a primary test For, in the first place, it is not easy to ascertain, or at least to settle absolutely, what truths may claim this common consent of humanity; and even though this were determined, still it might be urged, in the second place, that this does not prove that it is necessary or original, but simply that it is a native property,—like the appetite for food among all men,—and would still leave it possible for opponents to maintain that there may be intelligent beings in other worlds who accord no such assent, just as we can conceive beings in the other parts of the universe who have no craving for meat or drink. But while not inclined to use catholicity as a primary test, I think it may come in at times as an auxiliary one For what is in all men may most probably come from what is not only native, but necessary; and must also in all probability be self-evident, or at least follow very directly from what is self-evident. Catholicity, when conjoined with necessity, may determine very readily and precisely whether a conviction is intuitive.

Important purposes are served by the combination of these two tests, that is, necessity and catholicity By the first we have a personal assurance which can never be shaken, and of which no one can deprive us Though the whole world were to declare that we do not exist, or that a cruel action is good, we would not give up our own personal conviction in favour of their declaration By the other principle we have confidence in addressing our fellow-men, for we know that there are grounds of thought common to them and to us, and to these we can appeal in reasoning with them By the one I am enabled, yea, compelled, to hold by my personality, and maintain my independence, by the other I am made to feel that I am one of a large family, every member of which has the same principles of thought and belief as I myself have The one gives me the argument from private judgment, the other the argument from common or catholic consent The concurrence of the two should suffice to protect me from scepticism of every kind, whether it relate to the world within or the world without, whether to physical or moral truths.—*M'Cosh, 'Intuitions of the Mind,'* pp 31–33

The essential notes or characters by which we are enabled to distinguish our original from our derivative convictions may be reduced to four.—1. Their *Incomprehensibility.* A conviction is incomprehensible when there is merely given us in consciousness *that its object is,* and when we are unable to comprehend through a higher notion or belief, *Why or how it is* 2 Their *Simplicity.* It is manifest that if a cognition or belief can be analysed into a plurality of cognitions or beliefs, that, as compound, it cannot be original. 3. Their *Necessity* and *Absolute Universality* When a belief is necessary it is, *eo ipso,* universal; and that a belief is universal is a certain index that it must be necessary 4 Their *Comparative Evidence* and *Certainty* As Buffier says, they must be 'so clear, that if we attempt to prove or to disprove them this can be done only by propositions which are manifestly neither more evident nor more certain.'—*Hamilton, in Reid's 'Works,'* p 754.

Their Characteristics.

THEORETICAL

(*a.*) *Classified*

The intuitions may be considered, *first,* as laws, rules, principles regulating the original action and the primitive perceptions of the mind Or, *secondly,* they may be regarded as individual perceptions or convictions manifesting themselves in consciousness. Or, *thirdly,* they may be contemplated as abstract notions, or general rules, or Universal Truths elaborated out of the individual exercises. We cannot have a distinct or adequate view of our intuitions unless we carefully distinguish these the one from the other The whole of the confusion, and the greater part of the errors, which have appeared in the discussions about innate ideas and *à priori* principles, have sprung from neglecting these distinctions, or from not carrying them out consistently. In each of these sides the intuitions present distinct characters, and many affirmations may be properly made of the original principles of the mind under one of these aspects, which would by no means hold good of the others. For example:—

As Laws, Rules, or Principles guiding the Mind.

1. *They are native.* Hence they have been designated natural, innate, connate, connatural, implanted, constitutional. All these phrases point to the circumstance that they are not acquired by practice, nor the result of experience, but are in the mind naturally, as constituents of its very being, and involved in its higher exercises. In this respect they are analogous to universal gravitation and chemical affinity, which are not produced in bodies as they operate, but are in the very nature of bodies and the springs of their action.

2. *They are tendencies.* The intuitions operate on the appropriate objects being presented to call them forth; they fail only when there has been nothing suitable to evoke them.

3. *They are regulative.* They lead and guide the deeper mental action, just as the chemical and vital properties conduct and control the composition of bodies and the organisation of plants.

4. *They are catholic or common.* That is, they are in every human mind. Not that they are in all men as formalised principles; under this aspect they come before the minds of comparatively few. Some of them are perhaps not even manifested in all minds; certainly some of them are not manifested, in their higher forms, in the souls of all. In infants some of them have not yet made their appearance, and among persons low in the scale of intelligence they do not come out in their loftier exercises,—just as the plant does not all at once come into full flower, just as in unfavourable circumstances it may never come into seed at all. Still the capacity is there, needing only favourable circumstances—that is, the appropriate objects pressed on the attention—to foster it into developed forms.—*M'Cosh*, '*Intuitions of the Mind*,' pp. 35–37.

At the same time these are after all only the diverse aspects of one great general fact, and they have relations all to each and each to all. There is first a mind with its native capacities, each with its rule of action. In due time these come out into action, some of them at an earlier, and some of them at a later date, on the appropriate objects being presented, and the actions are before consciousness. As being before consciousness we can observe them by reflection, and discover the nature of the law which has all along been in the mind, and in its very constitution.—*M'Cosh*, '*Intuitions of the Mind*,' p. 46.

(*b.*) *Misapprehensions in regard to these.*

Looking on the above as the properties and marks of the intuitive convictions of the mind, we see that a wrong account is often given of them.

1. It is wrong to represent them *as unaccountable feelings, as blind instincts, as unreasonable impulses.* They have nothing whatever of the nature of those feelings or emotions which raise up excitement within us, and attach us to certain objects and draw us away from others.

2. It is wrong to represent man, so far as he *yields to these* convictions, *as being under some sort of stern and relentless fatality which compels him to go, without yielding him light of any kind.* No doubt they constrain him to acknowledge the existence of certain objects, and the certainty of special truths, but this, not by denying him light, but by affording him the fullest conceivable light, such light that he cannot possibly mistake the object or wander from the path.

3. It is wrong to represent these self-evident truths as being *truths merely to the individual, or truths merely to man, or beings*

constituted like man. There are some who speak and write as if what is truth to one man might not be truth to another man; as if what is truth to mankind might not be truth to other intelligent beings. But what we perceive by an original intuition is a reality, is a truth; we know it to be so, we judge it to be so. And it is a reality, a truth, whether others know and acknowledge it or no.

4. It is wrong to represent all *our intuitive convictions as being formed within us from our birth.*—*M'Cosh, 'Intuitions of the Mind,'* pp. 46–48.

PRACTICAL.

From the theoretical characters there flow some others of a more practical nature.

1. *All men who have had their attention addressed to the objects, are in fact led by these spontaneous convictions, and this, whatever be their professed speculative opinions.* This follows from the circumstance that they are self-evident, and that men, all men, must give their assent to them. The regulative principles being essential parts of man's nature, we find all human beings under their influence. Being irresistible, no man can deliver himself from them. They are ever operating spontaneously, and that whether men do or do not acknowledge them reflexly. In this respect the philosopher and the peasant, the dogmatist and the sceptic, are as one.

2. *These self-evident truths cannot be set aside by any other truth, real or pretended.* They could be overthrown only by some truth higher in itself, or carrying with it greater weight. But there is no such truth, there can be no such truth.—*M'Cosh, 'Intuitions of the Mind,'* pp. 49, 50.

Their Classification

According to what they reveal.

We classify the intuitions according to what they look at and reveal, as—

I. THE TRUE. II. THE GOOD.

Both TRUE and GOOD

CONTAIN

I. PRIMITIVE COGNITIONS. II. PRIMITIVE BELIEFS. III. PRIMITIVE JUDGMENTS.

—*M'Cosh, 'Intuitions of the Mind,'* p. 81.

According to relations perceived.

The mind seems capable of noticing intuitively the relations of—

I. IDENTITY AND DIFFERENCE.
II. WHOLE AND PARTS.
III. SPACE.
IV. TIME.
V. QUANTITY.
VI. RESEMBLANCE.
VII. ACTIVE PROPERTY.
VIII. CAUSE AND EFFECT.

—*M'Cosh, 'Intuitions of the Mind,'* p. 213.

According to their objects.

The intuitions may be divided into *the formal, the mathematical,* and *the real.* The *formal* are those which are necessarily involved in the act of knowledge, whatever be its objects-matter—whether they be real, imagined, or generalised—whether they be actually existing or purely mental creations. They are essential to the form or process of knowledge, and appear in all its objects or products. The *mathematical* are those which grow out of the existence of space and time and suppose these to be realities. The relations included under this definition are not exclusively used in the sciences of number and quantity, but inasmuch as they are fundamental to these sciences, we distinguish them by this epithet; using mathematical to designate all the time and space relations and those which are dependent upon them. The *real* are those which are ordinarily recognised as generic and fundamental to the so-called qualities and properties of existing things, both material and spiritual. We do not, however, by using the term *real*, imply or concede that the *formal* and the *mathematical* are any the less real—but that they are not limited so exclusively to objects really existing — *Porter*, '*Human Intellect*,' p. 514

Their Employment.

Method of it

To justify the application of them in philosophy, it is essential that their exact nature, and precise law and rule, be carefully determined.

1 *The spontaneous must always precede the reflex form* The generalised expression of them must always be later We cannot generalise them till we have observed them, and we cannot observe them till they are in exercise

2 *The intuition, in its reflex, abstract, or general form, is derived from, and is best tested by, the concrete spontaneous conviction* In order to the formation of the definition, maxim, or axiom, we must have objects or examples before us, and we must be careful to observe them, and note what is involved in them

3 *The expression of the abstract or general truth is more or less easy, and is likely to be more or less correct, according to the simplicity of the objects to which the spontaneous conviction is directed* It is evident that some of the intuitive principles of the mind are more difficult to detect and formalise than others. Those which are directed to sensible objects, and simple objects, will be found out more easily, and at an earlier date, than those which look to more complex or spiritual objects.

4 In their spontaneous action *the intuitions never err, properly speaking; but there may be manifold mistakes lurking in their reflex form and application* I have used the qualified language that *properly speaking* they do not err in their original impulses; for even here they may carry error with them They look to a representation given them, and this representation may be erroneous, and error will appear in the result. The mind intuitively declares that on a real quality presenting itself, it must imply a substance.

5 *The tests of intuitive convictions admit of an application to the abstract and general principle, only so far as the abstraction and generalisation have been properly performed.* —*M'Cosh*, '*Intuitions of the Mind*,' pp 51–57

Rules.

1 Those who *appeal to first truths must be prepared to show that they are first truths.*

2 *Those who employ intuitive principles in demonstration, speculation, or discussion of any kind, must see that they accurately express them*

The two rules now laid down may seem to some to be very hard ones; but they are very necessary ones to arrest those confused and confusing controversies which abound to such an extent in philosophy, in theology, and in other departments of investigation as well —*M'Cosh*, '*Intuitions of the Mind*,' pp 64–67.

Their Relation to Experience.

1 Let us consider the relation of Experience to Intuition, considered as a body of Regulative Principles In this sense intuition, being native and original, is prior to experience of every kind, personal or general So far from depending on what we have passed through, our intuitions are a powerful means of prompting to the acquisition of experience, for, being in the mind as natural inclinations and aptitudes, they are ever instigating to action. All of them seek for objects, and are gratified when the proper objects are presented. Just as the eye was given us to see, and light is felt to be pleasant to the eyes, so the cognitive powers were given us in order to lead to the acquisition of knowledge, and they are pleased when knowledge is furnished.—*M'Cosh*, '*Intuitions of the Mind*,' p 299

IV. IDEAS.

The Fortune of the Word

The fortune of this word is curious. Employed by Plato to express the real forms of the intelligible world, in lofty contrast to the unreal images of the sensible; it was lowered by Descartes, who extended it to the objects of our consciousness in general. When, after Gassendi, the school of Condillac had analysed our highest faculties into our lowest, the *idea* was still more deeply degraded from its high original. Like a fallen angel, it was relegated from the sphere of divine intelligence to the atmosphere of human sense; till at last *Idéologie* (more correctly *Idéalogie*), a word which could only properly suggest an *à priori* scheme, deducing our knowledge from the intellect, has in France become the name peculiarly distinctive of that philosophy of mind which exclusively derives our knowledge from the senses. Word and thing, *ideas* have been the *crux philosophorum*, since Aristotle sent them packing, to the present day.—*Hamilton*, '*Discussions*,' p. 69.

Classes of Ideas

Descartes affirms three sorts of ideas in my mind. 1. There are adventitious ideas, which come to me from without, through the agency of the senses. 2. There are factitious ideas, constructed by myself out of the materials furnished by sense. 3. There are those which are native-born, original or innate.—*Bowen*, '*Modern Philosophy*,' p. 28.

Of ideas Berkeley recognises three sorts:—(*a*) those 'actually imprinted on the senses,' called sensations—as when what we are conscious of is something coloured, or hard, or odorous, &c.; (*b*) 'passions or operations of the mind'—as when we are conscious of anger, or of exerting ourselves corporeally or intellectually; (*c*) mental images (to which last the name idea is popularly confined)—as when we remember a scene we have witnessed, or contemplate one of our own creation, or *universalise* what we thus imagine, in general or scientific knowledge.—*Fraser*, '*Selections from Berkeley*,' p. 30, *note*.

It is a curious omission on Hume's part that, while dwelling on two classes of ideas, *Memories* and *Imaginations*, he has not, at the same time, taken notice of a third group, of no small importance, which are as different from imaginations as memories are; though, like the latter, they are often confounded with pure imaginations in general speech. These are the ideas of expectation, or as they may be called for the sake of brevity, *Expectations;* which differ from simple imaginations in being associated with the idea of the existence of corresponding impressions in the future, just as memories contain the idea of the existence of the corresponding impressions in the past.—*Huxley*, '*Hume*,' p. 94.

Doctrine of Ideas, according to

Plato.

The Platonic philosophy centres in the Theory of Ideas. The Platonic Idea is the pure archetypal essence, in which those things which are together subsumed under the same concept participate. Æsthetically and ethically, it is the perfect in its kind, to which the given reality remains perpetually inferior. Logically and ontologically considered, it is the object of the concept. The idea is known through the concept. The idea is the archetype, individual objects are images.—*Ueberweg*, '*Hist. of Phil.*,' i. 115.

An idea, according to Plato, has always place wherever a general notion of species and genus has place. Thus he speaks of the idea of a bed, of a table, of strength, of health, of the voice, of colour, of ideas of mere relation and quality. In a word, there is always an idea to be assumed whenever a many is designated by the same appellative, by a common name; or as Aristotle has it, Plato assumed for every class of existence an idea.—*Schwegler*, '*Hist. of Phil.*,' p. 77.

In the Platonic sense, ideas were the patterns according to which the Deity fashioned the phenomenal or ectypal world. *Hamilton.*

Descartes.

Of my thoughts some are, as it were, images of things, and to these alone properly belongs the name *idea;* as when I think [represent to my mind] a man, a chimera, the sky, an angel, or God.—'*Meditations,*' iii p. 117.

Locke.

Whatsoever the mind perceives in itself, or is the immediate object of perception, thought, or understanding, that I call idea. The term stands for whatsoever is the object of the understanding, when a man thinks, whatever the mind can be employed about in thinking —'*Human Understanding,*' bk. ii., i. and viii.

Berkeley

By 'ideas' Berkeley, like Locke, means *whatever we are directly conscious of*—whether a real sensation, a real passion or operation of the mind, or a mental representation of either.—*Fraser*, '*Selections from Berkeley,*' p. 30, *note*

There exist, says Berkeley, only spirits and their functions (ideas and volitions). There are no abstract ideas; there is, for example, no notion of extension without an extended body, a definite magnitude, &c A singular or particular notion becomes general by representing all other particular notions of the same kind Thus, for example, in a geometrical demonstration a given particular straight line represents all other straight lines.—*Ueberweg,* '*Hist of Phil,*' ii 88.

James Mill

Ideas are what remains after the sensations are gone As our sensations occur either in the synchronous or successive order, so our ideas present themselves in either of the two. The preceding is called the suggesting, the succeeding is called the suggested idea. The antecedent may be either a sensation or an idea, the consequent is always an idea.—*Ueberweg,* '*Hist of Phil,*' ii. 423.

Reid

Dr Reid takes *idea* to mean something interposed between the mind and the object of its thought—a *tertium quid,* or a *quartum quid,* an independent entity different from the mind and from the object thought of —*Fleming,* '*Vocab of Phil,*' p. 226.

Origin of our Ideas, or Sources of Knowledge. (See INNATE IDEAS)

Classification of Theories.

As to the origin of our ideas, the opinions of metaphysicians may be divided into three classes. 1. Those who deny the senses to be anything more than instruments conveying objects to the mind, perception being active (Plato and others) 2 Those who attribute all our ideas to sense (Hobbes, Gassendi, Condillac, the ancient sophists). 3. Those who admit that the earliest notions proceed from the senses, yet maintain that they are not adequate to produce the whole knowledge possessed by the human understanding (Aristotle, Locke).—*Mill,* '*Essays,*' pp 314, 321

Importance in this investigation of the sense attached to "idea"

The question of the origin of our ideas is substantially the same with that of the sources of our knowledge; but, in discussing this second question, it is of all things essential to have it fixed what is meant by "idea." Plato, with whom the term originated as a philosophic one, meant those eternal patterns which have been in or before the Divine mind from all eternity, which the works of nature participate in to some extent, and to the contemplation of which the mind of man can rise by abstraction and philosophic meditation Descartes meant by it whatever is before the mind in every sort of mental apprehension Locke tells us that he denotes by the phrase "whatever is meant by phantasm, notion, species" Kant applied the phrase to the ideas of substance, totality of phenomena, and God, reached by the reason as a regulative faculty going out beyond the province of experience and objective reality. Hegel is for ever dwelling on an absolute idea, which he identifies with God, and represents as ever unfolding itself out of nothing into being, subjective and objective. Using the phrase in the Platonic sense, it is scarcely relevant to inquire into the origin of our ideas; it is clear, however, that Plato represented our recognition of eternal ideas as a high intellectual exercise, originating in the inborn power of the mind, and awakened by inward cogitation and reminiscence. In the Kantian and Hegelian systems the idea is supposed to be discerned by reason; Kant giving it no existence except in the mind, and Hegel giving it an existence both objective and subjective, but identifying the reason with the idea, and the objective with the subjective. Using the phrase in the Cartesian and Lockian sense, we can inquire into the origin of our ideas —*M'Cosh, 'Intuitions of the Mind,'* p. 289.

The Experience Theory.

(*a.*) *As held by Hobbes and Mill*—All knowledge grows out of sensations. After sensation, there remains behind the memory of it, which may reappear in consciousness —*Hobbes, in Ueberweg's 'Hist of Phil.,'* ii. 39.

The sensations which we have through the medium of the senses exist only by the presence of the object, and cease upon its absence. When our sensations cease, by the absence of their objects, something remains. After I have seen the sun, and by shutting my eyes see him no longer, I can still think of him. I have still a feeling, the consequence of the sensation, which, though I can distinguish it from the sensation, and treat it as not the sensation, but something different from the sensation, is yet more like the sensation than anything else can be; so like, that I call it a copy, an image of the sensation: sometimes a representation or trace of the sensation. Another name by which we denote this trace, this copy of the sensation, which remains after the sensation ceases, is IDEA.—*Mill, 'Analysis of the Human Mind,'* i. 51.

(*b.*) *By Hume*—He distinguishes between impressions and ideas or thoughts; under the former he understands the lively sensations which we have when we hear, see, feel, or love, hate, desire, will; and under the latter the less lively ideas of memory and imagination, of which we become conscious when we reflect on any impression. The creative power of thought extends no further than to the faculty of combining, transposing, augmenting, or diminishing the material furnished by the senses and by experience. All the materials of thought are given us through external or internal experience; only their combination is the work of the understanding or the will. All our ideas are copies of perceptions.—*Ueberweg, 'Hist. of Phil.,'* ii. 132.

(*c.*) *Objections to this theory*—There are three very flagrant oversights in the theory of those who derive all our ideas from sensation:—First, there is an omission of all such ideas as we have of spirit and of the qualities of spirit, such as rationality, free will, personality. Secondly, there is a neglect or a wrong account of all the further cognitive exercises of the mind by which it comes to apprehend such objects as infinite time, moral good, merit, and responsibility. Thirdly, there is a denial, or at least oversight, of the mind's deep convictions as to necessary and universal truth. Sensationalism, followed out logically to its consequences, would represent the mind as incapable of conceiving of a spiritual God, or of being convinced of the indelible distinction between good and evil; and make it illegitimate to argue from the effects in the world in favour of the existence of a First

Cause.—*M'Cosh, 'Intuitions of the Mind,'* p. 291.

Locke's Theory

The fountains of knowledge, from whence all the ideas we have or can naturally have do spring, are two. First, our senses, conversant about particular sensible objects, do convey into the mind several distinct perceptions of things, according to those various ways wherein those objects do affect them: and thus we come by those ideas we have, of yellow, white, heat, cold, soft, hard, bitter, sweet, and all those which we call sensible qualities; which when I say the senses convey into the mind, I mean they from external objects convey into the mind what produces there those perceptions. This great source of most of the ideas we have depending wholly upon our senses, and derived by them to the understanding, I call *Sensation*. Secondly, the other fountain from which experience furnisheth the understanding with ideas is the perception of the operations of our mind within us, as it is employed about the ideas it has got, which operations, when the soul comes to reflect on and consider, do furnish the understanding with another set of ideas, which could not be had from things without; and such are perception, thinking, doubting, believing, reasoning, knowing, willing, and all the different actings of our own minds, which we being conscious of, and observing in ourselves, do from these receive into our understandings as distinct ideas as we do from bodies affecting our senses. This source of ideas every man has wholly in himself, and though it be not sense as having nothing to do with external objects, yet it is very like it, and might properly enough be called internal sense. But as I call the other Sensation, so I call this *Reflection*, the ideas it affords being such only as the mind gets by reflecting on its own operations within itself.—*'Human Understanding,'* II. i. 3, 4.

It is to experience and to our own reflections that we are indebted for by far the most valuable part of our knowledge.—*Stewart, 'Works,'* ii. 405.

Experience with Locke was simply the experience of the individual. In order to acquire this experience it was indeed necessary that we should have certain 'inherent faculties.' But of these faculties he gives no other account than that God has 'furnished' or 'endued' us with them. Locke's system left so much unexplained that it was comparatively easy for Kant to show that the problem of the origin of knowledge could not be left where Locke had left it.—*Fowler, 'Locke,'* p. 143.

Kant's Theory.

(*a.*) *Knowledge begins with experience.*—That all our knowledge begins with experience there can be no doubt. For how should the faculty of knowledge be called into activity if not by objects which affect our senses, and which either produce representations by themselves, or rouse the activity of our understanding to compare, to connect, or to separate them; and thus to convert the raw material of our sensuous impressions into a knowledge of objects, which we call experience? In respect of time, therefore, no knowledge within us is antecedent to experience, but all knowledge begins with it.—*Kant, 'Critique,'* vol. i. p. 398.

(*b.*) *But does not all arise out of experience.*—Although all our knowledge begins with experience it does not follow that it arises from experience. For it is quite possible that even our empirical experience is a compound of that which we receive through impressions, and of that which our own faculty of knowledge (incited only by sensuous impressions) supplies from itself, a supplement which we do not distinguish from that raw material until long practice has roused our attention, and rendered us capable of separating one from the other.—*Kant, 'Critique,'* vol. i. p. 398.

The negative scepticism of Hume stimulated Kant to produce his great work, the 'Kritik of the pure Reason.' He saw, as Reid also did, that Locke's principle regarding the origin of knowledge naturally led to Hume's conclusion. If all our ideas are simply modified sensations, if all our knowledge arises out of experience, many of our most cherished and valuable beliefs must be undermined. Hence, Kant set himself to show that, although 'all our knowledge *begins with* experience,' yet 'it by no means follows that all *arises out* of our experience.' There are certain elements of our knowledge which could not be derived from experience. 'Experience, no doubt, teaches us that this or that object is constituted in such and such a manner, but not that it could not possibly exist otherwise. Now, if we have a proposition which contains the idea of necessity in its very conception, it is a judgment *à priori*; if, moreover, it is not derived from any other proposition, unless from one equally involving the idea of necessity, it is absolutely *à priori*. An empirical judgment never exhibits strict and absolute, but only assumed and comparative, universality.'—*Jardine*, '*Psychology of Cognition*,' p. 153.

The Intuitional Theory, as modified by M'Cosh.

The mind in its intelligent acts starts with knowledge. But let not the statement be misunderstood. I do not mean that the mind commences with abstract knowledge, or general knowledge, or indeed with systematised knowledge of any description. It acquires first a knowledge of individual things, as they are presented to it and to its knowing faculties, and it is out of this that all its arranged knowledge is formed by a subsequent exercise of the understanding. From the concrete the mind fashions the abstract, by separating in thought a part from the whole, a quality from the object. Starting with the particular, the mind reaches the general by observing the points of agreement. From premises involving knowledge, it can arrive at other propositions also containing knowledge.—*M'Cosh*, '*Intuitions of the Mind*,' p. 102.

V. INNATE IDEAS. (See INTUITIONS.)

What is meant by Innate Ideas.

General Statement.

Innate ideas are such as are inborn and belong to the mind from its birth, as the idea of God or of immortality. Cicero, in various passages of his treatise *De Natura Deorum*, speaks of the idea of God and of immortality as being inserted, or engraven, or inborn in the mind. In like manner, Origen (*Adv. Celsum*, i. 4) has said, "That men would not be guilty, if they did not carry in their mind common notions of morality, innate and written in divine letters."—*Fleming*, '*Vocab. of Phil.*,' p. 259.

There are three senses in which an idea may be supposed to be innate: (1) one, if it be something originally superadded to our mental constitution, either as an idea in the first instance fully developed, or as one undeveloped but having the power of self-development; (2) another, if the idea is a subjective condition of any other ideas, which we receive independently of the previous acquisition of this idea, and is thus proved to be in some way embodied in, or interwoven with the powers by which the mind receives those ideas; (3) a third, if, without being a subjective condition of other ideas, there be any faculty or faculties of the mind, the exercise of which would suffice, independently of any knowledge acquired from without, spontaneously to produce the idea. In the first case, the idea is given us at our first creation, without its bearing any special relation to our mental faculties; in the second case, it is given us as a form, either of thought generally or of some particular species of thought, and is therefore embodied in mental powers, by which we are enabled to receive the thought; in the third case, it is, as in the second, interwoven in the original constitution of some mental power or powers; not, however, as in the preceding case, simply as a pre-requisite to their exercise, but by their being so formed as by exercise spontaneously to produce the idea.—*Alliot*, '*Psychology and Theology*,' p. 93

Doctrine of Descartes.

I have never either thought or said that the mind has any need of innate ideas [*idées naturelles*] which are anything distinct from its faculty of thinking. But it is true that, observing that there are certain thoughts which arise neither from external objects nor from the determination of my will, but only from my faculty of thinking; in order to mark the difference between the ideas or the notions which are the forms of these thoughts, and to distinguish them from the others, which may be called extraneous or voluntary, I have called them innate. But I have used this term in the same sense as when we say that generosity is innate in certain families; or that certain maladies, such as gout or gravel, are innate in others; not that children born in these families are troubled with such diseases in their mother's womb, but because they are born with the disposition or the faculty of contracting them.—'*Œuvres*' (ed. Cousin), x. 71.

Descartes, the founder of modern philosophy, laid down that there are in the mind certain faculties or capacities for forming thoughts which are born with a man. These are not ideas, but powers to form ideas. But Descartes explains that he does not mean actual but potential ideas, latent capacities for having ideas, which we certainly have. They are 'forms of thought,' which require elements derived from sensation before they become actual ideas.—*Ryland*, '*Handbook of Psychology*,' p. 97.

Doctrine of Leibnitz.

I do not maintain that Innate Ideas are inscribed in the mind in such wise that one can read them there, as it were, *ad aperturam libri*, on first opening the book, just as the edict of the prætor could be read upon his *album*, without pains and without research; but only that one can discover them there by dint of attention, occasions for which are furnished by the senses. I have compared the mind rather to a block of marble, which has veins marked out in it, than to a block which is homogeneous and pure throughout, corresponding to the *tabula rasa* of Locke and his followers. In the latter case, the truths would be in us only as a statue of Hercules is in any block which is large enough to contain it, the marble being indifferent to receive this shape or any other. But if there were veins in the stone, which gave the outline of this statue rather than of any other figure, then it might be said that Hercules was in some sense innate in the marble, though the chisel were necessary to find him there by cutting off the superfluities. Hence to the well-known adage of Aristotle, *Nihil est in intellectu quod non fuit prius in sensu*, I have added this qualification,—*nisi intellectus ipse.*—*Leibnitz.*

The ideas of being, substance, identity, the true, the good, are innate in the mind, for the reason that the mind itself is innate in itself, and in itself embraces all these ideas.—*Leibnitz.*

Doctrine of Hume.

The word *idea* seems to be commonly taken in a very loose sense by Locke and others, as standing for any of our perceptions, our sensations, and passions, as well as thoughts. But understanding by *innate* what is original or copied from no precedent perception, then may we assert that all our impressions are innate, and our ideas not innate.—'*Essay concerning Human Understanding*,' sec. ii., *note.*

Recent Statements.

We are prepared to defend the following propositions in regard to innate ideas, or constitutional principles of the mind:—*First*,—Negatively, that there are no innate ideas in the mind—(1) as images or mental representations; nor (2) as abstract or general notions; nor (3) as principles of thought, belief, or action before the mind as principles. But, *second*,—Positively, (1) that there are constitutional principles operating in the mind, though not before the consciousness as principles; (2) that these come forth into consciousness as individual (not general) cognitions or judgments; and (3) that these individual exercises, when carefully inducted, but only when so, give us primitive or philosophic truths.—*M'Cosh*, '*Method of Divine Government*,' p. 508.

'Though the existence of God may be proved from reason and from lights of the natural order, it is certain that the knowledge of God's existence anticipated all such reasoning. The theism of the world was not a discovery. Mankind possessed it by primeval revelation, were penetrated and pervaded by it, before any one doubted of it; and reasoning did not precede, but followed the doubt. Theists came before philosophers, and Theism before Atheism, or even a doubt about the existence of God.'

This passage, as it seems to me, throws light on the manner in which *à priori* knowledge, or Innate Ideas, exist in the mind, before they are developed by experience or distinctly recognised and explicated by conscious exertion of the intellect. Certainly we have reason to believe that the ideas of a Divinity, of space, of time, of efficient causation, of substance, of right and wrong, and some others, are truly *à priori*, or in some way innate; that is, if not absolutely born with us, they are native to the mind, being inwrought into its inmost structure, and necessary in order to form the very experience which appears to develop them.—*Bowen*, '*Modern Philosophy*,' p. 42.

By innate knowledge is meant that which is due to our constitution as sentient, rational, and moral beings. It is opposed to knowledge founded on experience; to that obtained by *ab extra* instruction; and to that acquired by a process of research and reasoning.—*Hodge*, '*Syst. Theol.*,' i. 191.

The Controversy as to the Existence of Innate Ideas.

Locke's argument against them.

It is an established opinion amongst some men that there are in the understanding certain innate principles; some primary notions, characters, as it were, stamped upon the mind of man, which the soul receives in its very first being, and brings into the world with it.

But this supposition is false. For (1) this hypothesis of Innate Ideas is not required; men, barely by the use of their natural faculties, may attain to all the knowledge they have, without the help of any innate impressions, and may arrive at certainty without any such original notions or principles. (2) Universal Consent, which is the great argument, proves nothing innate. If there were certain truths wherein all mankind agreed, this would not prove them innate if the universal agreement could be explained in any other way. But these so-called innate propositions do not receive universal assent; since (3) such ideas are not perceived by children, but require reason to discover them. To imprint anything upon the mind, without the mind's perceiving it, seems hardly intelligible. (4) We are not conscious of them, and therefore they do not exist.—'*Human Understanding*,' II. ii. (condensed).

The most effective perhaps of Locke's arguments against this doctrine is his challenge to the advocates of Innate Principles to produce them, and show what and how many they are. Did men find such innate propositions stamped on their minds, nothing could be more easy than this. 'There could be no more doubt,' says Locke, 'about their number than there is about the number of our fingers. 'Tis enough to make one suspect that the supposition of such innate principles is but an opinion taken up at random, since those who talk so confidently of them are so sparing to tell us which they are.'—*Fowler*, '*Locke*,' p. 130.

The question at issue.

The real question at issue is, whether the mind is a *tabula rasa*, a perfectly blank surface on to which sensations are projected; or whether it has certain definite, inherited methods of reacting when impressions are felt.—*Ryland*, '*Handbook of Psychology*,' p. 98.

Setting aside, as irrelevant, those arguments which are little better than quibbles on the word *innate*, such as Locke's appeal to the consciousness of new-born children, the real point to be determined is this:—Are there any modes of human consciousness which are derived, not from the accidental experience of the individual man, but from the essential constitution of the human mind in general, and which thus naturally and necessarily grow up in all men, whatever may be the varieties of their several experiences?—*Mansel*, '*Metaphysics*,' p. 272.

The solution as offered by the Evolution Theory.

The evolutionist teaches us that these instinctive intellectual forms represent vast numbers of ancestral experiences, namely, such as have been uniform in their order through long ages of racial development. In this manner he is able to preserve for these innate intuitions the superior dignity previously accorded them, while he nevertheless assigns to them an origin in experience.—*Sully*, '*Sensation, &c.*,' p. 20.

What are the 'Innate Ideas' of the older philosophers, or the Forms and Categories of Kant, but certain *tendencies* of the mind to group phenomena, the 'fleeting objects of sense,' under certain relations, and regard them under certain aspects? And why should these tendencies be accounted for in any other way than that by which we are accustomed to account for the tendency of an animal or a plant belonging to any particular species, to exhibit, as it develops, the physical characteristics of the species to which it belongs? The existence of the various mental tendencies and aptitudes, so far as the individual is concerned, is, in fact, to be explained by the principle of hereditary transmission. But how have these tendencies and aptitudes come to be formed in the race? The most scientific answer is that which, following the analogy of the theory now so widely admitted with respect to the physical structure of animals and plants, assigns their formation to the continuous operation, through a long series of ages, of causes acting uniformly in the same direction—in one word, of Evolution. —*Fowler*, '*Locke*,' p. 145.

The general doctrine of evolution reconciles the experience-hypothesis and the intuition-hypothesis, each of which is partially true, neither of which is tenable by itself. In the nervous system certain *pre-established* relations, answering to relations in the environment, absolutely constant, absolutely universal, exist through transmission. In this sense there are 'forms of intuition,' that is, elements of thought infinitely repeated until they have become automatic, and impossible to get rid of. These relations are potentially present before birth in the shape of definite nervous connections, antecedent to and independent of individual experiences, but not independent of *all* experiences, having been determined by the experiences of preceding organisms. The human brain is an organised register of infinitely numerous experiences received during evolution, and successively bequeathed.—*Spencer*, '*Principles of Psychology*,' i. 467–470 (summarised).

VI.

KNOWLEDGE OF THE OUTER WORLD, OR PERCEPTION.

I. PERCEPTION

Perception Described

Perception is that act of consciousness whereby we apprehend external objects.

In its *wider* sense perception is nearly equivalent to Intuition or Presentation. The faculty of perception is that by which ideas first enter the mind, and it has two branches, External Perception and Internal Perception—the former again including the five senses. In a narrower sense perception is opposed to sensation, and is limited to the objective (as sensation is to the subjective) characteristics of the products of the faculty of perception. In this sense it seems to be exclusively applied to external perception, and what Hamilton speaks of as the various theories of perception are in fact theories of external perception only.—*Monck*, '*Sir W. Hamilton*,' p. 187.

Perception is that act of consciousness whereby we apprehend in our body, (*a*) Certain *special affections*, whereof as an animated organism it is contingently susceptible; and (*b*) Those *general relations of extension* under which as a *material* organism it necessarily exists. Of these Perceptions, the former is *Sensation* proper, the latter is *Perception* proper.—*Hamilton*, '*Reid's Works*,' p. 876.

Perception is limited to the apprehension of sense alone. This limitation was first formally imposed by Reid, and thereafter by Kant. A still more restricted meaning, through the authority of Reid, is perception in contrast to sensation. He defines perception simply as that act of consciousness whereby we apprehend in our body.—*Fleming*, '*Vocab. of Phil.*,' p. 374.

Perception, or properly perceptivity, is the faculty by which we perceive external objects. A perception is a taking notice of anything through the senses. That which is perceived is called the percept, object, or thing perceived. As the perceptive process appears before the consciousness, it may be described in such phrases as these—I see a mountain; I hear a cataract; I smell a rose; I perceive a man. This process is really simple.—*Murphy*, '*Human Mind*,' p. 44.

All perception or knowledge implies mind. To perceive is an act of mind; whatever we may suppose the thing perceived to be, we cannot divorce it from the percipient mind. To perceive a tree is a mental act; the tree is known *as perceived*, and not in any other way.—*Bain*, '*Mental Science*,' p. 197.

Perception is based on Sensation, from which, however, it must be carefully distinguished.

Sensation the basis of Perception

Every Perception proper has a Sensation proper as its condition. For we are only aware of the existence of our organism, in being sentient of it, as thus or thus affected.—*Hamilton's* '*Reid*,' p. 880.

Sensation and Perception distinguished

Perception is only a special kind of knowledge, and sensation only a special kind of feeling. Perception proper is the consciousness, through the senses, of the qualities of an object known as different from Self; Sensation proper is the consciousness of the subjective affection of pleasure or pain, which accompanies that act of knowledge. Perception is thus the objective element in the complex state—the element of cognition; Sensation is the subjective element,—the element of feeling.—*Hamilton*, '*Metaphysics*,' ii. 98.

Sensation proper is the consciousness of certain affections of our body as an animated organism. Perception proper is the consciousness of the existence of our body as a material organism, and therefore as extended.—*Mansel*, '*Metaphysics*,' p. 68.

It is necessary to make a clear distinction between the simple Sensation and the highly complex state called Perception, which commonly goes along with the simple Sensation. When I have certain visual sensations—say a yellowish colour and a round shape—I immediately *perceive* an orange. But the act of Perception embodies a great deal more than those two Sensations: a number of ideas or remembered Sensations, such as those of a peculiar odour and taste, of a certain degree of hardness and of weight, are called up; and I attribute these also to the object which I *infer* to exist before me at a certain distance, in a certain direction, and so on. It would have been quite possible for me to have those two Sensations of colour and form, and yet make a wrong inference. Suppose a waxen orange had been put on a plate to deceive me; or that owing to some disease of the optic nerves, the feelings had been called up without any external cause at all. In either case my classification or inference would have been wrong.—*Ryland*, '*Handbook, &c.*,' pp. 41, 42.

The law of their relation.

The law is simple and universal, and once enounced, its proof is found in every mental manifestation. It is this:—Perception and Sensation, though always coexistent, are always in the inverse ratio of each other. As a sense has more of the one element it has less of the other. Thus in Sight, there is presented to us, at the same instant, a greater number and a greater variety of objects and qualities, than any other of the senses. In this sense, therefore, perception, the objective element, is at its maximum. But sensation, the subjective element, is here at its minimum; for, in the eye, we experience less organic pleasure or pain from the impressions of its appropriate objects (colours), than we do in any other sense. On the other hand, in Taste and Smell, the degree of sensation, that is, of pleasure or pain, is great in proportion as the perception, that is, the information they afford, is small.—*Hamilton*, '*Metaphysics*,' ii. 99–101.

Spencer's criticism of the law.

It would seem, not that Sensation and Perception vary inversely, but that they exclude each other with degrees of stringency which vary inversely. When the sensations (considered simply as physical changes in the organism) are weak, the objective phenomenon signified by them is alone contemplated. The sensations, if not absolutely excluded from consciousness, pass through it so rapidly as not to form appreciable elements in it; and cannot be detained in it, or arrested for inspection, without a decided effort. When the sensations are rendered somewhat more intense, the perception continues equally vivid—still remains the sole occupant of consciousness; but it requires less effort than before to make them the subjects of thought. If the intensity of the sensations is gradually increased, a point is presently reached at which consciousness is as likely to be occupied by them as by the external thing they imply,—a point at which either can be thought of with equal facility, while each tends in the greatest degree to draw attention from the other. When further intensified, the sensations begin to occupy consciousness to the exclusion of the perception: which, however, can still be brought into consciousness by a slight effort. But, finally, if the sensations rise to extreme intensity, consciousness becomes so absorbed in them that only by great effort, if at all, can the thing causing them be thought about.—'*Principles of Psychology*,' ii. pp. 248, 249.

Perception and Conception contrasted.

In the act of Conception there are present only ideas, or remembered impressions;

while in Perception there are present, in addition to remembered impressions, at least one or two *actual* impressions, that is, Sensations.—*Ryland, 'Handbook, &c.,'* p. 81.

Perceptions embody inferences.

All perceptions embody inferences. 'Every complete act of perception implies an expressed or unexpressed assertory judgment' (Spencer). In such a case as the perception that a building before us is a cathedral, we have an immense number of inferences, some implicit, some explicit, but all involving remembered sensations. The position, size, shape, material, and hollowness of the edifice, are all inferences, and from these inferences we again infer its ecclesiastical uses, and so on.—*Ryland, 'Handbook, &c.,'* p. 79.

The Doctrine of Perception is a cardinal point in philosophy.

Perception, as matter of psychological consideration, is of the very highest importance in philosophy, as the doctrine in regard to the object and operation of this faculty affords the immediate data for determining the great question touching the existence or non-existence of an external world; and there is hardly a problem of any moment in the whole compass of philosophy of which it does not mediately affect the solution. The doctrine of philosophy may thus be viewed as a cardinal point of philosophy.—*Hamilton, 'Metaphysics,'* ii. 43.

Relation of Subject and Object—Professor Green's Idealism.

All knowing and all that is known, all intelligence and all intelligible reality, indifferently consist in a relation between subject and object. The generic element in the true idealist's definition of the knowable universe is that it is such a relation. Neither of the two correlata in his view has any reality apart from the other. Every determination of the one implies a corresponding determination of the other. The object, for instance, may be known, under one of the manifold relations which it involves, as matter, but it is only so known in virtue of what may indifferently be called a constructive act on the part of the subject, or a manifestation of itself on the part of the object. The subject in virtue of the act, the object in virtue of the manifestation, are alike, and in strict correlativity, so far determined. Of what would otherwise be unknown it can now be said either that it appears as matter, or that it is that to which matter appears. Neither is the matter anything without the appearance, nor is that to which it appears anything without the appearance to it. The reality of matter, then, as of anything else that is known, is just as little merely objective as merely subjective; while the reality of 'mind,' if by that is meant the 'connected phenomena of conscious life,' is not a whit more subjective than objective.—*Green, 'Philosophical Works,'* i. 387.

II. ILLUSION AND HALLUCINATION.

Illusion Defined.

An illusion, as the name implies, is a state of consciousness, in which, though apparently informed, one is not really so, but is rather *played with*, made sport of, befooled.—*Murray, 'Handbook of Psychology,'* p. 241.

Sources of Illusion.

Illusory cognitions may be distinguished according to the sources from which they arise. These are three. Sometimes it is the senses that are at fault in creating the illusory impression. At other times the mistake originates in an intellectual process erroneously interpreting a normal impression of sense; while in a third class of cases the error lies wholly in an irregular intellectual process. To the first of these mental states, the name *hallucination* is often given by recent psychologists; the third comprehends the *fallacies* commonly described in logical text-books; while for the second the term *illusion* is specifically reserved. This distinction is one which cannot always be rigidly carried out. The hallucinations, arising from the abnormal activities of sense, merge imperceptibly at times into the illusions which imply a misinterpretation of sensuous impressions; and these again are often indistinguishable from fallacious processes of reasoning.—*Murray*, '*Handbook of Psychology*,' p. 242.

Illusion and Hallucination distinguished.

That there are differences in the origin and source of illusion is a fact which has been fully recognised by those writers who have made a special study of sense-illusions. By these the term illusion is commonly employed in a narrow, technical sense, and opposed to hallucination. An illusion, it is said, must always have its starting-point in some actual impression, whereas an hallucination has no such basis. Thus it is an illusion when a man, under the action of terror, takes a stump of a tree, whitened by the moon's rays, for a ghost. It is an hallucination when an imaginative person so vividly pictures to himself the form of some absent friend that, for the moment, he fancies himself actually beholding him. Illusion is thus a partial displacement of external fact by a fiction of the imagination, while hallucination is a total displacement.

It is to be observed, however, that the line of separation between illusion and hallucination, as thus defined, is a very narrow one. In by far the largest number of hallucinations it is impossible to prove that there is no modicum of external agency co-operating in the production of the effect. It is presumable, indeed, that many, if not all, hallucinations have such a basis of fact. —*Sully*, '*Illusions*,' pp. 11, 12.

The Progress of Illusion towards Hallucination.

In its lowest stages illusion closely counterfeits correct perception in the balance of the direct factor, sensation, and the indirect factor, mental reproduction or imagination. The degree of illusion increases in proportion as the imaginative element gains in force relatively to the present impression, till in the wild illusions of the insane, the amount of actual impression becomes evanescent. When this point is reached, the act of imagination shows itself as a purely creative process, or an hallucination.—*Sully*, '*Illusions*,' p. 120.

Two Orders of Hallucination.

Hallucination, by which I mean the projection of a mental image outwards when there is no external agency answering to it, assumes one of two fairly distinct forms; it may present itself either as a semblance of an external impression with the minimum amount of interpretation, or as a counterfeit of a completely developed percept. Thus, a visual hallucination may assume the aspect of a sensation of light or colour, which we vaguely refer to a certain region of the external world, or of a vision of some recognisable object. All of us frequently have incomplete visual and auditory hallucinations of the first order, whereas the complete hallucinations of the second order are comparatively rare. The first I shall call rudimentary, the second developed hallucinations.—*Sully*, '*Illusions*,' p. 113.

Examples of Illusion of the Senses.

A stick is plunged half-way into water; it seems bent, though it is straight. But between the presence of the stick and my perception there are several intermediaries, the first of which is a pencil of luminous rays. In the most common case, that is, when the stick is wholly in the air or wholly in the water, if the rays from one half are inflected with reference to the rays from the other half, the stick is actually curved; but this is only the most common case. When by exception the straight stick is plunged into two unequally refracting media, although it is straight, the rays from one half will be inflected with reference to the rays from the other half, and I shall have the same perception as if the stick were bent.

. . Take the case of a person who has lost a leg and complains of tinglings in the heel. He actually experiences tinglings; but not in the heel he no longer possesses, only the feeling seems to be there . . Usually, when the sensation arises it is preceded by peripheral disturbance, but usually only. When by exception the central extremity existing after amputation enters into activity, the sensation will arise though the heel is destroyed, and the patient will form the same conclusion as when he still had his leg.—*Taine*, '*On Intelligence*,' pp. 219, 220.

Example of Hallucination.

A man sees, with eyes closed or open, the perfectly distinct head of a corpse three paces in front of him, though no such head is there. This means, just as in the previous instances, that between the actual presence of a corpse's head and the affirmative perception are a group of intermediaries, the last of which is a particular visual sensation of the nervous centres. Usually, this sensation has as its antecedents a certain molecular motion of the optic nerves, a certain infringement of luminous rays; lastly, the presence of the real head of a corpse. But it is usually only that these three antecedents precede the sensation. If the sensation is produced in their absence, the affirmative perception will arise in their absence, and the man will see a corpse's head which is not actually there. —*Taine*, '*On Intelligence*,' p. 220.

VII.

THEORIES OF KNOWLEDGE OF THE OUTER WORLD.

The Principal Point on which Opinions Differ.

The principal point, in regard to which opinions vary, may be stated in a few words:—Is our perception or our consciousness of external objects mediate or immediate? Philosophers may be divided into two main classes—those who do, and those who do not, hold in its integrity the fact that in external perception Mind and Matter are both given; who do, or do not, hold that the Existence of Matter is actually given us by Intuition, and has not to be inferred.—*Hamilton*, '*Metaphysics*,' ii. 29, i. 293 (condensed).

Two Points of View.

There are two distinct points of view from which the student of the process of perception may proceed in the examination of his knowledge. It is difficult to find any single unambiguous word which indicates these points of view respectively, and therefore, without in the meantime naming them, we shall proceed to describe them at length.

(1.) From the first standpoint, the psychologist regards the objects of the world of sense as having an existence independent of the mind; and the phenomena of the mind as having an existence independent of material objects. The trees, and stones, and other objects which we know, and as we know them, exist away outside of us, and the mind which knows exists somewhere within the body; and these two things, the external material bodies and the mind, are totally different in nature and independent in existence. And the problem of psychology is to determine how it is that the mind knows the objects of the material world, and what amount of confidence is to be placed in this knowledge. This is what we might call the standpoint of practical common sense. The practical man, with his sensitive organism completely matured and educated, sees objects in the world around him apparently existing independently of his mind; and when he becomes a philosopher his great question naturally is how these objects, which are extended, figured, and distant, can be perceived by his mind, which is an unextended spiritual substance. Thus there is assumed the existence of two worlds, differing in nature and independent in existence, and then the question is asked, how does the one come to know the other, how does mind know matter? For the sake of distinctness, and for want of a better name, we may call this the standpoint of *practical dualism*.

(2.) Those who adopt the second point of view assume nothing regarding the existence or nature of an external world, but analyse all their knowledge into its original elements, as found in consciousness; and, beginning with the simplest facts given in consciousness, seek to discover the manner in which the sphere of our knowledge and belief is gradually filled up. As a preliminary to the adoption of this method, it is necessary that nearly all our naturally acquired beliefs regarding the existence and nature of objects of sense should, for the time, be given up. The object of the psychologist is to determine the origin and process of the acquisition of knowledge, and, therefore, it is not legitimate to assume anything regarding the existence and nature of the objects of knowledge until it is seen *how they have become objects*. From this, which we may call the *philosophical* point of view, the student works his way from within outwards, beginning with those facts of consciousness, which, as far as he can discover, are elementary, endeavouring to discover what they reveal of the non-ego, and how they are combined or modified, and in no case assuming anything which they do not give.—*Jardine*, '*Psychology*,' pp. 94, 96.

I. CLASSIFICATION OF THEORIES.

Hamilton's Classification of Theories.

Sir W. Hamilton gives the following classification of theories of Perception (*Metaphysics*, i. 293–299).—

A. Natural Dualists, or Natural Realists.

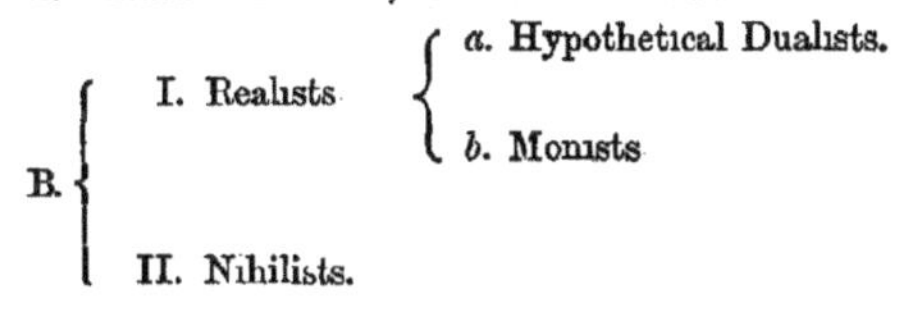

B. I. Realists — *a.* Hypothetical Dualists. *b.* Monists — i. Idealists. ii. Materialists. iii. Those who hold absolute identity of mind and matter.

II. Nihilists.

Natural Realists hold that the Existence of Matter is actually given us by Intuitions, and has not to be inferred.

Realists affirm that Matter or Mind, one or both, exists. They are divided into (1) *Dualists*, who affirm that Mind and Matter are ultimately distinct and independent, but that the existence of Matter is known to us only by Inference or Hypothesis; (2) *Monists*, who reject the testimony of consciousness to the ultimate duality of Subject and Object in Perception, but arrive at the assertion of their unity in different ways.

Like all other schemes of this sort, this classification sacrifices accuracy to clearness and symmetry. Philosophic thought does not grow up in straight lines. At the same time, it will serve as a valuable preliminary division, to help the beginner in understanding the somewhat confusing mutual relations of the different Theories of Perception.—*Ryland*, '*Handbook, &c.*,' pp. 82–84.

Professor Masson's Classification.

The mere distribution of philosophers into the two great orders of Realists and Idealists does not answer all the historical requirements. Each order has been subdivided, still on cosmological grounds, into two sections Among Realists, the *Materialists*, or *Materialistic Realists*, have been distinguished strongly from the *Dualistic Realists*, called also *Natural Realists*. Similarly, among Idealists there has been a large group of what may be called *Constructive Idealists*, distinguishable from the *Pure Idealists*. But this is not all. Not only by this subdivision of each of the orders, still on cosmological grounds, into two sects, are we provided with the four sects of *Materialists*, *Natural Realists*, *Constructive Idealists* and *Pure Idealists*; but (by bringing considerations into the classification which, I think, are not exclusively cosmological) these four sects have been flanked by two extreme sects, called respectively *Nihilists* and *Pantheists*. The doctrine of these last is called also, in recent philosophical language, the doctrine of *Absolute Identity*.—*Masson*, '*Recent British Philos.*,' pp 43, 44.

All possible forms of the representative hypothesis are reduced to three, and these have all been actually maintained.

1 The representative object not a modification of mind.

2. The representative object a modification of mind, dependent for its apprehension, but not for its existence, on the act of consciousness.

3 The representative object a modification of mind, non-existent out of consciousness;—the idea and its perception only different relations of an act (state) really identical.—*Hamilton*, '*Discussions*,' p 56

II REALISM OR DUALISM.

Statement of the Theory.

As generally held

Realism, as opposed to idealism, is the doctrine that in perception there is an immediate or intuitive cognition of the external object, while according to Idealism our knowledge of an external world is mediate and representative, *i.e.*, by means of ideas.—*Fleming*, '*Vocab. of Phil.*' p. 422

1. *Sir W. Hamilton's Natural Realism*

We may lay it down as an undisputed truth that consciousness gives, as an ultimate fact, a primitive duality;—a knowledge of the ego in relation and contrast to the non-ego, and a knowledge of the non-ego in relation and contrast to the ego. The ego and non-ego are thus given in an original synthesis; we are conscious of them in an indivisible act of knowledge together and at once,—but we are conscious of them as in themselves, different and exclusive of each other Again, they are not only given together, but in absolute co-equality. The one does not precede, the other does not follow. Realism accepts this fact as given in, and by consciousness in all its integrity.—*Hamilton*, '*Metaphysics*,' i. 292.

Hamilton's doctrine asserts that we have a direct and immediate consciousness of the external world as really existing, and are not left to infer its existence from the sensations which it is supposed to produce, or from the ideas which are supposed to resemble (or represent) it, or even from a blind faith in its existence, which says 'I believe,' but can give no reason for believing. I believe that it exists, says Hamilton, because I know it, I feel it, I perceive it, as existing According to him we have a direct intuitive perception of the qualities, attributes, or phenomena of matter, just as we have of the qualities, attributes, or phenomena of mind, the substances in both cases being equally unknown. (See RELATIVITY OF KNOWLEDGE) —*Monck*, '*Sir W. Hamilton*,' pp 23, 25

2. *Herbert Spencer's* '*Transfigured Realism.*'

In a long and elaborate argument Mr. Spencer defends Realism, but endeavours to 'purify' it 'from all that does not belong to it.' The result is what he calls 'Transfigured Realism'—'Realism contenting itself with affirming that the object of cognition is an independent existence.' He says, 'The Realism we are committed to is one which simply asserts objective existence as separate from, and independent of, subjective existence. But it affirms neither that any one mode of this objective existence is in reality that which it seems, nor that the connections among its modes are objectively what they seem. Thus it stands widely distinguished from Crude Realism; and to mark the distinction it may properly be called Transfigured Realism.—'*Principles of Psychology*,' ii. 494.

3. '*Reasoned Realism*' *of George H. Lewes*.

It is a doctrine which endeavours to rectify the natural illusion of Reason when Reason attempts to rectify the supposed illusion of sense. I call it Realism, because it affirms the reality of what is given in Feeling; and Reasoned Realism, because it justifies that affirmation through an investigation of the grounds and processes of Philosophy, when Philosophy explains the facts given in Feeling.—'*Problems of Life and Mind*,' First Series, i. 177.

4. *Intuitive Realism—M'Cosh.*

We know the object as existing or having being. This is a necessary conviction, attached to, or rather composing an essential part of, our concrete cognition of every material object presented to us, be it of our own frame or of things external to our frame; whether this hard stone, or this yielding water, or even this vapoury mist or fleeting cloud. We look on each of the objects thus presented to us, in our organism or beyond it, as having an existence, a being, a reality. Every one understands these phrases; they cannot be made simpler or more intelligible by an explanation. We understand them because they express a mental fact which everyone has experienced. We may talk of what we contemplate in sense-perception being nothing but an impression, an appearance, an idea, but we can never be made to give our spontaneous assent to any such statements. However ingenious the arguments which may be adduced in favour of the objects of our sense-perceptions being mere illusions, we find after listening to them, and allowing to them all the weight that is possible, that we still look upon bodies as realities next time they present themselves. The reason is, we know them to be realities by a native cognition which can never be overcome.—'*Intuitions of the Mind*,' p. 108.

III. THE CARTESIAN DOCTRINE.

Descartes.

It cannot be doubted that every perception we have comes to us from some object different from our mind; for it is not in our power to cause ourselves to experience one perception rather than another, the perception being entirely dependent on the object which affects our senses. It may, indeed, be matter of inquiry whether that object be God, or something different from God; but because we perceive, or rather, stimulated by sense, clearly and distinctly apprehend, certain matter extended in length, breadth, and thickness, the various parts of which have different figures and motions, and give rise to the sensations we have of colours, smells, pains, &c., God would, without question, deserve to be regarded as a deceiver if He directly and of Himself presented to our mind the idea of this extended matter, or merely caused it to be presented to us by some object which possessed neither extension, figure, nor motion. For we clearly conceive this matter as entirely distinct from God and from ourselves or our mind; and appear even clearly to discern that the idea of it is formed in us on occasion of objects existing out of our minds, to which it is in every respect similar. But, since God cannot deceive us, for this is repugnant to His nature, as has been already remarked, we must unhesitatingly conclude that there exists a certain object, extended in length, breadth, and thickness, and possessing all those properties which we clearly apprehend to belong to what is extended. And this extended substance is what we call body or matter.—'*Principles*,' part ii. i, *quoted by R. Jardine*, '*Elements of Psychology*,' pp. 100, 101.

Geulinx.—Doctrine of Occasional Causes.

It was Geulinx who first brought out, in its proper form, the celebrated doctrine of *occasional causes*, according to which God Himself is the direct agent in all the related movements of the soul and the body, while the affections of the latter afford the *occasion* upon which he produces the corresponding sensations in the former.—*Morell, 'Speculative Philosophy of Europe,'* 1 p. 178.

The external world cannot possibly act directly upon us. For, even if the external objects cause, in the act of vision, say, an image in my eye, or an impression in my brain, as if in so much wax, this impression or this image is still something corporeal or material merely; it cannot enter into my spirit, therefore, which is essentially disparate from matter. There is nothing left us, then, but to seek in God the means of uniting the two sides . . . Every operation that combines outer and inner, the soul and the world, is neither an effect of the spirit nor of the world, but simply an immediate act of God. When I exercise volition, consequently, it is not from my will but from the will of God that the proposed bodily motions follow. On *occasion* of my will, God moves my body; on *occasion* of an affection of my body, God excites an idea in my mind; the one is but the occasional cause of the other (and hence the name, *Occasionalism*, of this theory).—*Schwegler, 'Hist. of Phil.,'* p. 165.

Malebranche.—We see all things in God.

God, the absolute substance, contains all things in Himself, He sees all things in Himself according to their true nature and being. For the same reason in Him, too, are the ideas of all things; He is the entire world as an intellectual or ideal world. It is God, then, who is the means of mediating between the ego and the world. In Him we see the ideas, inasmuch as we ourselves are so completely contained in Him, so accurately united to Him, that we may call Him the place of spirits. Our volition and our sensation in reference to things proceed from Him; it is He who retains together the objective and the subjective worlds, which, in themselves, are separate and apart.—*Schwegler, 'Hist. of Phil.,'* p. 167.

IV. IDEALISM.

Its General Principle.

Idealism denies the existence or the immediate knowledge of the external world or matter, and maintains that nothing exists, or is known, except minds.—*Monck, 'Sir W. Hamilton,'* p. 179.

The idealist says, There is only one existence, the mind. Analyse the conception of matter, and you will discover that it is only a mental synthesis of qualities. Our knowledge is subjective.—*Ribot, 'Contemporary English Psychology,'* p. 280.

Idealism blots out matter from existence, and affirms that mind is the only reality.—*Calderwood, 'The Philosophy of the Infinite,'* p. 31.

Its Ruder and Finer Forms.

The ruder form of the doctrine holds that ideas are entities different both from the reality they represent and from the mind contemplating their representation. The finer form of the doctrine holds that all that we are conscious of in perception (of course also in imagination), is only a modification of the mind itself.—*Hamilton, in Reid's 'Works,'* p. 130.

Forms of Idealism, Historically Considered.

Ancient Idealism.

'Thought and the object of thought are one and the same'—so runs the celebrated line of the earliest of Greek Idealists—Parmenides. The sentence appears sufficient to stamp its author as the earliest of the metaphysicians. He threw down into the arena of controversy the first, the greatest, the most lasting of the discoveries of metaphysics. For assuredly there is no deeper principle than this, that the truth of things is not Matter, or Force, or Atoms, or Molecules, but the thinking intelligence. There is no rest in the vexed sea of speculation till this truth be secured. When we know that the deepest, ultimate ground of reality to which we can attain is just our true self of thought, then we gain not only peace but freedom.—*Courtney*, '*Studies in Philosophy*,' pp. 1, 21.

English Subjective Idealism—Berkeley.

The ideas imprinted on the senses by the Author of nature are called *real things*, and those excited in the imagination being less regular, vivid, and constant, are more properly termed *ideas*, or *images of things*, which they copy and represent. But then our sensations, be they never so vivid and distinct, are nevertheless ideas, that is, they exist in the mind, or are perceived by it, as truly as the ideas of its own framing. The ideas of sense are allowed to have more reality in them, that is, to be more strong, orderly, and coherent, than the creatures of the mind; but this is no argument that they exist without the mind. They are also less dependent on the spirit, or thinking substance which perceives them, in that they are excited by the will of another and more powerful spirit; yet still they are *ideas*, and certainly no idea, whether faint or strong, can exist otherwise than in a mind perceiving it.—'*Principles of Human Knowledge*,' Part I. 33.

Ideas imprinted on the senses are real things, or do really exist; this we do not deny, but we deny they can subsist without the minds which perceive them, or that they are resemblances of any archetypes existing without the mind; since the very being of a sensation or idea consists in being perceived, and an idea can be like nothing but an idea. Again, the things perceived by sense may be termed *external*, with regard to their origin—in that they are not generated from within by the mind itself, but imprinted by a Spirit distinct from that which perceives them. Sensible objects may likewise be said to be 'without the mind' in another sense, namely, when they exist in some other mind; thus, when I shut my eyes, the things I saw may still exist, but it must be in another mind.—'*Principles of Human Knowledge*,' Part I. 90.

'When,' says Berkeley, 'we do everything in our power to conceive the existence of external bodies, we are all the time doing nothing but contemplating our own ideas.' These objects and ideas are the same thing, then; nothing exists but what is perceived.—*Ribot*, '*English Psychology*,' p. 279.

Before we deduce results from such abstract ideas as cause, substance, matter, we must ask what in reality do these mean,—what is the actual content of consciousness which corresponds to these words? Do not all these ideas, when held to represent something which exists absolutely apart from all knowledge of it, involve a contradiction? Are they not truly, when so regarded, inconceivable, and mere arbitrary figments which cannot possibly be realised in consciousness? The essence of Berkeley's answer to this question is that the universe is inconceivable apart from mind,—that existence, as such, denotes conscious spirits and the objects of consciousness. Matter and external things, in so far as they are thought to have an existence beyond the circle of consciousness, are impossible, inconceivable, absurd.—*Adamson*, '*Encyclopædia Britannica*,' iii. 591 (ed. ix.)

Berkeley not only regarded the supposition that a material world really exists as not strictly demonstrable, but as false. There exist, says Berkeley, only spirits and their functions (ideas and volitions). We are immediately certain of the existence of our thoughts. We infer also that bodies different from our ideas exist. But this inference is deceptive; it is not supported by conclusive evidence, and it is refuted by the fact of the impossibility of explaining the co-working of substances completely heterogeneous. The *esse* of non-thinking things is *percipi*.—*Ueberweg*, '*Hist of Phil*,' ii. 88.

Independent matter — the unconscious substantial cause of our sensations, in the problematical material world of Locke and others—is melted down by Berkeley into the very sensations themselves which it was supposed to explain, whose existence, of course, cannot be doubted, for their reality consists simply in our being percipient or conscious of them. Perishable sensations are thus with Berkeley the atoms or constituent elements of matter. When we say that we see or touch a real material thing, our only intelligible meaning must be, he argues, that we are immediately percipient or conscious of real sensations, and not merely of imaginary ones. Conceivable matter is composed of sensations which depend on being perceived, in contrast with the matter feigned by philosophers to have an absolute and yet rational existence, apart from being perceived by any mind. We have the same sort of evidence for it that we have for our own existence.—*Fraser*, '*Selections from Berkeley*,' p. xxii.

Arthur Collier.

Arthur Collier published in 1713 his *Clavis Universalis; or, a New Inquiry after Truth, being a Demonstration of the Non-existence or Impossibility of an External World.* The following extract is taken from the introduction to the *Clavis* :—

'In affirming that there is no external world, I make no doubt or question of the *existence* of bodies, or whether the bodies which are seen exist or not. It is with me a first principle that *whatsoever is seen*, is. To deny or doubt of this is arrant scepticism, and at once unqualifies a man for any part or office of a disputant or philosopher; so that it will be remembered from this time that my inquiry is not concerning the existence, but altogether concerning the *extra*-existence of certain things or objects; or, in other words, what I affirm and contend for is not that bodies do not exist, or that the external world does not exist, but that such and such bodies, which are supposed to exist, do not exist externally; or in universal terms, that there is no such thing as an external world.'

Criticism of Berkeley's Idealism.

To say that the only matter that is conceivable consists of the transitory sensations (however real while they last) which succeed one another in sentient minds, is plainly no adequate or intelligible account of the external world. Even granting that a real or conscious knowledge of sensations *per se* is possible, such matter is not external; it must be somehow *externalised*. If the external world were resolved merely into actual sensations, the existence of the sensible things we see and touch would be intermittent and fragmentary, not permanent and complete. If external matter means only actual sensations, all visible qualities of things must relapse into nonentity when they are left in the dark; and thus tangible ones, too, unless a percipient is in contact with every part of them. The external world could not have existed millions of ages before men or other sentient beings began to be conscious of sensations, if this is what is meant by its real existence.—*Fraser*, '*Selections from Berkeley*,' xxiv.

Sensational Idealism.

It has lately become fashionable with Idealists, instead of denying the existence of an external world, to admit that in a certain sense it exists, and then to give an explanation which denies its existence in the only sense which the vulgar attach to it. Thus we are told [by Stuart Mill] that matter is admitted to exist in the sense of a Permanent Possibility, or Potentiality, of Sensations. This may mean, either Permanent Possibility of *producing* the sensations, or a Permanent Possibility of *feeling* them.—*Monck*, '*Sir W. Hamilton*,' p. 16.

J. S. Mill.

I see a piece of white paper on a table. I go into another room, and though I have ceased to see it, I am persuaded that the paper is still there. I no longer have the sensations which it gave me; but I believe that when I again place myself in the circumstances in which I had those sensations, that is, when I go again into the room, I shall again have them; and further, that there has been no intervening moment at which this would not have been the case. Owing to this property of my mind, my conception of the world at any given instant consists, in only a small proportion, of present sensations. Of those I may at the time have none at all, and they are in any case a most insignificant portion of the whole which I apprehend. The conception I form of the world existing at any moment, comprises, along with the sensations I am feeling, a countless variety of possibilities of sensation: namely, the whole of those which past observation tells me that I could, under any supposable circumstances, experience at this moment, together with an indefinite and illimitable multitude of others which, though I do not know that I could, yet it is possible that I might, experience in circumstances not known to me.—'*Examination of Sir W. Hamilton*,' pp. 192, 193.

A. Bain.

Professor Bain's view is practically the same as Berkeley's. He states it thus (*Mental Science*, p. 197):—'All Perception or Knowledge implies Mind. The prevailing doctrine is that a tree is something in itself apart from all perception. But the tree is known only through perception; what it may be anterior to, or independent of, perception, we cannot tell; we can think of it as perceived, but not as unperceived.' We thus see that the object world is a mere abstraction, to which we have no right to give an independent existence. It is simply a coherent series of thoughts and feelings.—*Ryland*, '*Handbook, &c.*,' p. 87.

The sense of the external is the consciousness of particular energies and activities of our own.

Sensation is never wholly passive, and in general is much the reverse. Moreover, the tendency to movement exists before the stimulus of sensation; and movement gives a new character to our whole percipient existence. The putting forth of energy, and the consciousness of that energy, are facts totally different in their nature from pure sensation; meaning thereby sensation without activity, of which we can form some approximate idea, from the extreme instances occurring to us of impressions languidly received.

It is in this exercise of force that we must look for the peculiar feeling of *externality* of objects, or the distinction that we make between what impresses us from without and impressions not recognised as *external*. Any impression on the senses that rouses muscular energy, and that varies with that energy, we call an *external* impression.—*Bain*, '*Senses and Intellect*,' pp. 376, 377.

Critical Idealism.

Kant.

Nothing is really given to us but perception, and the empirical progress from this to other possible perceptions. For by themselves phenomena, as mere representations, are real in perception only, which itself is nothing but the reality of an empirical representation, that is, phenomenal appearance. To call a phenomenon a real thing, before it is perceived, means either, that in the progress of experience we must meet with such a perception, or it means nothing. For that it existed by itself, without any reference to our senses and possible experience, might no doubt be said when we speak of a thing by itself. We here are speaking, however, of a phenomenon in space and time, which are not determinations of things by themselves, but only of our sensibility. Hence that which exists in them (phenomena) is not something by itself, but consists in representations only, which, unless they are given in us (in perception), exist nowhere.

The nonsensuous cause of these representations is entirely unknown to us, and we can never perceive it as an object, for such a cause would have to be represented neither in space nor in time, which are conditions of sensuous representation only, and without which we cannot conceive any intuition. We may, however, call that purely intelligible cause of phenomena in general, the transcendental object, in order that we may have something which corresponds to sensibility as a kind of receptivity. We may ascribe to that transcendental object the whole extent and connection of all our possible perceptions, and we may say that it is given by itself antecedently to all experience. Phenomena, however, are given accordingly, not by themselves, but in experience only, because they are mere representations which, as perceptions only, signify a real object, provided that the perception is connected with all others, according to the rules of unity in experience.—'*Critique of Pure Reason*,' vol. ii. 428, 429.

German Idealism.

Its Different Phases.

I see a tree. Certain psychologists tell me that there are three things implied in this one fact of vision, viz., a tree, an image of that tree, and a mind which apprehends that image. Fichte tells me that it is I alone who exist. The tree and the image of it are one thing, and that is a modification of my mind. This is *subjective idealism*. Schelling tells me that both the tree and my *ego* (or self) are existences equally real or ideal, but they are nothing less than manifestations of the absolute, the infinite, or unconditioned. This is *objective idealism*. But Hegel tells me that all these explanations are false. The only thing really existing (in this one fact of vision) is the idea, the relation. The ego and the tree are but two terms of the relation, and owe their reality to it. This is *absolute idealism*. The only real existences are certain ideas or relations. (See NIHILISM.)—*Lewes*, '*History of Philosophy*,' iii. 209.

German Subjective Idealism.

Fichte.

In every perception there are present at once an ego and a thing, or intelligence and its object. Which of the two sides shall be reduced to the other? Abstracting from the ego the philosopher obtains a thing-in-itself, and is obliged to attribute the ideas to the object; abstracting from the object again, he obtains only an ego in itself. The former is the position of dogmatism, the latter that of idealism. Both are incapable of being reconciled, and a third is impossible. We must choose one or the other then. To assist decision let us observe the following:—(1.) The ego is manifest in consciousness, but the thing-in-itself is a mere fiction, for what is in consciousness is only a sensation, a feeling. (2.) Dogmatism undertakes to explain the origin of an idea, but it commences this explanation with an object in itself; that is, it begins with something that is not and never is in consciousness. But what is materially existent produces only what is materially existent—being produces only being, not feeling. The right consequently lies with idealism, which begins not with being (material existence) but with intelligence. To idealism intelligence is only active, it is not passive, because it is of a primitive and absolute nature. For this reason its nature is not being (material outwardness) but wholly and solely action. The forms of this action, the necessary system of the act of intelligence, we must deduce from the principle (the essential nature) of intelligence itself. If we look for the laws of intelligence in experience, the source from which Kant (in a manner) took his categories, we commit a double blunder,—(1.) In so far as it is not demonstrated *why* intelligence must act thus, and *whether* these laws are also immanent in intelligence; and (2.) In so far as it is not demonstrated how the object itself arises. The objects, consequently, as well as the principles of intelligence, are to be derived from the ego itself.—*Schwegler*, '*Hist. of Phil.*,' pp. 259, 260.

Objective Idealism.

Schelling.

Perception generally is an identifying of thought and being. When I perceive an object, the being of this object and my thought of it are for me absolutely the same thing, but in ordinary perception unity is assumed between thought and some particular sensuous existence. In the perception of reason, intellectual perception, on the contrary, it is the absolute subject-object that is perceived, or identity is assumed between thought and being in general, all being. Intellectual perception is absolute cognition, and absolute cognition must be thought as such that in it thinking and being are no longer opposed. Intellectually to perceive directly within yourself the same indifference of ideality and reality which you perceive, as it were, projected out of you in time and space, this is the beginning and the first step in philosophy. This veritably absolute cognition is wholly and solely in the absolute itself. That it cannot be taught is evident. We do not see either why philosophy should be under any obligation to concern itself with this inability. It is advisable rather on all sides to isolate from common consciousness the approach to philosophy, and to leave open neither footpath nor highroad from the one to the other. Absolute cognition, like the truth it contains, has no true contrariety without itself, and admits not of being demonstrated to any intelligence, neither does it admit of being contradicted by any. It was the endeavour of Schelling then to reduce intellectual perception to a method, and this method he named construction. Of this method the possibility and necessity depended on this, that the absolute is in all, and all is the absolute. The construction itself was nothing else than a demonstration of how, in every particular relation or object, the whole is absolutely expressed. Philosophically to construe an object then is to point out that in it the entire inner structure of the absolute repeats itself.—*Schwegler*, '*Hist. of Phil.*,' pp. 301, 302.

Absolute Idealism.

Hegel.

To be in earnest with idealism, Hegel said to himself, is to find all things whatever but forms of thought. But how is that possible without a standard—without a form of thought, that, in application to things, will reduce them to itself? What, in fact, *is* thought—what is its ultimate, its principle, its radical? These questions led to the result that what was peculiar to thought, what characterised the function of thought, what constituted the special nerve of thought, was a triple *nisus*, the movement of which corresponded in its successive steps or moments to what is named in logic simple apprehension, judgment, and reason. Simple apprehension, judgment, and reason do indeed constitute chapters in a book, but they collapse in man into a single force, faculty, or virtue that has these three sides. That is the ultimate pulse of thought—that is the ultimate virtue into which man himself retracts. Let me but be able, then, thought Hegel, to apply this standard to all things in such a manner as shall demonstrate its presence in them, as shall demonstrate it to be their nerve also, as shall reduce all things into its identity, and I shall have accomplished the one universal problem. All things shall then be demonstratively resolved into thought, and idealism—absolute idealism—definitely established.—*Stirling*, '*Annotations to Schwegler's History of Philosophy*,' p. 431.

Defects of Idealism.

When the Idealist says that what he knows as an object is a cluster of sensations contained in his consciousness, the proposition has intrinsically the same character as that which asserts the equi-angularity of a sphere. The two terms, object and consciousness, are severally intelligible; and the relation of inclusion, considered apart, is intelligible. But the proposition itself, asserting that the object stands to consciousness in the relation of inclusion, is unintelligible; since the two terms cannot be combined in thought under this relation; no effort whatever can present or represent the one as within the limits of the other. And if it is not possible to conceive it within the limits, still less is it possible to believe it within the limits; since belief, properly so-called, presupposes conception. —*Spencer*, '*Principles of Psychology*,' ii. 501.

The argumentation by which Idealism seeks to disturb the belief in the existence of an external world, altogether independent of the perceiving subject, is vitiated by the assumption that our knowledge is the criterion of existence; this is conferring upon it an absolute value that it does not possess. —*Ribot*, '*English Psychology*,' p. 281.

Idealism in itself is an unphilosophic system, and, in the end, has a dangerous tendency. Its radical vice lies in maintaining that certain things, which we intuitively know or believe to be real, are not real I say certain things: for were it to deny that all things are real it would be scepticism. Idealism draws back from such an issue with shuddering. But, affirming the reality of certain objects, with palpable inconsistency it will not admit the existence of other objects equally guaranteed by our constitution. This inconsistency will pursue the system remorselessly as an avenger. Idealism commonly begins by declaring that external objects have no such reality as we suppose them to have, and then it is driven or led in the next age, or in the pages of the next speculator, to avow that they have no reality at all. At this stage it will still make lofty pretensions to a realism founded, not on the external phenomenon, but on the internal idea. But the logical necessity speedily chases the system from this refuge, and constrains the succeeding speculator to admit that self is not as it seems, or that it exists only as it is felt, or when it is felt; and the terrible consequence cannot be avoided, that we cannot know whether there be objects before us or no, or whether there be an eye or a mind to perceive them. There is no way of avoiding this black and blank scepticism but by standing up for the trustworthiness of all our original intuitions, and formally maintaining that there is a reality wherever our intuitions delare that there is.—*M'Cosh*, '*Intuitions of the Mind*,' p. 329.

V. NIHILISM.

The Doctrine.

Nihilism is Scepticism carried to the denial of all existence.—*Fleming*, '*Vocab. of Phil.*,' p. 345.

It is the doctrine which recognises nothing but passing mental modifications, and denies the independent existence of mind and matter, as well as of any higher substance.—*Monck*, '*Sir W. Hamilton*,' p. 185.

To deny any fact of consciousness as an actual phænomenon is utterly impossible. But though necessarily admitted as a present phænomenon, the import of this phænomenon,—all beyond our actual consciousness of its existence, may be denied. We are able, without self-contradiction, to suppose, and consequently, to assert, that all to which the phænomenon of which we are conscious refers, is a deception,—that, for example, the past, to which an act of memory refers, is only an illusion involved in our consciousness of the present,—that the unknown subject to which every phænomenon of which we are conscious involves a reference, has no reality beyond this reference itself,—in short, that all our knowledge of mind or matter is only a consciousness of various bundles of baseless appearances. This doctrine, as refusing a substantial reality to the phænomenal existence of which we are conscious, is called Nihilism.—*Hamilton*, '*Metaphysics*,' i. 293.

Nihilistic Philosophers.

Of positive or dogmatic Nihilism there is no example in modern philosophy, for Oken's deduction of the universe from the original nothing is only the paradoxical foundation of a system of realism; and in ancient philosophy, we know too little of the book of Gorgias, the Sophist, entitled 'Concerning Nature or the Non-Existent,' to be able to affirm whether it were maintained by him as a dogmatic and *bona fide* doctrine. But as a sceptical conclusion from the premises of previous philosophers, we have an illustrious example of Nihilism in Hume; and the celebrated Fichte admits that the speculative principles of his own idealism would, unless corrected by his practical, terminate in this result.—*Hamilton*, '*Metaphysics*,' i. 294.

Hume resolved the phenomena of consciousness into impressions and ideas. And as, according to Berkeley, sensitive impressions were no proof of external realities, so, according to Hume, ideas do not prove the existence of mind—so that there is neither matter nor mind, for anything that we can prove.—*Fleming*, '*Vocab. of Phil.*,' p. 346.

The Doctrine of Hume.

Since nothing is ever present to the mind but perceptions, and since all ideas are deriv'd from something antecedently present to the mind, it follows, that 'tis impossible for us so much as to conceive or form an idea of anything specifically different from ideas and impressions. Let us fix our attention out of ourselves as much as possible: Let us chace our imagination to the heavens, or to the utmost limits of the universe; we never really advance a step beyond ourselves, nor can conceive any kind of existence, but those perceptions, which have appear'd in that narrow compass. This is the universe of the imagination, nor have we any idea but what is there produc'd.

The farthest we can go towards a conception of external objects, when suppos'd *specifically* different from our perceptions, is to form a relative idea of them, without pretending to comprehend the related objects. Generally speaking we do not suppose them specifically different; but only attribute to them different relations, connections, and durations.—'*Treatise on Human Nature*,' pt. ii. sec. vi. vol. i. 371.

His Admission as to Reality of Things External.

Nature is always too strong for principle. And, though a Pyrrhonian may throw himself or others into a momentary amazement and confusion by his profound reasonings, the first and most trivial event in life will put to flight all his doubts and scruples, and leave him the same, in every point of action and speculation, with the philosophers of every other sect, or with those who never concerned themselves in any philosophical researches. When he awakes from his dream, he will be the first to join in the laugh against himself, and to confess that all his objections are mere amusement, and can have no other tendency than to show the whimsical condition of mankind, who must act, and reason, and believe, though they are not able, by their most diligent inquiry, to satisfy themselves concerning the foundation of these operations, or to remove the objections which may be raised against them.—'*Enquiry Concerning Human Understanding*,' pt. ii. sec. xii. vol. ii. 131.

VI. MONISM

The philosophical Unitarians or Monists reject the testimony of consciousness to the ultimate duality of the subject and object in perception, but they arrive at the unity of these in different ways. Some admit the testimony of consciousness to the equipoise of the mental and material phenomena, and do not attempt to reduce either mind to matter or matter to mind. They reject, however, the evidence of consciousness to their antithesis in existence, and maintain that mind and matter are only phenomenal modifications of the same common substance This is the doctrine of Absolute Identity,—a doctrine of which the most illustrious representatives among recent philosophers are Schelling, Hegel, and Cousin. Others again deny the evidence of consciousness to the equipoise of the subject and object as co-ordinate and co-original elements; and as the balance is inclined in favour of the one relative or the other, two opposite schemes of psychology are determined. If the subject be taken as the original and genetic, and the object evolved from it as its product, the theory of Idealism is established. On the other hand, if the object be assumed as the original and genetic, and the subject evolved from it as its product, the theory of Materialism is established.—*Hamilton*, '*Metaphysics*,' i. 296, 297.

Attempts at Philosophical Reconciliation

Transfigured Realism completes the differentiation of subject and object by definitely separating that which belongs to the one from that which belongs to the other It does not, with Idealism, say that the object exists only as perceived—does not abolish the line of demarcation between subject and object by bringing the object within consciousness; but it admits the independent existence of the object as unperceived. It does not, with crude Realism, hold that, apart from a perceiving consciousness, the object possesses those attributes by which it is distinguished in perception—does not ascribe to the object something which belongs to the subject. Asserting an impassable limit between the two, it recognises an external independent existence which is the cause of changes in consciousness, while the effects it works in consciousness constitute the perception of it; and it infers that the knowledge constituted by these effects cannot be a knowledge of that which causes them, but can only imply its existence.—*Spencer*, '*Principles of Psychology*,' ii. 505 xx.

We admit that matter does not exist *as matter*, save in relation to our intelligence, since what we mean by matter is a congeries of qualities—weight, resistance, extension, colour, &c.—which have been severally proved to be merely names for divers ways in which our consciousness is affected by an unknown external agency. Take away all these qualities, and we freely admit, with the idealist, that the *matter* is gone; for by *matter* we mean, with the idealist, the phenomenal thing which is seen, tasted, and felt. But we nevertheless maintain, in opposition to the idealist, that *something* is still there, which, to some possible mode of impressibility quite different from conscious intelligence, might manifest itself as something wholly different from, and incomparable with, matter, but which, to anything that can be called conscious intelligence, must manifest itself as matter. What we refuse to admit is the legitimacy of the idealist's inference that the Unknown Reality beyond consciousness does not exist.—*Fiske*, '*Cosmic Philosophy*,' pp. 80, 81.

Bain's theory of a 'double-faced unity.'

The arguments for the two substances have, we believe, now entirely lost their validity; they are no longer compatible with ascertained science and clear thinking The one substance, with two sets of properties, two sides, the physical and the mental—a *double-faced unity*—would appear to comply with all the exigencies of the case We are to deal with this, as in the language of the Athanasian Creed, not confounding the persons nor dividing the substance. The mind is destined to be a double study—to conjoin the mental philosopher with the physical philosopher.—'*Mind and Body*,' p. 196.

Mind-stuff the reality which we perceive as matter.

The actual reality which underlies what we call matter is not the same thing as the mind, is not the same thing as our perception, but it is made of the same stuff. . . .

That element of which even the simplest feeling is a complex I shall call *mind-stuff*. A moving molecule of inorganic matter does not possess mind or consciousness, but it possesses a small piece of mind-stuff. When molecules are so combined together as to form the film on the under side of a jelly-fish, the elements of mind stuff which go along with them are so combined as to form the faint beginnings of sentience. When the molecules are so combined as to form the brain and nervous system of a vertebrate, the corresponding elements of mind-stuff are so combined as to form some kind of consciousness; that is to say, changes in the complex which take place at the same time get so linked together that the repetition of one implies the repetition of the other. When matter takes the complex form of a living human brain, the corresponding mind-stuff takes the form of a human consciousness, having intelligence and volition.

The universe consists entirely of mind-stuff. Some of this is woven into the complex form of human minds containing imperfect representations of the mind-stuff outside them and of themselves also, as a mirror reflects its own image in another mirror, *ad infinitum*. Such an imperfect representation is called a material universe. It is a picture in a man's mind of the real universe of mind-stuff.

The two chief points of this doctrine may be thus summed up —

Matter is a mental picture in which mind-stuff is the thing represented.

Reason, intelligence, and volition are properties of a complex which is made up of elements themselves not rational, not intelligent, not conscious.—*Clifford*, '*Lectures and Essays*,' ii. pp. 64, 85, 87.

VII. SPACE AND TIME.

Consciousness has two formal modes, time and space, different but inseparable and simultaneous; the two senses which reveal space, sight and touch, exist simultaneously with those which reveal time by itself; hence their inseparability in any way except provisionally; and hence the difference in the modes of connection between them, namely, that in all time there is involved space as its accompaniment, in all space there is involved time as its element. — *Hodgson*, '*Time and Space*,' p. 117.

It is sometimes held that time and space are merely generalisations from experience. All abstract and general cognitions may be generalised from experience, and as those of time and space are general and abstract in the highest degree, they also may be generalised in the same way. But this property, which they possess in common with other general and abstract cognitions, does not prove that they do not possess other properties which are peculiar to themselves, and which distinguish them from others. And in point of fact they do possess such property, namely, that they alone of all abstract and general cognitions cannot be annihilated in or banished from thought. — *Hodgson*, '*Time and Space*,' p. 118.

The doctrine of Kant.

Space is not a discursive or so-called general concept of the relations of things in general, but a pure intuition. For, first of all, we can imagine one space only, and if we speak of many spaces, we mean part only of one and the same space. Nor can these parts be considered as antecedent to the one and all-embracing space and, as it were, its component parts out of which an aggregate is formed, but they can be thought of as existing within only. Space is essentially one; its multiplicity, and therefore the general concept of spaces in general, arises entirely from limitations. Hence it follows that, with respect to space, an intuition *à priori*, which is not empirical, must form the foundation of all conceptions of space.—'*Critique of Pure Reason*,' vol. ii. 22.

Time is not an empirical concept deduced from any experience, for neither co-existence nor succession would enter into our perception, if the representation of time were not given *à priori*. Only when this representation *à priori* is given, can we imagine that certain things happen at the same time (simultaneously) or at different times (successively).

Time is a necessary representation on which all intuitions depend. We cannot take away time from phenomena in general, though we can well take away phenomena out of time. Time therefore is given *à priori*. In time alone is reality of phenomena possible. All phenomena may vanish, but time itself (as the general condition of their possibility) cannot be done away with.—'*Critique of Pure Reason*,' vol ii. 27

Of Cousin.

As soon as you know that there are external objects, I ask you whether you do not conceive them in a place that contains them. In order to deny it, it would be necessary to deny that everybody is in a place, that is to say, to reject a truth of physics, which is at the same time a principle of metaphysics, as well as an axiom of common sense. But the place that contains a body is often itself a body, which is only more capacious than the first. This new body is in its turn in a place. Is this new place also a body? Then it is contained in another place more extended and so on; so that it is impossible for you to conceive a body which is not in a place, and you arrive at the conception of a boundless and infinite place, that contains all limited places and all possible bodies.—that boundless and infinite place is space.

As we believe that everybody is contained in a place, so we believe that every event happens in time. Can you conceive an event happening, except in some point of duration? This duration is extended and successively increased to your mind's eye, and you end by conceiving it unlimited like space. Deny duration, and you deny all the sciences that measure it, you destroy all the natural belief upon which human life reposes. It is hardly necessary to add that sensibility alone no more explains the notion of time than that of space, both of which are nevertheless inherent in the knowledge of the external world.—'*On the True, the Beautiful, and the Good*,' Lecture i., pp. 40, 41.

Of Shadworth Hodgson.

Time has one dimension—length. It is infinitely divisible in thought; it is infinitely extensible in thought. It admits of no minimum in division, and of no maximum in extension. For these reasons it contains everything; nothing is short enough to slip through it, nothing long enough to outrun it. It is one in nature, for all its parts are still time. It is incompressible, for no single part can be annihilated.

Space has three dimensions,—length, breadth, and depth. It is infinitely divisible in thought; it is infinitely extensible in thought. It admits of no minimum in division, and of no maximum in extension. For these reasons it contains everything; nothing is small enough to slip through it, nothing is great enough to outstand it. It is one in nature, for all its parts are still space. It is incompressible, for no single part can be annihilated.—'*Time and Space*,' pp. 121, 122.

Dr. Bain's theory of space.

I hold, as regards extension in general, that this is a feeling derived in the first instance from the locomotive or moving organs; that a definite amount of movement of these comes to be associated with the sweep and adjustment and other effects of the eye; and that the notion when full-grown is a compound of locomotion, touch, and vision, any one implying and recalling the others. A certain movement of the eye, as the sweep over a table, gives us the sense of that table's magnitude, when it recalls and revives the extent and direction of arm movement necessary to compass the length, breadth, and height of the table. Previous to this experience, the sight of the table would be a mere visible effect, differing consciously from other visible effects, and not suggesting any foreign effect whatever. It could not suggest magnitude, because magnitude is not magnitude, if it do not mean the extent of movement of the arms or limbs that would be needed to compass the object; and this can be joined in no way but through actual trial by these very organs.—'*Senses and Intellect*,' pp. 371, 372.

VIII. RELATIVITY OF KNOWLEDGE.

All our Knowledge is Relative.

'Man,' says Protagoras, 'is the measure of the universe;' and, in so far as the universe is an object of human knowledge, the paradox is a truth. Whatever we know, or endeavour to know, God or the world, mind or matter, the distant or the near, we know and can know only in so far as we possess a faculty of knowing in general, and we can only exercise that faculty under the laws which control and limit its operations. However great and infinite and various, therefore, may be the universe and its contents, these are known to us only as our mind is capable of knowing them.—*Hamilton*, '*Metaphysics*,' i 61.

When on the seashore we note how the hulls of distant vessels are hidden below the horizon, and how, of still remoter vessels, only the uppermost sails are visible, we realise with tolerable clearness the slight curvature of that portion of the sea's surface which lies before us. But when we seek in imagination to follow out this curved surface as it actually exists, slowly bending round until all its meridians meet in a point eight thousand miles below our feet, we find ourselves utterly baffled We cannot conceive in its real form and magnitude even that small segment of our globe which extends a hundred miles on every side of us, much less the globe as a whole. Yet we habitually speak as though we had an idea of the earth.—*Spencer*, '*First Principles*,' p. 25.

Forms of the Doctrine.

As stated by Sir W. Hamilton.

All our knowledge of mind and matter is relative—conditioned—relatively conditioned. Of things absolutely or in themselves, be they external, be they internal, we know nothing, or know them only as incognisable; and we become aware of their incomprehensible existence only as this is indirectly and accidentally revealed to us, through certain qualities related to our faculties of knowledge, and which qualities, again, we cannot think as unconditioned, irrelative, existent in and out of themselves. All that we know is therefore phenomenal.—'*Discussions*,' p 608

All our knowledge is only relative,—1. Because existence is not cognisable, absolutely and in itself, but only in special modes; 2 Because these modes can be known only if they stand in a certain relation to our faculties; and, 3 Because the modes, thus relative to our faculties, are presented to and known by the mind only under modifications determined by these faculties themselves.—'*Metaphysics*,' i 148

On 1. and 2. in the last extract, John Stuart Mill remarks, 'Whoever can find anything more in these two statements, than that we do not know all about a Thing, but only as much about it as we are capable of knowing, is more ingenious or more fortunate than myself' On 3. he says, 'The proposition that our cognitions of objects are only in part dependent on the objects themselves, and in part on elements superadded by our organs or by our minds, cannot warrant the assertion that all our knowledge, but only that the part so added, is relative.'—'*Examination of Hamilton*,' pp 30, 31.

As stated by Spencer.

'The reality existing behind all appearances is, and must ever be, unknown.'—'*First Principles*,' p 69

As held by Dr Bain.

Mr Stuart Mill says that 'Mr Bain habitually uses the phrase "relativity of knowledge" in this sense, that we only know anything, by knowing it as distinguished from something else; that all consciousness is of difference; that two objects are the smallest number required to constitute consciousness; that a thing is only seen to be what it is by contrast with what it is not.' Mr. Mill adds, 'I have no fault to find with this use of the phrase; it expresses a real and important law of our mental nature' (see '*Examination of Hamilton*,' p. 6). Dr. M'Cosh, however, regards it 'as destroying the simplicity of our mental operations, and reversing the order of nature;' and will not allow that we should not have known a sensation, say the feeling of a lacerated limb, to be painful, unless we had contrasted it with a pleasurable one; on the contrary, I maintain that in order to contrast the two we must have experienced them in succession.'—'*Examination of Mill*,' pp. 222, 225.

Form preferred by John Stuart Mill.

'Our knowledge of objects, and even our fancies about objects, consist of nothing but the sensations they excite, or which we imagine them exciting in ourselves.' 'This knowledge is merely phenomenal.' 'The object is known to us only in one special relation, namely, as that which produces, or is capable of producing, certain impressions on our senses; and all that we really know is these impressions.' 'This is the Doctrine of the Relativity of Knowledge to the knowing mind, in the simplest, purest, and, as I think, the most proper acceptation of the words.'—'*Examination of Hamilton*,' pp. 7–14.

What is implied by the Relativity of knowledge is, that we do not perceive things actually as they are in themselves, but only as conditioned by our faculties. Objects are to us bundles of sensations united in certain bonds we call relations. But the sensations of a starfish are probably quite different from our own, and so also are the relations which unite them. The same light-waves produce different colours in the case of persons afflicted with colour-blindness from those perceived by ordinary persons. The sun's rays produce in us feelings of heat and light according to the parts of the body on which they fall. From such facts we gather that our sensations bear no resemblance to the agencies in the external world which give rise to them; we can only know the phenomena, and not the underlying realities themselves.—*Rylands*, '*Handbook, &c.*,' p. 60.

I do not see that such a theory has any right to claim the title of 'knowledge,' or that it can get 'relations' when it has no things to bring into relation. The theory is simply that we know sensations, and possibilities of sensations, while we cannot be said to know what sensations are.—*M'Cosh*, '*Examination of Mill*,' p. 228.

As propounded by M'Cosh.

There is evidently a true doctrine of relativity, if only we could express it accurately. It should be admitted—(1.) That man knows only so far as he has the faculties of knowledge; (2.) That he knows objects only under aspects presented to his faculties; and (3.) That his faculties are limited, and consequently his knowledge limited, so that not only does he not know all objects, he does not know all about any one object. It may further be allowed—(4.) That in perception by the senses we know external objects in relation to the perceiving mind. But while these views can be established in opposition to the philosophy of the absolute, it should ever be resolutely maintained, on the other hand,—(1.) That we know the very thing; and (2.) That our knowledge is correct so far as it goes. We admit a subtle scepticism when we allow, with Kant, that we do not know the thing itself, but merely a phenomenon in the sense of appearance; or with Hamilton, that we perceive merely the relations of things. A still more dangerous error follows where it is affirmed that our knowledge is always modified by the percipient mind, and that we add to the object something which is not, or at least may not, be in it.—'*Intuitions of the Mind,*' p 344.

The Doctrine that Human Knowledge is Relative does not imply that it is Inaccurate.

It has been stated that human knowledge is relative. This is no doubt in some sense to be admitted. But we must beware of allowing this circumstance to detract from its reality or certainty. When I have a sensation, and thereupon perceive an object existing external to my sense, and displaying certain properties and relations, which I descry by intuition and distinguish by abstraction, you may fairly call the knowledge relative, namely, to the extent of my faculties and the opportunities of my position But, first, we remark, all knowledge, short of omniscience, may be called relative in the same sense. And next, human knowledge is clear, distinct, and adequate, as far as it goes, and therefore thoroughly trustworthy. And lastly, if we be true to ourselves, we may ascertain some very definite landmarks between that which may be known and that which is beyond the reach of our present powers of observation. Hence our knowledge is limited indeed; but it is not therefore inaccurate or at variance with the nature of things, and it is far from having reached the range which is possible to our intellectual powers.—*Murphy*, '*Human Mind,*' p. 56.

It is true that knowledge is relative; that is, that it is conversant with things or persons in relation to self, to other minds, to one another, and to God It is so because it is knowledge All knowledge is composed of judgment, and every judgment implies the relation of subject and object as necessarily as a magnet implies the relation between two poles But it is not true that this relativity of knowledge is any imperfection, circumscription, or disability; or that there is any conceivable or possible knowledge of *things in themselves*, as opposed to the knowledge of their properties and relations, which, if attainable, would be a higher kind of knowledge, and in comparison with which our actual knowledge is illusory. On the contrary, the inadequacy or limitation of our knowledge lies in the fact that comparatively few of the actual or possible relations of things to one another, to ourselves, and to God are as yet known to us. Illusion consists not in this limitation, but in believing these relations to be other than they are In a word, the relativity of knowledge consists in that correlation, mental and physical, of thought with being, and of being with thought, on which the possibility, certainty, and value of knowledge depend.—*Conder*, '*Basis of Faith,*' p 147.

VIII.

REPRESENTATIVE KNOWLEDGE.

I. IMAGES.

Definition of the Image.

We may define it as a repetition or revival of the sensation, while at the same time we distinguish it from the sensation; first, by its origin, since it has the sensation as its antecedent, while the sensation is preceded by an excitation of the nerve; and again, by its association with an antagonist, since it has several reductives, among others the special corrective sensation, while the sensation itself has no reductive.—*Taine*, '*On Intelligence,*' p. 73.

Distinct from the Percept and Concept

The term image in psychology points to a double distinction. On the one hand it is representative, whereas a percept is presentative (or largely so); on the other side it is a representation of a concrete object, or a mental picture, and is thus distinguished from a concept or general notion which typifies a class of things.—*Sully*, '*Outlines of Psychology*,' p. 219, note 2.

We have no difficulty in general in distinguishing between an actual perception and an imagination of a thing. We instantly feel the difference between looking at an object, as a horse, and forming a mental picture of it when it is absent. We roughly define the difference by saying that the image is the copy of the percept, that it is less vivid, and less distinct in its parts.—*Sully*, '*Outlines of Psychology*,' p. 224.

Automatic Character of the Image.

The recurrence of images is essentially *automatic*; but the mind can determinately place itself in the condition most favourable to their reproduction, and can project itself, as it were, in search of them. While some persons are obliged to wait until the memory supplies them with the image they desiderate, there are others who are distinguished by the exuberance of this reproductive power; so that they have only to ask themselves for an appropriate simile or metaphor, and it immediately occurs to them.—*Carpenter*, '*Mental Physiology*,' p. 489.

Mental Imagery.

I have many cases of persons mentally reading off scores when playing the pianoforte, or manuscript when they are making speeches. One statesman has assured me that a certain hesitation in utterance which he has at times, is due to his being plagued by the image of his manuscript speech with its original erasures and corrections. He cannot lay the ghost, and he puzzles in trying to decipher it.

Some few persons see mentally in print every word that is uttered; they attend to the visual equivalent and not to the sound of the words, and they read them off usually as from a long imaginary strip of paper, such as is unwound from telegraphic instruments. The experiences differ in detail as to size and kind of type, colour of paper, and so forth, but are always the same in the same person.—*Galton*, '*Inquiries into Human Faculty*,' p. 96.

The power of visualising is higher in the female sex than in the male, and is somewhat, but not much, higher in public schoolboys than in men. After maturity is reached, the further advance of age does not seem to dim the faculty, but rather the reverse, judging from numerous statements to that effect; but advancing years are sometimes accompanied by a growing habit of hard abstract thinking, and in these cases the faculty undoubtedly becomes impaired.—*Galton*, '*Human Faculty*,' pp. 99, 100.

II. ASSOCIATION OF IDEAS.

Defined.

The tendency which one thought has to introduce another.—*Stewart*, '*Works*,' ii. 257.

Association of ideas is that mental principle which enables one mental state to recall another to the memory. Thus the thought of Waterloo recalls to my memory at once the thoughts Napoleon and Wellington, together with several others. In this case the thoughts Napoleon and Wellington are both said to be *associated* with the thought Waterloo.—*Monck*, '*Sir W. Hamilton*,' p. 169.

Association of Ideas, or Mental Association, is a general name used in Psychology to express the conditions under which representations arise in consciousness, and also is the name of a principle put forward by an important school of thinkers to account generally for the facts of mental life. It is allowed on all hands that this phrase, Association of Ideas, contains too narrow a reference; association, in either of the senses above noted, extending beyond ideas or thoughts proper to every class of mental states.—*Robertson*, '*Encyclopædia Britannica*,' ii. 730.

The Doctrine

Some of our ideas have a natural correspondence and connection one with another. Ideas, that in themselves are not all of kin, come to be so united in some men's minds that it is very hard to separate them; they always keep in company, and the one no sooner at any time comes into the understanding but its associate appears with it; and if they are more than two which are thus united, the whole gang, always inseparable, show themselves together.—*Locke*, '*Human Understanding*,' book ii chap 33.

It is evident that there is a principle of connection between the different thoughts or ideas of the mind, and that, in their appearance to the memory or imagination, they introduce each other with a certain degree of method and regularity. In our more serious thinking or discourse, this is so observable that any particular thought which breaks in upon the regular tract or chain of ideas is immediately remarked and rejected. And even in our wildest and most wandering reveries, nay, in our very dreams, we shall find, if we reflect, that the imagination ran not altogether at adventures, but that there was still a connection upheld among the different ideas which succeeded each other. Were the loosest and freest conversation to be transcribed, there would immediately be observed something which connected it in all its transitions.—*Hume*, '*Essay on Human Understanding*,' sec iii

A determinate object being present in consciousness with its proper thought, feeling, or desire, it is not present, isolated and alone, but may draw after it the representation of other objects, with their respective feelings and desires.—*Hamilton*, '*Metaphysics*,' ii. 488.

When two or more ideas have been often repeated together, and the association has become very strong, they sometimes spring up in such close combination as not to be distinguishable. Some cases of sensation are analogous. For example, when a wheel, on the seven parts of which the seven prismatic colours are respectively painted, is made to revolve rapidly, it appears not of seven colours, but of one uniform colour—white. By the rapidity of the succession the several sensations cease to be distinguishable; they run, as it were, together, and a new sensation, compounded of all the seven, but apparently a single one, is the result. Ideas also, which have been so often conjoined, that whenever one exists in the mind the others immediately exist along with it, seem to run into one another—to coalesce, as it were, and out of many to form one idea; which idea, however in reality complex, appears to be no less simple than any of those of which it is compounded.—*Mill*, '*Analysis of the Human Mind*,' chap iii.

Origin of the Modern Doctrine of Association.

About eighteen years ago I was informed that the Rev. Mr Gay, then living, asserted the possibility of deducing all our intellectual pleasure and pains from association. This put me upon considering the power of association.

From inquiring into the power of association, I was led to examine both its consequences in respect of morality and religion and its physical cause. By degrees many disquisitions foreign to the doctrine of association, or at least not immediately connected with it, intermixed themselves.—*Hartley*, '*Observations on Man*,' preface.

Illustrations

'That one thought is often suggested to the mind by another, and that the sight of an external object often recalls former occurrences and revives former feelings, are facts which are perfectly familiar. In passing along a road which we have formerly travelled in the company of a friend, the particulars of the conversation in which we were then engaged are frequently suggested to us by the objects we meet with. In such a scene we recollect that a particular subject was started; and in passing the different houses and plantations and rivers the arguments we were discussing when we last saw them recur spontaneously to the memory . After time has, in some degree, reconciled us to the death of a friend, how wonderfully are we affected the first time we enter the house where he lived! Everything we see—the apartment where he studied, the chair upon which he sat—recall to us the happiness we have enjoyed together'—*Stewart*, '*Works*,' ii. 252 *seq.*

A note of music suggests the snatch of melody in which it has been heard, this suggests the air, till the whole tune is repeated to the ear of the mind. If a man sees a horse like one which he formerly owned, or a lady sees a dress which in material or colour is like one which she has worn, the horse or dress are instantly recalled. The heroic devotion of Florence Nightingale brings to view the relief and comfort of sick and wounded soldiers.—*Porter*, '*The Human Intellect*,' 277, 278.

We sleep in a strange bedroom, and getting up in the dark to reach the water bottle, recall at once the position of the washing-stand. We read a book, and without having specially observed the fact, remember that a passage we want to find lies near the bottom of a left-hand page. —*Spencer*, '*Psychology*,' i. 260.

Slight withal may be the things which bring
Back on the heart the weight which it would fling
Aside for ever it may be a sound,—
A tone of music,—summer's eve,—or spring,
A flower,—the wind,—the ocean,—which shall wound,
Striking the electric chain wherewith we are darkly bound
—*Byron*, '*Childe Harold*,' c iv. stanza 23.

Ultimate Ground of Association.

That Similarity is an ultimate ground of mental association cannot seriously be questioned, and to neglect or discount it, in the manner of the older representatives of the school, is to render the associationist theory quite inadequate for purposes of general psychological explanation. It is simply impossible to overrate the importance of this principle.—*Robertson*, '*Encyclopædia Britannica*,' ii 733.

Two Schools of Associationists

Those who apply the doctrine to explain mental reproduction and representation only. Of these Aristotle is the first.

When, therefore, we accomplish an act of reminiscence, we pass through a certain series of precursive movements, until we arrive at a movement on which the one we are in quest of is habitually consequent. Hence, too, it is that we hunt through the mental train, excogitating from the present or some other, and from similar or contrary or coadjacent. Through this process reminiscence takes place.—*Aristotle*, '*De Memoria*, &c'

Those who apply the doctrine to explain all mental acquisitions.

There has grown up, especially in England, a psychological school which aims at explaining all mental acquisitions, and the more complex mental processes generally, under laws not other than those determining simple reproduction. Hobbes is the first thinker of permanent note to whom the doctrine may be traced. Hartley and Priestley took it up. Its most modern representatives are Bain, J. S. Mill, and Herbert Spencer.—*Robertson*, '*Encyclopædia Britannica*,' ii 731.

But the principle of association will not explain all psychical processes.

To refer all pleasures to association is to acknowledge no sound but echo.—*Hare*, '*Guesses at Truth*,' p. 180.

The association of ideas can never account for the origin of a new notion, or of a pleasure essentially different from all others which we know. It presupposes, in every instance, the existence of those notions and those feelings which it is its province to combine.—*Stewart, 'Works,* ii 322.

The attempts that have been made to resolve all our mental pleasures and pains into Association, are guilty of a twofold vice For, in the first place, they convert a partial into an exclusive law; and, in the second, they elevate a subordinate into a supreme principle.—*Hamilton, 'Metaphysics,'* ii 489

The Influence of Associations.

To the power of association may be justly attributed most of the sympathies and antipathies observable in men, which work as strongly and produce as regular effects as if they were natural; and are therefore called so, though they at first had no other original but the accidental connexion of two ideas, which either the strength of the first impression or future indulgence so united, that they always afterwards kept company together in that man's mind, as if they were but one idea Many children imputing the pain they endured at school to their books they were corrected for, so join their ideas together that a book becomes their aversion, and they are never reconciled to the study and use of them all their lives after, and thus reading becomes a torment to them which otherwise possibly they might have made the great pleasure of their lives.—*Locke, 'Human Understanding,'* book ii. chap. 33.

All that strikes us in our friends or in our enemies is associated with the agreeable or the disagreeable feeling which we severally experience; the faults of the former borrow always something pleasing from their amiable qualities, whereas the amiable qualities of the latter seem always to participate of their vices. Hence it is that these associations exert a powerful influence on our whole conduct. They foster our love or hatred, enhance our esteem or contempt, excite our gratitude or indignation, and produce those sympathies, those antipathies, or those capricious inclinations for which we are sometimes sorely puzzled to render a reason.—*Hamilton, 'Logic,'* ii. 127.

The moral influence of accidental associations is well worthy of attention, for their power for evil as well as their capacity for good. Pleasing manners, high intellectual culture, the attractions of wealth and position may be combined with libertine principles and easy morals, and thus become powerful aids and instruments of vice and corruption. The easy manners, the gay life, and the generous hospitality of the cavaliers of Charles I. and of the courtiers of Charles II lent a charm to their cause and a fascination to their name and memory, while the unnatural strictness, the over-stiff manners, and the precise pedantry of the Puritans have caused their pure morals, their patriotic heroism, and their fervent piety to be odious in the minds of many noble men, and have burdened their very name with associations of contempt and reproach.—*Porter, 'The Human Intellect,'* p. 298.

III ASSOCIATION, LAWS OF

Defined.

The conditions or laws under which the mind recalls one object by means of another are called the laws of association.—*Porter, 'The Human Intellect,'* p. 254.

Classification of the Laws, by

Aristotle.

Aristotle recalled the laws to four, or rather to three: Contiguity in time and space, Resemblance, and Contrariety. He even seems to have thought they might all be carried up into the one law of Co-existence.—*Hamilton, 'Metaphysics,'* ii 231.

St. Augustine.

He reduces association to a single canon, viz, Thoughts which have once co-existed in the mind are afterwards associated.—*Hamilton, 'Metaphysics,'* ii. 231.

Hume.

Who first, among the moderns, enumerates distinct principles of association.

To me there appear to be only three principles of connection among ideas, namely, Resemblance, Contiguity in time or place, and Cause or Effect. A picture naturally leads our thoughts to the original (Resemblance). The mention of one apartment in a building naturally introduces an inquiry or discourse concerning the others (Contiguity). If we think of a wound we can scarcely forbear reflecting on the pain which follows it (Cause and Effect).—'*Essay on Human Understanding*,' sec. iii.

Dugald Stewart.

The relations, upon which some of the associations are founded, are perfectly obvious to the mind; those which are the foundation of others are discovered only in consequence of particular efforts of attention. Of the former kind are the relations of Resemblance and Analogy, of Contrariety, of Vicinity in time and place, and those which arise from accidental coincidence in the sound of different words. Of the latter kind are the relations of Cause and Effect, of Means and End, of Premises and Conclusion; and those others which regulate the train of thought in the mind of the philosopher when he is engaged in a particular investigation.—'*Philosophical Works*,' iii. 263.

Brown.

He divides the circumstances affecting association into primary and secondary. Under the primary laws of Suggestion he includes Resemblance, Contrast, Contiguity in time and place. By the secondary he means the vivacity, the recentness, and the frequent repetition of our thoughts. *Hamilton*, '*Metaphysics*,' ii. 232.

Sir W. Hamilton.

In his ultimate scheme he lays down four *General Laws* of mental succession concerned in reproduction:—(1) Associability or Possible Co-suggestion; (2) Repetition or Direct Remembrance; (3) Redintegration, Indirect Remembrance or Reminiscence; (4) Preference. To these he adds *Special Laws*, namely—(A.) Primary, modes of the laws of Repetition and Redintegration—(1) Law of Similars (Analogy and Affinity); (2) Law of Contrast; (3) Law of Coadjacency (Cause and Effect, Whole and Parts, &c.). (B.) Secondary, modes of the Law of Preference:—(1) Law of Immediacy; (2) Law of Homogeneity; (3) Law of Facility.—*Hamilton's* '*Reid*,' note D*** (abridged).

Bain.

Who lays down a law—(1) of Contiguity, (2) of Similarity, (3) of Compound Association.—'*Mental and Moral Science*,' bk. ii.

Herbert Spencer.

The fundamental law of all mental association is that each relation or feeling at the moment of presentation aggregates with its like in past experience. Besides this law of association there is no other; but all further phenomena of association are incidental. [See Association of Ideas, § iii.]—'*Psychology*,' i. 269.

Noah Porter.

The laws of association are divided into *higher* and *lower*. The lower are those which are presented to us in the acquisitions of sense and consciousness, and which are reproduced by the representative imagination or the uncultured memory. These are the relations of *time* and *space*. As they are more obvious and natural, they require little of higher culture or discipline. They are also developed earliest in the order of time, and are common to the whole race. The relations of likeness and of contrast form an intermediate class between the natural and the philosophical; being now present in the one, and then largely represented in the other. The higher are the relations of *cause* and *effect*; involving *means* and *end*, *premise* and *conclusion*, *datum* and *inference*, *genus* and *species*, *law* and *example*,—all, in short, of the so-called *philosophical* or *logical* relations. All these are present in and control the higher imagination and the more developed processes of thought.—'*Human Intellect*,' p. 296.

Statement of the Laws.

1. *Law of Associability*

All thoughts of the same mental subject are associable, or capable of suggesting each other

2. *Law of Repetition*

Thoughts co-identical in modification, but differing in time, tend to suggest each other. If A be recalled into consciousness, A will tend to reawaken B, B to reawaken C, and so on.

3. *Law of Redintegration*

Thoughts once co-identical in time are, however different as mental modes, again suggestive of each other, and that in the mutual order which they originally hold.

Bain's Law of Contiguity may be put by the side of this; Actions, Sensations, and States of Feeling occurring together, or in close succession tend to grow together, or cohere, in such a way that when any of them is afterwards presented to the mind the others are apt to be brought up in idea.

4. *Law of Preference.*

Thoughts are suggested, not merely by force of the general subjective relation subsisting between themselves, they are also suggested, in proportion to the relation of interest (from whatever source) in which these stand to the individual mind.

5 *Law of Similars.*

Things—thoughts resembling each other (be their semblance simple or analogical) are mutually suggestive

Compare Bain's statement:—*Present* Actions, Sensations, Thoughts, or Emotions tend to revive their *like* among previously occurring states.

6 *Law of Immediacy.*

Of two thoughts, if the one be immediately, the other mediately connected with a third, the first will be suggested by the third in preference to the second.

7 *Law of Homogeneity.*

A thought will suggest another of the same order in preference to one of a different order. Thus a smell will suggest a smell, a sight a sight, &c.

8. *Law of Facility.*

A thought easier to suggest will be roused in preference to a more difficult one. The easier are those more strongly impressed on the mind, or more recent, or more frequently repeated, or more interesting, &c.—The above laws are taken from *Hamilton's* '*Reid*,' note D***.

9 *Law of Compound Association.*

Past Actions, Sensations, Thoughts, or Emotions are recalled more easily when associated either through contiguity or similarity with more than one present object or impression. We may not be able to remember a mineral specimen by its being a certain ore of iron, but some local association in a museum or cabinet may complete the recall of its visible aspect.—*Bain*, '*Mental and Moral Science*,' p. 151

10. *Law of Inseparable Association.*

Some ideas are by frequency and strength of association so closely combined that they cannot be separated. If one exists, the other exists along with it, in spite of whatever effort we may make to disjoin them. It is not in our power to think of colour without thinking of extension, or of solidity without figure.—*Mill*, '*Analysis of the Human Mind*,' i. 93.

IV. REVERIE AND ABSTRACTION—DREAMS, &c.

Reverie and Abstraction.

When the mind is not following any definite direction of its own, one idea may be readily substituted for another by new suggestions from without; and thus the whole state of the convictions, the feelings, and the impulses to action, may be altered from time to time, without the least perception of the strangeness of the transition. Such are the characteristics of the states known as *Reverie* and *Abstraction*; which are fundamentally the same in their character, though the *form* of their products differs with the temperament and previous habits of the individual, and with the degree in which his consciousness may remain open to external impressions,—*Reverie* being the automatic mental action of the poet, *Abstraction* that of the Reasoner.—*Carpenter*, '*Mental Physiology*,' p 544

Dreaming.

Absence of control over the thoughts in dreaming.

With the absence of consciousness of external things, there may be a state of mental activity, of which we are more or less cognisant at the time, and of which our subsequent remembrance in the waking state varies greatly in completeness. The chief peculiarity of the state of *dreaming* appears to be, that there is an *entire* suspension of volitional control over the current of thought, which flows on automatically, sometimes in a uniform, coherent order, but more commonly in a strangely incongruous sequence. The former is most likely to occur, when the mind simply takes up the train of thought on which it had been engaged during the waking hours, not long previously; and it may even happen that, in consequence of the freedom from distraction resulting from the suspension of external influences, the reasoning processes may thus be carried on during sleep with unusual vigour and success, and the imagination may develop new and harmonious forms of beauty.

Thus, Condorcet saw in his dreams the final steps of a difficult calculation which had puzzled him during the day: and Condillac tells us that, when engaged in his 'Cours d'Étude,' he frequently developed and finished a subject in his dreams, which he had broken off before retiring to rest —*Carpenter*, '*Mental Physiology*,' p. 584.

The Materials of Dreams

There can be no doubt that the materials of our dreams are often furnished by the 'traces' left upon the brain by occurrences long since past, which have completely faded out of the *conscious* memory—*Carpenter*, '*Mental Physiology*,' p. 587.

Rapidity of thought in Dreams.

There would not appear to be any limit to the amount of thought which may pass through the mind of the dreamer, in an interval so brief as to be scarcely capable of measurement; as is obvious from the fact, that a dream involving a long succession of supposed events, has often distinctly originated in a sound which has also awoke the sleeper, so that the whole must have passed during the almost inappreciable period of transition between the previous state of sleep and the full waking consciousness.—*Carpenter*, '*Mental Physiology*,' p. 588.

Explanation of the origin of Dreams

It is known that the brain becomes comparatively bloodless in sleep, while there is a partial return of blood to its vessels when the sleep is disturbed by the imperfect consciousness of dreams; and the quantity of blood in its vessels becomes greatly increased with the perfect restoration of consciousness on awaking. Dreaming is, therefore, a state in which we are half-asleep and half-awake—sufficiently awake to have some consciousness. In this we have an explanation of the generally admitted fact, that most dreams take place at the transition from waking to sleep, or, perhaps more commonly, from sleep to waking.

The state of the dreamer's consciousness, then, is one in which the higher function of thought or comparison, implying voluntary control, is dormant, and only the more mechanical function of association active.—*Murray*, '*Psychology*,' pp. 254, 255.

Somnambulism.

It seems common to every phase of this condition that there is the same want of volitional control over the current of thought, and the same complete subjection of the consciousness to the idea which may for a time possess it, as in dreaming; but the somnambulist differs from the ordinary dreamer in possessing such a control over his nervo-muscular apparatus as to be enabled to execute, or at any rate to attempt, whatever it may be in his mind to do; while some of the inlets to sensation ordinarily remain open, so that the somnambulist may *hear*, though he does not *see* or *feel*, or may *feel*, while he does not *see* or *hear*. The Muscular Sense, indeed, seems always active; and many of the most remarkable performances, both of *natural* and of *induced* somnambulism, seem referable to the extraordinary intensity with which impressions on it are perceived, in consequence of the exclusive fixation of the attention on its guidance.—*Carpenter*, '*Mental Physiology*,' p. 591.

Induced Somnambulism—Hypnotism.

Method of producing Hypnotism.

The method, discovered by Mr. Braid, of producing this state of artificial somnambulism, which was appropriately designated by him as *Hypnotism*, consists in the maintenance of a fixed gaze, for several minutes consecutively, on a bright object placed somewhat above and in front of the eyes, at so short a distance that the convergence of their axes upon it is accompanied with a sense of effort, even amounting to pain.

In Hypnotism, as in ordinary somnambulism, no remembrance whatever is preserved in the waking state of anything that may have occurred during its continuance; although the previous train of thought may be taken up and continued uninterruptedly on the next occasion that the hypnotism is induced. And when the mind is not excited to activity by the stimulus of external impressions, the hypnotised subject appears to be profoundly asleep, a state of complete torpor, in fact, being usually the first result of the process just described, and any subsequent manifestation of activity being procurable only by the prompting of the operator.—*Carpenter*, '*Mental Physiology*,' pp. 601, 602.

The suggestion of ideas in Hypnotism.

By attitude or gesture.

If the hand be placed upon the top of the head, the somnambulist will frequently, of his own accord, draw his body up to its fullest height, and throw his head slightly back; his countenance then assumes an expression of the most lofty pride, and his whole mind is obviously possessed by that feeling. Where the first action does not of itself call forth the rest, it is sufficient for the operator to straighten the legs and spine, and to throw the head somewhat back, to arouse that feeling and the corresponding expression to its fullest intensity. During the most complete domination of this emotion, let the head be bent forward, and the body and limbs gently flexed, and the most profound humility then instantaneously takes its place.—*Carpenter*, '*Mental Physiology*,' p. 602.

Of the ideas connected with particular actions.

If the hand be raised above the head and the fingers be bent upon the palm, the notion of climbing, swinging, or pulling at a rope is called up; if, on the other hand, the fingers are bent when the arm is hanging at the side, the idea excited is that of lifting some object from the ground; and if the same be done when the arm is advanced forwards in the position of striking a blow, the idea of fighting is at once aroused, and the somnambulist is very apt to put it into immediate execution.—*Carpenter*, '*Mental Physiology*,' p. 605.

Influence upon Organic Functions—instance.

A female relative of Mr. Braid was the subject of a severe rheumatic fever, during the course of which the left eye became seriously implicated, so that after the inflammatory action had passed away there was an opacity over more than one half of the cornea, which not only prevented distinct vision, but occasioned an annoying disfigurement Having placed herself under Mr Braid's hypnotic treatment for the relief of violent pain in her arm and shoulder, she found, to the surprise alike of herself and Mr B., that her sight began to improve very perceptibly The operation was therefore continued daily, and in a very short time the cornea became so transparent that close inspection was required to discover any remains of the opacity.—('*Neurhypnology*,' p. 175.)

The writer has known other cases in which secretions that had been morbidly suspended have been reinduced by this process, and is satisfied that, if applied with skill and discrimination, it would take rank as one of the most potent methods of treatment which the physician has at his command The channel of influence is obviously the *vaso-motor* system of nerves, which, though not directly under subjection to the will, is peculiarly affected by emotional states —*Carpenter*, '*Mental Physiology*,' p 609.

V. MEMORY.

Its Nature

Definition.

Memory is an immediate knowledge of a *present* thought, involving an absolute belief that this thought represents another act of knowledge that *has been* —*Hamilton*, '*Discussions*,' p 51.

Consciousness testifies that when a thought has once been present to the mind it may again become present to it with the additional consciousness that it has formerly been present to it. When this takes place we are said to *remember*, and the faculty of which *remembrance* is the act, is *memory* —*Fleming*, '*Vocab of Phil.*,' p. 302.

To remember is to mind again, to have again before the mind a thing or event, knowing it to have been formerly experienced. I go through a house, walk into the adjacent garden, and observe the fields surrounding it on all sides. This is an act of perception. I retire to rest, rise the next morning, and survey the same scene. I recognise it as the same which I observed the day before. This is that form of memory which may be called recognition. I proceed to another house with its garden and adjoining scenery. I recall the former house and mark the points of difference. The former part of this act is pure memory. —*Murphy*, '*Human Mind*,' p. 89.

The word Memory always expresses some modification of that faculty which enables us to treasure up and to preserve for future use the knowledge which we acquire. This faculty implies two things, a capacity of retaining knowledge and a power of recalling it to our thoughts when we have occasion to apply it to use Sometimes our thoughts recur to us spontaneously, in other cases they are recalled by an effort of our will.—*Stewart*, '*Works*,' ii. 349, *seq.*

Essential elements.

It is not very easy to determine what bare memory consists in apart from its adjuncts. Writers on mental science have scarcely entered upon the subject, they have certainly not discussed it It is clear that in every act of memory proper there must be a recollection of self, and of self in a certain state, say perceiving, feeling, or thinking. When an external thing has been observed, or an occurrence witnessed, there will co-exist with the remembrance of self a recollection of the object or event Very frequently the thing perceived fills the mind, and the co-existing reminiscence of self is scarcely attended to. Such, I suppose, must be our original memory Such, I suppose, must be the whole memory of the infant, and hence its floating and uncertain character.—*M'Cosh*, '*Intuitions of the Mind*,' p 175.

An act or state of memory may be defined as that in which the essential elements of an act of previous cognition are more or less perfectly reknown, both objective and subjective, with the relations essential to each These elements are not all recalled with the same distinctness, and hence there are varieties of memory; but it is essential to an act of memory that some portion of each of these elements and relations should be recalled and reknown.

For example: I remember an event which occurred an hour ago—that a friend made me a call, or passed me, as I was walking in the street. What is involved in this act of memory? First of all, I must reproduce the image of my friend as before me, or as he passed; second, I must recall the image or recollection of myself as seeing or conversing with him, perhaps with more or less feeling. Unless both these elements are recalled, the object perceived or in some way cognised, and myself in the act of apprehending and perhaps of feeling—*i.e.*, the objective and subjective elements—the act cannot be an act of memory. If we recall or represent any event or object, and say we remember it, we must also recall ourselves in some act or state related to it. Third, the act of originally knowing the object or event was my act—*i.e.*, I, the same being who now recall and reknow it in the ways described, did know it before. The act of knowing the object, and of having known it, are acts of the *same* being. Fourth, the two acts are in this process also distinguished as before and after, the present as actual, the past, both act and object, as having been actual. This involves the distinctions of before and after, or the relations of succession involving time. Fifth, in the original act of observation I must have been in some place, and the object observed must have sustained some relation to attending or accompanying objects. Neither myself nor the object can ordinarily be recalled without some of these accompaniments involving relations to space. Sixth, the objective and subjective elements, and the relations which they involve, thus recalled as images, must be known to represent realities.—*Porter*, '*Human Intellect*,' p. 300.

Memory implies,—1. A mode of consciousness experienced. 2. The retaining or remaining of that mode of consciousness so that it may subsequently be revived without the presence of its object. 3. The actual revival of that mode of consciousness; and 4. The recognising that mode of consciousness as having formerly been experienced.—*Fleming*, '*Vocab. of Phil.*,' p. 303.

Memory is a complex idea made up of at least two constituents. In the first place, there is the idea of an object, and secondly, there is the idea of the relation of antecedence between that object and some present objects.—*Huxley*, '*Hume*,' p. 97.

It involves belief.

In memory of our own past experience, belief is involved. When I remember, I have present to consciousness ideas which represent past reality. To have ideas simply is to imagine; to have ideas which we are convinced represent past experience is to have imagination *plus* belief, *i.e.*, to remember. It should be observed that we are frequently said to trust our memory, to believe that what we remember is true. This phraseology is objectionable; we cannot properly be said to *trust* our memory, we simply use it. In the very fact of remembering is involved the reference to past reality which is the essence of belief. —*Adamson*, '*Encyclopædia Britannica*,' iii. 533 (ed. ix.).

It is based on consciousness.

It is manifest that the ground of memory is consciousness. The bare fact of memory may be expressed in the sentence, I saw the tree yesterday. But this statement gives rise to the question, How do you know now that you saw it then? The answer to this is not far to seek. I knew that I saw it then; and so I know now that I saw it then. Knowledge once acquired is a constant possession. This is the foundation of memory.—*Murphy*, '*Human Mind*,' p. 92.

Conditions of Memory.

Generally.

The circumstances which have a tendency to facilitate or insure the retention or the recurrence of anything by the memory, are chiefly—*Vividness, Repetition*, and *Attention*. When an object affects us in a pleasant or in a disagreeable manner—when it is frequently or familiarly observed—or when it is examined with attention and interest, it is more easily and surely remembered.—*Fleming*, '*Vocab. of Phil*,' p. 305.

The things which are best preserved by the memory are the things which *please* or *terrify*—which are *great* or *new*—to which much *attention* has been paid—or which have been oft *repeated*,—which are *apt to* the circumstances—or which have many things *related to them*.—*Herbert*, '*De Veritate*,' p. 156.

Vivid impressions.

It is a law of mind that the intensity of the present consciousness determines the vivacity of the future memory. Memory and consciousness are thus in the direct ratio of each other. On the one hand, looking from cause to effect,—vivid consciousness, long memory; faint consciousness, short memory; no consciousness, no memory; and on the other, looking from effect to cause,—long memory, vivid consciousness; short memory, faint consciousness; no memory, no consciousness.—*Hamilton*, '*Metaphysics*,' i. 368.

Attention and repetition.

The connection between memory and attention has been remarked by many authors. It is essential to memory, that the perception or the idea that we would wish to remember should remain in the mind for a certain space of time, and should be contemplated by it exclusively of everything else; and that attention consists partly (perhaps entirely) in the effort of the mind to detain the idea or the perception, and to exclude the other objects that solicit its notice.—*Steuart*, '*Works*,' ii. 123.

It is easier to get by heart a composition after a very few readings, with an attempt to repeat it at the end of each, than after a hundred readings without such an effort.—*Stewart*, '*Works*,' ii. 352.

Attention and repetition help much to the fixing any ideas in the memory; but those which naturally at first make the deepest and most lasting impression, are those which are accompanied with pleasure or pain. Those ideas which are oftenest refreshed by a frequent return of the objects or actions that produce them, fix themselves best in the memory and remain clearest and longest there.—*Locke*, '*Human Understanding*,' ii. x. 3, 6.

Association of Ideas. (See Laws of Association.)

If I think of any case of memory, I shall always find that the idea, or the sensation which preceded the memory, was one of those which are calculated, according to the laws of association, to call up the idea involved in that case of memory; and that it was by the preceding idea, or sensation, that the idea of memory was in reality brought into the mind. I have not seen a person with whom I was formerly intimate for a number of years; nor have I, during all that interval, had occasion to think of him. Some object which had been frequently presented to my senses along with him, or the idea of something with which I have strongly associated the idea of him, occurs to me; instantly the memory of him exists.—*Mill*, '*The Human Mind*,' p. 321.

What is the contrivance to which we have recourse for preserving the memory; that is, for making sure that it will be called into existence, when it is our wish that it should? All men invariably employ the same expedient. They endeavour to form an association between the idea of the thing to be remembered, and some sensation, or some idea, which they know beforehand will occur at or near the time when they wish the remembrance to be in their minds. If this association is formed, and the sensation or the idea, with which it has been formed, occurs; the sensation, or idea, calls up the remembrance; and the object of him who formed the association is attained. To use a vulgar instance; a man receives a commission from his friend, and, that he may not forget it, ties a knot on his handkerchief How is this fact to be explained? First of all, the idea of the commission is associated with the making of the knot. Next, the handkerchief is a thing which it is known beforehand will be frequently seen, and of course at no great distance of time from the occasion on which the memory is desired. The handkerchief being seen, the knot is seen, and this sensation recalls the idea of the commission, between which and itself the association had been purposely formed.—*Mill*, '*The Human Mind*,' p. 323.

Whensoever there is a desire to fix any train in the memory, all men have recourse to one and the same expedient. They practise what is calculated to create a strong association. The grand cause of strong associations is repetition. This, accordingly, is the common resource. If any man, for example, wishes to remember a passage of a book, he repeats it a sufficient number of times. To the man practised in applying the principle of association to the phenomena in which it is concerned, the explication of this process presents itself immediately. The repetition of one word after another, and of one idea after another, gives the antecedent the power of calling up the consequent from the beginning to the end of that portion of discourse, which it is the purpose of the learner to remember

That the remembrance is produced in no other way, is proved by a decisive experiment For, after a passage has been committed to memory in the most perfect manner, if the learner attempts to repeat it in any other order than that, according to which the association was formed, he will fail. A man who has been accustomed to repeat the Lord's Prayer, for example, from his infancy, will, if he has never tried it, find the impossibility of repeating it backwards, small as the number is of the words of which it consists.—*Mill*, '*The Human Mind*,' p. 326.

One of the most obvious and striking questions [in treating of memory] is, what the circumstances are which determine the memory to retain some things in preference to others? Among the subjects which successively occupy our thoughts, by far the greater number vanish, without leaving a trace behind them; while others become, as it were, a part of ourselves, and by their accumulations, lay a foundation for our perpetual progress in knowledge. . . . Memory depends upon two principles of our nature—Attention and the Association of Ideas.—*Stewart*, '*Works*,' ii. 352.

Good health and vigour.

No other mental power betrays a greater dependence on corporeal conditions than memory. Not only in general does its vigorous or feeble activity essentially depend on the health and indisposition of the body, more especially of the nervous system; but there is manifested a connection between certain functions of memory and certain parts of the cerebral apparatus. —*Schmid*, '*Versuch einer Metaphysik der inneren Natur*,' p. 235

How much the constitution of our bodies and the make of our animal spirits are concerned in the fading of our ideas, and whether the temper of the brain makes this difference, that in some it retains the characters drawn on it like marble, in others like freestone, and in others little better than sand, I shall not here inquire, though it may seem probable that the constitution of the body does sometimes influence the memory, since we oftentimes find a disease quite strip the mind of all its ideas, and the flames of a fever in a few days calcine all those images to dust and confusion which seemed to be as lasting as if graved in marble.—*Locke*, '*Human Understanding*,' ii. x. 5

Memory in its exercises is very dependent upon bodily organs, particularly the brain In persons under fever, or in danger of drowning, the brain is preternaturally excited; and in such cases it has been observed that memory becomes more remote and far-reaching in its exercise than under ordinary and healthy circumstances Several authentic cases of this kind are on record. And hence the question has been suggested whether thought be not absolutely imperishable, or whether every object of former consciousness may not, under peculiar circumstances, be liable to be recalled?—*Fleming*, '*Vocab of Phil.*,' p. 307

Loss of the Memory of Words

To this condition the term *Aphasia* has been recently applied. Sometimes the memory of words is impaired merely, so that the patient mistakes the proper terms And in some instances there is an obvious association, though an irrelevant one, between the word used and the word that ought to have been used; thus the case of a clergyman has been lately mentioned to the writer, who continually confuses 'father' and 'son,' 'brother' and 'sister,' 'gospel' and 'epistle,' and the like. But sometimes there is no recognisable relation, so that the patient speaks a most curious jargon. Again, the Memory of only *a particular class of words*, such as nouns or verbs, may be lost; or the patient may remember the letters of which a word is composed, and may be able to *spell* his wants though he cannot speak the *word* itself A very curious affection of the memory is that in which the *sound* of spoken words does not convey any idea to the mind; yet the individual may recognise in a written or printed list of words those which have been uttered by the speaker, the *sight* of them enabling him to understand their meaning Conversely, the sound of the word may be remembered, and the idea it conveys fully appreciated; but the visual memory of its written form may be altogether lost, although the component letters may be recognised —*Carpenter*, '*Mental Physiology*,' pp. 446, 447

Physical Cause of Aphasia

Aphasia follows upon damage to the outgoing fibres leading from the left Auditory and Visual through the Kinæsthetic Word-Centres to the great Motor Ganglion beneath, viz., the Corpus Striatum

It would seem that these two sets of outgoing channels are, at all events in some parts of their course, situated moderately close together, so that they may be destroyed simultaneously by some small lesion, and that too without the implication of outgoing fibres for limb-movements, and consequently without the association of a right-sided paralysis.—*Bastian*, '*The Brain, &c.*,' p. 648.

Mental Activity during Aphasia.

Although it is generally recognised that Aphasia, when serious and of long duration, is always accompanied by mental weakness, there can be no doubt that mental activity persists, even where there are no means of translating the ideas into words or gestures

Patients deprived of only a part of their vocabulary, but unable to find the proper word, replace it by a paraphrase or description For scissors they say 'the things that cut;' for window, 'what you see through.' They designate a man by the place where he lives, by his titles, his profession, inventions which he has made, or books that he has written In the most serious cases we sometimes find the patient able to play at cards with calculation and discretion; others are able to superintend their affairs.—*Ribot*, '*Diseases of Memory*,' p 157

Significance of Memory.

Empirical theory

The thread of consciousness which composes the mind's phenomenal life, consists not only of present sensations but likewise in part of memories and expectations Now what are these? In themselves, they are present feelings, states of present consciousness, and in that respect not distinguished from sensations. They all, moreover, resemble some given sensations or feelings, of which we have previously had experience. But they are attended with the peculiarity that each of them involves a belief in more than its own present existence A sensation involves only this; but a remembrance of sensation, even if not referred to any particular date, involves the suggestion and belief that a sensation, of which it is a copy or representation, actually existed in the past; and an expectation involves the belief, more or less positive, that a sensation or other feeling to which it directly refers, will exist in the future.—*Mill, 'Examination of Sir W. Hamilton,'* p. 241.

Mill's admission as to the ultimate fact in memory.

Our belief in the veracity of Memory is evidently ultimate; no reason can be given for it which does not presuppose the belief and assume it to be well-grounded.—*Mill, 'Examination of Sir W. Hamilton,'* p. 174.

Belief in Memory inconsistent with the empirical Theory of Mind.

Dr. Ward's criticism of J. S. Mill.

You make use of your own past experience,—you make use of other men's experience,—as part of the foundation on which you build. How can you even guess what your past experience has been? By trusting memory. But how do you prove that those various intuitive judgments, which we call acts of memory, *can* rightly be trusted? So far from this being provable by past experience, it must be in such case *assumed* and *taken for granted* before you can have any cognisance of your past experience.

I am at this moment comfortably warm, but I call to mind with great clearness the fact that a short time ago I was very cold. What datum does 'sensation' give me? Simply that I am now warm. What datum does 'consciousness' give? That I have the *present impression* of having been cold a short time ago. But both these data are altogether wide of the mark. The question which I would earnestly beg Mr. Mill to ask himself is this, What is my ground for believing that I *was* cold a short time ago? 'I have the present *impression* of having been cold a short time ago;' this is one judgment. 'I *was* cold a short time ago;' this is a totally distinct and separate judgment. There is no necessary, nor any even probable, connexion between these two judgments,—no ground whatever for thinking that the truth of one follows from the truth of the other,—except upon the hypothesis that my mind is so constituted as accurately to represent past facts. But how will either 'sensation' or 'consciousness,' or the two combined, in any way suffice for the establishment of any such proposition?—*'Nature and Grace,'* pp. 26–28.

Varieties of Memory.

With the progress and development of the powers and activities of the soul, the memory itself advances through separate stages, each of which prepares the way for that which follows, and occupies the place of its natural and logical condition. The memory of the infant differs from the memory of the child; the memory of the child differs from that of the youth; the memory of the man, in each of the several stages of active life, differs from that in the stage which succeeds it. In general, the memory of the person in active life differs from the memory of old age. This must necessarily follow from the very nature of memory when considered as to the materials on which it works, and the laws by which it acts. The memory of an individual can rise no higher than the intellectual and emotional life which furnish the objects which it has to recall. It can take no other direction than that which is indicated by the relations and connections in which these objects are habitually combined. As these objects and relations stand to all men in a certain common order of preparation and evolution, there must consequently be a certain similarity in the order of the stages through which the memory of all is evolved. As there are also special classes of objects and relations that are proper to different classes of men, arising from their peculiar employments and habits of thinking and feeling, each of these classes has a memory that is peculiar to itself. The memory of the artist is very unlike the memory of the mathematician. The memory of the erudite and disciplined thinker differs greatly in its objects and its laws from the memory of the person who has had little culture from reading or thought. Hence there exist many clearly distinguishable *varieties* of memory, if we make nothing of the fact that every individual must have a type of memory which arises from those individual habits of thought and feeling which he can share with no other person.—*Porter*, '*Human Intellect*,' p. 314.

Of all our faculties Memory is generally supposed to be that which nature has bestowed in the most unequal degrees on different individuals. However, the original disparities among men in this respect are by no means so immense as they seem to be at first view. Much is to be ascribed to different habits of attention, and to a difference of selection among the various objects and events presented to their curiosity.—*Stewart*, '*Works*,' ii. 362 *seq*.

Those individuals who possess unusual powers of memory with respect to any one class of objects, are commonly as remarkably deficient in some of the other applications of that faculty. One man is distinguished by a power of recollecting names and dates and genealogies; a second by the facility with which words and combinations of words seem to lay hold of his mind; a third by his memory for poetry; a fourth by his memory for music; a fifth by his memory for architecture, statuary, and painting, and all the other objects of taste which are addressed to the eye.—*Stewart*, '*Works*,' ii. 363.

Good and Bad Memory.

Memory is never perfectly accurate in details.

When complex impressions or complex ideas are reproduced as memories, it is probable that the copies never give all the details of the originals with perfect accuracy, and it is certain that they rarely do so. No one possesses a memory so good, that if he has only once observed a natural object, a second inspection does not show him something that he has forgotten. Almost all, if not all, our memories are therefore sketches, rather than portraits, of the originals—the salient features are obvious, while the subordinate characters are obscure or unrepresented.—*Huxley*, '*Hume*,' p. 94.

Good Memory.

a Its conditions, mental and moral.

To a good memory there are certainly two qualities requisite,—1. The capacity of Retention; and 2. The faculty of Reproduction. But the former quality is the principal one.—*Hamilton*, '*Metaphysics*,' ii. 218.

The qualities of a good memory are, in the first place, to be susceptible; secondly, to be retentive; and thirdly, to be ready. It is but rarely that these three qualities are united in the same person.—*Stewart*, '*Works*,' ii. 364.

It is natural, in this connection, to notice the moral conditions of a good memory. The man who would have a strong and trustworthy memory must always be true to it in his dealings with himself and with other men. He must paint to his own imagination, with scrupulous fidelity, whatever he has witnessed or experienced. He must never so yield to the bias of interest or passion as to strive to persuade himself, even for a moment, that events were different from what he knows they actually were. He must seek to repeat to others the precise words of what he has heard or read, whenever he makes communications by language. Such a moral discipline to internal and external honesty, both implies and enforces a mental discipline to earnest and wide-reaching attention—an attention which does complete justice to every object that comes before it, and which neither slights nor omits anything which ought to be brought to view. An intellect that is regulated and held to its duties by the tension of such a purpose, will act with the precision and certainty of clock-work. Its recollections will be trusted by others because they are trusted by the person himself, and for the best of reasons—because he is true to what he remembers.—*Porter*, '*Human Intellect*,' p. 324.

b. Method may aid memory.

If we wish to fix the particulars of our knowledge very permanently in the memory, the most effectual way of doing it is to refer them to general principles, to arrange them philosophically and associate them according to their relations, such as the relations of Cause and Effect, or of Premises and Conclusion. Ideas which are connected together merely by *casual* relations, present themselves with readiness to the mind, so long as we are forced by the habits of our situation to apply them daily to use; but when a change of circumstances leads us to vary the objects of our attention, we find our old ideas gradually to escape from the recollection; and if it should happen that they escape from it altogether, the only method of recovering them is by renewing those studies by which they were at first acquired. The differences between the philosophical and casual memory constitute the most remarkable of all the varieties.—*Stewart*, '*Works*,' ii. 367, 368, 371.

Sound logic, as the habitual subordination of the individual to the species, and of the species to the genus; a philosophical knowledge of facts under the relation of cause and effect; a cheerful and communicative temper, that disposes us to notice the similarities and contrasts of things, that we may be able to illustrate the one by the other; a quiet conscience; a condition free from anxieties; sound health, and above all (as far as relates to passive remembrance), a healthy digestion; *these* are the best—these are the only ARTS OF MEMORY.—*Coleridge*, '*Biog. Literaria*,' chap. vii.

c. Instances of good memory.

Leibnitz made extracts from every book he read, and added to them whatever reflections they suggested, after which he laid his manuscript aside, and never thought of it more. His memory, which was astonishing in its powers, did not, as in most men, feel itself disburdened of the knowledge which he had committed to writing, but, on the contrary, the exertion of writing seemed to be all that was requisite to imprint it on his memory for ever.—*Bailly*, '*Éloge de Leibnitz*.'

Hortensius, after sitting a whole day at a public sale, gave an account from memory in the evening of all the things sold, with the prices and the names of the purchasers; which account was found on examination to agree in every particular with what had been taken in writing by a notary.—*Stewart*.

There dwelt in the neighbourhood of Padua a young man, a Corsican by birth, and of a good family in that island, who had come thither for the cultivation of civil law. He was a frequent visitor at the house and gardens of Muretus, who, having heard that he possessed a remarkable art or faculty of memory, took occasion, though incredulous in regard to reports, of requesting from him a specimen of his power. He at once agreed; and having adjourned with a considerable party of distinguished auditors into a saloon, Muretus began to dictate words, Latin, Greek, barbarous, significant and non-significant, disjoined and connected, until he wearied himself, the young man who wrote them down, and the audience who were present. 'We were all,' he says, 'marvellously tired.' The Corsican alone was the one of the whole company alert and fresh, and continually desired Muretus for more words, who declared he would be more than satisfied if he could repeat the half of what had been taken down, and at length he ceased. The young man, with his gaze fixed upon the ground, stood silent for a brief season, and then says Muretus, 'Vidi facinus mirificissimum.' Having begun to speak, he absolutely repeated the whole words, in the same order in which they had been delivered, without the slightest hesitation; then, commencing from the last, he repeated them backwards till he came to the first. Then again, so that he spoke the first, the third, the fifth, and so on; did this in any order that was asked, and all without the smallest error. He assured Muretus that he could recite, in the manner I have mentioned, to the amount of thirty-six thousand words. And what is more wonderful, they all so adhered to the mind, that after a year's interval, he could repeat them without trouble.—*Hamilton*, '*Metaphysics*,' ii. 219.

d. Its advantages.

A great memory is the principal condition of bringing before the mind many different representations and notions at once, or in rapid succession.—*Diderot*, '*Lettres sur les Sourds et Muets*.'

A good spontaneous memory, or, as it is often called, a good memory for facts and dates, is generally and correctly regarded rather as a great intellectual convenience than as a decisive indication of intellectual power. It is doubtless true that many persons are distinguished by natural memory who are inferior in capacity for discrimination, judgment, and reasoning. It has become a common observation, Great memory, little common sense. In such cases the power of discerning the higher relations may be either originally deficient, or it may be neglected in consequence of the predominant use of the power to apprehend, and, of course, to recall, objects in the relations that are most obvious. A very energetic mind may be very limited in its apprehensions, and will, of course, be energetic though limited in its memory. It is noticeable also that persons who become eminent in those achievements which are proper to the higher intellectual powers and relations are in early life usually distinguished for the strength and reach of the memory of the eye and the ear. In many such cases extraordinary powers of this sort are observed in the person's own experience gradually to be diminished, till at last they entirely cease as the higher powers of the intellect are completely matured, or are more constantly—in a sense exclusively—exercised. This does not invariably occur. There are striking examples of persons who seem to forget nothing, neither in age nor in youth.—*Porter*, '*Human Intellect*,' p. 306.

e. A good memory is not incompatible with a high degree of intelligence.

There seems no valid ground for the belief that where there is great memory there is not sound judgment. The opinion is refuted by the slightest induction; for we immediately find that many of the individuals who towered above their fellows in intellectual superiority were almost equally distinguished for the capacity of their memory. For intellectual power of the highest order none were distinguished above Grotius and Pascal; and Grotius and Pascal forgot nothing they had ever read or thought. Leibnitz and Euler were not less celebrated for their intelligence than their memory, and both could repeat the whole of the *Æneid*. Ben Jonson tells us that he could repeat all he had ever written, and whole books that he had read. —*Hamilton*, '*Metaphysics*,' ii. 225.

Bad memory.

a. Ideas fade in the memory.

The pictures drawn in our minds are laid in fading colours, and if not sometimes refreshed, vanish and disappear. Thus the ideas, as well as children of our youth, often die before us; and our minds represent to us those tombs to which we are approaching, where, though the brass and marble remain, yet the inscriptions are effaced by time, and the imagery moulders away."—*Locke*, '*Human Understanding*, Bk. ii. c. 10.

b. Causes of the fading.

(1) *The crowding in of new ideas.*

New acquisitions are continually pressing in upon the old, and continually taking place along with them among the modifications of the ego; and so the old cognitions, unless from time to time refreshed and brought forward, are driven back and become gradually fainter and more obscure. The mind is only capable, at any one moment, of exerting a certain quantity or degree of force. In proportion to the greater number of activities in the mind, the less will be the proportion of force which will accrue to each; the feebler, therefore, each will be, and the fainter the vivacity with which it can affect self-consciousness. In these circumstances it is to be supposed that every new cognition, every newly-excited activity, should be in the greatest vivacity, and should draw to itself the greatest amount of force. This force will, in the same proportion, be withdrawn from the earlier cognitions; and it is they, consequently, which must undergo the fate of obscuration. Thus is explained the phenomenon of Forgetfulness or Oblivion.—*Hamilton*, '*Metaphysics*,' ii. 213.

(2.) *Defective attention to want of repetition.*

Some ideas have been produced in the understanding by an object affecting the senses once only, and no more than once; others, that have more than once offered themselves to the senses, have yet been little taken notice of: the mind, either heedless, as in children, or otherwise employed, as in men intent only on one thing, not setting the stamp deep into itself. In these cases ideas in the mind quickly fade, and often vanish quite out of the understanding, leaving no more footsteps or remaining characters of themselves than shadows do flying over fields of corn, and the mind is as void of them as if they had never been there.—*Locke*, '*Human Understanding*,' ii. x. 4.

(3.) *Dormancy of faculty.*

"I never yet heard of any old man whose memory was so weakened by time as to forget where he had concealed his treasure. The aged seem, indeed, to be at no loss in remembering whatever is the principal object of their attention. The faculties of the mind will preserve their powers in old age, unless they are suffered to lose their energy and become languid for want of due cultivation. When Cæcilius, therefore, represents certain veterans as fit subjects for the Comic Muse, he alludes only to those weak and credulous dotards whose infirmities of mind are not so much the natural effects of their years as the consequence of suffering their faculties to lie dormant and unexerted in a slothful and spiritless inactivity.'—*Cicero*, '*De Senectute*,' chap. xi.

c. Is entire forgetfulness possible?

(1.) *Forgotten knowledge may be recovered.*

It is questioned by many whether absolute forgetfulness is possible—whether, at least, we are authorised to affirm that the soul can lose beyond recovery anything which it has known. It is certain that knowledge which has remained out of sight for a long period has often been suddenly recovered. In the excitement of sickness or delirium, in moments of terror or joy, events that had been long unthought of have thronged in upon the memory with the vividness of recent occurrences. A language that had been disused for years, and supposed to be entirely forgotten, has come back to the tongue when the powers were weakened by disease and seemed to be returning to the simplicity of second childhood. Prayers and hymns, the lessons of earliest infancy, though forgotten for all the life since, are repeated at such times fluently and correctly. Even acquisitions that were the least likely to be remembered, and which previously were never known or suspected to have been made, come up as though the soul were inspired to receive strange revelations of its capacities and acquirements.—*Porter*, '*Human Intellect*,' p. 311.

When the mind once knows anything, an interval of duration has no power in itself to abolish the knowledge. This knowledge is, therefore, so far perpetual; and there is no reason whatever in the nature of duration why that which has once been within the experience of the mind may not be recalled at any distance of time, however great.—*Murphy*, '*Human Mind*,' p. 91.

(2.) *Singular instances of this recovery.*

Numerous examples of all these classes of facts have occurred within the observation of the curious, and not a few are recorded in history. The well-known and often-quoted story, which was originally published by Coleridge in his *Biographia Literaria*, is in substance as follows:—A servant girl in Germany was very ill of nervous fever accompanied with violent delirium. In her excited ravings she recited long passages from classical and rabbinical writers which excited the wonder and even terror of all who heard them, the most of whom thought her inspired by a good or evil spirit. Some of the passages which were written down were found to correspond with literal extracts from learned books. When inquiries were made concerning the history of her life, it was found that several years before she had lived in the family of an old and learned pastor in the country who was in the habit of reading aloud favourite passages from the very writers in whose works these extracts were discovered. These sounds, to her unintelligible, were so distinctly impressed upon her memory that, under the excitement of delirious fever, they were reproduced to her mind and uttered by her tongue.

Rev. Timothy Flint, in his *Recollections*, records of himself that, when prostrate by malarious fever, he repeated aloud long passages from Virgil and Homer which he had never formally committed to memory, and of which, both before and after his illness, he could repeat scarcely a line.

Dr. Rush, in his *Medical Inquiries*, says that he once attended an Italian who died in New York of yellow fever, who at first spoke English, at a later period of his illness French, and when near his end Italian only. He records also that he was informed by a Lutheran clergyman that old German immigrants whom he attended in their last illness often prayed in their native tongue, though some of them, he was certain, had not spoken it for many years.

A favourite pupil of the writer, the son of a missionary in Syria, who had spent much of his life in this country, died of yellow fever, and spoke in Arabic—an almost forgotten language—during his last hours.

Dr. Abercrombie tells us that a boy, at the age of four years, received an injury upon the head which made the operation of trepanning necessary. During the operation he was apparently in an unconscious stupor, and after his recovery it was never recalled to his recollection till he was fifteen years old, when, in a delirium occasioned by a fever, he gave to his mother a precise account of the whole transaction, describing the persons who were present, their dress, &c. &c., to the minutest particular.—*Murphy*, '*Human Mind*,' p. 313.

d. Explanation of mistakes of memory.

The question is started, Whence the seeming mistakes of memory? We find at times two honest witnesses giving different accounts of the same transaction. We have all found ourselves at fault in our recollections on certain occasions. I believe we must account for the seeming treachery of the memory in much the same way as we do for the deception of the senses. There ever mingle with our proper recollections more or fewer inferences, and in these there may be errors. In order to clear up the subject we must draw the distinction between our natural or pure reminiscences and those mixed ones in which there are processes of reasoning.—*M'Cosh*, '*Intuitions of the Mind*,' p. 175.

The Cultivation of Memory.

Its capability of improvement.

The improvement of which the mind is susceptible by culture is more remarkable, perhaps, in the case of memory than in that of any other of our faculties.—*Stewart*, '*Works*,' ii. 391.

Rules for its cultivation.

The cultivation of the memory is a subject which has been earnestly discussed by many writers, and is of practical interest to all those who are bent on self-improvement, or are devoted to the education of others. Many complain of a general defect of memory. Others are especially sensible of painful failures in respect to certain classes of objects, as names, dates, facts of history, sentences or passages from authors familiarly read. The question is often anxiously propounded, How can these general or special defects be overcome?

The only practical rules, which can be attained, may be summed up in the following comprehensive directions: 'To remember anything, you must attend to it; and in order to attend, you must either find or create an interest in the objects to be attended to This interest must, if possible, be felt in the objects themselves, as directly related to your own wishes, feelings, and purposes, and not to some remote end on account of which you desire to make the acquisition' For this reason, in entering upon a new study or course of reading, it is often essential to feel that the knowledge which they will give is necessary for ourselves, so that we may be eager to satisfy our minds upon the points which are involved, and may receive what is furnished, with freshness and zest It should never be forgotten, that in memory, what is reproduced is not the object as such, or the object in itself, but the object as apprehended and reacted on by the soul In other words, the soul can recall no more than it makes its own—no more than, in acquiring, it constructs or creates as a spiritual product by its own activity.—*Porter*, '*Human Intellect*,' p. 320

One mode of improving memory is mere exercise This effect of practice upon the memory seems to be an ultimate law of our nature. Another mode is the free use of the principles of association, so as to connect new facts and ideas with each other and with the former objects of our knowledge. Again the natural powers of the memory are greatly aided by habits of classification and arrangement. This is by far the most important improvement of which memory is susceptible A fourth mode is the practice of committing to writing our acquired knowledge —*Stewart*, '*Works*,' ii. 391–404.

We remember most vividly what we have seen; PAINT YOUR IDEAS *therefore, or at any rate* ACQUIRE *distinct and* CLEAR PERCEPTIONS *of them*, one great cause of our confused recollection is our very confused perception. If the eye beholds objects through a mist, how can we be expected to give any clear account of them? on the contrary, objects distinctly beheld are longest retained in the mind, and most vividly recalled; thus also it is with mental perception, and the reflection of the objects upon the understanding

Arrangement or METHOD *greatly assists the understanding and the memory* Sir James Mackintosh is said by Mr Hall to have had so wonderful a memory, that it appeared as if everything in his mind was arranged upon pegs;—an Historical peg, a Natural History peg, a peg for Natural Philosophy, another for Poetry, another for Theology; and he had only to lift his hand and take down the illustration he most needed; this seems very convenient, and there must have been in the man capable of this originally great power of retention, but it resulted also from habit—vigorous habit of arrangement How can there be in that mind selection, and compact and various orderliness, over which no supervision has been exercised? 'Marshal thy notions into a handsome method One will carry twice more weight trussed and packed up in bundles than when it lies untoward flapping and hanging about his shoulders.'

Again—REVIEW *your attainments*, RECALL *your ideas from time to time.* We should not make a sink or sewer of our memory—we must not make our books the sepulchre—the immuring tomb of the soul The miser counts his wealth, the landlord walks over his fields, should not you review the progress you have made from week to week, and from year to year? And review with the pen if you would remember set down upon paper the topics, writing calls forth the attention and elicits thought Dr. Watts has said, 'There is more gained by writing once than by reading five times.'—*Paxton Hood.*

The Benefits of Memory.

It is a source of new knowledge.

By memory we not only retain and recall former knowledge, but we also acquire new knowledge. It is by means of memory that we have the notion of continued existence or duration, and also the persuasion of our personal identity, amidst all the changes of our bodily frame, and all the alterations of our temper and habits.—*Fleming*, '*Vocab. of Phil.*,' p. 306.

Without it all knowledge would be impossible.

If we had no other state of consciousness than sensation we never could have any knowledge, excepting that of the present instant. The moment each of our sensations ceased it would be gone for ever, and we should be as if we had never been.

The same would be the case if we had only ideas in addition to sensations. The sensation would be one state of consciousness, the idea another state of consciousness. But if they were perfectly insulated, the one having no connection with the other, the idea, after the sensation, would give me no more information than one sensation after another. We should still have the consciousness of the present instant, and nothing more. We should be wholly incapable of acquiring experience, and accommodating our actions to the laws of nature. Of course we could not continue to exist.

Even if our ideas were associated in trains, but only as they are in Imagination, we should still be without the capacity of acquiring knowledge. One idea, upon this supposition, would follow another. But that would be all. Each of our successive states of consciousness, the moment it ceased, would be gone for ever. Each of those momentary states would be our whole being.

Such, however, is not the nature of man. We have states of consciousness which are connected with past states. I hear a musical air; I recognise it as the air which was sung to me in my infancy. I have an idea of a ghost; I recognise the terror with which, when I was alone in the dark, that idea, in my childish years, was accompanied. Uniting in this manner the present with the past, and not otherwise, I am susceptible of knowledge. This part of my constitution which is of so much importance to me is memory.—*Mill*, '*Human Mind*,' p. 318.

VI. EXPECTATION.

In the process of perception this plays a very important part. The different qualities of which an object of perception is composed have been so constantly found in our experience united together, that when we perceive any one of them we expect to find the others. . . . Whenever we see an orange we *expect* to find within it what our past experience tells us is likely to be there. Thus, expectation is founded upon memory; and upon the constancy and invariability of the experience with which memory furnishes us will depend the confidence of our expectation. The perfection of expectation is prevision.—*Jardine*, '*Elements of Psychology*,' p. 193.

In anticipation, as in memory, there is, first, the complex idea; next the passage of the mind forwards from the present state of consciousness, the antecedent, to one consequent after another till it comes to the anticipated sensation. Suppose that, as a punishment, a man is condemned to put his finger after two days in the flame of a candle; wherein consists his anticipation? The complex idea of the painful sensation, with all its concomitant sensations and ideas, is the first part of the process. The remainder is the association with this idea of the events, one after another, which are to fill up the intermediate time, and terminate with his finger placed in the flame of the candle. The whole of this association, taken together, comprises the idea of the pain as his pain, after a train of antecedents.

The process of anticipation is so precisely the same, when the sensation is of the pleasurable kind, that I deem it unnecessary to repeat it.—*Mill, 'Human Mind,'* ii. 197, 198.

Analysis of hope and fear.

When a pleasurable sensation is contemplated as future, but not certainly, the state of consciousness is called Hope. When a painful sensation is contemplated as future, but not certainly, the state of consciousness is called Fear. Again: when a pleasurable sensation is anticipated with certainty, we call the state of consciousness Joy. When a painful sensation is thus anticipated, we call it Sorrow. Neither of the two terms is good; because not confined to this signification.—*Mill, 'Human Mind,'* ii. 199, 200.

VII. IMAGINATION.

What is Imagination?

The term is ambiguous.

Imagination is an ambiguous word; it means either the *act* of imagining, or the *product*—*i.e.*, the image imagined.—*Hamilton, Reid's 'Works,'* p. 291.

Imagination has two meanings. It means either some one train, or the potentiality of a train. These are two meanings which it is very necessary not to confound.—*Mill, 'Human Mind,'* ii. 239.

Definitions of the Faculty.

Imagination, in its most extensive meaning, is the faculty *representative* of the phenomena both of the external and internal worlds.—*Hamilton, Reid's 'Works,'* p. 809.

Imagination is not a name of any one idea. I am not said to imagine unless I combine ideas successively in a less or greater number. An imagination, therefore, is the name of a *train*. I am said to have an imagination when I have a train of ideas; and when I am said to imagine, I have the same thing; nor is there any train of ideas to which the term imagination may not be applied.—*Mill, 'Human Mind,'* ii. 239.

The principal elements of Imagination are—(1.) Concreteness; it has for its objects the concrete, the real or the actual, as opposed to abstractions and generalities, which are the matter of science, and occasionally of the practical arts. (2.) Originality or Invention; it is not a mere reproduction of previous forms, but is a constructive process. (3.) The presence of an Emotion; all constructions are for some end, which must be a feeling in the last resort.—*Bain, 'Mental and Moral Science,'* p. 174.

Imagination is a complex power. It includes Conception or simple Apprehension, which enables us to form a notion of those former objects of perception or of knowledge out of which we are to make a selection; Abstraction, which separates the selected materials from the qualities and circumstances which are connected with them in nature; and Judgment or Taste, which selects the materials and directs their combination. To these we may add that particular habit of association to which I give the name of Fancy, as it is this which presents to our choice all the different materials which are subservient to the efforts of the Imagination, and which may, therefore, be considered as forming the groundwork of poetical genius.—*Stewart, 'Works,'* ii. 435 *seq.*

It implies belief.

The imagination of an object is necessarily accompanied with a belief of the existence of the mental representation.—*Hamilton, Reid's 'Works,'* p. 105.

The sphere of Imagination is the finite.

The sphere of the imagination is only the finite. All the pictures which it can construct are of limited objects. It is by means only of such pictures that it can imagine its concepts of the infinite, if it attempts to image them at all. That it attempts thus to image them is evident. That it can adequately picture them no man believes. What is embraced in the concept is the known likeness between the finite and infinite. What is pictured by the image is some limited example of the thought-relation which the image suggests. These pictures may be increased in number, extent, or energy, but this is all.—*—Porter, 'Human Intellect,'* p. 373.

Every one possesses this faculty.

In the comprehensive meaning of the word Imagination, there is no man who has not Imagination, and no man who has it not in an equal degree with any other. Every man imagines, nay, is constantly and unavoidably imagining. He cannot help imagining. He can no more stop the current of his ideas, than he can stop the current of his blood.—*Mill, 'Human Mind,'* ii. 239.

The Functions of Imagination.

It does not strictly speaking create, but it reproduces and combines.

The terms *productive* or *creative* are very improperly applied to Imagination, or the representative faculty of mind. It is admitted on all hands, that Imagination creates nothing, that is, produces nothing new; and the terms in question are, therefore, by the acknowledgment of those who employ them, only abusively applied to denote the operations of Fancy, in the new arrangement it makes of the old objects furnished to it by the senses. The imagination only builds up old materials into new forms.—*Hamilton, 'Metaphysics,'* ii. 262.

I can recall the joys, the hopes, the sorrows, the fears, which at some former time may have moved my bosom. I can do more: I can picture myself, or picture others, in new and unheard-of scenes of gladness or of grief. Not only can I represent to myself the countenance of my friend, I can have an idea of his character and dispositions. I can form a mental picture of the outward scenes in which Shakespeare or Walter Scott places his heroes or heroines; but I can also enter into their thoughts and feelings.

But all these ideas, in the sense of phantasms, are reproductions of past experience in the old forms or in new dispositions. He who has had the use of his eyes at any time can ever after understand what is meant by the colour of scarlet; but the person born blind has not the most distant idea of it in the sense of image; and if pressed for an answer to the question what he supposes it to be, he can come no nearer the reality than the man mentioned by Locke, who likened it to the sound of a trumpet; or than the blind boy of whom I have heard, who when asked whether he would prefer a lilac-coloured or a brown-coloured book, offered as a prize, decided for the lilac, as he supposed it must resemble the lilac-bush, whose odour had been so agreeable to him.—*M'Cosh, 'Intuitions, &c.,'* p. 12.

Modes of Reproduction.

We must distinguish between two chief uses of Imagination. There is the Reproductive Imagination, by which is meant only the power to *represent* past impressions, to hold up before the mind what has been remembered. And there is the Productive Imagination, by which is meant the power to form combinations of such impressions different from any combinations actually experienced. It is this latter which is usually meant by Imagination, when we are speaking of artistic creation; and it implies not only *representation*, but also constructiveness and originality, together with certain emotional elements, mainly æsthetic.—*Ryland, 'Handbook, &c.,'* p. 99.

Order of reproductions.

We may distinguish three principal orders in which Imagination represents ideas:—(1.) The Natural Order, which is that in which we receive the impression of external objects, or the order according to which our thoughts spontaneously group themselves. (2.) The Logical Order, which consists in presenting what is universal, prior to what is contained under it as particular, or in presenting the particulars first, and then ascending to the universal which they constitute. This order is a child of art, it is the result of our will. (3.) The Poetical Order, which consists in seizing individual circumstances, and in grouping them in such a manner that the imagination shall represent them so as they might be offered by the sense. The poetical order is exclusively calculated on effect.—*Ancillon*, '*Essais Philosophiques*,' ii. 152.

Modes of combination by the Imagination.

The following are the most important modes in which the constructive imagination is found to operate:—

1. In imagination, there may be a separation of the parts or qualities of which any object is made up. We can imagine a horse without its head; a flower without its colour or smell; a bird without its wings; a human being without some quality or character which he now possesses.

2. In imagination, parts or qualities thus separated from their natural relations may be recombined so as to form new objects. Centaurs, winged bulls, griffins, &c., are illustrations of this process.

3. In this reconstructive process, the elements of the new object may be greatly and variously modified, may be changed in shape, size, or excellence, either for improvement or deterioration. Conformity to the truth of nature is not at all an essential feature of the products of imagination.

4. In imagination, when we wish to represent to ourselves something unknown, we can do so only by employing elements taken from things known. We are frequently bound to believe in the existence of things which we have not directly known, and probably can never know. In this case the imagination clothes the unknown with forms taken from the known.

5. In the object which the imagination constructs there must be a certain congruity between the elements of which it is made up, in order to render the imaginative act possible. To imagine a square circle, for example, would be impossible.—*Jardine*, '*Psychology*,' p. 196.

There are three different acts in which its creative power is shown. (1.) The imagination can recombine and arrange the constituents of Nature in new forms and products. (2.) It can idealise and apply the relations of objects to extension and time. (3.) It can form and employ an ideal standard for the intensity and the direction of the activity of natural or spiritual agents, and for the material objects and acts which symbolise them.—*Porter*, '*Human Intellect*,' p. 357.

Activity of the Imagination.

In seeking to understand imaginative activity, one needs to distinguish three ingredients, namely, the intellectual, the emotional, and the active or volitional. First of all, imagination is obviously limited by experience and by association. Secondly, it involves the satisfaction of ideal longings, that is, the thirst begotten of the several emotions for a fuller and purer form of delight. Thirdly, it includes a pleasurable volitional activity, as manifested in the pursuit of a hidden meaning, in the anticipation of a coming issue, and so on.—*Sully*, '*Sensation, &c.*,' p. 344.

Products of Imagination.

These are ideals.

The ideals of science and of art, of achievement and of duty, are the products of that form of psychical activity which is properly called the creative imagination. It is *imaginative*, because the representative or imaging power is conspicuously prominent in its functions. It is *creative*, because there is no counterpart in nature from which its objects and products are literally transcribed or copied. It is to be observed, however, that imaging and images are not the sole elements in these processes or products. The imaging power, as such, is limited to the representation of the objects of actual experience, as wholes and as parts The rational and emotional natures are absolutely essential to its existence and its exercise There is properly no creative imagination in which the reason and the feelings are not conspicuous, and in which rational and emotional relations are not recognised and controlling Its *creative function* is rendered possible *by the union of the thinking power with the imaging power*; the joint action of both resulting in these ideal products which address the intellectual and emotional nature.—*Porter*, '*Human Intellect*,' p 361.

Founded on experience.

All ideas, however refined and elevated, are in some sense founded upon and related to the actual experience of each individual. A person born and nurtured upon a plain, who had never seen a hill or a mountain, can scarcely imagine the charm to the eye and the excitement to the mind which such scenery imparts, and would be quite incapable of creating ideal pictures suggested by such materials, or even of appreciating them when framed by others One who has never been upon the sea can neither picture to himself nor to others the wild sublimity of an ocean tempest The Oriental, basking in the heat of an equatorial sun, and always surrounded by the fruits, the foliage, and the flowers that such a sun alone can nourish, cannot form an ideal picture of an arctic winter. Nor can the Scandinavian, out of the pale sunlight of his brightest days, or the most luxuriant vegetation of his starveling summer, construct an adequate representation of the exuberant life and the glowing intensity of a tropical landscape.—*Porter*, '*Human Intellect*,' p. 363.

The Use and Abuse of Imagination.

Its utility is manifested in—

Art.

A strong imagination—that is, the power of building up any ideal object to the mind in clear and steady colours—is a faculty necessary to the poet and to the artist. The vigour and perfection of this faculty are seen not so much in the representation of individual objects as in the representation of systems In the better ages of antiquity the perfection, the beauty, of all works of taste, whether in Poetry, Eloquence, Sculpture, Painting, or Music, was principally estimated from the symmetry or proportion of all the parts to each other and to the whole which they together constituted; and it was only in subservience to the general harmony that the beauty of the several parts was appreciated The reason of this seems to be that in antiquity not the Reason but the Imagination was the more vigorous.—*Hamilton*, '*Logic*,' ii. 131.

Poetry, painting, sculpture, music, and architecture are the usually recognised fine arts. In the whole of these the imagination is exercised in calling up and combining images in the mind fitted to express or to excite some emotion The artist can only employ the materials which nature gives him; and whether he tries merely to imitate nature or to produce something better than nature, his imagination must be employed in moulding, reforming, or idealising natural things.—*Jardine*, '*Psychology*,' p. 201

When the designer cannot repeat his experiments, in order to observe the effect, he must call up in his imagination the scene which he means to produce, and apply to this imaginary scene his taste and his judgment, to ascertain beforehand the effect the objects would produce if they were actually exhibited to his senses. This power forms what Lord Chatham beautifully and expressively called *the prophetic eye of Taste*—that eye which, in the language of Gray, 'sees all the beauties that a place is susceptible of long before they are born; and when it plants a seedling, already sits under the shade of it, and enjoys the effect it will have from every point of view that lies in the prospect.'—*Stewart*, '*Works*,' ii. 437 *seq.*

Literature.

Imagination empowers us to traverse the scenes of all history, and force the facts to become again visible, so as to make upon us the same impression which they would have made if we had witnessed them and in the minor necessities of life to enable us, out of any present good, to gather the utmost measure of enjoyment by investing it with happy associations, and, in any present evil, to lighten it by summoning back the images of other hours, and also to give to all mental truths some visible type in allegory, simile, or personification which shall more deeply enforce them.—*Ruskin*, '*Modern Painters*,' iii, Pt iv. ch. iv. § 6

Our view of any transaction, especially one that is remote in time or place, will necessarily be imperfect, generally incorrect, unless it embrace something more than the bare outline of the occurrences; unless we have before the mind a lively idea of the scenes in which the events took place, the habits of thought and of feeling of the actors, and all the circumstances of the transaction; unless, in short, we can in a considerable degree transport ourselves out of our own age, and country, and persons, and imagine ourselves the agents and spectators.—*Whately*, '*Rhetoric*,' p. 124

The aim of the poet is, by means of words, to conjure up before the mind of his hearer or reader images of such a nature as will excite the special kind of emotion which he desires to excite. There are various species of poetry in which this is attempted, and perhaps it is difficult to find amongst them a common characteristic But, generally speaking, it appears essential to the production of the effect that there should be a certain *illusion* produced on the mind of the hearer. He must be made for the moment to believe in the reality of what he only imagines. The true artist *realises* the products of his imagination.—*Jardine*, '*Psychology*,' p. 202.

Science.

It may perhaps be thought somewhat incongruous to unite imagination with science, as science is usually supposed to deal only with known facts. But the truth is that nearly all the great discoveries of science have been the result of an effort of imagination; and many of the greatest men who have advanced scientific knowledge have been men gifted with a strong constructive imagination. Let us study the part which imagination plays in the progress of scientific discovery. Some phenomenon, say the fall of rain from the clouds, requires to be explained. It is observed that dark clouds appear in the sky; the lightning flashes, the thunder rolls, the rain falls in torrents. The cause of all this is unknown, and people set their imagination at work to think of what the cause may be. In other words they frame an hypothesis —*Jardine*, '*Psychology*,' p. 197

A strong imagination is requisite for the successful cultivation of every scientific pursuit; and, though differently applied, and different in the character of its representations, it may well be doubted whether Aristotle did not possess as powerful an imagination as Homer.—*Hamilton*, '*Logic*,' ii 131.

Invention and Discovery.

Discoverers and inventors have never attained to any high degree of excellence without a considerable share of the faculty of imagination You want to work the rod of a pump by means of a horizontal axis which revolves above it In considering how it is to be effected, innumerable ideas connected with machinery crowd into the mind. A thousand projects are proposed, examined, and rejected, till at last the idea of a crank is hit upon. Its relation to the other parts is immediately perceived, and it becomes a part of the machine.—*Sydney Smith*, '*Moral Phil.*,' p. 87.

There can be no question that to invention imagination is entirely essential, indeed, that, without an active imagination, philosophic invention and discovery are impossible. To invent or discover is always to recombine It is to adjust in new positions, objects or parts of objects which have never been so connected before. The discoverer of a new solution of a problem, or a new demonstration for a theorem in mathematics, the inventor of a new application of a power of nature already known, or the discoverer of a power not previously dreamed of, the discoverer of a new argument to prove or deduce a truth or of a new induction from facts already accepted, the man who evolves a new principle or a new definition in moral or political science—must all analyse and recombine in the mind things, acts, or events, with their relations, in positions in which they have never been previously observed or thought of. This recombination is purely mental. If there be a discovery or invention, there has never before been such a juxtaposition of the materials nor of their parts in the world of fact or in the thoughts of men. These objects and parts are now for the first time brought together in the mind—*i.e.*, the imagination of the discoverer. Every discovery is, in fact, a work of the creative imagination.—*Porter*, '*Human Intellect*,' p. 369.

Oratory.

Imagination is a most legitimate instrument of persuasion. It is an indispensable instrument. The minds of men are sometimes so sluggish that we cannot get them to listen to us unless our case is stated with a warmth and a vigour which the imagination alone can supply. There are many, again, who are not accessible to abstract argument, but who recognise truth at once when it assumes that concrete form with which imagination may invest it; they cannot follow the successive steps of your demonstration, but they admit the truth of your proposition the moment you show them your diagram. Then, again, there are some truths, and these among the greatest, which rest, not upon abstract reasoning, but upon facts. Imagination must make the facts vivid and real.—*Dale*, '*Lectures on Preaching*,' p. 48.

Ethics.

The *practical* or *ethical uses* of the imagination are numerous and elevated. These are sufficiently obvious from the single consideration, that the law of duty is and must be an ideal law: for whether it is or is not fulfilled, it must precede the act which reaches or falls short of itself. Every ethical rule must be a mental creation, an ideal formed by the creative power, and held before the soul as a guide and law. Asserting, as we do, that this law, in general, is the same in its import for all men—so that, in a certain sense, the imagination of every one must create the same general ideal rule, it remains true that the practical ideal of every one is peculiar to himself, and is shared by no other person. This ideal, so far as the particulars of his character and life are concerned, may vary both in its import and in the vividness with which this import is conceived. What each man may become in this and that respect, in wealth, position, knowledge, power, &c., is the romantic ideal of youth and the pleasant dream of later years. The aspirations of endeavour, the visions of hope, and the romances of pure reverie which express more than we dare aspire after or hope to effect, are obviously the work of the creative imagination. If these are conformed to a just ideal of life and character, they are most elevating in their influence. If they are consistent with the conditions of our human nature and our human life, if they are conformed to the physical and moral laws of our nature, and the government and will of God, they are healthful and ennobling. Such ideals can scarcely be too high, or too ardently and steadfastly adhered to. But if they are false in their theory of life and happiness, if they are untrue to the conditions of our actual existence, if they involve the disappointment of our hopes, and discontent with real life, they are the bane of all enjoyment, and fatal to true happiness.—*Porter*, '*Human Intellect*,' p. 371.

The faculty of imagination is a principal source of human improvement. As it delights in presenting to the mind scenes and characters more perfect than those we are acquainted with, it prevents us from ever being completely satisfied with our present conditions or with our past attainments, and engages us continually in the pursuit of some untried enjoyment or of some ideal excellence. Destroy this faculty and the condition of man will become as stationary as that of the brutes.—*Stewart*, '*Works*,' ii. 467.

Religion.

Imagination is the power of perceiving, or conceiving with the mind, things which cannot be perceived by the senses. Its first and noblest use is to enable us to bring sensibly to our sight the things which are recorded as belonging to our future state, or as invisibly surrounding us in this. It is given us that we may imagine the cloud of witnesses in heaven and earth, and see, as if they were now present, the souls of the righteous waiting for us; that we may conceive the great army of the inhabitants of heaven, and discover among them those whom we most desire to be with for ever; that we may be able to vision forth the ministry of angels beside us, and see the chariots of fire on the mountains that gird us round; but, above all, to call up the scenes and facts in which we are commanded to believe, and be present, as if in the body, at every recorded event of the history of the Redeemer.—*Ruskin*, '*Modern Painters*,' iii Pt. iv. ch. iv. § 6.

The imagination is sometimes a source of error and untruth.

Imagination is the source of error, both when it is too languid and when it is too vigorous. If the imagination be weak and languid, the objects represented by it will be given in such confusion and obscurity that their differences are either null or evanescent, and judgment thus rendered either impossible, or possible only with the probability of error. If there be a disproportioned vivacity of imagination, the renewed or newly modified representations make an equal impression on the mind as the original presentations, and are, consequently, liable to be mistaken for these. Even during the perception of real objects, a too lively imagination mingles itself with the observation, which it thus corrupts and falsifies.—*Hamilton*, '*Logic*,' ii. 131, 133.

The abuses of imagination are either in creating, for mere pleasure, false images, where it is its duty to create true ones; or in turning what was intended for the mere refreshment of the heart into its daily food, and changing the innocent pastime of an hour into the guilty occupation of a life.—*Ruskin*, '*Modern Painters*,' iii. pt. iv chap. iv § 6.

The Pleasures of Imagination.

Imagination multiplies the sources of innocent enjoyment. How much has the sphere of our happiness been extended by those agreeable fictions which introduce us to new worlds, and make us acquainted with new orders of being! Imagination loves to indulge herself likewise in painting future scenes, and her prophetic dreams are almost always favourable to happiness. Even when human life presents to us no object on which our hopes can rest, the imagination is invited beyond the dark and troubled horizon which terminates all our earthly prospects, to wander unconfined in the regions of futurity.—*Stewart*, '*Works*,' ii. 469 *sq.*

How happy is that mind in which the belief and reverence of a perfect all-governing mind casts out all fear but the fear of acting wrong; in which serenity and cheerfulness, innocence, humanity, and candour guard the imagination against the entrance of every unhallowed intruder, and invite more amiable and worthier guests to dwell. There shall the Muses, the Graces, and the Virtues fix their abode, for everything that is great and worthy in human conduct must have been conceived in the imagination before it was brought into act. The man whose imagination is occupied by these guests must be wise and he must be happy.—*Reid*, '*Works*,' p. 388.

The Imagination is Capable of Cultivation.

The imagination is capable of steady growth, and requires constant cultivation.

The creative imagination, when most gifted can at first only rise to a certain height above the materials which its experience gives. Its succeeding essays are founded upon those which have been made before, and it proceeds by successive steps, more or less long and high, till it attains the most consummate achievements that are ever reached by man. That there is a striking diversity of original endowment cannot be doubted; but that this is the common law of the development of this power cannot be denied. It is shown to be clearly true from the nature of the power itself, as well as from the history of those who have been most distinguished for their achievements in poetry, fiction, and art.—*Porter*, '*Human Intellect*,' p. 364.

IX.

THOUGHT.

I. THE TERM.

Variously applied.

The term *thought* is applied to a great variety of processes, which are familiarly known as *abstraction*, *generalisation*, *naming*, *judging*, *reasoning*, *arranging*, *explaining*, and *accounting for*. These processes are often grouped together, and called the logical or rational processes.—*Porter*, '*The Human Intellect*,' p. 377.

Two Senses.

The term *thought* is used in two significations of different extent. In the wider meaning, it denotes every cognitive act whatever; by some philosophers, as Descartes and his disciples, it is even used for every mental modification of which we are conscious, and thus includes the Feelings, the Volitions, and the Desires. In the more limited meaning, it denotes only the acts of the Understanding properly so-called. It is in this more restricted signification that thought is said to be the object-matter of Logic.—*Hamilton*, '*Logic*,' i. 12.

Thought is Mediate Knowledge.

There are a great many things which we know although they are not immediately under the observation of our senses; there are a great many things apparently very different from one another which we connect together in various ways in our minds; there are a great many things which we firmly believe although they have never been immediately known to us at all. Knowledge and belief of these various kinds are the result of a process which we have called Elaboration, and which has been variously denominated Thought, Reasoning, Reflection, and so on.—*Jardine*, '*Psychology*,' p. 225.

Nature of Thought according to

Hobbes.

All thinking is a combining and separating, an adding and subtracting of mental representations; to think is to reckon.—*Ueberweg*, '*Hist. of Phil.*,' ii. 40.

Hume.

The creative power of thought extends no further than to the faculty of combining, transposing, augmenting, or diminishing the material furnished by the senses and by experience. All the materials of thought are given us through external or internal experience, only their combination is the work of the understanding or the will.—*Ueberweg*, '*Hist. of Phil.*,' ii. 132.

Ulrici.

The question: What does thought mean? leads to the following propositions, in which the fundamental qualifications of thought are formulated. (1.) Thought is activity. But the conception of activity is a simple conception which cannot be defined. (2.) In addition to productivity, which is a mark of thinking, as of all activity, a specific mark of thought is the act of distinguishing, so that thought may be defined as distinguishing activity, though not as the mere act of distinguishing. (3.) To these may be added, as a third qualification, that thought, by exercising this distinguishing activity upon itself, becomes consciousness and self-consciousness, a result which may be reached either independently, or through the co-operation of others. (4.) Since thought is a distinguishing activity, fourthly, it can exist only in distinctions, *i.e.*, we can only have a thought when and in so far as we distinguish it from another thought; hence pure thought, *i.e.*, thought without content, is no thought, and all real thinking involves multiplicity in thought. (5.) Finally, in the fact of thought and of knowledge is contained the certainty that it is possible for thought to know in its true nature the object of thought (at least when this object is itself).—*Ueberweg*, '*Hist. of Phil.*,' ii. 300.

Sir W. Hamilton.

The distinctive peculiarity of thinking in general is that it involves the cognition of one thing by the cognition of another. All thinking is, therefore, a mediate cognition; we know one object only through the knowledge of another. As one object is only known through another, there must always be a plurality of objects in every single thought.—'*Logic*,' i. 75.

Mansel.

Thought proper, as distinguished from other facts of consciousness, may be adequately described as the act of knowing or judging of things by means of concepts.—'*Prolegomena Logica*,' p. 22.

We have in the complete exercise of thought three successive representations. The sign is representative of the notion; the notion is representative of the image; and the image is representative of the object from which the notion was formed. —'*Metaphysics*,' p. 39.

Forms of Thought, according to Kant (See CATEGORY).

The forms of thought are the twelve categories or original conceptions of the understanding, on which all the forms of our judgments are conditioned. They are: unity, plurality, totality,—reality, negation, limitation,—substantiality, causality, reciprocal action,—possibility, existence, necessity.—*Ueberweg*, '*Hist. of Phil.*,' ii. 157.

Formal Perfection of Thought

This is made up of the three virtues or characters:—(1.) Of Clearness; (2.) Of Distinctness; (3.) Of Harmony.—*Hamilton*, '*Logic*,' ii. 9.

Range and Dignity of Thought.

Its Range.

It is by thought only that we can form those conceptions of number and magnitude which are the postulates and the materials of mathematical science. By thinking, we both enlarge and rise above the limited and transient information which is gained by single acts of consciousness and sense-perception, as we lay hold of that in them which is universal and permanent. By thought we know effects by their causes, and causes through their effects, we believe in powers whose actings only we can directly discern, and infer powers in objects which we have never tested or observed; we explain what has happened by referring it to laws of necessity or reason, and we predict what will happen by rightly interpreting what has occurred. By thinking we rise to the unseen from that which is seen, to the laws of nature from the facts of nature, to the laws of spirit from the phenomena of spirit, and to God from the universe of matter and spirit, whose powers reveal His energy, and whose ends and adaptations manifest His thoughts and character.—*Porter, 'The Human Intellect,'* p. 377.

Its Dignity

Thought qualifies us for our noblest functions. It makes us capable of language, by which we communicate what we know and feel for the good of others, or record it for another generation; of science, as distinguished from and elevated above the observation and remembrance of single and isolated facts; of forecast, as we learn wisdom by experience; of duty, as we exalt ourselves into judges and lawgivers over the inward desires and intentions; of law, as we discern its importance and bow to its authority; and of religion, as we believe in and worship the Unseen, whose existence and character we interpret by His works and learn from His Word.—*Porter, 'The Human Intellect,'* p. 378.

Theory that Thought is Transformed Sensation.

If a multitude of sensations operate at the same time with the same degree of vivacity, or nearly so, man is then only an animal that feels; experience suffices to convince us that then the multitude of impressions takes away all activity from the mind. But let only one sensation subsist, or without entirely dismissing the others, let us only diminish their force; the mind is at once occupied more particularly with the sensation which preserves its vivacity, *and that sensation becomes attention*, without its being necessary for us to suppose *anything else in the mind*. If a new sensation acquire greater vivacity than the former, it will become in its turn attention. But the greater the force which the former had, the deeper the impression made on us, and the longer it is preserved. Experience proves this. Our capacity of sensation is therefore divided into the sensation we have had and the sensation which we now have; we perceive them both at once, but we perceive them differently: the one seems as past, the other as present. The name of *sensation* designates the impression actually made upon our senses; and it takes that of *memory* when it presents itself to us as a sensation which has formerly been felt. Memory is only the transformed sensation. When there is double attention there is *comparison*, for to be attentive to two ideas and to compare them is the same thing. But we cannot compare them without perceiving some difference or some resemblance between them; to perceive such relations is *to judge*. The act of comparing and judging are therefore only attention; it is thus that sensation becomes successively attention, comparison, judgment.—*Condillac, quoted by Lewes, 'History of Philosophy,'* ii. 351.

II. ABSTRACTION.

Definitions.

Abstraction is the power of considering certain qualities or attributes of an object apart from the rest.—*Stewart, 'Works,'* ii. 162.

Abstraction means etymologically the active withdrawal (of attention) from one thing in order to fix it on another thing (Lat. *ab* and *traho*). Although we commonly speak of abstraction in reference to turning away from differences to similarities, the same process shows itself in other forms. Thus, in looking at a face we may withdraw attention from the eyes and fix it on some less impressive feature. If two things (*e.g.*, two sheep) are very like, we need to make an effort of abstraction in order to overlook the similarities and attend to the differences.—*Sully, 'Outlines of Psychology,'* p. 343.

Process.

Archbishop Thomson analyses the process into several steps, the name of the principal act being given to the whole:—(1.) 'Comparison or the act of putting together two or more single objects with a view to ascertain how far they resemble each other. (2.) Reflection or the ascertainment of their points of resemblance and their points of difference. (3.) Abstraction or the separation of the points of agreement from those of difference, that they may constitute a new nature, different from, yet including, the single objects.'—'*Laws of Thought*,' p. 75.

Bain states it thus:—'The first stage in abstraction is to identify and compare a number of objects possessing similarity in diversity. The second is to attend to the points of agreement of resembling things, and to neglect the points of difference, as when we think of the light of the heavenly bodies.'—'*Mental and Moral Science*,' p. 176.

Abstraction as a Mental Process is the Correlative of Attention.

Abstraction is exclusive attention. When things are found to agree or to disagree in certain respects, the consciousness is, by an act of volition, concentrated upon the objects which thus partially agree, and in them, upon those qualities in or through which they agree. This concentration constitutes an act of attention. The result of attention, by concentrating the mind upon certain qualities, is thus to withdraw or abstract it from all else. Attention fixed on one object is tantamount to a withdrawal, to an abstraction, of consciousness from every other.—*Hamilton*, '*Logic*,' i. 123.

Hence Abstraction is of two kinds.

Dobrisch observes that the term *abstraction* is used sometimes in a psychological, sometimes in a logical sense. In the former we are said to abstract the attention from certain distinctive features of objects presented. In the latter, we are said to abstract certain portions of a given concept from the remainder.—*Mansel*, '*Prolegomena Logica*,' note; p. 26, p. 30 in Ed. ii.

The Power of Abstraction separates Man from Brutes.

Brutes abstract not. This, I think, I may be positive in, that the power of abstracting is not at all in them, and that the having of general ideas is that which puts a perfect distinction betwixt man and brutes, and is an excellency which the faculties of brutes do by no means attain to; for it is evident we observe no footsteps in them of making use of general signs for universal ideas; from which we have reason to imagine that they have not the faculty of abstracting, or making general ideas, since they have no use of words, or any other general signs.—*Locke*, '*Human Understanding*,' Book ii. chap. xi. sect. 10.

Uses of Abstraction.

Abstraction tends to the increase of knowledge.

If we will warily attend to the motions of the mind, and observe what course it usually takes in its way to knowledge, we shall, I think, find that the mind having got an idea which it thinks it may have use of either in contemplation or discourse, the first thing it does is to abstract it, and get a name to it, and so lay it up in its storehouse, the memory, as containing the essence of a sort of things, of which that name is always to be the mark. If the mind should proceed by and dwell only upon particular things, its progress would be very slow, and its work endless; therefore, to shorten its way to knowledge and make each perception more comprehensive, the mind binds the things into bundles, and ranks them so into sorts that what knowledge it gets of any of them it may thereby with assurance extend to all of that sort, and so advance by larger steps in that which is its great business, knowledge.—*Locke*, '*Human Understanding*,' Book ii. chap. xxxii. sect. 6.

It avails in both arts and sciences.

A carpenter considers a log of wood with regard to hardness, firmness, colour, and texture; a philosopher, neglecting these properties, makes the log undergo a chemical analysis, and examines its taste, its smell, and component principles; the geometrician confines his reasoning to the figure, the length, breadth, and thickness.

Thus the process of abstraction is familiar to most minds —*Kames, 'Elements of Criticism,'* ii 533

Abstractions have no separate existence apart from the mind

There is a strong tendency in the mind to ascribe separate existence to abstractions; the motive resides in the Feelings, and is favoured by the operation of language We are apt to expect every word to have a thing corresponding —*Bain, 'Mental and Moral Science,'* p 180

The idea of their separate existence is favoured by the ordinary conception of the process.

It is agreed on all hands that 'the qualities' or modes of things do never really exist each of them apart by itself, and separated from all others, but are mixed, as it were, and blended together, several in the same object. But, we are told, the mind being able to consider each quality singly, or abstracted from those other qualities with which it is united, does by that frame to itself abstract ideas For example, there is perceived by sight an object extended, coloured, and moved: this mixed or compound idea the mind resolving into its simple, constituent parts, and viewing each by itself, exclusive of the rest, does frame the abstract ideas of extension, colour, and motion. Not that it is possible for colour or motion to exist without extension, but only that the mind can frame to itself by *abstraction* the idea of colour exclusive of extension, and of motion exclusive of both colour and extension —*Berkeley, 'Principles of Human Knowledge,'* intro 7.

Abstract ideas so conceived do not exist

Whether others have this wonderful faculty of abstracting their ideas, they best can tell For myself, I find indeed I have a faculty of imagining, or representing to myself, the idea of those particular things I have perceived, and of variously compounding and dividing them I can imagine a man with two heads, or the upper parts of a man joined to the body of a horse I can consider the hand, the eye, the nose, each by itself abstracted or separated from the rest of the body But then whatever hand or eye I imagine, it must have some particular shape and colour Likewise the idea of a man that I frame to myself must be either of a white, or a black, or a tawny, a straight, or a crooked, a tall, or a low, or a middle-sized man I cannot by any effort of thought conceive the abstract idea of man And it is equally impossible for me to form the abstract idea of motion distinct from the body moving, and which is neither swift nor slow, curvilinear nor rectilinear, and the like may be said of all other abstract general ideas whatsoever To be plain, I own myself able to abstract in one sense, as when I consider some particular parts or qualities separated from others, with which though they are united in some object, yet it is possible they may really exist without them But I deny that I can abstract from one another, or conceive separately, those qualities which it is impossible should exist so separated; or that I can frame a general notion, by abstracting from particulars in the manner aforesaid—which last are the two proper acceptations of *abstraction.* And there is ground to think most men will acknowledge themselves to be in my case.—*Berkeley, 'Principles of Human Knowledge,'* intro 10.

Bishop Berkeley's argument is, as far as it goes, irrefragable —*Hamilton, 'Lectures,'* ii 298

Locke practically admits the absurdity of this doctrine, although he pleaded for it He says, 'General ideas are fictions and contrivances of the mind that carry difficulty with them, and do not so easily offer themselves as we are apt to imagine. For example, does it not require some pains and skill to form the general idea of a triangle? (which is yet none of the most abstract, comprehensive, and difficult) for it must be neither oblique nor rectangle, neither equilateral, equicrural, nor scalenon, but all and none of these at once.'—*Locke,*

'*Human Understanding*,' bk. iv. chap. vii. § 9.

'If any man has the faculty of framing in his mind such an idea of a triangle as is here described, it is in vain to pretend to dispute him out of it, nor would I go about it.'—*Berkeley*, '*Principles of Human Knowledge*,' introd. 13.

III. ABSTRACT IDEAS.

Their Nature.

The generic ideas which are formed from several similar but not identical complex experiences, are what are commonly called *abstract* or *general* ideas. Berkeley endeavoured to prove that all general ideas are nothing but particular ideas annexed to a certain term which gives them a more extensive signification and makes them recall, upon occasion, other individuals which are similar to them. Hume says that he regards this as 'one of the greatest and most valuable discoveries that has been made of late years in the republic of letters,' and endeavours to confirm it in such a manner that it shall be 'put beyond all doubt and controversy.' I may venture to express a doubt whether he has succeeded in his object.—*Huxley*, '*Hume*,' pp. 95, 96.

An abstract notion is a consciousness of some quality or aspect of an object considered without reference to others. When a quality of which an abstract notion might be formed is cognised in actual connection with a certain set of other phenomena the cognition is a perception; the notion of the quality loses its abstractness, it becomes concreted with the other phenomena. The notion of a quality loses its abstractness also when it becomes general, but in this case it is conceived as in possible connection with numerous sets of phenomena. Thus the cognition expressed in 'I perceive this quadruped,' implies the connection of four-footedness with an individual set of phenomena; while the cognition, 'I conceive a quadruped' implies the connection of the same quality, not with any definite set of actual phenomena but with an indefinite number of possible phenomena. In other words, the notion of a quality which in itself is an abstract notion becomes general when it is thought as applying to various individuals, as it is singular when it applies only to one.—*Clark Murray*, '*Psychology*,' pp. 190, 191.

How they are formed.

The mind has the high capacity of forming abstract and general notions. Out of the concrete it can form the abstract notion. I can see or image a lily only as with both a shape and colour, but I can in thought contemplate its whiteness apart from its form. Having seen a number of beasts with four limbs, I can think about a class of animals agreeing in this that they are all quadrupeds. It appears then that the mental image and the abstract or general notion are not the same. The former is an exercise of the reproductive powers, recalling the old or putting the old in new collocations. The other is the result of an exercise of thought, separating the part from the whole, or contemplating an indefinite number of objects as possessing common qualities. If the one may be called the phantasm, the other, in contradistinction, may be denominated the notion or concept, or, to designate it more unequivocally, the logical notion or concept. —*M'Cosh*, '*Intuitions of the Mind*,' p. 14.

When several complex impressions which are more or less different from one another (let us say that out of ten impressions in each six are the same in all, and four are different from all the rest) are successively presented to the mind, it is easy to see what must be the nature of the result. The repetition of the six similar impressions will strengthen the six corresponding elements of the complex idea, which will, therefore, acquire greater vividness while the four differing impressions of each will not only acquire no greater strength than they had at first but, in accordance with the law of association, they will all tend to appear at once, and will thus neutralise one another.

This mental operation may be rendered

comprehensible by considering what takes place in the formation of compound photographs, when the images of the faces of six sitters, for example, are each received on the same photographic plate, for a sixth of the time requisite to take one portrait. The final result is that all those points in which the six faces agree are brought out strongly, while all those in which they differ are left vague, and thus what may be termed a *generic* portrait of the six, in contradistinction to a *specific* portrait of any one, is produced.

Thus our ideas of single complex impressions are incomplete in one way, and those of numerous, more or less similar, complex impressions are incomplete in another way; that is to say, they are *generic*, not *specific*. —*Huxley*, '*Hume*,' p. 94.

Their Relation to General Notions.

Every abstract notion implies a process of separation, every general notion implies a process of comparison; and both one and other proceed on a previous knowledge which has come within the range of our consciousness.—*M'Cosh*, '*Intuitions of the Mind*,' p. 16.

Some of the laws involved in the formation both of the Abstract and General Notion are these. In regard to the former, (1) the Abstract implies the Concrete, (2) when the Concrete is real the Abstract is also real; (3) when the Abstract is an attribute it has no independent reality, its reality is simply in the Concrete objects. Again in regard to the General Notion, (1) The Universal implies the Singulars; (2) when the Singulars are real the Universal is also real, (3) the reality of the Universal consists in the objects possessing common marks.—*M'Cosh*, '*Intuitions of the Mind*,' p. 446.

IV. GENERALISATION.

Two Meanings.

The term generalisation, as commonly used, includes two processes which are of different character, but are often closely associated together. In the first place, we generalise when we recognise even in two objects a common nature. We cannot detect the slightest similarity without opening the way to inference from one case to the other. Drops of water scattered by the oar in the sun, the spray from a water-wheel, the dewdrops lying on the grass in the summer morning, all display a similar phenomenon. No sooner have we grouped together these apparently diverse instances than we have begun to generalise. A second process, to which the name of generalisation is often given, consists in passing from a fact or partial law to a multitude of unexamined cases which we believe to be subject to the same conditions. Having observed that many substances assume, like water and mercury, the three states of solid, liquid, and gas, and having assured ourselves by frequent trial that the greater the means we possess of heating and cooling, the more substances we can vaporise and freeze, we pass confidently in advance of fact, and assume that all substances are capable of these three forms.—*Jevons*, '*Principles of Science*,' p. 597.

Distinguished from

Abstraction.

Generalisation implies abstraction; but it is not the same thing, for there may be abstraction without generalisation. When we are speaking of an individual, it is usually an abstract notion that we form; *e.g.*, suppose we are speaking of the present King of France, he must *be* either at Paris or elsewhere; sitting, standing, or in some other posture, and in such and such a dress, &c. Yet many of these circumstances, which are regarded as *non-essential to the individual*, are quite disregarded by us; and we abstract from them what we consider as essential, thus forming an abstract notion of the individual. Yet there is here no generalisation.—*Whately*, '*Logic*,' p. 84.

On this passage Archbishop Thomson remarks: 'A great error lies hid in it—

that of not perceiving that the power of separating circumstances, called essential to the individual, from those which are not so, results from former generalisations. How do we know that 'sitting' or 'standing' is not essential to a king? By prior generalisation, by the help of the conception we have formed of a king already.—'*Laws of Thought*,' p. 105.

Analogy.

There is no distinction but that of degree between what is known as reasoning by generalisation and reasoning by analogy. In both cases, from certain observed resemblances, we infer, with more or less probability, the existence of other resemblances. In generalisation the resemblances have great extension and usually little intension, whereas in analogy we rely upon the great intension, the extension being of small amount. In analogy we reason from likeness in many points to likeness in other points.—*Jevons*, '*Principles of Science*,' p. 596.

Results of Generalisation.

Concepts or general notions.

Generalisation is the process through which we obtain what are called general or universal notions. A general notion is nothing but the abstract notion of a circumstance in which a number of individual objects are found to agree, that is, to resemble each other. In so far as two objects resemble each other, the notion we have of them is identical, and, therefore, to us the objects may be considered as the same. Accordingly, having discovered the circumstance in which objects agree, we arrange them by this common circumstance into classes, to which we also usually give a common name,—*Hamilton*, '*Metaphysics*,' ii. 294.

Laws.

The law of gravitation is exemplified in the fall of a single stone to the ground. But many stones and other heavy bodies must have been observed to fall before the fact was generalised and the law stated. And in the process of generalising there is involved a principle which experience does not furnish. Experience, how extensive soever it may be, can only give the particular, yet from the particular we rise to the general, and affirm not only that all heavy bodies which have been observed, but that all heavy bodies, whether they have been observed or not, gravitate. This is a principle furnished by reason.—*Fleming*, '*Vocab. of Phil.*,' p. 206.

Value of Generalisation.

As an Art of Discovery.

The Arts and Methods of Discovery embrace Facts and Reasonings on Facts, which are all comprehended in the one process, *generalisation*. A number of individual observations being supposed, the next thing is to discover agreements among them—to strike out identities wherever there are points to be identified; those identities ending either in Notions or in General Principles.—*Bain*, '*Logic, Induction*,' p. 414.

For the furtherance of knowledge.

It might seem that if we know particular facts there can be little use in connecting them together by a general law. The particulars must be more full of useful information than an abstract general statement. But in reality we never do obtain an adequate knowledge of particulars until we regard them as cases of the general. Not only is there a singular delight in discovering the many in the one, and the one in the many, but there is a constant interchange of light and knowledge. The undulatory theory of light might have been unknown at the present day had not the theory of sound supplied hints by analogy.—*Jevons*, '*Principles of Science*,' p. 599.

V. CONCEPTION.

Its Nature as a Mental Operation.

The term is frequently used both for a mental operation and its product. For the product, however, the term 'concept' is now generally employed. The mental operation alone will be considered in this section. See CONCEPT.

Conception means a taking up in bundles, or grasping into unity.—*Hamilton*, '*Metaphysics*,' ii. 262.

The word *Conception* is often used not only for the act of *forming* a concept but for the act of individualising it, or calling up in imagination an object which exemplifies it. This seems to be in fact the ordinary application of the verb to *conceive* as well as of the adjectives *conceivable* and *inconceivable*.—*Monck*, '*Sir W. Hamilton*,' p. 172.

Stewart usurps the word *conception* in a very limited meaning, in a meaning which is peculiar to himself, viz., for the simple and unmodified representation of an object presented in Perception. Reid again vacillates in the signification he attaches to this term,—using it sometimes as a synonym for Imagination, sometimes as comprehending not only Imagination, but Understanding and the object of Understanding. In this latter relation alone is found its correct and genuine signification. It means the act of conceiving.—*Hamilton*, '*Logic*,' i. 40.

Conception consists in a conscious act of the understanding, bringing any given object or impression into the same class with any number of other objects or impressions, by means of some character or characters common to them all. We *comprehend* a thing when we have learnt to comprise it in a known class.—*Coleridge*, '*Church and State*,' p. 4.

Conception is the forming or bringing an image or idea into the mind by an effort of will. It is distinguished from *Sensation* and *Perception*, produced by an object present to the senses; and from *imagination*, which is the joining together of ideas in new ways; it is distinguished from *memory* by not having the feeling of past time connected with the idea.—*Taylor*, '*Elements of Thought*.'

VI. CONCEPT.

The Term.

Its meaning.

Concept signifies that which is grasped or held together, and refers us to the act by which different similar attributes are treated as one, or the same act by which separate individual beings are united as one by their common attribute or attributes. If ten patches of red colour, of the same form and dimensions, were presented to the eye, the mind might gather, or conceive, or grasp them together, by their common redness, and form a general notion or concept of them.—*Porter*, '*The Human Intellect*,' pp. 391, 388.

Defined.

A concept is a collection of attributes, united by a sign, and representing a possible object of intuition.—*Mansel*, '*Prolegomena Logica*,' p. 60.

A concept is the cognition or idea of the general character or characters, point or points, in which a plurality of objects coincide.—*Hamilton*, '*Logic*,' i. 122.

Concept is convertible with *general notion*, or more correctly, *notion* simply.—*Hamilton*, '*Discussions, &c.*'

But though the words *concept* and *notion* are convertible with each other, they denote a different aspect of the same simple operation. Notion denotes being relative to and expressing the apprehension—the remarking, the taking note of, the resembling attributes in objects; *concept*, the grasping up or synthesis of these in the unity of thought. —*Hamilton*, '*Logic*,' i. 130.

A concept, which is defined by Sir W. Hamilton as 'a bundle of attributes,' does not signify the mere fact of resemblance between objects; it signifies our mental representation of that in which they resemble. —*Mill*, '*Examination of Hamilton*,' p. 375.

The term concept should be reserved to express what we comprehend but cannot picture in imagination, such as a relation, a general term, &c.—*Reid*, '*Works*,' p. 291.

What it includes.

The Class-Notion always includes both objects and attributes, objects having a resemblance, and common attributes possessed by them. So far as it embraces objects, it is said to have Extension. So far as it contains attributes, it is said to have Comprehension or Intension. As we multiply the marks or attributes, there must be fewer objects possessing them. As we multiply the objects, they must have fewer common marks. [Thus the term *element* may be applied to a larger number of objects than the term *metal*, because it possesses fewer attributes or common marks than *metal*.]—*M'Cosh*, '*Examination of Mill*,' p. 274.

Classification of Concepts

As Concrete and Abstract.

Concepts are distinguished as concrete and abstract. The concrete notion contemplates attributes, and is applied to beings existing. The abstract notion treats an attribute as though it were itself such a being. *Man* and *human* are concrete; *humanity* is an abstract notion.—*Porter*, '*The Human Intellect*,' p. 394.

A distinction of some importance may be drawn between two kinds of Concepts. In the one the class is determined by a single attribute, or by it together with the attributes implied in it. Such are the classes designated by adjectives, as generous, faithful, virtuous—pointing to one quality of an object, along with those that may be involved in that quality. In other cases the Comprehension of the class consists of an aggregate of attributes. Thus we cannot fix on any one attribute of the class Man, and derive all the others from it. Rationality is one quality, but he has many others. The one kind of notions I would be inclined to call the Generalised Abstract. The other I call the Generalised Concrete.—*M'Cosh*, '*Examination of Mill*,' p. 282.

As Pure, Empirical, and Mixed.

Kant and his followers applied the word *concept* to notions which are general without being absolute. They say these are of three kinds:—1. *Pure concepts*, which borrow nothing from experience; as the notions of cause, time, and space. 2. *Empirical concepts*, which are altogether derived from experience; as the notion of colour or pleasure. 3. *Mixed concepts*, composed of elements furnished partly by experience, and partly by the pure understanding.—*Fleming*, '*Vocab. of Phil.*,' p. 99.

General Characters of Concepts

A concept affords only inadequate knowledge.

A concept involves the representation of a part only of the various attributes or characters of which an individual object is the sum; and, consequently, affords only a one-sided and inadequate knowledge of the things which are thought under it. It is evident that when we think of Socrates by any of the concepts—*Athenian*, *Greek*, *European*, *man*, *biped*, *animal*, *being*—we throw out of view the far greater number of characters of which Socrates is the complement, and those, likewise, which more proximately determine or constitute his individuality.—*Hamilton*, '*Logic*,' i. 127.

A concept cannot be depicted to sense or imagination.

A mental picture of a mountain is one thing, and a general notion of the class mountain is a very different thing. All our cognitions by the senses or the consciousness, and all our subsequent images of them in memory or imagination, are singular and concrete; that is, they are of individual things, and of things with an aggregate of qualities. I can see or picture to myself an individual man of a certain form or character, but I cannot perceive nor adequately represent in the phantasy the class man. I can see or imagine a piece of magnetised iron, but I cannot see or imagine the polarity of the iron apart from the iron.—*M'Cosh*, '*Intuitions of the Mind*,' p. 16.

A concept is dependent on language.

The concept, formed by an abstraction of the resembling from the non-resembling qualities of objects, would fall back into the confusion and infinitude from which it has been called out, were it not rendered permanent for consciousness by being fixed and ratified in a verbal sign.—*Hamilton*, '*Logic*,' i. 137.

No one, without the aid of symbols, can advance beyond the individual objects of sense or imagination. In the presence of several individuals of the same species, the eye may observe points of similarity between them; and in this no symbol is needed; but every feature thus observed is the distinct attribute of a distinct individual, and however similar, cannot be regarded as identical. For example: I see lying on the table before me a number of shillings of the same coinage. Examined severally, the image and superscription of each is undistinguishable from that of its fellow; but in viewing them side by side, *space* is a necessary condition of my perception; and the difference of locality is sufficient to make them distinct, though similar, individuals. To find a representative which shall embrace them all at once, I must divest it of the condition of occupying space; and this, experience assures us, can only be done by means of *symbols*, verbal or other, by which the concept is fixed in the understanding. Such, for example, is a verbal description of the coin in question, which contains a collection of attributes freed from the condition of locality, and hence from all resemblance to an object of sense.—*Mansel*, '*Prolegomena Logica*,' pp. 15–17.

General notions require to be fixed in a representative sign. The general notion, as such, is not a sensible image, but an intelligible relation; and such a relation, as far as our experience can testify, cannot be apprehended without the aid of *language*—*i.e.*, of some system of signs, verbal or other. Language in this sense appears to be necessary, not merely to the communication, but even to the formation of thought. —*Mansel*, '*Metaphysics*,' p. 39.

A concept is known by means of some individual example.

The mind cannot conceive and acquire knowledge of the import of any concept, except by means of some individual example of the qualities or relations which it includes. We cannot know what single sensible attributes signify, as *red*, *sweet*, *smooth*, &c., without the actual experience of the sensation which each occasions, or of one that is analogous. So it is with the concepts of simple acts and states of the soul, as *to perceive*, *to imagine*, *to love*. The same is true of the concepts that are clearly complex, as *house*, *meadow*, *township*, *legislature*, *wealth*, *wages*, *civilisation*. Of all these concepts, the elements must first have been made intelligible to the mind by their application—*i.e.*, by being observed, experienced, or thought, in some individual being or agent.—*Porter*, '*The Human Intellect*,' p. 416.

To be perfect, concepts must be clear and distinct.

There are two degrees of the logical perfection of concepts,—viz., their *Clearness* and *Distinctness*. A concept is said to be *clear*, when the degree of consciousness is such as enables us to distinguish it as a whole from others; and *distinct*, when the degree of consciousness is such, as enables us to discriminate from each other the several characters, or constituent parts of which the concept is the sum.—*Hamilton*, '*Logic*,' i. 158.

In order that a conception may be clear the only requisite is that we shall know exactly in what the agreement among the phenomena consists; that it shall have been carefully observed and accurately remembered. The clearness of our conceptions chiefly depends on the carefulness and accuracy of our observing and comparing faculties. — *Mill*, '*Logic*,' ii. 201–203.

How Concepts are Formed.

Out of concrete notions.

Out of the concrete, the mind can form the abstract notion I can see or image a lily only as with both a shape and colour, but I can in thought contemplate its whiteness apart from its form. Having seen a number of beasts with four limbs, I can think about a class of animals agreeing in this, that they are all quadrupeds. The general notion is the result of an exercise of thought, separating the part from the whole, or contemplating an indefinite number of objects as possessing common qualities.—*M'Cosh*, '*Intuitions of the Mind,*' p. 17.

Process of formation.

A concept or notion arises from considering or attending to some parts of an object, or of several resembling objects, to the exclusion of the remaining parts When we consider separately the (subjective) parts in which two or more objects resemble each other, to the exclusion of those in which they differ, we form a general concept, general notion, or general idea, which includes the points of agreement to the exclusion of the points of difference. Thus in forming the general concept of a square, I take several square objects and withdrawing my attention from the materials of which they are composed, the positions which they occupy, and even their magnitudes, and attending only to their figure, and form a notion of that in which alone they agree, and am thus enabled to regard any of them (or any similar figure that I may meet with thereafter) as a square.—*Monck*, '*Sir W. Hamilton,*' p. 172.

We are so constantly forming general notions, that it should not be difficult to evolve the processes involved in it. The two first steps are,—(1) That we observe a resemblance among objects; (2) That we fix on the points of resemblance. The first is accomplished by the mind's power of perceiving agreements, and the second by an operation of abstraction. No absolute rule can be laid down as to which of these processes is the prior.—*M'Cosh*, '*Examination of Mill,*' p. 270

In the formation of a concept, the process may be analysed into four momenta In the first place, we must have a plurality of objects presented or represented by the subsidiary faculties. In the second place, the objects thus supplied are, by an act of the understanding, compared together, and their several qualities judged to be similar or dissimilar In the third place, an act of volition, called Attention, concentrates consciousness on the qualities thus recognised as similar. In the fourth place, the qualities, which by comparison are judged similar, and by attention are constituted into an exclusive object of thought, are already, by this process, identified in consciousness.—*Hamilton*, '*Logic,*' i. 132.

When formed they become types

We compare phenomena with each other to get the conception, and we then compare those and other phenomena *with* the conception. We get the conception of an animal (for instance) by comparing different animals, and when we afterwards see a creature resembling an animal we compare it with our general conception of an animal; and if it agrees with that general conception we include it in the class. The conception becomes the type of comparison.—*Mill*, '*Logic,*' ii. 196.

Is the Term a Valuable One

I think that the words Concept, General Notion, and other phrases of like import, convenient as they are for the lighter and everyday uses of philosophical discussion, should be abstained from where precision is required. Above all, I hold that nothing but confusion ever results from introducing the term Concept into Logic, and that instead of the Concept of a class, we should always speak of the signification of a class name.—*Mill*, '*Examination of Hamilton,*' p 388.

But surely it is desirable to have a word

to express the 'mental modification' when we contemplate a 'class,' and Conception or General Notion seems appropriate enough I also think it desirable to have a phrase to denote, not the 'signification of a class name,' but the thing signified by the class name; and the fittest I can think of is Concept.—*M'Cosh, 'Examination of Mill,'* p 276.

VII. THEORIES OF THE CONCEPT—REALISM, NOMINALISM, CONCEPTUALISM.

PRELIMINARY

Much Controversy as to the Nature of the Concept.

As a metaphysical and logical question the nature of the concept has been fruitful of discussion in the schools of ancient and modern philosophy. From Plato to John Stuart Mill it has been the perpetual theme for discussion and controversy The history of the various theories which have been held is not merely interesting as a subject of curious speculation, and as the key to much of the history of philosophy; but it is most instructive as enabling us to understand the nature and reach of language, as well as the grounds of our faith in philosophy itself, and in the special sciences of which philosophy is the foundation.—*Porter, 'The Human Intellect,'* p. 403.

Reason for it.

It is very common to think and speak with wonder, if not with contempt, of the strife between the Nominalists and Realists The modern critic often congratulates the men of his own times that they are not distracted by controversies at once so trivial and fruitless He asks himself how it could be possible, that what seems to him only a metaphysical subtlety or a trivial logomachy, should have occasioned so great acrimony between the parties and schools concerned, and should have even embroiled their rulers, in both church and state, with one another in bitter and bloody contention. The proper answer to this question is found in the consideration that the logical opinions taught were immediately applied to theological doctrines, and the inferences which the opposite opinions warranted in fact, or were supposed to warrant, in respect of the received doctrines of the church, invested them with the supremest importance Viewed in this light, the earnestness and bitterness with which these disputes were conducted should occasion no surprise; certainly no greater surprise than that the philosophy of Mr Hume, Mr. J S Mill, Mr. Herbert Spencer, or Mr Mansel should now be judged by its relations to theological opinion.—*Porter, 'The Human Intellect,'* p. 407.

Essential Point of the Controversy.

The question, broadly stated, to the neglect of many nice subtleties and shades of opinion brought out in the history of the controversy is this—Are these Universals [General Notions or Ideas, Concepts] real existences, apart from the mind that has formed them by abstraction, and independently of the things in which alone they appear to us,—or are they mere modes of intellectual representation that have no real existence except in our thoughts? The various opinions upon this question are indicated by the names Realism, Nominalism, and Conceptualism.—*Thomson, 'Laws of Thought,'* p. 97.

1 REALISM.

Doctrine of.

Realists believed that there were real things which corresponded to our general ideas or concepts—these real things not being the individual things contained in the extension of the concept, but universals. They seem to have been what Plato called Ideas, so that in this meaning of Realism and the Platonic meaning of Idea, Realism and Idealism would coincide instead of being opposed —*Monck, 'Sir W. Hamilton,'* p. 184.

Realists held that Genus and Species are some real *things*, existing independently of our conceptions and expressions, and that, as in the case of Singular-terms, there is some real individual corresponding to each, so, in Common-terms also, there is some Thing corresponding to each; which is the object of our thoughts when we employ any such term.—*Whately,* '*Logic,*' p. 182.

Realists maintained that General Names are the names of General Things. Besides individual things, they recognised another kind of Things, not individual, which they technically called Second Substances, or Universals *a parte rei.* Over and above all individual men and women, there was an entity called Man—Man in general, which inhered in the individual men and women, and communicated to them its essence. These Universal Substances they considered to be a much more dignified kind of beings than individual substances, and the only ones the cognisance of which deserved the names of Science and Knowledge. Individual existences were fleeting and perishable, but the beings called Genera and Species were immortal and unchangeable.—*Mill,* '*Examination of Hamilton,*' p. 364.

Varieties of Realism.

Extreme Realism.

The doctrine (of Plato, or at least the doctrine ascribed to him by Aristotle) that universals have an independent existence apart from individual objects, and that they exist before the latter (whether merely in point of rank and in respect of the causal relation, or in point of time also), is extreme Realism, which was afterwards reduced to the formula: *universalia ante rem.*—*Ueberweg,* '*Hist. of Phil.,*' i. 366.

Moderate Realism.

The (Aristotelian) opinion, that universals, while possessing indeed a real existence, exist only *in* individual objects, is the doctrine of Moderate Realism, expressed by the formula: *universalia in re.*—*Ueberweg,* '*Hist. of Phil.,*' i. 366.

Origin of Realism.

What kind of existences correspond to the universal cognitions? That was the puzzle. If the analysis of cognition be a division into kinds, and if the particular cognitions are distinct from the universal, and have their appropriate objects—to wit, particular things—the universal cognitions must, of course, be distinct from the particular, and must have *their* appropriate objects. What then are these objects? What is the nature and manner of their existence? Those who, to their misunderstanding of Plato, united a reverence for his name, and for what they conceived to be his opinions, maintained that the universals—such genera and species as man, animal, and tree—had an actual existence in nature, distinct, of course, from all particular men, animals, or trees. Whether these genera and species were corporeal or incorporeal, they were somewhat at a loss to determine; but that they were real they entertained no manner of doubt. And accordingly the doctrine known in the history of philosophy under the name of Realism was enthroned in the schools, and being supported by the supposed authority of Plato, and in harmony with certain theological tenets then dominant, it kept its ascendancy for a time.—*Ferrier,* '*Institutes of Metaphysic,*' p. 178.

Is the Universal—that whole, that unity which we must attribute to a family, a nation, a race—merely *attributed?* Is it not there? Thus did the controversy respecting Universals become the controversy respecting the Real and the Nominal.—*Maurice,* '*Moral and Metaphysical Phil.,*' i. 554.

The development of these doctrines was connected with the study of Porphyry's Introduction to the logical writings of Aristotle, in which Introduction the conceptions: *genus, differentia, species, proprium,* and *accidens* are treated of; the question was raised whether by these were to be understood five realities or only five words.—*Ueberweg,* '*Hist. of Phil.,*' i. 365.

The Truth and Error in Realism.

The truth.

The Realist asserts for the concept a still higher import and use. The truth which is the basis of his theory is that every real concept should suggest or express some one or more of the *essential properties* and *unchanging laws* of individual beings. He insists that the concept ought to signify and represent the most important of all descriptions of knowledge, the knowledge of that which is permanent and universal.—*Porter*, '*The Human Intellect*,' p. 422.

The error

The mistakes of the Realists have been twofold. They have both in language and thought confounded the subjective concept, which is a purely psychological product, with its objective correlate — the related elements which it represents or indicates; and have often called both by the same name, and invested them with the same properties. They have used a highly metaphoric terminology to express the nature of universals and their relations to individual beings.—*Porter*, '*The Human Intellect*,' p. 424.

Nothing so much conduces to the error of Realism as the transferred and secondary use of the words 'same,' 'one and the same,' 'identical,' &c., when it is not clearly perceived and carefully borne in mind that they *are* employed in a secondary sense, and *that* more frequently even than in the primary. Suppose, *e.g.*, a thousand persons are thinking of the sun: it is evident that it is one and the same individual object on which all these minds are employed. But suppose all these persons are thinking of a Triangle,—not any individual triangle, but Triangle in general; it would seem as if, in this case also, their minds were all employed on 'one and the same' object: and this object of their thoughts, it may be said, cannot be the *mere word* Triangle, but that which is *meant* by it: nor, again, can it be everything that the word will apply to; for they are not thinking of *triangles*, but of *one* thing.—*Whately*, '*Logic*,' p. 184.

An Abandoned Doctrine

This, the most prevalent philosophical doctrine of the Middle Ages, is now universally abandoned, but remains a fact of great significance in the history of philosophy; being one of the most striking examples of the tendency of the human mind to infer difference of things from difference of names,—to suppose that every different class of names implied a corresponding class of real entities to be denoted by them.—*Mill*, '*Examination of Hamilton*,' p. 365.

2. NOMINALISM.

Doctrine of.

Nominalism is the doctrine that general notions, such as the notion of a tree, have no realities corresponding to them, and have no existence but as names or words. The doctrine immediately opposed to it is Realism. To the intermediate doctrine of Conceptualism, Nominalism is closely allied.—*Fleming*, '*Vocab. of Phil.*,' p. 346.

In the later Middle Ages there grew up a rival school of metaphysicians, termed Nominalists, who, repudiating Universal Substances, held that there is nothing general except names. A name, they said, is general if it is applied in the same acceptation to a plurality of things; but every one of the things is individual.—*Mill*, '*Examination of Hamilton*,' p. 365.

Nominalism maintains that every notion, considered in itself, is singular, but becomes as it were general, through the intention of the mind to make it represent every other resembling notion, or notion of the same class. Take, for example, the term *man*. Here we can call up no notion, no idea corresponding to the universality of the class or term. This is manifestly impossible. The class *man* includes individuals, male and female, white and black and copper-coloured, tall and short, fat and thin, straight and crooked, whole and mutilated, &c. &c.; and the notion of the class must therefore at once represent all and none of these. It is therefore evident that we cannot represent to ourselves the class *man* by any equivalent notion or idea. All that we can do is to call up some individual image and consider it as representing, though inadequately representing, the generality.—*Hamilton*, '*Metaphysics*,' ii. 297.

Varieties of Nominalism.

Moderate Nominalism.

Moderate Nominalists hold that Universals exist as a product of the mind only; they are formal representations of things, constructed by the mind through the assistance of language.—*Thomson*, '*Laws of Thought*,' p. 98.

Ultra-Nominalism.

The doctrine of the Ultra-Nominalists is that Universals are mere names; and the only realities are individual things which we group together by the aid of names alone.—*Thomson*, '*Laws of Thought*,' p. 99.

Origin of Nominalism.

Nominalism, as the conscious and distinct stand-point of the opponents of Realism, first appeared in the second half of the eleventh century, when a portion of the scholastics ascribed to Aristotle the doctrine that logic has to do only with the right use of words, and that genera and species are only (subjective) collections of the various individuals designated by the same name, and disputed the interpretations which gave to universals a real existence. The most famous among the Nominalists of this time is Roscellinus, Canon of Compiègne, who, by his application of the nominalistic doctrine to the dogma of the Trinity, gave great offence.—*Ueberweg*, '*Hist. of Phil.*,' ii. 371.

The Real Point in Dispute.

I venture to think that the interminable contest between Platonist and Aristotelian, Realist and Nominalist, is, at bottom, not so much a question of what Universals are as of how they shall be treated, not so much a question of metaphysics as of method. Upon the *nature* of general notions there is a large amount of agreement between the parties. The Realist believes with the Nominalist that they are in the human mind, whilst, if the Nominalist believes at all that the world was created by design, he can scarcely escape from recognising the Realist's position that such ideas as animal, right, motion, must have had their existence from the beginning in the creative mind.—*Thomson*, '*Laws of Thought*,' p. 99.

The Conflict continues.

The controversy, treated by some modern writers as an example of barbarous wrangling, was in truth an anticipation of that modern dispute which still divides metaphysicians, whether the human mind can form general ideas, and whether the words which are supposed to convey such ideas be not general terms, representing only a number of particular perceptions? questions so far from frivolous that they deeply concern both the nature of reasoning and the structure of language.—*Mackintosh*, '*Progress of Ethical Phil.*,' p. 328.

3. CONCEPTUALISM. (See ABSTRACT IDEAS.)

Doctrine of.

A third doctrine arose which endeavoured to steer between the two [Realism and Nominalism]. According to this, which is known by the name of Conceptualism, generality is not an attribute solely of names but also of thoughts. External objects indeed are all individual, but to every general name corresponds a General Notion or Conception, called by Locke and others an Abstract Idea. General Names are the names of these Abstract Ideas.—*Mill*, '*Examination of Hamilton*,' p. 365.

Conceptualism maintained that the general existences had no reality in nature, but only an ideality in the mind—that they existed only as abstractions and were not independent of the intelligence which fabricates them.—*Ferrier*, '*Institutes of Metaphysics*,' p. 188.

That universality which the Realists held

to be in things themselves, Nominalists in names only, the Conceptualists held to be neither in things nor in names only, but in our conceptions.—*Reid*, '*Works*,' p. 406.

Origin of Conceptualism.

The actual independent existence of genera and species [Realism] was too ridiculous and unintelligible an hypothesis to find favour with those who deferred more to reason than to authority. They accordingly surrendered universals considered as independent entities; and now, inasmuch as the old sources of our universal cognitions were thus extinguished with the extinction of the realities from which they had been supposed to proceed, these philosophers, in order to account for them, were thrown upon a new hypothesis, which was this: they held that all existences are particular, and also, that all our knowledge is, in the first instance, particular; that we start from particular cognitions; but that the mind, by a process of abstraction and generalisation, which consists in attending to the resemblances of things, leaving out of view their differences, subsequently constructs conceptions or general notions, or universal cognitions, which, however, are mere *entia rationis*, and have no existence out of the intelligence which fabricates them. These genera and species were held to have an ideal, though not a real, existence, and to be the objects which the mind contemplates when it employs such words as man, tree, or triangle.—*Ferrier*, '*Institutes of Metaphysics*,' p. 180.

Sir W. Hamilton holds that—

The whole disputes between the Conceptualists and the Nominalists (to say nothing of the Realists) have only arisen from concepts having been regarded as affording an irrespective and independent object of thought. This illusion has arisen from a very simple circumstance. Objects compared together are found to possess certain attributes, which, as producing indiscernible modifications in us, are to us absolutely similar. They are, therefore, considered the same. The relation of similarity is thus converted into identity, and the real plurality of resembling qualities in nature is factitiously reduced to a unity in thought; and this unity obtains a name in which its relativity, not being expressed, is still further removed from observation.—'*Logic*,' i. 128.

The whole controversy of Nominalism and Conceptualism is founded on the ambiguity of the terms employed. The opposite parties are substantially at one. Had we, like the Germans, different terms, like *Begriff* and *Anschauung*, to denote different kinds of thought, there would have been as little difference of opinion in regard to the nature of general notions in this country as in the Empire. With us, *Idea*, *Notion*, *Conception*, &c., are confounded, or applied by different philosophers in different senses.—*Note to Reid's* '*Works*,' p. 412.

John S. Mill says of this that while Hamilton's 'general mode of thought and habitual phraseology are purely Conceptualist,' his doctrine is that of 'pure Nominalism.'—'*Examination of Hamilton*,' chap. xvii.

The Difficulty of Conceptualism.

Conceptualism is bound to show—if she would make good her scheme—that just as the particular cognitions stand distinct from the general cognitions, so the latter stand distinct from the former. The question, therefore, with which Conceptualism has to deal is this: does the mind know or think of the universal without thinking of the particular; of the genus without taking into account any of the singulars which compose it; of the resemblance among things without looking, either really or ideally, to the things to which the resemblance belongs? In a word, can the conceptions be objects of the mind *without* the intuitions,—just as, according to conceptualism, the intuitions can be objects of the mind without the conceptions? That is the only question for conceptualism to consider, and to answer in the affirmative, *if she can.*—*Ferrier*, '*Institutes of Metaphysics*,' p. 183.

VIII. JUDGMENT

The Nature of Judgment as a Mental Act.

Defined.

Judgment, in the limited sense in which it is distinguishable from consciousness in general, is an act of comparison between two given concepts, as regards their relation to a common object.—*Mansel*, '*Metaphysics*,' p. 220.

In judgment, say the philosophers, there must be two objects of thought compared, and some agreement or disagreement, or, in general, some relation discerned between them; in consequence of which there is an opinion or belief of that relation which we discern. The definition commonly given of judgment, by the more ancient writers, was that it is 'an act of the mind, whereby one thing is affirmed or denied of another.' I believe this is as good a definition of it as can be given. It is true that it is by affirmation or denial that we express our judgments; but there may be judgment which is not expressed. It is a solitary act of the mind, and may be tacit. The definition must be understood of mental affirmation or denial.—*Reid*, '*Works*,' pp. 243, 413.

The faculty of judgment consists in determining whether anything falls under a given rule or not.—*Kant*, '*Critique*,' ii. 116.

Judgment is the faculty by which we perceive a relation of any kind subsisting between one thing and another. It comes into exercise on the comparison of things, and therefore presupposes observation, memory, and imagination. By it we become acquainted with the numerous tribe of relations in which things and their qualities stand to one another. The sources from which the decisions of the judgment come are intuition, experience, and reasoning.—*Murphy*, '*Human Mind*,' p. 136.

Criticism of Definitions by Associational School.

Professor Bain says ('Senses and Intellect,' p. 329), 'What is termed judgment may consist in discrimination on the one hand, or in the sense of agreement on the other: we determine two or more things either to differ or to agree. It is impossible to find any case of judging that does not, in the last resort, mean one or other of these two essential activities of the intellect.' This account tends very much to narrow the capacities of the human mind. Mr. Bain, in his view of the intellect, mixes up together what the Scottish metaphysicians have carefully separated, the mind's power of discovering relations with the laws of the succession of our mental state.—*M'Cosh*, '*Intuitions of the Mind*,' p. 214.

A judgment is usually defined as a comparison of two notions. Upon which Mr. J. S. Mill remarks that 'propositions (except where the mind itself is the subject treated of) are not assertions respecting our ideas of things, but assertions respecting things themselves;' adding, 'My belief has not reference to the ideas, it has reference to the things' ('Logic,' i. v. 1). There is force in the criticism, yet it does not give the exact truth. In propositions about extra-mental objects, we are not comparing the two notions as states of mind; so far as logicians have proceeded on this view, they have fallen into confusion and error. But still, while it is true that our predications are made, not in regard to our notions, but of things, it is in regard to things apprehended, or of which we have a notion, as Mr. Mill admits: 'In order to believe that gold is yellow, I must indeed have the idea of gold and the idea of yellow, and something having reference to those ideas must take place in my mind.'—*M'Cosh*, '*Intuitions of the Mind*,' p. 208.

Its relation to apprehension.

We can neither judge of a proposition nor reason about it, unless we conceive or apprehend it. We may distinctly conceive a proposition without judging of it at all.

We may have no evidence on one side or the other; we may have no concern whether it be true or false. In these cases we commonly form no judgment about it, though we perfectly understand its meaning.—*Reid, 'Works,'* p. 375.

Apprehension is as impossible without judgment as judgment is impossible without apprehension. The apprehension of a thing or notion is only realised in the mental affirmation that the *concept* ideally exists, and this affirmation is a judgment. In fact all consciousness supposes a judgment, as all consciousness supposes a discrimination. —*Hamilton, Reid's 'Works,'* p. 243.

Its relation to necessary existence.

The necessity attached to our Judgments is exactly coincident with them. These imply objects on which they are pronounced. At the same time, the judgment, with its adhering necessity, has a regard not to the objects directly but to the relation of the objects. These objects may be real or they may be imaginary. I may pronounce Chimborazo to be higher than Mont Blanc, but I may also affirm of a mountain 100,000 feet high that it is higher than one 50,000 feet high. As to whether the objects are or are not real, this is a question to be settled by our cognitions and beliefs, original and acquired, and by inferences from them. But it is to be carefully observed that, even when the object is imaginary, the judgment proceeds on a cognition of the elements of the objects. Thus, having known what is the size of a man, we affirm of a giant who is greater than a common man, that he is greater than a dwarf who is smaller than ordinary humanity. Still, the necessity in the judgment does not of itself imply the existence of the objects, still less any necessary existence; all that it proclaims is that the objects might exist out of materials which have fallen under our notice, and that the objects, being so and so, must have such a relation.

In a sense, then, our primitive judgments are hypothetical, the objects being so must have a particular connexion. There may be, or there may never have been, two exactly parallel lines, what our intuitive judgment declares is, that if there be such, they can never meet. A similar remark may be made of every other class of intuitive comparisons. There may or there may not be a sea in the moon, but if there be its waters must be extended and can resist pressure. There may or there may not be inhabitants in the planet Jupiter, but if there be they must have been created by a power competent to the operation. But it is to be borne in mind that when the objects exist, the judgments, with their accompanying necessity, apply to them.—*M'Cosh, 'Intuitions of the Mind,'* p. 305.

It is the source of certain ideas.

There are notions or ideas that ought to be referred to the faculty of judgment as their source, because if we had not that faculty they could not enter into our minds; and to those that have that faculty and are capable of reflecting upon its operations they are obvious and familiar. Among these we may reckon the notion of judgment itself; the notions of a proposition —of its subject, predicate, and copula, of affirmation and negation, of true and false; of knowledge, belief, disbelief, opinion, assent, evidence. From no source could we acquire these notions but from reflecting upon our judgments.—*Reid, 'Works,'* p. 414.

The Results (Judgments) are of Various Kinds.

Aristotle's division.

Our judgments, according to Aristotle, are either *problematical, assertive,* or *demonstrable;* or, in other words, the results of opinion, of belief, or of science. We cannot show that the problematical judgment truly represents the object about which we judge. It is a mere opinion. The assertive judgment is one of which we are fully persuaded ourselves, but cannot give grounds for our belief that shall compel men in general to coincide with us. The demonstrative judgment is certain in itself or capable of proof.—*Fleming*, '*Vocab. of Phil.*,' p. 274.

Kant's distinction of (a) Analytical and Synthetical.

In all judgments in which there is a relation between subject and predicate, that relation can be of two kinds. Either the predicate B belongs to the subject A as something contained (though covertly) in the concept A; or B lies outside the sphere of the concept A, though somehow connected with it. In the former case I call the judgment Analytical, in the latter Synthetical. If I say, for instance, all bodies are extended, this is an analytical judgment. I need not go beyond the concept connected with the name of body in order to find that extension is connected with it. I have only to analyse that concept and become conscious of the manifold elements always contained in it, in order to find that predicate. This is, therefore, an analytical judgment. But if I say all bodies are heavy, the predicate is something quite different from what I think as the mere concept of body. The addition of such a predicate gives us a synthetical judgment. —*Kant*, '*Critique of Pure Reason*,' ii. 6.

Æsthetic and Teleological.

I experience pleasure or pain directly on the presentation of an object, and before I have formed any notion of it. An emotion of this nature can be referred only to a harmonious relation subsisting between the form of the object and the faculty that perceives it. Judgment in this subjective aspect is *æsthetic judgment*. In the second case I form first of all a notion of the object, and then decide whether the object corresponds to this notion. That my perception should find a flower beautiful, it is not necessary that I should have formed beforehand a notion of this flower. But to find contrivance in the flower, to that a notion is necessary. Judgment, as the faculty cognisant of objective adaptation, is named *teleological judgment*.—*Schwegler*, '*Hist. of Phil.*,' p. 241.

IX. SYLLOGISM.

What a Syllogism is.

Syllogism may be defined as the act of thought by which from two given propositions we proceed to a third proposition, the truth of which necessarily follows from the truth of these given propositions. When the agreement is fully expressed in language, it is usual to call it concretely a syllogism.—*Jevons*, '*Logic*,' p. 127.

A syllogism is a speech (or enunciation) in which certain things (the premises) being supposed, something different from what is supposed (the conclusion) follows of *necessity*, and this solely in virtue of the suppositions themselves.—*Aristotle*, '*Prior. Analyt.*,' lib. i., cap. i., § 7.

Its Three Parts.

In a syllogism, the first two propositions are called the *premises*, because they are the things premised or put before; they are also called the *antecedents*: the first of them is called the *major* and the second the *minor*. The third proposition, which contains the thing to be proved, is called the *conclusion* or *consequent*, and the particle which unites the conclusion with the premises is called the *consequentia* or *consequence*. Thus:—

Every virtue is laudable (major premise).
Diligence is a virtue (minor premise).
Therefore diligence is laudable (conclusion).—*Fleming*, '*Vocab. of Phil.*,' p. 500.

Two Kinds of Syllogisms.

According to the different kinds of propositions employed in forming them, syllogisms are divided into Categorical and Hypothetical.

1. In the Categorical syllogism, the two premises and the conclusion are all categorical propositions.

2. In a Conditional syllogism, one premiss is a conditional proposition; the other premiss is a categorical proposition, and either asserts the antecedent or denies the consequent. Thus, 'If what we learn from the Bible is true, we ought not to do evil that good may come; but what we learn

from the Bible is true, therefore we ought not to do evil that good may come'

Categorical syllogisms are divided into Pure and Modal. Hypothetical syllogisms into Conditional and Disjunctive.—*Fleming*, '*Vocab. of Phil.*,' p. 501

(This usage of 'Hypothetical' and 'Conditional' is reversed by some logicians).

Value of the Syllogism.

All that may rightly be claimed for the syllogism is, that by conveniently exhibiting the data, it enables us deliberately to verify an inference already drawn; provided this inference belongs to a particular class. I add this qualification because its use, even for purposes of verification, is comparatively limited. To a large class of the cases commonly formulated in syllogisms, there applies the current criticism that *a petitio principii* is involved in the major premiss; since no test of the *objective* reality of the alleged correlation is yielded, unless the *all* asserted can be asserted absolutely; the implication being that the syllogism here serves simply to aid us in re-inspecting our propositions; so that we may see whether we have asserted much more than we absolutely know, and whether the conclusion is really involved in the premisses as we supposed.—*Spencer*, '*Principles of Psychology*,' ii. 99.

X. METHOD.

Explanatory.

Defined.

Method is 'a procedure *according to principles*.'—*Kant*, '*Critique*,' ii. 733.

Method in general is the regulated procedure towards a certain end; that is, a progress governed by rules which guide us by the shortest way straight towards a certain point, and guard us against devious aberrations.—*Hamilton*, '*Logic*,' ii. 3.

Method means the way or path by which we proceed to the attainment of some object or aim. In its widest acceptation, it denotes the means employed to obtain some end. Every art and every handicraft has its method. Scientific or philosophical method is the march which the mind follows in ascertaining or communicating truth. It is the putting of our thoughts in a certain order with a view to improve our knowledge or to convey it to others.—*Fleming*, '*Vocab. of Phil.*,' p. 316.

Method implies a progressive transition, and it is the meaning of the word in the original language. The Greek is literally a way or path of transit. Thus we extol the Elements of Euclid, or Socrates' discourse with the slave in the Menon of Plato, as methodical, a term which no one, who holds himself bound to think or speak correctly, would apply to the alphabetical order or arrangement of a common dictionary. But as without continuous transition there can be no method, so without a preconception there can be no transition with continuity. The term 'method' cannot therefore, otherwise than by abuse, be applied to a mere dead arrangement, containing in itself no principle of progression.—*Coleridge*, '*The Friend*,' iii. 122.

Method may be called, in general, the art of disposing well a series of many thoughts, either for the discovering truth when we are ignorant of it, or for proving it to others when it is already known.—'*Port Royal Logic*,' part iv. chap. 2.

Distinguished from Order.

Method differs from Order in that Order leads us to learn one thing *after* another, and Method, one thing *through* another.—*Facciolati*, '*Rudimenta Logicæ*.'

Method in Reasoning.

All things, in us and about us, are a chaos, without method. and so long as the mind is entirely passive, so long as there is an habitual submission of the understanding to mere events and images, as such, without any attempt to classify and arrange them, so long the chaos must continue. There may be transition, but there can never be progress; there may be sensation, but there cannot be thought: for the total absence of method renders thinking impracticable; as we find that partial defects of method proportionably render thinking a trouble and a fatigue. But as soon as the mind becomes accustomed to contemplate, not *things* only, but likewise *relations* of things, there is immediate need of some path or way of transition from one to the other of the things related;—there must be some law of contrast or of agreement between them; there must be some mode of comparison; in short, there must be method. We may, therefore, assert that the *relations of things* form the prime objects, or, so to speak, the *materials of Method*. and that the contemplation of those relations is the indispensable condition of thinking methodically.—*Coleridge*, '*Treatise on Method, Intro. to Encyclopædia Metropolitana*,' Sect. i.

Enumeration of Methods.

Method in general.

We ought to proceed from the better known to the less known, and from what is clearer to us to that which is clearer in nature. But those things are first known and clearer which are more complex and confused, for it is only by subsequent analysis that we attain to a knowledge of the facts and elements of which they are composed. We ought, therefore, to proceed from universals to singulars; for the whole is better known to sense than its parts; and the universal is a kind of whole, as the universal comprehends many things as its parts. Thus it is that names are at first better known to us than definitions; for the name denotes a whole, and that indeterminately; whereas the definition divides and explicates its parts. Children, likewise, at first call all men fathers, and all women mothers; but thereafter they learn to discriminate each individual from another.—*Aristotle*, '*Phys. Ausc.*' i. 1.

The true method which would furnish demonstrations of the highest excellence, if it were possible to employ the method fully, consists in observing two principal rules. The first rule is not to employ any term of which we have not clearly explained the meaning; the second rule is never to put forward any proposition which we cannot demonstrate by truths already known; that is to say, in a word, *to define all the terms* and *to prove all the propositions*.—*Pascal*, '*Pensées*,' pt. i. art. ii. p. 10.

Method of Analysis and Synthesis.

Method consists of two processes, correlative and complementary of each other. For it proceeds either from the whole to the parts, or from the parts to the whole. As proceeding from the whole to the parts, that is, as resolving, as unloosing, a complex totality into its constituent elements, it is Analytic; as proceeding from the parts to the whole, that is, as recomposing constituent elements into their complex totality, it is Synthetic. These two processes are not, in strict propriety, two several methods, but together constitute only a single method. Each alone is imperfect. Analysis and Synthesis are as necessary to themselves and to the life of science as expiration and inspiration in connection are necessary to each other and to the possibility of animal existence.—*Hamilton*, '*Logic*,' ii. 4.

Newton demands that Analysis always precede Synthesis; he expresses the belief that the Cartesians have not sufficiently observed this order, and have deluded themselves with mere hypotheses. The analytical method, he explains, proceeds from experiments and observations to general conclusions; it concludes from the compound to the simple, from motions to moving forces, and, in general, from effects to causes, from the particular causes to the more general, and so on to the most general; the synthetic method, on the contrary, pronounces from an investigation of causes the phenomena which will flow from them.—*Ueberweg*, '*Hist. of Phil.*,' ii. 89.

Method of Discovery and Instruction.

We must distinguish—1. The Method of Discovery; 2. The Method of Instruction. The method of discovery is employed in the acquisition of knowledge, and really consists in those processes of inference and induction by which general truths are ascertained from the collection and examination of particular facts. The second method only applies when knowledge has already been acquired and expressed in the form of general laws, rules, principles, or truths, so that we have only to make ourselves acquainted with these and observe the due mode of applying them to particular cases, in order to possess a complete acquaintance with the subject. A student, for example, in learning Latin, Greek, French, or any well-known language, receives a complete grammar and syntax setting forth the whole of the principles, rules, and nature of the language. He takes these instructions to be true on the authority of the teacher or writer, and after rendering them familiar to his mind, he has nothing to do but to combine and apply the rules in reading or composing the language. He follows, in short, the method of Instruction. But this is an entirely different and opposite process to that which the scholar must pursue who has received some writings in an unknown language, and is endeavouring to make out the alphabet, words, grammar, and syntax of the language. He pursues the method of discovery, consisting in a tedious comparison of letters, words, and phrases, such as shall disclose the more frequent combinations and forms in which they occur. The methods of Analysis and Synthesis closely correspond to this distinction between the methods of Discovery and Instruction.—*Jevons*, '*Logic*,' 202, 203.

In prosecuting science with the view of extending our knowledge of it, or the limits of it, we are said to follow the method of investigation or inquiry, and our procedure will be chiefly in the way of analysis. But in communicating what is already known, we follow the method of exposition or doctrine, and our procedure will be chiefly in the way of synthesis.—*Fleming*, '*Vocab of Phil.*,' p. 318.

Rules of Method, as given by

Descartes.

a. Never accept anything as true which is not clearly known to be such; that is to say, carefully avoid precipitancy and prejudice, and comprise nothing more in the judgment than what is presented to the mind so clearly and distinctly as to exclude all ground of doubt.

b. Divide each of the difficulties under examination into as many parts as possible.

c. Commence with the simplest objects and those easiest to know, and ascend little by little and as it were step by step to the knowledge of the more complex.

d. Make enumerations so complete, and reviews so general, as to be assured that nothing is omitted.—'*Discourse on Method*,' p. 19.

Pascal.

a. Admit no terms in the least obscure or equivocal without defining them.

b. Employ in the definitions only terms perfectly known or already explained.

c. Demand as axioms only truths perfectly evident.

d. Prove all propositions which are at all obscure, by employing in their proof only the definitions which have preceded, or the axioms which have been accorded, or the propositions which have been already demonstrated, or the construction of the thing itself which is in dispute, when there may be any operation to perform.

e. Never abuse the equivocation of terms by failing to substitute for them, mentally, the definitions which restrict and explain them.—'*Port Royal Logic*,' pt. iv. chap. iii. p. 317.

Observation the Condition of Method.

The relations of objects are prime materials of method, and the contemplation of relations is the indispensable condition of thinking methodically. The absence of method which characterises the uneducated, is occasioned by an habitual submission of the understanding to mere events and images as such, and independent of any power in the mind to classify or appropriate them. The general accompaniments of time and place are the only relations which persons of this class appear to regard in their statements. As this constitutes their leading feature, the contrary excellence, as distinguishing the well-educated man, must be referred to the contrary habit. Method, therefore, becomes natural to the mind which has been accustomed to contemplate not things only, or for their own sake alone, but likewise and chiefly the relations of things, either their relations to each other, or to the observer, or to the state and apprehension of the hearers. To enumerate and analyse these relations, with the conditions under which alone they are discoverable, is to teach the science of method.—*Coleridge*, '*The Friend*,' iii. 124, 112.

Importance of Method.

A good method gives the mind such power that it can to some extent take the place of talent. It is a lever giving to even a weak man who uses it a strength which the most powerful man without it cannot command.—*Comte*, '*Traité de la Legislation*,' lib. i., c. i.

Marshal thy notions into a handsome method. One will carry twice as much weight, trussed and packed up in bundles, as when it lies untoward, flapping and hanging about his shoulders.—'*Pleasures of Literature*,' p. 104.

From the cotter's hearth or the workshop of the artisan to the palace or the arsenal, the first merit, that which admits of neither substitute nor equivalent is, that everything be in its place. Where this charm is wanting, every other merit either loses its name, or becomes an additional ground of accusation and regret. Of one, by whom it is eminently possessed, we say proverbially, he is like clockwork. The resemblance extends beyond the point of regularity and yet falls short of the truth. Both do, indeed, at once divide and announce the silent and otherwise indistinguishable lapse of time. But the man of methodical industry and honourable pursuits does more; he realises its ideal divisions, and gives a character and individuality to its moments. He organises the hours and gives them a soul.—*Coleridge*, '*The Friend*,' iii. 110.

XI. LAWS OF THOUGHT.

Their Nature and Number.

By *law of thought*, or by logical necessity, we do not mean a physical law, such as the law of gravitation, but a general precept which we are able certainly to violate, but which, if we do not obey, our whole process of thinking is suicidal, or absolutely null. These laws are consequently the primary conditions of the possibility of valid thought.

The Fundamental Laws of Thought or the conditions of the thinkable, as commonly received, are three:—(1.) The Law of Identity; (2.) The Law of Contradiction; (3.) The Law of Exclusion, or Excluded Middle.—*Hamilton*, '*Logic*,' i. 78 and 86, note *a*.

These laws describe the very simplest truths, in which all people must agree, and which at the same time apply to all notions which we can conceive. It is impossible to think correctly and avoid evident self-contradiction unless we observe the Three Primary Laws of Thought.

These laws then, being universally and necessarily true, to whatever things they are applied, become the foundation of reasoning. All acts of reasoning proceed from certain judgments, and the act of judgment consists in comparing two things or ideas together and discovering whether they agree or differ, that is to say, whether they are identical in any qualities. The laws of thought inform us of the very nature of this identity with which all thought is concerned.—*Jevons*, '*Logic*,' pp. 117, 121.

The following are the General Laws of Thought:—

I. *The Law of Identity* is popularly expressed in the formula, *Whatever is, is;*

more technically in the formula, *A is A* Its purport as a law of thought will probably be better understood by the following statement:—*Whatever is thought must be thought to be that which it is thought*

II. The *Law of Contradiction*, as it is commonly called, or the *Law of Non-Contradiction*, as it has been perhaps more appropriately called, is expressed in the popular formula, *It is impossible for a thing to be and not to be at the same time*, sometimes in the technical formula *A is not non-A* The purport of the law may be more clearly indicated by the statement:—*Whatever is thought cannot be thought not to be that which it is thought*

III The *Law of Excluded Middle* is so called because by it a middle or third alternative is excluded between two contradictory judgments, inasmuch as one of these must always be in thought affirmed, the other in thought denied Its technical expression is the formula, *A either is or is not B*, but perhaps the following formula may explain it more distinctly:—*Of whatever is thought anything else that is thinkable must either be or not be thought.*—*Murray*, '*Handbook of Psychology*,' pp. 107, 108.

The Law of Identity

Statement of the Law.

This law expresses the relation of total sameness in which a concept stands to all, and the relation of partial sameness in which it stands to each, of its constituent characters In other words, it declares the impossibility of thinking the concept and its characters as reciprocally unlike. It is expressed in the formula, A is A, or A = A; and by A is denoted every logical thing, every product of our thinking faculty,—concept, judgment, reasoning, &c.—*Hamilton*, '*Logic*,' i 79.

The Law of Identity *Whatever is, is.*

This statement may perhaps be regarded as a description of Identity itself, if so fundamental a notion can admit of description. A thing at any moment is perfectly identical with itself, and, if any person were unaware of the meaning of the word 'identity,' we could not better describe it than by such an example —*Jevons*, '*Principles of Science*,' p. 5.

The axiom of Identity should be thus expressed: A is A, *i.e.*, everything is what it is In a wider sense the axiom of Identity may apply to the agreement of all knowledge with itself, as the (necessary though insufficient) condition of its agreement with actual existence.—*Ueberweg*, '*Logic*,' p. 232.

What is at the bottom of 'principles of logical affirmation' is, that Logic postulates to be allowed to assert the same meaning in any words which will, consistently with their signification, express it. Looked at in this light, the Principle of Identity ought to have been expressed thus. Whatever is true in one form of words is true in every other form of words which conveys the same meaning Thus worded, it fulfils the requirements of a First Principle of Thought, for it is the widest possible expression of an act of thought which is always legitimate, and continually has to be done —*Mill*, '*Examination of Hamilton*,' p 466.

Its logical importance

The logical importance of the law of Identity lies in this,—that it is the principle of all logical affirmation and definition.—*Hamilton*, '*Logic*,' i 80.

The Law of Contradiction

Stated.

The Law of Contradiction: *A thing cannot both be and not be.* The meaning of this law is that nothing can have at the same time and at the same place contradictory and inconsistent qualities. A piece of paper may be blackened in one part while it is white in other parts, or it may be white at one time and afterwards become black, but we cannot conceive that it should be both white and black at the same place and time. A door after being open may be shut, but it cannot at once be shut and open. Water may feel warm to one hand and cold to another hand, but it cannot be both warm and cold to the same hand. No quality can both be present and absent at the same time; and this seems to be the most simple and general truth which we can assert of all things. It is of the very nature of existence that a thing cannot be otherwise than it is; and it may be safely said that all fallacy and error may arise from unwittingly reasoning in a way inconsistent with this law. All statements or inferences which imply a combination of contradictory qualities must be taken as impossible and false, and the breaking of this law is the mark of their being false.—*Jevons*, '*Logic*,' p. 118.

The highest of all logical laws, in other words, the supreme law of thought, is what is called the principle of Contradiction, or more correctly the principle of Non-Contradiction. When an object is determined by the affirmation of a certain character, this object cannot be thought to be the same when such character is denied of it. Assertions concerning a thing are mutually contradictory, when the one asserts that the thing possesses the character which the other asserts that it does not. This law is logically expressed in the formula, What is contradictory is unthinkable. A = not A = O, or A − A = O.—*Hamilton*, '*Lectures*,' ii. 368, iii. 81.

The axiom of (the avoidance of) Contradiction is—Judgments opposed contradictorily to each other cannot both be true. The one or the other must be false. From the truth of the one follows the falsehood of the other. The double answer, Yes and No, to one and the same question, in the same sense, is inadmissible.—*Ueberweg*, '*Logic*,' p. 235.

Its logical importance.

The logical import of this law lies in its being the principle of all logical negation and distinction.—*Hamilton*, '*Logic*,' i. 82.

We must hold the principle of contradiction to be the universal and fully sufficient principle of all analytical cognition; but, as a sufficient criterion of truth, it has no further utility or authority.—*Kant*, '*Critique of Reason*,' p. 115.

Thoroughgoing consistency requires that when we affirm a certain thing to be a straight line we must be prepared also to deny that it is a bent line; when we call this man wise we must also deny that he is foolish. This is an equivalent form that plays a great part in Logic. Viewed thus, the Law of Contradiction has a pregnant meaning.—*Bain*, '*Logic, Deduction*,' p. 16.

The Law of Contradiction is a principle of Reasoning in the same sense, and in the same sense only, as the Law of Identity is. It is the generalisation of a mental act which is of continual occurrence and which cannot be dispensed with in reasoning. As we require the liberty of substituting for a given assertion the same assertion in different words, so we require the liberty of substituting, for any assertion, the denial of its contradictory. The affirmation of the one and the denial of the other are logical equivalents which it is allowable and indispensable to make use of as mutually convertible.—*Mill*, '*Examination of Hamilton*,' p. 471.

Aristotle truly described this law as the first of all axioms,—one of which we need not seek for any demonstration. All truths cannot be proved, otherwise there would be an endless chain of demonstration; and it is in self-evident truths like this that we find the simplest foundations.—*Jevons*, '*Principles of Science*,' p. 6.

The Law of Excluded Middle.

Stated.

The principle of Contradiction, viewed in a certain aspect, is called the principle of Excluded Middle, or more fully, the principle of Excluded Middle between two Contradictions. *A thing either is or it is not;* there is no medium; one must be true, both cannot.—*Hamilton*, '*Metaphysics*,' ii. 368.

The axiom of Excluded Third or Middle is thus stated: Judgments opposed as contradictions (such as A is B, and A is not B) can neither both be false nor can admit the truth of a third or middle judgment, but the one or the other must be true, and the truth of the one follows from the falsehood of the other —*Ueberweg*, '*Logic*,' p 260

The third of these laws completes the other two—*a thing must either be or not be* It asserts that at every step there are two possible alternatives—presence or absence, affirmation or negation Hence I propose to name this law the Law of Duality, for it gives to all the formulæ of reasoning a dual character It asserts also that between presence and absence, existence and non-existence, affirmation and negation, there is no third alternative As Aristotle said, there can be no mean between opposite assertions we must either affirm or deny. Rock must be either hard or not-hard, gold must be either white or not-white, an action must be either virtuous or not-virtuous Hence the inconvenient name by which it has been known—the Law of Excluded Middle.—*Jevons*, '*Principles of Science*,' p. 6.

Its logical importance

The Law of Excluded Middle is the principle of Disjunctive Judgments, that is, of judgments in which a plurality of judgments are contained, and which stand in such a reciprocal relation that the affirmation of the one is the denial of the other. —*Hamilton*, '*Logic*,' i. 84.

Limits of the argument from Contradiction

The argument from Contradiction is omnipotent within its sphere, but that sphere is narrow It has the following limitations :—

(1.) It is negative, not positive; it may refute, but it is incompetent to establish It may show what is not, but never, of itself, what is

(2.) It is dependent; to act, it pre-supposes a counter-proposition to act from

(3.) It is explicative, not ampliative; it analyses what is given, but does not originate information, or add anything, through itself, to our stock of knowledge

(4.) But, what is its principal defect, it is partial, not thorough-going It leaves many of the most important problems of our knowledge out of its determination, and is, therefore, all too narrow in its application as a universal criterion or instrument of judgment.—*Hamilton*, '*Metaphysics*,' ii 524

These Laws are Variously Regarded, as

Rules of Evidence

Viewed as instruments for judging of material truth, they sink into mere rules for the reception of evidence The Principle of Contradiction is a caution against receiving into our notion of a subject any attribute that is irreconcilable with some other, already proved upon evidence we cannot doubt. The Principle of Identity is a permission to receive attributes that are not thus mutually opposed, or a hint to seek for such only The Principle of Excluded Middle would compel us to reconsider the evidence of any proposition, when other evidence threatened to compel us to accept its contradictory —*Thomson*, '*Laws of Thought*,' p. 214

Laws of Consistency

To call them the fundamental laws of Thought is a misnomer; but they are the laws of Consistency All inconsistency is a violation of some one of these laws, an unconscious violation, for knowingly to violate them is impossible.—*Mill*, '*Examination of Hamilton*,' p. 464

Yet on page 475, Stuart Mill says: 'I readily admit that these three general propositions are universally true of all phænomena I also admit that if there are any inherent necessities of thought, these are such . . They may or may not be capable of alteration by experience, but the conditions of our existence deny to us the experience which would be required to alter them Any assertion, therefore, which conflicts with one of these laws—any proposition, for instance, which asserts a contradiction, though it were on a subject wholly removed from the sphere of our experience, is to us unbelievable. The belief in such a proposition is, in the present constitution of nature, impossible as a mental fact.'

Three Aspects of the same Truth.

It may be allowed that these laws are not three independent and distinct laws; they rather express three different aspects of the same truth, and each law doubtless presupposes and implies the other two. But it has not been found possible to state these characters of identity and difference in less than the threefold formula.—*Jevons*, '*Principles of Science*,' p. 6.

Value of these Laws

General Influence on Thought.

No thought can pretend to validity and truth which is not in consonance with, which is not governed by, them. For man can recognise that alone as real and assured which the laws of his understanding sanction; and he cannot but regard that as false and unreal which these laws condemn. —*Hamilton*, '*Logic*,' i. 105.

Denial of them subverts the reality of Thought.

To deny the universal application of the first three laws is, in fact, to subvert the reality of thought, and as this subversion is itself an act of thought, it in fact annihilates itself. When, for example, I say that A is, and then say that A is not, by the second assertion I sublate or take away what, by the first assertion, I posited or laid down; thought, in the one case, undoing by negation what in the other it had by affirmation done. This is tantamount to saying that truth and falsehood are merely empty sounds.—*Hamilton*, '*Logic*,' i 99

XII. UNDERSTANDING AND REASON.

1 Understanding.

Definitions of it are various.

Philosophical.

The understanding comprehends our *contemplative powers*; by which we perceive objects; by which we conceive or remember them; by which we analyse or compound them; and by which we judge and reason concerning them.—*Reid*, '*Works*,' p. 242

The understanding, taken in the most comprehensive sense, is the faculty of knowing and conceiving. It includes understanding proper, the apprehending or empirical faculty; reason, the intuitive faculty; and imagination, the conceptive faculty. By it we observe, remember, know, imagine, judge, and reason. We observe, when we feel, discern, perceive, or are conscious of anything. We imagine, when we conceive or construct.—*Murphy*, '*The Human Mind*,' p. 22.

The understanding, considered exclusively as an organ of human intelligence, is the faculty by which we reflect and generalise. Take, for instance, any object consisting of many parts, a house or a group of houses; and if it be contemplated as a whole, that is, as many constituting a one, it forms what, in the technical language of psychology, is called a total impression. Among the various component parts of this, we direct our attention especially to such as we recollect to have noticed in other total impressions. Then, by a voluntary act, we withhold our attention from all the rest to reflect exclusively on these; and these we henceforward use as common characters, by virtue of which the several objects are referred to one and the same sort. Thus the whole process may be reduced to three acts, all depending on and supposing a previous impression on the senses: first, the appropriation of our attention; second (and in order to the continuance of the first), abstraction, or the voluntary withholding of the attention; and, third, generalisation. And these are the proper functions of the understanding: and the power of so doing is what we mean when we say we possess understanding, or are created with the faculty of understanding.—*Coleridge*, '*Aids to Reflection*,' p. 169.

As all acts of the understanding can be reduced to judgments, the *understanding* may be defined as *the faculty of judging*.—*Kant*, '*Critique*,' ii. 61.

Popular.

In its popular sense, understanding seems to be very nearly synonymous with *reason*, when that word is used most comprehensively, and is seldom or never applied to any of our faculties, but such as are immediately subservient to the investigation of truth or to the regulation of our conduct In this sense it is so far from being understood to comprehend the powers of Imagination, Fancy, and Wit that it is often stated in direct opposition to them, as in the common maxim, that a sound understanding and a warm imagination are seldom united in the same person. But philosophers, without rejecting this use of the word, very generally employ it, with far greater latitude, to comprehend Imagination, Memory, and Perception, as well as the faculties to which it is appropriated in popular discourse, and which, it seems, indeed, most properly to denote.—*Stewart*, '*Works*,' iii 13

Understanding and Reason are often distinguished from each other.

The Reason and the Understanding have not been steadily distinguished by English writers. The most simple way to use the substantive *Understanding* in a definite sense, is to make it correspond, in its extent, with the verb *understand* To understand anything is to apprehend it according to certain *assumed* ideas and rules; we do not include, in the meaning of the word, an examination of the ground of the ideas and rules, by reference to which we understand the thing We understand a language when we apprehend what is said, according to the established vocabulary and grammar of the language; without inquiring how the words came to have their meaning, or what is the ground of the grammatical rules. We *understand* the sense without *reasoning* about the etymology and syntax.

Reason may be requisite to understanding. We may have to reason about the syntax, in order to understand the sense. But understanding leaves still room for reasoning, we may understand the elliptical theory of Mars' motions, and may still require a reason for the theory. Also we may understand what is not conformable to Reason; as when we understand a man's arguments, and think them unfounded in Reason. The Reason includes both the Faculty of seeing First Principles, and the Reasoning Faculty by which we obtain other Principles which are derivative. The Understanding is the Faculty of applying Principles, however obtained.—*Whewell*, '*Elements of Morality*,' p 24.

Comparison will show the difference :—

Understanding.	*Reason.*
1 Understanding is discursive.	1. Reason is fixed.
2. The Understanding in all its judgments refers to some other faculty as its ultimate authority.	2. The Reason in all its decisions appeals to itself as the ground and *substance* of their truth.
3. Understanding is the faculty of reflection.	3 Reason of contemplation. Reason, indeed, is much nearer to Sense than to Understanding, for Reason (says our great Hooker) is a direct aspect of truth, an inward beholding, having a similar relation to the intelligible or spiritual, as Sense has to the material or phenomenal —*Coleridge*, '*Aids to Reflection*,' p 168.

Milton draws the distinction between reason 'intuitive' and 'discursive.' Reid and Beattie represent Reason as having two degrees: in the former, reason sees the truth at once; in the other, it reaches it by a process. There is evidently ground for these distinctions But the distinction I am now to examine was first drawn in a formal manner by Kant, and has since assumed divers shapes in Germany and in this country. According to Kant, the mind has three general intellectual powers, the Sense, the Understanding (Verstand), and the Reason (Vernunft); the Sense giving us presentations or phenomena; the Understanding binding these by categories; and the Reason bringing the judgments of the Understanding to unity by three Ideas—of Substance, Totality of Phenomena, and Deity—which are especially the Ideas of Reason. The distinction was introduced among the English-speaking nations by Coleridge, who, however, modified it. 'Reason,' says he, 'is the power of universal and necessary convictions, the source and substance of truths above sense, and having their evidence in themselves. Its presence is always marked by the necessity of the position affirmed' ('Aids to Reflection,' i. 168). It has become an accepted distinction among a certain class of metaphysicians and divines all over Europe and the English-speaking people of the great American continent These parties commonly illustrate their views in some such way as the following:—The mind, they say, must have some power by which it gazes immediately on the true and the good But sense, which looks only to the phenomenal and fluctuating, cannot enable us to do so As little can the logical understanding, whose province it is to generalise the phenomena of sense, mount into so high a sphere. We must, therefore, bring in a transcendental power—call it Reason, or Intellectual Intuition, or Faith, or Feeling—to account for the mind's capacity of discovering the universal and the necessary, and of gazing at once on eternal Truth and Goodness, on the Infinite and the Absolute.

Now there is great and important truth aimed at and meant to be set forth in this language. The speculators of France, who derive all our notions from sense, and those of Britain, who draw all our maxims from experience, are overlooking the most wondrous properties of the soul, which has principles at once deeper and higher than sense, and the faculty which compounds and compares the material supplied by sense. And if by Reason is meant the aggregate of Regulative Principles, I have no objections to the phrase, and to certain important applications of it, but then we must keep carefully in view the mode in which these principles operate.

Moreover each of the divisions, the reason and the understanding, comprises powers which run into the other This distinction is at the best confusing, and it is often so stated as to imply that the reason, without the use of the understanding processes of abstraction and generalisation, can rise to the contemplation of the true, the beautiful, and the good.—*M'Cosh*, '*Intuitions of the Mind*,' pp 310, 61.

Function of the Understanding.

The function of the Understanding may, in general, be said to bestow on the cognitions which it elaborates the greatest possible compass, the greatest possible clearness and distinctness, the greatest possible certainty and systematic order.—*Hamilton*, '*Metaphysics*,' ii 501.

Possession of Understanding is necessary to Moral Freedom.

The Liberty of a Moral Agent supposes him to have Understanding and Will; for the determinations of the will are the sole object about which this power is employed; and there can be no will without such a degree of understanding at least as gives the conception of that which we will.—*Reid*, '*Works*,' p. 599.

2. Reason.

The term 'Reason' is used in Various Senses.

The word Reason has been employed in a great diversity of significations Sometimes it stands for the faculty which reasons or draws inferences. With other writers, reason, as distinguished from the understanding, denotes the power which sees necessary truth at once without an intermediate process. With certain English writers it stands for that aggregate of qualities (unspecified) which distinguishes man from brutes Very often it is a general name for intelligence, or for the cognitive powers of man. When persons compare or contrast the exercises of reason with those of faith they should be careful to understand for themselves and to signify to others the sense in which they employ the phrases.—*M'Cosh, 'Intuitions of the Mind,'* p. 375.

This word is liable to many ambiguities 1. Sometimes it is used to signify all the intellectual powers collectively. 2. Frequently it is employed to denote those intellectual powers exclusively in which man differs from brutes 3. It is often used for the Faculty of carrying on the operation of *Reasoning* or Ratiocination. 4. It is also employed to signify the Premiss or Premises of an Argument, especially the Minor Premiss; and it is from Reason in this sense that the word 'Reasoning' is derived. 5. It is also very frequently used to signify a *Cause*, as when we say, in popular language, that the 'Reason of an eclipse of the sun is that the moon is interposed between it and the earth.' This should be strictly called the *cause*.—*Whately, 'Logic,'* p 223.

The Offices of Reason considered as Intelligence in general.

To regulate Belief and Conduct.

That talent which we call *Reason*, by which men that are adult and of a sound mind are distinguished from brutes, idiots, and infants, has in all ages, among the learned and unlearned, been conceived to have two offices, *to regulate our belief and to regulate our actions and conduct.*—*Reid, 'Works,'* p 579.

To act as Judge.

There is nothing that can pretend to judge of Reason but itself; and, therefore, they who suppose they can say aught against it are forced (like jewellers who beat true diamonds to powder to cut and polish false ones) to make use of it against itself. But in this they cheat themselves as well as others; for if what they say against Reason be without Reason they deserve to be neglected, and if with Reason they disprove themselves For they use it while they disclaim it, and with as much contradiction as if a man should tell me that he cannot speak.—*Butler, 'Reflections on Reason.'*

To seek after Truth.

The whole interest of my reason, whether speculative or practical, is concentrated in the three following questions:—1. What can I know? 2. What should I do? 3. What may I hope? The first question is purely speculative The second question is purely practical The third question, namely, What may I hope for if I do what I ought to do? is at the same time practical and theoretical; the practical serving as a guidance to the answer to the theoretical, and, in its highest form, speculative questions.—*Kant, 'Critique,'* ii. 690, 691.

Its relation to Faith.

It is wrong to represent faith as in itself opposed to reason in any of its forms Faith may go far beyond intelligence, but it is not in itself repugnant to it. There is belief involved in all kinds of intelligence except the primary ones, those in which we look on the object as now present; and in all the higher exercises of reason there is a large faith-element which could be taken out of reason only with the certain penalty that reason would thereby be clipped of all its soaring capacities. What could cognition say of duration, expansion, substance, causation, beauty, moral good, infinity, God, were faith denied its proper scope and forbidden to take excursions in its native element?

But if reason is not independent of faith, so neither should faith proceed without reason. In particular, it would be far wrong to insist on any one believing in the existence of any object, or in any truth, without a warrant True, the mind is led to believe in much intuitively, but it is because the objects or verities are self-evident and reflexly can stand the tests of intuition. And in all cases in which we have not this self-evidence it is entitled to demand mediate evidence and should not concede credence till this is furnished. It is not indeed justified in insisting that all darkness be dispelled, but it is abandoning its prerogative when it declines to demand that light be afforded, either direct light, which is the most satisfactory, or reflected light where direct light cannot be had.—*M'Cosh*, '*Intuitions of the Mind*,' p. 375.

The Difficulties of Reason

Arise often from the limitation and imperfection of our nature.

No sooner do we depart from Sense and Instinct to follow the light of a superior principle—to reason, meditate, and reflect on the nature of things, but a thousand scruples spring up in our minds concerning those things which before we seemed fully to comprehend. Prejudices and errors of sense do from all parts discover themselves to our view; and endeavouring to correct these by Reason, we are insensibly drawn into uncouth paradoxes, difficulties, and inconsistencies, which multiply and grow upon us as we advance in speculation, till at length, having wandered through many intricate mazes, we find ourselves just where we were, or which is worse, set down in a forlorn Scepticism.—*Berkeley*, '*Principles of Human Knowledge*,' intro. 1.

Yet too much is frequently laid to the charge of this.

The cause of this is thought to be the obscurity of things, or the natural weakness and imperfection of our understandings. It is said the faculties we have are few, and those designed by nature for the support and pleasure of life, and not to penetrate into the inward essence and constitution of things. Besides, the mind of man being finite, it is not to be wondered at if it run into absurdities and contradictions, it being of the nature of the infinite not to be comprehended by that which is finite. But upon the whole, I am inclined to think that far the greater part, if not all, of those difficulties which have hitherto amused philosophers, and blocked up the way to knowledge, are entirely owing to ourselves—that we have first raised a dust and then complain we cannot see.—*Berkeley*, '*Principles of Human Knowledge*,' intro. 2, 3.

3. Reasoning.

As a Mental Act.

Reasoning is the process by which we pass from one judgment to another, which is the consequence of it. Accordingly our judgments are distinguished into intuitive, which are not grounded upon any preceding judgment, and discursive, which are deduced from some preceding judgment by reasoning.—*Reid*, '*Works*,' p. 475.

In the Logical Sense.

Reasoning is an act of comparison between two concepts, and only differs from judgment in that the two concepts are not compared together directly in themselves, but indirectly by means of their mutual relation to a third. As the concept furnishes the materials for the act of judging, so the judgment furnishes the materials for the act of reasoning.—*Mansel*, '*Metaphysics*,' p. 227.

Reasoning is drawing from two judgments, called the premises, a third called the conclusion, which is involved in the other two. The simple principle of all reasoning is, that whatever applies to the whole of a class applies to that which is known to be a part of it, and likewise whatsoever does not apply to the whole does not apply to any known part of it. In the natural order, the first or minor premise assigns the part to the whole, and in the second or major, some attribute is declared to apply or not, as the case may be, to the whole: whence it is gathered in the conclusion that this attribute applies or does not apply to the part already assigned to the whole. Thus—

These men are unjust; all the unjust are to be condemned:

∴ These men are to be condemned.—*Murphy*, '*Human Mind*,' p. 142

To this view of Reasoning, John Stuart Mill strongly objects. He says :—

'It is impossible rationally to hold that reasoning is the comparison of two notions through the medium of a third, and that reasoning is the source from which we derive new truths And the truth of the latter proposition being indisputable, it is the former which must give way The theory of Reasoning which attempts to unite them both has this defect :—it makes the process consist in eliciting something out of a concept which never was in the concept, and if it ever finds its way there, does so after the process, and as a consequence of its having taken place.' 'The principle of reasoning is not, a part of the part is a part of the whole, but, a mark of the mark is a mark of the thing marked It means, that two things which constantly coexist with the same third thing, constantly coexist with one another, the things meant not being our concepts, but the facts of experience on which our concepts ought to be grounded '—'*Examination of Hamilton*,' pp. 429, 426.

Reasoning is Founded on First or Assumed Principles.

Reasoning proceeds on principles which cannot be proved by reasoning, but must be assumed, and assumed as seen intuitively to be true In all ratiocination there must be something from which we argue That from which we argue is the premise; in the Aristotelian analysis of argument it is the two premises. But as we go back and back we must at length come to something which cannot be proven.—*M'Cosh*, '*Intuitions of the Mind*,' p. 24.

"I hold it to be certain, and even demonstrable, that all knowledge got by reasoning must be built upon first principles This is as certain as that every house must have a foundation. The power of reasoning, in this respect, resembles the mechanical powers or engines; it must have a fixed point to rest upon, otherwise it spends its force in the air and produces no effect. When we examine, in the way of analysis, the evidence of any proposition, either we find it self-evident or it rests upon one or more propositions that support it. The same thing may be said of the propositions that support it, and of those that support them, as far back as we can go But we cannot go back in this track to infinity. Where, then, must the analysis stop? It is evident that it must stop only when we come to propositions which support all that are built upon them, but are themselves supported by none,—that is, to self-evident propositions.—*Reid*, '*Works*,' p. 435.

Reasoning may be—

À priori or à posteriori.

In the ancient meaning of the terms, reasoning *à priori* is from the essential nature of the cause, prior to an experience of its effects; reasoning *à posteriori* is based upon observation of the effects which issue from the cause. The premises of the former are principles; those of the latter, facts The method of the former is deductive; that of the latter inductive.—*Fraser*, '*Selections from Berkeley*,' p. 43, note.

Probable or Demonstrative.

The most remarkable distinction of reasonings is, that some are probable, others demonstrative. In every step of demonstrative reasoning the inference is necessary, and we perceive it to be impossible that the conclusion should not follow from the premises. In probable reasoning the connection between the premises and the conclusion is not necessary, nor do we perceive it to be impossible that the first should be true while the last is false.—*Reid*, '*Works*,' p. 476.

The Power of Reasoning.

Its Utility.

Without the power of reasoning we should have been limited to a knowledge of what is given by immediate intuition; we should have been unable to draw any inference from this knowledge, and have been shut out from the discovery of that countless multitude of truths which, though of high, of paramount importance, are not self-evident This faculty is likewise of peculiar utility in order to protect us in our cogitations from error and falsehood, and to remove these if they have already crept in For every, the most complex, web of thought may be reduced to simple syllogisms; and when this is done their truth or falsehood, at least in a logical relation, flashes at once into view —*Hamilton*, '*Logic*,' i 277

It is rarely absent in Man, but it is sometimes a dormant faculty

It is nature, undoubtedly, that gives us the capacity of reasoning When this is wanting, no art nor education can supply it But this capacity may be dormant through life, like the seed of a plant which, for want of heat and moisture, never vegetates This is probably the case of some savages —*Reid*, '*Works*,' p 476

This power is strengthened by exercise.

Although the capacity be purely the gift of nature, and probably given in very different degrees to different persons, yet the power of reasoning seems to be got by habit, as much as the power of walking or running Its first exertions we are not able to recollect in ourselves, or clearly to discern in others. They are very feeble, and need to be led by example and supported by authority By degrees it acquires strength, chiefly by means of imitation and exercise.—*Reid*, '*Works*,' p. 476

XIII. CONCEIVABILITY REGARDED AS A TEST OF TRUTH

Forms of the Doctrine.

What we can distinctly conceive we may conclude to be true

As I observed that in the words *I think, hence I am*, there is nothing at all which gives me assurance of their truth beyond this, that I see very clearly that in order to think it is necessary to exist, I concluded that I might take, as a general rule, the principle that all the things which we very clearly and distinctly conceive are true, only observing, however, that there is some difficulty in rightly determining the objects which we distinctly conceive —*Descartes*, '*Discourse on Method*,' p 34

The criterion of true knowledge is only to be looked for in our knowledge and conceptions themselves, for the entity of all theoretical truth is nothing else but clear intelligibility, and whatever is clearly conceived is an entity and a truth; but that which is false, Divine power itself cannot make it to be clearly and distinctly understood. A falsehood can never be clearly conceived or apprehended to be true —*Cudworth*, '*Eternal and Immutable Morality*,' chap v sec 5

Of that which neither does nor can exist we can have no idea —*Bolingbroke*

What we can distinctly conceive we may conclude to be possible

The bare having an idea of the proposition proves the thing not to be impossible; for of an impossible proposition there can be no idea —*Clarke*.

The measure of impossibility to us is inconceivableness: that of which we can have no idea, but that reflecting upon it, it appears to be nothing, we pronounce it to be impossible —*Abernethy*.

It is an established maxim in metaphysics, that whatever the mind conceives, includes the idea of possible existence, or in other words, that nothing we imagine is absolutely impossible —*Hume*

The impossibility of conceiving the negative of a proposition shows that the proposition is true

If, having touched a body in the dark, and having become instantly conscious of some extension as accompanying the resistance, I wish to decide whether the proposition, 'Whatever resists has extension,' expresses a cognition of the highest certainty, how do I do it? I endeavour to think away the extension from the resistance I think of resistance, I endeavour to keep extension out of thought. I fail absolutely in the attempt. I cannot conceive the negation of the proposition that whatever resists is extended; and *my failure to conceive the negation*, is the discovery that along with the subject (something resisting) there *invariably exists* the predicate (extension). Hence the inconceivableness of its negation is that which shows a cognition to possess the highest rank—is the criterion by which its unsurpassable validity is known.—*Spencer*, '*Principles of Psychology*,' ii. 406.

Necessary truths are those in which we cannot, even by an effort of imagination, or in a supposition, conceive the reverse of that which is asserted. They are those of which we cannot even distinctly conceive the contrary.—*Whewell*, '*Phil. of Induc. Sciences*,' i. 55, 59.

A common account is that we cannot 'conceive' the contradictory of necessary truth. But the word 'conceive' is ambiguous, and in itself means nothing more than 'image' or 'apprehend,' that is, have a notion; and certainly we are not entitled to appeal to a mere phantasm or concept as a test of ultimate truth. The exact account is that we cannot be convinced of the opposite of the intuitive conviction. But our intuitive convictions may take the form of cognitions, or beliefs, or judgments; and, according to the nature of the intuition, that is, according as it is knowledge, or faith, or comparison, is the nature of the necessity attached. Whatever we *know* intuitively as existing, we cannot be made to know as not existing. Whatever we intuitively *believe*, we cannot be made not to believe. When we intuitively discover a relation in objects, we cannot be made to *judge* that there is not a relation. From neglecting these distinctions, which are very obvious when stated, manifold errors have arisen, not only in the application of the test of necessity, but in the general account given of primary truths.—*M'Cosh*, '*Intuitions of the Mind*,' p. 304.

Objections to the Doctrine.

Inconceivability is no test of truth or possibility.

We cannot conclude anything to be impossible, because its possibility is inconceivable to us, for two reasons. First, what seems to us inconceivable, and, so far as we are personally concerned, may really be so, usually owes its inconceivability only to a strong association. There is no need to go further for an example than the case of the Antipodes. This physical fact was, to the early speculators, inconceivable; not, of course, the fact of persons in that position—this the mind could easily represent to itself—but the possibility that, being in that position, and not being nailed on, nor having any glutinous substance attached to their feet, they could help falling off. Because inconceivable it was unhesitatingly believed to be impossible. But, secondly, even assuming that inconceivability is not solely the consequence of limited experience, but that some incapacities of conceiving are inherent in the mind, and inseparable from it; this would not entitle us to infer that what we are thus incapable of receiving cannot exist. Such an inference would only be warrantable, if we could know *à priori* that we must have been created capable of conceiving whatever is capable of existing. What is inconceivable, then, cannot therefore be inferred to be false. —*Mill*, '*Examination of Hamilton*,' pp. 80–82.

There is no ground for inferring a certain fact to be impossible, merely from our inability to conceive its possibility.—*Hamilton*, '*Discussions*,' p. 596.

As observation of objects affords the materials for our conceptions of them, the external association of qualities in an object may have an exact counterpart in the conception of these qualities associated in the mind. If our observation of trees has uniformly involved the recognition of trunk, branches, and green leaves, these three characteristics will be associated in our conception of a tree. We could not on this ground, however, warrantably maintain the physical impossibility of any variation. The sight of a black beech gives external diversity, and introduces a new association True, then, as it is in the history of mind, that external facts or phenomena answering to ideas constantly associated within, come at last to be regarded by us as in reality inseparable, such an inference from internal association to external reality is logically incompetent. The possibilities of existence are not restricted by the range of our conceptions Conceivableness is not the test of truth; nor is inconceivableness the test of the false. As a test of *possible existence*, conceivability is the least reliable that can be used The conceivable may be only what we have known, the inconceivable, nothing more than what we have never known. The tendency to employ inconceivableness as a test of truth has involved philosophical inquiry in confusion, and has led to the egregious assumption that our thoughts are the measure of reality.—*Calderwood*, '*Moral Philosophy*,' p 117.

Conceivability no test of truth or possibility.

Man's capability of imagining an object is no proof of its existence I can picture a hobgoblin without supposing it to be a reality I can form a notion of a class of mermaids without being convinced that mermaids were ever seen by any human being.—*M'Cosh*, '*Examination of Mill*,' p 236

Reply to the objections

Mr Mill objects that propositions once accepted as true because they withstood the test of the inconceivability of their negation, have since been proved to be false, as in the instance of the antipodes To this criticism my reply is that the propositions erroneously accepted because they seemed to withstand the test, were not simple propositions but complex to which the test is inapplicable, and that no errors arising from its illegitimate application can be held to tell against its legitimate application If the question be asked—How are we to decide what is a legitimate application of the test? I answer, by restricting its application to propositions which are not further decomposable. Further, Mr Mill tacitly assumes that all men have adequate powers of introspection; whereas many are incapable of correctly interpreting consciousness in any but its simplest modes, and even the remainder are liable to mistake for dicta of consciousness what prove on closer examination not to be its dicta.—*Spencer*, '*Principles of Psychology*,' ii. 409–413 (condensed).

Conceivability and inconceivability can be employed as a test of truth only in the third meaning of the term conceive [the two other meanings being, (1) image or represent, (2) have a general notion] as signifying 'construe in thought,' judge or decide In the case of the antipodes given by Mr Mill, it is evident our fathers could have little difficulty in imagining to themselves a round globe with persons with their feet adhering to it all around Their difficulty lay in deciding it to be true, because the alleged fact seemed contrary to a law of nature established by observation As a narrow experience had created the difficulty, so it could remove it by giving us a view of the earth as a mass of matter causing human beings to adhere to it over its whole surface. Such a case does not in the least tend to prove that truths which are seen to be truths at once, and without a gathered experience, could ever be set aside by a further experience; that a conscious intelligent being could be made to regard himself as non existing; or that he could be led to allow that two straight lines might enclose a space in the constellation Orion.—*M'Cosh*, '*Examination of Hamilton*,' pp. 236, 240.

XIV. BELIEF.

The Term.

Its manifold senses

By a singular freak of language we use the word *belief* to describe our state of mind with reference both to those propositions of the truth of which we are least certain, and to those of the truth of which we are most certain We apply it to states of mind which have nothing in common, except that they cannot be justified by a chain of logical proofs. For example, you believe perhaps that all crows are black, but, being unable to furnish absolutely convincing demonstration of this proposition, you say that you believe it, not that you know it You also believe in your own personal existence, of which, however, you can furnish no logical demonstration, simply because it is an ultimate fact in your consciousness which underlies and precedes all demonstration.—*Fiske.*

The word belief is used in a variety of relations which seem at first to have but little in common We are said to believe in what lies beyond the limits of our temporal experience, in the supersensible, in God and a future life Again, we are said to believe in the first principles or ultimate verities from which all trains of demonstration must start, as conditions of demonstration, these are themselves undemonstrable and are therefore objects of belief We receive by belief perceptions of simple matters of fact, which, from their very nature, cannot be demonstrated We believe from memory the facts of past experience, we have expectation or belief in future events We accept truths on the evidence of testimony; and, finally, we believe that our actual consciousness of things is in harmony with reality.—*Adamson, 'Encyclop. Brit.,'* iii. 532.

It cannot be defined.

Every man that has any belief—and he must be a curiosity that has none—knows perfectly what belief is, but can never define it Belief is a word not admitting of logical definition, because the operation of mind signified by it is perfectly simple and of its own kind.—*Reid, 'Works,'* pp 108, 327.

It may be laid down with some confidence that no logical definition of the process of belief is possible.—*Adamson, 'Encyclop. Brit.,'* iii. 532.

Relation of Belief to Knowledge

The ordinary distinction between them.

In common language, when Belief and Knowledge are distinguished, Knowledge is understood to mean complete conviction, Belief a conviction somewhat short of complete, or else we are said to believe when the evidence is probable (as that of testimony), but to know, when it is intuitive or demonstrative from intuitive premises we believe, for example, that there is a continent of America, but know that we are alive, that two and two make four, and that the sum of any two sides of a triangle is greater than the third side. This is a distinction of practical value.—*Mill, 'Examination of Hamilton,'* p. 75.

Other distinctions drawn by philosophers.

Herein lies the difference between probability and certainty, faith and knowledge, that in all the parts of knowledge there is intuition; each immediate idea, each step has its visible and certain connexion; in belief not so That which makes me believe is something extraneous to the thing I believe; something not evidently joined on both sides to, and so not manifestly showing the agreement or disagreement of those ideas that are under consideration.—*Locke, 'Essay,'* bk iv chap. xv sect. 3.

The notion of Sir W. Hamilton that we have two convictions on the same point, one guaranteeing the other—our knowledge of a truth, and our belief in the truth of that knowledge—seems to me a piece of false philosophy We do not know a truth and believe it besides; the belief *is* the knowledge. Belief altogether is a genus which includes knowledge; according to the usage of language we believe whatever we assent to, but some of our beliefs are knowledge, others are only belief. The first requisite which, by universal admission, a belief must possess to constitute it knowledge, is that it be true. The second is that it be well-grounded, for what we believe by accident or on evidence not sufficient we are not said to know When a belief is true, is held with the strongest conviction we ever have, and held on grounds sufficient to justify that strongest conviction, most people would think it worthy of the name of knowledge, whether it be grounded on our personal investigations or on the appropriate testimony, and whether we know only the fact itself or the manner of the fact —*Mill*, '*Examination of Hamilton*,' p 78, note

We can hardly consider Stuart Mill's view satisfactory, since it makes the objective truth of the proposition believed, rather than the manner in which it is held by the mind, the distinguishing characteristic of Knowledge as opposed to Belief; while it overlooks the fact that Belief includes certain important non-intellectual elements which are not existent, or not prominent, in Knowledge.—*Ryland*, '*Psychology and Ethics*,' p. 100

Knowledge precedes Belief.

In the order of nature, belief always precedes knowledge,—it is the condition of instruction. The child (as observed by Aristotle) must believe in order that he may learn, and even the primary facts of intelligence,—the facts which precede, as they afford the conditions of, all knowledge,—would not be original were they revealed to us under any other form than that of natural or necessary beliefs —*Hamilton*, '*Metaphysics*,' i. 44.

The Relation of Belief to Activity

This is expressed by saying, that what we believe we act upon. In the practice of everyday life, we are accustomed to test men's belief by action, 'faith by works.' If a politician declares free trade to be good, and yet will not allow it to be acted on, people say he does not believe his own assertion. A general affirming that he was stronger and better entrenched than the enemy, and yet acting as if he were weaker, would be held as believing not what he affirmed, but what he acted on Any one pretending to believe in a future life of rewards and punishments, and acting precisely as if there were no such life, is justly set down as destitute of belief in the doctrine —*Bain*, '*Mental and Moral Science*,' p 372.

Analysis of Belief

It is a highly composite state of mind.

Belief, however simple a thing it appears at first sight, is really a highly composite state of mind, or at least involves the presence of numerous other forms of consciousness. Thus, to give but one example, it is easily seen that every belief implies an idea, and that the laws of the one must somehow or other be influenced by the laws of the other. Consequently the science of ideas, their formation, and the order of their recurrence, has to precede the science of belief —*Sully*, '*Sensation*,' p. 74.

The analysis of James Mill.

Belief of every kind : *e.g.*, 1 Belief in events, *i.e.*, real existences; 2 Belief in testimony; 3. Belief in the truth of propositions—including belief in cause and effect, *i.e.*, of antecedence and consequence, in substance, and in personal identity—is resolved into some form of inseparable association —*Ueberweg*, '*Hist of Phil.*,' ii. 424.

The analysis of Professor Bain.

The mental foundations of Belief are to be sought (1) in our Activity, (2) in the Intellectual Associations of our Experience, and (3) in the Feelings.

It is here affirmed, not only that Belief in its essence is an active state, but that its foremost generating cause is the Activity of the system, to which are added influences Intellectual and Emotional.—'*Mental and Moral Science*,' p. 376.

Criticism of these analyses. Belief is not resolvable into inseparability of association (James Mill's theory).

If belief were nothing but a transformation of inseparably associated ideas, then every case of such association would develop belief But as a matter of fact we are frequently compelled, as in the case of the apparent motion of the sun, to conceive events in one way and to believe them in another This view ignores the difference between imagination and belief.—*Sully*, '*Sensation, &c.*,' p 76.

Readiness to act (Bain's theory).

Just as we do not find belief involved in activity, so we can conceive, and may find belief without any accompanying activity. No doubt, in the structure of our mental constitution belief is most intimately connected with action, yet there is surely no contradiction in conceiving of a mind, perfectly destitute of action, participating in this feeling. We can readily represent to ourselves the case of a helpless paralytic, carefully tended by nurses, who might come to anticipate periodic recurrence of his comforts, and feel at the signs of their approach what is implied in belief.—*Sully*, '*Sensation*,' p 78.

Bain's whole theory seems but an instance of a not uncommon error in psychology,—the confusion of the test or measure of a thing with the thing itself Belief is truly a motive of action, and all that has been said of it by Professor Bain would hold good of it in this relation to identify the two is to run together two totally distinct processes.—*Prof R Adamson*, '*Encyclop. Brit*,' iii. 534.

Belief is the primary condition of reason.

St. Austin accurately says, 'We know what rests upon *reason*; but believe what rests upon *authority*.' But reason itself must rest at last upon authority; for the original data of reason do not rest on reason, but are necessarily accepted by reason on the authority of what is beyond itself. These data are, therefore, in rigid propriety, Beliefs or Trusts Thus it is that in the last resort we must perforce philosophically admit that belief is the primary condition of reason, and not reason the ultimate ground of belief. We are compelled to surrender the proud *Intellige ut credas* of Abelard, to content ourselves with the humble *Crede ut intelligas* of Anselm.—*Hamilton, Reid's* '*Works*,' p. 760.

The Grounds and Motives of Belief.

In general

It is necessary, of course, to distinguish between the grounds and motives of belief; the *cause* of a belief may not be exactly a *reason* for it. But if we include both causes and reasons under the title principles of belief, these may be divided into three classes:—(1.) *Testimony*. Our natural tendency is to accept all testimony as true; it is experience alone that teaches caution The majority of men would be astonished to find how much their belief depends upon the society into which they have been born and in which they live. (2.) *Feelings, Desires, or Wishes*. It has always been a popular saying that 'The wish is father to the thought.' We believe that without which our nature would be dissatisfied. (3.) *Evidence of Reason*. Wherever our knowledge is incomplete, belief is ready to step in and fill up the gap. Great portions of our so-called scientific knowledge are nothing but rational belief,—hypotheses unverified, perhaps even unverifiable.—*Adamson*, '*Encyclop. Brit.*,' iii 535.

Belief may be influenced by

Feeling.

'The powerful influence of feeling on belief has long been recognised The *first* thing to be remarked is, that whenever an emotion attaches to itself distinct ideas, they tend to become very intense,—to brighten, so to speak, in the glow of the emotional surroundings, and to attain a vivacity and a persistency which assimilate them more or less completely to external sensations. The mind of the observer looks at the object through an emotional medium, and so fails to discern the true relations of things. Feeling interferes, in some slight measure at least, with the just perception of truth The *second* point to be noticed is the direction which a ruling emotion gives to the thoughts. Every feeling tends, according to what may be called a law of self-conservation, to sustain itself in consciousness, and to oppose the entrance of heterogeneous and hostile feelings. To this end it welcomes and retains all ideas fitted to intensify it, and excludes others which would serve to introduce an opposite state of feeling. For example, whenever the impulse of tender regard is strongly excited, the mind is quick to spy qualities fitted to gratify the feeling, and slow to detect the presence of adverse qualities. — *Sully*, '*Sensations, &c.*,' p. 100–104.

Habit.

The effect of habit on belief appears to be twofold. It tends to reduce the believing process to a rapid and fugitive mental state; for habitual conduct tends to become less and less a conscious process, and so to leave but little room for the distinct intellectual conditions of belief. At the same time it immensely deepens the potential tenacity of belief, for the habit of practically carrying out a conviction has a reflex effect in strengthening it. Religious conviction illustrates the tendency of any idea long cherished and acted upon to become a necessity of the mental organisation, to tear up which would be to strike deep down towards the roots of mental life.—*Sully*, '*Sensations, &c.*,' p. 114.

Will.

The mode in which the will most certainly affects belief is through the activities of voluntary attention. Whenever the impression or idea is a pleasurable one, it calls forth the energies of attention, and thus rises into greater distinctness and acquires greater permanence. All the pleasurable emotional susceptibilities may thus, through the stimulation of attention, exert an appreciable effect on belief. . . . Another mode in which the will may indirectly affect belief is through a restraining of the emotional impulses. This exercise of the will may either directly modify the strength of the feeling itself, or, by a direction of attention to other ideas, indirectly discourage the feeling.—*Sully*, '*Sensations, &c.*,' p. 115.

The personal equation in Belief.

The mind of each one of us, at any given time, possesses in its peculiar intellectual structure a clearly-defined framework into which all new convictions have to be fitted. The range of observation in past individual experience, the habit of supplementing this knowledge by learning what others have experienced too, and the discipline of the conceptive and reasoning powers, serve to determine the capacities of credence in relation to any new proposition submitted for examination. And the intellectual idiosyncrasy thus established forms one side of what has been well termed the 'personal equation,' or variable individual factor in human belief.—*Sully*, '*Sensation, &c.*,' p. 99.

Disbelief is Belief.

It is most important to keep in mind the self-evident, but often-forgotten maxim, that Disbelief is Belief; only they have reference to *opposite conclusions*. For example, to disbelieve the real existence of the city of Troy, is to believe that it was feigned. So also, though the terms 'infidel' and '*un*believer' are commonly applied to one who rejects Christianity, it is plain that to *dis*believe its divine origin is to believe its human origin. The proper opposite to Belief is either conscious *Ignorance* or *Doubt.* —*Whately's* '*Rhetoric*,' p. 51.

XV. PROBABILITY.

Its Nature.

Probability is the quantity or degree of belief, or more truly, the quantity of information concerning an uncertain event, measured by the ratio of the number of cases favourable to the event to the total number of cases which are possible.—*Jevons*, '*Logic*,' p. 339.

What happens, not always, but sometimes,—as that the sun rises in a cloudless sky, that men live seventy years—is not certain. Neither the fact, nor the failure of the fact, is certain. To this situation is applied the term Probability.—*Bain, 'Logic, Induction,'* p 90.

'Probability' is not always used in its proper meaning, namely, the expression of what is true, not in every case, but in *most.* Not unfrequently, the two sets of cases, *pro* and *con,* are called the probabilities for and against a thing The wind blows from the east, say three days in seven, and from the west four days in seven, the proper expression then is, there is a probability of four to three in favour of west wind on a given day To say that the probabilities are four in favour of, and three against a west wind, leads to a confounding of the probable with the improbable. A vacillation between the meanings is observable in Butler's Introduction to his 'Analogy'—*Bain, 'Logic, Induction,'* p. 388.

Does probability exist in the things which are probable, or in the mind which regards them as such? The etymology of the name lends us no assistance; for, curiously enough, *probable* is ultimately the same word as *provable,* a good instance of one word becoming differentiated to two opposite meanings But every one sees, after a little reflection, that it is in our knowledge the deficiency lies, not in the certainty of nature's laws. There is no doubt in lightning as to the point it shall strike; in the greatest storm there is nothing capricious; not a grain of sand lies upon the beach but infinite knowledge would account for its lying there.—*Jevons, 'Principles of Science,'* p 197.

Two Kinds

Probability is of two kinds; either when the object is itself uncertain, and to be determined by chance, or when, though the object be already certain, yet it is uncertain to our judgment, which finds a number of proofs or presumptions on each side of the question.—*Hume, 'Dissertation on the Passions,'* sec. i. 5.

Analogy is the Great Rule of Probability

We see animals are generated, nourished, and move; the loadstone draws iron; and the parts of a candle, successively melting, turn into flame, and give us both light and heat. These and the like effects we see and know; but the causes that operate, and the manner they are produced in, we can only guess and probably conjecture For these and the like, coming not within the scrutiny of human senses, cannot be examined by them, or be attested by anybody, and therefore can appear more or less probable, only as they more or less agree to truths that are established in our minds, and as they hold proportion to other parts of our knowledge and observation. Analogy in these matters is the only help we have, and it is from that alone we draw all our grounds of probability.—*Locke, 'Essay,'* bk. iv. chap xvi. sec. 12.

Probability admits of Degrees.

Probable evidence is essentially distinguished from demonstrative by this, that it admits of degrees; and of all variety of them, from the highest moral certainty, to the very lowest presumption We cannot indeed say a thing is probably true upon one very slight presumption for it; because, as there may be probabilities on both sides of a question, there may be some against it; and though there be not, yet a slight presumption does not beget that degree of conviction, which is implied in saying a thing is probably true But that the slightest possible presumption is of the nature of a probability, appears from hence, that such low presumption often repeated, will amount even to moral certainty. Thus a man's having observed the ebb and flow of the tide to-day, affords some sort of presumption, though the lowest imaginable, that it may happen again to-morrow But the observation of this event for so many days and months and ages together, as it has been observed by mankind, gives us a full assurance that it will.—*Butler, 'Analogy,'* introd.

Theory of Probability.

What it is.

The theory of probability consists in putting similar cases on a par, and distributing equally among them whatever knowledge we possess Throw a penny into the air, and consider what we know with regard to its way of falling We know that it will certainly fall upon a side, so that either head or tail will be uppermost; but as to whether it will be head or tail, our knowledge is equally divided. Whatever we know concerning head, we know also concerning tail, so that we have no reason for expecting one more than the other. Our state of knowledge will be changed should we throw up the coin many times and register the results. Every throw gives us some slight information as to the probable tendency of the coin, and in subsequent calculations we must take this into account. If we have the slightest reason for suspecting that one event is more likely to occur than another, we should take this knowledge into account. This being done, we must determine the whole number of events which are, so far as we know, equally likely. Thus, if we have no reason for supposing that a penny will fall more often one way than another, there are two cases, head and tail, equally likely But if from trial or otherwise, we know or think we know, that of 100 throws 55 will give tail, then the probability is measured by the ratio of 55 to 100.—*Jevons*, '*Principles of Science*,' pp. 200–202.

Calculation of Probabilities

The mode of calculation is too complicated to be explained here. The reader may be referred to De Morgan 'On the Theory of Probabilities,' Venn's 'Logic of Chance,' Whitworth's 'Choice and Chance,' Jevons' 'Principles of Science,' Bain's 'Logic,' Induction, bk. iii. chap ix.

Probability is the Guide of Life.

Nothing which is the possible object of knowledge, whether past, present, or future, can be probable to an infinite Intelligence; since it cannot but be discerned absolutely as it is in itself, certainly true, or certainly false But to us, probability is the very guide of life —*Butler*, '*Analogy*,' introd.

In actual life the most momentous decisions have frequently to be made on probable grounds. A statesman may feel the greatest uncertainty respecting the policy he ought to adopt in a great crisis; he may hesitate months before deciding, but when the decision has been made, he will, if he be a wise man, devote his whole energies and all the power he wields to carry it into effect. The conduct of a friend or child often renders it imperative for a man to interpose and to act; and he may find it a most difficult matter, needing the anxious consultation of friends, to decide what course it is his duty to take. But he must decide, and decide promptly; and having decided, he must do what he considers his duty without hesitation. For the purpose of our moral responsibility, whether in great matters or in small, Butler's statement is impregnable that 'to us probability is the very guide of life.'—*Wace*, '*Christianity and Morality*,' p. 183.

It is the necessary basis of the judgments we make in the prosecution of science, or the decisions we come to in the conduct of ordinary affairs. In nature perfect knowledge would be infinite knowledge, which is clearly beyond our capacities. All our inferences concerning the future are merely probable.—*Jevons*, '*Principles of Science*,' p. 197.

XVI. THE CATEGORIES.

The Term

Its twofold meaning

In a philosophical application, it has two meanings, or rather it is used in a general and in a restricted sense In its general sense, it means simply a *predication* or *attribution*, in its restricted sense, it has been deflected to denote predications or attributions of a very lofty generality, in other words, certain classes of a very wide extension. In modern philosophy it has been very arbitrarily, in fact very abusively, perverted from both its primary and its secondary signification among the ancients —*Hamilton*, '*Logic*,' i. 197.

Exemplified in Aristotle and Kant

The Categories of Aristotle and other philosophers were the highest classes (under Being) to which the objects of our knowledge could be generalised. Kant contorted the term from its proper meaning of attribution; and from an objective to a subjective application; bestowing this name on the ultimate and necessary laws by which thought is governed in its manifestations. The term, in this relation, has, however, found acceptation; and been extended to designate, in general, all the *à priori* phenomena of mind, though Kant himself limited the word to a certain order of these —*Hamilton, Reid's 'Works,'* p. 762.

Definition

The categories are the highest classes to which all the objects of knowledge can be reduced, and in which they can be arranged in subordination and system.—*Fleming, 'Vocab. of Phil.,'* p. 73.

Origin of the Categories.

Philosophy seeks to know all things But it is impossible to know all things individually. They are, therefore, arranged in classes, according to properties which are common to them. And when we know the definition of a class, we attain to a formal knowledge of all the individual objects of knowledge contained in that class This attempt to render knowledge in some sense universal has been made in all ages of philosophy, and has given rise to the *categories* which have appeared in various forms —*Fleming, 'Vocab. of Phil.,'* p. 73.

Aim.

The intention of the Categories is to muster every object of human apprehension under heads; for they are given as a complete enumeration of everything which can be either the subject or the predicate of a proposition. So that, as every soldier belongs to some company, and every company to some regiment, in like manner every thing that can be the object of human thought has its place in one or other of the categories, and by dividing and subdividing properly the several categories, all the notions that enter into the human mind may be mustered in rank and file, like an army in the day of battle.

There are two ends that may be proposed by such divisions The first is, to methodise or digest in order what a man actually knows. The second is, to exhaust the subject divided, so that nothing that belongs to it shall be omitted.—*Reid, 'Works,'* pp. 687, 688.

And use.

A regular distribution of things under proper classes or heads is, without doubt, a great help both to memory and judgment. —*Reid, 'Works,'* p. 688.

The Categories as Arranged by Various Philosophers.

Aristotle's Ten Categories or Predicaments.

1. *Essence* or *Substance;* such as man, horse. 2 *How much* or *Quantity;* such as, two cubits long, three cubits long 3 *What manner of* or *Quality;* such as, white, erudite. 4. *Ad aliquid—To something* or *Relation;* such as, double, half, greater 5. *Where,* such as in the market-place, in the Lykeium 6. *When,* such as, yesterday, last year. 7. *In what posture;* such as, he stands up, he is sitting down. 8 *To have;* such as, to be shod, to be armed 9. *Activity,* such as, he is cutting, he is burning. 10 *Passivity;* such as, he is being cut, he is being burned —*Grote, 'Aristotle,'* pp. 65, 66.

Mill's criticism of the Aristotelic Categories.

(1.) The list is unphilosophical and superficial, being a mere catalogue of the distinctions rudely marked out by the language of familiar life, without any attempt to penetrate to the rationale of even these common distinctions

(2.) It is redundant: Action, Passion, Position, Place, Time, and Possession are cases of Relation; Position and Place are the same, viz., position in space.

(3.) It is defective: having no head, or *summum genus,* under which *States of Con-*

ousness can be classed.—*Killick*, '*Handbook to Mill's Logic*,' p. 16.

The Stoics.

These reduce the ten Categories of Aristotle to four:—The Substance or Substratum, the Essential Quality, Manner of Being, and Relation.

Kanada (Hindu Philosopher).

He has six Categories:—Substance, Quality, Action, Genus, Individuality, and Concretion or Co-inherence. Under these six classes Kanada ranges the facts of the universe.

Plotinus.

Plotinus subjects the Aristotelian and also the Stoic doctrine of Categories to a minute criticism, of which the fundamental idea is that the *ideal* and the *sensible* do not fall under the same categories. He thus offers a twofold list:—(1.) Fundamental Forms of the Ideal are Being, Rest, Motion, Identity, and Difference. (2.) Categories of the Sensible are Substance, Relation, Quality, Quantity, and Motion.

Descartes.

Who arranged all things under two great Categories, the Absolute and the Relative.

Kant.

I. *Of Quantity.* Unity, Plurality, Totality.
II. *Of Quality.* Reality, Negation, Limitation.
III. *Of Relation.* Of Inherence and Subsistence (*substantia et accidens*).
" " Of Causality and Dependence (cause and effect).
" " Of Community (reciprocity between the active and the passive).
IV. *Of Modality.* Possibility, Impossibility, Existence, Non-existence, Necessity, Contingency.
—'*Critique*,' ii. p. 71.

John S. Mill.

We obtain the following as an enumeration and classification of all Nameable Things:—(1.) Feelings, or States of Consciousness. (2.) The Minds which experience these feelings. (3.) The Bodies or external objects which excite certain of those feelings, together with the powers or properties whereby they excite them. (4.) The Successions and Co-existences, the Likenesses and Unlikenesses, between feelings or states of consciousness.—'*Logic*,' i. 83.

Professor Adamson remarks justly that 'this classification proceeds on a quite peculiar view of the categories.'

Noah Porter.

The categories or intuitions may be divided into (1) *the formal*, which are those that are necessarily involved in the act of knowledge—essential to the form or process of knowledge; (2) *the mathematical*, those which grow out of the existence of space and time; (3) *the real*, those ordinarily recognised as generic and fundamental to the so-called qualities and properties of existing things.—'*Human Intellect*,' p. 514.

Substance.

Locke's account of the origin of the idea.

The mind being furnished with a great number of the simple ideas conveyed in by the senses, as they are found in exterior things, or by reflection on its own operations, takes notice also that a certain number of these simple ideas go constantly together; which being presumed to belong to one thing, and words being suited to common apprehensions, and made use of for quick dispatch, are called, so united in one subject, by one name; which, by inadvertency, we are apt afterwards to talk of and consider as one simple idea, which indeed is a complication of many ideas together; because, as I have said, not imagining how these simple ideas can subsist by themselves, we accustom ourselves to suppose some substratum wherein they do subsist, and from which they do result; which, therefore, we call substance.—'*Human Understanding,*' bk ii ch. xxiii. sec. 1.

Cousin's criticism of Locke's theory.

Admitting only ideas explicable by sensation or reflection, and being able to explain the idea of substance by neither, it was necessary for him to deny it, to reduce it to qualities which are easily attained by sensation or reflection. Hence the systematic confusion of qualities and substance, of phenomena and being, that is, the destruction of being, and consequently of beings. Nothing, therefore, substantially exists, neither God nor the world, neither you nor I; all is resolved into phenomena, into abstractions, into words; and, strange enough, it is the very fear of abstraction and verbal entities, it is the badly understood taste for reality which precipitates Locke into an absolute nominalism, which is nothing else than an absolute nihilism.—'*History of Modern Philosophy,*' ii 205.

Hume denies existence of substance.

I would fain ask those philosophers, who found so much of their reasonings on the distinction of substance and accident, and imagine we have clear ideas of each, whether the idea of *substance* be deriv'd from the impressions of sensation or of reflection? If it be convey'd to us by our senses, I ask, which of them; and after what manner? If it be perceiv'd by the eyes, it must be a colour; if by the ears, a sound; if by the palate, a taste; and so of the other senses. But I believe none will assert, that substance is either a colour, or sound, or a taste. The idea of substance must therefore be deriv'd from an impression of reflection, if it really exist. But the impressions of reflection resolve themselves into our passions and emotions, none of which can possibly represent a substance. We have, therefore, no idea of substance, distinct from that of a collection of particular qualities, nor have we any other meaning when we either talk or reason concerning it.—'*Human Nature,*' part i. sec. vi.

Substance is apprehended by the Mind.

Consciousness, in the first place, tells us that no sensible quality can be perceived or conceived by itself, but that each is necessarily accompanied by an intellectual apprehension of its relation to space, as occupying it and contained in it. Colour cannot be perceived without extension; nor extension without solidity; and solidity is not a single attribute, but includes in its comprehension the three special dimensions of length, breadth, and thickness. In the second place, it tells us that all sensitive perception is a relation between self and not-self; that all sensible objects are apprehended as occupying space, and thus as distinct from the apprehending mind, whether distinct or not from the bodily organism. Every attribute is thus intuitively perceived, and, consequently, is also reflectively conceived, as accompanied by other attributes, and as constituting, in conjunction with those attributes, a *non-ego* or sensible thing; but of an insensible substratum consciousness tells us and can tell us nothing; nor do we feel any necessity of believing in its existence, when the question is distinctly put before us, disentangled from its usual associations.—*Mansel,* '*Metaphysics,*' pp. 262, 263.

If you think of a quality, attribute, or phenomenon, you must think of a substance that has it: the idea is of *a relation,* as much as the idea of father and child, of back and front; but, in the absence of phenomenon or quality, there is no need and no room for substance in our thought, any more than for a back where there is no front, or likeness where there is but unity.

When you have said that substance is *the ground of quality,* you have assigned to it its *only predicate;* there is no more to be said about it; nor is this proposition fruitful of ulterior ones, unless you like to take it in the inverse direction, and say that quality inheres in substance.—*Martineau,* '*Types of Ethical Theory,*' i. 267.

Cause Defined

Generally.

The general idea of *cause* is, that without which another thing, called the *effect*, cannot be.—*Monboddo*, '*Ancient Metaphysics*,' bk. i. ch. iv.

As an invariable antecedent.

A cause is that which immediately precedes any change, and which, existing at any time in similar circumstances, has been always, and will be always, immediately followed by a similar change.—*Thomas Brown*, '*Inquiry, &c.*,' part i.

A cause is that assemblage of phenomena, which occurring, some other event follows invariably and unconditionally.—*Killick*, '*Handbook to Mill*,' p. 103.

As a productive power.

A cause is that which, of itself, makes anything begin to be.—*Irons*, '*Final Causes*,' p. 74.

A cause is something which not only *precedes*, but has power to *produce* the effect.—*Fleming*, '*Vocab. of Phil.*,' p. 78.

A cause is the sum or aggregate of all such accidents, both in the agents and the patients, as concur in the producing of the effect propounded; all which existing together, it cannot be understood but that the effect existeth with them, or that it can possibly exist if any of them be absent.—*Hobbes.*

Source of the Idea of Cause. Opinions of

Locke.

Who refers this idea to sensation or reflection. We see that one thing has the power to create, or generate, or make, or alter another thing, and such powers we call *causing*, and the things that have them are causes.—'*Human Understanding*, ii. 26, § 2.

Hume.

He rejects the notion that the fact which we call a cause exercises any power whatever over the effect. But from constantly observing the association or sequence of two facts, we begin to see their invariable connection, and to represent one as the cause of the other. A number of observations is thus a necessary condition of our forming the idea.—'*Essay on Human Understanding*,' sec. vii. pt. ii.

Leibnitz.

Who assigns to everything that exists a certain force or power, and thus constitutes it a cause. Power and causation are attributes of all being, not inferred from but implied by it.—'*Nouveaux Essais*,' bk. ii.

Kant.

He considered the notion of cause and effect as one of the forms of the understanding, one of the conditions under which we must think. We are compelled by a law of our mind to arrange the impressions of our experience according to this form, making one thing a cause and another an effect.—'*Critique, Transcendental Analytic.*'

Maine de Biran.

The notion of cause originates with our consciousness of the power of will, which recognises the will as the cause of our actions; and we transfer this personal power by a kind of analogy to all the operations of nature.

Sir W. Hamilton.

He traces the idea of causality to that limitation of our faculties which prevents us from realising an *absolute* commencement or an absolute termination of being. When we think of a thing, we know that it has come into being as a phenomenon, but we are forced to believe that the elements and facts that produced the phenomenon existed already in another form. In the world to which our observations are confined, being does not *begin*; it only changes its manifestations.—*Thomson's* '*Laws of Thought*,' pp. 194, 195.

Four Kinds of Causes.

Aristotle divides into four kinds, known by the name of the *material*, the *formal*, the *efficient*, and the *final*. The first is that of which any thing is made. Thus brass or marble is the *material* cause of a statue; earth, air, fire, and water, of all natural bodies. The *formal cause* is the form, idea, archetype, or pattern of a thing; for all these words Aristotle uses to express it. Thus the idea of the artist is the formal cause of the statue. The *efficient cause* is the principle of change or motion which produces the thing. In this sense the statuary is the cause of the statue, and the God of nature the cause of all the works of nature. And lastly, the *final* cause is that for the sake of which any thing is done. Thus the statuary makes the statue for pleasure or for profit, and the works of nature are all for some good end.—*Monboddo*, '*Ancient Metaphysics*,' bk. i. chap. iv.

It is possible that one object may combine all the kinds of causes. Thus in a house, the *principle of movement* is the art and the workmen, the *final* cause is the work, the *matter* the earth and stones, and the plan is the *form*.—*Aristotle*, '*Metaphysics*,' lib. iii. cap. 2.

First Causes, the Search of Philosophy.

Philosophical knowledge, in the widest acceptation of the term, and as synonymous with science, is the knowledge of effects as dependent on their causes. The aim of philosophy is to trace up the series of effects and causes, until we arrive at causes which are not also themselves effects. These first causes do not indeed lie within the reach of philosophy. But as philosophy is the knowledge of effects in their causes, the tendency of philosophy is ever upwards; and philosophy can, in thought, in theory, only be viewed as accomplished when the ultimate causes—on which all other causes depend—have been attained and understood.—*Hamilton*, '*Metaphysics*,' i. 58.

The First Cause.

An infinite chain of causes is impossible.

The series of causes and effects can neither recede *in infinitum*, nor return like a circle into itself; it must, therefore, depend on some necessary link, and this link is the first being. This first being exists necessarily; the supposition of its non-existence involves a contradiction. It is uncaused, and needs in order to its existence no cause external to itself. It is the cause of all that exists.—*Alfarabius*, '*Fontes Quaestionum*,' chap. 3.

It is said, in a loose way, that every object must have a cause; and then, as this cause must also have a cause, it might seem as if we were compelled to go on for ever from one link to another. We must then seek for a cause not only of the world, but of the Being who made the world. Kant endeavours to escape from this by declaring that the law of cause and effect, which thus required an infinite *regressus*, was a law of thought and not of things. But all inquiry into causation conducts us to substance; but it does not compel us to go further, or to go on for ever. If we find no signs of that Being who made the world being an effect, our intuition regarding causation would be entirely satisfied in looking on that Being as uncaused, as self-existent, as having power in Himself.—*M'Cosh*, '*Intuitions of the Mind*,' p. 271.

The principle of causation does not, when properly interpreted, necessitate us to look for an infinite series of causes. The intuition is satisfied when it reaches a Being with power adequate to the whole effect. It feels restless indeed till it attains this point. As long as it is mounting the chain, it is compelled to go on; it feels that it cannot stop, and yet is confidently looking for a termination; but when it reaches the All-Powerful Being, it stays in comfort, as feeling that it has reached an unmovable resting-place.—*M'Cosh*, '*Intuitions of the Mind*,' p. 434.

Cause implies a First Cause of all.

Cause implies a Substance with Potency. This doctrine was explicitly stated and defended by Leibnitz. We never know of a causal influence being exercised, except by an object having being and substantial existence. We decide, I must decide, that every effect proceeds from one or more substances having potency. If a tree is felled to the ground, if the salt we saw dry a minute ago is now melted, if a limb of man or animal is broken, we not only look for a cause, but we look for a cause in something that had being and property, say in the wind blowing on the tree, or in water mingling with the salt, or in a blow being inflicted by a stick or other hard substance, on the limb If this world be an effect, we look for its cause in a Being possessed of power.—*M'Cosh*, '*Intuitions of the Mind*,' p. 263.

A First Cause demanded by

a. Reasoning.

Every event must have a cause, and that cause again a cause, until we are lost in the obscurity of the past, and are driven to the belief in one First Cause, by whom the course of nature was determined.—*Jevons*, '*Principles of Science*,' p. 221.

b. Philosophy.

Philosophy, as the knowledge of effects in their causes, necessarily tends, not towards a plurality of ultimate or first causes, but towards one alone—the Creator Unless all analogy be rejected, unless our intelligence be declared a lie, we must, philosophically, believe in an ultimate or primary unity —*Hamilton*, '*Metaphysics*,' i. p. 60.

c. The impulses of the soul.

Our conviction of substance is not content till it comes to one who has all power in himself. Infinite time and space are felt, after all, to be only infinite emptiness till we fill them up with a living and loving Being. All the beautiful relationships in nature, all the order in respect of form, time, and quantity, all the adaptations of means to ends, seem but the scattered rays from an original and central wisdom. The impulse which prompts us to search after causes will not cease its cravings till it carries us up to a first cause in a self-acting substance. Earthly beauty is so evanescent that we rejoice to learn that there is a Divine beauty of which the other is but a flickering reflection. Our moral convictions especially mount towards God as their proper sphere, their source and their home. We cannot be satisfied till we learn that we hang on a Great Central Power and Light, round which we should revolve, as the earth does round the sun.—*M'Cosh*, '*Intuitions of the Mind*,' p. 477.

Final Cause

Definition.

The term final cause (*causa finalis*) was introduced into the language of philosophy by scholasticism. It signifies the end (*finis*) for which one acts, or towards which one tends, and which may consequently be considered as a cause of action, or of motion. Aristotle explains it thus: Another sort of cause is the end, that is to say, *that on account of which* (τὸ οὗ ἕνεκα) the action is done; for example, in this sense, health is the cause of walking exercise. Why does such a one take exercise? We say it is *in order* to have good health; and, in speaking thus, we mean to name the cause.—*Janet*, '*Final Causes*,' p. 1.

When we see means independent of each other conspiring to accomplish certain ends, we naturally conclude that the ends have been contemplated and the means arranged by an intelligent agent; and, from the nature of the ends and the means, we infer the character or design of the agent Thus, from the ends answered in creation being wise and good, we infer not only the existence of an Intelligent Creator, but also that He is a Being of infinite wisdom and goodness. This is commonly called the argument from design or from final causes.—*Fleming*, '*Vocab. of Phil*,' p. 81.

Occasional causes.

This theory was devised by the Cartesians to explain the action of the soul on the body Geulinx held that neither does the soul act directly on the body, nor the body directly on the soul There is thus nothing left but to seek in God the means of uniting the two sides Hence the theory that on the *occasion* of the bodily change God calls forth the corresponding idea in the soul, and that on the *occasion* of our willing God moves the body in accordance with our will.—*Ueberweg and Schwegler.*

According to this theory, the admirable structure of the body and its organs is useless, as a dull mass would have answered the purpose equally well.—*Fleming*, '*Vocab of Phil.*,' p. 83

XVII. CAUSATION.

Importance of the Question.

Of all questions in the history of philosophy, that concerning the nature and genealogy of the notion of Causality is, perhaps, the most famous —*Hamilton*, '*Metaphysics*,' ii. 376.

When we look into the idea of Cause, we find immediately that it involves the most astonishing thoughts and conceptions We cannot help ourselves having it, we cannot help ourselves being bound by the necessity of it, we cannot release ourselves from its grasp; but it is, at the same time, such an unfathomable idea that we pause under the impress of it, and feel ourselves under some great solemnising shadow as soon as we enter into this region of thought As soon as the gates of the awful kingdom of Causation have unclosed, we are instantly upon, I will not say magic ground, for that is to convey a sense of illusion and unreality, but upon mysterious ground; and we are in company with majestic, inconceivable ideas, which we cannot grasp, and yet cannot do else than accept.—*Mozley*, '*Faith and Free Thought*,' p. 7.

Causation as a Law and a Principle.

The relation of causality is sometimes called *the Principle*, at other times *the Law* of causality, causation, or cause and effect. The first of these appellations is *subjective* and *logical*, and designates the place which the relation or the proposition in which it is expressed holds in the systematic arrangement of our knowledge. The other is *objective* and *real*, and indicates its universal prevalence among objects actually existing. *Causation as a principle* is placed first or highest with reference to the other concepts or truths which depend upon or are derived from it—either relatively or absolutely, according as the truth is received as original or derived Causation as *a law* is viewed as a relation actually prevailing in or ruling over the finite universe of physical and spiritual being

Causation as a *law* may be stated thus: Every finite event is a caused event, or, more briefly, is an effect. Causation, as a *principle*, may be thus expressed: Every finite event may be accounted for by referring it to a cause as the ground or reason of its existence.—*Porter*, '*Human Intellect*,' p 569.

The belief that every exchange implies a cause, or that every change is produced by the operation of some power, is regarded by some as a primitive belief, and has been denominated by the phrase, the principle of causality.—*Fleming*, '*Vocab of Phil.*,' p. 78.

Nature of the Causal Relation.

Two schools of explanation

We have only two positive notions of causation: one, the exertion of power by an intelligent being, the other, the uniform sequence of phenomenon B from A. *Mansel*, '*Prolegomena Logica*,' App. D.

Theories of Causation.

a Theory of Sequence.

The history of speculation abounds in attempts to explain the relation of causality by some relation of time This is not surprising The relations of time pertain to all objects whatever. If objects are connected by the relation of causality, the same objects must be united to observation, either as co-existent or as successive. The most conspicuous advocates of this disposition or solution of the causal relation are *David Hume, Dr. Thomas Brown*, and *John Stuart Mill.*—*Porter*, '*Human Intellect*,' p. 573.

'The first time a man saw the communication of motion by impulse, as by the shock of two billiard-balls, he could not pronounce that the one event was *connected*, but only that it was *conjoined* with the other. After he has observed several instances of this nature, he then pronounces them to be *connected*. What alteration has happened to give rise to this new idea of *connexion*? Nothing but that he now *feels* these events to be *connected* in his imagination, and can readily foretell the existence of one from the appearance of the other. When we say, therefore, that one object is connected with another, we mean only that they have acquired a connection in our thought, and give rise to this inference, by which they become proofs of each other's existence, — a conclusion which is somewhat extraordinary, but which seems founded on sufficient evidence.' . . . 'We may define a cause to be an object followed by another, and where all the objects, similar to the first, are followed by objects similar to the second. Or, in other words, where, if the first object had not been, the second never had existed. The appearance of a cause always conveys the mind, by a customary transition, to the idea of the effect. Of this we have experience. We may, therefore, suitably to this experience, form another definition of cause, and call it, an object followed by another and whose appearance always conveys the thought to that other.' —*Hume*, '*Essay on Human Understanding*,' § 7, pt. ii.

A cause, therefore, in the fullest definition which it philosophically admits, may be said to be that which immediately precedes any change, and which, existing at any time in similar circumstances, has been always and will be always immediately followed by a similar change. Priority in the sequence observed, and invariableness of antecedence in the past and future sequences supposed, are the elements and the only elements combined in the notion of a cause. By a conversion of terms we obtain a definition of the correlative *effect*, and *power*, as I have before observed, is only another word for expressing abstractly and briefly the antecedence itself and the invariableness of the relation.—*Brown*, '*Inquiry into the Relation of Cause and Effect*,' pt. 1. sec. 1. Cf. '*Lectures*,' lec. vii.

The theory of Dr. Thomas Brown is closely assimilated with the theory of Hume in certain features, though it is far removed from it in others. Brown agrees with Hume that the relation of cause and effect is nothing more than the constant and invariable connexion of two objects in time,—the one as antecedent and the other as consequent. Brown differs from Hume in holding that two objects need only be conjoined in a single instance in order to be known as cause and effect respectively, while the theory of Hume requires that they must be frequently conjoined in order to be causally connected. Indeed, the whole force and meaning of Hume's causal connection depends upon the tendency of the mind to think of those objects together which have been observed to be conjoined in fact. Brown contends that the only use of repeated observations is to enable the mind to analyse or separate complex objects into their ultimate elements; for a single conjunction of any two clearly distinguished objects gives their causal connexion. Hume makes our conviction of the reality of this connexion to consist in and depend upon the mind's tendency to associate objects customarily united. Brown resolves this conviction into *an original necessity or law of our nature.*—*Porter*, '*Human Intellect*,' p. 575.

The law of causation, the recognition of which is the main pillar of inductive philosophy, is but the familiar truth that invariability of succession is found by observation to obtain between every fact in nature and some other fact which has preceded it . . . To certain facts certain facts always do and, as we believe, always will succeed. The invariable antecedent is termed the cause; the invariable consequent, the effect; and the universality of the law of causation consists in this, that every consequent is connected in this manner with some particular antecedent or set of antecedents Let the fact be what it may, if it has begun to exist it was preceded by some fact or facts with which it is invariably connected.—*Mill*, '*System of Logic*,' bk. iii. chap. v. § 2.

b. Theory of power excited by an agent

We assert that the mind intuitively believes that every event is caused, *i.e.*, every event is produced by the action of some agent or agents, which, with respect to the effect, are called its cause or its causes.

The reasons for this view are the following:—

(*a.*) All that we do in common or practical life rests upon and is directed by the assumption of this truth Our explanations of events that have occurred would have no meaning without it. They consist in referring these phenomena to the beings or the agencies which have occasioned them When these producing agents are discovered, and the modes and laws of their action are referred to or unfolded for the first time, the process of explanation is complete.

(*b.*) When an event has occurred which is not yet accounted for, the mind is aroused to the effort to solve or explain its occurrence; it believes firmly that it can be accounted for.—*Porter*, '*Human Intellect*,' p. 572.

Cause implies a Substance with Potency. This doctrine was explicitly stated and defended by Leibnitz, and has been incidentally admitted by many who were not prepared to adhere to the general statement We never know of a causal influence being exercised except by an object having being and substantial existence. We decide and must decide that every effect proceeds from one or more substances having potency. If a tree is felled to the ground, if the salt we saw dry a minute ago is now melted, if a limb of man or animal is broken, we not only look for a cause but we look for a cause in something that had being and property, say in the wind blowing on the tree, or in water mingling with the salt, or in a blow being inflicted on the limb by a stick or other hard substance. When we discover effects produced by light, heat, electricity, or similar agents, whose precise nature has not been discovered, we regard them either as separate substances, or, if this seems (as it does) highly improbable, we regard them as properties or affections of substances If this world be an effect, we look for its cause in a Being possessed of power —*M'Cosh*, '*Intuitions of the Mind*,' p. 232

When we analyse the meaning which we can attribute to the word *cause*, it amounts to the existence of suitable portions of matter endowed with suitable quantities of energy —*Jevons*, '*Principles of Science*,' p. 226.

Tabular view of Theories.

The following is a tabular view of the theories in regard to the principles of Causality:—

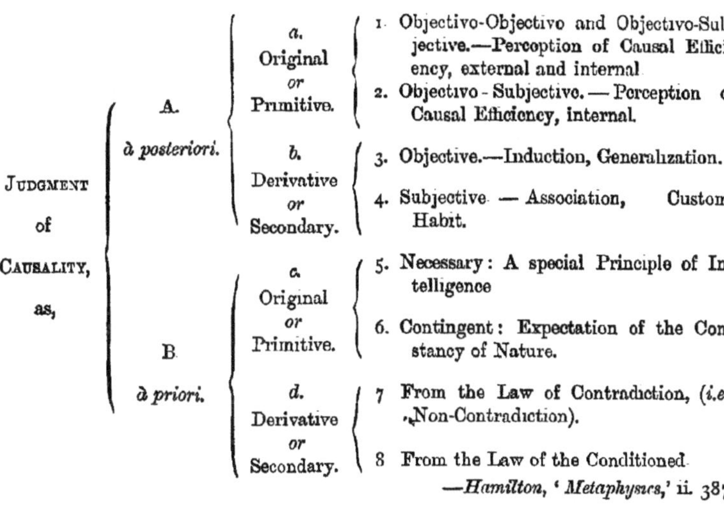

JUDGMENT of CAUSALITY, as,

- A. *à posteriori.*
  - *a.* Original *or* Primitive.
    1. Objectivo-Objectivo and Objectivo-Subjective.—Perception of Causal Efficiency, external and internal
    2. Objectivo-Subjectivo.—Perception of Causal Efficiency, internal.
  - *b.* Derivative *or* Secondary.
    3. Objective.—Induction, Generalization.
    4. Subjective—Association, Custom, Habit.
- B. *à priori.*
  - *c.* Original *or* Primitive.
    5. Necessary: A special Principle of Intelligence
    6. Contingent: Expectation of the Constancy of Nature.
  - *d.* Derivative *or* Secondary.
    7. From the Law of Contradiction, (*i.e.*, Non-Contradiction).
    8. From the Law of the Conditioned.

—*Hamilton*, '*Metaphysics*,' ii. 387.

This table is more ingenious than sound in its classified subdivisions.—*Porter*, '*Human Intellect*,' p. 579.

e. Causes and conditions distinguished.

We distinguish between the cause of an event and the conditions of its actually producing the effect. The stroke of a hammer is the cause of the fracture of a stone, of the flattening of a leaden bullet, of the heating of a bit of iron. The conditions of the effect would, in such a case, be said to be the properties of the stone, the bullet, or the iron. If the breaking, the flattening, or the heating of the mass are the several effects of the common cause, the varying effects are ascribed to the varying conditions under which, or the objects upon which, it acts.—*Porter*, '*Human Intellect*,' p. 572.

On the other hand, Professor Jevons held that 'a cause is not to be distinguished from the group of positive or negative conditions which, with more or less probability, precede an event.'—'*Principles of Science*,' p. 226.

Law of Universal Causation.

Every phenomenon which has a beginning must have a cause; and it will invariably arise whenever that certain combination of positive facts which constitutes the cause exists, provided certain other positive facts do not exist also.—*Killick*, '*Handbook to Mill*,' p. 103.

The Idea of Causation is Opposed to Atheism

The idea of causation applied to this universe takes us up to an Eternal, Original, Self-existent Being. For 'how much thought soever,' says Clarke, 'it may require to demonstrate the other attributes of such a Being, yet as to its existence, that there is somewhat eternal, infinite, and self-existing, which must be the cause and original of all other things; this is one of the first and most natural conclusions that any man who thinks at all can form in his mind. All things cannot possibly have arisen out of nothing, nor can they have depended on one another in an endless succession. We are certain, therefore, of the being of a Supreme Independent Cause; that there is something in the Universe, actually existing without, the supposition of whose not-existing plainly implies a contradiction.'—*Mozley*, '*Faith and Free Thought*,' pp. 29, 30.

In observing them, he discovers phenomena which bear all the marks of being effects. Everywhere are there traces of plan and purpose; heterogeneous elements and diverse agencies conspire to the accomplishment of one end. They are made, for example, in the organs of plants and of animals, to take typical forms, which it is interesting to the eye, or rather the intellect, to contemplate, and which look as if they were built up by a skilful and tasteful architect. Then every member of the animal body has a purpose to serve, and is so constructed as to promote, not merely the being, but the well-being of the whole. Even in the soul itself there are traces of structure and design. Man's faculties are suited to one another, and to the state of things in which he is placed; the eye seems given him to see, and the memory to remember, and the laws of the association of his ideas are suited to his position, and his disposition to generalise and his capacity of grouping enable him to arrange into classes, in due subordination, the infinite details of nature. If once it be admitted that these are effects, it will not be difficult to prove that they do not proceed from the ordinary powers working in the cosmos. No doubt there are natural agencies operating in the production of every natural phenomenon which may be pressed into the theistic argument, but the agencies are acting only as they operate in those works of human skill, which are most unequivocally evidential of design. In the construction and movements of a chronometer there is nothing, after all, but natural bodies, and the action of mechanical forces, but there is room for the discovery of high purpose in the collocation and concurrence of the various parts to serve an evident end. It is in the same way that we are led to discover traces of design in the works of nature; we see physical agents made to combine and work, to accomplish what is obviously an intended effect. Just as in the construction of a time-piece we discern traces of an effect not produced by the mere mechanical laws of the parts, so in the construction of the eye we find marks of plan and adaptation which do not proceed from the potency of the coats and humours and muscles and nerves, but which must come from a power above them, and using natural agencies merely as a means to accomplish its end.—*M'Cosh, 'Intuitions of the Mind,'* p. 382.

X.

KNOWLEDGE OF MIND, FINITE AND INFINITE.

I. KNOWLEDGE OF OTHER MINDS.

Mr. Spencer says, 'I can construe the consciousness of other minds only in terms of my own.' Is this so? I think it can be shown that it is not so. First as to the child. At a very early age the feeling of being alone distresses and terrifies him, and what he evidently longs for is not the reappearance of certain phenomena, but the sense of a protecting presence. He is, moreover, an instinctive physiognomist, and can read the expression of faces,—that is to say, the hidden feelings of which changes of countenance are the natural signs—before he is able accurately to discriminate the features. His intuition of personality is, in fact, so strong that it overruns its bounds. He attributes personality to inanimate objects and cannot help feeling as if the chairs and tables could see and hear him, and as if his warm bed loved and took care of him.

Neither is it true of the mature mind that it can construe the consciousness of ther minds only in terms of its own I now that some minds possess an intensity f passion, others a positive vigour and on stiffness of will, others an intuitive elicacy and prompt accuracy in discerning orm and colour, or melody and harmony; thers a power of sympathy with every orm of humanity, others an acerbity and apacity of hatred and revenge; none of hich I am able to construe in terms of y own consciousness. The phenomena resent to the consciousness of those minds an no more come within the range of my onsciousness than their sense of personal dentity can be interchanged with mine. f it be replied—'You are still employing ere *terms of your own consciousness*, only aised to a very high power,' I answer—That is true, if you choose so to express t;—but why? Only because my reason ranscends phenomena, and assures me of he real existence of other minds generically alike, but specifically unlike, my own, o whom a consciousness which I can dimly or not at all imagine is a living experience. —*Conder*, '*Basis of Faith*,' Lect. iv., pp. 181, 182, abridged.

II. THE CONDITIONED AND THE UNCONDITIONED.

The Conditioned Defined and Explained.

Hamilton seems to have used the term 'condition,' with its various cognates, in a sort of twofold reference, both of which, however, are justified by common language. Thus we say that one thing is a condition of another, or that one thing is conditioned by another, meaning that the two are related, or perhaps specially related by way of causation, for though a condition is not equivalent to a cause, the cause must be regarded as the sum-total of the conditions. Again, we say that a thing is in a certain condition, meaning that it is in some particular state or mode—as, for instance, we say that matter can exist in three conditions, the solid, the fluid, and the gaseous. This latter meaning of the word condition —which Mr. Mill does not notice—was, I think, that which was most prominently present to the mind of Sir William Hamilton. If I know a thing only in a certain condition, mode, or state, and that thing is capable of existing in other conditions, modes, or states, my knowledge of it is not absolute—meaning by absolute 'finished, perfected, completed.' The statement that we know nothing but the Conditioned, would thus seem to be equivalent to stating that we know existence only in certain special modes related to our faculties.—*Monck*, '*Sir W. Hamilton*,' pp. 81–83.

A condition is that which is pre-requisite in order that something may be, and especially in order that a cause may operate. A condition does not operate but by removing some impediment, as opening the eyes to see. A condition is prior to the production of an effect; but it does not produce it. It is fire that burns; but, before it burns, it is a condition that there be an approximation of the fire to the fuel, or the matter that is burned. The impression on the wax is the *effect*—the seal is the *cause;* the pressure of the one substance upon the other, and the softness or fluidity of the wax, are *conditions*. The condition is the ground which must be pre-supposed; and what pre-supposes a condition is the conditioned, conditionate, or conditional.—*Fleming*, '*Vocab. of Phil.*,' p. 105.

The Law of the Conditioned.

Sir W. Hamilton thus enunciates it:—All positive thought lies between two extremes, neither of which we can conceive as possible, and yet as mutual contradictions, the one or the other we must recognise as necessary.—*Reid*, '*Works*,' p. 911.

He expands the law thus:—The Conditioned is the mean between two extremes —two inconditionates, exclusive of each other, neither of which can be conceived as possible, but of which, on the principles of contradiction and excluded middle, one must be admitted as necessary.—'*Discussions*,' p. 14.

He illustrates it by Extension:—Let

us take body, or rather, since body as extended is included under extension, let us take extension itself, or space. Space, it is evident, must either be limited, that is, have an end and circumference, or unlimited, that is, have no end, no circumference. These are contradictory suppositions; both therefore cannot, but one must, be true. Now let us try positively to comprehend, positively to conceive, the possibility of either of these two mutually exclusive alternatives. Can we represent, or realise in thought, extension as absolutely limited? In other words, can we mentally hedge round the whole of space, conceive it absolutely bounded, that is, so that beyond its boundary there is no outlying, no surrounding space? This is impossible. Let us consider its contradictory: Can we comprehend the possibility of infinite or unlimited space? To suppose this is a direct contradiction in terms; it is to comprehend the incomprehensible. We think, we conceive, we comprehend a thing, only as we think it as within or under something else; but to do this of the infinite is to think the infinite as finite, which is contradictory and absurd.—'*Logic*,' i. 100, *et seq.*

Of this law John Stuart Mill says that it rests on no rational foundation. The proposition that the Conditioned lies between two hypotheses concerning the Unconditioned, neither of which hypotheses we can conceive as possible, must be placed in that numerous class of metaphysical doctrines, which have a magnificent sound, but are empty of the smallest substance.—'*Examination of Hamilton*,' p. 104.

The reader who desires further information may be referred to 'Hamilton's Lectures,' vols. ii. and iii., 'Discussions,' and Reid's 'Works,' on the one side, and to Mill's 'Examination of Hamilton,' ch. vi., on the other.

The Unconditioned.

The Unconditioned will, of course, be the opposite of the Conditioned. The Conditioned, Hamilton otherwise designates as the conditionally limited, the contradictory of which—the not-conditionally limited—will evidently include two cases, viz., the unconditionally limited (or Absolute), and unconditionally unlimited (or Infinite).—*Monck*, '*Sir W. Hamilton*,' p. 83.

This term has been employed in a twofold signification, as denoting either the entire absence of all *restriction*, or more widely, the entire absence of all *relation*. The former we regard as its only legitimate application.—*Calderwood*, '*Philosophy of the Infinite*,' p. 36.

The Unconditioned embraces both Absolute and Infinite, and indicates entire freedom from every restriction, whether in its own nature or in relation to other beings. I think it were well that the term Unconditioned were altogether abandoned, as there is no special need for its use, and it is very apt to mislead.—*Calderwood*, '*Philosophy of the Infinite*,' p. 179.

It seems rather an arbitrary use of language on the part of Sir W. Hamilton ('Metaphysics,' Lect. 38) to make the Unconditioned a genus including two species, the Infinite and Absolute. When the Unconditioned is referred to, let us always understand whether it means unconditioned in thought or existence.—*M'Cosh*, '*Intuitions of the Mind*,' p. 342.

Leibnitz complained of Sophie Charlotte of Prussia that she asked the *why* of the *why*. There are some truths in regard to which we are not warranted to ask the why. They shine in their own light; and we feel that we need no light, and we ask no light wherewith to see them, and any light which might be brought to aid would only perplex us. In all such cases the mind asks no *why*, and is amazed when the *why* is asked; and feels that it can give no answer, and ought not to attempt an answer. Other truths may be known only mediately, or by means of some other truth coming between as evidence. I need no mediate proof to convince me that I exist, or that I hold an object in my hand which I call a pen; but I need evidence to convince me that there are inhabitants in India, or that there is a cycle of spots presented in the sun's rotation. In regard to this class of truths I am entitled—nay, required—to ask the *why*. Not only so; if the truth urged as evidence is not self-evident, I may ask the *why* of the *why*, and the *why* of that *why*, on and on, till we come to a self-evident truth, when the *why* becomes unintelligible. Now we may say of the one class of truths that they depend (to us) on no condition, and call them Unconditioned; whereas we must call the other Conditioned, for our rational nature demands another truth as a condition of our assenting to them.

But this is not precisely what is meant, or all that is meant, by conditioned and unconditioned in philosophic nomenclature We find that not only does one truth depend on another as *evidence* to our minds, but one thing as an *existence* depends on another. Everything falling under our notice on earth is dependent on some other thing as its cause All physical events proceed from a concurrence of previous circumstances All animated beings come from a parentage But is everything that exists thus a dependent link in a chain which hangs on nothing? There are intellectual instincts which recoil from such a thought There are intuitions which, proceeding on facts ever pressing themselves on the attention, lead to a very different result. By our intuitive conviction in regard to substance we are introduced to that which has power of itself True, we discover that all mundane substances, spiritual and material, have in fact been originated, and have proceeded from something anterior to them. But then intuitive reason presses us on, and we seek for a cause of that cause which is furthest removed from our view Pursuing various lines, external and internal, we come to a substance which has no mark of being an effect; to a substance who is the cause, and, as such, the intelligent cause, of all the order and adaptation of one thing to another in the universe; who is the founder of the moral power within us, and the sanctioner of the moral law to which it looks, and who seems to be that Infinite Existence to which our faith in infinity is ever pointing,—and now the mind in all its intuitions is satisfied The intuitive belief as to power in substance is satisfied; the intuitive belief in the adequacy of the cause to produce its effect is satisfied; the native moral conviction is satisfied; and the belief in infinity is satisfied. True, every step in this process is not intuitive or demonstrative—there may be more than one experiential link in the chain; but the intuitive convictions enter very largely; and when experience has furnished its quota, they are gratified, and feel as if they had nothing to demand beyond this One Substance possessed of all power and of all perfection.

If we would avoid the utmost possible confusion of thought, we must distinguish between these two kinds of conditioned and unconditioned; the one referring to human knowledge, and the discussion of it falling properly under Gnosiology; the other to existence, and so falling under Ontology. The conditional, in respect of knowledge, does, if we pursue the conditioned sufficiently far, conduct at last to primary truths, which are to us unconditioned.—*M'Cosh, 'Intuitions of the Mind,'* p. 339 *et seq*

The Conditioned and Unconditioned regarded as Objects of Knowledge.

Various opinions on the Unconditioned.

Four opinions may be entertained regarding the Unconditioned as an immediate object of knowledge and of thought: 1. The Unconditioned is incognisable and inconceivable; its notion being only negative of the Conditioned, which last can alone be positively known or conceived. 2. It is not an object of knowledge; but its notion as a regulative principle of the mind itself is more than a mere negation of the conditioned 3. It is cognisable, but not conceivable; it can be known by a sinking back into identity with the absolute, but is incomprehensible by consciousness and reflection, which are only of the relative and the different 4. It is cognisable and conceivable by consciousness and reflection, under relation, difference, and plurality. — *Hamilton*, '*Discussions*,' p 12.

The Unconditioned is unthinkable

Thought is only of the conditioned, because to think is simply to condition Thought cannot transcend consciousness; consciousness is only possible under the antithesis of a subject and object of thought, known only in correlation, and mutually limiting each other; while all that we know of subject and object is only a knowledge in each of the different, of the modified, of the phenomenal —*Hamilton*, '*Discussions*,' p 14.

A thought involves *relation*, *difference*, *likeness*. Whatever does not present each of these does not admit of cognition. Hence we may say that the Unconditioned, as presenting none of them, is trebly unthinkable —*Spencer*, '*First Principles*,' p. 82.

The Conditioned is held to be the sole sphere of thought.

The conditionally limited (which we may briefly call the *Conditioned*) is the only possible object of knowledge and of positive thought — thought necessarily supposes conditions *To think* is *to condition*, and conditional limitation is the fundamental law of the possibility of thought For as the greyhound cannot outstrip his shadow, nor (by a more appropriate simile) the eagle outsoar the atmosphere in which he floats, and by which alone he may be supported, so the mind cannot transcend that sphere of limitation within and through which exclusively the possibility of thought is realised Thought is only of the conditioned.—*Hamilton*, '*Discussions*,' p. 14

The philosophy of the Conditioned.

The philosophy of the Conditioned denies to man a knowledge of either the Absolute or the Infinite, and maintains all which we immediately know, or can know, to be only the Conditioned, the Relative, the Phenomenal, the Finite The doctrine of the Conditioned is a philosophy professing relative knowledge, but confessing absolute ignorance.—*Hamilton*, '*Discussions*,' p. 584.

III. THE ABSOLUTE.

Meanings of the Term.

The term absolute is of a twofold ambiguity, corresponding to the double signification of the word in Latin.

1. *Absolutum* means what is *freed* or *loosed*, in which sense the Absolute will be what is aloof from relation, comparison, limitation, condition, dependence, &c. In this meaning the Absolute is not opposed to the Infinite.

2. *Absolutum* means *finished*, *perfected*, *completed*. in which sense the Absolute will be what is out of relation, &c., as finished, perfect, complete. In this acceptation, the Absolute is diametrically opposed to, is contradictory of, the Infinite. [And in this sense Sir W Hamilton exclusively uses it: with him the absolute is 'the unconditionally limited']—*Hamilton*, '*Discussions*,' p. 13.

1. As meaning what is complete or perfect in itself, as a man, a tree, it is opposed to what is relative.

2. As meaning what is free from restriction, it is opposed to what exists *secundum quid*. The *soul* of man is immortal *absolutely*; *man* is immortal *only* as to his soul.

3. As meaning what is underived, it denotes self-existence, and is predicable only of the first cause

4. It signifies not only what is free from external cause, but also free from *condition*.—*Fleming*, '*Vocab of Phil.*,' pp. 2, 3

The absolute is another term which is often interchanged with the infinite and the unconditioned. Originally and etymologically, it signifies *freed from*, or severed.

This signification is purely negative, and waits to be explained by that from which it is freed. Thus it was applied, to mean *the finished or completed*, even as the Latin word *absolutus*, as is thought, was originally used of the web when ready to be taken from the loom. Both these senses have passed into the modern uses of the term, and determined the varieties of its application. *First* of all, absolute and absolutely is applied to any thought or thing as viewed apart from any of its relations—regarded simply by itself. This meaning is near akin to that under which it is viewed as *complete within or by itself*. *Next*, it is applied to that which is complete of itself so far as the relations of *dependence* are concerned; to that which is necessarily dependent on nothing besides itself. In this sense it is very near in meaning to the *primary* sense of the *unconditioned* already explained. *Still further* it is used in the sense of severed or separated from all relations whatever, or *not related*—*i.e.*, not admitting of any relations. This sense is the same with that which Hamilton and Mansel give to the unconditioned and the infinite. *Still again*, it is applied to relations of *quantity*, and here the signification of *complete* or *finished* is applied to the greatest possible or conceivable whole, to *the total* of all existence, whether limited or unlimited in extent and duration.—*Porter*, '*Human Intellect*,' p. 650.

The term 'absolute' simply stands for an intellectual generalisation. It expresses an attribute, and is therefore a relative term, standing for a thought and nothing but a thought. We may say that God exists absolutely, or is the absolute Being, if we are careful to explain that we oppose 'absolute' to 'dependent.' God alone has being in Himself. But 'absolute existence,' if we do not explain what kind of existence we are speaking of, is a phrase absolutely without meaning. And if we take 'absolute' to mean 'without relation,' then it is not simply unmeaning, but untrue, to say that God exists absolutely.—*Cowler*, '*Basis of Faith*,' Lecture IV.

Absolute is a word of several meanings. In the sense in which it stands related to Infinite it means that which is finished or completed. In this sense the relation between the Absolute and the Infinite is a tolerably close one, namely, that of contrariety. For example, to assert an absolute minimum of matter is to deny its infinite divisibility. Again, we may speak of absolutely but not of infinitely pure water. The purity of water has an absolute limit. By Absolute is often meant the opposite of Relative; and this is rather many meanings than one. In another of its senses, Absolute means that which is independent of anything else; which exists and is what it is by its own nature and not because of any other thing. In this signification it is synonymous with the First Cause. It may also mean the *whole* of that to which it is applied. In this acceptation there is no inconsistency or incongruity in predicating both 'absolute' and 'infinite' of God.—*Mill*, '*Examination of Hamilton*,' pp. 46–8.

Formal definitions.

By the Absolute is meant that which exists in and by itself, having no necessary relation to any other being.—*Mansel*, '*Limits of Religious Thought*,' Lecture ii., p. 31.

The Absolute is that which is free from all *necessary* relation; that is, which is free from every relation *as a condition of existence*; but it may exist in relation, provided that relation be not a necessary condition of its existence; that is, provided the relation may be removed without affecting its existence.—*Calderwood*, '*Philosophy of the Infinite*,' p. 36.

Is there an Absolute?

The questions concerning the finite and its relations, the conditioned and its dependence upon the absolute, are the most vexed and the most unsettled of any in modern speculation. Can the infinite be conceived or known by a finite intellect? Can the unconditioned be brought under those relations which are appropriate only to the conditioned? What are the finite and the infinite—the conditioned and the absolute? These inquiries, and such as these, are discussed in various forms and phrases in all modern treatises and histories of philosophy. They force themselves into psychology as they compel us to inquire: By what powers and processes of the intellect do we form, or essay to form, conceptions of these objects? Do we believe that such objects exist? Who and what are time, space, and God? Do we only *believe* them to exist? If so, by what process and on what grounds? Is it a process of intuition, knowledge, or faith? What relations do they hold to one another? Are time and space infinite in every sense in which God is infinite? These questions we must attempt to answer, if we would analyse all the powers and explain all the products of the human intellect. We can do this most successfully if we consider the finite and the conditioned apart from the infinite and the absolute.—*Porter*, '*Human Intellect*,' p. 645.

Every one of the arguments by which the relativity of our knowledge is demonstrated distinctly postulates the positive existence of something beyond the relative. To say that we cannot know the Absolute is, by implication, to affirm that there *is* an Absolute. In the very denial of our power to learn *what* the Absolute is there lies hidden the assumption *that* it is.—*Spencer*, '*First Principles*,' p. 88.

Absolute Being may be, very possibly, that which we are ignorant of. Our ignorance is excessive—it is far more extensive than our knowledge. After we have fixed the meaning, the conditions, the limits, the extent, and the capacities of knowledge, it still seems quite possible, indeed highly probable, that absolute existence may escape us by throwing itself under the cover or within the pale of our ignorance! We may be altogether ignorant of *what is*, and may thus be unable to predicate anything at all about it. This difficulty is to be surmounted not by denying or blinking our ignorance but by facing it.—*Ferrier*, '*Institutes of Metaphysics*,' p. 47.

All Philosophy aims at a Knowledge of the Absolute.

All philosophy aims at a knowledge of the Absolute under different phases. In Psychology, the fundamental question is, have we ideas that are *à priori* and *absolute?* —in Logic, is human knowledge *absolute?* —in Ethics, is the moral law *absolute* rectitude?—and in metaphysics, what is the ultimate ground of all existence or *absolute* being?—*Fleming*, '*Vocab. of Phil.*,' p. 5.

Modes in which Philosophers attempt to reach the Absolute.

Some carry the absolute by assault,—by a single leap,—place themselves at once in the absolute,—take it as a datum; others climb to it by degrees,—mount to the Absolute from the conditioned,—as a result. Plotinus and Schelling do the former; Hegel and Cousin are examples of the latter.

Some place cognition of the Absolute above, and in opposition to, Consciousness, —conception,—reflection, the conditions of which are difference, plurality, and in a word, limitation. Others do not, but reach it through consciousness, &c.,—the consciousness of difference, contrast, &c., giving, when sifted, a cognition of identity (absolute).—*Hamilton*, '*Metaphysics*,' ii. 529.

Is the Absolute Thinkable or Knowable?

Sir W. Hamilton, Dean Mansel, and Herbert Spencer (with qualifications) say No.

The unconditionally limited, or the Absolute, cannot positively be construed to the mind: it can be conceived only by a thinking away from, or abstraction of, those very conditions under which thought itself is realised. For example: on the one hand we can positively conceive neither an absolute whole, that is, a whole so great that we cannot also conceive it as a relative part of a still greater whole; nor an absolute part, that is, a part so small that we cannot also conceive it as a relative whole divisible into smaller parts The result is the same whether we apply the process to limitation in space, in time, or in degree.—*Hamilton, 'Discussions,'* p 13.

To be conscious of the Absolute as such, we must know that an object, which is given in relation to our consciousness, is identical with one which exists in its own nature, out of all relation to consciousness But to know this identity, we must be able to compare the two together; and such a comparison is itself a contradiction. We are in fact required to compare that of which we are conscious with that of which we are not conscious; the comparison itself being an act of consciousness, and only possible through the consciousness of both its objects. It is thus manifest that, even if we could be conscious of the absolute, we could not possibly know that it *is* the absolute; and, as we can be conscious of an object as such, only by knowing it to be what it is, this is equivalent to an admission that we cannot be conscious of the absolute at all.—*Mansel, 'Limits of Religious Thought,'* p. 75

Herbert Spencer maintains that we are compelled by the necessities of finite and conditioned thinking to assume an Absolute and Infinite, and also compelled to form some definite notions of the same, although these of necessity are only approximative and therefore doomed to be set aside by those which shall be subsequently evolved. —*Ueberweg, 'Hist. of Phil.,'* ii 419.

John Stuart Mill and Calderwood (from different standpoints) say Yes, but admit that the conception may not be ADEQUATE.

Most of the arguments for the incognoscibility and inconceivability of the Absolute lose their application by simply substituting for the metaphysical abstraction 'The Absolute,' the more intelligible concrete expression 'Something absolute.' When we are told of an 'Absolute' in the abstract, or of an Absolute Being, even though called God, if we would know what we are talking about, we are bound to ask, absolute in *what?* The word 'absolute' is devoid of meaning unless in reference to predicates of some sort. What is absolute must be absolutely something; absolutely this or absolutely that. 'Absolute,' in reference to any given attribute, signifies the possession of that attribute in finished perfection and completeness A Being absolute in knowledge, for example, is one who knows, in the literal meaning of the term, everything Who will pretend that this conception is negative, or unmeaning to us? We cannot indeed form an *adequate* conception of a being as knowing every thing, since to do this we must have a conception, or mental representation, of all that he knows But neither have we an adequate conception of any person's finite knowledge. I have no adequate conception of a shoemaker's knowledge, since I do not know how to make shoes: but my conception of a shoemaker and of his knowledge is a real conception. If I talk of a Being who is absolute in wisdom and goodness, that is, who knows everything, and at all times intends what is best for every sentient creature, I understand perfectly what I mean: and however much the fact may transcend my conception, the shortcoming can only consist in my being ignorant of the details of which the reality is composed. —*Mill, 'Examination of Hamilton,'* pp. 55, 60.

Philosophy of the Absolute.

How held by many philosophers.

There have been thinkers from the earliest times, who, in different ways, and more or less explicitly, allow of no such restriction upon knowledge [*i.e.*, that of the absolute there is no knowledge], or at least consciousness, but on the contrary, starting from a notion, by the latter among them called the absolute, which includes within it the opposition of subject and object, pass therefrom to the explanation of all the phenomena of nature and of mind. In earlier days the Eleatics, Plato, and Plotinus, in modern times Spinoza, Leibnitz, Fichte, Schelling, Hegel, and Cousin, all have joined, under whatever different forms, in maintaining this view Kant, while denying the absolute or unconditioned as an object of knowledge, leaves it conceivable, as an idea regulative of the mind's intellectual experience It is against any such absolute, whether as real or conceivable, that Hamilton and Mansel have taken ground — *Robertson*, '*Encyclopædia Britannica*,' i 58

Two classes of philosophers of the Absolute.

Some explicitly hold that, as the Absolute is absolutely one, cognition and existence must coincide, to know the absolute is to be the absolute,—to know the absolute is to be God Others do not explicitly assert this, but only hold the impersonality of reason,—a certain union with God, in holding that we are conscious of eternal truths as in the divine mind (Augustine, Malebranche, Price, Cousin) — *Hamilton*, '*Metaphysics*,' ii 529

Doctrine of German Mysticism in the fourteenth and fifteenth centuries

In the doctrine of Eckhart, the Absolute, or Deity, remains as such, without personality and without work, concealed in itself Enveloped in it is God, who is from eternity, and who has the power of revealing Himself. He exists as the one divine nature, which is developed into a trinity of persons in the act of self-knowledge The Subject in this knowledge is the Father, the Object is the Son, the love of both for each other is the Spirit — *Ueberweg*, '*Hist of Phil*,' i 469

Doctrine of Hegel

The Absolute is, firstly, pure immaterial thought; secondly, it is heterisation of pure thought, disruption of thought into the infinite atomism of time and space—nature, thirdly, it returns out of this its self-externalisation and self-alienation back into its own self, it resolves the heterisation of nature, and only in this way becomes at last actual, self-cognisant thought, Spirit —*Schwegler*, '*Hist. of Phil*,' p 323

In the Hegelian terminology, the absolute takes a special signification from the fundamental assumptions of the Hegelian system. When the notion, *der Begriff*, has completed every possible form of development, and, as it were, done its utmost possible by the force of the movement essential to itself, the absolute is reached This absolute completes every possible form of development, and represents every kind of object conceivable and knowable by the mind, from the undetermined notion with which it begins, up to the highest form of development, when it becomes self-conscious in the human spirit by distinguishing itself from the material universe The conscious spirit thus evolved, and reflecting in itself all these lower forms of existence, is, with these forms, *the absolute* This is perpetually reproduced by the lower forces of the universe, and itself perpetually reproduces all these by its own reflective thinking — *Porter*, '*Human Intellect*,' p 650

The German Philosophy of the Absolute admits an attempted twofold refutation

Various and conflicting as are the theories of modern German philosophy, one common error may be detected as pervading all of them—that of identifying Reality with the Absolute or Unconditioned Instead of examining the conception of the real as it is formed under the necessary conditions of human thought, and inquiring what is the object which corresponds to the conception so conditioned, they assume at the outset that real existence means existence dependent upon nothing but itself, and that the conception of real existence is a conception determined by no antecedent. Being and knowledge are necessarily one and the same thing Absolute knowledge is thus possible only on the condition that the act of thought itself creates its own object and subject

The philosophy of the Absolute thus admits of a twofold refutation, in the consequences to which it leads, and in the premises from which it starts In its consequences it admits of no alternatives but

Atheism or Pantheism; atheism, if the absolute reality or creative thought is identified with myself; pantheism, if it is identified with anything beyond myself. Religion is equally annihilated under both suppositions; for if there is no God, whom are we to worship? and if all things are God, who is to worship Him? The premises from which these consequences issue are equally untenable. The primary testimony of consciousness affirms the existence of an *ego* and a *non-ego*, related to and limiting each other. Pantheism contradicts the first element of consciousness, by denying the real existence of myself. Egoism contradicts the second element, by denying the real existence of anything distinct from myself. —*Mansel*, '*Metaphysics*,' pp. 321–323

As a matter of fact, the hardiest and most consistent reasoners who have attempted a philosophy of absolute existence—Parmenides, Plotinus, Spinoza, Fichte, Schelling, Hegel—have one and all attained to their conclusions by dropping out of their philosophy the attribute of personality, and exhibiting the absolute existence as an impersonal abstraction, or as an equally impersonal universe of all existence.—*Mansel*, '*Limits of Religious Thought*,' p. x.

History is a progressive Revelation of the Absolute.

History, as a whole, is a progressive and gradual revelation of the Absolute. No single passage in history can be pointed out where the trace of God Himself is really visible; it is only through history as a whole. Schelling distinguishes three periods in this revelation of the Absolute, or in history, which he characterises as the periods respectively of fate, nature, and Providence.—*Ueberweg*, '*Hist. of Phil.*,' ii. 218.

IV. THE INFINITE.

The Subject is Profound and not to be evaded.

The subject now opening before us is a profound one. In meditating upon it we feel as we do when we look into the blue expanse of heaven, or when from a solitary rock we gaze on a shoreless ocean spread all around us. The topic has exercised the profoundest minds since thought began the attempt to solve the problems of the universe, and has been specially discussed since Christian theology made men familiar with the idea of an eternal and omnipresent God.—*M'Cosh*, '*Intuitions of the Mind*,' p. 187.

Beyond the starry firmament, what is there? More skies and stars. And beyond these? The human mind, impelled by an irresistible power, will never cease to ask itself, What lies beyond? Time and space arrest it not. At the furthest point attained is a finite boundary, enlarged from what preceded it; no sooner is it reached than the implacable question returns, returns for ever in the curiosity of man. It is vain to speak of space, of time, of size unlimited. These words pass the human understanding. But he who proclaims the existence of the Infinite—and no man can escape from it—comprehends in that assertion more of the Supernatural than there is in all the miracles of all religions; for the conception of the Infinite has the twofold characters, that it is irresistible and incomprehensible. We prostrate ourselves before the thought, which masters all the faculties of the understanding, and threatens the springs of intellectual life like the sublime madness of Pascal.—*M. Pasteur*, '*Discourse in French Academy, April 27, 1882*.'

The Meaning of the Phrase.

By the *Infinite* is meant that which is free from all possible limitation; that than which a greater is inconceivable; and which, consequently, can receive no additional attribute or mode of existence which it had not from all eternity.—*Mansel*, '*Limits of Religious Thought*,' p. 45.

The Infinite, like the Absolute, is a phrase of no meaning, except in reference to some particular predicate; it must mean the infinite in something, as in size, in duration, or in power These are intelligible conceptions.—*Mill*, '*Examination of Hamilton*,' p. 58

Infinite signifies, literally, that which is not bounded or terminated It is primarily applied to spatial quantity Everything which has extent is terminated or bounded by some other object or objects which are also extended The line or surface which divides one surface or solid from another, is called its *limit*, and the surface or solid, as necessarily thus terminated or terminable, is called finite or limited. In like manner, the mathematical point is conceived as terminating or limiting the mathematical line, and the line itself is limited or finite. By an obvious transference of signification from the objects of space to those of time, the first and last of any succession of events or series of numbers is called its limit, and every series of numbers, numbered objects, or events and portions of time, is finite or limited

The terms originally appropriate to extension, duration, and number, are still further applied to the exercise of power by material and spiritual agents. The exercise of power by man, whether spiritual or material, is possible only in certain places, at certain times, and with respect to a certain number of objects, or a measured quantity or mass of matter, and thus power itself becomes measurable by the relations of quantity and number as applied to its effects and the means by which they are caused. Man can only accomplish certain effects in *limited* places, times, and number, and hence he is said to be limited in his powers He can only know and do certain things under all these favouring circumstances, and is therefore a finite being. The word *finite* is, therefore, *originally a term of quantity*, and *secondarily of causal or productive agency* *The infinite*, in the general sense, is the *not*-finite Logically conceivable, there are as many sorts of the not-finite or infinite as there are senses of the finite.—*Porter*, '*Human Intellect*,' p 648

We look on infinity as an attribute of an object The infinite is not to be viewed as having an independent being, it is not to be regarded as a substance or a separate entity; it is simply the quality of a thing, very possibly the attribute of the attribute of an object Thus we apply the phrase to the Divine Being to denote a perfection of His nature; we apply it also to all His perfections, such as His wisdom and goodness, which we describe as infinite. It is the more necessary to insist on this view, from the circumstance that metaphysicians are very much tempted to give an independent being to abstractions, and, in particular, some of them write about the infinite in such a way as to make their readers look upon it as a separate existence. I stand up for the reality of infinity, but I claim for it a reality simply as an attribute of some existing object.—*M'Cosh*, '*Intuitions of the Mind*,' p. 197.

On the other hand, Dr. Calderwood holds that, 'The term Infinite is not a mere form of expression to indicate our inability to think in a certain manner; but, on the contrary, is exclusively applicable to one great Being, whom we adore as Supreme. This completely sweeps away Sir W Hamilton's distinction of the unconditioned into the infinite and the absolute'

The infinite expresses the entire absence of all limitation, and is applicable to the one Infinite Being in all His attributes.—'*Philosophy of the Infinite*,' pp. 76, 37.

When we assert that God is infinite, we mean,—first, literally, that God is present wherever space extends; secondly, figuratively, that every attribute which can be thought of as limited (that is, which admits of degrees) is possessed by God in perfection which has no limits; the word 'limit' being used in a varying sense according to the nature of each attribute.—*Conder*, '*Basis of Faith*,' p. 65.

Our Knowledge of the Infinite.

Many philosophers hold that the Infinite is altogether inconceivable.

a. They maintain that it cannot be known.

We know that there is such a thing as infinity, but we are ignorant of its nature. For instance we know it to be false that numbers are finite; there must, therefore, be an infinity in number. But what this is we know not. It can neither be odd nor even, because unity, added to it, does not change its nature. Thus we may very well know that there is a God, without comprehending what God is; and you ought by no means to conclude against the existence of God, from your imperfect conceptions of his nature.—*Pascal, 'Pensées.'*

Views of Kant, Hamilton, and Mansel.

Kant, Hamilton, and Mansel all hold that we cannot know, though we may believe that the infinite exists, simply because the conception of the infinite is not within the grasp of the finite. Kant teaches that the reason why we cannot know the infinite, is, that our faculties of knowing both the finite and the infinite have merely a subjective necessity and validity, and therefore we cannot trust these results as objectively true. Moreover, if we apply them to the infinite, we are involved in perpetual *antinomies* or *contradictions*. Our only apprehension of the absolute is, therefore, by the practical reason, and comes in the way of a moral necessity through the categorical imperative, which requires us to receive certain verities as true. Jacobi, Schleiermacher, and others say, that we reach these by faith or feeling, and not by knowledge. Hamilton says that we find ourselves impotent to know them, in consequence of the contradictions which the attempt involves. But he expressly asserts 'that the sphere of our belief is much more extensive than the sphere of our knowledge; and therefore, when I deny that the infinite can by us be *known*, I am far from denying that by us it is, must, and ought to be believed. This I have indeed anxiously evinced, both by reasoning and authority.' (*Letter to Calderwood.*) 'Thus, by a wonderful revelation, we are thus in the consciousness of our inability to conceive aught above the relative and finite, inspired with the belief in the existence of something unconditioned, beyond the sphere of all comprehensible reality.' (*Rev. of Cousin.*) It will be noticed, that what Hamilton *teaches here is not that the absolute cannot be adequately known, but that it cannot be known at all, because it cannot be conceived.* A similar doctrine was taught by Peter Browne in his 'Procedure and Limits of the Human Understanding,' and 'Things Divine and Supernatural,' &c.

Of this view, by whomsoever it may be held, it is enough to say, at this point, that it is impossible to conceive of an act of faith or belief which does not include the element of knowledge. Faith, or belief, may exclude definite knowledge, reasoned knowledge, &c., but it cannot exclude some kind of intellectual apprehension.—*Porter, 'Human Intellect,'* p. 655.

The unconditionally unlimited, or the Infinite, the unconditionally limited, or the Absolute, cannot positively be construed to the mind; they can be conceived only by a thinking away from, or abstraction of, those very conditions under which thought itself is realised; consequently, the notion of the unconditioned is only negative,—negative of the conceivable itself. For example, on the one hand, we can positively conceive, neither an absolute whole, that is, a whole so great, that we cannot also conceive it as a relative part of a still greater whole; nor an absolute part, that is, a part so small, that we cannot also conceive it as a relative whole, divisible into smaller parts. On the other hand, we cannot positively represent or realise, or construe to the mind an infinite whole, for this could only be done by the infinite synthesis in thought of finite wholes, which would itself require an infinite time for its accomplishment; nor, for the same reason, can we follow out in thought an infinite divisibility of parts. The result is the same whether we apply the process to limitation in *space*, in *time*, or in *degree*.—*Hamilton*, '*Discussions*,' pp. 12, 13

Nothing can be presented in Intuition, or represented in thought, except as *finite*. So long as the relation between subject and object exists in consciousness, so long must each limit the other. The subject is distinct from the object, and neither can be the universe. The infinite cannot be an object of human consciousness at all; and it appears to be so only by mistaking the negation of consciousness for consciousness itself. The *infinite*, like the *inconceivable*, is a term which expresses only the negation of human thought.—*Mansel*, '*Metaphysics*,' p. 277

To be conscious we must be conscious of something, and that something can only be known as that which it is by being distinguished from that which it is not. But distinction is necessarily limitation, for if one object is to be distinguished from another it must possess some form of existence which the other has not, or it must not possess some form which the other has. But it is obvious that the Infinite cannot be distinguished as such from the Finite by the absence of any quality which the Finite possesses, for such absence would be a limitation. Nor yet can it be distinguished by the presence of an attribute which the Finite has not, for, as no finite part can be a constituent of an infinite whole, this differential characteristic must itself be infinite, and must at the same time have nothing in common with the finite. A consciousness of the Infinite as such thus necessarily involves a self-contradiction; for it implies the recognition by limitation and difference of that which can only be given as unlimited and indifferent.—*Mansel*, '*Limits of Religious Thought*,' p. 70.

We have, it is true, conquered the earth, measured the track of the planets, analysed the stars, solved the nebulæ, and followed the eccentric course of comets; but, beyond those stars, whose light is centuries in reaching us, there are other orbs whose rays are lost in space; and further, further still, beyond all limits and all computation, are suns which we shall not behold and innumerable worlds hidden from our eyes. After two thousand years of efforts, if we reach the utmost extremity of the universe, which is but a point in the immensity of space, we are arrested on the threshold of the Infinite, of which we know nothing.—*Pasteur*, '*Discourse, &c.*'

b. But must be believed.

The Infinite does exist and must exist, though of the manner of that existence we can form no conception. In this impotence of Reason we are compelled to take refuge in Faith, and to believe that an Infinite Being exists though we know not how. The shadow of the Infinite still broods over the consciousness of the finite; and we wake up at last from the dream of absolute wisdom to confess, 'Surely the Lord is in this place, and I knew it not.'—*Mansel*, '*Limits of Religious Thought*,' pp. 120, 121.

Everywhere I see the inevitable expression of the infinite in the world. By it the supernatural is seen in the depths of every heart. The idea of God is a form of the idea of the Infinite. As long as the mystery of the Infinite weighs on the human mind, temples will be raised to the worship of the Infinite, whether the God be called Brahma, Allah, Jehovah, or Jesus; and on the floor of those temples you will see kneeling men absorbed in the idea of the Infinite. Metaphysics do but translate within us the paramount notion of the Infinite. The faculty which, in the presence of beauty, leads us to conceive of a superior beauty,—is it not, too, the conception of a never-realised ideal? Are science and the passion for comprehending, anything else than the effect of the stimulus exercised upon our mind by the mystery of the universe? Where are the real springs of woman's dignity, of modern liberty and democracy, unless in the notion of the Infinite, before which all men are equal?—*Pasteur*, '*Discourse, &c.*'

Others assert that the Infinite is Conceivable, though not Adequately.

In place of 'the Infinite' put the idea of Something infinite, and the argument [of Sir W. Hamilton] collapses at once. 'Something infinite' is a conception which, like most of our complex ideas, contains a negative element, but which contains positive elements also. Infinite space, for instance; is there nothing positive in that? The negative part of this conception is the absence of bounds. The positive are the idea of space, and of space greater than any finite space. So of infinite duration. True, we cannot have an *adequate* conception of space or duration as infinite; but between a conception which, though inadequate, is real, and correct as far as it goes, and the impossibility of any conception, there is a wide difference.—*Mill, 'Examination of Hamilton,'* p. 59.

Though our conception of infinite space can never be adequate, since we can never exhaust its parts, the conception as far as it goes is a real conception. We realise in imagination the various attributes composing it. We realise it as space. We realise it as greater than any given space. We even realise it as endless, in an intelligible manner; that is, we clearly represent to ourselves that, however much of space has been already explored, and however much more of it we may imagine ourselves to traverse, we are no nearer to the end of it than we were at first; since, however often we repeat the process of imagining distance extending in any direction from us, that process is always susceptible of being carried further. This conception is both real and perfectly definite.—*Mill, 'Examination of Hamilton,'* p. 101.

The idea of the Infinite is very clear and very distinct, since all that my mind clearly and distinctly conceives as real and true, or as having any perfection, is wholly wrapped up and contained in this idea.—*Descartes.*

I. Two Negative Propositions may be established.

(*a*.) *The mind can form no adequate apprehension of the infinite, in the sense of image or phantasm.* In saying so I do not mean merely that we cannot construct a mental picture of the infinite as an attribute. Of no quality can the mind fashion a picture; it cannot have a mental representation of transparency, apart from a transparent substance; and just as little can it picture to itself infinity apart from an infinite duration, or infinite extension, or an infinite God. But it is not in this sense simply that the mind cannot apprehend the infinite, it cannot have before it an apprehension of an infinite object, say of an infinite space or an infinite God. For to image a thing in our mind is to give it an extent and a boundary. When we would imagine unlimited space, we swell out an immense volume, but it has after all a boundary, commonly a spherical one. When we would picture unlimited time, we let out an immense line behind and before, but the rope is after all cut at both ends. When we would represent to ourselves almighty power, we call up some given act of God, say creating or annihilating the universe; but, after all, the work has a measure, and may be finished. In the sense of image, then, the mind cannot have any proper apprehension of infinity as an attribute, or of an infinite object.

(*b*.) *The mind can form no adequate logical notion of an infinite object.* We cannot accomplish this by abstraction or generalisation, or addition or multiplication, or composition or any intellectual process. So much may be alleged to those British philosophers who have been at pains to show that we can form no conception of the infinite, or that the notion is at best negative. But, on the other hand, I am prepared to maintain that the mind has some positive apprehension and belief in regard to infinity; otherwise, why do meditative minds find the thought so often pressing itself upon them? why has it such a place in our faith in God? why is it ever coming up in theology? And if we have an idea and conviction, it is surely possible to determine what they are by a careful observation of what passes through the mind when it would muse on the eternal, the omnipresent, the perfect.

II Two Positive Propositions may be laid down.

(1.) *The mind apprehends and believes that there is and must be something beyond its widest image and concept.* Let us follow the mind in its attempt to grasp infinity. I have allowed that we cannot have an idea of infinite space and time, in the sense of imaging, picturing, or representing them. Stretch itself as it may, the imaging power of the mind can never go beyond an expansion with a boundary, commonly a globe or sphere of which self is the centre, and duration stretching along like a line, but with a beginning and an end. In respect, then, of the mental picture or representation, the apprehension is merely of the very large or the very long, but still of the finite, of what might be called the indefinite, but not the infinite. But any account of our conviction as to infinity which goes no further leaves out the main, the peculiar element. The sailor is not led by any native instinct to believe that the ocean has no bottom, simply because in letting down the sounding-line he has not reached the ground. When the astronomer has gauged space as far as his telescope can penetrate, he finds that there are still stars and clusters of stars, but he is not necessitated to believe that there must be star after star on and for ever. The geologist in going down from layer to layer still finds signs of the existence of a previous earth, but he is not obliged to conclude that there must have been stratum before stratum from all eternity. But man is constrained to believe that whatever be the point of space or time to which his eye or his thoughts may reach, there must be a space and time beyond. Whence this belief of the mind, on space and time being presented to it? Whence this necessity of thought or belief? This is the very phenomenon to be accounted for; and yet the British school of metaphysicians can scarcely be said to have contemplated it seriously or steadfastly, with the view of unfolding the depth of meaning embraced in it. This intuitive belief, accompanied as it is with a stringent necessity of feeling, is the very peculiarity of the mind's conviction in regard to infinity, as it is one of the grandest characteristics of human intelligence.

(2.) *We apprehend and are constrained to believe in regard to the objects which we look upon as infinite that they are incapable of augmentation.* Here, as in every apprehension which we have of infinity, the imaging power of the mind fails and must fail; still we have an image and an intellectual conception; say, an image with a notion of extension, or duration, or Deity. Or we represent to ourselves the Divine Being, with certain attributes,—say, as wise or as good,—and our belief as to Him and these attributes is, that He cannot be wiser or better. This aspect may be appropriately designated as the Perfect. In regard, indeed, to the moral attributes of Deity, it is this significant word Perfect, rather than infinite, which expresses the conviction which we are led to entertain in regard, for example, to the wisdom, or benevolence, or righteousness of God.—*M'Cosh, 'Intuitions of the Mind,'* pp. 187–193.

The two ideas, the Finite and the Infinite, are logically co-related. The one is impossible without the other. So soon as we have the idea of the finite and the imperfect, we have immediately and necessarily the idea also of the Infinite and Perfect. But the Infinite and the Perfect is God.—*Cousin, 'Elements of Psychology.'*

Our Knowledge is at best Indefinite.

Our knowledge of the Infinite, however far extended, must be equally indefinite. From its very commencement our knowledge must be *clear*, that is it must involve a recognition of the Infinite God, as quite apart from, and altogether above, every other being; in proportion as our knowledge extends it becomes more and more *distinct*, that is, it involves a more ample recognition of the various attributes of the Deity, in their nature, their distinction from each other, and their mutual relation to each other; but however it may extend, it will continue indefinite in exactly the same degree as before, and from exactly the same cause—that there are no limits discovered or discoverable which could give definiteness to our knowledge.—*Calderwood* '*Phil. of the Infinite*,' p. 226.

The nature of man's conviction in regard to infinity, is fitted to impress us, at one and the same time, with the strength and the weakness of human intelligence, which is powerful in that it can apprehend so much, but feeble in that it can apprehend no more. The idea entertained is felt to be inadequate, but this is one of its excellencies, that it is felt to be inadequate; for it would indeed be lamentably deficient if it did not acknowledge of itself that it falls infinitely beneath the magnitude of the object. The mind is led by an inward tendency to stretch its ideas wider and wider, but is made to know at the most extreme point which it has reached that there is something further on. It is thus impelled to be ever striving after something which it has not yet reached, and to look beyond the limits of time into eternity beyond, in which there is the prospect of a noble occupation in beholding, through ages which can come to no end, and a space which has no bounds, the manifestations of a might and an excellence of which we can never know all, but of which we may ever know more. It is an idea which would ever allure us up towards a God of infinite perfection, and yet make us feel more and more impressively the higher we ascend, that we are, after all, infinitely beneath Him.—*M'Cosh*, '*Intuitions of the Mind*,' p. 201.

XI.

ANCIENT SCHOOLS OF PHILOSOPHY.

I. THE PRE-SOCRATIC SCHOOLS.

Ionian, Pythagorean, Eleatic, Atomistic, and Sophistic.

The three oldest schools of philosophy—the Ionian, the Pythagorean, and the Eleatic—are not only very near to each other in respect of time, but are much more alike in their scientific character than might at first be supposed. While they agree with the whole of the early philosophy in directing their inquiries to the explanation of nature, this tendency is in their case more particularly shown in a search for the substantial ground of things: in demanding what things are in their proper essence, and of what they consist; the problem of the explanation of Becoming, and passing away, of the movement and multiplicity of phenomena is not as yet distinctly grasped. Thales makes all things originate and consist in water, Anaximander in infinite matter, Anaximenes in air; the Pythagoreans say that everything is number, the Eleatics that the All is one invariable Being.—*Zeller*, '*Pre-Socratic Philosophy*,' i. 202.

The Ionians.

Thales (b. 640 B.C.). Thales is reputed to be the founder of the Ionian Naturalistic Philosophy. He is the first whom we know to have instituted any general inquiry into the natural causes of things, in contradistinction to his predecessors, who contented themselves partly with mythical cosmogonies, and partly with isolated ethical reflections. In answer to this inquiry, he declared water to be the matter of which all things consist, and from which they must have arisen. As to the reasons of this theory, nothing was known by the ancients from historical tradition.—*Zeller*, '*Pre-Socratic Philosophy*,' i. pp. 211, 216, 217.

Anaximander (b. 611 B.C.). He teaches 'All things must in equity again decline into that whence they have their origin; for they must give satisfaction and atonement for injustice, each in the order of time.' Anaximander first expressly gave to the assumed original material substance of things the name of principle (ἀρχή). As such principle he posits a matter, undetermined in quality (and infinite in quantity), the ἄπειρον. From it the elementary contraries, warm and cold, moist and dry, are first separated, in such manner that homogeneous elements are brought together. Through an eternal motion, there arise, as condensations of air, innumerable worlds, heavenly divinities, in the centre of which rests the earth, a cylinder in form, and unmoved on account of its equal remoteness from all points in the celestial sphere. The earth has been evolved from an originally fluid state. Living beings arose by gradual development out of the elementary moisture under the influence of heat. Land animals had, in the beginning, the form of fishes, and only with the drying up of the surface of the earth did they acquire their present form. Anaximander is said to have described the soul as aeriform.—*Ueberweg*, '*Hist. of Phil.*,' i. p. 35.

Anaximenes. All things, says Anaximenes, spring from the air by rarefaction or by condensation. These processes he seems to have regarded as resulting from the movement of the air. Rarefaction he makes synonymous with heating, and condensation with cooling. The stages through which matter has to pass in the course of these transformations he describes somewhat unmethodically. By rarefaction air changes into fire; by condensation it becomes wind, then clouds, then water, then earth, lastly stones. From these simple bodies compound bodies are then formed. —*Zeller*, '*Pre-Socratic Philosophy*,' i. 271, 272.

The Pythagoreans.

The doctrine that number is the essence of all things.

All is number, *i.e.*, all consists of numbers; number is not merely the form by which the constitution of things is determined, but also the substance and the matter of which they consist. It is one of the essential peculiarities of the Pythagorean standpoint that the distinction of form and matter is not as yet recognised.

All numbers are divided into odd and even, to which, as a third class, the even-odd (ἀρτιο-πέριττον) is added, and every given number can be resolved either into odd or even numbers. From this the Pythagoreans concluded that the odd and the even are the universal constituents of numbers, and furthermore, of all things. They identified the uneven with the limited, and the even with the unlimited, because the uneven sets a limit to bi-partition, and the even does not. Thus they arrived at the proposition that all consists of the limited and the unlimited. With this proposition is connected the following observation, that everything unites in itself opposite characteristics.—*Zeller*, '*Pre-Socratic Philosophy*,' i. 275, 277–280.

The ten fundamental opposites.

(1) Limited and Unlimited; (2) Odd and Even; (3) One and Many; (4) Right and Left; (5) Masculine and Feminine; (6) Rest and Motion; (7) Straight and Crooked; (8) Light and Darkness; (9) Good and Evil; (10) Square and Oblong. —*Zeller*, '*Pre-Socratic Philosophy*,' i. p. 381.

The Pythagorean doctrine of Transmigration.

The Pythagorean doctrine was, according to the most ancient authorities, essentially the same that we afterwards find associated with other Pythagorean notions, in Plato; and which is maintained by Empedocles, viz., that the soul on account of previous transgressions is sent into the body, and that after death each soul, according to its deserts, enters the Cosmos or Tartarus, or is destined to fresh wanderings through human or animal forms.—*Zeller*, '*Pre-Socratic Philosophy*,' i. 384.

The Eleatics.

The development of the Eleatic philosophy was completed in three generations of philosophers, whose activity extended over about a century. Xenophanes, the founder of the school, first expresses their general principle in a theological form. In opposition to Polytheism, he declares the Deity to be the One, underived, all-embracing Being; and in connection with this, the universe to be uniform and eternal. At the same time, however, he recognises the many and the mutable as a reality. Parmenides gives to this principle its metaphysical basis and purely philosophic expression; he reduces the opposites of the One and the Many, the Eternal and the Become, to the fundamental opposite of the Existent and the non-Existent; derives the qualities of both from their concept, and proves the impossibility of Becoming, Change, and Plurality in a strictly universal sense. Lastly, Zeno and Melissus maintain the propositions of Parmenides as against the ordinary opinion; but carry the opposition between them so far that the inadequacy of the Eleatic principle for the explanation of phenomena becomes clearly apparent.—*Zeller*, '*Pre-Socratic Philosophy*,' i. pp. 355, 356.

Zeno's Four Arguments against Motion.

1. Motion cannot begin because a body in motion cannot arrive at another place until it has passed through an unlimited number of intermediate places. 2. Achilles cannot overtake the tortoise, because as often as he reaches the place occupied by the tortoise at a previous moment the latter has already left it. 3. The flying arrow is at rest, for it is at every moment only in one place. 4. The half of a division of time is equal to the whole, for the same point, moving with the same velocity, traverses an equal distance (*i.e.*, when compared, in the one case, with a point at rest, in the other with a point in motion) in the one case in half of a given time, in the other the whole of that time.—*Ueberweg*, '*Hist. of Phil.*,' i. 57, 58.

The Atomists.

Leucippus of Abdera (or Miletus, or Elea) and Democritus of Abdera, the latter, according to his own statement, forty years younger than Anaxagoras, were the founders of the Atomistic philosophy. These philosophers posit, as principles of things, the 'full' and the 'void,' which they identify respectively with being and non-being, or something and nothing; the latter as well as the former having existence. They characterise the 'full' more particularly as consisting of indivisible primitive particles of matter or atoms, which are distinguished from one another, not by their intrinsic qualities but only geometrically, by their form, position, and arrangement. Fire and the soul are composed of round atoms. Sensation is due to material images, which come from objects and reach the soul through the senses. The ethical end of man is happiness, which is attained through justice and culture. — *Ueberweg*, '*Hist. of Phil.*,' i. 67.

The Sophists.

a. Their philosophy.

In the doctrine of the Sophists the transition was effected from philosophy as cosmology to philosophy as concerning itself with the thinking and willing subject. Yet the reflection of the Sophists extended only to the recognition of the subject in his immediate individual character, and was incompetent, therefore, to establish on a scientific basis the theory of cognition and science of morals, for which it prepared the way. The chief representatives of this tendency were Protagoras the Individualist, Gorgias the Nihilist, Hippias the Polymathist, and Prodicus the Moralist.

These men were followed by a younger generation of Sophists, who perverted the philosophical principle of subjectivism more and more, till it ended in mere frivolity. — *Ueberweg, 'Hist. of Phil.,'* i 72.

b Their historical importance.

The Sophists are the 'Illuminators' of their time, the encyclopædists of Greece, and they share in the advantages as well as the defects of that position. It is true that the lofty speculation, the moral earnestness, the sober scientific temperament entirely absorbed in its object, which we have such frequent occasion to admire both in ancient and modern philosophers, all this is wanting in the Sophists Their whole bearing seems pretentious and assuming, their unsettled wandering life, their money-making, their greediness for scholars and applause, their petty jealousies among themselves, their vain-gloriousness, often carried to most ridiculous lengths, form a striking contrast to the scientific devotion of an Anaxagoras or a Democritus, to the unassuming greatness of a Socrates, or the noble pride of a Plato. . . . We must not, however, forget that these defects are only in the main the reverse side, the degradation of a movement that was both important and justifiable; and that we equally fail to recognise the true character of the Sophists, or to do justice to their real services, whether we regard them merely as destroyers of the ancient Greek theory of life or with Plato as its representatives. — *Zeller, 'Pre-Socratic Philosophy,'* ii. 500, 503

The Sophists are historically important not only as rhetoricians, grammarians, and diffusers of various forms of positive knowledge, but also as representatives of a relatively legitimate philosophical standpoint. Their philosophical reflection centred in man, was subjective rather than objective in direction, and thus prepared the way for ethics and logic.—*Ueberweg, 'Hist. of Phil.,'* i. 72.

II. THE SOCRATIC SCHOOL.

Socrates. Born B C 469.

His conception of philosophy.

Human wisdom is patchwork; the gods have reserved what is greatest to themselves. The wisdom of Socrates was the consciousness of not knowing, and not the consciousness of a positive gradual approximation to the knowledge of truth.—*Ueberweg, 'Hist of Phil.,'* i 3

The direction he gave to philosophical inquiry was expressed in the saying that he brought 'Philosophy down from Heaven to Earth.' His subjects were Man and Society He entered a protest against the inquiries of the early philosophers as to the constitution of the Kosmos, the nature of the Heavenly Bodies, the theory of Winds and Storms. He called these Divine things; and in a great degree useless, if understood. The Human relations of life, the varieties of conduct of men towards each other in all capacities, were alone within the compass of knowledge, and capable of yielding fruit. —*Bain, 'Mental and Moral Science,'* p. 460.

His method of philosophising

The Socratic method has two sides, the one negative and the other positive. (1.) The negative one is what is known as the Socratic *irony*. Making believe to be ignorant, namely, and seeming to elicit information from those with whom he conversed, the philosopher would unexpectedly turn the tables on his seeming instructors, and confound their supposed knowledge, as well by the unlooked-for consequences which he educed by his incessant questions, as by the glaring contradictions in which they were in the end by their own admissions landed. Thus their supposed knowledge brought about its own refutation. (2.) The positive side of the Socratic method is the *maieutic* or obstetric art. Socrates likened himself to his mother Phœnarete, who was a midwife, because, if no longer able to bear thoughts himself, he was still quite able to help others to bear them, as well is to distinguish those that were sound from those that were unsound. The philosopher, by means of his incessant questioning and the resultant disentanglement of ideas, possessed the art of eliciting from him with whom he conversed a new and previously unknown thought, and so of helping to a birth his intellectual throes. A chief means here was his method of induction. To find the notion of justice, of fortitude, for instance, departure was taken from several particular examples of justice, of fortitude, and from them the universal *nature*, the notion of these virtues, was abstracted.—*Schwegler*, '*Hist. of Phil.*,' pp. 49, 50.

The mastery over words was the great art which the Athenian youth cultivated. It seems to have been the first observation of Socrates, when he began earnestly to meditate on the condition of his countrymen, that those who wished to rule the world by the help of words were themselves in the most ignominious bondage to words. The wish to break this spell seems to have taken strong possession of his mind. As he reflected, he began more and more clearly to perceive that words, besides being the instruments by which we govern others, are means by which we may become acquainted with ourselves. In trying really to understand a word, to ascertain what was the *bonâ fide* meaning which he himself gave it, he found that he gained more insight into his own ignorance, and at the same time that he acquired more real knowledge, than by all other studies together. In this work he knew that he was really honest; he was breaking through a thousand trickeries and self-deceptions. If, then, he was to deliver his countrymen from that miserable shallowness into which they had been betrayed by the ambition of wisdom and depth,—this must be his means. In every case he must lead his disciples to inquire what they actually meant by the words of the propositions which they were using, and must consider no time wasted which they honestly spent in this labour.—*Maurice*, '*Moral and Metaphysical Philosophy*,' i. 126.

His doctrine.

Socrates made all virtue dependent on knowledge, *i.e.*, on moral insight; regarding the former as flowing necessarily from the latter. He was convinced that virtue was capable of being taught, that all virtue was in truth only one, and that no one was voluntarily wicked, all wickedness resulting merely from ignorance. The good is identical with the beautiful and the useful. Self-knowledge is the condition of practical excellence. External goods do not advance their possessor.—*Ueberweg*, '*Hist. of Phil.*,' i. 80, 85.

To do right was the only way to impart happiness, or the least degree of unhappiness compatible with any given situation; now, this was precisely what every one wished for and aimed at—only that many persons, from ignorance, took the wrong road; and no man was wise enough always to take the right. But as no man was willingly his own enemy, so no man ever did wrong willingly; it was because he was not fully or correctly informed of the consequences of his own actions; so that the proper remedy to apply was enlarged teaching of consequences and improved judgment. To make him willing to be taught, the only condition required was to make him conscious of his own ignorance; the want of which consciousness was the real cause both of indocility and of vice.—*Grote*, '*History of Greece*,' pt. ii. ch. lxviii. vol. viii. p. 262.

Well-doing consisted in doing well whatever a man undertook. 'The best man,' he said, 'and the most beloved by the gods is he that, as a husbandman, performs well the duties of husbandry; as a surgeon, the duties of a medical art; in political life, his duty towards the commonwealth. The man that does nothing well is neither useful nor agreeable to the gods.' And as knowledge is essential to all undertakings, knowledge is the one thing needful.—*Bain*, '*Mental and Moral Science*,' p. 462.

Leading peculiarities of Socrates.

Three peculiarities distinguish the man 1. His long life passed in contented poverty, and in public apostolic dialectics. 2. His strong religious persuasion—or belief of acting under a mission and signs from the gods; especially his Dæmon or Genius—the special religious warning of which he believed himself to be frequently the subject 3. His great intellectual originality, both of subject and of method, and his power of stirring and forcing the germ of inquiry and ratiocination in others. Though these three characteristics were so blended in Sokrates that it is not easy to consider them separately—yet in each respect he stood distinguished from all Greek philosophers before or after him.—*Grote*, '*Hist. of Greece*,' pt. ii. ch. lxviii. vol. 8, p. 211

Xenophon on the method of Socrates

Sokrates continued incessantly discussing *human* affairs, investigating—What is piety? What is impiety? What is the honourable and the base? What is the just and the unjust? What is temperance or unsound mind? What is courage or cowardice? What is a city? What is the character fit for a citizen? What is authority over men? What is the character befitting the exercise of such authority? and other similar questions. Men who knew these matters he accounted good and honourable; men who were ignorant of them he assimilated to slaves.—Quoted by *Grote*, '*Hist of Greece*,' pt. ii. ch. lxviii. vol. 8, p. 228.

Plato Born 429 B.C.

Plato, the complete Socratic.

The complete Socrates was understood and represented by only one of his disciples, Plato. Proceeding from the Socratic idea of knowledge, he collected into a single focus all the elements and rays of truth which lay scattered, not only in his master, but in the philosophers before him, and made of philosophy a whole, a system The Platonic system is the objectivised Socrates, the conciliation and fusion of all previous philosophy, the first type and pattern of all higher speculation, of all metaphysical as well as of all ethical idealism.—*Schwegler*, '*Hist of Phil.*,' pp. 57, 93.

In the Socratic principle of knowledge and virtue, the problem for the successors of Socrates was the development of dialectic and ethics Of his immediate disciples, the larger number, as 'partial disciples of Socrates,' turned their attention predominantly to the one or other part of this double problem; the Megaric and Elean schools occupying themselves almost exclusively with dialectical investigations, and the Cynic and Cyrenaic schools treating, in different senses, principally of ethical questions. It was Plato, however, who first combined and developed into the unity of a comprehensive system the different sides of the Socratic spirit, as well as all the legitimate elements of earlier systems.—*Ueberweg*, '*Hist. of Phil.*,' i. 88.

His Doctrine.

a. Of Ideas.

The Platonic philosophy centres in the Theory of Ideas The Platonic Idea is the pure archetypal essence, in which those things which are together subsumed under the same concept, participate. Æsthetically and Ethically, it is the perfect in its kind, to which the given reality remains perpetually inferior. Logically and ontologically considered, it is the object of the concept. As the objects of the outer world are severally known through corresponding mental representations, so the idea is known through the concept. The Idea is not the essence immanent in the various similar individual objects as such, but rather this essence conceived as perfect in its kind, immutable, unique, and independent, or existing *per se*. The Idea respects the universal; but it is also represented by Plato as a spaceless and timeless archetype of individuals. The Idea is the archetype, individual objects are images of this. Independent singular existence was attributed to the Ideas, and even movement, life, animation, and reason were said to belong to them. Plato assumed a plurality of Ideas and held that the highest idea is the Idea of the Good.—*Ueberweg*, '*Hist. of Phil.*,' i. 115, 116.

The doctrine of Ideas constitutes the most native and peculiar portion of Plato's philosophy. The whole of the education and discipline of Socrates had been to lead his disciples away from appearances to realities. But one man has one notion of the things which he beholds and meditates upon; another man, another. Any one of these notions may be as right as another. Thus the notions which the mind forms respecting that which the bodily eye sees; or that which its own inward eye sees, seem confused, fluctuating, contradictory. But my notion of the flower is not the very flower; my notion of what is just is not the very just. These notions are indexes, guiding-posts to that which is not false, or confused, or contradictory. This notion of the flower and of justice proves that there is a very flower—a very justice. Again the mind is capable of beholding the Being, the One. But of this Being, of this One, all the notions, imaginations, premonitions of the sensual understanding offer most miserable and counterfeit resemblances. Yet there is that in this Being, this One, which does and must answer to these notions; that which they are trying, however vainly, however awkwardly to express.

Hence there are forms permanent and unchangeable in which that which is, manifests itself as it is; in which we behold it as it is. Therefore Plato speaks of the actual flower and tree that we behold, as well as of Justice, Goodness, and Beauty, as having a primary form or idea. He believes that in the minutest thing there is a reality, and therefore in some sense an archetypal form or idea; he believes also, just as firmly, that every idea has its ground and termination in one higher than itself, and that there is a supreme idea, the foundation and consummation of all these, even the idea of the absolute and perfect Being, in whose mind they all dwelt, and in whose eternity alone they can be thought or dreamed of as eternal. These ideas are the witnesses in our utmost being that there is something beyond us and above us; when we enter into the idea of anything, we abdicate our own pretensions to be authors or creators, we become mere acknowledgers of that which is.—*Maurice*, '*Moral and Metaphysical Philosophy*,' i. 147–150 (abridged).

Plato included under the expression *idea* everything stable amidst the changes of mere phenomena, all really and unchangeable definitudes, by which the changes of things and our knowledge of them are conditioned, such as the ideas of genus and species, the laws and ends of nature, as also the principles of cognition, and of moral action, and the essences of individual, concrete, thinking souls.—*Brandis, in* '*Dict. of Biog. and Myth.*,' iii. 401.

b. Of Ethics.

The highest good is, according to Plato, not pleasure, nor knowledge alone, but the greatest possible likeness to God, as the absolutely good. The virtue of the human soul is its fitness for its proper work. The virtue of the cognitive part of the soul is the knowledge of the good, or wisdom; that of the courageous part is valour, which consists in preserving correct and legitimate ideas of what is to be feared and what is not to be feared; the virtue of the appetitive part is temperance (moderation or self-control, self-direction), which consists in the agreement of the better and worse parts of the soul as to which should rule; justice, finally, is the universal virtue, and consists in the fulfilment by each part of its peculiar function. Virtue should be desired, not from motives of reward and punishment, but because it is in itself the health and beauty of the soul. To do injustice is worse than to suffer injustice.—*Ueberweg*, '*Hist. of Phil.*,' i. 128.

Not life in the perishableness, the changefulness of sensuous existence, but exaltation into true, into ideal being, is that which is the good absolutely. The task and destiny of the soul is flight from the inward and outward evils of sense, purification and emancipation from corporeal influence, the striving to become pure, just, and like withal to God; and the path to this is withdrawal from sensuous imaginations and appetites, retirement into thought, into the cognition of truth, in a word, philosophy.—*Schwegler*, '*Hist. of Phil.*,' p. 86.

Aristotle. Born 384 B.C.

His relation to Plato.

As Plato was the only true disciple of Socrates, so in turn the only true disciple of Plato was Aristotle.—*Schwegler*, '*Hist. of Phil.*,' p. 94.

In the Platonic philosophy the opposition between the real and the ideal had completely developed itself. The external and sensible world was looked upon as a world of appearance, in which the ideas cannot attain to their true and proper reality. Plato accordingly made the external world the region of the incomplete and bad, of the contradictory and false, and recognised absolute truth only in the eternal immutable ideas. Now this opposition, which set fixed limits to cognition, was surmounted by Aristotle.—*Stahr, in 'Dict. of Biog. and Myth.*,' i. 334.

His method.

The method of Aristotle is different from that of Plato. He proceeds, not synthetically and dialectically, like the latter, but almost always analytically and regressively, that is to say, passing ever backwards from what is concrete to its ultimate grounds and principles. His method, therefore, is induction, that is, the derivation of general inferences and results from a sum of given facts and phenomena. He bears himself mostly only as a thoughtful observer. Renouncing any expectation of universality and necessity in his conclusions, he is contented to have established an approximate truth, and pleased to have reached the greatest possible probability. Philosophy has consequently for him the character and the value of a calculation of probabilities, and his mode of exposition assumes not unfrequently only the form of a dubious counting up. Hence his dislike to imaginative flights and poetic figures in philosophy, his invariable submission to the existent fact. —*Schwegler*, '*Hist. of Phil.*,' p. 97.

The peculiar method of Aristotle stands in close connection with the universal direction which he gave to his intellectual exertions, striving to penetrate into the whole compass of knowledge. In this endeavour he certainly sets out from experience, in order first to arrive at the consciousness of *that which really exists*, and so to grasp in thought the multiplicity and breadth of the sensible and spiritual world. Thus he always first lays hold of his subject externally, separates that in it which is merely accidental, renders prominent the contradictions which result, seeks to solve them and to refer them to a higher idea, and so at last arrives at the cognition of the ideal intrinsic nature, which manifests itself in every separate object of reality. In this manner he consecutively develops the objects as well of the natural as of the spiritual world, proceeding *genetically* from the lower to the higher, and from the known to the less known, and translates the world of experience into the Idea.—*Stahr, in 'Dict. of Greek and Roman Biog.*,' i. 333.

His divisions of Philosophy.

The primary distinction and classification recognised by Aristotle among sciences or cognitions, is that of (1) Theoretical, (2) Practical, (3) Artistic or Constructive. Of these three divisions the second and third alike comprise both intelligence and action, but the two are distinguished from each other by this, that in the Artistic there is always some assignable product which the agency leaves behind independent of itself, whereas in the Practical no such independent result remains, but the agency itself, together with the purpose (or intellectual and volitional condition) of the agent is everything The division named Theoretical comprises intelligence alone—intelligence of *principia*, causes and constituent elements Here, again, we find a tripartite classification. The highest and most universal of all Theoretical Sciences is recognised by Aristotle as Ontology (First Philosophy, sometimes called by him Theology) which deals with all *Ens* universally, *quatenus Ens*, and with the *Prima Moventia*, themselves immovable, of the entire Kosmos The two other heads of Theoretical Science are Mathematics and Physics; each of them special and limited as compared with Ontology —*Grote*, '*Aristotle*,' p. 423

His Doctrine.

a. Metaphysics.

The first philosophy or Metaphysics is the science of the first principles and causes of things There are four first principles or causes of things:—(1) The substance and the idea; (2) the subject and the matter; (3) the principle of motion; (4) the purpose and the good.—*Stahr, in 'Dict. of Greek and Roman Biog.*,' i. 336.

The principles common to all spheres of reality are considered. These are Form or Essence, Matter or Substratum, Moving or Efficient Cause, and End. The principle of Form or Essence is the Aristotelian substitute for the Platonic Idea —*Ueberweg*, '*Hist. of Phil.*,' i. 157.

b. Ethics.

The highest and last purpose of all action, according to Aristotle, is *happiness*. This he defines to be the energy of life existing for its own sake (perfect life), according to virtue existing by and for itself (perfect virtue). As the highest good it must be pursued for its own sake Virtues are of two kinds, either intellectual virtues (dianoetic), or moral virtues (ethical), according to the distinction between the reasoning faculty and that in the soul which obeys the reason The intellectual virtues may be learnt and taught, the ethical virtues are acquired by practice. Virtue is based upon free self-conscious action —*Stahr, in 'Dict. of Greek and Roman Biog.*,' i. 340.

Socrates had set virtue and knowledge as one. But, in the opinion of Aristotle, it is not reason that is the first principle of virtue, but the natural sensations, inclinations, and appetites of the soul, without which action were not to be thought. Aristotle also disputes the teachableness of virtue. It is not through cultivation of knowledge, according to him, but through exercise that virtue is realised. We become virtuous through the practice of virtue, as through the practice of music and architecture we become musicians and architects. Man is good through three things: through nature, through habit, and through reason —*Schwegler*, '*Hist of Phil.*,' p. 116.

c. His doctrine of the relations of soul and body

'The soul,' says Aristotle, 'is not any variety of body, but it cannot be without a body; it is not a body, but it is something belonging to or related to a body, and for this reason it is *in* a body, and in a body of such or such potentialities.'

The animated subject is thus a form immersed or implicated in matter, and all its actions and passions are so likewise Each of those has its formal side as concerns the soul, and its material side as concerns the body. When a man or animal is angry, for example, this emotion is both a fact of the soul and a fact of the body; in the first of these two characters it may be defined as an appetite for hurting some one who has hurt us; in the second of the two it may be defined as an ebullition of the blood and heat round the heart. The emotion belonging to the animated subject or aggregate of soul and body is a complex fact having two aspects, logically distinguishable from each other, but each correlating and implying the other. This is true not only in regard to our passions, emotions, and appetites, but also in regard to our perceptions, phantasms, reminiscences, reasonings, efforts of attention in learning, &c.—*Grote*, '*Aristotle*,' pp. 458, 459.

d. His doctrine of Happiness or the highest good.

What is the business and peculiar function of man as man? Not simply Life, for that he has in common with the entire vegetable and animal world; nor a mere sensitive Life, for that he has in common with all animals: it must be something which he has apart both from plants and animals, viz., an active life in conformity with reason; or the exercise of Reason as a directing and superintending force, and the exercise of the appetite, passions, and capacities in a manner conformable to Reason. This is the special and peculiar business of man: it is what every man performs either well or ill: and the *virtue* of a man is that whereby he is enabled to perform it well. The Supreme Good of humanity, therefore, consisting as it does in the due performance of this special business of man, is to be found in the virtuous activity of our rational and appetitive soul, assuming always a life of the ordinary length, without which no degree of mental perfection would suffice to attain the object. The full position will then stand thus: 'Happiness, or the highest good of a human being, consists in the working of the soul and in a course of action, pursuant to reason and conformable to virtue, throughout the whole continuance of life.'—*Grote*, '*Aristotle*,' pp. 502, 503.

Want of harmony in his philosophy.

We observe the disjointed nature of his writings, their want of any systematic classification and division. Always advancing from particular fact to particular fact, he takes each region of reality by itself, and makes it the object of a special treatise; but he omits for the most part to demonstrate the threads by which the facts might mutually cohere and clasp together into a system. He obtains thus a plurality of co-ordinated sciences, each of which has its independent foundation, but no highest science which should comprehend all.—*Schwegler*, '*Hist. of Phil.*,' p. 97.

III. THE 'ONE-SIDED SOCRATICISTS.'

The Cynic and Cyrenaic Schools.

Several points these two opposite schools seem to have had in common. (1.) They started from a common principle, namely, the assertion of the individual consciousness and will, as being above all outward convention and custom, free and self-responsible. (2.) They agreed in disregarding all the sciences, which was a mistaken carrying out of the intentions of Socrates. (3.) They stood equally aloof from society and from the cares and duties of a citizen. (4.) They seem both to have upheld the ideal of a wise man, as being the exponent of universal reason and the only standard of right and wrong.—*Grant*, '*Aristotle's Ethics*,' i. 172.

The Cynics.

Cynicism implies sneering and snarling at the ways and institutions of society, it implies discerning the unreality of the shows of the world, and angrily despising them; it implies a sort of embittered wisdom, as if the follies of mankind were an insult to itself.

We may ask, How far did the procedure of the early Cynics justify this implication? On the whole, very much. The anecdotes of Antisthenes and Diogenes generally describe them as being true 'Cynics,' in the modern sense of the word. Their whole life was a protest against society. They lived in the open air; they slept in the porticos of temples; they begged; Diogenes was sold as a slave. They despised the feelings of patriotism, war and its glory they held in repugnance.

Their hard and ascetic life set them above all wants. 'I would rather be mad,' said Antisthenes, 'than enjoy pleasure.' They broke through the distinction of ranks by associating with slaves. And yet under this self-abasement was greater pride than that against which they protested. Socrates is reported to have said, 'I see the pride of Antisthenes through the holes in his mantle.' And when Diogenes exclaimed, while soiling with his feet the carpet of Plato, 'Thus I tread on Plato's pride,' 'Yes,' said Plato, 'with greater pride of your own.'—*Grant, 'Aristotle's Ethics,'* i. 173

The Cyrenaics

Personally, the Cyrenaics were not nearly so interesting as the Cynics. Their position was not to protest against the world, but rather to sit loose upon the world. Aristippus, who passed part of his time at the court of Dionysius, and who lived throughout a gay, serene, and refined life, avowed openly that he resided in a foreign land to avoid the irksomeness of mixing in the politics of his native city Cyrene. But the Cyrenaic philosophy was much more of a system than the Cynic. Like the *ethics* of Aristotle, this system started with the question, What is happiness? only it gave a different answer.

Cyrenaic morals began with the principle, taken from Socrates, that happiness must be man's aim. Next they start a question, which is never exactly started in Aristotle, and which remains an unexplained point in his system, namely, 'What is the relation of the parts to the whole, of each successive moment to our entire life?' The Cyrenaics answered decisively, 'We have only to do with the present. Pleasure is μονόχρονος, μερική, an isolated moment, of this alone we have consciousness. Happiness is the sum of a number of these moments. We must exclude desire and hope and fear, which partake of the nature of pain, and confine ourselves to the pleasure of the present moment.'—*Grant, 'Aristotle's Ethics,'* i. 174–176.

The Cyrenaic system a philosophy of despair.

The profound joylessness which there is at the core of the Cyrenaic system showed itself openly in the doctrines of Hegesias, the principal successor of Aristippus. Hegesias, regarding happiness as impossible, reduced the highest good for man to a sort of apathy; thus, at the extremest point, coinciding again with the Cynics.—*Grant, 'Aristotle's Ethics,'* i. 178.

IV. STOIC

Founders

The founder of the Stoic school is Zeno, born in Citium, a town of Cyprus, about the year 340 B.C.; not of pure Greek, but of Phœnician extraction. He was pupil first of Crates the Cynic, then of Stilpo the Megaric, and lastly of Polemo the Academic. Convinced at length of the necessity of a new philosophy, he opened, in an arcade at Athens, a school of his own. This arcade was named, from the paintings of Polygnotus, with which it was decorated, the 'many-coloured portico' (Stoa Pœcilè); whence those who attended the new school were called 'philosophers of the Porch.' Zeno's successor in the school was Cleanthes of Assos, in Asia Minor, a faithful follower of the tenets of his master. Cleanthes was succeeded by Chrysippus, who was born in Soli in Cilicia, and died about the year 208 B.C. He was so pre-eminently the support of the Stoa, that it used to be said, 'If Chrysippus were not, the Stoa were not.' At all events, as, for all the later Stoics, he was an object of exalted veneration, and almost infallible authority, he must be regarded as the most eminent originator of their doctrine.—*Schwegler, 'Hist. of Phil.,'* p. 123.

Zeno was probably of Shemitic race, for he is commonly styled 'the Phœnician.' Babylon, Tyre, Sidon, Carthage, reared some of his most illustrious successors. Cilicia, Phrygia, Rhodes were the homes of others. Not a single Stoic of any name was a native of Greece proper.—*Lightfoot, 'Philippians,'* p 271.

Origin of

The theory

The Stoical *theory* has deduced from an observation how much power a man possesses who is not the victim of pleasures or of pains. The endurance of pain, the contempt of it, seemed to the Stoic the signs of a man. He exaggerated the notion, till pain itself acquired a glory in his eyes, till he thought himself grand for hating pleasure. He dwelt in a magnificent self-sufficiency, believing that pain had some virtue or excellence of its own.—*Maurice, 'The Conscience,'* p. 79.

Like all the later systems of Greek philosophy, Stoicism was the offspring of despair Of despair in religion, for the old mythologies had ceased to command the belief or influence the conduct of men Of despair in politics; for the Macedonian conquest had broken the independence of the Hellenic States, and stamped out the last sparks of corporate life Of despair even in philosophy itself; for the older thinkers, though they devoted their lives to forging a golden chain which should link earth to heaven, appeared now to have spent their strength in weaving ropes of sand The sublime intuitions of Plato had been found too vague and unsubstantial, and the subtle analyses of Aristotle too hard and cold, to satisfy the natural craving of man for some guidance which should teach him how to live and to die.—*Lightfoot, 'Philippians,'* p. 269.

Of the practice.

We do not drop into Stoicism naturally. A few may have some bias to it from education; a few may be drawn into it by arguments, or the example of others The doctrine is much more commonly embraced by one who has for a long time acted on the maxim that pleasure is the supreme power which he must obey. He has had some stern and clear intimations of the effects which come from subjection to this ruler The consequence is a violent quarrel with himself, or the tendencies to which he has passively yielded. He gnashes his teeth at the things which have been the occasion of his distress and humiliation; he denounces pleasure as pleasure; he greedily seizes upon pain as if by enduring it he could take some revenge upon himself for that avoidance of it in times past which now seems to him feeble and cowardly.—*Maurice, 'The Conscience,'* p. 83.

Stoic Division of Philosophy

Three main divisions of philosophy were universally acknowledged by the Stoics—Logic, Natural Science, and Ethics. As regards the relative worth and sequence of these divisions, very opposite views may be deduced from the principles of the Stoic teaching. There can be no doubt that in position logic was subservient to the other two branches of science, logic being only regarded as an outpost of the system.—*Zeller, 'Stoics, Epicureans, &c.,'* p. 65.

Doctrine of

First Cause.

In the order and harmony of universal nature there are signs enough, Stoics argued, of a First Cause and Governing Mind. A little thought upon the matter shows us that there must be a power inherent in the world to move it as the soul can move the body. That power must have consciousness and reason, else how can we explain the being of conscious creatures like ourselves? Of God the Stoics speak in the language of devotional fervour, not only as an abstract Reason, but as a happy and beneficent Creator. But if we ask what were the real features of their creed, we shall find to our surprise that it was one of Pantheism undisguised. God is the eternal substance which is always varying its moods, and passing into different forms as the creative work is going forward, and may be alike conceived therefore as the primary matter and the efficient force which shapes the derivative materials of which all things are made From God all things proceed, and to Him they will all return at last when each cycle of time has run its course.—*Capes, 'Stoicism,'* p. 37

The Stoics did not think of God and the world as different beings. Their system was therefore strictly pantheistic. The world is the sum of all real existence, and all real existence is originally contained in God, who is at once universal matter and the creative force which fashions matter into the particular materials of which things are made. We can, therefore, think of nothing which is not either God or a manifestation of God. In point of Being, God and the world are the same, the two conceptions being declared by the Stoics to be absolutely identical.—*Zeller, 'Stoics, Epicureans, &c.,'* p. 149

They called God, now the spiritual breath that permeates nature, now the art-subserving fire that forms or creates the universe, and now the ether, which, however, was not different to them from the principle of fire. In consequence of this identification of God and the world, all in the world appears to them inspired by the divine life, coming into special existence out of the divine whole, and returning into it again.—*Schwegler, 'Hist. of Phil.,'* p 126

The fundamental and invincible error of Stoic philosophy was its theological creed. Though frequently disguised in devout language which the most sincere believer in a personal God might have welcomed as expressing his loftiest aspirations, its theology was nevertheless, as dogmatically expounded by its ablest teachers, nothing better than a pantheistic materialism. This inconsistency between the philosophic doctrine and the religious phraseology of the Stoics is a remarkable feature, which perhaps may be best explained by its mixed origin. The theological language would be derived in great measure from Eastern (I venture to think from Jewish) affinities, while the philosophic dogma was the product of Hellenised thought. Heathen devotion seldom or never soars higher than in the sublime hymn of Cleanthes. 'Thine offspring are we,' so he addresses the supreme Being, 'therefore will I hymn Thy praises and sing Thy might for ever Thee all this universe which rolls about the earth obeys, wheresoever Thou dost guide it, and gladly owns Thy sway.' 'No work on earth is wrought apart from Thee, nor through the vast heavenly sphere, nor in the sea, save only the deeds which bad men in their folly do.' If these words might be accepted in their first and most obvious meaning, we could hardly wish for any more sublime and devout expression of the relations of the creature to his Creator and Father. But a reference to the doctrinal teaching of the school dispels the splendid illusion. This Father in heaven, we learn, is no personal Being, all righteous and all holy, of whose loving care the purest love of an earthly parent is but a shadowy counterfeit. He—or It—is only another name for nature, for necessity, for fate, for the universe.—*Lightfoot, 'Philippians,'* p. 317.

Of Ethics.

Its place in their system.

The Eastern origin of Stoicism combined with the circumstances and requirements of the age to give it an exclusively ethical character. Consciously and expressly they held physical questions and the systematic treatment of logic to be valueless except in their bearing on moral questions. Representing philosophy under the image of a field, they compared physics to the trees, ethics to the fruit for which the trees exist, and logic to the wall or fence which protects the enclosure. Or again, adopting another comparison, they likened logic to the shell of an egg, physics to the white, and ethics to the yolk.—*Lightfoot, 'Philippians,'* p. 272.

Statement of it.

These ethics assert the supreme good, or the supreme end of our endeavours, to be an adaptation of our life to the universal law, to the harmony of the world, to nature. 'Follow nature,' or 'live in agreement with nature,' this is the moral principle of the Stoics More precisely: live in agreement with thy own rational nature, so far as it is not corrupted and distorted by art, but remains in its natural simplicity; be knowingly and willingly that which by nature thou art, a rational part of the rational whole; be reason and in reason, instead of following unreason and thy own particular self-will Here is thy destination, here thy happiness, as on this path thou avoidest every contradiction to thy own nature and to the order of things without, and providest thyself a life that glides along undisturbed in a smooth and even stream.—*Schwegler*, '*Hist. of Phil.*,' p 127

This leading principle of the Stoics was carried out to its conclusions with an exclusive and uncompromising rigour, and the startling paradoxes which they held seemed to follow naturally enough from their one-sided treatment of great truths. Good, in its wider sense, was commonly defined in the earlier schools as that which satisfies a natural want, but the essential element, the true nature of man as distinct from other creatures, is his reason; and his real good, therefore, lies in rational action, or in virtue There is no good independently of virtue Bodily advantages and gifts of fortune have no abiding character of good, satisfy no permanent want of reason So even health and wealth must be counted as indifferent, that is, with no distinctive character of good, for they may be and are sadly abused. Still less must pleasure be the object of pursuit Pleasure there is indeed in virtuous conduct, a cheerful serenity so sweet that we may say that only the wise man knows true pleasure, but we must not make that our aim and object. Virtue should be its own reward, and cannot need extraneous conditions to complete the happiness of those who have it For a man's true self vice alone was evil Hardship, poverty, disgrace, pain, sickness, death, seem evils to the beings who are content to live upon a lower level. The wise man alone is free, for he can make himself independent of the whims of fortune and enjoy the bliss of an unruffled calm.—*Capes*, '*Stoicism*,' pp 44–46.

Happiness, the Stoics said, can be sought only in rational activity or virtue. Speaking more explicitly, the primary impulse of every being is towards self-preservation and self-gratification. It follows that every being pursues those objects which are most suited to its nature, and that such objects alone have for it any value Hence the highest good—the end-in-chief, or happiness—can only be found in what is conformable to nature

The happiness of the virtuous man—and this is a peculiar feature of Stoicism—is thus far more negative than positive It consists more in independence and peace of mind than in the enjoyment which moral conduct brings with it In mental disquietude, says Cicero, speaking as a Stoic, consists misery; in composure, happiness The doctrine of the apathy of the wise man is alone enough to prove that freedom from disturbances, an unconditional assurance, and self-control, are the points on which these philosophers lay especial value, as constituting the happiness of the virtuous man.—*Zeller*, '*Stoics, Epicureans, &c.*,' pp 213 and 225

Its defects

The ethics of the Stoical school have vital defects The fundamental maxim of conformity to nature, though involving great difficulties in its practical application, might at all events have afforded a starting-point for a reasonable ethical code. Yet it is hardly too much to say that no system of morals, which the wit of man has ever devised, assumes an attitude so fiercely defiant of nature as this. It is mere folly to maintain that pain and privation are no evils. The paradox must defeat its own ends. Stoicism is pervaded by want of sympathy. Pity, anger, love, are ignored by the Stoic, or at least recognised only to be crushed. The Stoic ideal is stern, impassive, immovable. As a natural consequence, the genuine Stoic is isolated and selfish.—*Lightfoot, 'Philippians,'* p. 319.

Illustrations of Stoical Teaching.

Individual morality and self-examination.

'As far as thou canst, accuse thyself, try thyself: discharge the office, first of a prosecutor, then of a judge, lastly of an intercessor.—*'Seneca,' quoted by Lightfoot, 'Philippians,'* p. 279.

'We have all sinned, some more gravely, others more lightly, some from purpose, others by chance impulse, or else carried away by wickedness external to them; others of us have wanted fortitude to stand by our resolutions, and have lost our innocence unwillingly and not without a struggle. Not only we *have* erred, but to the end of time we shall continue to err. Even if any one has already so well purified his mind that nothing can shake or decoy him any more, it is through sinning that he has arrived at this state of innocence.—*'Seneca,' quoted by Grant, 'Aristotle's Ethics,'* i. 357.

Religious character of Stoical teaching.

'God has a fatherly mind towards good men, and loves them stoutly; and, saith He, Let them be harassed with toils, with pains, with losses, that they may gather true strength.' 'Those therefore whom God approves, whom He loves, them He hardens, He chastises, He disciplines.' 'It is best to endure what you cannot mend, and without murmuring to attend upon God, by whose ordering all things come to pass. He is a bad soldier who follows his captain complaining.'—*'Seneca,' quoted by Lightfoot, 'Philippians,'* pp. 277, 278.

The philosophers say that we ought first to learn that there is a God, and that He provides for all things; also that it is not possible to conceal from Him our acts, or even our intentions and thoughts. The next thing is to learn what is the nature of the gods; for such as they are discovered to be, he, who would please and obey them,' must try with all his power to be like them.—*Epictetus, 'Discourses,'* bk. ii. chap. xiv. p. 141.

Independence of circumstances.

'Varro thought that nature, Brutus that the consciousness of virtue, were sufficient consolations for any exile. How little have I lost in comparison with these two fairest possessions which I shall everywhere enjoy—nature and my own integrity! Whoever or whatever made the world,—whether it were a deity, or disembodied reason, or a divine interfusing spirit, or destiny, or an immutable series of connected causes, the result was that nothing, except our very meanest possessions, should depend on the will of another. Man's best gifts lie beyond the power of man either to give or to take away. This Universe, the grandest and loveliest work of nature, and the Intellect, which was created to observe and to admire it, are our special and eternal possessions which shall last as long as we last ourselves. Cheerful, therefore, and erect, let us hasten with undaunted footsteps whithersoever our fortunes lead us.

'What though fortune has thrown me where the most magnificent abode is but a cottage? the humblest cottage, if it be but the home of virtue, may be more beautiful than all temples; no place is narrow which may contain the crowd of glorious virtues; no exile severe into which you may go with such a reliance.'—*'Seneca,' quoted by F. W. Farrer, 'Seekers after God,'* pp. 93, 94.

Freedom and Slavery,—the one is the name of virtue and the other of vice; and both are acts of the will. But where there is no will, neither of them touches (affects) these things. But the soul is accustomed to be master of the body, and the things which belong to the body have no share in the will, for no man is a slave who is free in his will.—*Epictetus, 'Fragments,'* viii.

It is an evil chain, fortune (a chain) of the body and vice of the soul. For he who is loose (free) in the body but bound in the soul, is a slave; but, on the contrary, he who is bound in the body but free (unbound) in the soul is free.—*Epictetus*, '*Fragments*,' ix.

Benevolence.

Begin the morning by saying to thyself, I shall meet with the busybody, the ungrateful, arrogant, deceitful, envious, unsocial. All these things happen to them by reason of their ignorance of what is good and evil. But I, who have seen the nature of the good that it is beautiful, and of the bad that it is ugly, and the nature of him who does wrong that it is akin to me, not (only) of the same blood or seed, but that it participates in (the same) intelligence and (the same) portion of the divinity. I can neither be injured by any of them, for no one can fix on me what is ugly nor can be angry with my kinsman, nor hate him. For we are made for co-operation, like feet, like hands, like eyelids, like the rows of the upper and lower teeth. To act against one another, then, is contrary to nature, and it is acting against one another to be vexed and to turn away.—*Aurelius*, '*Thoughts*,' ii. 1.

Men exist for the sake of one another. Teach them then or bear with them.—*Aurelius*, '*Thoughts*,' viii. 59.

Suicide as an act of self-abnegation.

The culminating point of self-abnegation with the Stoics was suicide. The first leaders of the school, by their precept and example, recommended the wise, on occasion, to 'usher themselves out' of life. If suicide, thus dignified by a name, were an escape from a mere pain or annoyance, it would be an Epicurean act; but, as a flight from what is degrading,—as a great piece of renunciation, it assumes a Stoical appearance. The passion for suicide reached its height in the writings of Seneca, under the wretched circumstances of the Roman despotism; but, on the whole, it belongs to immature Stoicism. Epictetus and Marcus Aurelius dissuaded from it.—*Grant*, '*Aristotle's Ethics*,' i. 334, 335.

Its Characteristic Features.

The characteristic features of the system consist in three points: a pre-eminently practical tendency, the shaping of practical considerations by the notions of the good and virtue, the use of logic and natural science as a scientific basis.—*Zeller*, '*Stoics, Epicureans, &c.*,' p. 359.

Intense moral earnestness was the most honourable characteristic of Stoicism. The ever-active conscience is its glory, and proud self-consciousness is its reproach. Stoicism breathes the religious atmosphere of the East, which fostered on the one hand the inspired devotion of a David or an Isaiah, and on the other the self-mortification and self-righteousness of an Egyptian therapeutic or an Indian fakir. It might with great truth be described as the contact of Oriental influences with the world of classical thought.—*Lightfoot*, '*Philippians*,' p. 271.

Its Productive Element.

The productive element in the Stoic philosophy is not to be deemed insignificant, especially in the field of ethics, where their vigorous discrimination and severance of the morally good from the agreeable, and the rank of indifference to which they reduced the latter, mark at once the merit and the one-sidedness of the Stoics.—*Ueberweg*, '*Hist. of Phil.*,' i. 187.

Meagre results of Stoicism.

Our first wonder is that, from a system so rigorous and unflinching in its principles, and so heroic in its proportions, the direct results should have been marvellously little. It produced, or at least it attracted, a few isolated great men; but on the life of the masses and on the policy of states it was almost wholly powerless. Stoicism has no other history except the history of its leaders. It was a staff of professors without classes.—*Lightfoot*, '*Philippians*,' pp. 307, 317.

Its Relation to Christianity.

One of opposition.

Nothing can well be imagined more contrary to the spirit of Christianity. Nothing could be more repugnant to the Stoic than the news of a 'Saviour' who has atoned for our sin, and is ready to aid our weakness. Christianity is the school of Humility, Stoicism was the education of Pride. Christianity is a discipline of life; Stoicism was nothing better than an apprenticeship for death. In its full development Stoicism was utterly opposed to Christianity.—*Conybeare and Howson*, '*Life of St. Paul*,' i. 433.

Yet of preparation for the Gospel.

To the language of Stoicism was due a remarkable development of moral terms and images. St. Paul found in the ethical language of the Stoics expressions more fit than he could find elsewhere to describe in certain aspects the duties and privileges, the struggles and the triumphs, of the Christian life. But though the words and symbols remained substantially the same, yet in their application they became instinct with new force and meaning.—*Lightfoot*, '*Philippians*,' p. 300.

On this subject see the whole of Bishop Lightfoot's admirable Dissertation on St Paul and Seneca ('Epistle to the Philippians'), so frequently quoted in this article, and concerning which Mr. Capes rightly observes that it 'has left nothing further to be said upon the question.'

V. EPICUREAN.

The Founder—Epicurus, born 342 B.C.

The founder of the Epicurean school was Epicurus, the son of an Athenian who had emigrated to Samos. In his thirty-sixth year he opened at Athens a philosophical school, over which he presided till his death (in the year 270 B.C.). Epicurus's moral character has been frequently assailed; but his life, according to the most credible testimony, was in every respect blameless, and he himself alike amiable and estimable. Much of what is reported about the offensive sensuality of the Epicurean sty is in general considered to be calumny.—*Schwegler*, '*Hist. of Phil.*,' p. 131.

Epicurus had not the obtrusive idiosyncrasy of the Cynic, nor the severe and strict austerity of the Stoic. Philosophy with him did not mean speculation, nor yet an isolated seclusion; neither was its effect to be seen in the outward clothing, or want of clothing, of a Diogenes. Philosophy was 'a daily business of speech and thought, to secure a happy life.' It was not necessary to have read deeply or thought profoundly. One study, however, for a philosopher was absolutely necessary, the study of nature. The personal kindliness, the sympathy, the generosity, the sweetness of Epicurus's character stand out clearly.—*Courtney*, '*Studies in Philosophy*,' p. 30.

Epicurus, we are told, liked to hear anecdotes respecting the indifference and apathy of Pyrrho. But Epicurus was no doubter; he was the most imperious of dogmatists. No one had ever such entire faith in his own conclusions; no one more thoroughly and heartily rejected all conclusions but his own, as absurd, even as impossible. Unless he had attained to this perfect satisfaction in his own judgment, he would have missed the main object which he proposed to himself. A man must be brought into a peculiar condition of mind before he can believe that the universe and all that it contains exist only that they may tell him how he is to be comfortable; but when once he has believed this, it will be wonderful indeed if his ears ever catch any sound which is not an echo to his demand, or some fragment of an answer to it.—*Maurice*, '*Moral and Metaphysical Philosophy*,' i. 235.

Doctrine.

Its general character.

Epicurus denominated philosophy an activity which realises a happy life through ideas and arguments. It has essentially for him, therefore, a practical object, and it results, as he desires, in ethics which are to teach us how to attain to a life of felicity. The Epicureans did, indeed, accept the usual division of philosophy into logic (called canonic by them), physics, and ethics. But logic, limited to the investigation of the criteria of truth, was considered by them only as ancillary to physics. Physics, again, existed only for ethics, in order to secure men from those vain terrors of empty fables, and that superstitious fear which might obstruct their happiness. In Epicureanism, we have still, then, the three ancient parts of philosophy, but in reverse order, logic and physics being only at the service of ethics.—*Schwegler*, '*Hist. of Phil.*,' p. 131.

No other system troubled itself so little about the foundation on which it rested; none confined itself so exclusively to the utterances of its founder. Such was the dogmatism with which Epicurus propounded his precepts, such the conviction he entertained of their usefulness, that his pupils were required to commit summaries of them to memory; and the superstitious devotion for the founder was with his approval carried to such a length, that not the slightest deviation from his tenets was on a single point permitted. Probably it was easier for an Epicurean to act thus than it would have been for any other thinker. The aim of philosophy was, with them, to promote human happiness. Indeed, philosophy is nothing else but an activity helping us to happiness by means of speech and thought. All science which does not serve this end is superfluous and worthless. Hence Epicurus despised learning and culture, the researches of grammarians and the lore of historians, and declared that it was most conducive to simplicity of feeling to be uncontaminated by learned rubbish.—*Zeller*, '*Stoics, Epicureans, &c.*,' pp. 394–396.

His doctrine of atoms.

Every body is composed of a greater or smaller number of atoms, or indivisible particles, in various degrees of proximity to each other. What appears to be solid is never absolutely so. The air, the water, the fruit, the rock, have all an atomic or molecular constitution. The tiny particles of which they are composed float in an ocean of empty space, where they are forced into closer or laxer proximity to each other. How small these atoms are we cannot tell. They are cognisable by reason and thought, but they are beneath the power of sense, at least of unassisted sense.—*Wallace*, '*Epicureanism*,' p. 97.

Ethics.

In the Epicurean Ethics the highest good is defined as happiness. Happiness, according to Epicurus, is synonymous with pleasure, for this is what every being naturally seeks to acquire. Pleasure may result either from motion or from rest. The pleasure of rest is freedom from pain. Pleasure and pain, further, are either mental or bodily. The most powerful sensations are not, as the Cyrenaics affirmed, bodily, but mental; for while the former are confined to the moment, the latter are connected with the past and future, through memory and hope, which thus increase the pleasure of the moment. Not every species of pleasure is to be sought after, nor is every pain to be shunned; for the means employed to secure a certain pleasure are often followed by pains greater than the pleasure produced, or involve the loss of other pleasures; and that, whose immediate effect is painful, often serves to ward off greater pain, or is followed by a pleasure more than commensurate with the pain immediately produced. Whenever a question arises as to the expediency of doing or omitting any action, the degrees of pleasure and pain, which can be foreseen as sure to result from the act, must be weighed and compared, and the question must be decided according to the preponderance of pleasure or pain in the foreseen result. The correct insight necessary for this comparison is the cardinal virtue. From it flow all other virtues. The virtuous man is he who is able to proceed rightly in the quest of pleasure.—*Ueberweg*, '*Hist. of Phil.*,' i. 208.

'The end and aim of all action,' says Epicurus, 'is that we may neither suffer nor fear. When once this end is realised, all the tempest of the soul subsides, for animal nature has then no need to satisfy, nothing is wanting to the full completion of good, whether of body or soul. For we want pleasure when we feel pain at its absence; when we feel no pain we want no pleasure. It is for this reason that we say that pleasure is the beginning and end of a happy life.' Again he says, 'I can conceive of no good remaining if you take from me the pleasures of taste, the pleasures of love, and the pleasures of ear and eye.' But he adds, 'When we say that pleasure is the end, we do not mean the pleasures of the libertine and the pleasures of mere enjoyment, as some critics, either ignorant, or antagonistic, or unfriendly, suppose, but the absence of pain in the body and trouble in the mind.' 'Philosophy has no more priceless element than prudence, from which all other virtues flow, teaching us that it is not possible to live pleasantly without also living sensibly, honourably, and justly.' —*Courtney*, '*Studies in Philosophy*,' pp. 35–38.

Epicurus demands not for a happy life the most exquisite pleasures, he recommends, on the contrary, sobriety and temperance, contentment with little, and a life generally in accord with nature. He boasts to be willing to vie with Jupiter himself in happiness, if allowed only plain bread and water. The wise man can dispense with finer enjoyments, for he possesses within himself the greatest of his satisfactions, he enjoys within himself the truest and the most stable joy,—tranquillity of soul, impassibility of mind. The theory of Epicurus ends in the recommendation of negative pleasure through the avoidance of the disagreeable. But he knows nothing of a moral destiny in man.—*Schwegler*, '*Hist. of Phil.*,' p. 133.

His hedonism is of a sober and reflective kind. It rests on the assumption that pleasure is the end or natural aim, but, it adds, that the business of philosophy is to show within what limits that end is attainable. Thus if, on one hand, it declares against the philosophers that pleasure is the law of nature, and that ideal ends ought to promote the welfare of humanity, it declares on the other against the multitude that the ordinary pursuit of pleasure, and the common ideas of its possibilities, are erroneous. True pleasure is satisfaction, and not a yearning, which, though momentarily stilled, bursts forth again.—*Wallace*, '*Epicureanism*,' p. 147.

Theology of Epicurus.

Careless opponents have described Epicurus as an Atheist. But the existence of the gods is what he never denies: what he, on the contrary, asserts as a fundamental truth. The question on which he diverges from popular faith is not whether there are gods, but what is their nature and relation to man. His special tenet is a denial of the creative and providential functions of deity. The gods are away from the turmoil and trouble of the world. Going a step beyond Aristotle, he assigns them an abode in the vacant spaces between the worlds. In a place of calm, where gusty winds, and dank clouds and mists, and wintry snow and frost never come. Its smiling landscapes are bathed in perpetual summer light. There the bounties of nature know no end, and no troubles mar the serenity of the mind. Such was the Epicurean heaven: there was no Epicurean hell.—*Wallace*, '*Epicureanism*,' pp. 202, 203.

Compared with Stoic.

Epicurus and Zeno strove in different ways to solve the problem which the perplexities of their age presented. Both alike, avoiding philosophy in the proper sense of the term, concentrated their energies on ethics: but the one took happiness, the other virtue, as his supreme good, and made it the startingpoint of his ethical teaching Both alike contrasted with the older masters in building their systems on the needs of the individual and not of the State: but the one strove to satisfy the cravings of man as a being intended by nature for social life, by laying stress on the claims and privileges of friendship, the other by expanding his sphere of duty and representing him as a citizen of the world or even of the universe Both alike took conformity to nature as their guiding maxim: but nature with the one was interpreted to mean the equable balance of all the impulses and faculties of man, with the other the absolute supremacy of the reason, as the ruling principle of his being And, lastly, both alike sought refuge from the turmoil and confusion of the age in the inward calm and composure of the soul. If Serenity was the supreme virtue of the one, her twin sister Passionlessness was the sovereign principle of the other. — *Lightfoot, 'Philippians,'* p 270.

The Epicurean sage was not a hero, not a statesman, not even a philosopher, but a quiet, humane, and prudent man,—'a hero,' as Seneca says, 'disguised as a woman' Epicureanism was undoubtedly not a speculative success, but as a practical code of life it suited the world far more than its rival Stoicism, and lasted longer. It could not produce martyrs or satisfy the highest aspirations of mankind, but it made men fall back on themselves and find contentment and serenity in a life at once natural and controlled. — *Courtney, 'Studies in Philosophy,'* p 54.

The Epicureans stood aloof from practice to a far greater extent than the Stoics. The end of their system looked to life and not to business: the end of their wisdom was to enjoy life. They did not profess, like the Stoics, that their wise man was capable of doing well any of the innumerable vocations in life which he might choose to adopt. They claimed that he would live like a god amongst men and conquer mortality by his enjoyment at every instant of an immortal blessedness While the Stoic represented man as the creature and subject of divinity, the Epicurean taught him that he was his own master. While the Stoic rationalised the mythology of their country into a crude and fragmentary attempt at theology, the Epicurean rejected all the legends of the gods, and denied the deity any part in regulating the affairs of men. Both agreed in founding ethics on a natural as opposed to a political basis, but they differed in their application of the term nature To the Stoic it meant the instinct of self-conservation—the maintenance of our being in its entirety—acting up to our duty. To the Epicurean it meant having full possession of our own selves, enjoying to the full all that the conditions of human life permit.— *Wallace, 'Epicureanism,'* pp 18, 19.

Transmission of the System.

Epicurus has had many resurrections; his spirit has lived again in Gassendi, in La Rochefoucauld, in Saint-Evremond, in Helvetius, and in Jeremy Bentham. — *Courtney, 'Studies in Philosophy,'* p. 53.

VI. SCEPTIC

Three Schools.

There appeared in succession three Sceptical schools or groups of philosophers:—(1) Pyrrho of Elis (in the time of Alexander the Great) and his earliest followers; (2) the so-called Middle Academy, or the second and third Academic Schools; (3) the Later Sceptics, beginning with Ænesidemus, who again made the teaching of Pyrrho the basis of their own teaching. — *Ueberweg, 'Hist. of Phil.,'* i. 212.

Doctrine.

The tendency of these sceptical philosophers was, like that of the Stoics and Epicureans, proximately a practical one; philosophy shall conduct us to happiness. But, to live happy, we must know how things are, and how, consequently, we must relate ourselves to them. They answered the first question in this way: What things really are lies beyond the sphere of our knowledge, since we perceive not things as they are but only as they appear to us to be; our ideas of them are neither true nor false; anything definite of anything cannot be said. Neither our perceptions nor our ideas of things teach us anything true; the opposite of every proposition, of every enunciation, is still possible. In this impossibility of any objective knowledge of science, the true relation of the philosopher to things is entire suspense of judgment, complete reserve of all positive opinion. In this suspense of judgment, they believed their practical end, happiness, attained; for, like a shadow, imperturbability of soul follows freedom from judgment, as if it were a gift of fortune. He who has adopted the sceptical mood of thought lives ever in peace, without care and without desire, in a pure apathy that knows neither of good nor evil. —*Schuegler*, '*Hist of Phil.*,' p. 135.

Pyrrho's teaching may be summed up in the three following statements: (1.) We can know nothing about the nature of things. (2.) Hence the right attitude towards them is to withhold judgment. (3.) The necessary result of suspending judgment is imperturbability.—*Zeller*, '*Stoics, Epicureans, &c.*,' p. 492.

Causes producing it.

Not seldom do sceptical theories follow times of great philosophical originality. The impulse which emanated from the Stoic and Epicurean systems was strong. Related as these systems are to Scepticism by their practical tone, it was natural that they should afford fresh fuel to Scepticism. At the same time the unsatisfactory groundwork upon which they were built, and the contrast between their statements regarding morality and nature, promoted distinctive criticism. The important back-influence of Stoicism and Epicureanism in producing Scepticism may be best gathered from the fact that Scepticism only attained a wide extension of a more comprehensive basis after the appearance of those systems.—*Zeller*, '*Stoics, Epicureans, &c.*,' p. 488.

Its Relation to Theology.

The Scepticism of the Academy sought to demonstrate that the idea of God itself was an untenable one. The line of argument which Carneades struck out for this purpose is essentially the same as that used in modern times to deny the personality of God. The ordinary view of God regards Him as infinite, but at the same time, as an individual Being, possessing the qualities and living the life of an individual. But to this view Carneades objected, on the ground that the first assertion contradicts the second; and argues that it is impossible to apply the characteristics of personal existence to God without limiting His infinite nature.—*Zeller*, '*Stoics, Epicureans, &c.*,' p. 515.

The close connection between the general principles of the Sceptics and those of modern Agnostics will not escape the notice of the student. Compare Article on *Agnosticism*.

VII. ECLECTIC.

The Term.

We ordinarily understand by an eclectic one who, with different philosophies before him, chooses portions out of each which he embraces and portions which he rejects.—*Maurice*, '*Moral and Metaphysical Philosophy*,' ii 581.

Eclectic in philosophy denotes a thinker whose views are borrowed partly from one, partly from another of his predecessors. It perhaps requires to be noted that, where the characteristic doctrines of a philosophy are not thus merely adopted, but are the modified products of a blending of the systems from which it takes its rise, the philosophy is not properly eclectic.—'*Encyclop. Brit.*,' vii 643.

Rise of Eclecticism

In the second century B.C., a remarkable tendency toward eclecticism began to manifest itself. The longing to arrive at the one explanation of all things which had inspired the older philosophers became less earnest; the belief, indeed, that any such explanation was attainable began to fail; and the men, not feeling the need of one complete logical system, came to adopt from all systems the doctrines which best pleased them. In Panætius we find one of the earliest examples of the modification of Stoicism by the eclectic spirit, and about the same time the same spirit displayed itself among the Peripatetics.—'*Encyclop. Brit.*,' vii. 643.

Its Causes and Representatives.

When criticism had demonstrated the presence of untenable elements in all the great systems, the ineradicable need of philosophical convictions could not but lead either to the construction of new systems, or to Eclecticism. In the latter it would necessarily end, if the philosophising subject retained a naïve confidence in the directness of his natural perceptions of truth or in his sagacious tact in the appreciation of philosophical doctrines, while yet lacking the creative power requisite to the founding of a system. In particular, Eclecticism would naturally find acceptance with those who sought in philosophy not knowledge as such, but rather a general theoretical preparation for practical life and the basis of rational convictions in religion and morals, and for whom, therefore, rigid unity and systematic connection in philosophical thought were not unconditionally necessary. Hence the philosophy of the Romans was almost universally eclectic. The most important and influential representative of this tendency is Cicero, who, in what pertains to the theory of cognition, confessed his adhesion to the scepticism of the Middle Academy, took no interest in physics, and in ethics wavered between the Stoic and the Peripatetic doctrines.—*Ueberweg*, '*Hist. of Phil.*,' i. 218.

Its Method.

Eclectics gathered from every system what was true and probable. In this process of selection their decision was swayed by regard to the practical wants of man, and the ultimate standard of truth was placed in our own immediate consciousness, everything being referred to the subject as its centre. For their ethics and natural theology the Eclectics were also greatly indebted to the Stoics.—*Zeller*, '*Stoics, Epicureans, &c.*,' p. 23.

Its Results.

The popular philosophy of Cicero and other thinkers of a similar bent is not, despite its want of originality, independency, and rigour, to be too lightly estimated; for it led to the introduction of philosophy as a constituent element in culture generally.—*Schwegler*, '*Hist. of Phil.*,' p. 138.

The Right and Wrong of Eclecticism.

The Eclectic did not care for the opinions and conflicts of the schools; he found in each hints of the precious truths of which he desired to avail himself. He would gather the flowers without asking in what garden they grew; the prickles he would leave for those who had a fancy for them. Eclecticism in this sense seems only like another name for catholic wisdom. A man conscious that everything in nature and art was given for his learning, had a right to such honey wherever it was to be found. But once let it be fancied that the philosopher was not a mere receiver of treasures which had been provided for him, but an ingenious chemist and compounder of various naturally unsociable ingredients, and the eclectical doctrine would lead to mere self-conceit, would be more unreal and heartless, than any one of the sectarian elements out of which it was fashioned. It would want the belief and conviction which dwell, with whatever unsuitable companions, even in the narrowest theory. Many of the most vital characteristics of the original dogmas would be effaced, under pretence of taking off their rough edges and fitting them into each other. In general, the superficialities and formalities of each creed would be preserved in the new system; its original and essential characteristics sacrificed.—*Maurice, 'Moral and Metaphysical Philosophy,'* i. 315.

Later Eclectics.

Among the early Christians, Clement of Alexandria, Origen, and Synesius were Eclectics in philosophy. The Eclectics of modern philosophy are almost too numerous to name. Of Italian philosophers the Eclectics form a large proportion. Among the Germans we may mention Wolf and his followers, as well as Mendelssohn, Eberhard, Platner, and to some extent Schelling. The name is appropriately given to the French school, of which the most distinguished members are Victor Cousin, Théodore Jouffroy, Damiron, St. Hilaire, Rémusat, Garnier, and Ravaisson.—*'Encyc. Brit.,'* vii. 643.

VIII. NEO-PLATONIC.

Its Founder.

Plotinus (204–269 A.D.), who first developed the Neo-Platonic doctrine in systematic form, or at least was the first to put it into writing, was educated at Alexandria under Ammonius Saccas, and afterwards (from A.D. 240 on) taught at Rome.—*Ueberweg, 'Hist. of Phil.,'* i. 240.

Character of its Teaching.

Theory of Emanation.

Every such theory, and the Neo-Platonic as well, assumes the world to be an effluence or eradiation of God, in such manner that the remoter emanation possesses ever a lower degree of perfection than that which precedes it, and represents consequently the totality of existence as a descending series. Fire, says Plotinus, emits heat, snow cold, fragrant bodies exhale odours, and every organised being, so soon as it has reached maturity, generates what is like it. In the same manner, the all-perfect and eternal, in the exuberance of its perfection, permits to emanate from itself what is equally everlasting and next itself the best,—reason, which is the immediate reflection, the ectype of the primeval one.—*Schwegler, 'Hist. of Phil.,'* p. 141.

Doctrine of the soul and the body.

The individual souls, like the soul of the world, are amphibia between the higher element of reason and the lower of sense, now involved in the latter, and now turning to their source, reason. From the world of reason, which is their true and proper home, they have descended, each at its appointed time, reluctantly obedient to an inner necessity, into the corporeal world, without, however, wholly breaking the world of ideas: rather they are at once in both, even as a ray of light touches at once the sun and the earth. Our vocation, therefore, can only be a turning of our senses and our endeavours to our home in the world of the ideas, emancipation of our better self from the bondage of matter, through mortification of sense, through *ascesis*. Once in the ideal world, however, that reflection of the primal beautiful and good, our soul reaches thence the ultimate end of every wish and longing, ecstatic vision of the one, union with God, unconscious absorption—disappearance—in God.—*Schwegler, 'Hist. of Phil.,'* p. 142.

Religious Aspect of Neo-Platonism.

'As sun and moon, sky, earth, and sea, are common to all, while they have different names among different nations; so likewise, though there is but one system of the world which is supreme, and one governing providence, whose ministering powers are set over *all* men, yet there have been given to these, by the laws of different nations, different names and modes of worship; and the holy symbols which these nations used were, in some cases, more obscure, in others clearer; but in all cases alike failed of being perfectly safe guides in the contemplation of the divine. For some, wholly mistaking their import, fell into superstition; while others, in avoiding the quagmire of superstition, plunged unawares into the opposing gulf of infidelity.'

As Zeus is the beginning and centre of all, everything has sprung from Zeus, men should first correct and improve their ideas of the gods, if anything impure or wrong has found its way into them. But, if this is beyond their power, they should then leave every one to that mode in which he finds himself placed by the laws and religious traditions of his country.—*Plutarch, quoted by Neander, 'Church History,'* i. 27, 28.

XII.

MEDIÆVAL SCHOLASTIC PHILOSOPHY.

Origin of the Name 'Scholastic.'

The name of Scholastics (*doctores scholastici*) which was given to the teachers of the *septem liberales artes* (grammar, dialectic, rhetoric, in the *Trivium*; arithmetic, geometry, music, and astronomy in the *Quadrivium*), or at least of some of them, in the cloister-schools founded by Charlemagne, as also to teachers of theology, was afterwards given to all who occupied themselves with the sciences, and especially with philosophy, following the tradition and example of the schools.—*Ueberweg, 'Hist. of Phil.,'* i. 356.

Period of the Duration of Scholastic Philosophy.

It is not possible to define with accuracy the duration of the empire of scholastic philosophy. It began in the ninth century, and has in some degree survived to our own days; but the revival of classical literature and the Reformation deprived it for ever of that unlimited authority which it possessed before.—*Tennemann, 'Hist. of Phil.,'* p. 211.

Character of Scholasticism.

The character of scholasticism is conciliation between dogma and thought, between faith and reason. When the dogma passes from the Church, where it took birth, into the school, and when theology becomes a science treated in universities, the interest of thought comes into play, and asserts its right of reducing into intelligibleness the dogma which has hitherto stood above consciousness as an external, unquestionable power. A series of attempts is now made to procure for the doctrines of the Church the form of a scientific system.—*Schwegler, 'Hist. of Phil.,'* p. 144.

Scholasticism was philosophy in the service of the established and accepted theological doctrines, or, at least, in such subordination to them, that, when philosophy and theology trod on common ground, the latter was received as the absolute norm and criterion of truth. More particularly, scholasticism was the reproduction of ancient philosophy, under the control of ecclesiastical doctrine, with an accommodation, in case of discrepancy between them, of the former to the latter.—*Ueberweg, 'Hist. of Phil.,'* i. 355.

Scholasticism a Link between Ancient and Modern Philosophy.

The human mind was not, as has been imagined, asleep during the thousand years of mediævalism; still less was it sunk in the rigidity of death. There was development, albeit the slow development of autumn, when all the juices are transformed into food and garnered up to nourish in the coming spring the fresh green, luxuriant growth, and supply material for a new and blooming world.

Any one who surveys with comprehensive gaze the development of philosophy as the thought of the world in its relation to mankind, will see in the tranquil intellectual industry of the Middle Ages a great and significant mental crisis, an important and indispensable link between ancient and modern philosophy.—*Noiré, 'Historical Introduction to Professor Max Muller's Kant,'* pp. 67, 68.

The Scholastic Philosophy was mainly a Controversy of Nominalism and Realism.

Hand in hand with the development of Scholasticism in general, proceeded that of the antithesis between *nominalism* and *realism*, an antithesis the origin of which is to be found in the relation of Scholasticism to the philosophy of Plato and Aristotle. The nominalists were those who held universal notions (*universalia*) to be mere names, *flatus vocis*, empty conceptions without reality. With nominalists there are no general notions, no *genera*, no *species*: all that is, exists only as a singular in its pure individuality; and there is no such thing as pure thought, but only natural conception and sensuous perception. The realists again, by example of Plato, held firmly by the objective reality of the universals (*universalia ante res*). The antithesis of these opinions took form first as between *Roscelinus* and *Anselm*, the former as nominalist, the latter as realist; and it continues henceforth throughout the whole course of scholasticism.—*Schwegler*, '*Hist. of Phil.*,' p. 145.

The conflict between ideas and things forms the real substance of the debates and investigations of scholasticism.—*Noiré*, '*Introduction to Kant*,' p. 88.

The Four Epochs of Scholasticism.

Four epochs may be defined in the history of this philosophy, deducible from the history of the question concerning the *Reality* of Conceptions, and the relations of Philosophy to Theology. *First period*, down to the eleventh century: a blind *Realism*, with scattered attempts to apply the elements of Philosophy to Theology. *Second period*, from *Roscellin* to *Alexander of Hales* or *Alesius*, at the commencement of the thirteenth century. The first appearance of Nominalism and of a more liberal system of inquiry, quickly repressed by the ecclesiastical authorities, which established the triumph of Realism. An alliance was brought about between philosophy and theology in generals. *Third period*, from *Alexander* and *Albert*, surnamed the Great, to *Occam*: thirteenth and fourteenth centuries. During this period, Realism had exclusive dominion; the system of instruction adopted by the Church was consolidated by the introduction of the Arabic-Aristotelian system; and philosophy became still more closely connected with theology. The age of *St. Thomas Aquinas* and *Scotus*. *Fourth period*, from *Occam* to the sixteenth century. A continued contest between Nominalism and Realism, wherein the former obtained some partial successes. Philosophy was gradually detached from Theology, through the renewal of their old debates.—*Tennemann*, '*Hist. of Phil.*,' p. 212.

The Results of Scholasticism.

Among its good results were a dialectic use of the understanding, a great subtilty of thought, an extension of the domain of Dogmatical Metaphysics, and a rare sagacity in the development and distinction of ontological notions, with individual efforts on the part of several men of genius, notwithstanding the heavy bondage in which they were held. The ill effects were, the dissemination of a minute and puerile spirit of speculation, the decay of sound and practical sense, with a neglect of the accurate and real sciences and the sources whence they are to be derived, that is:—Experience, History, and the Study of Languages.

To these must be added the prevalence of the dominion of authority, and prescription; bad taste; and a rage for frivolous distinctions and subdivisions, to the neglect of the higher interests of science.—*Tennemann,* '*Hist. of Phil.,*' p. 213

The most important conception which mediæval philosophy was to originate and bequeath to modern times was that of the *concept* (*conceptus*) itself; something purely intellectual, an object born of the mind itself, which, nevertheless, has marvellous unexplained relations to reality, the full elucidation of which remained for a still remote future To discover these relations began henceforward to count as the chief business of philosophy. All the controversies of Scholasticism turn upon the Universals; these Universals are represented in modern philosophy by concepts or general ideas.—*Noiré,* '*Introd. to Kant,*' pp. 92, 93.

XIII.

MODERN PHILOSOPHICAL SCHOOLS.

Modern Philosophy has its Roots in the 'Revival of Learning.'

Among the events which introduced the transition from the Middle Ages to modern times, the earliest was the revival of classical studies This revival was negatively occasioned by the one-sided character and the gradual self-dissolution of scholasticism, and positively by the remains of ancient art and literature in Italy—which were more and more appreciated as material prosperity increased—and by the closer contact of the Western world, especially of Italy with Greece, particularly after the flight of large numbers of learned Greeks to Italy, at the time when the Turks were threatening Europe and had taken Constantinople The invention of the art of printing facilitated the spread of literary culture. The first important result in the field of philosophy of the renewed connection of Western Europe with Greece was the introduction of the Platonic and Neo-Platonic philosophies into the West, their enthusiastic reception, and the attempt by means of these to supplant the scholastic-Aristotelian philosophy. —*Ueberweg,* '*Hist of Phil,*' ii 5

With the revival of learning, after the fall of Constantinople, came fresh streams of Grecian influence. The works of Plato became generally known; under Marsilio Ficino, to whom we owe the Latin translation of Plato, a school of Platonists was formed, which continued to divide with the school of Aristotle the supremacy of Europe under new forms, as before it had divided it under the form of Realism The effect of this influx of Grecian influence, at a period when Philosophy was emancipating itself from the absolute authority of the Church, was to transfer the allegiance from the Church to antiquity.—*Lewes,* '*Hist. of Phil.,*' ii. 89.

Descartes and Cartesianism (See also Sec. vii. iii.)

At the head of the dogmatic (or rationalistic) development-series in modern philosophy stands the Cartesian doctrine. René Descartes (1596–1650) was educated in a Jesuits' school, was led, by comparing the different notions and customs of different nations and parties, by general philosophical meditations, and more especially by his observations of the great remoteness of all demonstrations in philosophy and other disciplines from mathematical certainty, to doubt the truth of all propositions received at second-hand The only thing, reasoned Descartes, which, though all else be questioned, cannot be doubted, is doubt itself; and, in general, thought viewed in its widest sense as the complex of all conscious psychical processes. But my thinking presupposes my existence: *cogito, ergo sum.* I find in me the notion of God, which I cannot have formed by my own power, since it involves a higher degree of reality than belongs to me; it must have for its author God Himself, who stamped it upon my mind, just as the architect impresses his stamp on his work. God's existence follows also from the very idea of God, since the essence of God involves existence—eternal and necessary existence. Among the attributes of God belongs truthfulness (*veracitas*). God cannot wish to deceive me; therefore, all that which I know clearly and distinctly must be true. All error arises from my misuse of the freedom of my will, in that I prematurely judge of that which I have not clearly and distinctly apprehended. I can clearly and distinctly apprehend the soul as a thinking substance, without representing it to myself as extended; thought involves no predicates that are connected with extension. I must, on the other hand, conceive all bodies as extended substances, and as such believe them to be real, because I can by the aid of mathematics obtain a clear and distinct knowledge of extension, and am at the same time clearly conscious of the dependence of my sensations on external corporeal causes. The soul and the body are connected, and they interact, the one upon the other, only at a single point, a point within the brain, the pineal gland. Descartes considered body and spirit as constituting a dualism of perfectly heterogeneous entities, separated in nature by an absolute and unfilled interval. Hence the interaction between soul and body, as asserted by him, was inconceivable, although supported in his theory by the postulate of divine assistance.—*Ueberweg*, '*Hist. of Phil.*,' ii. 41, 42.

Descartes' four principles of Method.

1. To receive nothing as true which is not evidently known to be such, by its presenting itself to the mind with a clearness and distinctness which exclude all doubt.

2. To divide, as far as possible, every difficult problem into its natural parts.

3. To conduct one's thoughts in due order, advancing gradually from the more simple and easy to the more complex and difficult, and to suppose a definite order, for the sake of the orderly progress of the investigation, even where none such is supplied in the nature of the subject investigated.

4. By completeness in enumeration and completeness in reviews, to make it sure that nothing has been overlooked.—*Ueberweg*, '*Hist. of Phil.*,' ii. 46.

His doctrine of Substance.

That is Substance which requires for its existence the existence of nothing else. In this (highest) sense only God is substance. God as infinite substance has the ground of His existence in Himself, is the cause of Himself. The two created substances, on the contrary—thinking substance and bodily substance, mind and matter—are substances only in the less restricted sense of the term; they may be placed under the common definition that they are things requiring for their existence only the co-operation of God. Each of these two substances has an attribute constitutive of its nature and being, to which all its other characteristics may be collectively reduced. Extension is the attribute and being of matter; thought is the being of spirit.—*Schwegler*, '*Hist. of Phil.*,' p. 161.

Spinoza.

The identity of Nature, God, and Substance.

Though identical in their application, they differ somewhat in their inner meaning; under 'nature' we are expected to think of the continuous *source of birth*, under 'God,' of the *universal cause* of created things; under 'Substance,' of the permanent reality behind phenomena.—*Martineau*, '*Study of Spinoza*,' p. 169.

Spinoza starts from the Cartesian doctrine of substance: substance is that which, for its existence, stands in need of nothing else. This notion of substance being assumed, there can exist, according to Spinoza, only a single substance. What is through its own self alone is necessarily infinite, unconditioned and unlimited by anything else. Spontaneous existence is the absolute power to exist, which cannot depend on anything else, or find in anything else a limit, a negation of itself; only unlimited being is self-subsistent, substantial being. A plurality of infinites, however, is impossible; for one were indistinguishable from the other. A plurality of substances, as assumed by Descartes, is necessarily therefore a contradiction. It is possible for only one substance, and that an absolutely infinite substance, to exist. This one substance is named by Spinoza God.—*Schwegler*, '*Hist. of Phil.*,' p. 169.

By God I understand a being absolutely infinite, that is, substance consisting of infinite attributes, whereof each one expresses eternal and infinite being.—Ethic i. Def. 6, quoted by *Pollock*, '*Spinoza*,' p. 159.

His definitions of Substance, Attribute, Mode.

By *Substance* I understand that which is in itself and is conceived by itself; that is, whose concept needs not the concept of another thing for it to be formed from.

By *Attribute* I understand that which intellect perceives concerning substance, as constituting the essence thereof.

By *Mode* I understand the affections of Substance, or that which is in somewhat else, through which also it is conceived.—*Pollock*, '*Spinoza*,' p. 159.

Monism of Spinoza.

The first and leading idea in Spinoza's philosophy—the only part of it, in fact, which has at all entered into the notion commonly formed of his system—is that of the unity and uniformity of the world. Nature, as conceived by him, includes thought no less than things, and the order of nature knows no interruption. Again, there is not a world of thought opposed to or interfering with a world of things; we have everywhere the same reality under different aspects. Nature is one as well as uniform. Now there is a thing to be well marked about this conception of Spinoza's; it is itself two-sided, having an ideal or speculative, and a physical or scientific aspect. On the one hand we find a line of reasoning derived from the metaphysical treatment of theology; in other words, a philosophy starting from the consideration of the nature and perfection of God. On the other hand, we find a view of the existing universe guarded by the requirements of exact natural science, so that the philosopher who follows this track is bound over to see that his speculation, whatever flights it may take, shall at all events not contradict physics. The combination of these two elements is one of the most characteristic features of Spinoza's philosophy. No one had before him attempted such a combination with anything like the same knowledge of the conditions of the task. Few have even after him been so courageous and straightforward in the endeavour. The pantheist or mystical element, as we may call it (though both terms are ambiguous and liable to abuse), is not merely placed beside the scientific element, but fused into one with it.—*Pollock*, '*Spinoza*,' pp. 84, 85.

Among the equivalent terms by which Spinoza designates the first principle of things, *substance* and *God* emphasise its absolute unity of Ground, while *natura* and *causa sui* connote what issues thence: the former make us think of τὸ ἕν, the latter of τὸ πᾶν. The paradox contained in the last is intended to make it serve both purposes, to distinguish and yet to identify the efficient and the effect. The 'Causa' makes us expect something else to come: the '*sui*' says, 'No, it is nothing else but a reappearance of the same.' The phrase thus prepares the way for a similar resolution of the remaining term *Nature* into duplicate form by appended epithets, marking respectively the causative essence and the modal expression of one and the same infinite existence. *Natura naturans* denotes 'that which exists in itself and is conceived of itself, or, such attributes of substance as express an infinite and eternal essence; *i.e.*, God, considered as *libera causa* (purely out of intrinsic nature). '*Natura naturata* denotes all that follows from the necessity of the Divine nature, or of any one of the attributes of God; *i.e.*, all modes of God's attributes, considered as things which exist in God, and without God can neither exist nor be conceived.'—*Martineau*, '*Study of Spinoza*,' pp. 224, 225.

Leibnitz.

The fundamental characteristic of the teaching of Leibnitz is its difference from that of Spinoza. Spinoza had made the one universal substance the single *positive* element in existence. Leibnitz, too, takes the notion of substance for the foundation of his philosophy, but he defines it differently; conceiving substance as eminently the living activity, the working force, and adducing as example of this force a bent bow, which asserts its power so soon as all external obstacles are withdrawn. That active force constitutes the quality of substance, is a proposition to which Leibnitz always returns, and with which the other elements of his philosophy most intimately cohere. This is applicable at once to the two further determinations of substance, firstly, that substance is individual, a monad; and, secondly, that there is a plurality of monads. Substance, in exercising an activity similar to that of an elastic body, is essentially an excludent power, repulsion: but what excludes others from itself is a personality, an individuality or *individuum*, a monad. But this involves the second consideration, that of the plurality of the monads. The notion of an *individuum* postulates *individua*, which as excluded from it, stand over against it. In antithesis to the philosophy of Spinoza, therefore, the fundamental thesis of that of Leibnitz is this: there is a plurality of monads which constitutes the element of all reality, the fundamental being of the whole physical and spiritual universe.—*Schwegler*, '*Hist. of Phil.*,' pp. 194, 195.

Bacon and the new Experimental Method.

Limitation of human knowledge.

Man, as the minister and interpreter of nature, does and understands as much as his observations on the order of nature, either with regard to things or the mind, permit him, and neither knows nor is capable of more.—'*Nov. Org.*, *Aph.*,' bk. i., i.

Knowledge and human power are synonymous, since the ignorance of the cause frustrates the effect; for nature is only subdued by submission, and that which in contemplative philosophy corresponds with the cause in practical science becomes the rule.—'*Nov. Org.*, *Aphorisms*,' bk. i., iii.

The Inductive Method of Inquiry.

There are and can exist but two ways of investigating and discovering truth. The one hurries on rapidly from the senses and particulars to the most general axioms, and from them, as principles and their supposed indisputable truth derives and discovers the intermediate axioms. This is the way now in use. The other constructs its axioms from the senses and particulars by ascending continually and gradually till it finally arrives at the most general axioms, which is the true but unattempted way.—'*Nov. Org.*, *Aph.*,' bk. i., xix.

Each of these two ways begins from the senses and particulars, and ends in the greatest generalities. But they are immeasurably different, for the one merely touches cursorily the limits of experiment and particulars, whilst the other runs duly and regularly through them,—the one from the very outset lays down some abstract and useless generalities, the other gradually rises to those principles which are really the most common in nature.—'*Nov. Org.*, *Aph.*,' bk. i., xxii.

The true order of investigation.

The signs for the interpretation of nature comprehend two divisions, the first regards the eliciting or creating of axioms from experiment, the second the deducing or deriving of new experiments from axioms. The first admits of three subdivisions into ministrations :—1. To the senses 2. To the memory. 3 To the mind or reason.

For we must first prepare, as a foundation for the whole, a complete and accurate natural and experimental history. We must not imagine or invent, but discover the acts and properties of nature.—'*Nov. Org., Aph.*,' bk ii., x.

The 'Idols' of the mind.

Idols are imposed upon the understanding either, (1) by the general nature of mankind; (2) the nature of each particular man; or (3) by words, or communicative nature The first kind we call idols of the tribe, the second kind, idols of the den; and the third kind, idols of the market. There is also a fourth kind which we call idols of the theatre, being superinduced by false theories, or philosophies, and the perverted laws of demonstration.—*Bacon*, '*Advancement of Learning*,' bk. v chap. iv.

The English Sensational Schools.

Hobbes.

His definition of Philosophy

It is the knowledge of effects or of appearances acquired from the knowledge we have first of their causes, and conversely of possible causes from their known effects, by means of true ratiocination. All reasoning, however, is computation; and, accordingly, ratiocination may be resolved into addition and subtraction. — *Quoted by Lange*, '*Hist. of Materialism*,' i. 275.

His sensationalism.

In his theory of *sensation*, we have already in germ the sensationalism of Locke. Hobbes supposes that the movements of corporeal things communicate themselves to our senses by transmission through the medium of the air, and from thence are continued to the brain, and from the brain finally to the heart. To every movement corresponds an answering movement in the organism, as in external nature. From this principle of reaction Hobbes derives sensation, but it is not the immediate reaction of the external organ that constitutes sensation, but only the movement that starts from the heart and then returns from the external organ by way of the brain, so that an appreciable time always elapses between the impression and the sensation. By means of this regressiveness of the movement of sensation, which is an 'endeavour' (*conatus*) towards the objects, is explained the transposition outwards of the images of sense. The sensation is identical with the image of sense (*phantasma*), and this again is identical with the motion of the '*conatus*' towards the objects, not merely *occasioned* by it.—*Lange*, '*Hist of Materialism*,' i. 289

Nominalism of Hobbes.

Of names, some are *common* to many things, as a *man*, a *tree*; others *proper* to one thing, as he *that writ the Iliad*, *Homer*, *this man*, *that man*. And a common name, being the name of many things severally taken, but not collectively of all together (as man is not the name of all mankind, but of every one, as of Peter, John, and the rest severally), is therefore called an *universal name*; and therefore this word *universal* is never the name of anything existent in nature, nor of any idea or phantasm formed in the mind, but always the name of some word or name; so that when *a living creature*, *a stone*, *a spirit*, or any other thing, is said to be *universal*, it is not to be understood that any man, stone, &c., ever was or can be universal, but only that these words, *living creature*, *stone*, &c., are universal names, that is, names common to many things; and the conceptions answering to them in our mind are the images and phantasms of several living creatures or other things And, therefore, for the understanding of the extent of an universal name we need no other faculty but that of our imagination, by which we remember that such names bring sometimes one thing, sometimes another into our mind.—*Hobbes*, '*De Corpore*,' c. 2, § 10.

Locke.

No Innate Ideas.

It is an established opinion amongst some men that there are in the understanding certain innate principles; some primary notions, characters, as it were, stamped upon the mind of man, which the soul receives in its very first being, and brings into the world with it. It would be sufficient to convince unprejudiced readers of the falseness of this supposition if I should only show how men, barely by the use of their natural faculties, may attain to all the knowledge they have without the help of any innate impressions, and may arrive at certainty without any such original notions or principles.—'*Essay Concerning Human Understanding*,' bk. i. c. ii. 1.

All Ideas come from Sensation and Reflection.

Let us then suppose the mind to be, as we say, white paper, void of all characters, without any ideas; how comes it to be furnished? Whence comes it by that vast store which the busy and boundless fancy of man has painted on it with an almost endless variety? Whence has it all the materials of reason and knowledge? To this I answer in one word, from experience; in that all our knowledge is founded, and from that it ultimately derives itself. Our observation employed either about external sensible objects, or about the internal operations of our minds, perceived and reflected on by ourselves, is that which supplies our understandings with all the materials of thinking. These two are the fountains of knowledge from whence all the ideas we have or can naturally have do spring.

If it shall be demanded, then, when a man begins to have any ideas, I think the true answer is, when he first has any sensation; for since there appear not to be any ideas in the mind before the senses have conveyed any in, I conceive that ideas in the understanding are coeval with sensation, which is such an impression or motion made in some part of the body as produces some perception in the understanding. It is about these impressions made on our senses by outward objects that the mind seems first to employ itself in such operations as we call perception, remembering, consideration, reasoning, &c.

In time the mind comes to reflect on its own operations about the ideas got by sensation, and thereby stores itself with a new set of ideas which I call ideas of reflection. These are the impressions that are made on our senses by outward objects that are extrinsical to the mind and its own operations, proceeding from powers intrinsical and proper to itself; which, when reflected on by itself, becoming also objects of its contemplation, are the original of all knowledge.—'*Essay Concerning Human Understanding*,' bk. ii. c. i. 2, 23, 24.

Criticism of Locke's Philosophy.

Origin of 'inherent faculties' not explained by Locke.

Locke derived all our knowledge from experience. But experience, with him, was simply the experience of the individual. In order to acquire this experience, it was indeed necessary that we should have certain 'inherent faculties.' But of these 'faculties' he gives no other account than that God has 'furnished' or 'endued' us with them. Thus, the *Deus ex machina* was as much an acknowledged necessity in the philosophy of Locke, and was, in fact, almost as frequently invoked, as in that of his antagonists. Is there any natural account to be given of the way in which we came to have these 'faculties,' of the extraordinary facility we possess of acquiring simple and forming complex ideas? is a question which he appears never to have put to himself.—*Fowler*, '*Locke*,' pp. 143, 144.

What is the 'tablet' impressed?

It is not the impression upon, or a motion in, the outward parts, as Locke admits, that constitutes the idea of sensation. It is not an agitation in the tympanum of the ear, or a picture on the retina of the eye, that we are conscious of when we see a sight or hear a sound. The motion or impression, however, has only, as he seems to suppose, to be 'continued to the brain,' and it becomes an idea of sensation. Notwithstanding the rough line of distinction between soul and body, which he draws elsewhere, his theory was practically governed by the supposition of a cerebral something, in which, as in a third equivocal tablet, the imaginary mental and bodily tablets are blended. If, however, the idea of sensation, as an object of the understanding when a man thinks, differs absolutely from 'a motion of the outward parts,' it does so no less absolutely, however language and metaphor may disguise the difference, from such motion as 'continued to the brain.' An instructed man, doubtless, may come to think about a motion in his brain as about a motion of the earth round the sun, but to speak of such motion as an idea of sensation or an immediate object of intelligent sense, is to confuse between the object of consciousness and a possible physical theory of the conditions of that consciousness. It is only, however, by such an equivocation that any idea, according to Locke's account of the idea, can be described as an 'impression' at all, or that the representation of the mind as a tablet, whether born blank or with characters stamped on it, has even an apparent meaning. A metaphor, interpreted as a fact, becomes the basis of his philosophical system.—*Green*, '*Introduction to Hume*,' vol. 10, 11.

Ambiguities in regard to Sensation and Reflection.

Taking Locke at his word, we find the beginning of intelligence to consist in having an idea of sensation. This idea, however, we perceive, and to perceive is to have an idea, *i.e.*, to have an idea of an idea of sensation. But of perception, again, we have a simple or primitive idea. Therefore the beginning of intelligence consists in having an idea of an idea of an idea of sensation.

By insisting on Locke's account of the relation between the ideas of sensation and those of reflection we might be brought to a different but not more luminous conclusion. '*In time* the mind comes to reflect on its own operations about the ideas got by sensation, and thereby stores itself with a new set of ideas, which I call ideas of reflection.' Of these only two are primary and original, viz., motivity or power of moving, perceptivity or power of perception. But, according to Locke, there cannot be any, the simplest, idea of sensation without perception. If, then, the *idea* of perception is only given later and upon reflection, we must suppose perception to take place without any idea of it. But, with Locke, to have an idea and to perceive are equivalent terms. We must thus conclude that the beginning of knowledge is an unperceived perception, which is against his express statement elsewhere (bk. ii. chap. xxvii. sec. 9), that it is 'impossible for any one to perceive without perceiving that he does perceive.'—*Green*, '*Introd. to Hume*,' vol. i. pp. 9, 10.

Professed reconciliation by evolutionism between the Empirical and Transcendental theories.

The existence of the various mental tendencies and aptitudes, so far as the individual is concerned, is to be explained by the principle of hereditary transmission. But how have these tendencies and aptitudes come to be formed in the race? The most scientific answer is that which, following the analogy of the theory now so widely admitted with respect to the physical structure of animals and plants, assigns their formation to the continuous operation through a long series of ages, of causes acting uniformly, or almost uniformly, in the same direction,—in one word, of evolution.

According to this theory there is both an *à priori* and an *à posteriori* element in our knowledge, or, to speak more accurately, there are both *à priori* and *à posteriori* conditions of our knowing, the *à posteriori* condition being, as in all systems, individual experience, the *à priori* condition being inherited mental aptitudes which, as a rule, become more and more marked and persistent with each successive transmission.—*Fowler*, '*Locke*,' pp. 145, 146.

Berkeley.

General outline of his philosophy.

The ascertainment by reflection of the contents and relations of purely visual consciousness is one of the three problems professedly solved in Berkeley's metaphysical account of the material world. That visible objects are a system of arbitrary signs of tangible matter is the conclusion of the *Essay*, that objects, visible and tangible, are a system of sensible signs of absent objects of sense, is the conclusion of the *Principles of Human Knowledge*, and especially of the *Dialogues of Hylas and Philonous*; and that this arbitrary system of signs, which cannot exist without a percipient, is a sensible expression of the Divine ideas presence, and providence, is the conclusion common to all the three treatises.—*Fraser*, '*Berkeley's Works*,' i. 4.

The six theses regarding the relation of Sight to Extension.

1. (Sect. 2–51.) Distance, or the fact of an interval between two points in the line of vision, in other words externality in space, in itself invisible, is, in all cases in which we appear to see it, only suggested to our imagination by certain visible phenomena and visual sensations, which are its arbitrary signs.

2. (Sect. 52–87.) Magnitude, or the external space that objects occupy, is absolutely invisible, all that we can see is merely a greater or less quantity of colour, and our apparently visual perceptions of real magnitude are interpretations of the tactual meaning of colours and other sensations in the visual organ.

3. (Sect. 88–120.) The situation of objects, or their relation to one another in space, is invisible, all that we can see is variety in the relations of quantities of colour to one another, our supposed pure vision of actual locality being an interpretation of visual signs.

4. (Sect. 121–146.) There is no sensible object common to sight and touch; space or extension, which has the best claim to this character, and which is nominally the object of both, is specifically as well as numerically different in each,—externality in space, or distance, being absolutely invisible, while size and situation, as visible, have nothing in common with size and situation as tangible.

5. (Sect. 147–148.) The explanation of the unity which we attribute to sensible things, as complements of visible and tangible qualities of one and the same substance, is contained in the theory that visible ideas and visual sensations, arbitrary signs in a Divine Language, are significant of distances, and of the real sizes and situations of distant things, while the constant association in nature of the two worlds of vision and touch, has so associated them in our thoughts, that visible and tangible extension are habitually regarded by us as specifically and even numerically one.

6. (Sect. 149–160.) The proper object of geometry is the kind of Extension given in our tactual experience, and not the kind of Extension given in our visual experience; and neither real solids nor real planes can be seen—real Extension in all its phases being invisible, and colour in its modifications of quantity being the only proper object of sight, while colour, being a pure sensation, cannot exist extra-organically in space.—*Fraser*, '*Berkeley's Works*,' i. 6, 7.

Is Matter or Intelligence the supreme reality?

Is an unknowing and unknown something, called Matter, or is Intelligence the supreme reality; and are men the transient results of material organisation, or are they immortal beings? This is Berkeley's implied question. His answer to it, although, in his own works, it has not been thought out by him into its primary principles, or sufficiently guarded in some parts, nevertheless marks the beginning of the second great period in modern thought, that in which we are living. The answer was virtually reversed in Hume, whose exclusive phenomenalism, reproduced in the Positivism of the nineteenth century, led to the Scotch conservative psychology, and to the great German speculation which Kant inaugurated.—*Fraser, 'Berkeley's Works,'* vol. i. pref. p. viii.

Matter is dependent upon Intelligence.

The dependent, *sui generis*, existence of space and the sensible world, in which we nevertheless become aware of what is external to our own subjective personality, is with Berkeley a datum of intuitive experience; the independent or absolute existence of matter is, on the contrary, an unintelligible hypothesis. He was the first in modern times to attack the root of what has been called Cosmothetic Idealism, and to lay the foundation, however indistinctly, of a reasoned Natural Realism—by discarding representative images in sense, and accepting instead what he believed to be the facts of consciousness. He maintains, accordingly, the certainty of sense perceptions, in opposition to ancient and modern sceptics, who dispute the possibility of any ascertainable agreement between our perceptions and reality; and, however defectively, in opposition also to a merely subjective Idealism, like Fichte's, which refers the orderly succession of sensible change to the laws of the individual mind in which they are perceived.—*Fraser, 'Berkeley's Works,'* vol. i. pref. p. x.

Hume.

His doctrine of the origin of Ideas.

All the perceptions of the human mind resolve themselves into two distinct kinds, which I shall call Impressions and Ideas. The difference betwixt these consists in the degrees of force and liveliness with which they strike upon the mind, and make their way into our thought or consciousness. Those perceptions, which enter with most force and violence, we may name *impressions*; and under this name I comprehend all our sensations, passions, and emotions, as they make their first appearance in the soul. By *ideas* I mean the faint images of these in thinking and reasoning.—*'Treatise on Human Nature,'* bk. i. pt. i. sect. 1.

Of Causation.

Surely, if there be any relation among objects, which it imports to us to know perfectly, it is that of cause and effect. On this are founded all our reasonings concerning matter of fact or existence. By means of it alone we attain any assurance concerning objects which are removed from the present testimony of our memory and senses. The only immediate utility of all sciences is to teach us how to control and regulate future events by their causes. Our thoughts and inquiries are, therefore, every moment employed about this relation. Yet so imperfect are the ideas which we form concerning it, that it is impossible to give any just definition of cause, except what is drawn from something extraneous and foreign to it. Similar objects are always conjoined with similar. Of this we have experience. Suitably to this experience, therefore, we may define a cause to be *an object followed by another, and where all the objects similar to the first are followed by objects similar to the second.*—*'Enquiry Concerning Human Understanding,'* sect. vii. pt. ii.

Of Cause and Effect.

The idea of causation must be derived from some relation among objects. I find, in the first place, that whatever objects are considered as causes or effects are *contiguous*; and that nothing can operate in a time or place which is ever so little removed from those of its existence.

The second relation I shall observe as essential to causes and effects is not so universally acknowledged, but is liable to some controversy. 'Tis that of PRIORITY of time in the cause before the effect.

An object may be contiguous and prior to another without being considered as its cause. There is a NECESSARY CONNECTION to be taken into consideration, and that relation is of much greater importance than any of the other two above mentioned.—'*Treatise of Human Nature*,' bk. i. pt. iii. sect. ii.

Reaction against Sensationalism.

In Germany.—The Transcendental Philosophy.

Kant. Pure and empirical knowledge.

We shall understand by knowledge *à priori* knowledge which is *absolutely* independent of all experience, and not of this or that experience only. Opposed to this is empirical knowledge, or such as is possible *à posteriori* only, that is, by experience. Knowledge *à priori*, if mixed up with nothing empirical, is called *pure*. Thus the proposition, for example, that every change has its cause, is a proposition *à priori*, but not pure; because change is a concept which can only be derived from experience.—'*Critique of Pure Reason*,' intro. i. vol. i. p. 399.

His opposition to Hume's empiricism.

In opposition to Hume, Kant had to show that the theory of receptivity as the one function of mind omitted the factor which alone rendered cognition of phenomena possible. A stream of conscious states, which to Hume makes up the substance of mind and experience, is to Kant pure abstraction, arrived at by thrusting out of sight the nature and significance of consciousness itself. It may be possible to speak of such a stream, but it is impossible to regard it as matter of knowledge; it is not to be known on any terms by any intelligence. Thus, with regard to Hume's empiricism, the Kantian problem becomes the quite general question as to the conditions necessarily involved in knowledge as such. With Hume, Kant recognises the distinction between the individual fleeting elements contained in experience and the general thoughts which unite with them in order to form a coherent context; as against Hume, he has to show that these universal elements are neither abstracted from the particular nor surreptitiously added to them, but are necessarily implicated in the particulars, which, apart from them, became pure abstractions, things in themselves, empty husks of thought.—*Adamson*, '*Kant*,' pp. 30, 31.

Kant proves that experience itself is impossible without the category of causality, and, of course, without several other categories also which Hume had overlooked, though they possess exactly the same character as the concept of causality. The gist of Kant's philosophy, as opposed to that of Hume, can be expressed in one line: that without which experience is impossible cannot be the result of experience, though it must never be applied beyond the limits of possible experience.—*Max Muller*, '*Kant's Critique*,' vol. i. p. xxvi.

Sensation not sufficient for Knowledge.

The secret of the objectivity of phenomena, and their connection as parts of one world, must obviously be sought, not without but within, not in what is simply given to the mind, but in what is produced by it. What comes from without is at the most a sensation or impression, which is itself but a passing phase of our inner life, and has no reference to anything but itself, no connection with other sensations, and no relation to an object as such. If out of such sensations a world of objects is made, it must be made by some mental activity.—*Caird*, '*Philosophy of Kant*,' p. 198.

À priori synthesis necessary.

What is this activity? (see above) Kant's answer is that it is synthesis. Mere impressions are isolated and unconnected. They have no relation to each other, and hence no relation to any object more permanent than themselves. Only so far as we relate them to each other, recognise them as repetitions of each other, and connect them with each other in definite and unchanging ways, can the shifting phases of our sentient life be to us the representation of a world of objects, which we distinguish from ourselves, yet conceive to be permanent with the permanence of the self. Nay, it is only in so far as we thus determine the data of sense, that we can exist for ourselves as permanent individual objects among the other objects of the world. Synthesis is necessary for objectivity, and as there can be no synthesis without some link of connection by which the different elements are brought together, so the activity of the mind must bring with it certain principles of relation, under which the manifold of sense must be brought, and to which it must conform.—*Caird, 'Philosophy of Kant,'* p. 199.

Kant's Two Factors of Knowledge.

Our knowledge springs from two fundamental sources of our soul; the first receives representations (receptivity of impressions), the second is the power of knowing an object by these representations (spontaneity of concepts). By the first an object is given us, by the second the object is *thought*, in relation to that representation which is a mere determination of the soul. Intuition therefore and concepts constitute the elements of all our knowledge, so that neither concepts without an intuition corresponding to them, nor intuition without concepts, can yield any real knowledge.

Both are either pure or empirical. They are empirical when sensation, presupposing the actual presence of the object, is contained in it. They are pure when no sensation is mixed up with the representation. The latter may be called the material of sensuous knowledge. Pure intuition therefore contains the form only by which something is seen, and pure conception the form only by which an object is thought. Pure intuitions and pure concepts only are possible, *à priori*, empirical intuitions and empirical concepts, *à posteriori*.

We call *sensibility* the *receptivity* of our soul, or its power of receiving representations whenever it is in any wise affected, while the *understanding*, on the contrary, is with us the power of producing representations, or the spontaneity of knowledge. We are so constituted that our intuition must always be sensuous, and consist of the mode in which we are affected by objects. What enables us to think the object of our sensuous intuition is the understanding. Neither of these qualities or faculties is preferable to the other. Without sensibility objects would not be given to us, without understanding they would not be thought by us. *Thoughts without contents are empty, intuitions without concepts are blind.*—*'Critique,'* pt. ii. intro i. vol. ii. 44, 45.

Results of Kant's Critique.

The result of Kant's *Critique* is, *in the first place*, to destroy the one-sided Individualism which prevailed during the second period of the history of modern philosophy; or perhaps we should rather say, to correct and transform that Individualism, by the aid of ideas ultimately derived from the equally one-sided Universalism of the first period. Thus Kant endeavoured to show that consciousness transcends the opposition of self and not-self; or, what is the same thing, that self-consciousness contains the unity to which, not merely the phenomena of inner experience, but also the phenomena of outer experience, are referred. In order to maintain this position, however, he was obliged, *in the second place*, to show that the understanding is not purely analytic, but that it is the source of certain conceptions, which, in their application to the perceptions of sense, are principles of *à priori* synthesis. These principles are of objective validity, because they are the principles which constitute the objective consciousness. On the other hand, the effect of Kant's reassertion of the synthetic principle in thought was to some extent neutralised by his denial that thought is *in itself* synthetic. For, if pure thought in itself is not synthetic but analytic, it follows necessarily that *the ideal* of knowledge derived from pure thought, and the *reality* which is known by the application of the pure thought to the form and the matter of sensuous experience, are at variance with each other. Hence, *in the third place*, Kant maintains that the universality of consciousness is limited to experience, and that there is an impassable gulf between things as they are known, and things as they are in themselves.—*Caird*, '*Philosophy of Kant*,' pp. 668, 669.

In Britain—Thomas Reid

The Reality of the objects of perception.

First, It is impossible to perceive an object without having some notion or conception of that which we perceive. We may, indeed, conceive an object which we do not perceive; but when we perceive the object we must have some conception of it at the same time; and we have commonly a more clear and steady notion of the object while we perceive it than we have from memory or imagination when it is not perceived.

Secondly, In perception we not only have a notion more or less distinct of the object perceived, but also an irresistible conviction and belief of its existence. This is always the case when we are certain that we perceive it. There may be a perception so faint and indistinct as to leave us in doubt whether we perceive the object or not.

Thirdly, This conviction is not only irresistible, but it is immediate, that is, it is not by a train of reasoning and argumentation that we come to be convinced of the existence of what we perceive.—'*On the Intellectual Powers*,' ii. chap. v. p. 258.

'*Common-Sense' Theory of Ideas, in opposition to that of Locke, Berkeley, and Hume.*

The *first* reflection I would make on this philosophical opinion is, that it is directly contrary to the universal sense of men who have not been instructed in philosophy. When we see the sun or moon, we have no doubt that the very objects which we immediately see are very far distant from us and from one another. We have not the least doubt that this is the sun and moon which God created some thousands of years ago, and which have continued to perform their revolutions in the heavens ever since. A *second* reflection upon this subject is, that the authors who have treated of ideas have generally taken their existence for granted, as a thing that could not be called in question, and such arguments as they have mentioned incidentally, in order to prove it, seem too weak to support the conclusion.

A *third* reflection is, that philosophers, notwithstanding their unanimity as to the existence of ideas, hardly agree in any one thing else concerning them. If ideas be not a mere fiction, they must be, of all objects of human knowledge, the things we have best access to know and to be acquainted with; yet there is nothing about which men differ so much.

A *fourth* reflection is, that ideas do not make any of the operations of the mind to be better understood, although it was probably with that view that they have been first invented, and afterwards so generally received.—'*On the Intellectual Powers*,' ii., chap. xiv. p. 298.

In France—Victor Cousin

Empiricism cannot abolish universal and necessary principles.

Not only is empiricism unable to explain universal and necessary principles, but we maintain that without these principles empiricism cannot even account for the knowledge of the sensible world.

Take away the principle of causality, and the human mind is condemned never to go out of itself and its own modifications. All the sensations of hearing, of smell, of taste, of touch, of feeling even, cannot inform you what their cause is, nor whether they have a cause. But give to the human mind the principle of causality, admit that every sensation, as well as every phenomenon, every change, every event, has a cause, as evidently we are not the cause of certain sensations, and that especially these sensations must have a cause, and we are naturally led to recognise for those sensations causes different from ourselves, and that is the first notion of an external world The universal and necessary principle of causality alone gives it and justifies it. Other principles of the same order increase and develop it.—*Cousin*, '*On the True, the Beautiful, and the Good*,' Lect. i p 40.

We possess these principles, but we are not their author.

We conceive them and apply them, we do not constitute them. Let us interrogate our consciousness Do we refer to ourselves, for example, the definitions of geometry as we do certain movements of which we feel ourselves to be the cause? If it is I who make these definitions, they are therefore mine, I can unmake them, modify them, change them, even annihilate them. It is certain that I cannot do it. I am not, then, the author of them It has also been demonstrated that the principles of which we have spoken cannot be derived from sensation, which is variable, limited, incapable of producing and authorising anything universal and necessary. I arrive, then, at the following consequence, also necessary:—truth is in me, and not by me. As sensibility puts me in relation with the physical world, so another faculty puts me in communication with the truths that depend upon neither the world nor me, and that faculty is Reason.—'*On the True, &c.*,' Lect i pp 42, 43.

Theory of their origin—Spontaneity and Reflection.

Is it not evident that we do not begin by reflection, that reflection supposes an anterior operation, and that this operation, in order not to be one of reflection, and not to suppose another before it, must be entirely spontaneous; that thus the spontaneous and instinctive intuition of truth precedes its reflection and necessary conception?—'*On the True, &c.*,' Lect. 1 p. 52.

God the Principle of Principles.

Truth necessarily appeals to something beyond itself. As every phenomenon has its subject of inherence, as our faculties, our thoughts, our volitions, our sensations, exist only in a being which is ourselves, so truth supposes a being in which it resides, and absolute truths suppose a being absolute as themselves, wherein they have their final foundation. We come thus to something absolute, which is no longer suspended in the vagueness of abstraction, but is a being substantially existing This being, absolute and necessary, since it is the subject of necessary and absolute truths, this being which is at the foundation of truth as its very essence, in a single word, is called God.—'*On the True, &c.*,' Lect. i. p. 80.

Modern Tendencies.

POSITIVISM.

The Philosophy of M. Comte.

The doctrine of Auguste Comte, the product at once of the mathematical and positive sciences and of Saint-Simonism, is a combination of empiricism and socialism, in which the scientific standpoint constantly gained in prominence, in comparison with the socialistic standpoint. There are in Positivism, as in all doctrines, two parts, a destructive part and a constructive part. (*a*.) The former part contains the denial of all metaphysics and all search for first or for final causes The beginning and the end of things, it says, are unknowable for us. It is only what lies between these two that belongs to us. Positivism repudiates all metaphysical hypotheses. It accepts neither atheism nor theism Nor does it accept pantheism, which is only a form of atheism (*b*.) In its constructive part, Positivism may be reduced, in the main, to two ideas. (1.) A certain historic conception, which is that the human mind passes necessarily through three stages—the theological, the metaphysical, and the positive. In the first state, man explains the phenomena of nature by reference to supernatural causes, by personal or voluntary interferences, by prodigies, miracles, &c. In the second period, supernatural and anthropomorphic causes give place to abstract, occult causes, scholastic entities, realised abstractions, and nature is interpreted *à priori*: the attempt is made to construe nature subjectively. In the third state, man contents himself with ascertaining by observation and experiment the connections of phenomena, and so learning to connect each fact with its antecedent conditions. This is the method which has founded modern science, and which must take the place of metaphysics. Whatever is not capable of experimental verification must be rigorously excluded from science. (2.) The second conception of Positivism is the classification and co-ordination of the sciences. The theory of this classification requires us to advance from the simple to the complex. At the basis are Mathematics; then come, in turn, Astronomy, Physics, Chemistry, Biology, and Sociology. These are the six fundamental sciences, each of which is necessary to the next following one. The Psychology of Positivism is a part of physiology. Its doctrine of morals is in no respect original; it rejects the doctrine of personal interest.—*Ueberweg*, '*Hist. of Phil.*,' ii. 344.

The three stages of development in Human Intelligence.

From the study of the development of human intelligence in all directions and through all times, the discovery arises of a great fundamental law to which it is necessarily subject, and which has a solid foundation of proof both in the facts of our organisation and in our historical experience. The law is this: that each of our leading conceptions,—each branch of our knowledge passes successively through three different theoretical conditions,—the theological or fictitious, the metaphysical or abstract, and the scientific or positive. In other words, the human mind, by its nature, employs in its progress three methods of philosophising, the character of which is essentially different and even radically opposed, viz., the theological method, the metaphysical, and the positive. Hence arise three philosophic or general systems of conceptions on the aggregate of phenomena, each of which excludes the others. The first is the necessary point of departure of the human understanding, and the third is its fixed and definite state; the second is merely a state of transition.—*Comte*, '*Positive Philosophy*,' i. 1, 2.

All knowledge is virtual Feeling.

Knowledge is simply virtual Feeling, the stored-up accumulations of previous experiences, our own and those of others; it is a vision of the unapparent relations which will be apparent when the objects are presented to Sense. Hence the imperious desire to find out how the thing *came to be*, what it is, and what it *will be* under other circumstances. Our sensible experiences grow into knowledge by a twofold process of grouping and classification; Feeling is added to feeling, quality to quality, each group enlarging with every fresh experience; and this process of incorporation henceforward causes any one of the feelings to revive the others, so that the sight will revive the taste or smell, and the name will revive the image. Nay, more, the process also causes any one of these feelings to be detached from those to which originally it cohered and to enter into some new group, thus linking the two groups together and revealing them as *like* one another. Every perception is felt to be at once like and unlike others. It is a cluster of feelings and images of past feelings.—*Lewes*, '*Problems of Life and Mind*,' ii. 23.

Comte's definition of Religion.

It is 'that state of complete harmony peculiar to human life, in its collective as well as in its individual form, when all the parts of life are ordered in their natural relations to each other. This definition, which alone embraces equally all the different phases of Religion, applies equally to the heart and to the intellect, for both of these must concur to produce any true unity of life. Religion, therefore, gives a natural harmony to the soul exactly analogous to that which Health gives to the Body. The union of the moral and the physical nature is so close, and the relation which these two states hold to one another is so intimate, that we may regard the Harmony of the Soul as virtually embracing the health of the Body.'—'*System of Positive Polity*,' ii. p. 8.

The functions of religion, according to Comte, are to *regulate* individual life and to *combine* collective lives.

The primary elements of Religion.

To constitute any true religious state there must be a concurrence of two primary elements, the one objective and essentially intellectual, the other subjective and essentially moral. Thus Religion exerts an influence at once over the understanding and the feelings, neither of which separately would suffice to establish a true unity, either for individual or collective life. On the one hand, it is requisite that our minds should conceive a Power without us, so superior to ourselves as to command the complete submission of our entire life; but, on the other hand, it is equally indispensable that our moral nature should be inspired within by our affection, capable of habitually combining all the rest. These two essential conditions naturally tend to work as one, since the sense of submission to a Power without necessarily seconds the discipline of the moral nature within; and this in turn prepares the way for the spirit of submission.—'*System of Positive Polity*,' ii. p. 11.

'Religion,' says Comte, 'is the complete harmony proper to human existence, individual and collective, when all its parts are brought into due relation to one another.' It is for the soul, in other words, what health is for the body; and as health is essentially one, though in all cases variously and imperfectly realised, so too religion is essentially one, though it is attained in various forms and in different degrees. Even to the last it is an ideal to which each specific type is an approximation. The object of religion, corresponding to this definition, is set forth as twofold. It is destined at once to discipline the individual, and to unite the separate individuals in a harmonious whole. It aims at personal unity and social unity. As the aim of religion is twofold, so also is its base. It reposes on an objective and on a subjective foundation. Without, there is the external order, in itself independent of us, which necessarily limits our thoughts and actions and feelings. Within, there is a principle of benevolent sympathy, which prompts us to look beyond our own wants and wishes, and to seek in a wider harmony the satisfaction of the deepest instincts of our nature.—*Westcott*, '*The Gospel of the Resurrection*,' p. 254.

The Positivist system of doctrine is simply the outline of the hierarchy of the sciences, which are severally subordinated one to another, and each regulated by its peculiar laws. . . . The Positivist view of the dependence of religion on science errs by defect, and not in principle. It requires to be supplemented, and not overthrown. . . . The grand and far-reaching ideas of the continuity, the solidarity, the totality of life, which answer equally to the laws of our being and the deepest aspirations of our souls, are not only reconcilable with Christianity, but they are essentially Christian. The Positivist theory, so far from advancing anything novel in such teaching, simply places us once again in the original Christian point of view of the Cosmos. . . . But Christianity does not pause where Positivism pauses,—in the visible order. It carries the unity of being yet further, and links all that is seen with that unseen which can only be figured to us in parables. An imperious instinct asserts that our individual existence is not closed by what falls here under our senses, and every indication of the intimate relationship of man with man, and of age with age, confirms the belief in the further extension of this law of dependence to an order of being beyond the present.—*Westcott*, '*The Gospel of the Resurrection*,' pp. 259, 261, 271, 273.

God.

Positivism says to us, 'Agnosticism is necessary and inevitable. About God nothing can be known. All the systems which human thought has devised to account for the universe, whether theistic, pantheistic, or atheistic, are a mere Babel of unmeaning words. On the side of heaven there is nothing for man but an absolute blank. But be of good cheer. Listen to me, and you shall not be without a Supreme Object to which your worship may ascend, and around which your holiest affections and dearest hopes may cluster with satisfaction and joy. Accept the religion of *Humanity*, and be happy.' We are bidden to call the idealising faculty into play. We are to think, not of individual men and women as we know them in our experience, but of the *Race*. 'Conceive of Humanity as a vast Whole,' it is urged. 'Imagine it as a mighty stream, of which all human beings, past, present, and to come, are the component drops; and see this majestic Flood emerging out of the bosom of the eternal Past, and ever swelling into grander proportions as it rolls onward to the unbounded Future. There is the true Supreme, the source of all goodness, the object of all worship, the sovereign ruler of destiny, the living force of the great drama of Evolution.—*Maitland*, '*Theism or Agnosticism*,' p. 233.

M. Comte, an acute philosopher, a disciple of the school of St. Simon, discovered that the divine belongs wholly to the early ages of the world. Worship, it seemed, was for ever to be banished from the world; all questions that have ever troubled men about their own spiritual condition were to disappear with it. But M. Comte proved a rebel to his own decrees. Positive philosophy, he found, wanted the completion of love, and love must bring back worship. All acknowledgment of any absolute Being is indeed dead. *That* belongs to the old times; but the goddess of humanity must be enthroned in our day. She requires a priesthood, and to that it would seem that men can only be initiated through some painful inward conflicts. A result surely to be considered and reflected upon for what it declares and for what it indicates.—*Maurice*, '*Moral and Metaphysical Philosophy*,' ii. 663.

Humanity the central point of Positivism.

In the conception of Humanity the three essential aspects of Positivism, its subjective principle, its objective dogma, and its practical object, are united. Towards Humanity, who is for us the only true great Being, we, the conscious elements of whom she is composed, shall henceforth direct every aspect of our life, individual or collective. Our thoughts will be devoted to the knowledge of Humanity, our affections to her love, our actions to her service.—'*Positive Polity*,' i. p. 264.

Positivism aims at the reorganisation of society.

It cannot be necessary to prove to anybody who reads this work that Ideas govern the world or throw it into chaos; in other words, that all social mechanism rests upon Opinions. The great political and moral crisis that societies are now undergoing is shown by a rigid analysis to arise out of intellectual anarchy. Till a certain number of general ideas can be acknowledged as a rallying-point of social doctrine, the nations will remain in a revolutionary state, whatever palliatives may be devised; and their institutions can be only provisional.

Now, the existing disorder is abundantly accounted for by the existence, all at once, of three incompatible philosophies,—the theological, the metaphysical, and the positive. Any one of these might alone secure some sort of social order; but while the three co-exist, it is impossible for us to understand one another upon any essential point whatever. If this is true, we have only to ascertain which of the philosophies must, in the nature of things, prevail; and, this ascertained, every man, whatever may have been his former views, cannot but concur in its triumph. The problem once recognised cannot remain long unsolved; for all considerations whatever point to the Positive Philosophy as the one destined to prevail.—*Comte*, '*Positive Philosophy*,' i. 12, 13.

The Religion of Humanity.

Love is our principle; Order our basis; and Progress our end. Such is the essential character of the system of life which Positivism offers for the definite acceptance of society; a system which regulates the whole course of our public and private existence, by bringing Feeling, Reason, and Activity into permanent harmony. In this final synthesis, all essential conditions are far more perfectly fulfilled than in any other. Each special element of our nature is more fully developed, and at the same time the general working of the whole is more coherent. Greater distinctness is given to the truth that the affective element predominates in our nature. Life in all its actions and thoughts is brought under the control and inspiring charm of Social Sympathy.

By the supremacy of the Heart, the Intellect, so far from being crushed, is elevated; for all its powers are consecrated to the service of the social instincts, with the purpose of strengthening and of directing their influence. By accepting its subordination to Feeling, Reason adds to its own authority.—'*Positive Polity*,' i. p. 257.

Criticism.

Professing to be a philosophy of the universe, Positivism has not provided a philosophy of human nature. It may be true that men from early times have concerned themselves with explanations of the phenomena of the outer world; but the first necessity was to guide their own life. If they were intellectually interested in physical events, they were practically concerned in human actions. If they gave some thought to the rising and setting of the sun, the flowing of the waters, and the growth of the trees,—they must have given more thought to the direction of their own energies. How did they recognise a rule of personal conduct? Positivism gives no answer. And while constructing a Sociology, with professed denial of the possibility of knowing causes, it fails to account for the most conspicuous fact in the procedure of Society, that it has always regarded men as the causes of their own actions, and has punished them for their evil deeds.—*Calderwood*, '*Moral Philosophy*,' p. 68.

Among the forces arrayed against Christianity at this hour, the most formidable, because the most consistent and the most sanguine, is that pure materialism, which has been intellectually organised in the somewhat pedantic form of Positivism. To the Positivist the most etherealised of deistic theories is just as much an object of pitying scorn as the creed of a St. John and a St. Athanasius. Both are relegated to 'the theological period' of human development.—*Liddon*, '*Bampton Lectures*,' p. 445.

Auguste Comte detected the simple laws of the course of development through which nations pass. There are always three phases of intellectual condition,—the theological, the metaphysical, and the positive; applying this general law of progress to concrete cases, Comte was enabled to predict that in the hierarchy of European nations, Spain would necessarily hold the highest place. Such are the parodies of Science offered to us by the positive philosophers.—*Jevons*, '*Principles of Science*,' p. 761.

M. Comte was certainly a man of some mathematical and scientific proficiency, as well as of quick but biassed intelligence. A member of the *Aufklarung*, he had seen the immense advance of physical science since Newton, under, as is usually said, the method of Bacon; and, like Hume, like Reid, like Kant, *who had all anticipated him in this,* he sought to transfer that method to the dominion of mind. In this he failed, and though in a sociological aspect he is not without true glances into the present disintegration of society and the conditions of it, anything of importance cannot be claimed for him. There is not a sentence in his book that, in the hollow elaboration and windy pretentiousness of its build, is not an exact type of its own constructor. On the whole, indeed, when we consider the little to which he attained, the empty inflation of his claims, the monstrous and maniacal self-conceit into which he was *exalted*, it may appear, perhaps, that charity to M. Comte himself, to say nothing of the world, should induce us to wish that both his name and his works were buried in oblivion.—*Stirling, 'As Regards Protoplasm,'* p. 5.

The true interpretation of altruism includes not merely a regard for our fellow-men, but a distinct ignoring of our Creator. It would be easy to show that a community in which every member of society should lose all thought and renounce all care of himself, would become utterly disorganised. Comte was very well aware of this; he knew that it is only by the due combination of prudence with benevolence that human well-being is secured. His vanity led him to exalt his own moral axioms above those accepted in Christendom. Yet an impartial student of religion and of morals cannot but regard the Christian law as superior to that of Comte. '*Thou shalt love the Lord thy God with all thy heart . . and thy neighbour as thyself,*' is a wise and practical principle of human conduct; it presumes as natural and right a regard to our own interest, but directs us to make this regard the measure of our interest in our fellow-men. Eighteen centuries before Comte's day, Christ had inculcated the duty of unselfishness and benevolence. But whilst Comtism relies only on the feeling of human community and sympathy as the motive power to compliance with its law, Christianity derives the love of man from the love of God, and supplies in the revelation of Divine compassion and mercy the spiritual impulse which is mighty to prompt man to benevolence.—*Thomson, 'Auguste Comte and the Religion of Humanity,'* pp. 49, 50.

The German Psychologists — Herbart, Lotze.

Herbart.

Philosophy is defined by Herbart as the elaboration of conceptions. Logic aims at clearness in conceptions, metaphysics at the correction of them, and æsthetics, in that wider sense in which it includes ethics, as the completion of them, by the addition of qualifications of worth.—*Ueberweg, 'Hist. of Phil.,'* ii. 264.

The soul originates ideas.

The soul is a simple, spaceless essence, of simple quality. It is located at a single point within the brain. When the senses are affected, and motion is transmitted by the nerve to the brain, the soul is penetrated by the simple, real essences which immediately surround it. Its quality then performs an act of self-preservation in opposition to the disturbance which it would otherwise suffer from the—whether partially or totally—opposite quality of each of these simple essences. Every such act of self-preservation on the part of the soul is an idea. All ideas (representations) endure, even after the occasion which called them forth has ceased. When there are at the same time in the soul several ideas, which are either partially or totally opposed to each other, they cannot continue to subsist together without being partially arrested; they must be arrested, *i.e.*, become unconscious, to a degree measured by the sum of the intensities of all these ideas with the exception of the strongest. This quantum of arrest is termed by Herbart the 'sum of arrest.' The part of each idea in this sum of arrest is greater, the less intense the idea is. On the intensive relations of ideas, and on the laws of the change of these relations, are founded the possibility and the scientific necessity of applying mathematics to psychology.—*Ueberweg*, '*Hist. of Phil.*,' ii. 265, 266.

Lotze.

Sensations arise in the soul.

The wooden notes of the musical instrument do not themselves contain the tones which, when struck, they draw forth from the chords, it is only the tension of the latter that by means of this propulsion can pass into tone-producing vibrations. In like manner, all bodily impressions are for the soul but strokes, drawing forth from its own nature the internal phenomena of sensation, that never can be communicated to it from without. For even if it were not the motion of the notes, but a veritable wave of sound, that brought the tone from the chord, yet that could only reproduce the tone by its own tension, no matter whether what set it in vibration were a process similar or dissimilar to that wave. The case would not be different if we chose anyhow to look on sensation as a state already existing in the nerves; it would still have to originate afresh in the soul through some excitation conveyed to it by the sensory nerve, and it could never arise through external impressions, were its own nature not in itself capable of evolving this peculiar form of internal action. Accordingly, every theory that takes for granted that what is to be manifested in the soul already exists outside of it, is yet forced to come back to this conception, and to view the external as merely an occasion, and the inner event, on the other hand, as proceeding from the nature of that in which it takes place.—'*Microcosmus*,' i. 282.

Things are acts of the Infinite wrought in minds.

All individual things are thinkable only as modifications of one single Infinite Being. . . . Manifesting itself in the individual mind, and being in it and in all its like the efficient source of their life, the Infinite develops a series of activities as to which *how* they take place remains incomprehensible to finite consciousness, which intuits their products as they occur, under the form of a multiform and changing world of sense.—'*Microcosmus*,' ii. 640, 641.

The finite a reflection of the Infinite.

Of the full personality which is possible only for the Infinite a feeble reflection is given also to the finite; for the characteristics peculiar to the finite are not producing conditions of self-existence, but obstacles to its unconditioned development, although we are accustomed, unjustifiably, to deduce from these characteristics its capacity of personal existence. The finite being always works with powers with which it did not endow itself, and according to laws which it did not establish,—that is, it works by means of a mental organisation which is realised not only in it, but also in innumerable similar beings. Hence in reflecting on self, it may easily seem to it as though there were in itself some obscure and unknown substance—something which is in the ego though it is not the ego itself, and to which, as to its subject, the whole personal development is attached.—'*Microcosmus*,' ii. 685, 686.

Perfect Personality is in God only, to all finite minds there is allotted but a pale copy thereof; and the finiteness of the finite is not a producing condition of this Personality but a limit and a hindrance of its development.—'*Microcosmus*,' p. 688.

Evolution.

Definition.

Evolution includes all theories respecting the origin and order of the world which regard the higher or more complex forms of existence as following and depending on the lower and simpler forms, which represent the course of the world as a gradual transition from the indeterminate to the determinate, from the uniform to the varied, and which assume the cause of this process to be immanent in the world itself that is thus transformed. All theories of evolution, properly so called, regard the physical world as a gradual progress from the simple to the complex, look upon the development of organic life as conditioned by that of the inorganic world, and view the course of mental life both of the individual and of the race as correlated with a material process.—*Sully*, '*Encyclop. Brit.*,' *art.* '*Evolution*,' viii. 751.

Mr. Herbert Spencer's definition.

Evolution is an integration of matter and concomitant dissipation of motion, during which the matter passes from an indefinite, incoherent homogeneity to a definite, coherent heterogeneity; and during which the retained motion undergoes a parallel transformation.—'*First Principles*,' p. 396.

Mental Evolution.

If the doctrine of Evolution is true, the inevitable implication is that Mind can be understood only by observing how much is evolved. If creatures of the most elevated kinds have reached those highly integrated, very definite, and extremely heterogeneous organisations they possess, through modifications upon modifications accumulated during an immeasurable past—if the developed nervous systems of such creatures have joined their complex structures and functions little by little, then, necessarily, the involved forms of consciousness which are the correlatives of these complex structures and functions must have arisen by degrees. And as it is impossible truly to comprehend the organisation of the body in general, or of the nervous system in particular, without tracing its successive stages of complication, so it must be impossible to comprehend mental organisation without similarly tracing its stages.—*Spencer*, '*Principles of Psychology*,' i. 292.

Regarded under every variety of aspect, intelligence is found to consist in the establishment of correspondences between relations in the organism and relations in the environment; and the entire development of intelligence may be formulated as the progress of such correspondences in space, in time, in speciality, in generality, in complexity.—*Spencer*, '*Principles of Psychology*,' i. 385.

Bodily and Mental Evolution harmonious.

From the lowest to the highest forms of life, the increasing adjustment of inner to outer relations is one indivisible progression. Just as, out of the homogeneous tissue with which every organism commences, there arises, by continuous differentiation and disintegration, a congeries of organs performing separate functions, but remaining mutually dependent, so the correspondence between the actions going on inside of the organism and those going on outside of it, beginning with some simple homogeneous correspondence, gradually becomes differentiated into various orders of correspondences, which, though constantly more and more subdivided, maintain a reciprocity of aid that grows ever greater. These two progressions are in truth parts of the same progression. The primordial tissue displays the several forms of irritability in which the senses originate; and the organs of sense, like all other organs, arise by differentiation of this primordial tissue. The impressions received by these senses form the raw materials of intelligence, which arises by combination of them, and must therefore conform to their law of development. Intelligence advances *pari passu* with the advance of the nervous system, and the nervous system has the same law of development as the other systems. Without dwelling on these facts, it is sufficiently manifest that, as the progress of organisation and the progress of correspondence between the organism and its environment are but different aspects of the evolution of Life in general, they cannot fail to harmonise. In this organisation of experiences which constitutes evolving Intelligence, there must be that same continuity, that same subdivision of function, that same mutual dependence, and that same ever-advancing *consensus* which characterise the physical organisation —*Spencer*, '*Principles of Psychology*,' i 387, 388, abridged

Criticism of Mr Spencer's philosophy.

Mr Spencer is a thoroughgoing realist From his general scheme of evolution one would be prepared to find him avowing himself a materialist. Yet he seeks to avoid this conclusion by saying that it is one unknowable reality which manifests itself alike in the material and in the mental domain At the same time, this unknowable is commonly spoken of as force, and in many places seems to be identified with material force Mr Spencer makes little use of his metaphysical conception in accounting for the evolution of things He tells us neither why the unknowable should manifest itself in time at all, nor why it should appear as a material world before it appears under the form of mind or consciousness Indeed, Mr. Spencer's doctrine of evolution cannot be said to have received from its author an adequate metaphysical interpretation The idea of the unknowable hardly suffices to give to his system an intelligible monistic basis In truth, this system seems in its essence to be dualistic rather than monistic.—*Sully*, *art* '*Evolution*,' '*Encyc Brit*,' viii. p. 765.

Criticism of the Evolution theory in general

This theory, philosophically or in ultimate analysis, is an attempt to prove that design, or the objective idea, especially in the organic world, is developed *in time* by natural means . . .

The only agency postulated by Mr Darwin is time—infinite time; and as regards actually existent beings and actually existent conditions, it is hardly possible to deny any possibility whatever to infinitude . . . But we can also say that any fruitful application even of *infinite time* to the *general problem of difference* in the world is inconceivable

In known geological eras, let us calculate them as liberally as we may, there is not time enough to account for the presently-existing varieties, from one or even several primordial forms Did light, or did the pulsations of the air, ever by any length of time, indent into the sensitive cell, eyes, and a pair of eyes—ears, and a pair of ears? Light conceivably might shine for ever without such a wonderfully complicated result as an eye. Similarly, for delicacy and marvellous ingenuity of structure, the ear is scarcely inferior to the eye; and surely it is possible to think of a whole infinitude of those fitful and fortuitous air-tremblings, which we call sound, without indentation into anything whatever of such an organ *Stirling*, '*As Regards Protoplasm*,' pp 56–59, abridged

Evolutional Religion—Religion as an adjustment

Not only have we seen that scientific inquiry, proceeding from its own resources and borrowing no hints from theology, leads to the conclusion that the universe is the manifestation of a Divine Power that is in no wise identifiable with the universe, or interpretable in terms of 'blind force,' or of any other phenomenal manifestation; but we have also seen that the ethical relations in which man stands with reference to this Divine Power are substantially the same, whether described in terms of modern science or in terms of ancient mythology. Not only does the Doctrine (of Evolution) show that the principles of action which the religious instincts of men have agreed in pronouncing sacred, are involved in the very nature of life itself, regarded as a continuous adjustment; but it shows that the obligation to conform to these principles, instead of deriving its authority from the arbitrary command of a mythologic quasi-human Ruler, derives it from the innermost necessities of that process of evolution which is the perpetual revelation of Divine

Power. He to whom the theory of Evolution, in all its details, has become as familiar as the saws and maxims of the old mythology are to him who still accepts it, will recognise that to be untrue to the highest attainable ethical code is to be untrue to philosophy, untrue to science, untrue to himself.—*Fiske*, '*Cosmic Philosophy*,' ii. 467, 468.

AGNOSTICISM.

Statement of the doctrine.

In science.

Agnosticism in science is the doctrine that 'ultimate scientific ideas are all representative of realities that cannot be comprehended.' 'Alike in the external and the internal worlds, the man of science sees himself in the midst of perpetual changes of which he can discover neither the beginning nor the end. If, tracing back the evolution of things, he allows himself to entertain the hypothesis that the Universe once existed in a diffused form, he finds it utterly impossible to conceive how this came to be so. In like manner, if he looks inward, he perceives that both ends of the thread of consciousness are beyond his grasp; nay, even beyond his power to think of as having existed or as existing in time to come. When, again, he turns from the succession of phenomena, external or internal, to their intrinsic nature, he is just as much at fault. Objective and subjective things he thus ascertains to be alike inscrutable in their substance and genesis. In all directions his investigations eventually bring him face to face with an insoluble enigma; and he ever more clearly perceives it to be an insoluble enigma. He, more than any other, truly *knows* that in its ultimate essence nothing can be known.'—*Spencer*, '*First Principles*,' pp. 66, 67.

In Theology.

Agnosticism in theology is the doctrine 'that the Power which the Universe manifests to us is utterly inscrutable.' 'Such a Power exists, but its nature transcends Intuition, and is beyond imagination.' God is 'unknown and unknowable.'—*Spencer*, '*First Principles*,' pp. 45, 46, 108.

Ultimate religious ideas and ultimate scientific ideas alike turn out to be merely symbols of the actual, not cognitions of it. —*Spencer*, '*First Principles*,' p. 68.

The unknowableness of God has been formulated as a Philosophy. It has even been defended as a Theology and hallowed as a Religion. The sublimation of rational piety has been gravely set forth as that blind wonder which comes from the conscious and necessary ignorance of God. In contrast with this new form of worship, the confident joyousness of the Christian faith has been called 'the impiety of the pious,' and the old saying has almost reappeared in a new guise, that even for a philosopher 'ignorance is the mother of devotion.'—*Porter*, '*Agnosticism*.'

Sir W. Hamilton's Doctrine.

True, therefore, are the declarations of a pious philosophy: 'A God understood would be no God at all;' 'To think that God is as we can think Him to be, is blasphemy.' The Divinity, in a certain sense, is revealed; in a certain sense is concealed. He is at once known and unknown. But the last and highest consecration of all true religion must be an altar—Ἀγνώστῳ Θεῷ—'To the unknown and unknowable God.'—'*Discussions*,' p. 15.

Dean Mansel's Doctrine.

The various mental attributes which we ascribe to God — Benevolence, Holiness, Justice, Wisdom, for example—can be conceived by us only as existing in a benevolent, and holy, and just, and wise Being, who is not identical with any one of His attributes, but the common subject of them all; in one word, in a *Person*. But Personality, as we conceive it, is essentially a limitation and a relation. . . . To speak of an Absolute and Infinite Person is simply to use language which, however true it may be in a superhuman sense, denotes an object inconceivable under the conditions of human thought.—'*Limits of Religious Thought,*' pp. 59, 60.

Of the nature and attributes of God in His Infinite Being Philosophy can tell us nothing; of man's inability to apprehend that nature, and why he is thus unable, she tells us all that we can know, and all that we need to know.—'*Limits of Religious Thought,*' p. 185.

Agnosticism not a new doctrine.

As a speculation Agnosticism is not new. It is as old as human thought. The doubts and misgivings from which it springs are older than the oldest fragment of human literature. The questions which it seeks to answer are as distinctly uttered in the book of Job as are the replies of sneering despair which are paraded in the last scientific periodical. Modern science and philosophy have not answered these questions. It may be doubted whether they have shed any light upon them. They have simply enlarged man's conceptions of the finite, and thus made it more easy for him to overlook or deny his power and his obligation to know the Infinite and the Self-existent.—*Porter*, '*Agnosticism,*' p. 29.

Criticism of Agnosticism.

Men have not listened to the voice of Mr Spencer. They proceed to look at the limits which he calls the Unknowable, and to look at the action of the force he has labelled the "Inscrutable." And they have found open paths, and the known forces of intelligence, will, and freedom at work everywhere in the sphere which Mr. Spencer calls the unknowable. They find that when they apply the forces they know in themselves and in history to the problems of nature and to the problems of our knowledge of God, they are fit and adequate for the explanation of them. While Mr. Spencer is telling us that we shall never know anything save the known manifestations of the unknowable force, behold this unknowable force has become known to us, and we find that our own personality is akin to Him who is the maker and upholder of the worlds. It is certainly not easy to understand how the inscrutable force which lies at the basis of existence according to Mr. Spencer should become the self-conscious force which I recognise in myself. On the other hand, if we take the Christian conception of God, as One who can be in some measure the known and obeyed and loved, we will fill up the dark inscrutable background of being with the living God, who has come forth to manifest Himself to us, and to speak to us words we can understand, and do deeds of kindness and of love.—*Iverach,* '*Is God Knowable,*' pp. 222, 223.

Agnosticism is the most refined of all Atheism, and that which most directly mocks and insults the dignity of human nature. It shrinks from avowed Atheism, and will not dare to say there is no God. It shrinks from Materialism, and will not dare to say that the forces of matter account for all phenomena. It simply declares the impossibility of knowing what the tremendous *Force* is that controls all things. There is no more deadly form of the great error of mankind than this which undermines every foundation.—*Pope,* '*Christian Theology,*' i. 389.

Agnostic Atheism first weakens and shatters our ideal of excellence; next, it denies the freedom by which we may rise, and, finally, it withdraws the inspiration which is ministered by our personal friend and deliverer. It weakens man's ideal. It cannot do otherwise, for it derives the law of duty from the changing feelings of our fellow-men. It degrades the law of duty into a shifting product of society; it resolves conscience with its rewards and penalties into the outgrowth of the imagined favour or dislike of men as unstable as ourselves, when this is fixed and transmitted by hereditary energy. Such an ideal, or law, or tribunal, can be neither sacred nor quickening, nor binding, because it has no permanence. To be a good or perfect man in one æon is not the same thing as to be a good man in another It is altogether a matter of taste or fashion, and each age under the law of development sets a new fashion for itself. —*Porter*, '*Agnosticism*,' pp 13, 14

Fatal to any real belief in God

The belief that there is an unknown subject of attributes absolutely unknown is a very innocent doctrine If this could once make its way and obtain in the world, there would be an end of all natural or rational religion, which is the basis both of the Jewish and the Christian for he who comes to God, or enters himself in the Church of God, must first believe that there is a God in some intelligible sense, and not only that there is *something in general* without any proper notion, though never so inadequate, of any of its qualities or attributes for this may be fate or chaos, or plastic nature, or anything else as well as God.—*Berkeley*, '*Alciphron, Fourth Dialogue*,' 17, 18

Fatal to Faith

An entirely unknown God cannot even engage faith —*Fraser*, '*Selections from Berkeley*,' p 235, note

There is neither inspiration nor hope for such a man in the help of God He certainly needs help from some one greater than himself If his moral ideals are not fixed, and he has no freedom with which to follow or reject such as he has, he is like a man who is bidden to walk in the sand that fails beneath his tread, and whose limbs are at the same time frozen with paralysis Or he is like a bird with stiffened wings when dropped into an exhausted receiver God cannot encourage or help him To him there is no God, or none of whom he can know that He can or will give him aid He has no God to whom to pray.—*Porter*, '*Agnosticism*,' p 14

To no purpose do the irrepressible instincts of man's soul cry out for communion with the unseen and the spiritual, above him he knows no mind to answer to his own, no God to whom his worship may ascend, no Father in whom his affections can find repose Hope dies within his breast, for he has no future Conscience becomes but a voice crying in the wilderness, for why should he toil and suffer for right, when right and wrong are but the dreams of a day? 'Let us eat and drink, for to-morrow we die!'—*Maitland*, '*Theism or Agnosticism*,' p 17

It abandons hope.

So far as man denies God, or denies that God can be known, he abandons hope of every kind—that intellectual hope which is the life of scientific thought; hope for his own moral progress; hope for the progress of society; hope for guidance and comfort in his personal life; and hope for that future life for which the present is a preparation As he lets those hopes go one by one, his life loses its light and its dignity; morality loses its enthusiasm and its energy, science has no promise of success, sin gains a relentless hold, sorrow and darkness have no comfort, and life becomes a worthless farce or a sad tragedy, neither of which is worth the playing, because both end in nothing Sooner or later this agnostic without hope will become morose and surly, or sensual and self-indulgent, or avaricious and churlish, or cold and selfish, or cultured and hollow,—in a word, a theoretical or a practical pessimist, as any man must who believes the world as well as himself to be without any worthy end for which one man or many men should care to live —*Porter*, '*Agnosticism*,' p 27

It is unfavourable to science

Our newly-fledged agnostics are apt to forget that all our modern science has been prosecuted in the broad and penetrating sunlight of faith in one living and personal God—that not a single theory has been proposed or experiment tried in nature, except with the distinct recognition of the truth that a wise and loving Mind at least *may* uphold and direct the goings-on of nature. The most passionate atheist cannot deny that this is the conviction of most of the living and breathing men about him The most restrained agnostic cannot but know and feel that the theory which he strives to cherish is rejected by most of the women and children in Christendom who look up into the sky and walk upon the earth The simple teachings of Christian theism are capable of being expanded into the grandest conceptions that science ever attempted to formulate—conceptions so grand that human reason is overwhelmed with their sublime relationships, and the human imagination is dazed to blindness when it would make them real.—*Porter*, '*Agnosticism*,' p. 6.

Fallacy of Agnosticism

The principle against which we protest may be expressed as follows:—Knowledge must be based on logical proofs; the knowable and the demonstrable are identical; whatever cannot be shown by strict inductive reasoning to exist must be dismissed from the region of science and consigned to the dream-land of the speculative imagination. Our contention is that as soon as this principle, which is really the stronghold of agnosticism, is tried at the bar of the practical reason, and brought face to face with the realities of human life, it must be convicted of monstrous absurdity

Nothing is more certain than that every train of reasoning must have some premiss from which to start. Arguments cannot sustain themselves in the air, without any basis to rest upon, real or assumed. Logical processes without materials to work upon can no more bring forth results in the shape of knowledge than a mill can grind out flour without being supplied with grist But whence shall we fetch the indispensable premisses to set our arguments agoing? If it be said they are furnished by previous trains of argument by means of which they have been established, we must again ask whence the premisses for these were obtained; nor can we cease reiterating the question until in each case we reach some premiss which was antecedent to every logical process, and was the original material on which the reasoning faculty began to operate And how did we get these? Not by reasoning, for the argument could not begin until the mind was in possession of them They were the primitive elements of thought, the starting-point of knowledge, the foundation of all the science of which man is capable. And they were not the result of any process of reasoning. If they were trustworthy and true, then we possess real knowledge, which was not derived from reasoning and is not capable of logical demonstration. If they were not trustworthy and true, then none of our pretended knowledge is trustworthy and true, for upon them every particle of it ultimately depends. So that we are driven perforce to choose between these alternatives; either we know nothing at all or we know more than we can prove.—*Maitland*, '*Theism, &c*,' pp. 49-51

All this life, this reality, rest on knowledge which is prior to logical processes and is obtained through our consciousness We do not reason it out; it comes to us, and we possess it and live by it. We trust our intuitions, our perceptions, our experience, that is the secret of our practical, our human life In the sphere of this life, the question, Can you prove demonstratively the grounds on which you act? turns out to be an idle one. Were we to wait till we could answer it in the affirmative, death would overtake us before we had begun to live —*Maitland*, '*Theism, &c.*,' p. 57

God may be known, seeing—

He is suggested by our own personality.

Man asks earnestly, Is there nothing more in this wide universe than force and law? If there is nothing more, no man is so much to be pitied as he—the man of scientific knowledge and scientific imagination, for no man feels so lonely and helpless as he. He is alone! alone! as he muses upon the vastness of this great solitude, peopled though it be with the enormous agents that haunt and overmaster him with their presence, but are without a thought or care for his personal life. Could he but see behind these forces a personal being like himself and capable of directing both force and law to issues of blessings to men, how welcome would that knowledge be to his lonely heart. That God he may see and find if he will. He is suggested by his own personality, which is his nobler, nay, his essential self. He is demanded by the weakness and limitations of his own nature. Why should there not be a personal and living God behind this machinery of force and law which we call nature? Why should I not know a living Spirit, as well as unknown force and definite law? and why should I not accept personality in God as the best explanation of both? There is, there must be such a Person; He fills this vast solitude by His immanent presence and His animating life.—*Porter, 'Agnosticism,'* p. 20.

And testified to by our consciousness.

The whole of the practical knowledge on which human life is based rests on no logical foundation, but on the trustworthiness of our instinctive consciousness and intuitive perceptions. We do trust these, and it is only through trusting them that we are enabled to live human lives. We have no other ground for our belief in the physical world, in our fellow-men, or even in our own permanent personality. Why, then, should we begin to distrust our consciousness and cast doubts on its veracity, as soon as it begins to witness to us of God? If our souls are conscious of him, why should we not believe that He really exists? Experience proves that there is a vision of God by the purified soul, just as truly as there is a vision of the beauteous face of nature by the sensitive eye. The consciousness of God is one of the primary and fundamental intuitions of human nature.—*Maitland, 'Theism, &c.,'* p. 163.

MATERIALISM.

Definition and Statement.

Materialism is the theory of perception according to which the perceiver and the perceived are alike material—mind being only a kind of matter, or a product of matter.—*Monck, 'Sir W. Hamilton,'* p. 184.

There is nothing but matter, no spirit separate from matter—such is its fundamental maxim. Materialists teach that matter is everything, and that there is nothing else; it is eternal and imperishable, 'the primary cause of all existence, all life and all forms are but modifications of matter,' it is only form which is perishable and mutable.—*Luthardt, 'Fundamental Truths,'* p. 83.

Materialism, both ancient and modern, adduces two propositions: (1) That sensuous perception is the source of all knowledge; and (2) That all mental action is nothing more than the activity of matter, and therefore the soul itself is material and mortal.—*Christlieb, 'Modern Doubt,'* p. 148.

The materialistic hypothesis—that material changes cause mental changes, is one which presents great fascination to the student of science. By laborious investigation physiology has established the fact that there is constant relation of concomitancy between cerebral action and thought. That is to say, mind is found in constant and definite association with the brain, the size and elaboration of which throughout the animal kingdom stand in conspicuous proportion to the degree of intelligence displayed, and the impairment of which by anæmia, mutilation, decay, or appropriate poison, entails corresponding impairment of mental processes. This constant and concomitant relation is regarded as a causal relation. It is said that the evidence of causation between neurosis and psychosis is quite as valid as that of any other case of recognised causation.—*Romanes, 'Nineteenth Century,'* December 1882.

Origin of Materialism explained.

When we pass over from the study of matter to the study of spirit, we are at once confronted with new and strange objects. Though the states of the soul have been the nearest to our experience and the most familiar to our enjoyment, they have been removed the farthest from our observation and study. We ask, Are they real? Are they actual and substantial? Surely they are not like those phenomena which we see and hear, which we handle and taste. But allowing that they are actual phenomena, are they distinct and definite? Can we compare and class them? To what substance do they pertain? The readiest answer is, To some material substance. Hence the soul is readily resolved into some form of attenuated matter. Its functions are explained by the action of the animal spirits, or by chemical or electrical changes in the nervous substance. Perception is explained by impressions on the eye and the ear, which impressions are referred to motions in a vibrating fluid without, which in turn are responded to by motions aroused in a vibrating agent within. Memory and association are explained by the mutual attractions or repulsions of ideas, similar to those to which the particles of matter are subjected by cohesion or electricity. Generalisation and judgment, induction and reasoning, are resolved by the frequent and often-repeated deposits of impressions that have affinity for one another, and are thus transformed into general conceptions and relations.

From these tendencies and prepossessions have resulted the various schemes of materialism, the grosser and the more refined. By these influences we can account for the ready acceptance of phrenology, with its more or less decided material affinities. To the same we refer the occasional semi-materialistic solutions of psychical phenomena, which occur in many treatises and systems which are far from being avowedly materialistic. By them we can easily explain those modes of thinking and speaking in respect to the soul in which resort is had to some law or principle of matter to explain a phenomenon which is simply and purely spiritual. Even those who on moral or religious grounds believe most firmly in the spiritual and immortal existence of the soul, often fall, in the scientific conceptions which they form of its essence and its actings, into modes of thinking and reasoning which are more or less plainly material. Especially are they easily puzzled by objections which derive their sole plausibility from material analogies. These phenomena are not at all surprising. The mind that is trained by the most liberal culture, or that is schooled to the most complete self-control, cannot easily divest itself of the prejudices and prepossessions which have been contracted by previous studies.—*Porter*, '*Human Intellect*,' p. 18.

The intellectual habits formed by exclusive attention to external nature lead many to attribute their very conscious life itself, as well as all mind in the universe, to unconscious material power—the dead substance to which Locke referred his sensations. It is thought that unconscious matter may be the source of all that happens in consciousness, as well as all that happens in external nature.—*Fraser*, '*Selections from Berkeley*,' p. xvii.

Found in many systems.

We find Materialism in the Buddhism of ancient India; in Greece, among the Atomists and Sophists, the Epicureans and the Sceptics; we find it in the Middle Ages, when the Roman Church clearly betrayed her tendency to the worship of matter, and even at times among the occupants of the Papal throne, of whom, for instance, John XXIII. and Paul III publicly denied the immortality of the soul; we find it in the seventeenth and eighteenth centuries, as the ultimate result of the long protracted doubts as to revelation.—*Christlieb*, '*Modern Doubt*,' p. 145.

Materialism is as old as philosophy, but not older. The physical conception of nature, which dominates the earliest periods of the history of thought, remains ever entangled in the contradictions of Dualism and the fantasies of personification The first attempt to escape from these contradictions, to conceive the world as a unity, and to rise above the vulgar errors of the senses, lead directly into the sphere of philosophy, and amongst these first attempts Materialism has its place.—*Lange, 'History of Materialism,'* i. 3.

Although modern Materialism appeared as a system first in France, yet England was the classic land of Materialistic modes of thought Here the ground had already been prepared by Roger Bacon and Occam; Bacon of Verulam, who lacked almost nothing but a little more consistency and clearness in order to be a Materialist, was wholly the man of his age and nation, and Hobbes, the most consequent of the modern Materialists, is at least as much indebted to English tradition as to the example and precedence of Gassendi.—*Lange, 'History of Materialism,'* ii 3

'The world consists of atoms and empty space.' In this principle the Materialistic systems of antiquity and of modern days are in harmony, whatever differences may have gradually developed themselves in the notion of the atom, and however different are the theories as to the origin of the rich and varied universe from such simple elements. . . The atomic doctrine of to-day is still what it was in the time of Democritus. It has still not lost its metaphysical character; and already in antiquity it served also as a scientific hypothesis for the explanation of the observed facts of nature.—*Lange, 'History of Materialism,'* ii. 351

French Materialism of the Eighteenth Century

De la Mettrie's 'Natural History of the Soul.'

Identity of soul and matter.

Soul without body is like matter without any form . it cannot be conceived. Soul and body have been formed together, and in the same instant. He who wishes to learn the qualities of the soul must previously study those of the body, whose active principle the soul is.—*Lange, 'History of Materialism,'* ii. 57.

Matter only becomes a definite substance through form, but whence does it receive the form? From another substance which is also material in its nature This again from another, and so on to infinity, that is, we know the form only in its combination with matter. In this indissoluble union of form and matter things react and form each other, and so it is also with motion Only the abstract, separately conceived matter is that passive thing: the concrete, actual matter is never without motion, as it is never without form; it is, then, in truth identical with substance. Where we do not perceive motion it is yet potentially present, just as matter also contains potentially all forms in itself There is not the slightest reason for assuming that there is an agent outside the material world.—*Lange, 'History of Materialism,'* ii. 58

Holbach's 'System of Nature' (1770)

What distinguishes the "System of Nature" from most materialistic writings is the outspokenness with which the whole second part of the book, which is still stronger than the first, in fourteen chapters, combats the idea of God in every possible shape. Regarding religion as the chief source of all human corruption, he tries to eradicate all foundation for this morbid tendency of mankind, and therefore pursues the deistic and pantheistic idea of God, that were yet so dear to his age, with no less zeal than the ideas of the Church.—*Lange, 'Hist. of Materialism,'* ii. 115, 116.

German Materialism.

Moleschott.

In *Der Kreislauf des Lebens*, the whole order of things is conceived as a continual flux and exchange of material elements, which accounts for all psychic life no less than for bodily life, and of which man, equally with the lower animals, is a temporary product.—*Sully, art.* '*Evolution,*' '*Enc. Brit.*,' vol. viii. 767.

Ohne Phosphor kein Gedanke, "No Thought without Phosphorus."—*Moleschott.*

No force without matter, no matter without force! Neither can be thought of *per se*, separated, they become empty abstractions.—*Buchner*, '*Force and Matter,*' p. 2.

Those who talk of a creative power which is said to have produced the world out of itself or out of nothing, are ignorant of the first and most simple principle, founded upon experience and the contemplation of nature. How could a power have existed, not manifested in material substance, but governing it arbitrarily according to individual views? Neither could separately existing forces be transferred to chaotic matter and produce the world in this manner; for a separate existence of either is an impossibility. The world, or matter with its properties, which we term forces, must have existed from eternity and must last for ever—in one word, the world cannot have been created.—*Buchner*, '*Force and Matter,*' p. 5.

Matter is uncreatable as it is indestructible.—*Carl Vogt.*

A spirit without body is as unimaginable as electricity or magnetism without metallic or other substances on which these forces act. The animal soul is a product of external influences, without which it would never have been called into existence. Unprejudiced philosophy is compelled to reject the idea of an individual immortality, and of a personal continuance after death. With the decay and dissolution of its material substratum, through which alone it has acquired a conscious existence and became a person, and upon which it was dependent, the spirit must cease to exist. All knowledge which this being has acquired relates to earthly things; it has become conscious of itself in, with, and by these things; it has become a person by its being opposed against earthly limited individualities. How can we imagine it to be possible that, torn away from these necessary conditions, this being should continue to exist with self-consciousness and as the same person?—*Buchner*, '*Force and Matter,*' p. 196.

Arguments against Materialism.

It does not explain the facts to be accounted for.

The theory of materialism can never be accepted by any competent mind as a final *explanation* of the facts with which it has to deal. Useful as a fundamental hypothesis in physiology and medicine, it is wholly inadequate as a hypothesis in philosophy. A very small amount of thinking is enough to show that what I call my knowledge of the external world is merely a knowledge of my own mental modifications. My idea of causation as a principle in the external world is derived from my knowledge of this principle in the internal world. Thus, in the very act of thinking the evidence, we are virtually denying its possibility as evidence; for as evidence it appeals only to the mind, and since the mind can know only its own sequences, the evidence must be presenting to the mind an account of its own modifications. The evidence is proved to be illusory.—*Romanes*, 1882.

Such a theory is insufficient as an explanation of the most commonly recognised facts. Without touching the multitude of complex questions involved in any theory which would attempt to explain the present condition of the universe, with unorganised matter as its sole cause or source, there are two considerations which are fatal to its logical claims: (1.) Unorganised matter is inadequate as the cause of the various forms of organised existence. (2.) We recognise in our own consciousness a form of existence higher than the material. Explanation of the higher by the lower is achieved only by the reversal of Logic.—*Calderwood*, '*Moral Philosophy,*' p. 235.

Especially Self-consciousness.

If the difference between the merely animal and the human soul-life consists essentially in self-consciousness, then *no explanation can be given as to the origin of self-consciousness in man.* Granted that the individual acts of our soul-life all resulted from nothing but chemico-physical causes, it can never be denied that these acts are all rooted in a certain fixed, permanent centre, in 'the idea of the Ego as the basis of all thought;' that is, in self-consciousness Whence, then, is this? This centre is *not identical with the individual acts of thought;* for it is not an isolated act, but a continuous condition. Materialism, it is true, would fain make it identical with thought, but again in opposition to all experience For do we not clearly distinguish ourselves in self-consciousness from any definite act of thought? Are there not conditions in which correct reasoning is coexistent with perturbed consciousness? And, *vice versâ*, is there not sometimes a continuance of consciousness notwithstanding the cessation of intellectual activity? The materialist, who will hear of no operative factor except the individual agencies —brain, muscles, nerves, &c.—and who denies as an empty abstraction the bond which unites these separate agents, and preserves its own unity amid all the changes of thought and perception—that is, the self-consciousness, or the personality as such—makes out man to be a 'purely mechanical lay-figure,' or, as Czolbe openly admits, 'a piece of mosaic, mechanically constructed from various atoms,'—a theory which explains absolutely nothing of the practical phenomena of soul-life.—*Christlieb, 'Modern Doubt,'* p. 155

The facts of consciousness are utterly destructive of materialistic opinions. The first fact is that of thought, and especially of self-consciousness. If all thought is but the brain's own product, how does it set itself thinking? The brain is but an organ; who puts this organ in motion? To do this a power is needed, which is not itself of a kind appreciable by the senses. This motive power must be of a kind corresponding to its effect, i e, it must be of a mental kind. The highest effect produced by this mental power is *self-consciousness.* How can this be designated a mere action of the brain, when it is rather a mental act of man entirely unparalleled in the whole remaining terrestrial creation? Something answering to reflection and judgment is found even among animals; but self consciousness, that most purely mental act, by which man separates himself from all that is about him and comprehends and thinks of himself in his oneness with himself, is specific; it is an absolutely new principle, and one which raises man far above all other living beings And this self-consciousness remains the same under all changes, whether external or internal, which may happen to man. It is absurd to call that which is an abstraction from all matter a product of matter.—*Luthardt, 'Fundamental Truths,'* p. 135.

Moral consciousness.

The second fact is *moral consciousness* For my conscience, or moral consciousness, is as much a fact as my body It is not a result of persuasion, education, or cultivation, but an inward moral voice which perceptibly echoes every moral testimony from without Wherever a human being is found, we find in him this moral consciousness. It may be obscured or perverted, yet it still exists, it is still the foundation in the midst of all its perversion.—*Luthardt, 'Fundamental Truths,'* p. 136.

Religious consciousness.

Religious consciousness,—that inward attraction of man towards a higher power, reflected and attested by his consciousness —an attestation which can neither be refuted nor avoided wherever man exists,—is no less a fact of his mental life And, even if it be declared an error, the fact of its existence must be acknowledged and its possibility accounted for. It is, however, an impossibility, if nothing exists but what is a product of matter. Materialism denies the higher life of man and gives us in exchange a brutalisation of humanity.—*Luthardt, 'Fundamental Truths,'* p. 136.

Organisation.

The materialistic view is utterly annihilated by the fact of organisation. If none but merely mechanical combinations were found, we might be contented to accept a force merely mechanical. But what produced organisms? Utterly futile has been the attempt to refer them to a merely physical process. Whatever conceptions we may form of atoms, they are insufficient to explain organisation. There is an essential difference between the formation of a crystal and the formation of an organised being. That which distinguishes an organism is the vital interaction of its component parts, and the mutual relations into which it enters with the bodies which surround it, by which processes a constant alteration of its condition is kept up. Moreover, every organism is founded on an idea. This idea existed prior to its realisation; indeed, the whole realm of organised nature is governed by its idea. This idea works for the future. The eye is made for light, the ear for sound. We have here a designing agency pointing past all external causes,—back to a fashioning and designing mind. How is this fact to be explained, if we admit only matter and force, or nature acting unconsciously, and not the *creative power* of the Intelligence that fashioned the world?—*Luthardt, 'Fundamental Truths,'* p. 87.

The mind distinguishes itself from matter.

The acting *ego* is not only not known to be in any way material, but it distinguishes its own actings, states, and products, and even itself, from the material substance with which it is most intimately connected, from the very organised body on whose organisation all its functions, and the very function of knowing or distinguishing, are said to depend. First, it distinguishes from this body all other material things and objects, asserting that the one are not the other. Second, it just as clearly, though not in the same way or on the same grounds, distinguishes itself and its states from the material objects which it discerns. It knows that the agent which sees and hears is not the matter which is seen and heard. Third, the soul also distinguishes itself and its inner states from the organised matter, *i.e.*, its own bodily organs, by means of which it perceives and is affected by other matter. Fourth, it resists the force and actings of its own body, and, in so doing, distinguishes itself as the agent most emphatically from that which it resists. By its own activity it struggles against and opposes the coming on of sleep, of faintness, and of death. Even in those conscious acts in which it feels itself most at the disposal and control of the body, it recognises its separate existence and independent energy.—*Porter, 'Human Intellect,'* p. 23.

Materialism assumes mind.

You cannot get mind as an ultimate product of matter, for in the very attempt to do so you have already begun with mind. The earliest step of any such inquiry involves categories of thought, and it is in terms of thought that the very problem you are investigating can be so much as stated. You cannot start in your investigations with a bare, self-identical, objective fact, stripped of every ideal element or contribution from thought. The least and lowest part of outward observation is not an independent entity—fact *minus* mind, and out of which mind may somewhere or other be seen to emerge, but it is fact or object as it appears to an observing mind, the medium of thought, having mind or thought as an inseparable factor of it. To make thought a function of matter is thus, simply, to make thought a function of itself.—*Caird.*

Matter is not a sufficient cause of mind.

If we could see any analogy between thought and any one of the admitted phenomena of matter, we should be justified in the conclusion of materialism as the simplest, and as affording a hypothesis most in accordance with the comprehensiveness of natural laws; but between thought and the physical phenomena of matter there is not only no analogy, but no conceivable analogy; and the obvious and continuous path which we have hitherto followed up in our reasonings from the phenomena of lifeless matter through those of living matter, here comes suddenly to an end. The chasm between unconscious life and thought is deep and impassable, and no transitional phenomena can be found by which, as by a bridge, we may span it over.—*Allman, 'Presidential Address.'*

The passage from the physics of the brain to the corresponding facts of consciousness is unthinkable. Granted that a definite thought and a definite molecular action in the brain occur simultaneously, we do not possess the intellectual organ, nor apparently any rudiment of the organ, which would enable us to pass, by a process of reasoning, from the one phenomenon to the other. Were our minds and senses so expanded, strengthened, and illuminated as to enable us to see and feel the very molecules of the brain; were we capable of following all their motions, all their groupings, all their electrical discharges, if there be such; and were we intimately acquainted with the corresponding states of thought and feeling, the chasm between the two classes of phenomena would still remain intellectually impassable.—*Tyndall.*

If we suppose causation to proceed from brain to mind, we must, according to the doctrine of the Conservation of Energy, suppose the essential requirement of equivalence between the cerebral causes and the mental effects to be satisfied somewhere. But where are we to say that it is satisfied? The brain of a Shakespeare probably did not, as a system, exhibit so much energy as does the brain of an elephant. Many a man must have consumed more than a thousand times the brain-substance and brain energy that Shelley expended over his 'Ode to a Skylark,' and yet as a result have produced an utterly worthless poem. In what way are we to estimate the 'work done' in such cases? What becomes of the evidence of equivalency between the physical causes and the psychical effects?—*Romanes*, 1882.

Materialism does not solve the difficulties which it is supposed to solve.

The existence of a Universal Will and the existence of Matter stand upon exactly the same basis—of certainty if you trust, of uncertainty if you distrust, the *principia* of your own reason. If I am to see a ruling Power in the world, is it folly to prefer a man-like to a brute-like power, a seeing to a blind? The similitude to man means no more and goes no further than the supremacy of intellectual insight and moral ends over every inferior alternative; and how it can be contemptible and childish to derive everything from the highest known order of power rather than the lowest, and to converse with nature as embodied Thought, instead of taking it as a dynamic engine, it is difficult to understand. Is it absurd to suppose mind transcending the human? or, if we do so, to make our own Reason the analogical base for intellect of wider sweep? —*Martineau, 'Modern Materialism,'* pp. 59, 60.

Effect of Materialistic views upon Study of Nature.

It is a strange and yet an intelligible pride that our scientific *illuminati* take in requiring for the explanatory reconstruction of reality in thought no other postulates than an original store of matter and force, and the unshaken authority of a group of universal and immutable laws of nature. Strange, because after all these are no trifling postulates, and because it might be expected to be more in accordance with the comprehensive spirit of the human reason to acknowledge the unity of a creative cause than to have imposed on it as the starting-point of all explanation the promiscuous variety of merely actually existent things and notions. And yet intelligible; for in return for this single sacrifice the finite understanding may now enjoy the satisfaction of never again being overpowered by the transcendent significance and beauty of any single phenomenon. However wondrous and profound may appear to it any work of nature, those universal laws, which are to it perfectly transparent, give it the means of warding off a disagreeable impression, and, while proving how perfectly it understands that even this phenomenon is but an incidental result of a well-known order of nature, it succeeds in drawing within the limits of its own finitude what to the unprejudiced mind is conceivable only as a product of infinite wisdom.—*Lotze*, '*Microcosmus*,' i. 375.

Consequences of Materialism

First and foremost, it is clear that materialistic principles do away with the immortality of the soul and all belief in another world. For he who does not acknowledge any immaterial principles in man will not allow the existence of an absolute Spirit, *i.e.*, of God, either in or above the world. Every one sees what questionable results follow from the negation of our immortality, even as regards *this life*, and the moral order of the present world. With shameless audacity Materialism would destroy all the moral faculties of our life. Moleschott, for instance, says that 'sin lies in the unnatural, and not in the will to do evil.' 'The brain alters with the ages; and with the brain custom, which is the standard of morals, is altered also.' 'To understand everything is to tolerate everything.' The man who robs and murders is no worse than the falling stone which crushes a man. In good sooth, the materialists are the most dangerous enemies of progress that the world has ever seen.—*Christlieb*, '*Modern Doubt*,' p. 156.

Its relation to Atheism.

Materialism is the true brother of Atheism. They must necessarily be simultaneous; for he who desires the existence of God is unable to maintain the spiritual personality of man. Historically it invariably either proceeds from or closely follows Atheism. The two play into one another's hands, and, in fact, amount to the same thing. For Atheism must ultimately believe in the eternity of matter, and, just like Materialism, must make it its God.—*Christlieb*, '*Modern Doubt*,' p. 145.

Materialism is the modern form of Atheism which seems to threaten the hold of religion on men's minds. It is the last and most uncompromising of its enemies: never during earlier ages having risen with anything like strength, it seems now to be encouraged to assault the Faith by the aid of physical science. But sound science must sooner or later utterly disavow a system that abolishes the notions of cause and effect, of all final causes and ends, and asserts, in the face of evidence most absolute, the spontaneous origin of life.—*Pope*, '*Christian Theology*,' i. 150.

Pantheism.

Pantheism considers God as the Soul of the world, and material nature as His body only. Materialism merges God in matter, for according to it nothing at all exists but matter. Materialism may well be called the gospel of the flesh.—*Christlieb*, '*Modern Doubt*,' p. 145.

Pantheism makes the universe only and all the universe God; Materialism makes all the universe only matter. Thus Materialism stands at the opposite pole of Pantheism, as the philosophical or scientific antagonist of the Scriptural doctrine of the Creator and creation: opposite poles, however, of one and the same sphere of thought. Pantheism gives the notion of God the pre-eminence, all things phenomenal being His eternal but ever-changing vesture; Materialism gives matter the pre-eminence, as the only substance that is, and regards what men call God as the unknown law by which that substance is governed in all its evolutions.—*Pope, 'Christian Theology,'* i. 385

Truth in Materialism.

Doubtless there is something true and justifiable in Materialism. It calls our attention more closely than in former days to the profound interpenetration of our soul-life and our bodily condition, and to the fact that the activity of our mind and will is partly determined by bodily functions,—the circulation of the blood, the action of the nerves, &c.; in a word, to the unquestionably very important influence exercised by material agents, both within and without us, on our mental condition. Materialism may thus teach a lesson to those one-sided idealists, who look upon their reason as absolutely free in its nature, without believing in their dependence on material influences.—*Christlieb, 'Modern Doubt,'* p. 160.

Absurdities of Materialism.

The following extracts may serve as an illustration of the ridiculous conclusions drawn from this theory, as well as of the manner in which its advocates can unconsciously disprove it by a *reductio ad absurdum*:—

'Man is produced from wind and ashes. The action of vegetable life called him into existence. Man is the sum of his parents and his wet nurse, of time and place, of wind and weather, of sound and light, of food and clothing; his will is the necessary consequence of all these causes, governed by the laws of nature, just as the planet in its orbit, and the vegetable in its soil.

'Thought consists in the motion of matter, it is a translocation of the cerebral substance; without phosphorus there can be no thought; and consciousness itself is nothing but an attribute of matter.'—*Moleschott, 'Der Kreislauf des Lebens.'*

'We are what we eat.'—*Feuerbach.*

A constant danger.

Materialism is a danger to which individuals and societies will always be more or less exposed. The present generation, however, and especially the generation which is growing up, will obviously be very specially exposed to it; as much so perhaps as any generation in the history of the world. Within the last thirty years the great wave of spiritualistic or idealistic thought has been receding and decreasing, and another, which is in the main driven by materialistic forces, has been gradually rising behind, vast and threatening. It is but its crest that we at present see; it is but a certain vague shaking produced by it that we at present feel; but we shall probably soon enough fail not both to see and feel it fully and distinctly.—*Flint, 'Antitheistic Theories,'* p. 99.

PANTHEISM.

Its leading Idea.

Pantheism supposes God and nature, or God and the whole universe, to be one and the same substance—one universal being; insomuch that men's souls are only modifications of the Divine substance.—*Waterland, 'Works,'* viii. 81.

The forms of Pantheism are various, yet it has but a single fundamental notion, and this fundamental notion from which all these forms proceed is, that there is at the root of the infinite variety of this world, and its individual phenomena, a common principle which constitutes its unity, and that this common principle is God. This is, however, no conscious, personal God; it is but the common life which lives in all the common existence which is in all, or the reason in all things. We only call it God. This God has no independent being, he exists only in the world, the world is his reality, and he is only its truth.—*Luthardt, 'Fundamental Truths,'* p. 65.

The leading idea of Pantheism is, that God is everything, and everything is God. Though all mind, whether of men or animals, is God; yet no individual mind is God; and so all distinct personality of the Godhead is lost. The supreme being of the Hindoos is therefore neither male nor female, but neuter. All the numberless forms of matter are but different appearances of God; and though He is invisible, yet everything you see is God. Accordingly, the Deity Himself becomes identified with the worshipper. 'He who knows that Deity, is the Deity itself.'—*Brown, 'Thirty-nine Articles,'* p. 14.

Pantheism derives its name from the motto, ἓν καὶ πᾶν, *i.e.*, One and all, which was first brought into vogue by the Greek philosopher Xenophanes. According to this view, God is the universe itself; *beyond* and *outside* the world He does not exist, but only *in* the world. He is the Soul, the Reason, and the Spirit of the world, and all nature is His body. In reality, God is everything, and beside Him there is nothing. Thus making God the Soul of the world, Pantheism is distinguished, on the one hand, from Materialism, according to which God and nature are immediately identical; and, on the other hand, from Theism, that is, from the belief in a self-conscious, personal God, who created the world, and guides even its most minute details. For the main point of pantheistic belief is that this soul of the world is not a personal, self-conscious Being, who appears in his totality in any one phenomenon or at any one moment, so as to comprehend himself or become comprehensible for us, but that it is only the One ever same essence which, filling everything and shaping everything, lives and moves in all existing things, and is revealed in all that is visible, yet is Itself never seen.—*Christlieb, 'Modern Doubt, &c.,'* p. 161.

Two main forms of Pantheism.

Heyder calls attention to the fact that Pantheism is divided into two main forms, the occidental and the oriental. The former merges the world in God, the latter merges God in the world. In that, God is rest, in this, He is motion; there, God is being, here, He is development, process.—*Luthardt, 'Fundamental Truths,'* p. 356.

Pantheism is that system of thought, which loses sight of the wide gulf which separates God and man—the Creator and the created—the finite and the Infinite. There are two sides, therefore, from which this error may arise; either the Creator may be brought down to the level of His works, or the creature lifted up to the level of the Creator. The first has been the more besetting error of ancient, the last of modern days.—*Wilberforce, 'Doctrine of the Holy Eucharist,'* p. 423.

But many shapes.

Pantheism has assumed an immense number of shapes, if shape it can be said to have, whose very nature is to be shapeless. The following seem to be the more decided:—

(1.) There is *Material Pantheism.* According to this, it is the mere matter of the universe, with its forces, its life, its thought, as the result of organism, which constitutes the One All, that may be called God. This is the lowest sort of Pantheism.

(2.) There is *Organic or Vital Pantheism.* The difficulty which we have in defining life, or in apprehending it, holds out a temptation to many to explain all things by it, which, in fact, is to explain the *ignotum per ignotius.* All nature, they say, is full of life. This idea that all nature has life, comes out in the writings of certain physical speculators of the school of Schelling, and in all cases tends to substitute some sort of impersonal power for a personal God.

3. There is the *One Substance Pantheism.* Persons begin first by declaring that the material universe is the body, and God the soul. This prepares the way for pantheism, which maintains that there is a spiritual power acting in the material form, the two being all the while one substance. We

owe the introduction of this system, as a system, to Spinoza. According to this shy, thought-bewildered man, there is but one substance, which substance has attributes which the mind can conceive as its essence and modes, being the affections of the substance This substance is infinite, a part of it is substance finite, and man is such a part of the Divine substance

4. There is *Ideal Pantheism.* Kant began with making time and space subjective forms, and Fichte went on to make matter and God Himself a subjective creation of the mind. Schelling sought to enlarge the system by making mind and matter, God and the universe, at one and the same time ideal and real,—ideal on the one side, and real on the other; and Hegel came forward with an artificial dialectic, to show how nothing could become something, and how God becomes conscious in humanity. —*M'Cosh, 'Intuitions of the Mind,'* pp 449–452.

Pantheistic doctrine of Spinoza.

'The foundation of all that exists,' taught Spinoza, 'is the one eternal substance which makes its actual appearance in the double world of thought, and of matter existing in space. Individual forms emerge from the womb of this substance as of ever-fertile nature, to be again swallowed up in the stream of life. As the waves of the sea rise and sink, so does individual life arise, to sink back again into that common life which is the death of all individual existence.—*Luthardt 'Fundamental Truths,'* p. 65.

'To my mind,' says Spinoza, 'God is the immanent (that is, the intra-mundane), and not the transcendent (that is, the supramundane) Cause of all things; that is, the totality of finite objects is posited in the Essence of God, and not in His *Will.* Nature, considered *per se,* is one with the essence of God' According to Spinoza, God is the one universal Substance, in which all distinctions and all isolated qualifications are resolved into unity, to which *per se* we cannot therefore ascribe either understanding or will. 'God does not act in pursuance of a purpose, but only according to the *necessity* of His nature. Everything follows from nature with the same logical necessity as that by which the attributes of a thing follow from its idea, or from the nature of a triangle that its three angles are equal to two right angles.' This expresses the fundamental view of every form of Pantheism.—*Christlieb, 'Modern Doubt,'* p. 163.

Schelling.

Eternal absolute being is continually separating in the double world of mind and nature. It is one and the same life which runs through all nature, and empties itself into man. It is one and the same life which moves in the tree and the forest, in the sea and the crystal, which works and creates in the mighty forces and powers of natural life, and which, enclosed in a human body, produces the thoughts of the mind.—*Schelling, quoted in Luthardt, 'Fundamental Truths,'* p 66.

Hegel.

The absolute is the universal reason, which, having first buried and lost itself in nature, recovers itself in man, in the shape of self-conscious mind, in which the absolute, at the close of its great process, comes again to itself, and comprises itself into unity with itself This process of mind is God Man's thought of God is the existence of God. God has no independent being or existence; He exists only in us. God does not know Himself; it is we who know Him. While man thinks of and knows God, God knows and thinks of Himself and exists. God is the truth of man, and man is the reality of God.—*Hegel, quoted in Luthardt, 'Fundamental Truths,'* p. 66

Difficulties of Pantheism.

Philosophical

Want of connection between facts and theory

The special difficulty of a Pantheistic theory is to connect the facts with the doctrine by any competent philosophic process It first presupposes a conception of Deity, such as belongs to the Theistic doctrine; and secondly, a theoretic affirmation that all known finite existence belongs, either essentially or in a phenomenal sense, to the Divine nature. Both of these are positions which need to be established by a distinct philosophic process. Without this, Pantheism merely accepts the Theistic doctrine in the first stage of its development, in order to violate it in the second, thus becoming self-contradictory. To make good its claim to a place among philosophic theories, it must show first, how it reaches its theism, and next how it lifts up the 'all' into its theism, for legitimate construction of a Pantheism. — *Calderwood*, '*Handbook of Moral Philosophy*,' p. 238.

It contradicts the testimony of consciousness

The primary testimony of consciousness affirms the distinct existence of an *ego* and a *non-ego*, relating to and limiting each other. I know myself as existing in the midst of certain phenomena which I did not create and can only partially control Pantheism contradicts the first element of consciousness by denying the real existence of myself.—*Mansel*, '*Metaphysics*,' p. 323.

Pantheism is inconsistent with the consciousness of self, with the belief in our personality It may seem a doctrine at once simple and sublime to represent the universe as Ἓν καὶ πᾶν, but it is inconsistent with one of the earliest and most ineradicable of our primary convictions If it can be shown that there are two or more persons, it follows that all is not one, that all is not God According to every scheme of Pantheism, I, as a part of the universe, am part of God, part of the whole which constitutes God In all consciousness of self we know ourselves as persons; in all knowledge of other objects we know them as different from ourselves, and ourselves as different from them Every man is convinced of this, no man can be made to think otherwise. If there be a God, then, as all His works proclaim, He must be different from at least one part of His works, He must be different from me —*M'Cosh*, '*Intuitions of the Mind*,' p. 453.

And is contradicted by consciousness

If there is one dream of a godless philosophy to which, beyond all others, every moment of our consciousness gives the lie, it is that which subordinates the individual to the universal, the person to the species, which regards the living and conscious man as a wave on the ocean of the unconscious infinite; his life a momentary tossing to and fro on the shifting tide; his destiny to be swallowed up in the formless and boundless universe —*Mansel*, '*Limits of Religious Thought*,' p. 62

Moral

Pantheism has only one way in which to escape from the mystery of evil, and that is to deny all distinction between right and wrong, between moral good and moral evil. Of course, there can be no such thing as sin for the pantheist, because all, according to his creed, is nature, and development, and necessity The ontology and ethics of Pantheism may be summed up in one sentence, "Whatever is, is; and there is neither right nor wrong, but all is fate and nature."—*Rigg*, '*Modern Scepticism*,' p. 70.

The Pantheistic idea of God cannot afford any support to our moral life, inasmuch as it is unable either to explain the moral law or enforce it It must lead even to the destruction of all morality The reason is this, that Pantheism (just as Materialism) is at last compelled, if consistent with its own principles, to deny the freedom of man, his responsibility, and even the distinction between good and evil, by which means all morality is done away with. According to the pantheistic view, the world is moving in a circle formed by an inexorably firm chain of cause and effects, one thing resulting from another with iron necessity. Man is no exception to this rule. He stands, according to Spinoza, as a link in the endless series of determining causes. In his spirit there is no such thing as freedom; for each act of his will is determined by some other cause, and this again by another, and so on *ad infinitum* Whatever the will does, it cannot help doing These utterances of Spinoza completely destroy all morality Whatever I do, I do it of necessity, and so it is right, seemly, and profitable for the whole!—*Christlieb, 'Modern Doubt,'* p. 185.

Pantheism abolishes the very postulates of morality; for all the distinctions of good and evil are but different manifestations of one absolute principle. Consequently, they cease to be actual moral contrasts What we call evil is in truth as necessary as what we call good; how, then, can we condemn what is necessary?—*Luthardt, 'Fundamental Truths,'* p. 67.

Theological

Pantheism, a more difficult belief than Theism.

It is much simpler and easier to believe in a personal God than in such an impersonal divinity as this Protean force Every difficulty which belongs to the thought of God's existence belongs to this also This force must be self-originated; must be the source of all intelligence, though itself unintelligent; of all sympathy, although itself incapable of sympathy; must have formed the eye, though it cannot see, and the ear, though it cannot hear; must have blossomed and developed into personal intelligences, although personal intelligence is a property which cannot be attributed to it Surely no contradiction could be greater.—*Rigg, 'Modern Scepticism,'* p. 47

And reducible to Atheism

An impersonal Deity, however tricked out to usurp the attributes of the Godhead, is no God at all, but a mere blind and immovable law or destiny, with less than even the divinity of a fetish, since *that* can at least be imagined as a being who may be offended or propitiated by the worshipper. —*Mansel, 'Metaphysics,'* p. 372.

Pantheism agrees with atheism in its denial of a personal Deity. Its divinity of the universe is a divinity without will and without conscious intelligence In what respect then does Pantheism really differ from atheism? Atheism denies that in, or over, or with nature there is anything whatever besides nature. Does not Pantheism do the very same? If not, what is there, let the pantheist tell us, in nature besides nature? What sort of divinity is that which is separate from conscious intelligence and from voluntary will and power? Is it said that though there be no Deity in the universe, yet there is a harmony, a unity, an unfolding plan and purpose, which must be recognised as transcending all limitation, as unerring, inexhaustible, infinite, and therefore as divine? Let us ask ourselves what unity that can be which is above mere nature, as such, and yet stands in no relation to a personal Lord and Ruler of the Universe; what plan and purpose that can be which is the product of no intelligence, which no mind ever planned; what infinite and unerring harmony can mean, when there is no harmonist to inspire and regulate the life and movement of the whole—*Rigg, 'Modern Scepticism,'* p 41.

Pantheism annihilates religion. For its God is not a personal God, to whom I can occupy a personal relation, whom I can love, in whom I can trust, to whom I can pray, whom I may approach and address as my Friend, but only the power of necessity beneath which I must bow, the universal life in which I may lose myself—*Luthardt, 'Fundamental Truths,'* p 67.

See how much falls to the ground if the personality of God be given up In the first place, we can no longer acknowledge a creation of the world as a free act of the Divine Will; since things are 'posited in the nature of God, not in His will.' Miracles and Providence must fare in like manner, and especially the incarnation of God in Christ is left without any basis. It can no longer be looked upon as a fact which took place in this particular Individual, but only as a universal, everlasting, and daily-renewed process. There is no longer any place for the free will of man, and for the ordinary distinction between good and evil. Finally, it is patent that the immortality of man, and the continuance of personal existence after death, are ideas which must henceforth be rejected. All personal life *must* again resolve itself into the impersonal primal cause. Religion itself can no longer be considered a reality.—*Christlieb*, '*Modern Doubt*,' p. 165.

Such divinity as Pantheism can ascribe to Christ is, in point of fact, no divinity at all. When God is nature and nature is God, everything indeed is divine, but also nothing is divine; and Christ shares this phantom-divinity with the universe, nay, with the agencies of moral evil itself. In truth our God does not exist in the apprehension of Pantheistic thinkers; since, when such truths as creation and personality are denied, the very idea of God is fundamentally sapped; and although the prevailing belief of mankind may still be humoured by a discreet retention of its conventional language, the broad practical result is in reality neither more nor less than Atheism. —*Liddon*, '*Bampton Lectures*,' p. 28.

The Pantheistic idea of God labours under great difficulties. It cannot be understood how *personality* can proceed from an *impersonal* principle. We ourselves are persons, that is, we can conceive and determine ourselves; for in this personality consists. Whence then is this self-consciousness supposed to proceed, if the soul of the world, from which we ourselves have emanated, has no consciousness? Can God communicate that which he does not Himself possess, and create forms of existence which transcend His own? Can the effect contain anything which does not exist in the cause? To this one simple question no pantheist has as yet been able to give a satisfactory answer.—*Christlieb*, '*Modern Doubt*,' p. 168.

Pantheism shows us a beautiful mansion, but the sight is melancholy; we have no desire to enter the building, for it is without an inhabitant; there is no warm heart to beat, and no just mind to rule, in these large but tenantless halls. It gives us illusions which serve to alleviate nothing, to solve nothing, to illuminate nothing; they are vapours which may indeed show bright and gaudy colours when seen at a great distance, but in the bosom of which, if one enters, there is nothing but chill and gloom. —*M'Cosh*, '*Method of Divine Government*,' p. 215.

Christian Pantheism.

Christian Pantheism sees God in everything, and is taught, in part by the beauty of the world, to think of Him as the splendour of all things, gathered into unity and expanded to infinite totality. Pantheism does not mean that God is this or that, but that He is all in all. And conversely, we cannot, and ought not, to say of a mountain or a tree, or even of a good man, or of the starry heavens, that this is God. For all of these are only fragmentary phenomenal manifestations of God.

A spiritual Pantheism need not find anything incongruous in the idea of Christ's special divinity, or in the conception of a supreme manifestation of God in Him. For, as we say of scenes in nature peculiarly suggestive of the all-embracing Life that they are divinely fair, and as we say of thoughts instinct with moral grandeur that they are divinely great or good, so we must say of Him whose spiritual majesty is enthroned for ever in the gateways of eternity, 'Truly this man is the Son of God.'—*Picton*, '*Mystery of Matter*,' pp. 405, 419, 427.

Element of Truth in Pantheism.

Pantheism would never have attained to so strong a position as that which it actually holds in European as well as in Asiatic thought, unless it had embodied a great element of truth, which is too often ignored by some arid Theistic systems. To that element of truth we Christians do justice when we confess the Omnipresence and Incomprehensibility of God, and still more, when we trace the gracious consequences of His actual Incarnation in Jesus Christ. —*Canon Liddon, 'Bampton Lectures,'* p. 29

It cannot be denied that Pantheism is founded upon a great idea, an exalted sentiment; and that this idea, this sentiment, is moreover a true one, viz., that there is a unity in existence, a connection between our life and the universal life around us.—*Luthardt, 'Fundamental Truths,'* p. 66.

Unquestionably there is something true even in Pantheism. There is something grand in the idea of the *unity of all being*, and of the connection of our life with the whole life of the universe. And this fundamental view is by no means entirely unjustifiable. — *Christlieb, 'Modern Doubt,'* p. 188.

Best safeguard against Pantheism.

The doctrine of the Incarnation, as being a perpetual witness that by supernatural gift alone can God and man be united, is the best safeguard against confounding the Creator with His works. The Second Person in the Blessed Trinity, God the Word, vouchsafed to enter into relation with the beings whom He had created, through the taking of the manhood into God. Through this act the Creator and the creature were brought into relation. Thus Eternal Goodness united men by the law of love, without superseding the law of personality. So that the Deity is not lowered to the level of His works, nor the creature lifted up to the Creator; but two natures, the Infinite and the finite, have been joined together, in order that the perfections of the one might correct the deficiencies of the other. —*Wilberforce, 'Doctrine of the Holy Eucharist,'* p. 426.

Its Connection with Polytheism.

The fact that the Pantheistic view of the world is first met with among nations with polytheistic religions, such as the Hindoos and the Greeks, points to an internal relationship between Polytheism and Pantheism which is often overlooked. The two seem opposed, but, when accurately considered, they are in principle the same. Just as, *e.g.*, the ordinary Greeks believed that there was a nymph or a naiad in every tree and in every fountain, and, in addition to the Olympian gods, peopled all nature with innumerable demigods, so also in every being and in every phenomenon the Greek pantheistic philosopher saw a manifestation of the Deity. Pantheism and Polytheism are but a higher and lower form of one and the same view of the world. The former is the refined, the latter the vulgar mode of deifying nature; the former seeks after unity amid the individual phenomena, the latter stops short at and personifies them.—*Christlieb, 'Modern Doubt,'* p. 162.

Pantheism has been the prevailing Esoteric doctrine of all Paganism, and, with various modifications, the source of a great deal of ancient philosophy. Thales and the Eleatic school expressed it distinctly, and in the definite language of philosophy. There can be little doubt that it was the great doctrine revealed in the mysteries. The Egyptian Theology was plainly based upon it. It was at the root of the Polytheism of the Greeks and Romans; and their gross idolatry was probably but an outward expression of its more mystic refinements. The Brahmins and Buddhists, though exoterically gross Polytheists, are yet in their philosophy undisguised Pantheists.—*Browne, 'Thirty-nine Articles,'* p. 14.

MYSTICISM.

Definitions

A mystic—according to the Greek etymology—should signify one who is initiated into mysteries; one whose eyes are open to see things which other people cannot see. And the true mystic in all ages and countries has believed that this was the case with him. He believes that there is an invisible world as well as a visible one; so do most men; but the mystic believes also that this same invisible world is not merely a supernumerary one world more, over and above the earth on which he lives, and the stars over his head, but that it is the cause of them and the ground of them; that it was the cause of them at first, and is the cause of them now, even to the budding of every flower and the falling of every pebble to the ground; and, therefore, that, having been before this visible world, it will be after it, and endure just as real, living, and eternal, though matter were annihilated to-morrow.—*Kingsley*, '*Miscellanies*,' i. 328.

Mysticism is that system 'which, refusing to admit that we can gain truth with absolute certainty, either from sense or reason, points us to faith, feeling, or inspiration as its only valid source.'—*Morell*, '*Speculative Philosophy of Europe*,' ii. 332.

Mysticism, whether in religion or philosophy, is that form of error which mistakes for a divine manifestation the operations of a merely human faculty.—*Vaughan*, '*Hours with the Mystics*,' i. 22.

Mysticism is the *romance of religion*.—*Vaughan*, '*Hours with the Mystics*,' i. 27.

Three classes of Mysticism.

It arises—

1. When truth is supposed to be gained in pursuance of some regular law or fact of our inward sensibility; this may be variously termed a mode of faith or of intuition.

2. When truth is supposed to be gained by a fixed supernatural channel.

3. When truth is supposed to be gained by extraordinary supernatural means.—*Morell*, '*Speculative Philosophy*,' ii. 341.

Mysticism not necessarily unpractical.

The greatest and most prosperous races of antiquity—the Egyptians, Babylonians, Hindoos, Greeks—had the mystic element as strong and living in them as the Germans have now; and certainly we cannot call them unpractical people. Our forefathers were mystics for generations; they were mystics in the forests of Germany and in the dales of Norway; they were mystics in the convents and the universities of the middle ages; they were mystics, all the deepest and noblest minds of them, during the Elizabethan era.

Even now the few mystic writers of this island are exercising more influence on thought than any other men, for good or for evil. Coleridge and Alexander Knox have changed the minds, and with them the acts of thousands.—*Kingsley*, '*Miscellanies*,' i. 326.

Causes of Mysticism.

First of all, the reaction against the frigid formality of religious torpor; then heart-weariness, the languishing longing for repose,—the charm of mysticism for the selfish or the weak; and last, the desire, so strong in some minds, to pierce the barriers that hide from man the unseen world—the charm of mysticism for the ardent and strong.—*Vaughan*, '*Hours with the Mystics*,' i. 28.

Jacob Bohme, his life and doctrines.

The most profound, and at the same time the most unaffected of all the mystics of the sixteenth century, was Jacob Bohme, who was born in 1575, and who died in 1624. He was a poor shoemaker of Gorlitz, without any literary attainments, for which reason he remained for a long time in obscurity, occupied solely with two studies, which every Christian and every man may always pursue, the study of nature ever spread out before his eyes, and that of the sacred Scriptures. He is called the Teutonic philosopher. He wrote a multitude of works, which afterwards became the gospel of mysticism. One of the most celebrated, published in 1612, is called 'Aurora.' The fundamental points of the doctrine of Bohme are—1st, the impossibility of arriving at truth by any other process than illumination; 2d, a theory of the creation; 3d, the relations of man to God; 4th, the essential identity of the soul and of God, and the determination of their difference as to form; 5th, the origin of evil; 6th, the reintegration of the soul; 7th, a symbolical exposition of Christianity.—*Cousin*, '*Hist. of Phil.*,' ii 59, 60

Emanuel Swedenborg

The doctrine of Correspondence is the central idea of Swedenborg's system. Everything visible has belonging to it an appropriate spiritual reality. The history of man is an acted parable; the universe, a temple covered with hieroglyphics. Behmen, from the light which flashes on certain exalted moments, imagines that he receives the key to these hidden significances,—that he can interpret the *Signatura Rerum*. But he does not see spirits, or talk with angels. According to him, such communications would be less reliable than the intuition he enjoyed. Swedenborg takes opposite ground. 'What I relate,' he would say, 'comes from no such mere inward persuasion. I recount the things I have seen. I do not labour to recall and to express the manifestation made me in some moment of ecstatic exaltation. I write you down a plain statement of journeys and conversations in the spiritual world, which have made the greater part of my daily history for many years together. I take my stand upon experience. I have proceeded by observation and induction as strict as that of any man of science among you. Only it has been given to me to enjoy an experience reaching into two worlds—that of spirit as well as that of matter.'

A mysticism like that of Swedenborg clothes every spiritual truth in some substantial envelope, and discerns a habitant spirit in every variety of form.—*Vaughan*, '*Hours with the Mystics*,' ii. 321.

The faith of the new heaven and the new church.

It is called the faith of the new heaven and the new church, because heaven, which is the abode of angels, and the church, which is constituted by men on earth, are one in operation, like the internal and external of man. Hence every member of the church, who is in the good of love derived from the truths of faith, and in the truths of faith derived from the good of love, is, with regard to the interiors of his mind, an angel of heaven; and therefore after death he enters into heaven, and enjoys happiness therein, according to the state of the conjunction subsisting between his love and faith.—*Swedenborg*, '*True Christian Religion*,' 1.

GNOSTICISM.

Hegel.

General statement.

Hegelianism is the Philosophy that professes to have rid the earth for ever of the fancied necessity of Agnosticism as to all that lies beyond the commencement of perceptibility, and to have brought the Absolute strictly within ken. This it does through its famous principle of the identity of Knowing and Being, held no longer as a postulate, or act of faith, or intellectual intuition, as it was in Schelling's preparatory theory, but as, by Hegelian demonstration, a fact. By this principle the rule of the Thinking Microcosm called Mind is the rule of the Universal Macrocosm or All of Existence; nay, the All of Being is reproduced in every atom of Thinking Self-consciousness is the Absolute in miniature; nay, every throb of self-consciousness, every minutest act of thought, is a nerve of the Absolute, in which the whole substance of the Absolute is repeated in reduction, and may be thoroughly studied.—*Masson*, '*Recent British Philosophy*,' pp 294, 295

The Hegelian system was the first attempt to display the organisation of thought, pure and entire, as a whole and in all its details. This organisation of thought, as the living reality or gist of the external world and the world within us, is termed the Idea. The Idea is the 'reality' and the 'ideality' of the world or totality, considered as a process beyond time. The reality because every element is expressly included. The ideality because whatever is has been denuded of its immediacy, crushed in the winepress, and only the spirit remains.

In the study of mind and its works, such

as the State, Art, and Religion, as well as in the study of Nature, the several phenomena can only be successfully apprehended when they are known to evince the same real development as in the abstract medium of thought. Classes of living beings, and faculties of mind, instead of being treated in co-ordination on one level, are looked at as successive points emphasised and defined in the course of development.

The whole of Philosophic Science is divided into three heads. Logic, the Philosophy of Nature, and the Philosophy of Mind. The first branch might also be termed Metaphysics; the second is a systematic arrangement of the several Physical Sciences and their results; the third includes anthropology and psychology, as well as the theory of Ethics and Jurisprudence, the Philosophy of Art, of History, and of Religion.—*Wallace, 'Logic of Hegel,'* Proleg clxxv.

The Universe as Thought.

Thought is the real contents of the universe: in Nature it is but as other, and in a system as other, in Spirit it returns from Nature, its other, into its own self, is by its own self, and is its own energy. The Absolute Spirit, then, God, is the first and last, and the universe is but His difference and system of differences, in which individual subjectivities have but their part and place. Subjectivity, however, is the principle of central energy and life,—it is the Absolute Form. The thought of subjectivity, again, that is, the thought it thinks, just amounts to the whole system of objective notions which are in the absolute contents. Thus is man, as participant in the absolute form and the absolute matter, raised to that likeness to God of which the Bible speaks; but God Himself is not detracted from or rendered superfluous. Pantheism is true of Hegel's system, just as it is true of all others, Christianity and Materialism included, and there is nothing in the system to disprove or discountenance a personal God, but on the contrary.—*Sterling, 'Secret of Hegel,'* i. 165.

Being and not-Being.

'Being and not-Being are identical' This mysterious utterance of Hegel, round which so much controversy has waged, and which has seemed to many but a caprice of metaphysics run mad, does not mean that Being and not-Being are not also distinguished, but it does mean that the distinction is not absolute, and that, if it is made absolute, at that very moment it disappears. The whole truth, therefore, cannot be expressed either by the simple statement that Being and not-Being are identical, or by the simple statement that they are different. But the consideration of what these abstractions are in themselves, when we isolate them from each other, just as a scientific man might isolate a special element in order to find the essential relativity or energy that lies in it, shows that their truth is not *either* their identity or their difference, but is their *identity in difference*.—*Caird, 'Hegel,'* pp. 162, 163.

'Being makes the beginning.'

When we begin to think, we have nothing but thought in its merest indeterminateness and absence of specialisation; for we cannot specialise unless there is both one and another, and in the beginning there is yet no other. The indeterminate, as we have it, is a primary and underived absence of characteristics; not the annihilation or elimination of all character, but the original and underived indeterminateness, which is previous to all definite character and is the very first of all. And this is what we call Being. It is not something felt, or perceived by spiritual sense, or pictured in imagination; it is only and merely thought, and as such it forms the beginning.—*Hegel's 'Logic'* (Wallace's transl.), p. 136.

Development from Kant to Hegel.

The metaphysical position of Hegel may be summarily distinguished from that of Kant, by saying that in the later philosophy thought is recognised as absolute or self-conditioning—as the unity in other words, within which all oppositions are only relative Thought is, therefore, the source of all the distinctions which make up the knowable universe—even of the distinction between the individual self and the objective world to which it is related Thought itself becomes the object of philosophy, and the search for something 'real,' beyond and apart from thought is definitely abandoned The business of philosophy is henceforth the explication of the distinctions which belong to the nature of thought, and this is otherwise definable for Hegel as the 'Explication of God.'—*Seth, 'From Kant to Hegel,'* pp. 145, 146

Hegel's Philosophy of Religion.

God is recognised, Hegel says, 'not as a Spirit beyond the stars, but as spirit in all spirits;' and so the course of human history is frankly identified with the course of divine self-revelation. The culmination of this religious development is reached in Christianity, and Christianity reveals nothing more than that God is essentially this revelation of Himself In this connection it is that a new significance is given to the doctrine of the Trinity, which thereby becomes fundamental for the Hegelian Philosophy of Religion This attitude towards the course of history, and towards Christianity in particular, is the only one which is permissible to an absolute philosophy However fenced about with explanations, the thesis of such a philosophy must always be—'The actual is the rational.'—*Seth, 'From Kant to Hegel,'* p. 166.

Hegelianism in Britain

Hegelianism, more or less, modified or unmodified, is now running its course rather briskly in Britain In 1865 we had to name Dr Hutchison Stirling as the solitary British Hegelian,—substantially the first importer of Hegelianism or any adequate knowledge of Hegel into the British Islands. But Dr. Stirling does not now stand alone. There have been recent translations from Hegel and commentaries on Hegel besides his; Hegelianism, or a Hegelian vein of thought, appears strongly in several of the recent British philosophical treatises reckoned among the most important, or lies yet half announced in British thinkers of known promise; and it is within my cognisance that not a few of the young men of the English and Scottish universities are at present discontented with the old native cisterns, and trying, directly or indirectly, what they can make of Hegel.—*Masson, 'Recent British Philosophy,'* pp 295, 296

B.—PSYCHOLOGY AND PHILOSOPHY OF FEELING.

XIV.

CHARACTER AND LAWS OF FEELING AS DISTINCT FROM KNOWING.

Meaning of the Word.

The expression *feeling*, like all others of a psychological application, was primarily of a purely physical relation, being originally employed to denote the sensations we experience through the sense of Touch, and in this meaning it still continues to be employed. From this, its original relation to matter and the corporeal sensibility, it came by a very natural analogy to express our conscious states of mind in general, but particularly in relation to the qualities of pleasure and pain, by which they are characterised. Such is the fortune of the term in English; and precisely similar is that of the cognate term *Gefuhl* in German. The same, at least a similar, history might be given of the Greek term *αἴσθησις*, and of the Latin *sensus, sensatio*, with their immediate and mediate derivatives in the different Romanic dialects of modern Europe—the Italian, Spanish, French, and English dialects.—*Hamilton*, '*Metaphysics*,' ii. 419

Definition and Description of Feeling.

By feeling is meant any state of consciousness which is pleasurable or painful. The feelings are pleasures and pains of various sorts, agreeable and disagreeable states of mind. Every feeling is either pleasurable or painful, agreeable or disagreeable, in some degree. At the same time, there are many mixed states of feeling, such as grief, anger, and so on, which are partly the one and partly the other, and it is sometimes difficult to say which element preponderates.

In the second place, feeling includes pleasures and pains of all kinds. Thus the term covers, first of all, those simple mental effects which are the direct result of nerve-stimulation, and which are commonly marked off as 'sensations' of pleasure and pain, such as the pains of hunger and thirst, and the corresponding pleasure. In the second place, the term feeling comprehends the more complex effects which depend on mental activity of some kind, and which are marked off as emotions, such as fear, hope, admiration, and regret. —*Sully*, '*Outlines of Psychology*,' pp. 449, 450.

Positively, Feeling comprehends pleasures and pains, and states of excitement that are neither. Negatively, it is opposed to Volition and to Intellect.—*Bain*, '*Mental Science*,' p. 215

Characters of Feeling.

The characters of Feeling are—(1) Those of Feeling proper (Emotional); (2) those referring to the Will (Volitional); (3) those bearing upon Thought (Intellectual); and (4) certain mixed properties, including Forethought, Desire, and Belief.—*Bain*, '*Mental Science*,' p. 217.

Fundamental Character of Feeling

Not recognised by ancient philosophers.

Until a very recent epoch, the feelings were not recognised by any philosopher as the manifestations of any fundamental power. The distinction taken in the Peripatetic school, by which the mental modifications were divided into Gnostic or Cognitive, and Orectic or Appetent, and the consequent reduction of all the faculties to the *Facultas cognoscendi* and the *Facultas appetendi*, was the distinction which was long most universally prevalent, though under various, but usually less appropriate, denominations.—*Hamilton*, '*Metaphysics*,' ii. 415.

The ancient division (of mental phenomena) as fixed by Aristotle was a bipartite or twofold one, intellect and will, or, according to Aristotle, thought (νοῦς) and desire (ὄρεξις). This remained the customary division in the Middle Ages. It survives in the classification of Reid, (1) Intellectual Powers and (2) Active Powers. Here feeling is subsumed under one or both of the other divisons.—*Sully*, '*Psychology*,' p. 687

Introduced by German psychologists.

J. N. Zetens (1736–1805) 'was the first to co-ordinate feeling as a fundamental faculty with the understanding and the will, but he included in "feeling," as the receptive faculty, not only pleasure and pain, but also the sensuous perceptions and the "affections" or impressions which the mind produces on itself.'—*Ueberweg*, '*Hist. of Phil.*,' ii. 119.

It remained for Kant to establish, by his authority, the decisive trichotomy of the mental powers. In his *Critique of Judgment* ('Kritik der Urtheilskraft'), and, likewise, in his *Anthropology*, he treats of the capacities of Feeling apart from, and along with, the faculties of Cognition and Conation.—*Hamilton, 'Metaphysics,'* ii. 416.

But not admitted by all philosophers.

Supposing it to be allowed that feeling, intellect, and volition are perfectly distinct groups of mental states, there remains the question whether they are equally fundamental, primordial, or independent. This question has been answered in different ways. Thus Leibnitz, Wolff, Herbart and his followers, regard intellect or the power of presentation (Wolff's *vis repræsentiva*) as the fundamental one out of which the others are derived. Hamilton, who strongly insists on the generic distinctness of the three classes, feeling, knowing, and willing, goes a certain way in the same direction when he says that 'the faculty of knowledge is certainly the first in order, inasmuch as it is the *conditio sine qua non* of the others.' By this he means that we have only feelings or desires in so far as we are conscious of them, and that consciousness is knowledge.—*Sully, 'Psychology,'* p. 68.

Relation of Feeling to Knowing.

I am able to discriminate in consciousness certain states, certain qualities of mind, which cannot be reduced to those either of Cognition or Conation; and I can enable others, in like manner, to place themselves in a similar position, and observe for themselves these states or qualities which I call *Feelings.*—*Hamilton, 'Metaphysics,'* ii. 420.

We find, in actual life, the Feelings intermediate between the Cognitions and the Conations, and this relative position of these several powers is necessary; without the previous cognition, there could be neither feeling nor conation; and without the previous feeling there could be no conation. Without some kind or another of complacency with an object, there could be no tendency, no protension of the mind to attain this object as an end; and we could, therefore, determine ourselves to no overt action. The mere cognition leaves us cold and unexcited; the awakened feeling infuses warmth and life into us and our action; it supplies action with an interest, and, without an interest, there is for us no voluntary action possible. Without the intervention of feeling, the cognition stands divorced from the conation, and, apart from feeling, all conscious endeavour after anything would be altogether impossible.—*Biunde, quoted by Sir W. Hamilton, 'Metaphysics,'* ii. 425, 426.

It is a Relation at once one of Mutual Opposition and of Reciprocal Aid.

In the first place, feeling and knowing are in a manner opposed. The mind cannot at the same moment be in a state of intense emotional excitement and of close intellectual application. All violent feeling takes possession of the mind, masters the attention, and precludes the due carrying out of the intellectual processes. Nice intellectual work, such as discovering unobtrusive differences or similarities among objects, or following out an intricate chain of reasoning, is impossible except in a comparatively calm state of mind. Even when there is no strong emotional agitation present, intellectual processes may be interfered with by the subtle influence of the feelings on the thoughts working in the shape of bias.

On the other hand, all intellectual activity, since it implies interest, depends on the presence of a certain moderate degree of feeling. It may be said, indeed, that all good and effective intellectual work involves the presence of a gentle wave of pleasurable emotion. Attention is more lively, images recur more abundantly, and thought traces out its relations more quickly, when there is an undercurrent of pleasure. Hence rapid intellectual progress is furthered by lively intellectual feelings.—*Sully, 'Psychology,'* pp. 451, 452.

Feeling gives Variety to Knowledge.

To each simple sensation, each colour, each tone, corresponds originally a special degree of pain or pleasure; but, accustomed as we are to note these impressions only in their significance as marks of objects, whose import and notion are of consequence to us, we observe the worth of these simple objects only when we throw ourselves with concentrated attention into their content. Every form of composition of the manifold produces in us, along with a perception, a slight impression of its agreement with the usages of our own development, and it is these often obscure feelings that give to each several object its special complexion for each several temperament, so that, with the same complement of properties for all, it yet seems to each of us different. Even the simplest and apparently driest notions are never quite destitute of this attendant feeling; we cannot grasp the conception of unity without experiencing a pleasant satisfaction that is part of its content, or that of antagonism without participating in the pain of conflictive opposition; we cannot observe in things or evolve within ourselves such conceptions as *rest*, *motion*, *equilibrium*, without throwing ourselves into them with all our living strength, and having a feeling of the kind and degree of resistance or assistance which they might bring to bear on us. A considerable part of our higher human culture is the result of this pervading presence of feelings; it is the basis of imagination, whence spring works of art, and which makes us capable of entering into natural beauty; for productive and reproductive power consists in nothing else than the delicacy of apprehension by which the mind is able to clothe the *world of values* in the *world of forms*, or to become instinctively aware of the happiness concealed under the enveloping form.—*Lotze*, '*Microcosmus*,' i. 243, 244.

But it is insufficient to constitute knowledge.

For a merely sentient being—for one who did not think upon his feelings—the oppositions of inner and outer, of subjective and objective, of fantastic and real, would not exist; but neither would knowledge or a world to be known. That such oppositions, misunderstood, may be a heavy burden on the human spirit, the experience of current controversy and its spiritual effects might alone suffice to convince us; but the philosophical deliverance can only lie in the recognition of thought as their author, not in the attempt to obliterate them by the reduction of thought and its world to feeling,—an attempt which contradicts itself, since it virtually admits their existence while it renders them unaccountable.—*Green*, '*Introduction to Hume*,' p. 142.

Ideas, such as Causation and Identity explicable only as data of Thought, not as data of sense.

Identity and Causation can only be claimed for sense, if sense is so far one with thought,—one not by conversion of thought into sense but by taking of sense into thought, as that Hume's favourite appeals to sense against the reality of intelligible relations become unmeaning. They may be 'impressions,' there may be 'impressions of them,' but only if we deny of the impression what Hume asserts of it, and assert of it what he denies; only if we understand by 'impression' *not* an 'internal and perishing existence,' *not* that which, if other than taste, colour, sound, smell, or touch, must be a 'passion or emotion,' *not* that which carries no reference to an object other than itself, and which must either be single or compound; but something permanent and constituted by permanently co-existing parts,—something that may be 'conjoined with' any feeling, because it is none, that always carries with it a reference to a subject which it is not, but of which it is a quality; and that is both many and one, since 'in its simplicity it contains many different resemblances and relations'—*Green*, '*Introduction to Hume*,' p. 239.

The Reality of Objects depends not upon Feeling, but upon the Relations which Thought prescribes.

So soon, in short, as reality is ascribed to a system, which cannot be an 'impression,' and of which consequently there annot be an 'idea,' the first principle of Hume's speculation is abandoned. The truth is implicitly recognised, that the reality of an individual object consists in that system of its relations which only exists for a conceiving, as distinct from a feeling, subject, even as the unreal has no meaning except as a confused or inadequate conception of such relations; and that thus the 'present impression' is neither real nor unreal in itself, but may be equally one or the other according as the relations, under which it is conceived by the subject of it, correspond to those by which it is determined for a perfect intelligence.—*Green, 'Introduction to Hume,'* p. 281.

Mr. Spencer maintains

That Feeling and Knowing cannot be dissociated.

In our ordinary experiences, the impossibility of dissociating the psychical states classed as intellectual from those seemingly most unlike psychical states classed as emotional, may be discerned. While we continue to compare such extreme forms of the two as an inference and a fit of anger, we may fancy that they are entirely distinct. But if we examine intermediate modes of consciousness, we shall quickly find some which are both cognitive and emotive. Take the state of mind produced by seeing a beautiful statue. Primarily, this is a co-ordination of the visual impressions which the statue gives, resulting in a consciousness of what they mean; and this we call a purely intellectual act. But usually this act cannot be performed without some pleasurable feeling of the emotional order. . . . Not only does the state of consciousness produced by a melody show us cognition and emotion inextricably entangled, but the state of conciousness produced by a single beautiful tone does so. Not only is a combination of colours, as in a landscape, productive of a pleasurable feeling beyond that due to mere sensations, but there is pleasure accompanying the perception of even one colour when of great purity or brilliance. Nay, the touch of a perfectly smooth or soft surface causes an agreeable consciousness. In all these cases the simple distinct feeling directly aroused by the outer agent, is joined with some compound vague feeling indirectly aroused.

The materials dealt with in every cognitive process are either sensations or the representations of them. These sensations, and by implication the representations of them, are habitually in some degree agreeable or disagreeable. Hence only in those rare cases in which both its terms and its remote associations are absolutely indifferent, can an act of cognition be *absolutely* free from emotion. Conversely, as every emotion involves the presentation or representation of objects and actions, and as the perceptions, and by implication the recollections, of objects and actions, all imply cognitions; it follows that no emotion can be *absolutely* free from cognition.—*Spencer, 'Principles of Psychology,'* i. 473, 474.

Feeling not produced but roused by representation.

The capacity of feeling pleasure and pain must be originally inherent in the soul; the separate events of the train of ideas, reacting on the nature of the soul, do not produce the capacity, but only rouse it to utterance . We should be by no means content to accept in place of this conviction the concession with which we might be met,—that to be sure any actual state of the train of ideas is not itself the feeling of pain or pleasure or the effort flowing from it, but yet that feeling and effort are nothing else than the forms under which that state is apprehended by consciousness. We should have, on the other side, to add that these forms of apprehension are themselves not unimportant accessories, to be referred to by the way, as merely occurring along with the facts of the train of ideas in which alone the kernel of the matter lay; on the contrary, the essential part of the phenomenon is just this mode of manifestation. It is as feelings and efforts, that feelings and efforts are of consequence in mental life, the significance of which lies not in the fact that all kinds of complications of ideas occur, of which men may incidentally become conscious under the form of feeling and effort, but in the fact that the nature of the soul renders it capable of bringing anything before itself *as* feeling and effort.—*Lotze*, '*Microcosmus*,' i. 179, 180.

Feeling regarded as the primordial type of mental manifestation.

An attempt has recently been made by Horwicz to regard it as the primordial type of mental manifestation. This assertion is based on the fact that in the early stages of mental development, both of the individual and of the animal series, the element of feeling (sense feeling) is conspicuous and predominant. To this argument Schneider replies that in the simplest sensational consciousness, there is involved a rudiment of intellection in the shape of the discrimination of a state as favourable or unfavourable.—*Sully*, '*Psychology*,' p. 688.

Development of Feeling.

An outburst of feeling passes through the stages of rise, culmination, and subsidence.

What we call a state of feeling, or emotion, is a transitory outburst from a permanent condition approaching to indifference. There is every variety of mode as respects both degree and duration. A feeble stimulus can be continued longer than a powerful one; while every intense display must be rendered short by exhaustion.

Practically, the moment of culmination of feeling, or passion, is the moment of perilous decisions and fatal mistakes.—*Bain*, '*Mental Science*,' p. 224.

The Laws of Feeling.

1. *According to James Sully.*

The Law of Stimulation or Exercise.

The principal law may be called the Law of Stimulation or the Law of Exercise. All pleasure is the accompaniment of the activity of some organ which is connected with the nerve-centres or the seat of conscious life. Or, since this activity has its physical concomitant, we may say that all pleasure is connected with the exercise of some capability, faculty, or power of the mind. And it will be found in general that all moderate stimulation of an organ, or all moderate exercise of a capability, produces pleasure.—'*Psychology*,' p. 457.

The Law of Change or Contrast.

Pleasure involves change or contrast of mental condition for a double reason: (1) because all the more powerful modes of pleasurable stimulation need to be limited in duration if they are not to fatigue and produce pain instead of pleasure; and (2) because change, variety, or contrast of impression, is a condition of that vigorous activity of attention on which all vivid states of mind depend. The greater the amount of change involved (provided it is not *violent*, that is so great and sudden as to produce the disagreeable effect of shock) the more intense in general will be the resulting pleasure.—'*Psychology*,' p. 464.

2. *According to A. Bain.*

The Law of Diffusion.

According as an impression is accompanied with Feeling, the aroused currents *diffuse* themselves freely over the brain, leading to a general agitation of the moving organs, as well as affecting the viscera.—'*Emotions, &c.*,' p. 4.

The Law of Relativity.

Change is necessary to feeling; we are unconscious of unremitted impressions; the degree of feeling is proportioned to the change; abruptness or suddenness of transition is one mode of enhancing the effect. —'*Emotions, &c.*,' p. 78.

Mutual Furtherance and Hindrance of Activities.

It follows from the close connection of the several nerve structures or organs that the condition of one affects that of the others. When the vital processes of digestion and circulation go on well the cerebral activities are furthered, the thoughts flow freely, and the mind takes on a cheerful tone. Conversely, when the mind is cheered by happy thoughts, the organic processes are promoted. On the other hand, an over-tasking or impeding of the activities of any organ, not only leads to a painful feeling in connection with that organ, but interferes with the due pleasurable exercise of the other organs. A striking example of this law is seen in the prostrating effects of intensely painful emotion as terror and passionate grief. These distressing forms of mental activity enfeeble not only the powers of the brain but those of the muscular and internal organs.—*Sully*, '*Psychology*,' pp. 471–72.

Classification of Feelings.

The division into centrally-initiated feelings, called emotions, and peripherally-initiated feelings, called sensations; and the subdivision of these last into sensations that arise on the exterior of the body and sensations that arise in its interior; respectively refer to differences among the parts in action. Whereas the division into vivid or real feelings and faint or ideal feelings, cutting across the other divisions at right angles, as we may say, refers to a difference of amount in the actions of these parts. The first classification has in view unlikeness of kind among the feelings, and the second, a marked unlikeness of degree common to all kinds.—*Spencer*, '*Principles of Psychology*,' i. 167.

Feelings of pleasure and pain fall into two main divisions, those arising immediately from a process of nervous stimulation, more particularly the excitation of sensory (incarrying) nerves, and those depending on some mode of mental activity. The first (popularly marked off as bodily feelings), as involving processes in the outlying parts of the organism, may be called peripherally excited feelings, or more briefly sense-feelings. The second, being connected with central nerve processes (in the brain), may be described as centrally excited feelings or as emotions.—*Sully*, '*Psychology*,' p. 475.

Feelings originating in the Periphery.

The peripherally-initiated feelings, or sensations, may be grouped into those which, caused by disturbances at the ends of nerves distributed on the outer surface, are taken to imply outer agencies, and those which, caused by disturbances at the ends of nerves distributed within the body, are not taken to imply outer agencies; which last, though not peripherally initiated in the ordinary sense, are so in the physiological sense. But as between the exterior of the body and its interior there are all gradations of depth, it results that this distinction is a broadly marked one, rather than a sharply marked one.—*Spencer*, '*Principles of Psychology*,' i. 166.

The sense-feelings may arise from certain changes or disturbances in some part of the organism itself. These are the organic sense-feelings, such as hunger, thirst, feelings connected with increase and decrease of temperature in the skin, &c. Since the sensations of which these feelings are the immediate accompaniments are to a large extent wanting in definiteness of character and in susceptibility of distinct localisation, the several elements of feeling are not easily distinguishable one from another.

The second group of sense-feelings consists of the pleasures and pains connected with the stimulation of the special senses. To these may be added the pleasures and pains of muscular sensation, pleasures of movement, pain of prolonged effort, and so forth. These are much more definitely distinguishable than the organic pleasures and pains, and they are susceptible of localisation.—*Sully*, '*Psychology*,' p. 476.

Their effect on the Emotional Life.

Owing to the close connection between body and mind, the organic feelings have a far-reaching effect on the higher emotional life. An uneasy attitude of body, the pressure or chafing of a garment, or the chilliness of a limb, is quite enough to depress the mental powers, to induce irritability of temper, a disposition to peevishness, and to outbreaks of angry passion. On the other hand, pleasurable states of the body lead to a cheerful, hopeful state of mind. The sum of all the imperfectly discriminated organic feelings at any time constitutes the basis of what is known as the cœnæsthesis or general feeling of well-being, or its opposite, *malaise*, which has much to do with determining the dominant mental tone or mood of cheerfulness, or depression.

Finally, the sense-feelings as a whole will be found to supply important elements out of which the emotions proper are developed. Thus fear and anger have their rise in the mental reproduction of some organic pain (*e.g.*, the effect of a burn or of a blow). So noble a feeling as love itself may have as its humble origin in the infant's mind a memory of numerous organic pleasures (satisfactions of appetites, of warmth, &c.). The pleasures of the higher senses are taken up into the emotions of beauty.—*Sully*, '*Psychology*,' pp. 477, 478.

XV.

THE EMOTIONS.

I. DEFINITIONS, CLASSIFICATIONS, &c.

Definition of Emotion.

Perhaps the nearest approach to a positive definition of the Emotions may be found in the language of Aristotle, who describes them as *those states of mind which are accompanied by pleasure or pain*, but the definition requires some explanation before it can be accepted as satisfactory. A toothache is accompanied by pain; but a toothache is not an emotion. The pursuit and acquisition of knowledge is a source of pleasure: but neither the pursuit nor the acquisition can be classed among the emotions. The *desire* of knowledge, and the *pleasure* which it imparts, are emotions: the act of pursuit and the state of possession are not so. We may, with tolerable accuracy, define the emotions or passions as *those states of mind which consist in the consciousness of being affected agreeably or disagreeably*.—*Mansel*, '*Metaphysics*,' p. 152.

Susceptibility is the capacity of the mind to be affected, in the way of pleasure or pain, by that which is before it. An emotion is the thrill or flutter of excitement which attends almost every object of experience or consideration. It stands to the estimate we spontaneously form of the object in much the same relation as the sensation to the perception of the same. It is a rude stroke, felt, but not yet fully construed by the mind. It is the emotional, as distinguished from the sensible feeling of the object.—*Murphy*, '*Human Mind*,' p. 169.

Analysis of Emotion.

Four persons of very much the same age and temperament are travelling in the same vehicle. At a particular stopping-place it is announced to them that a certain individual has just died suddenly and unexpectedly. One of the company looks perfectly stolid, a second comprehends what has taken place, but is in no way affected; the third looks and evidently feels sad; the fourth is overwhelmed with grief, which finds expression in tears, sobs, and exclamations. Whence the difference of the four individuals before us? In one respect they are all alike,—an announcement has been made to them. The first is a foreigner, and has not understood the communication. The second had never met with the deceased, and could have no special regard for him. The third had often met with him in social intercourse and business transactions, and been led to cherish a great esteem for him. The fourth was the brother of the departed, and was bound to him by native affection and a thousand interesting ties, earlier and later. From such a case we may notice that in order to emotion there is need, first, of some understanding or apprehension. The foreigner had no feeling, because he had no idea or belief. We may observe further that there must be, secondly, an affection of some kind, for the stranger was not interested in the occurrence. The emotion flows forth from a well, and it is strong in proportion to the waters,—is stronger in the brother than in the friend. It is evident, thirdly, that the persons affected are in a moved or excited state. A fourth peculiarity has appeared in the sadness of the countenance and the agitations of the bodily frame. Four elements have thus come forth to view.

First, there is the affection, or what I prefer calling the motive principle, or the appetence. In the illustrative case, there are the love of a friend and the love of a brother. But the appetence, to use the most unexceptionable phrase, may consist of an immense number and variety of other motive principles, such as the love of pleasure, the love of wealth, or revenge, or moral approbation. These appetences may be original, such as the love of happiness; or they may be acquired, such as the love of money, or of retirement, or of paintings, or of articles of *vertu*, or of dress. These moving powers are at the basis of all emotion. Without the fountain there can be no flow of waters.

Secondly, there is an idea of something, of some object or occurrence, as fitted to gratify or disappoint a motive principle or appetence. When the friend and brother of the departed did not know of the occurrence, they were not moved. But as soon as the intelligence was conveyed to them and they realised the death, they were filled with sorrow. The idea is thus an essential element in all emotion. But ideas of every kind do not raise emotion. The stranger had a notion of a death having occurred, but was not moved. The idea excited emotion in the breasts of those who had the affection, because the event apprehended disappointed one of the cherished appetences of their minds.

Thirdly, there is the conscious feeling. The soul is in a moved or excited state,—hence the phrase emotion. Along with this there is an attraction or repulsion: we are drawn toward the objects that we love, that is, for which we have an appetence, and driven away from those which thwart the appetence. To use looser phraseology, we cling to the good, and we turn away from the evil. This excitement, with the attractions and repulsions, is the conscious element in the emotion. Yet it all depends on the two other elements, on the affection and the idea of something fitted to gratify or disappoint it.

Fourthly, there is an organic affection. The seat of it seems to be somewhere in the cerebrum, whence it influences the nervous centres, producing soothing or exciting and at times exasperating results. This differs widely in the case of different individuals. Some are hurried irresistibly into violent expressions or convulsions. Others, feeling no less keenly, may appear outwardly calm, because restrained by a strong will; or they may feel repressed and oppressed till they have an outlet in some natural flow or outburst. But it is to be observed that this organic affection is not the primary nor the main element in anything that deserves the name of emotion.—*M'Cosh, 'The Emotions,'* pp. 1–3.

Classification of Emotions.

According to their quality.

An eminent modern philosopher [Jouffroy] has observed that there are, strictly speaking, but two passions,—the one arising from the consciousness of pleasure, manifesting itself in the successive stages of joy, love, and desire; the other arising from the consciousness of pain, and exhibiting the successive forms of grief, hate, and aversion. The various subdivisions of these two classes are, properly, not so much distinctions in the nature of the emotion itself as in that of the objects upon which it is exercised.—*Mansel*, '*Metaphysics*,' p. 154.

Emotions are of three kinds, some of them agreeable, some disagreeable, and some indifferent. The agreeable and disagreeable may be said to be of one genus, running through all possible degrees, from the highest intensity of the agreeable to the like extreme of the disagreeable.—*Murphy*, '*Human Mind*,' p. 169.

Some emotions are not immediately connected with outward action, while others are. Of the first sort are simple Joy and Grief, Cheerfulness, Melancholy, Beauty, Sublimity, &c. These, like every feeling, nay, like every thought, *may* lead to outward action; but they may not, and they never immediately precede it; whereas Desire and Fear, in some form or other, directly urge to action, and when this takes place they are always the immediate antecedents. This distinction seems sufficiently well defined and sufficiently important for the purposes of classification.

Agreeably to this view, our primary division will be into the PASSIVE and the ACTIVE emotions.—*Ramsay*, '*Analysis of the Emotions*,' p. 2.

As they proceed from simple to complex.

Herbert Spencer.

Feelings are divisible into four subclasses.

Presentative feelings, ordinarily called sensations, are those mental states in which, instead of regarding a corporeal impression as of this or that kind, or as located here or there, we contemplate it in itself as pleasure or pain; as, when inhaling a perfume.

Presentative-representative feelings, embracing a great part of what we commonly call emotions, are those in which a sensation or group of sensations, or group of sensations and ideas, arouses a vast aggregation of represented sensations; partly of individual experience, but chiefly deeper than individual experience, and consequently indefinite.

Representative feelings, comprehending the ideas of the feelings above classed, when they are called up apart from the appropriate external excitements. Instances of these are the feelings with which the descriptive poet writes, and which are aroused in the minds of his readers.

Re-representative feelings, under which head are included those more complex sentient states that are less the direct results of external excitements than the indirect or reflex results of them.—'*Principles of Psychology*,' ii. 514.

Professor Bain.

We cannot, in classifying the emotions, comply with the rules of logical division. The nature of the case admits of but one method—to proceed from the simpler to the more complex.

The arrangement is as follows:—

1. Emotions of Relativity: Novelty, Wonder, Liberty.
2. Emotion of Terror.
3. Tender Emotion: Love, Admiration, Reverence, Esteem.
4. Emotions of Self: Self-gratulation, Self-esteem, Love of Approbation.
5. Emotion of Power.
6. Irascible Emotion—Anger.
7. Emotions of Action—Pursuit.
8. Emotions of Intellect.
9. Æsthetic Emotions.
10. The Moral Sense.—'*Mental Science*,' p. 227, 228.

Spinoza's Enumeration of the Emotions.

1. Desire. 2. Pleasure. 3. Pain. 4. Wonder. 5. Contempt. 6. Love. 7. Hate. 8. Inclination. 9. Aversion. 10. Devotion. 11. Derision. 12. Hope. 13. Fear. 14.

Confidence 15. Despair. 16 Joy 17. Disappointment (or grief). 18. Pity 19 Approval. 20. Indignation. 21. Over-esteem. 22. Disparagement. 23. Envy. 24. Mercy (or goodwill). 25. Self-contentment. 26. Humility. 27. Repentance 28. Pride. 29. Dejection. 30. Honour. 31. Shame. 32. Regret. 33. Emulation. 34. Thankfulness. 35 Benevolence 36. Anger 37. Revenge. 38. Cruelty. 39. Fear. 40 Daring. 41. Cowardice 42 Consternation. 43. Civility (or deference). 44. Ambition 45. Luxury 46 Drunkenness. 47. Avarice 48 Lust.—*Pollock's* '*Spinoza*,' ch. vii.

J. H Godwin.

1 *Simple Emotions.*

Joy, Grief, Surprise, Wonder.

2. *Propensities and Passions.*

Desires, Aversions, Hope, Fear.
Primary and Secondary.

3 *Social Affections.*

Pleasant and Attractive, Painful and Repulsive.
Composite Affections.

4 *Other Affections.*

Reflective, Religious, Indefinite (æsthetic).—'*Active Principles*,' p. 6.

In their relation to Time.

The Emotions are classed by Thomas Brown as Immediate, Retrospective, and Prospective. The immediate emotions are subdivided into those which do not, and those which do, involve moral affections. Under the first are Cheerfulness and Melancholy, Wonder at what is strange, Languor at what is tedious, Beauty and Deformity, Sublimity, Ludicrousness. Under the second are feelings distinctive of Vice and Virtue, Love and Hate, Sympathy, Pride and Humility. The Retrospective Emotions having relations to others are Anger and Gratitude. The Retrospective Emotions which have reference to ourselves are Regret and its opposite, and Remorse and its opposite The Prospective Emotions comprehend the desire for Continued Existence, the desire of Pleasure, the desire of Action, the desire of Society, the desire of Knowledge, the desire of Power, in the two forms of Ambition and of Power, the desire of Affection of others, the desire of Glory, the desire of the Happiness of others, the desire of Evil to others.—*Ueberweg*, '*Hist. of Phil.*,' ii. 413.

Sources of Emotion.

Mental representations.

The idea which calls forth emotion is of an object fitted to gratify or to disappoint an appetence of the mind The mere existence of the appetence as a tendency or disposition is not sufficient to call forth feeling, though I have no doubt it is ever prompting it, or rather by the law of association stirring up the idea which gives it a body. There must always be an idea carrying out the appetence to call the emotion into actual exercise. If the object be before us, of course we have a perception of it by the senses, or we are conscious of it within our minds If it be not present we have a remembrance of it, or we have formed an imagination of it That object may be mental or material, may be real or imaginary, may be in the past, the present, or the future; but there must always be a representation of it in the mind Let a man stop himself at the time when passion is rolling like a river, he will find that the idea is the channel in which it flows. An idea is as much needed as a pipe is to conduct gas and enable it to flame; shut up the conduit and the feeling will be extinguished.—*M'Cosh*, '*The Emotions*,' p. 42

Working through association.

An idea which has no emotion attached may come notwithstanding to raise up feeling through the idea with which it is associated, and which never can come without sentiment Thermopylæ, Bannockburn, and Waterloo look uninteresting enough places to the eye, and to those who may be ignorant of the scenes transacted there;

but the spots and the very names stir up feeling like a war-trumpet in the breasts of all who know that freedom was there delivered from menacing tyranny Thus it is that the buds and blossoms of spring, and the prattle of boys and girls, call forth a hope as fresh and lively as they themselves are. Thus it is that the leaves of autumn, gorgeous though they be in colouring, and the graveyard where our forefathers sleep, clothed though it be all over with green grass, incline to musing and to sadness.—*M'Cosh*, '*Intuitions, &c*,' p 323.

But not through abstract truths.

It may be doubted whether any abstract truth or general principle is fitted to kindle emotion. Analysis and classification are intended to deepen and amplify our intellectual conceptions, but are by no means fitted to rouse feeling It is not by dwelling on the grand ideas of the lovely and the good that sentiment is evoked, but by the contemplation of a lovely object or a good individual These ideas may serve to widen our views and raise our minds above a weak superstition, but they are not fitted nor intended by Him who hath given us the capacity to form them, to create and cherish affection in our bosoms.—*M'Cosh*, '*Intuitions, &c*,' p. 405.

Manifestation of Emotion

How the strength of Emotion is determined.

It is always to be taken into account that the emotive susceptibility is naturally stronger in some minds than in others, is stronger at one period of life, or even one day or hour, than another; but making due allowance for this variable element, the intensity of feeling is determined by the strength of the motive principle, its native strength or its acquired strength, and by the extent of the appetible or inappetible embraced within the mental apprehension of the object or end fitted to gratify or disappoint the appetency There are thus three elements determining the emotion, and these varying in the case of different individuals, and of the same individual at different times. There is the emotional susceptibility, depending largely on the state of the brain or particular organs of it. There is the mental appetency, natural or acquired. There is the mental apprehension of an object or event as tending to content or gratify the appetence.—*M'Cosh*, '*Intuitions, &c*.,' p. 248

Influence of Emotion on the body.

The powerful part which the passions were intended to act in our constitution, is clearly evinced by those rapid and dreadful effects which they frequently commit upon the body. Instances are very numerous of persons who have been driven mad by joy,—who have dropped down dead from anger or grief. Great numbers of people die every year, pining away from deranged circumstances, or from disgrace, or disappointed affection, in a state which we call broken-hearted. The passions kill like acute diseases, and like chronic ones too Every physician who knows anything of the science, has seen innumerable cases of all the disorders of the body, originating from disturbed emotion, and totally inaccessible to all the remedies by which mere animal infirmities are removed.—*Smith*, '*Moral Philosophy*,' p 336.

Influence of Emotion on the organic functions.

The secretion of Tears, which is continually being formed to an extent sufficient to lubricate the surface of the eyes, is poured out in great abundance under the moderate excitement of the emotions, either of joy, tenderness, or grief. It is checked, however, by violent grief; and it is a well-known indication of moderated sorrow, when tears 'come to the relief' of the sufferer.

So, the Salivary secretion may be suspended by strong emotion: a fact of which advantage is taken in India for the discovery of a thief among the servants of a family, each of them being required to hold a certain quantity of rice in his mouth during a few minutes, and the offender being generally distinguished by the dryness of his mouthful.

That the gastric secretion may be entirely suspended by powerful emotion, clearly appears as well from the results of experiments on animals, as from the well-known influence exerted by a sudden mental shock (whether painful or pleasurable) in dissipating the appetite for food, and in suspending the digestive process when in active operation.—*Carpenter*, '*Mental Physiology*,' pp. 677, 678.

While we cannot at present specify scientifically the precise influence exercised on the body by the various kinds of emotion, we can enumerate a few laws, chiefly of an empirical character, but full of interest and importance

The emotions through the nerves act particularly on the heart and lungs, and thence on the organs of breathing, the nerves of which spread over the face, which may thus reveal the play of feeling Every sudden emotion quickens the action of the heart and consequently the respiration, which may produce involuntary motions. If our organs of respiration and circulation had been different, our expression would also have been different. 'Dr. Beaumont had the opportunity of experimenting for many months on a person whose stomach was exposed to inspection by accident, and he states that mental emotion invariably produced indigestion and disease of the lining membrane of the stomach—a sufficient demonstration of the direct manner in which the mind may disorder the blood.'[1] Certain emotions, such as sudden fear, increase the peristaltic action, whereas anxiety and grief diminish it. Sorrow of every kind, sympathy, and pity act on the bowels. All strong passions are apt to make the muscles tremble; this is especially the case with all aggravated forms of fear, with terror and rage, but is also so with anger, and even joy The action of the heart is increased by anger. In fear, the blood is not transferred with the usual force Settled malice and envy give rise to jaundice, it is said, by causing the matter secreted to be reabsorbed into the capillary blood-vessels of the liver, instead of being carried out by the branches of the bile-duct. The idea of the ludicrous raises a mental emotion which bursts out in laughter, grief finds an outlet in tears Complacency with those we converse with is manifested in smiles. We read, in various languages, of lightness of heart, of the paleness of fear, of the breathlessness of surprise, of the trembling with passion, of bowels of compassion, of the jaundiced eye of envy, and all these figures embody truths recognised in universal experience It is a curious circumstance that young infants do not shed tears, though they utter screams and fall into convulsions. These last are the effects of pain, but they do not shed tears till they have an emotion, with its idea of the appetible and inappetible.—*M'Cosh*, '*The Emotions*,' p 91.

[1] Moore on 'The Power of the Soul over the Body,' pt. iii. ch. viii.

Emotions regarded as restraints upon action.

Besides the restraint upon activity, arising (1) from the natural laws of exercise, and (2) from the application of moral law, there are certain natural forces whose primary, though not exclusive, function it is to restrain from action These are Emotions, of which the chief are Wonder, Grief, and Fear.—*Calderwood*, '*Moral Philosophy*,' p 161.

The muscular expression of Emotion.

Visible muscular expression is to passion what language or audible muscular expression is to thought. Bacon rightly, therefore, pointed out the advantage of a study of the forms of expression. 'For,' he says, 'the lineaments of the body do disclose the disposition and inclination of the mind in general; but the motions of the countenance and facts do not only so, but do further disclose the present humour and state of the mind or will' The muscles of the countenance are the chief exponents of human feeling, much of the variety of which is due to the action of the orbicular muscles with the system of elevating and depressing muscles. The manifold shades and kinds of expression which the lips present—the gibes, gambols, and flashes of merriment; the quick language of a quivering nostril, the varied waves and ripples of beautiful emotion which play on the human countenance, with the spasms of passion that disfigure it—all which we take such pains to embody in art—are simply effects of muscular action. —*Maudsley*, '*Mind and Body*,' p 28

The close connection between mind and body is nowhere more plainly illustrated than in the correlation between states of feeling and certain bodily accompaniments Feeling is accompanied by well-marked physical changes, including those external manifestations which are commonly called expression, facial movements, gestures, modifications of vocal utterance, &c, together with certain internal organic effects. Pleasure and pain, and to some extent the several kinds of pleasurable or painful feelings, as anger, fear, love, reverence, have their distinct or characteristic expression —*Sully*, '*Psychology*,' p 454

Mr Darwin, by his own observations, and by the answers given to queries which he issued as to the various races of mankind, especially those who have associated but little with Europeans, seems to have established the following points, some of them, perhaps, only provisionally and partially. Astonishment is expressed by the eyes and mouth being opened wide, and by the eyebrows being raised. Shame excites a blush when the colour of the skin allows it to be visible When a man is indignant or defiant he frowns, holds his body and head erect, squares his shoulders, and clenches his fists When considering deeply on any subject, or trying to understand any puzzle, he is apt to frown and wrinkle the skin beneath the lower eyelids When in low spirits the corners of the mouth are depressed, and the inner corner of the eyebrows are raised by that muscle which the French call the "grief muscle" The eyebrow in this state becomes slightly oblique, with a little swelling at the inner end, and the forehead is transversely wrinkled in the middle part, but not across the whole breadth, as when the eyebrows are raised in surprise. When persons are in good spirits the eyes sparkle, the skin is a little wrinkled round and under them, and the mouth a little drawn back at the corners. When a man sneers or snarls at another the corner of the upper lip over the canine or eye tooth is raised on the side facing the man whom he addresses A dogged or obstinate expression may often be recognised, being chiefly shown by the mouth being firmly closed, by a lowering brow, and a slight frown. Contempt is expressed by a slight protrusion of the lips and by turning up the nose with a slight expiration Disgust is shown by the lower lip being turned down, the upper lip slightly raised, with a sudden expiration something like incipient vomiting, or like something spit out of the mouth Laughter may be carried to such an extreme as to bring tears into the eyes. When a man wishes to show that he cannot prevent something being done, or cannot himself do something, he is apt to shrug his shoulders, turn inwards his elbows, extend outwards his hands, and open the palms, with the eyebrows raised. Children when sulky are disposed to pout, or greatly protrude the lips. The head is nodded vertically in affirmation, and shaken laterally in negation —*M'Cosh*, '*The Emotions*,' p 95

The feelings have in common the character that they cause bodily action which is violent in proportion as they are intense We have the set teeth, distorted features, and clenched hands accompanying bodily pain, as well as those accompanying rage There is a tearing of the hair from fury as well as despair. There are the dancings of joy, as well as the stampings of anger There is the restlessness of moral distress, and there is the inability to sit still which ecstasy produces —*Spencer*, '*Psychology*,' ii. 541.

The emotional manifestations are often complicated by restraints intentionally put on the actions of the external organs, for the purpose of hiding or disguising the feelings. The secondary feelings prompting this concealment have a natural language of their own; which in some cases is easily read even by those of ordinary intelligence, and is read by those of quick insight in cases where it is comparatively unobtrusive. Some of the most common are those in which the hands play a part. Often an agitation not clearly shown in the face is betrayed by fumbling movements of the fingers—perhaps in twisting or untwisting the corner of an apron. Or again, a state of *mauvaise honte*, otherwise tolerably well concealed, is indicated by an obvious difficulty in finding fit positions for the hands. Similarly pain or anger, the ordinary signs of which are consciously suppressed, may be indicated by a clenching of the fingers.—*Spencer*, '*Psychology*,' p. 551.

Theories of the expression of Emotion

Sir C. Bell

If we attend to the evidence of the anatomical investigation, we shall perceive a remarkable difference between the provision for giving motion to the features in animals and that for bestowing expression in man. In the lower creatures there is no expression but what may be referred, more or less plainly, to their acts of volition or necessary instincts; while in man there seems to be a special apparatus for the purpose of enabling him to communicate with his fellow-creatures by that natural language which is read in the changes of his countenance. There exist in his face not only all those parts, which by their action produce expression in the several classes of quadrupeds, but there is added a peculiar set of muscles to which no other office can be assigned than to serve for expression.—'*Anatomy of Expression*,' p. 113.

Spencer

Every feeling, peripheral or central, sensational or emotional, is the concomitant of a nervous disturbance and resulting nervous discharge, that has on the body both a special effect and a general effect.

The general effect is this. The molecular motion disengaged in any nerve-centre by any stimulus tends ever to flow along lines of least resistance throughout the nervous system, exciting other nerve-centres and setting up other discharges. The feelings of all orders, moderate as well as strong, which from instant to instant arise in consciousness, are the correlatives of nerve-waves continually being generated and continually reverberating throughout the nervous system,—the perpetual nervous discharge constituted by these perpetually generated waves affecting both the viscera and the muscles, voluntary and involuntary.

At the same time, every particular kind of feeling, sensational or emotional, being located in a specialised nervous structure that has relations to special parts of the body, tends to produce on the body an effect that is special. The speciality may be very simple and constant, as in a sneeze, or it may be much involved and variable within wide limits, as in the actions showing anger. But all qualifications being made, it is undeniable that there is a certain specialisation of the discharge, giving some distinctiveness to the bodily changes by which each feeling is accompanied.—'*Principles of Psychology*,' ii. 540.

Darwin.

The general principles of expression.

1. *The principle of serviceable associated Habits.*—Certain complex actions are of direct or indirect service under certain states of the mind in order to relieve or gratify certain sensations, desires, &c., and whenever the same state of mind is induced, however feebly, there is a tendency through the force of habit and association for the same movements to be performed, though they may not then be of the least use.

2. *The principle of Antithesis.*—Certain states of the mind lead to certain habitual

actions which are of service, as under our first principle. Now, when a directly opposite state of mind is induced, there is a strong and involuntary tendency to the performance of movements of a directly opposite nature, though these are of no use; and such movements are in some cases highly expressive.

3. *The principle of actions due to the constitution of the nervous system, independently from the first of the Will, and independently to a certain extent of Habit.*—When the sensorium is strongly excited, nerve-force is generated in excess, and is transmitted in certain definite directions, depending on the connection of the nerve-cells and partly on habit; or the supply of nerve-force may, as it appears, be interrupted. Effects are thus produced which we recognise as expressive. This third principle may, for the sake of brevity, be called that of the direct action of the nervous system.—'*Expression of the Emotions*,' pp. 28, 29.

The vocal expression of Emotion.

We have the words 'growling' and 'grumbling,' commonly used to describe the vocal expression of more or less decided anger. Oaths, when uttered with much depth of passion, are uttered in the deepest bass. A curse, muttered between set teeth, is always in a low pitch. And in masses of people indignation habitually vents itself in groans. That anger also expresses itself vocally in screaming notes, is doubtless true. A rising tide of feeling, causing increased muscular strain, may adjust the vocal apparatus to tones increasingly higher or increasingly lower—either of these implying muscular strain that is greater as departure from the medium tones is wider. Possibly the reason why anger that is beginning uses the lower tones, and when it becomes violent uses tones of high pitch, is that tones much below the middle voice are made with less effort than tones much above it; and that hence, implying as they do a greater excess of nervous discharge, the higher tones are natural to the stronger passion.—*Spencer*, '*Psychology*,' ii. 549.

The Pleasure of Excited Emotion

Young men turn soldiers and sailors from the love of being agitated; and for the same reason, country gentlemen leap over stone walls. This—and not avarice—is the explanation of gaming. Men who game, are, in general, very little addicted to avarice; but they court the conflict of passions which gaming produces, and which guards them from the dulness of *ennui* to which they would otherwise feel themselves exposed. The love of emotion is the foundation of tragedy; and so pleasant is it to be moved, that we set off for the express purpose of looking excessively dismal for two hours and a half interspersed with long intervals of positive sobbing. The taste for emotion may, however, become a dangerous taste; and we should be very cautious how we attempt to squeeze out of human life, more ecstasy and paroxysm than it can well afford. It throws an air of insipidity over the greater part of our being, and lavishes on a few favoured moments the joy which was given to season our whole existence. It is to act like schoolboys,—to pick the plums and sweetmeats out of the cake, and quarrel with the insipidity of the batter: whereas the business is, to infuse a certain share of flavour throughout the whole of the mass; and not so to habituate ourselves to strong impulse and extraordinary feeling, that the common tenor of human affairs should appear to us incapable of amusement, and devoid of interest. The only safe method of indulging this taste for emotion, is by seeking for its gratification, not in passion, but in science, and all the pleasures of the understanding; by mastering some new difficulty; by seeing some new field of speculation open itself before us; by learning the creations, the divisions, the connections, the designs, and contrivances of nature.—*Smith*, '*Moral Philosophy*,' p. 343.

Relation of Passion to Emotion.

The popular word for affections in their highest degree, is *passion*, and the objection to using it, is, that it only means the *excess* of the feeling: for instance, we could not say that a man experienced the passion of anger who felt a calm indignation at a serious injury he had received; we should only think ourselves justifiable in applying the term *passion* if he were transported beyond all bounds, if his reason were almost vanquished, and if the bodily signs of that passion were visible in his appearance.—*Smith*, '*Moral Philosophy*,' p 288

Origin of the Emotions

Sensation and Perception

We may safely assume it to be admitted as a general truth that Emotions of various kinds gradually manifest themselves and gain in strength as the sensorial endowments of animals, and their relational correspondence with their environment, increase in definiteness and complexity. 'Pleasures' and 'pains' soon begin to be realised as direct results of their various movements and sensorial activities; and from the traces of these which survive in the form of nascent and clustered memories of many related sensations, those numerous, vague, but all-powerful modes of Feeling, commonly known as Emotions, take their origin, and often seem to increase in strength as the wealth of associations from which they are derived becomes organised and widened in successive generations of animals. The revival of such vague clustered memories of 'pleasures' or 'pains' usually follows as a direct result of some Perception An impression made upon some organ of sense may thence reverberate through the brain so as to produce a Perception of the corresponding object, and may simultaneously evoke some distinctly related Emotion.—*Bastian*, '*The Brain, &c.*,' p. 184

By Evolution and Inheritance

The law of development of the mental activities, considered under their cognitive aspect, equally applies to them considered under their emotional aspect. That gradual organisation of forms of thought which results from the experience of uniform external relations is accompanied by the organisation of forms of feeling similarly resulting. Given a race of organisms habitually placed in contact with any complex set of circumstances, and if its members are already able to co-ordinate the impressions made by each of the various minor groups of phenomena composing this set of circumstances, there will slowly be established in them a co-ordination of these compound impressions corresponding to this set of circumstances The constant experiences of successive generations will gradually strengthen the tendency of all the component clusters of psychical states to make one another nascent And when ultimately the union of them, expressed in the inherited organic structure, becomes innate, it will constitute what we call an emotion or sentiment, having this set of circumstances for its object.—*Spencer*, '*Principles of Psychology*,' i. 491.

II GENERAL FEELINGS.

Pleasure and Pain.

Definition

Pleasure, strictly so called, is the emotion of comfort or delight that accompanies certain states of the body and conditions of the things around us, as well as the different objects and frames of the mind.—*Murphy*, '*Human Mind*,' p. 172.

Pain is the opposite of this state of mind Pleasure is a reflex of the spontaneous and unimpeded exertion of a power, of whose energy we are conscious. Pain, a reflex of the overstrained or repressed exertion of such a power.—*Hamilton*, '*Metaphysics*,' ii 440

By pleasure and pain I must be understood to mean whatsoever delight or uneasiness is felt by us, whether arising from any grateful or unacceptable sensation or reflection.—*Locke*, '*Human Understanding*,' II. xx. 15

Different Kinds

Pleasures differ in kind according to the capacities or faculties on whose exercise they attend, and they vary in quality according to the quality of mental exercise, of which they are the natural accompaniment.

In accordance with the first statement, we speak of the pleasures of the senses, of the affections, of the intellect, of the imagination. In accordance with the second, we speak of the pleasures of the senses as lower than those of the intellect, and sensualism is a term of reproach applied to the indulgence of the appetites, in neglect of the restraints of understanding and conscience. As the active transcends the passive, so does the happiness of activity surpass in value all the pleasures which spring from mere sensibility. And, as among the active powers, some transcend others, the attendant pleasures are graduated accordingly.—*Calderwood*, '*Moral Philosophy*,' p. 125.

There are different kinds of pleasure, and different kinds of pain. In the first place, these are twofold, inasmuch as each is either Positive and Absolute, or Negative and Relative. In regard to the former, the mere negation of pain does, by relation to pain, constitute a state of pleasure. Thus, the removal of the toothache replaces us in a state which, though one really of indifference, is, by contrast to our previous agony, felt as pleasurable. This is negative or relative pleasure. Positive or absolute pleasure, on the contrary, is all that pleasure which we feel above a state of indifference, and which is therefore prized as a good in itself, and not simply as the removal of an evil. On the same principle, pain is divided into Positive or Absolute, and into Negative or Relative.—*Hamilton*, '*Metaphysics*,' ii. 442.

On the side of Pleasure, we have, as leading elements:—Muscular Exercise, Rest after Exercise; Healthy Organic Sensibility in general, and Alimentary Sensations in particular; Sweet Tastes and Odours; Soft and Warm Touches; Melody and Harmony in Sound; Cheerful Light and Coloured Spectacle; the Sexual feelings; Liberty after Constraint; Novelty and Wonder; the warm Tender Emotions; Sexual, Maternal, and Paternal Love; Friendship, Admiration, Esteem, and Sociability in general; Self-complacency and Praise; Power, Influence, Command; Revenge; the Interest of Plot and Pursuit; the charms of knowledge and Intellectual Exertion; the cycle of the Fine Arts, culminating in Music, Painting, and Poetry, with which we couple the enjoyment of Natural Beauty; the satisfaction attainable through Sympathy and the Moral Sentiment.

The Pains are mostly implied in the negation of the pleasures:—Muscular Fatigue, Organic derangements and diseases, Cold, Hunger, Ill Tastes, and Odours; Skin Lacerations; Discords in Sound; Darkness, Gloom, and excessive glare of Light; ungratified Sexual Appetite; Restraint after Freedom; Monotony; Fear in all its manifestations; privation in the Affections; Sorrow; Self-humiliation and Shame; Impotence and Servitude; disappointed Revenge; baulked Pursuit or Plot; Intellectual Contradictions and Obscurity; the Æsthetically Ugly; Harrowed Sympathies; an Evil Conscience.—*Bain*, '*Mental and Moral Science*,' Appendix, p. 76.

The pleasures which are received through the emotional faculty may be arranged, according to the sources from which they spring, under the following heads:—

I. Pleasures of Sense	1. Appetite. 2. Health. 3. Taste.
II. Pleasures of Intellect	4. Utility. 5. Knowledge. 6. Imagination.
III. Pleasures of Conscience	7. The Right. 8. The True. 9. The Good.
IV. Pleasures of the Will.	10. Volition. 11. Liberty. 12. Sociality.
V. Pleasures of Power.	13. Action. 14. Courage. 15. Success. 16. Rest.

—*Murphy*, '*Human Mind*,' p. 179.

Diverse Quality of Pleasures

Mr. John S. Mill has insisted, with peculiar felicity, on the diversity of quality among pleasures. It is one of his highest distinctions, as an expounder of Utilitarianism and a leader of thought, that he has given prominence to the superior quality of some pleasures in comparison with others. Thus he has dwelt upon the important fact that 'a being of higher faculties requires more to make him happy . . . than one of an inferior type.' So also he points to the fact that those equally capable of appreciating and enjoying all pleasures 'give a most marked preference to the manner of existence which employs their higher faculties.'—*Calderwood, 'Moral Philosophy,'* p. 125.

It would be absurd that while, in estimating all other things, quality is considered as well as quantity, the estimation of pleasures should be supposed to depend on quantity alone. Now it is an unquestionable fact that those who are equally acquainted with, and equally capable of appreciating and enjoying both, do give a most marked preference to the manner of existence which employs their higher faculties. Few human creatures would consent to be changed into any of the lower animals for a promise of the fullest allowance of a beast's pleasures; no intelligent human being would consent to be a fool, no instructed person would be an ignoramus, no person of feeling and conscience would be selfish and base, even though they should be persuaded that the fool, the dunce, or the rascal is better satisfied with his lot than they are with theirs. . . . It is better to be a human being dissatisfied than a pig satisfied; better to be a Socrates dissatisfied than a fool satisfied. And if the fool or the pig is of a different opinion, it is because they only know their own side of the question.—*Mill, 'Utilitarianism,'* pp. 11, 14.

Theories of Pleasure and Pain.

The rise of pleasure, as connected with the functions of our life, admits of a twofold explanation. It is the natural accompaniment of our Sensations or of the exercise of our energies. In the one case, it attends upon our 'Passivity or Receptivity,' as in the warmth of the body or the cooling influence of the breeze. In the other case, it attends upon our Activity or Voluntary use of powers, as in the exercise of our muscles or of our reasoning power. The former belongs to sentient existence; the latter to active existence, whether physical or intellectual, or both combined.

Besides these forms of pleasure there is another which does not here call for special note, namely, pleasure in the possession of objects of value.

Pain comes either through injury inflicted upon the Sentient organism or through unnatural restraint upon the energies when brought into exercise. Pain is not merely a negation or want of pleasure, but a positive experience, opposite in kind. —*Calderwood, 'Moral Philosophy,'* p. 124.

Plato is the first philosopher who can be said to have attempted the generalisation of a law which regulates the manifestation of pleasure and pain. The sum of his doctrine on the subject is this,—that Pleasure is nothing absolute, nothing positive, but a mere relation to, a mere negation of pain. Pain is the root, the condition, the antecedent of pleasure, and the latter is only a restoration of the feeling subject from a state contrary to nature to a state conformable with nature. Pleasure is the mere replenishing of a vacuum, the mere satisfying of a want. A state of pleasure is always preceded by a state of pain.

Aristotle first refutes the Platonic theory that pleasure is only the removal of a pain. He then proposes his own doctrine. Pleasure, he maintains, is the concomitant of energy,—of perfect energy, whether of the functions of Sense or Intellect; and perfect energy he describes as that which proceeds from a power in health and vigour, and exercised upon an object relatively excellent that is suited to call forth the power into unimpeded activity.

To these two theories we find nothing

added, worthy of commemoration, by the succeeding philosophers of Greece and Rome, nay, we do not find that in antiquity these doctrines received any farther development or confirmation A host of commentators in the Lower Empire, and during the middle ages, were content to repeat the doctrines of Aristotle and Plato. The philosopher next in order is Descartes; and his opinion is deserving of attention His philosophy of the pleasurable is promulgated in one short sentence of the sixth letter of the First Part of his 'Epistles.' It is as follows —'All our pleasure is nothing more than the consciousness of some one or other of our perfections'

The Kantian doctrine is this:—'Pleasure is the feeling of the furtherance, pain of the hindrance of life. In a state of pain, life appears long, in a state of pleasure, it seems brief, it is only, therefore, the feeling of the promotion,—the furtherance of life, which constitutes pleasure.'—*Hamilton*, '*Metaphysics*,' ii. sect xlıı. (abridged)

The Guidance afforded by Pleasure and Pain.

They are the index of the natural and un natural.

Pleasure, being a form of experience naturally attendant upon the use of our sensibilities or energies, is not the end of their use. Pain, being attendant upon the injury or restraint of our powers, is not the product of their natural use Pleasure and pain are the index of the natural and the unnatural in the use of powers, of conformity with the law of their exercise, or violation of that law As Feuchtersleben has said, 'Beauty is in some degree the reflection of health,' so pleasure is the symbol of natural exercise Pleasure and pain are respectively as the smooth play or the irksome fretting of machinery, but neither is the end for which it is kept moving Consciousness of simple pleasure and nothing more, is unknown A capacity or faculty whose function it is to produce pleasure and nothing more, is unknown. Pleasure may thus be generalised as the common accompaniment of all natural exercise —*Calderwood*, '*Moral Philosophy*,' p 124.

They lead to Self-conservation

The connection of feelings with physical states may be summed up, for one large class of the facts, in the law of self-conservation :—States of pleasure are concomitant with an increase, and states of pain with an abatement, of some or all, of the vital functions. Muscular exertion, when pleasurable, is the outpouring of exuberant energy; muscular fatigue is the result of exhaustion. Laughter is a joyful expression; and, in all its parts, it indicates exalted energy. In the convulsive outburst of grief nearly everything is reversed, the features are relaxed, the whole body droops —*Bain*, '*Mental Science*,' pp. 75, 77.

Generally speaking, pleasures are the concomitants of medium activities, where the activities are of kinds liable to be in excess or defect, and where they are of kinds not liable to be excessive, pleasure increases as the activity increases, except where the activity is either constant or involuntary.—*Spencer*, '*Psychology*,' i. 272.

Three Psychological Facts

Mr Spencer notices three psychological facts, to which the student's attention may be directed.

1 Pleasures to a great extent, and pains to some extent, are separate from, and additional to, the feelings with which we habitually connect them

2 Pleasures and pains may be acquired, may be, as it were, superinduced on certain feelings which did not originally yield them.

3 Pleasures are more like one another than are the feelings which yield them, and among pains we may trace a parallel resemblance.—*Spencer*, '*Psychology*,' i 286–288.

Pain

In relation to moral evil.

There is as close a connection between sin and pain as there is between virtue and happiness. There may indeed be happiness, and there may be suffering, where there is neither virtue nor the opposite, as, for example, among the brute creation; but we decide that, wherever there is virtue, it merits happiness, and wherever there is sin, that it deserves suffering, and we are led to anticipate that the proper consequences will follow under the government of a good and a holy God. But as the intellectual intuition of causation, while it constrains us to look for a cause, does not make known the precise cause, so our moral conviction of merit, while it leads us to look for the punishment of sin, does not specify where, or when, or how the penalty is to be inflicted: all that it intimates is that it should and shall come. This conviction keeps alive in the breasts of the wicked, at least an occasional fear of punishment, even in the midst of the greatest outward prosperity, and points very emphatically, if not very distinctly, to a day of judgment and of righteous retribution.—*M'Cosh, 'Intuitions of the Mind,'* p. 268.

As a source of fear.

Pain is the teacher of fear. Before pain there is *no* fear; and when that passion exists, however great the distance, and however circuitous the course, *there* is the fountain-head from which it sprang.—*Smith, 'Moral Philosophy,'* p. 294.

The Indifferent Feelings.

Their existence asserted.

Besides the sensations that are either agreeable or disagreeable, there is still a greater number that are indifferent. To these we give so little attention, that they have no name, and are immediately forgot, as if they had never been; and it requires attention to the operations if one minds to be convinced of their existence.—*Reid, 'Intellectual Powers,'* p. 311.

We may feel, and yet be neither pleased nor pained. A state of feeling may have considerable intensity, without being either pleasurable or painful; such states are described as neutral or indifferent. Surprise is a familiar instance. There are surprises that delight us, and others that cause suffering; but many surprises do neither. We are awakened, roused, stirred, made conscious; on the physical side there is a diffused wave shown in lively demonstrations of feature, gesture, voice, and oral expression. The attention is detained upon some object, the source of feeling; if a sudden clap of thunder, or flash of lightning, excited the feeling, the mind is for the moment occupied with the sensation, and withdrawn from other objects of thought.

Almost every pleasurable and painful sensation and emotion passes through a stage or moment of indifference.—*Bain, 'Emotions, &c.,'* p. 13.

Their existence disputed.

Sir W. Hamilton says that the existence of the indifferent feelings 'is a point in dispute among philosophers.'—*Hamilton's 'Reid,'* p. 311, note.

It may be questioned whether any feeling as such can be indifferent.—*Sully, 'Psychology,'* p. 449.

Joy, or Mental Pleasure.

Its causes.

The primary causes of joy are (1) pleasant sensations and their objects; (2) knowledge of any kind; (3) every description of exercise; and (4) every degree of effectiveness.

The secondary causes of joy are Riches, Authority, Society, Superiority. These please because they contain the primary causes of pleasure, or because previously connected with them.—*Godwin, 'Active Principles,'* pp. 9, 18.

Is not a sensation.

The pleasant *emotion* is very different from any pleasant *sensation*. The highest joy is felt without any agreeable sensation, and when all sensations are disagreeable —*Godwin, 'Active Principles,'* p. 9

Surprise and Wonder.

Their causes.

Surprise is caused by *contrariety* to expectation, not by what is merely unexpected We are surprised on meeting a friend whom we supposed to be in a distant country; on hearing that any one said or did what seems contrary to his known ways and character; when persons fail whom we expected to succeed, or succeed when we expected they would fail; when any objects appear to be different from what they were thought to be, when any events occur which are deemed unnatural

Wonder is awakened by greatness of any kind, material or mental We view with wonder the height of a lofty mountain, the expanse of the ocean, the number of the stars, buildings of extraordinary dimensions The same emotion is caused by considering the magnitudes, distances, and movements of the heavenly bodies; the force of gravitation, steam, electricity, the unseen power which regularly renews the verdure and fruitfulness of the earth, and sustains every living thing Wonder is produced by what is mental and moral—by large attainments in knowledge, great intellectual ability, much energy of will in doing or suffering —*Godwin, 'Active Principles,'* pp. 23, 24.

Emotions of Action—Pursuit and Plot-interest.

In working to some end, as the ascent of a mountain, or in watching any consummation drawing near, as a race, we are in a peculiar state of arrested attention, which, as an agreeable effect, is often desired for itself

On the PHYSICAL side, the situation of pursuit is marked by (1) the intent occupation of some one of the senses upon an object, and (2) the general attitude or activity harmonising with this; there being, on the whole, an energetic muscular strain.

On the MENTAL side, Pursuit supposes (1) a motive in the interest of an end, heightened by its steady approach; (2) the state of engrossment in object regards, with remission of subject regards —*Bain, 'Mental Science,'* p. 268

III THE ÆSTHETIC FEELINGS

ÆSTHETICS.

The Term

Its first application.

Alex. Gottlieb Baumgarten (1714–1762) wrote, among other things, a work entitled 'Æsthetica,' in which he systematically developed this branch of philosophy, to which he first gave the name of Æsthetics, on the ground of his definition of beauty as perfection apprehended through the senses. —*Ueberweg, 'Hist. of Phil.,'* ii 117

Its meaning

Etymologically, the term comes from a Greek word signifying sensation or perception Æsthetics, then, should be that science which treats of sensations and perceptions All of them, or only some of them? In the former case, we should have a complete system of philosophy In the latter case, the term is wanting in precision; because it does not tell us with which perceptions or sensations it is concerned. The word, in fine, is ill made But it has passed into use, and we must put up with it for want of a better.—*Véron, 'Æsthetics,'* p. 95.

Definition

We may preserve the definition of æsthetics which usage has sanctioned—*The Science of Beauty.* For the sake of clearness, however, and to prevent confusion, we prefer to call it the *Science of Beauty in Art* Or we may put it thus:—Æsthetics is the science whose object is the study and elucidation of the manifestations of artistic genius —*Véron, 'Æsthetics,'* p. 109.

Æsthetics is the term now employed to designate the theory of the fine arts—the Science of the Beautiful, with its allied conceptions and emotions. The province of the science is not, however, very definitely fixed.—'*Encyclop Brit.*,' i. 212.

The Chief Problem of Æsthetics

Its first and foremost problem is the determination of the nature and laws of beauty, including along with the beautiful, in its narrower signification, its kindred subjects, the sublime and the ludicrous. To discover what it is in things which makes them beautiful or ugly, sublime or ludicrous, is one constant factor in the æsthetic problem.—'*Encyclop. Brit.*,' i. 212.

Two methods of approaching it.

We find two diametrically opposed methods of approaching the subject-matter of æsthetics, which distinctly colour all parts of the doctrine arrived at. The first is the metaphysical or *à priori* method; the second, the scientific or empirical method. The one reasons deductively from ultra-scientific conceptions respecting the ultimate nature of the universe and human intelligence, and seeks to explain the phenomena of Beauty and Art by help of these. The others proceed inductively from the consideration of these phenomena, as facts capable of being compared, classified, and brought under certain uniformities. It must not be supposed that either method is customarily pursued in complete independence of the other.—'*Encyclop. Brit.*,' i. 212.

For the various theories of the beautiful, see "BEAUTY."

ART.

What it is—opinions of philosophers

Art is free production. Mechanical art executes those actions, which are prescribed by our knowledge of a possible object, as necessary to the realisation of the object. Æsthetic art has immediately in view the feeling of pleasure, either as mere sensation (agreeable art) or as pleasure in the beautiful and implying judgment (fine art).—*Kant (summarised by Ueberweg).*

Art is conscious imitation of the unconscious ideality of nature, imitation of nature in the culminating points of its development; the highest stage of art is the negation of form through the perfect fulness of form; the annihilation of form through the perfection of form. Through ever higher combination and final blending of manifold forms, the artist who emulates nature must attain to the greatest beauty, in forms of the highest simplicity and of infinite meaning.—*Schelling (summarised by Ueberweg).*

Art, the work of genius, repeats the eternal Ideas apprehended in pure contemplation, the essential and the permanent in all the phenomena of the world. Its only aim is the communication of this knowledge. According to the material in which it repeats, it is plastic art, poetry, or music.—*Schopenhauer (summarised by Ueberweg).*

The essence of Art.

The essence of art may be defined as the production of some permanent object or passing action which is fitted not only to supply an active enjoyment to the producer, but to convey a pleasurable *impression* to a number of spectators or listeners, quite apart from any personal advantage to be derived from it. This conception obviously excludes all hypotheses of some one eternally fixed quality of art, some essence of beauty.—*Sully*, '*Sensation, &c.*,' p. 341.

Doctrines of various philosophers on Art.

In the State, that Art alone should find a place which consists in the imitation of the good. In this category are included philosophical dramas, the narration of myths (expurgated and ethically applied), and in particular, religious lyrics (containing the praises of gods and also of noble men). All art which is devoted to the imitation of the phenomenal world, in which good and bad are commingled, is excluded.—*Plato (summarised by Ueberweg)*

Art, in the wider sense of the term, as signifying that skill in giving form to any material, which results from, or at least depends on the knowledge of rules, has a twofold object: it has either to complete what nature has been unable to complete, or it may imitate. Art attains its end by imitation. That which it imitates, however, is not so much the particular as the essence of the particular object; in other words, art must idealise its subjects, each in its peculiar character. Imitative art serves three ends: recreation and (refined) entertainment, temporary emancipation from the control of certain passions by means of their excitation and subsequent subsidence, and, last and chiefly, moral culture.—*Aristotle (summarised by Ueberweg)*

Art is the one and the eternal revelation; there is no other, it is the miracle that must convince of the absolute reality of that supreme principle which never becomes objective itself, but is the cause nevertheless of all that is objective. Art is what is highest for the philosopher, for it opens as it were the holy of holies to him, where in eternal and primæval union there burns as in a flame what in nature and history is separated, and what in life and action, as well as in thought, must be eternally divided.—*Schelling (summarised by Schwegler)*

Schelling, who was a Pantheist, here elevates Art as the only true religion; he has had many followers, who have damaged the cause of Art by their gross exaggeration of its functions.

Characteristics of Fine Art productions

The productions of Fine Art appear to be distinguished by these characteristics:—(1) They have pleasure for their immediate end; (2) they have no disagreeable accompaniments; (3) their enjoyment is not restricted to one or a few persons. A picture or a statue can be seen by millions; a great poem reaches all that understand its language; a fine melody may spread pleasure over the habitable globe. The sunset and the stars are veiled only from the prisoner and the blind.—*Bain, 'Mental and Moral Science,'* p. 290.

It is a principle of the utmost importance, that, outside the material conditions that relate to optics and acoustics, that which dominates in a work of art and gives it its special character is the personality of the author. The value of the work of art rests entirely upon the degree of energy with which it manifests the intellectual character and æsthetic impressions of its author. An artist of true feeling has but to abandon himself to his emotion, and it will become contagious.—*Véron, 'Æsthetics,'* p. vi and vii.

Qualities of Art—how estimated

The æsthetic value of a poem or a painting may be viewed in one of two lights. One may regard the work either as relatively and subjectively beautiful, that is to say, as fitted to delight the order of minds for which it is produced, or as absolutely and objectively beautiful, that is to say, as capable of delighting all minds alike. Thus a Pieta of Francia possesses a relative beauty in its power of satisfying the dominant religious emotions of the age, an objective beauty in a universally impressive representation of human suffering and of the affectionate tendency which it customarily calls forth.—*Sully, 'Sensation, &c.,'* p. 345.

The alpha and omega of Art

These are Truth and Personality; *truth* as to facts, and the *personality* of the artist. But if we look more closely, we shall see that these two terms are in reality but one. Truth as to fact, so far as art is concerned, is above all the truth of our own sensations, of our own sentiments. It is truth as we see it, as it appears modified by our own temperament, preferences, and physical organs. It is, in fact, our personality itself.—*Véron, 'Æsthetics,'* p. 389.

Greatness in Art.

The art is greatest which conveys to the mind of the spectator, by any means whatsoever, the greatest number of the greatest ideas; and I call an idea great in proportion as it is received by a higher faculty of the mind, and as it more fully occupies, and in occupying, exercises and exalts the faculty by which it is received.—*Ruskin*, '*Modern Painters*,' I. pt. i. sec. i. ch. ii.

Great art dwells on all that is beautiful; but false art omits or changes all that is ugly. Great art accepts Nature as she is, but directs the eyes and thoughts to what is most perfect in her; false art saves itself the trouble of direction by removing or altering whatever it thinks objectionable —*Ruskin*, '*Modern Painters*,' III. pt. iv. ch. iii.

Art leaves something to the Imagination.

To leave something to the Imagination is better than to express the whole. What is merely suggested is conceived in an ideal form and colouring. Thus in a landscape, a winding river disappears from sight; the distant hazy mountains are realms for the fancy to play in. Breaks are left in the story, such as the reader may fill up.—*Bain*, '*Mental and Moral Science*,' p. 300.

Epochs of liberty are epochs of Art.

All the great art epochs have been epochs of liberty. In the time of Pericles, as in that of Leo X., in the France of the thirteenth century as in the Holland of the seventeenth, artists were able to work after their own fancies. No æsthetic dogmas confused their imaginations, no official corporations claimed any art dictatorship, or thought themselves responsible for the direction taken by the national taste.—*Véron*, '*Æsthetics*,' p. xi.

TASTE.

A man of taste.

He who has followed up the natural laws of aversion and desire, rendering them more and more authoritative by constant obedience, so as to derive pleasure always from that which God originally intended should give him pleasure, and who derives the greatest possible sum of pleasure from any given object, is a man of taste. Perfect taste is the faculty of receiving the greatest possible pleasures from those material sources which are attractive to our moral nature in its purity and perfection. He who receives little pleasure from these sources wants taste; he who receives pleasure from any other sources has false or bad taste.—*Ruskin*, '*Modern Painters*,' I. pt. i. sec. i. ch. vi.

Right taste—how formed.

The temper by which right taste is formed is characteristically patient. It dwells upon what is submitted to it. It does not trample upon it, lest it should be pearls, even though it looks like husks. It is a good ground, soft, penetrable, retentive; it is hungry and thirsty too, and drinks all the dew that falls upon it.—*Ruskin*, '*Modern Painters*,' II. pt. iii. ch. iii.

The Science of Æsthetics.

Its aim.

Æsthetics seeks a final standard of art value, and aims at subsuming all possible effects of art under the most general conceptions.—*Sully*, '*Sensation, &c.*,' p. 371.

Its unsatisfactory condition at present.

No science has suffered more from metaphysical dreaming than that of Æsthetics. From the doctrines of Plato to those of our present official teachers, art has been turned into an amalgam of transcendental mysteries and fancies, finding their final expression in that absolute conception of ideal Beauty which is the unchangeable and divine prototype of the real things around us.—*Véron*, '*Æsthetics*,' p. v.

The chaotic state of opinion on all matters relating to the Fine Arts seems to indicate that we are still far from the construction and even from the conception of an Æsthetic Science. Art has stubbornly sought to exclude the cold, grey dawn of scientific inquiry. With a special tenacity indeed she has wrapped herself about in the grateful gloom of a mystic twilight. For is it not her peculiar office to minister to the imagination, drawing the contemplative soul high above the region of fact and law? and would not any attempt to investigate her processes with the keen measuring eye of science be an outrage on this supreme right of phantasy to live apart, undisturbed by thought of what is, and must be? It is scarcely to be wondered at that so many of her worshippers have clung to the idea that all her power on the human soul is an insoluble mystery.—*Sully*, '*Sensation, &c.*,' p. 336.

As there is no such thing as abstract art, *l'art en soi*, because absolute beauty is a chimera, so neither is there any definitive and final system of Æsthetics.—*Véron*, '*Æsthetics*,' p. viii.

How a theory might be formed.

A theory of Æsthetics would have to proceed by means of historical research, supplemented by psychological explanation. The widest possible knowledge of all that art has done and sought to do would need to be completed by an inquiry into the law and tendency of these variations, on the supposition of a general progress in intellectual and other culture.—*Sully*, '*Sensation, &c.*,' p. 340.

Growth of Æsthetic Feelings.

Æsthetic feelings, first of all, grow in number, subtlety, and variety, that is, become more refined and frequent enjoyments, *pari passu* with the development of the Discriminative and the Assimilative functions. The artist's eye notes myriads of points of diversity and of resemblance among visual forms and shades of tint which wholly escape the attention of ordinary men. The poet finds shades of the admirable and beautiful where the uncultivated person fails to find them. In the second place, these feelings grow in range or amplitude with the development of the Retentive power of the mind, that is to say, its capability of ideal aggregation and of ideal revival.—*Sully*, '*Sensation, &c.*,' pp. 356, 357.

The Æsthetic Characteristics of Nations.

The idea of the colossal may be assigned to the Orient, the idea of sublimity to the Hebrews, the idea of beauty to the Greeks, elegance and dignity to the Romans, the characteristic and fantastic to the Middle Ages, and the ingenious and critical to modern times.—*Rudolph Hermann Lotze* (*from Ueberweg*).

IV. THE SUBLIME

Described.

I mean by the sublime, as I meant by the beautiful, a feeling of mind; though, of course, a very different feeling. It is a feeling of pleasure, but of exalted tremulous pleasure, bordering on the very confines of pain, and driving before it every calm thought and every regulated feeling. It is the feeling which men experience when they behold marvellous scenes of nature; or when they see great actions performed. Such feelings as come on the top of exceeding high mountains, or the hour before a battle, or when a man of great power and of an unyielding spirit is pleading before some august tribunal against the accusations of his enemies. These are the hours of sublimity, when all low and little passions are swallowed up by an overwhelming feeling; when the mind towers and springs above its common limits, breaks out into larger dimensions, and swells into a nobler and grander nature.—*Smith*, '*Moral Philosophy*,' p. 214.

The Sublime is the sympathetic sentiment of superior Power in its highest degrees. The objects of sublimity are, for the most part, such aspects and appearances as betoken great might, energy, or vastness, and are thereby capable of imparting sympathetically the elation of superior power.—*Bain*, '*Mental Science*,' p. 301.

Analysed

The results of the analysis of the Sublime are very various. Its essential elements, according to various philosophers, are :—

1. *Terror and Wonder.*

A mixture of wonder and terror almost always excites the feeling of the sublime. Extraordinary power generally excites the feeling of the sublime by these means,—by mixing wonder with terror. A person who has never seen anything of the kind but a little boat, would think a sloop of eighty tons a goodly and somewhat of a grand object, if all her sails were set and she were going gallantly before the wind, but a first-rate man-of-war would sail over such a sloop and send her to the bottom without any person on board the man-of-war perceiving that they had encountered any obstacle. Such power is wonderful and terrible, therefore sublime. —*Smith*, '*Moral Philosophy*,' p 217.

The passion caused by the great and sublime in *nature*, when those causes operate most powerfully, is astonishment; and astonishment is that state of the soul, in which all its motions are suspended, with some degree of horror. In this case the mind is so entirely filled with its object, that it cannot entertain any other, nor by consequence reason on that object which employs it. Hence arises the great power of the sublime, that far from being produced by them, it anticipates our reasonings, and hurries us on by an irresistible force. Astonishment is the effect of the sublime in its highest degree; the inferior effects are admiration, reverence, and respect.

No passion so effectually robs the mind of all its powers as fear. Whatever therefore is terrible, with regard to sight, is sublime too. Indeed, terror is in all cases whatsoever, either more openly or latently, the ruling principle of the sublime.—*Burke*, '*The Sublime, &c.*,' pt ii sects i ii

The Element of Terror denied by Mr. Ruskin.

A little reflection will easily convince any one that, so far from the feelings of self-preservation being necessary to the sublime, their greatest action is totally destructive of it; and that there are few feelings less capable of its perception than those of a coward. But the simple conception or idea of greatness of suffering or extent of destruction is sublime, whether there be any connection of that idea with ourselves or not. If we were placed beyond the reach of all peril or pain, the perception of these agencies, in their influence on others, would not be less sublime, not because peril or pain are sublime in their own nature, but because their contemplation, exciting compassion or fortitude, elevates the mind and renders meanness of thought impossible.—'*Modern Painters*,' pt. i. sect. ii ch iii.

And by Professor Bain

There is an incidental connection of the Sublime with Terror. Properly, the two states of mind are hostile and mutually destructive; the one raises the feeling of energy, the other depresses it. In so far as a sublime object gives us the sense of personal or of sympathetic danger, its sublimity is frustrated. The two effects were confounded by Burke in his 'Theory of the Sublime.'—'*Mental Science*,' p. 302

2. *Magnitude.*

Sublimity requires magnitude as its condition; and the formless is not unfrequently sublime. That we are at once attracted and repelled by sublimity, arises from the circumstance that the object which we call *sublime* is proportioned to one of our faculties, and disproportioned to another; but as the degree of pleasure transcends the degree of pain, the power whose energy is promoted must be superior to that power whose energy is repressed The Sublime may be divided into the Sublime of Space, the Sublime of Time, and the Sublime of Power.—*Hamilton*, '*Metaphysics*,' ii. 513

The sublimity of inanimate forms seems to arise chiefly from two sources; firstly, from the nature of the objects distinguished by that form; and, secondly, from the quantity or magnitude of the form itself. There are other circumstances in the nature of forms, which may extend or increase this character, but I apprehend, that the two now mentioned are the only ones which of themselves constitute sublimity.—*Alison*, '*Essays on Taste*,' II. ch. iv. sect. 1.

3. *Height a source of Sublime Emotion.*

Sublimity in its primitive sense carries the thoughts in a direction opposite to that in which the great and universal Law of terrestrial gravitation operates. Hence it is, that while motion downward conveys the idea only of a passive obedience to the laws of nature, motion *upwards* always produces, more or less, a feeling of pleasing surprise, from the comparative rarity of the phenomenon.—*Stewart*, '*Essays*, p. 280.

4. *Sublimity is Elevation of the Mind.*

Sublimity is not a specific term,—not a term descriptive of the effect of a particular class of ideas. Anything which elevates the mind is sublime, and elevation of mind is produced by the contemplation of greatness of any kind; but chiefly, of course, by the greatness of the noblest things. Sublimity is, therefore, only another word for the effect of greatness upon the feelings. Greatness of matter, space, power, virtue, or beauty, are thus all sublime; and there is perhaps no desirable quality of a work of art, which in its perfection is not, in some way or degree, sublime.—*Ruskin*, '*Modern Painters*,' I. pt. i. sec. ii. ch. iii. § 1.

5. *The Infinite, the source of the Sublime.*

Every one feels that the sentiment of the sublime differs from that of the beautiful. The one pleases and delights, the other overawes and yet elevates.

It seems to me that whatever tends to carry away the mind into the Infinite raises that idea and feeling which are called the sublime. The idea embraces two elements, or, rather, has two sides. First the infinite is conceived as something beyond our largest phantasm, that is, image, and beyond our widest concept or general notion. We exert our imaging and conceiving power to the utmost; but as we do so we are led to perceive that there is vastly more beyond. Whatever calls forth this exercise is sublime, that is, excites that special feeling which we have all experienced, and which we call sublime.

It is not all that I see of the British that so impresses me, said Hyder Ali, but what I do not see, the power beyond the seas, the power in reserve. It was his belief in a power beyond, in a power unseen, which so struck the mind of the Mahratta chief. The feeling of sublimity is always called forth in this way, that is, by whatever fills its imaging power and yet suggests something farther, something greater and higher. A great height, such as a great mountain, Mont Blanc, Monte Rosa, Chimborazo, raises the idea, and with it the corresponding feeling. The discoveries of astronomy stir up the emotion, because they carry the mind into the immeasurable depths of space while yet we feel that we are but at its verge. The discoveries of geology exalt the mind in much the same way, by the long vistas opened of ages of which we cannot detect the beginning. Every vast display of power calls forth the overawing sentiment; we notice agencies which are great, arguing a power which is greater. It is thus that we are moved by the howl of the tempest and the raging of the sea, both, it may be, producing terrible havoc, in the prostration of the trees of the forest or in the wreck of vessels. The roar of the waterfall, the musical crash of the avalanche, the muttering and the prolonged growl of the thunder, the sudden shaking of the stable ground when the earth quakes, all these fill our minds, in our endeavour to realise them, and raise apprehension of unknown effects to follow. The forked lightning raises the thought of a bolt shot by an almighty hand. Thick masses of cloud or of darkness may become sublime by suggesting depths which we cannot sound. The vault of heaven is always a grand object when serene; as we look into it we feel that we are looking into the boundless. A clear, bright space in the sky, whether in a natural scene or in a painting, is an outlet, by which the mind may go out into the limitless. We are exhilarated by the streaks of light in the morning sky, partly, no doubt, from the associated hope of the coming day, but still more because of the suggested region beyond, from which the luminary of day comes. I explain in much the same way the feeling of grandeur awakened by the sun setting in splendour in the evening sky, our souls go after him into the region to which he is going. In much the same way there is always a profound feeling of awe associated with the serious contemplation of the death of a fellow-man; it is, if we view it aright, the departure of a soul into an unending eternity.

But there is a second element in infinity. It is such that nothing can be added to it, and nothing taken from it; in other words, incapable of augmentation or diminution. Under this aspect it is the perfect. As an example we have 'the law of the Lord, which is perfect.' Kant's language has often been quoted, as to the two things which impressed him with sublimity, the starry heavens and the law of God.—*M'Cosh*, '*Emotions*,' p. 189–191.

The Sublime in Morals.

Firmness and constancy of purpose, that withstands all solicitation, and, in spite of all danger, goes on straightly to its object, is very often sublime. The resolution of St. Paul, in going up to Jerusalem, where he has the firmest conviction that he shall undergo every species of persecution, quite comes within this description of feeling. 'What mean ye to weep and break my heart? I am ready, not to be bound only, but to die, at Jerusalem, for the name of Jesus.'

There is something exceedingly majestic in the steadiness with which the Apostle points out the single object of his life, and the unquenchable courage with which he walks towards it. 'I know I shall die, but I have a greater object than life,—the zeal of an high duty. Situation allows some men to think of safety; I not only must not consult it, but I must go where I know it will be most exposed. I must hold out my hands for chains, and my body for stripes, and my soul for misery. I am ready to do it all!' These are the feelings by which alone bold truths have been told to the world; by which the bondage of falsehood has been broken, and the chains of slavery snapped asunder! It is in vain to talk of men numerically; if the passions of a man are exalted to a summit like this, he is a *thousand* men!—*Smith*, '*Moral Philosophy*,' p. 225.

There are still grander scenes presented in the moral world, raising the feeling of sublimity, because revealing an immense power and suggesting an immeasurable power. We are affected with a feeling of wonder and awe when we contemplate Abraham lifting the knife to slay his son, and the old Roman delivering his son to death because guilty of a crime, we think of, and yet cannot estimate, the strong moral purpose needed to overcome the natural affection which was burning all the while in the bosoms of the fathers. The commander burning his ships that he may have no retreat, tells of a will and a purpose which cannot be conquered. We feel overawed, and yet exalted, when we read of the Hollanders being ready to open the sluices which guard their country and let in the ocean to overflood it, and of the Russians setting fire to their capital, rather than have their liberties trampled on. Who can read the account in Plato's 'Phædo' of the death of Socrates without saying, How grand, how sublime! and we do so because we would estimate, and yet cannot estimate, the grand purpose which enabled him to retain such composure amidst scenes so much fitted to agitate and to overwhelm. History discloses a yet more sublime scene in Jesus, patient and benignant under the fearful and mysterious load laid upon Him. —*M'Cosh*, '*The Emotions*,' p. 191.

Pleasure in the Sublime Contrasted with Pleasure in Beauty.

The feeling of pleasure in the Sublime is essentially different from our feeling of pleasure in the Beautiful. The beautiful awakens the mind to a soothing contemplation; the sublime rouses it to strong emotion. The beautiful attracts without repelling; whereas the sublime at once does both; the beautiful affords us a feeling of unmingled pleasure, in the full and unimpeded activity of our cognitive powers; whereas our feeling of sublimity is a mingled one of pleasure and pain,—of pleasure in the consciousness of the strong energy, of pain in the consciousness that this energy is vain.—*Hamilton*, '*Metaphysics*,' ii. 512.

V. THE BEAUTIFUL.

Its Sources.

Not one but manifold.

The source of Beauty is not to be sought in any single quality, but in a circle of effects. The search after some common property applicable to all things named beautiful is now abandoned. Every theorist admits a plurality of causes. The common attribute resides only in the emotion, and even that may vary considerably without passing the limits of the name.—*Bain*, '*Mental and Moral Science*,' p. 292.

The unity of Beauty is questioned. It is asked whether all objects which appear beautiful are so because of some one ultimate property, or combination of properties, running through all examples of Beauty, or whether they are so called simply because they produce some common pleasurable feeling in the mind. This is a question of induction from facts. It has been most vigorously disputed by British writers on the subject, and many of them have decided in favour of the plurality and diversity of elements in Beauty.—'*Encyclop. Brit.*,' i. 213.

There are moral beauties as well as natural; beauties in the objects of sense, and in intellectual objects; in the works of men, and in the works of God; in things inanimate, in brute animals, and in rational beings; in the constitution of the body of man, and in the constitution of his mind. There is no real excellence which has not its beauty to a discerning eye when placed in a proper point of view; and it is as difficult to enumerate the ingredients of beauty as the ingredients of real excellence. —*Reid*, '*Works*,' 491.

Its Nature.

Generally.

Beauty is perfection unmodified by a predominating expression.'—'*Guesses at Truth*,' p. 79.

Beauty is truth, truth beauty,—that is all
Ye know on earth, and all ye need to know.—*Keats*, '*Ode on a Grecian Urn*.'

Beauty is indeed in the mind, in the feelings: were there not the idea of Beauty in the beholder, associated with the feeling of pleasure, nothing would be beautiful or lovely to him. But it is also in the object; and the union and communion of the two is requisite to its full perception.—'*Guesses at Truth*,' p. 386.

Theories of the Beautiful.

The best-known theories of the Beautiful may be thus classified. But it will be noticed that it is not easy, if it be possible, to avoid all cross division.

1. *The Theological theory*: that beautiful qualities are transcriptions of the Divine attributes (Ruskin).

2. *The Metaphysical theory*, closely allied with the former: that objects, attributes, and actions are beautiful, through participating in and embodying certain original ideas or archetypes (Plato, Modern German Transcendentalists).

3. *The Mathematical theory*: that the beautiful is to be found in proportion and symmetry, ultimately resolvable into spatial and numerical relations (M'Vicar, &c. Applied to the human figure and to colours by Hay).

4. *The Special Sense theory*: that the beautiful, like the good, is immediately discovered by an original faculty (Hutcheson).

5. *The Qualities theory*: that beauty lies in a combination of qualities characterising the object (Burke, Hogarth).

6. *The Association theory*: that nothing is beautiful in itself, but only through what it suggests (Alison, Jeffrey).

7. *The Physiological theory*: that the æsthetically beautiful is that which affords the maximum of stimulation with the minimum of fatigue or waste, in processes not directly connected with the vital functions (Grant Allen, developing hints of Bain and Spencer).—*J. Radford Thomson.*

Doctrines of Philosophers.

Socrates.

He holds that the beautiful and the good or useful are the same; a dung-basket, if it answers its end, may be a beautiful thing, while a golden shield, not well formed for use, is an ugly thing.—'*Memorabilia,*' iii. 8.

Plato.

Plato leaned decidedly to a theory of an absolute Beauty. It is only this absolute Beauty, he tells us, which deserves the name of Beauty; and this is beautiful in every manner, and the ground of Beauty in all things. It is nothing discoverable as an attribute in another thing, whether living being, earth, or heaven, for these are only beautiful things, not the Beautiful itself. It is the eternal and perfect existence, contrasted with the oscillations between existence and non-existence in the phenomenal world. So far as his writings embody the notion of any distinguishing element in beautiful objects, it is proportion, harmony, or unity among the parts of an object.—'*Encyclop. Brit.*,' i. 215.

Aristotle.

Aristotle ignores all conceptions of an absolute Beauty, and at the same time seeks to distinguish the Beautiful from the Good. The universal elements of Beauty, Aristotle finds to be order, symmetry, and definiteness or determinateness: he adds that a certain magnitude is desirable. Hence an animal may be too small to be beautiful; or it may be too large, when it cannot be surveyed as a whole.—*Aristotle,* '*Metaphysics and Poetics.*'

Plotinus.

The essence of Beauty consists not in mere symmetry but in the supremacy of the higher over the lower, of the form over matter, of the soul over the body, of reason and goodness over the soul. The beauty of human reason is the highest.—'*Enneades.*'

Relativity of Beauty.

Hutcheson.

'All Beauty is relative to the sense of some mind perceiving it.' The cause of Beauty is not any simple sensation from an object, as colour, tone, but a certain order among the parts, or 'uniformity amidst variety.' The faculty by which this principle is known is an internal sense which is defined as 'a passive power of receiving ideas of Beauty from all objects in which there is uniformity in variety.—'*Encyclop. Brit.*,' i. 221.

Diderot.

Beauty consists in the perception of Relations.—'*Encyclopédie,*' *art.* '*Beau.*'

Beauty typical (see also Sir J. Reynolds' Theory).

Buffier.

It is the *type* of a species which gives the measure of Beauty. Among faces there is but one beautiful form, the others being not beautiful. But while only a few are modelled after the ugly forms, a great many are modelled after the beautiful form.—*Bain,* '*Mental and Moral Science,*' p. 305.

Reid.

I apprehend that it is in the moral and intellectual perfections of the mind, and in its active powers, that Beauty originally dwells; and that from this as the fountain all the Beauty which we perceive in the visible world is derived. This was the opinion of Akenside.

'Mind, mind alone, bear witness, earth and heav'n!
The living fountains in itself contains
Of beauteous and sublime. Here, hand in hand,
Sit paramount the graces. Here, enthron'd,
Celestial Venus, with divinest airs,
Invites the soul to never-fading joy.'

All the objects we call beautiful agree in two things, which seem to concur in our sense of beauty:—(1) When they are perceived, or even imagined, they produce a certain agreeable emotion or feeling in the mind; (2) this agreeable emotion is accompanied with an opinion or belief of their having some perfection or excellence belonging to them.—'*Works*,' 503, 499.

Sir Joshua Reynolds.

The deformed is what is *uncommon*; Beauty is what is above 'all singular forms, local customs, particularities, and details of every kind.' 'Perfect beauty in any species must combine all the characters which are beautiful in that species.'—*Bain*, '*Mental and Moral Science*,' p. 306.

Hogarth.

The elements of visible beauty are six. —(1) *Fitness* of the parts to some design; twisted columns are elegant if not required to bear too great a weight; (2) *Variety* in form, length, line, magnitude, &c.; *e.g.*, the gradual lessening of a pyramid; (3) *Uniformity*, regularity, or symmetry, which is only beautiful when it helps to preserve the character of fitness; (4) *Simplicity*, or distinctness, because it enables the eye to enjoy the variety with ease; (5) *Intricacy*, because the unravelling of it gives the interest of pursuit, providing employment for the active energies. Waving and serpentine lines lead the eye a wanton kind of chase; (6) *Magnitude*, or quantity, which produces admiration and awe. The serpentine line is the Line of Grace.—'*Analysis of Beauty*.'

Smoothness and Softness.

Burke.

He finds the elements of Beauty to be—(1) Smallness of size; (2) smoothness of surface; (3) gradual variation of direction of outline, by which he means gentle curves; (4) delicacy, or the appearance of fragility; (5) brightness, purity, and softness of colour. He says that beautiful objects have the tendency to produce an *agreeable relaxation of the fibres*. Thus '*smooth* things are relaxing; *sweet* things, which are the *smooth* of taste, are relaxing too; and *sweet smells*, which bear a great affinity to sweet tastes, relax very remarkably.' Hence he proposes 'to call sweetness the beautiful of taste.' 'In trees and flowers smooth leaves are beautiful; smooth slopes of earth in gardens; smooth streams in landscapes; smooth coats of birds and beasts in animal beauty.'—See '*The Sublime and Beautiful*.'

Kant.

He attempts, in a somewhat strained manner, to define the Beautiful by the help of his four categories. (1.) In *quality*, Beauty is that which pleases without interest or pleasure in the existence of the object. This distinguishes it from the simply Agreeable and the Good, the former stimulating desire, and the latter giving motive to the will. (2.) In *quantity*, it is a universal pleasure. As regards the Agreeable, every one is convinced that his pleasure in it is only a personal one; but whoever says, 'This picture is beautiful,' expects every one else to find it so. (3.) Under the aspect of *relation*, the Beautiful is that in which we find the *form* of adaptation without conceiving at the same time any particular *end* of this adaptation. (4.) In *modality*, the Beautiful is a *necessary* satisfaction. The Agreeable actually does cause pleasure, but the Beautiful *must* cause pleasure.—See '*The Critique of Judgment*.'

Hegel.

The Beautiful is defined as the shining of the idea through a sensuous medium (as colour or tone) He defines the form of the Beautiful as unity of the manifold.—'*Encyclop. Brit.*,' i. 218.

Association Theory of Beauty.

Alison.

The emotion of Beauty is not a Simple, but a Complex Emotion involving—(1) The production of some Simple Emotion or the exercise of some moral affection; and (2) a peculiar operation of the Imagination, namely, the flow of a train of ideas through the mind, which ideas are not arbitrarily determined, but always correspond to that simple affection or emotion (as cheerfulness, sadness, awe) awakened by the object. He thus makes association the sole source of the Beautiful. The Oak suggests Strength, the Myrtle Delicacy, the Violet Modesty; there is an analogy between an ascending path and ambition; Blue, the colour of the Heavens in serene weather, is associated with serenity of mind, Green with the delights of spring.—*Alison*, '*Essay on Taste.*'

Jeffrey.

It appears to us that objects are sublime or beautiful, *first*, when they are the natural signs and perpetual concomitants of pleasurable sensations, or, at any rate, of some lively feeling or emotion in ourselves or in some other sentient beings; or, *secondly*, when they are the arbitrary or accidental concomitants of such feelings; or, *thirdly*, when they bear some analogy or fanciful resemblance to things with which these emotions are necessarily connected.—'*Essay on Taste.*'

Our sense of beauty depends entirely on our previous experience of simple pleasures or emotions, and consists in the *suggestion* of agreeable or interesting sensations with which we had formerly been made familiar by the direct and intelligible agency of our common sensibilities; and that vast variety of objects, to which we give the common name of beautiful, become entitled to that appellation, merely because they all possess the power of recalling or reflecting those sensations of which they have been the accompaniments, or with which they have been associated in our imagination by any other more casual bond of connection. According to this view of the matter, therefore, beauty is not an inherent property or quality of objects at all, but the result of the accidental relations in which they may stand to our experience of pleasures or emotions, and does not depend upon any particular configuration of parts, proportions, or colours, in external things, nor upon the unity, coherence, or simplicity of intellectual creations,—but merely upon the associations which, in the case of every individual, may enable these inherent, and otherwise indifferent qualities, to suggest or recall to the mind emotions of a pleasurable or interesting description.—'*Essay on Taste.*'

Mathematical basis of Beauty.

D. R. Hay.

His theory is based upon the Pythagorean system of harmonic number.

Æsthetic science, as the science of beauty is now termed, is based upon that great harmonic law of nature which pervades and governs the universe. It is in its nature neither absolutely physical, nor absolutely metaphysical, but of an intermediate nature, assimilating in various degrees, more or less, to one or other of those opposite kinds of science. It specially embodies the inherent principles which govern impressions made upon the mind through the senses of hearing and seeing. Thus, the æsthetic pleasure derived from listening to the beautiful in musical composition, and from contemplating the beautiful in works of formative art, is in both cases simply a response in the human mind to artistic development of the great harmonic law upon which the science is based.—'*The Science of Beauty*,' p. 15.

Sir W. Hamilton.

Not variety alone, and not unity alone, but variety combined with unity, is that quality in objects, which we emphatically denominate *beautiful.*—'*Metaphysics,*' ii 449.

Theological basis of Beauty.

John Ruskin.

He divides Beauty into Typical and Vital Beauty The forms of Typical Beauty are—(1) Infinity, the type of the Divine incomprehensibility; (2) Unity, the type of the Divine comprehensiveness; (3) Repose, the type of the Divine permanence; (4) Symmetry, the type of the Divine justice; (5) Purity, the type of the Divine energy, and (6) Moderation, the type of government by law.—'*Modern Painters,*' vol ii

Physical basis of Beauty.

Grant Allen.

My object is to exhibit the purely physical origin of the sense of beauty, and its relativity to our nervous organisation Modern scientific Psychology, based upon an accurate Physiology, has roughly demonstrated that all mental phenomena are the subjective sides of what are objectively cognised as nervous functions; and that they are in consequence as rigorously limited by natural laws as the physical processes whose correlatives they are. But while this truth has been abundantly illustrated with regard to those physical functions (such as sensations and voluntary motions) which are ordinarily regarded as of purely bodily origin, it has not been carried out into full detail in the case of the intellectual faculties and the higher emotions, which, until the rise of Physiological Psychology, were usually considered as purely and exclusively mental I wish, therefore, to examine the æsthetic feelings as an intermediate link between the bodily senses and the higher emotions—'*Physiological Æsthetics,*' p 2.

When we exercise our limbs and muscles, not for any ulterior life-serving object, but merely for the sake of the pleasure which the exercise affords us, the amusement is called play. When we similarly exercise our eyes or ears, the resulting pleasure is called an Æsthetic Feeling. In both cases the pleasure is a concomitant of the activity of a well-fed and under-worked organ, but in the latter instance it is on the receptive side, in the former on the re-active, so that Æsthetic Pleasure may be provisionally defined as the subjective concomitant of the normal amount of activity, not directly connected with life-serving function, in the peripheral end-organs of the cerebro-spinal nervous system —'*Physiological Æsthetics,*' p 34

The Pleasure of Beauty.

It is mental

There is nothing that makes its way more directly to the Soul than Beauty, which immediately diffuses a secret satisfaction and complacency through the Imagination, and gives a finishing to anything that is great or uncommon. The very first discovery of it strikes the mind with an inward joy, and spreads a cheerfulness and delight through all its faculties —*Addison,* '*Spectator,*' No. 412

A beautiful thing is one whose form occupies the Imagination and Understanding in a free and full, and consequently in an agreeable activity.—*Hamilton,* '*Metaphysics,*' ii 512.

And contemplative.

The gratification we feel in the beautiful, the sublime, the picturesque is purely contemplative, that is, the feeling of pleasure which we then experience arises solely from the consideration of the object, and altogether apart from any desire of, or satisfaction in, its possession —*Hamilton,* '*Metaphysics,*' ii 507

It sustains the soul.

Beauty has been appointed by the Deity to be one of the elements by which the human soul is continually sustained; it is therefore to be found more or less in all natural objects, but in order that we may not satiate ourselves with it, and weary of it, it is rarely granted to us in its utmost degrees. When we see it in those utmost degrees, we are attracted to it strongly, and remember it long, as in the case of singularly beautiful scenery, or a beautiful countenance. On the other hand, absolute ugliness is admitted as rarely as perfect beauty.—*Ruskin*, '*Architecture and Painting*,' Lect. i.

It affords relief from the miseries of life.

Whenever (natural beauty) discloses itself suddenly to our view, it almost always succeeds in delivering us, though it may be only for a moment, from subjectivity, from the slavery of the will, and in raising us to the state of pure knowing. This is why the man who is tormented by passion, or want, or care, is so suddenly revived, cheered, and restored by a single free glance into nature: the storm of passion, the pressure of desire and fear, and all the miseries of willing are then at once, and in a marvellous manner, calmed and appeased. For at the moment at which, freed from the will, we give ourselves up to pure will-less knowing, we pass into a world from which everything is absent that influenced our will and moved us so violently through it. This feeling of knowledge lifts us as wholly and entirely away from all that, as do sleep and dreams; happiness and unhappiness have disappeared; we are no longer individual; the individual is forgotten; we are only pure subject of knowledge; we are only that *one* eye of the world which looks out from all knowing creatures, but which can become perfectly free from the service of will in man alone. Thus all difference of individuality so entirely disappears, that it is all the same whether the perceiving eye belongs to a mighty king or to a wretched beggar; for neither joy nor complaining can pass that boundary with us.—*Schopenhauer*, '*The World as Will and Idea*,' i. 255, 256.

It is a growth.

Æsthetic impressions are a growth, rising, with the advance of intellectual culture, from the crude enjoyments of sensation to the more refined and subtle delights of the cultivated mind.—'*Encyclop. Brit.*,' i. 214.

Permanent.

A thing of beauty is a joy for ever:
Its loveliness increases; it will never
Pass into nothingness.
—*Keats*, '*Endymion*.'

The source of Beauty's power.

Beauty of all kinds gives us a peculiar delight and satisfaction; as deformity produces pain, upon whatever subject it may be placed, and whether surveyed in an animate or inanimate object. It would seem that the very essence of beauty consists in its power of producing pleasure. All its effects, therefore, must proceed from this circumstance.—*Hume*, '*Philosophical Works*,' iv. 148.

The Power of Beauty

To exact homage.

There is but one power to which all are eager to bow down, to which all take pride in paying homage, and that is the power of Beauty.—*Hare*, '*Guesses at Truth*,' p. 354.

To influence.

Beauty has been the delight and torment of the world ever since it began. The philosophers have felt its influence so sensibly, that almost every one of them has left us some saying or other, which has intimated that he too well knew the power of it. One [Aristotle] has told us that a graceful person is a more powerful recommendation than the best letter that can be writ in your favour. Carneades called it Royalty without force.—*Steele*, '*Spectator*,' No. 144.

Its moral effects.

Let our artists be those who are gifted to discern the true nature of beauty and grace; then will our youth dwell in the land of health, amid fair sights and sounds; and beauty, the effluence of fair works, will visit the eye and ear, like a healthful breeze from a purer region, and insensibly draw the soul even in childhood into harmony with the beauty of reason.—*Plato, 'The Republic,'* iii. 401.

I believe that it is not good for man to live among what is most beautiful;—that he is a creature incapable of satisfaction by anything upon earth; and that to allow him habitually to possess, in any kind whatsoever, the utmost that earth can give, is the surest way to cast him into lassitude or discontent.—*Ruskin, 'Modern Painters,'* IV. pt. v. ch. xi.

Beauty of character.

A beautiful character is he who with ease exercises the virtues which circumstances require of him: righteousness, benevolence, moderation, fidelity; and who in a happy and contented existence, finds his joy in the exercise of these duties. Who but must find such a man amiable, and love him in whom we meet the full unison of the natural impulses and the prescriptions of reason?—*Martensen, 'Christian Ethics,'* ii. 47.

Beauty, if it light well, maketh virtues shine, and vices blush.—*Bacon, 'Essays,'* xliii.

Artistic Beauty.

The academic theory of Beauty.

This abstract term has an air of Platonic entity which, like everything touched by metaphysical philosophy, refuses to submit to analysis. From ancient days down to our own, almost all the æsthetic doctrines founded upon the 'beauty' theory, have considered it as something abstract, divine, with an absolute and distinct reality quite apart from man. The small number of metaphysicians who have held a different view has exercised a very restricted influence over art, to which we need not refer here.—*Véron, 'Æsthetics,'* p. 96.

The Line of Beauty.

The curve soothes and pleases us by the variety of its impressions, and by the easy gradation which permits of an almost unconscious passage from one impression to another; just as the gentle progression of melody has a peculiar charm for the ear. The serpentine line, so extolled by Hogarth, unites, we may say, the two elements of variety and unity: it combines rigidity and softness, and produced a superior harmony which is, in fact, what is called grace. This 'line of beauty,' as it has been called, joins to its other advantages that of being the line of life *par excellence.* All living things, whether animal or vegetable, display more or less the serpentine line; when it is not in their shape, it is to be found in their movements.—*Véron, 'Æsthetics,'* pp. 40, 41.

Is Beauty imparted by the Artist?

The only beauty in a work of art is that placed there by the artist. It is both the result of his efforts and the foundation of his success. As often as he is struck by any vivid impression—whether moral, intellectual, or physical,—and expresses that impression by some outward process—by poetry, music, sculpture, painting, or architecture,—in such a way as to cause its communication with the soul of spectator or auditor; so often does he produce a work of art the beauty of which will be in exact proportion to the intelligence and depth of the sentiment displayed, and the power shown in giving it outward form.—*Véron, 'Æsthetics,'* p. 108.

That is the best part of Beauty, which a picture cannot express; no, nor the first sight of the life.—*Bacon, 'Essays,'* xliii.

Natural Beauty.

Of clouds.

It is a strange thing how little in general people know about the sky. It is the part of creation in which nature has done more for the sake of pleasing man, more for the sole and evident purpose of talking to him and teaching him, than in any other of her works, and it is just the part in which we least attend to her. There are not many of her other works in which some more material or essential purpose than the mere pleasing of man is not answered by every part of their organisation, but every essential purpose of the sky might, so far as we know, be answered, if once in three days or thereabouts, a great, ugly black rain cloud were brought up over the blue, and everything well watered, and so all left blue again till next time, with perhaps a film of morning and evening mist for dew. And instead of this, there is not a moment of any day of our lives, when nature is not producing scene after scene, picture after picture, glory after glory, and working still upon such exquisite and constant principles of the most perfect beauty, that it is quite certain it is all done for us, and intended for our perpetual pleasure. And every man, wherever placed, however far from other sources of interest or of beauty, has this doing for him constantly. The noblest scenes of the earth can be seen and known but by few; it is not intended that man should live always in the midst of them, he injures them by his presence, he ceases to feel them if he be always with them; but the sky is for all; bright as it is, is not "too bright, nor good, for human nature's daily food," it is fitted in all its functions for the perpetual comfort and exalting of the heart, for the soothing it and purifying it from its dross and dust. Sometimes gentle, sometimes capricious, sometimes awful, never the same for two moments together; almost human in its passions, almost spiritual in its tenderness, almost divine in its infinity, its appeal to what is immortal in us, is as distinct as its ministry of chastisement or of blessing to what is mortal is essential.—*Ruskin*, '*Modern Painters*,' I. pt. ii. sc. iii. ch. i.

Beauty of Sunset.

Nature has a thousand ways and means of rising above herself, but incomparably the noblest manifestations of her capability of colour are in these sunsets among the high clouds. I speak especially of the moment before the sun sinks, when his light turns pure rose colour, and when this light falls upon a zenith covered with countless cloud-forms of inconceivable delicacy, threads and flakes of vapour, which would in common daylight be pure snow white, and which give therefore fair field to the tone of light. There is then no limit to the multitude, and no check to the intensity of the hues assumed. The whole sky, from the zenith to the horizon, becomes one molten, mantling sea of colour and fire; every black bar turns into massy gold, every ripple and wave into unsullied, shadowless crimson, and purple, and scarlet, and colours for which there are no words in language, and no ideas in the mind,—things which can only be conceived while they are visible,—the intense hollow blue of the upper sky melting through it all,—showing here deep, and pure, and lightless, there, modulated by the filmy, formless body of the transparent vapour, till it is lost imperceptibly in its crimson and gold.—*Ruskin*, '*Modern Painters*,' I. pt. ii. sc. ii. ch. ii.

VI. MORAL AND RELIGIOUS FEELINGS

Distinguished from Moral Intelligence.

There is in man a moral law,—a law of duty, which unconditionally commands the fulfilment of its behests. This supposes that we are able to fulfil them, or our nature is a lie; and the liberty of human action is thus, independently of all direct consciousness, involved in the datum of the law of duty. Inasmuch also as moral intelligence unconditionally commands us to perform what we are conscious to be our duty, there is attributed to man an absolute work,—an absolute dignity. The feeling which the manifestation of this work excites is called Respect. With the consciousness of the lofty nature of our moral tendencies, and our ability to fulfil what the law of duty prescribes, there is connected the feeling of self-respect, whereas from a consciousness of the contrast between what we ought to do, and what we actually perform, there arises the feeling of self-abasement The sentiment of respect for the law of duty is the moral feeling, which has by some been improperly denominated the Moral Sense; for through this feeling we do not take cognisance whether anything be morally good or morally evil, but when, by our intelligence, we recognise aught to be of such a character, there is herewith associated a feeling of pain or pleasure which is nothing more than our state in reference to the fulfilment or violation of the law.—*Hamilton*, '*Metaphysics*,' ii. 520.

The Moral Sense in Animals.

Of these elementary moral feelings, those of the lower animals which associate most closely with man are obviously capable. The *sense of duty* towards a being of a higher nature, which shows itself in the *actions* of the young Child towards its Parent or Nurse, long before any Ideational comprehension of it can have been attained, is exactly paralleled by that of the Dog or Horse towards its master 'Man,' as Burns truly said, 'is the God of the Dog.' It is the substituting of the *superior* for the *inferior* directing principle, the distinct Intellectual comprehension of it, and the volitional direction of the attention to it, which constitutes the essential difference between the most conscientious effort of the enlightened Christian, and the honest and self-sacrificing response to his sense of Duty, which is seen in the Horse that falls down dead from exhaustion after putting forth his utmost power at the behest of his rider, or in the Dog who uses his utmost skill and intelligence in seeking and collecting his master's flock.—*Carpenter*, '*Mental Physiology*,' p. 212.

Experience shows, as Dr. J. D Morell justly remarks, 'that an instinctive *apprehension* of "right" and "wrong," as attached to certain actions, precedes in the child any distinct *comprehension* of the language by which we convey Moral truths. Moreover, the power and purity of moral feeling not unfrequently exist even to the highest degree amongst those who never made the question of Morals in any way the object of direct thought, and may perchance be unconscious of the treasure they possess in their bosoms.'—*Carpenter*, '*Mental Physiology*,' p 212.

Evolutional Theory of the Moral Sense.

Darwin.

The following proposition seems to me in a high degree probable—namely, that any animal whatever, endowed with well-marked social instincts, the parental and filial affections being here included, would inevitably acquire a moral sense or conscience, as soon as its intellectual powers had become as well, or nearly as well, developed, as in man. For, *firstly*, the social instincts lead an animal to take pleasure in the society of its fellows, to feel a certain amount of sympathy with them, and to perform various services for them. *Secondly*, As soon as the mental faculties had become highly developed, images of all past actions and motives would be incessantly passing through the brain of each individual, and that feeling of dissatisfaction, or even misery, which invariably results from any unsatisfied instinct, would arise, as often as it was perceived that the enduring and always present social instinct had yielded to some other instinct, at the same time stronger, but neither enduring in its nature, nor leaving behind it a very vivid impression *Thirdly*, After the power of language had been acquired, and the wishes of the community could be expressed, the common opinion how each member ought to act for the public good, would naturally become in a paramount degree the guide to action. *Lastly*, Habit in the individual would ultimately play a very important part in guiding the conduct of each member; for the social instinct, together with sympathy, is like any other instinct, greatly strengthened by habit, and so consequently would be obedience to the wishes and judgment of the community.—'*Descent of Man*,' pp. 98, 99.

Herbert Spencer.

I believe that the experiences of utility organised and consolidated through all past generations of the human race, have been producing corresponding modifications, which, by continued transmission and accumulation, have become in us certain faculties of moral intuition—certain emotions responding to right and wrong conduct, which have no apparent basis in the individual experiences of utility.—*Letter to Mr Mill, in Bain's 'Mental and Moral Science*,' p. 722.

The Religious Feelings.

There are religious *thoughts*, *feelings*, and *actions*; the first giving rise to the second, and the second to the third. As it is with the social affections, so it is with the religious; the *object* must be known in part before any *feeling* is excited, and then it is more fully known.

The religious affections are Fear, Adoration, Gratitude, Faith. These are in nature like the social affections; but they are distinguished by their unlimited character. Their objects are invisible, *indefinitely* great, and so approach towards the Infinite.—*Godwin, 'Active Principles*,' pp. 99, 100.

Distinction between Moral and Religious Feelings

Are religious and *moral* feelings identical? They are certainly closely related, and touch upon and interpenetrate each other. It is possible, however, to distinguish the two in thought, for the purpose of scientific inquiry, in the same way as has been done with religion and morality themselves. The *moral* feeling manifests itself more particularly in its negative aspects as tact, and on the positive side as impulse or instinct. The substance in which it inheres is conduct—the doing of things, or leaving them undone. It impels or restrains. *Religious* feeling is self-centred, and finds its satisfaction in itself. It is, in short, the *sacred chamber of our inner being*, that ἄδυτον of the soul, in which all earthly changes cease to agitate, together with all opposition of desire and aversion, within whose limits the merely sensuous has its range. This inner sanctuary, which is first disclosed to the *penitent* alone—this heaven in the soul, whence shine the stars of faith, and love, and hope, to cheer the darkness of our night—this anchor that holds firm, upon which everything depends and must depend if it shall not founder in the current of fleeting time—is *religious feeling*.—*Crooks and Hurst, 'Theol. Encyclop*.,' pp 35, 36.

Religious Feeling is not Conscience, but is Established by it.

Religious feeling should be firm and steadfast. As it develops into definite convictions, it should also become a settled disposition. In this regard the *conscience* renders the service in practice which *reason* performs in theory. As the religious feeling is *enlightened* by reason, so it is *established* and morally *strengthened* by the conscience. In practical matters *law* stands related to *conscience* as the understanding to reason in the domain of theory. In the latter province, that is, theory, the cognitions, being merely logically arranged and combined by the understanding, may harden into a lifeless dogma, and become rigid; and, in like manner, the law of outward morality may become a dead statute, for the letter of the law kills, the spirit makes alive. A conscience enlightened by reason will doubtless be one in which religious feeling manifests and approves itself. But as feeling could not be resolved into reason, *so here it cannot be resolved into conscience.*—*Crooks and Hurst, 'Theol. Encyclop.*' p. 40.

C.—PSYCHOLOGY AND PHILOSOPHY OF THE WILL.

XVI.

THE WILL.

I THE NATURE OF THE WILL.

It is the faculty of control

Will is a power of control over the other faculties and capacities of our nature, by means of which we are enabled to determine personal activity

It is to be carefully observed that Will is control of our own powers, *not of external things.* Edwards has quite overlooked this in his definition, 'Will is that which chooses anything' ('Freedom of Will,' i 1). And, again, he extends its application to '*things* present and absent' Locke had said ('Essay,' ii 21, sec 15), with more accuracy, '*Volition* is an act of the mind knowingly exerting that dominion it takes itself to have over any part of the man by employing it in, or withholding it from any particular action And what is the *Will* but the faculty to do this?' So Reid makes Will 'a power to determine, in things which he conceives to depend upon his determinations' ('Active Powers,' ii 1) From the time of Kant, the doctrine of the Will has generally had the leading place in the Ethical systems of Germany.—*Calderwood*, '*Moral Philosophy*,' p 165

We find in ourselves a power to begin or forbear, continue or end, several actions of our minds and motions of our bodies, barely by a thought or preference of the mind ordering, or, as it were, commanding the doing or not doing such or such a particular action. This power, which the mind has thus to order the consideration of any idea, or the forbearing to consider it, or to prefer the motion of any part of the body to its rest, and *vice versâ*, in any particular instance, is that which we call the will—*Locke*, '*Human Understanding*,' II. xxi. 5.

According to the Sensational theory it is action excited by Desire

There appears no circumstance by which the cases called voluntary are distinguished from the involuntary, except that in the voluntary there exists a Desire. Shedding tears at the hearing of a tragic story, we do not desire to weep; laughing at the recital of a comic story, we do not desire to laugh. But when we elevate the arm to ward off a blow, we desire to lift the arm; when we turn the head to look at some attractive object, we desire to move the head. I believe that no case of voluntary action can be mentioned in which it would not be an appropriate expression to call the action desired.

In a voluntary action we recognise two Ideas: first, the idea of the sensation or exemption, which two, for shortness, we shall call by one name, Pleasure, secondly, the idea of an action of our own as the cause of the pleasure It is also easy to see how the Idea of a pleasure should excite the idea of the action which is the cause of it; and how, when the Idea exists, the action should follow —*Mill*, '*Analysis, &c*' ii. 350.

It is an Essential Feature in the Moral Personality

Will is an essential and prominent feature of Personality A person is a Self-conscious Intelligence capable of self-determination If Intelligence is needful to make knowledge of Moral Law possible, Will, or power of self-determination is needful to make obedience to that law possible Power of self-determination is thus essential to the nature of a moral being Kant says of man that 'his will' is his 'proper self' ('Metaph of Ethics,' 3d ed 71) —*Calderwood*, '*Moral Philosophy*,' p 166

Moral good lies in the region of the will. By this I mean that every truly virtuous act must be a voluntary one. In saying so, I do not mean to assert that every morally good act must be a volition contemplating or performing some outward deed. The will of man exists in other forms than in a resolution to act. Wherever there is choice, I hold that there is will. Whenever I adopt any particular object presented, or prefer any one object to another, there is choice. There is also the exercise of choice, and therefore of will, in all cases in which we deliberately reject any object or proposal made to us. I hold then that there is choice—not only in volition, or resolution, or the final determination to act—there is choice in wish or in voluntary aversion. When we wish that our friends may prosper and be in health, that God's name may be hallowed, there is will. These wishes and volitions and rejections may unite themselves with any one of our feelings, and even with our intellectual exercises. Using 'will' in this wide sense, I say that it is the region, and the exclusive region, of moral good. It is in voluntary acts that the conscience discerns a moral quality, and it is upon such acts, and no others, that it pronounces its decisions. It is upon acts which we were free to perform, but from which also we were free to abstain, that all the judgments of conscience are declared.—*M'Cosh*, '*Intuitions*,' p 259

Volition is not, indeed, the whole of personality, but it is one necessary element of it;—the consciousness of the one rising and falling with the consciousness of the other; both more or less vividly manifested, as is the case with all consciousness, according to the less or greater familiarity of particular instances; but never wholly obliterated in any,—capable at any moment of being detected by analysis, and incapable of being annihilated by any effort of thought.—*Mansel*, '*Metaphysics*,' p 362.

Will and Volition Distinguished

Will is an ambiguous word, being sometimes put for the *faculty* of willing; sometimes for the *act* of that faculty, besides other meanings. But *volition* always signifies the *act of willing*, and nothing else.—*Reid*

The correlative terms, *will* and *volition*, are usually distinguished, in the language of philosophy, as applying the one to the general faculty, the other to the special acts in which it manifests itself. A volition is an act of the will.—*Mansel*, '*Metaphysics*,' p 171

Will is distinct from all other Powers.

Will is a power distinct from all the other powers already named. Intellect is knowing power, Will is controlling power. Affection is inclination towards another person, Will is guidance of our own activity. Desire is craving of what we have not, Will is use of what belongs to us as part of our own nature. Emotion is excitement of feeling in contemplation of an object, Will is energy from within, directing us in our relations to external objects. Affection, Desire, and Emotion, are all concerned with external objects, Will is concerned with the management of affections, desires, and emotions. Intellect, besides being occupied with the objects and occasions which awaken affections, desires, and emotions, is capable of making these exercises of feeling themselves the matter of observation, but it is the function of Will, under fixed laws, to determine in the case of all these, including Intellect, the time, manner, and measure of exercise.—*Calderwood*, '*Moral Philosophy*,' p 166.

Its Relation to Intelligence

Will holds a double relation to Intelligence, (1) a relation of *superiority* in respect of control; and (2) a relation of *dependence* in respect of need for guidance in the government of the subordinate powers. The former is the common relation of Will to all other powers of personal activity. The latter is a special relation subsisting between Will and Intellect, by reason of which self-control in human experience is a Rational Self-control.

Reason is the 'legislator and governor of Will' (Kant, 'Metaph of Ethics,' p 18) The term 'governor' must, however, be interpreted in harmony with legislation or discovery of law, which is the proper function of intelligence.

Intellect has superiority of teaching power, without controlling power, Will has superiority of controlling power, without teaching power. The grand distinction of man as an active being is recognised when the harmony of these two is such as to secure unity of force and unity of result — *Calderwood*, '*Moral Philosophy*,' p 167.

Physical Side of Volition.

The Volitional exertion really consists in an intensification of the hyperæmic state of the Ideational centre, which will produce an augmented tension of its nerve-force, whose discharge through the *motor* centres calls forth the muscular movement. And this may take place without a corresponding intensification of the *idea* itself, if, according to the doctrine previously advanced, we only become *conscious* of Cerebral changes as Ideas, when their influence has been reflected downwards to the Sensorium. —*Carpenter*, '*Mental Physiology*,' p. 425.

The Power of the Will

It is of obvious practical importance to ascertain precisely how far the power of the will actually extends. The effects which it is possible to cause by human volition seem to be of three kinds: (1.) Changes in the external world consequent upon muscular contractions. (2.) Changes in the train of ideas and feelings that constitutes our conscious life. (3.) Changes in the tendencies to act hereafter in certain ways under certain circumstances.—*Sidgwick*, '*Methods of Ethics*,' p. 66.

Some psychologists confine the sphere of the Will to mere muscular movements, this view is adopted by Professor Bain. 'The control of Feeling and of Thought is through the muscles. The intervention of the Will being restricted to movements, the voluntary control of the Feelings hinges on the muscular accompaniments' In the same way the control of Will over Thought is due to the 'local identity of actual and ideal movements:' hence the control over actual movements leads on to control over ideal movements. It will be noticed that Professor Bain does not very clearly point out how a control of the Will over ideas of movement is developed into a control over ideas of other kinds, not 'occupying the same parts' as those of muscular movements. And further, it should be remembered that the 'local identity' of ideal sensations with actual sensations is only a hypothesis, more or less plausible.—*Ryland*, '*Handbook, &c.*,' p. 113.

In so far as the Will cannot originate all actions, and cannot altogether prevent the rise of impulses, it has only a restricted control. Within these natural limits, however, the control exercised by the Will is rational self-control, inasmuch as the exercise of intellectual power is constantly under command of the Will, for the guidance of our activity.—*Calderwood*, '*Moral Philosophy*,' p 171.

The Idea of Freedom proceeds from the Will. (See FREEWILL.)

It is from the exercise of will that we get our very idea of freedom. As we survey the external world, including even our own bodily frame, we find it bound in the chain of physical causation, in which every movement of an object is determined from without. Even our very intellectual and emotive states are under laws of association and potencies which control them. It is in the sanctuary of the will that freedom alone is to be found.—*M'Cosh*, '*Intuitions, &c.*,' p. 271.

II. THEORIES OF THE WILL.

Professor Bain.

Professor Bain states the primitive elements of the Will to be, first, the existence of a spontaneous tendency to execute movements independent of the stimulus of sensations or feelings; and, secondly, the link between a present action and a present feeling, whereby the one comes under the control of the other.

There is in the constitution a store of nervous energy, accumulated during the nutrition and repose of the system, and proceeding into action with or without the application of outward stimulants or feelings anyhow arising. Spontaneity, in fact, is the response of the system to nutrition, —an effusion of power of which the food is the condition.

We suppose movements spontaneously begun, and accidentally causing pleasure; we then assume that with the pleasure there will be an increase of vital energy, in which increase the fortunate movements will share, and thereby increase the pleasure. Or, on the other hand, we suppose the spontaneous movements to give pain, and assume that with the pain there will be a decrease of energy, extending to the movements that cause the evil, and thereby providing a remedy. A few repetitions of the fortuitous concurrence of pleasure and a certain movement will lead to the forging of an acquired connection, so that at an after time the pleasure or its idea shall evoke the proper movement at once. —'*The Emotions and the Will*,' pp. 303, 304, 315.

The Will as Reflex Action.

Hartmann.

It is scarcely to be doubted that what we regard as immediate cause of our action, and call Will, is to be found in the consciousness of animals as causal moment of their action, and must also be called Will, if we cease to give ourselves airs of superiority by employing different names for the very same things. The dog *will* not separate from its master; it *wills* to save the child which has fallen into the water from the well-known death; the bird *will* not let its young be injured; the cock *will* not share his hen with another, &c. I know there are many people who think they elevate man when they ascribe as much as possible in the life of animals, especially the lower ones, to 'reflex action.' If these persons have in their minds the ordinary physiological sense of the term reflex action, involuntary reaction on an external stimulus, it may safely be said that either they have never observed animals, or that they have eyes but they see not. If, however, they extend the meaning of reflex action beyond its usual physiological acceptation, they are assuredly right; but then they forget—firstly, that man, too, lives and moves in pure reflex actions, that every act of will is a reflex action; and, secondly, that *every* reflex action is an act of will.—*Hartmann*, '*Philosophy of the Unconscious*,' i. 60.

Professor Green's Doctrine

Is there a single principle which manifests itself under endless diversity of circumstance and relation in all the particular desires of a man, and is thus, in virtue of its own nature, designated by a single name? And are our acts of intelligence and will severally the expression of a single principle, which renders each group of acts possible, and is entitled in its own right to the single name it bears? We shall find reason to adopt this view. The meaning we attach to it, however, is not that in one man there are three separate or separable principles or agents severally underlying his acts of desire, understanding, and will. We adopt it in the sense that there is one subject or spirit, which desires in all a man's experiences of desire, understands in all operations of his intelligence, wills in all his acts of willing; and that the essential character of his desires depends on their all being desires of one and the same subject which also understands, the essential character of his intelligence on its being an activity of one and the same subject which also desires, the essential character of his acts of will on their proceeding from one and the same subject which also desires and understands. —'*Prolegomena to Ethics*,' p 122.

The Will is the Man himself.

The will is simply the man Any act of will is the expression of the man as he at the time is The motive issuing in his act, the object of his will, the idea which for the time he sets himself to realise, are but the same thing in different words. Each is the reflex of what for the time, as at once feeling, desiring, and thinking, the man is In willing he carries with him, so to speak, his whole self to the realisation of the given idea All the time that he so wills he may feel the pangs of conscience, or (on the other hand) the annoyance, the sacrifice, implied in acting conscientiously He may think that he is doing wrong, or that it is doubtful whether after all there is really an objection to his acting as he has resolved to do He may desire some one's good opinion which he is throwing away, or some pleasure which he is sacrificing. But for all that it is only the feeling, thought, and desire, represented by the act of will, that the man recognises as for the time himself The feeling, thought, and desire with which the act conflicts are influences that he is aware of influences to which he is susceptible, but they are not *he* —'*Prolegomena to Ethics*,' pp 158, 159.

Autonomy of the Will the Supreme Principle of Morality.

Autonomy of the will is that property of it by which it is a law to itself (independently on any property of the objects of volition). The principle of autonomy then is: Always so to choose that the same volition shall comprehend the maxims of our choice as a universal law We cannot prove that this practical rule is an imperative, *i e.*, that the will of every rational being is necessarily bound to it as a condition, by a mere analysis of the conceptions which occur in it, since it is a synthetical proposition; we must advance beyond the cognition of the objects to a critical examination of the subject, that is, of the pure practical reason, for this synthetic proposition which commands apodictically must be capable of being cognised wholly *à priori* But that the principle of autonomy in question is the sole principle of morals can be readily shown by mere analysis of the conceptions of morality For by this analysis we find that its principle must be a categorical imperative, and that what this commands is neither more nor less than this very autonomy.—*Kant*, '*Theory of Ethics*,' p 59

Will gives Man Authority over his Desires and Inclinations

The claims to freedom of will made even by common reason are founded on the consciousness and the admitted supposition that reason is independent on merely subjectively determined causes which together constitute what belongs to sensation only, and which consequently comes under the general designation of sensibility Man considering himself in this way as an intelligence, places himself thereby in a different order of things, and in a relation to determining grounds of a wholly different kind, when on the one hand he thinks of himself as an intelligence endowed with a will, and consequently with causality, and when on the other he perceives himself as a phenomenon in the world of sense (as he really is also), and affirms that his causality is subject to external determination according to laws of nature Now he soon becomes aware that both can hold good, nay, must hold good, at the same time.

Hence it comes to pass that man claims the possession of a will which takes no account of anything that comes under the head of desires and inclinations, and on the contrary conceives actions as possible to him, nay, even as necessary, which can only be done by disregarding all desires and sensible inclinations The causality of such actions lies in him as an intelligence, and in the laws of effects and actions (which depend) on the principles of an intelligible world, of which indeed he knows nothing more than that in it pure reason alone independent on sensibility gives the law; moreover, since it is only in that world, as an intelligence, that he is his proper self (being as man only the appearance of himself), those laws apply to him directly and categorically, so that the incitements of inclinations and appetites (in other words, the whole nature of the world of sense) cannot impair the laws of his volition as an intelligence.—*Kant*, '*Theory of Ethics*,' pp. 77, 78.

XVII

RELATIONS OF THE WILL TO:

I. DESIRE.

The Nature of Desire.

Described.

The uneasiness a man finds in himself upon the absence of anything whose present enjoyment carries the idea of delight with it, is what we call desire; which is greater or less, as that uneasiness is more or less vehement.—*Locke*, '*Human Understanding*,' II. xx. 6.

Desire is more comprehensive than appetite. It is drawn forth by all that produces mere pleasure or personal gratification. Hence it denotes the liking or longing we have for that which pleases, or for anything in so far as it gives pleasure. The foundation of all desire, then, is the sense of pleasure, and, we may add, of pain. We wish for that which causes pleasure, and we wish away that which creates pain. —*Murphy*, '*Human Mind*,' p. 232.

Desire is a state of mind where there is a motive to act—some pleasure or pain, actual or ideal—without the ability. It is thus a state of interval, or suspense between motive and execution. Walking at a distance from home, the air suddenly cools to the chilling point. We have no remedy at hand. The condition thus arising, a motive without the power of acting, is Desire.—*Bain*, '*Mental Science*,' p. 366.

Man has a nature and his nature has an end. This end is indicated by certain tendencies. He feels inclination or *desire* towards certain objects, which are suited to his faculties and fitted to improve them. The attainment of these objects gives pleasure, the absence of them is a source of uneasiness. Man seeks them by a natural and spontaneous effort.—*Fleming*, '*Vocab. of Phil.*,' p. 135.

Distinguished from Will.

The distinction between desire and will is, that what we will must be an action and our own action; what we desire may not be our own action; it may be no action at all.—*Reid.*

[But the Will has power over thought as well as action. See under *Will*.]

By will is meant a free and deliberate, by desire a blind and fatal tendency to act. —*Hamilton*, '*Metaphysics*,' i. 185.

That volition is not identical with desire was one of the earliest results of psychological analysis, and is, indeed, obvious to the consciousness of every man who has experienced the two, however much they may have been confounded together by the perversity of a few unscrupulous system-makers. A man may be thirsty and yet refuse to drink; his desire drawing him one way, and his will determining him in the other.—*Mansel*, '*Metaphysics*,' p. 171.

Desiring and willing are two distinct acts of the mind, and the will is perfectly distinguished from desire, which in the very same action may have a quite contrary tendency from that which our will sets us upon A man whom I cannot deny, may oblige me to use persuasions to another, which, at the same time I am speaking, I may wish may not prevail on him In this case, it is plain the will and desire run counter —*Locke*, '*Human Understanding*,' II. xxi 30

Appetite is the will's solicitor, and the will is appetite's controller; what we covet according to the one, by the other we often reject.—*Hooker*, '*Eccles. Pol.*,' bk i.

Illusion of Desire.

It is hard to resist the illusion that a thing will happen because we desire it.—*Stephen*, '*The Science of Ethics*,' p 55

Thy wish was father to that thought —*Shakespeare*, '*Hen. IV.*,' pt ii act iv. sc 4

Variety in Desire.

Number of Desires

The number of our desires is the same with that of our pleasurable sensations. [But see below.]—*Mill*, '*Analysis*,' ii. 193.

Springing from the pleasures and pains of which we find ourselves susceptible, our desires are no less numerous and diversified in their character They multiply also as our wants increase by experience, by habit, by education, and by general culture. They differ in their nature according to the source from which they come.—*Murphy*, '*Human Mind*,' p. 233.

Two classes.

Under the general head of Desires may be specified (1) the *appetites*, which take their rise from bodily conditions, and are common to men and brutes,—comprising the feelings of hunger, thirst, and sexual instinct; and (2) the *desires*, as they are sometimes called in a special sense, such as the desire of knowledge, of society, of esteem, of power, and of superiority, together with the counter-feelings of repugnance to the opposite class of objects.—*Mansel*, '*Metaphysics*,' p 157.

The Growth of Desire.

Through consideration of a proposed benefit.

By a due consideration, and examining any good proposed, it is in our power to raise our desires in a due proportion to the value of that good, whereby in its turn and place, it may come to work upon the will, and be pursued Due contemplation brings it nearer to our mind, gives some relish of it, and raises in us desire —*Locke*, '*Human Understanding*,' II. xxi. 45, 46

By the sense of need and the expectation of pleasure

The provocatives of desire are (1) the actual wants and deficiencies of the system, and (2) the experience of pleasure The first class correspond with the appetites and with those artificial cravings of the system generated by physical habits An interval or delay in the gratification of our natural wants brings in the state of craving or longing The main provocative of desire is the experience of pleasure. When any pleasure has once been tasted, the recollection is afterwards a motive to regain it. Desire comes in with new pleasures.—*Bain*, '*Mental Science*,' p 369

The rise of desire is not within our control.

Desires are not under our own control; they arise naturally and necessarily on the occasion of the presence of objects which affect us agreeably or disagreeably We cannot help being so constituted as to derive pleasure from certain objects; we cannot help feeling attracted to pleasant objects, for the pleasure constitutes the attraction. But we can help yielding to the attraction of desire when felt; and we can help putting ourselves in the way of feeling it.—*Mansel*, '*Metaphysics*,' p. 172.

Men differ according to the strength of their desires

Men differ as their desires are vehement or weak. Some can hardly be said to have any desires at all, others would overturn kingdoms and mingle heaven with earth, to effect the least of all their desires.

Another variety in human character is the length or continuation of desire, which, united with vehemence of desire, makes, I believe, what we call strength of character: for we could not deny to any man that attribute who wished anything vehemently and continued in the pursuit of it steadily —*Smith*, '*Moral Philosophy*,' p. 349.

The Object of Desire

James Mill and others hold that this is always some pleasure.

In the case of a pleasurable sensation, the state of consciousness under the sensation, that is, the sensation itself, differed from other sensations in that it was agreeable. A name was wanted to denote this peculiarity, to mark, as a class, the sensations which possess it. The term Pleasure was adopted I revive the sensation; in other words, have the idea; and, as I had occasion for a name to class the sensations, I have occasion for a name to class the ideas. My state of consciousness under the sensation I call a Pleasure; my state of consciousness under the idea, that is, the idea itself, I call a Desire. The term 'Idea of a pleasure,' expresses precisely the same thing as the term Desire It does so by the very import of the words The idea of a pleasure is the idea of something as good to have. But what is a desire other than the idea of something as good to have; good to have, being really nothing but desirable to have? The terms, therefore, 'idea of pleasure' and 'desire' are but two names; the thing named, the state of consciousness, is one and the same.—*Mill*, '*Analysis*,' i. 191.

Desiring a thing and finding it pleasant are, in the strictness of language, two modes of naming the same psychological fact.—*Mill.*

II. MOTIVES.

Their Nature.

They are incentives to action.

Motives are inducements to act in a certain way. It is evident that the motives to act are the inclinations of the will, in their various forms and in the widest import which can be given to the term.—*Murphy*, '*Human Mind*,' p. 231.

Motives are not like physical causes, constraining and necessitating; they are only incentives, disposing, not compelling. —*Martensen*, '*Christian Ethics*,' i. 117.

The objects of the intention.

In common language the term *Motive* is rather used to designate the special object of the intention than the general desire which impels us to intend When a man labours hard for gain, his spring of action being the desire of having, his motive is to get money. But he may do the same thing his motive being to support his family, and then his spring of action is his family affections.—*Whewell*, '*Elements of Morality*,' p. 28.

According to the Sensational School, they consist solely of our Pleasures and Pains.

The Motives or Ends of Action are our Pleasures and Pains. The pleasures and pains of the various Senses (with the Muscular Feelings), and of the Emotions, are in the last resort, the stimulants of our activity, the objects of pursuit and avoidance.—*Bain*, '*Mental Science*,' p. 346

When the idea of the Pleasure is associated with an action of our own as its cause; that is, contemplated as the consequent of a certain action of ours and incapable of otherwise existing; or when the cause of a Pleasure is contemplated as the consequent of an action of ours and not capable of otherwise existing; a peculiar state of mind is generated which, as it is a tendency to action, is properly denominated MOTIVE

The word MOTIVE is by no means steadily applied to its proper object. The pleasure, for example, which is the consequent of the act, is apt to be regarded as alone the impelling principle, and properly entitled to the name of *Motive* It is obvious, however, that the idea of the pleasure does not constitute the motive to action without the idea of the action as the cause; that it is the association, therefore, to which alone the name belongs.—*Mill*, '*Analysis*,' ii. 258.

A motive is that which moves to action. But that which moves to action is the end of the action, that which is sought by it; that for the sake of which it is performed. Now that, generically speaking, is the pleasure of the agent. Motive, then, taken generically, is pleasure. The pleasure may be in company or connection with things infinite in variety. But these are the accessaries; the essence is the pleasure. Thus, in one case, the pleasure may be connected with the form, and other qualities of a particular woman; in another, with a certain arrangement of colours in a picture; in another, with the circumstances of some fellow-creature. But in all these cases, what is generical, that is the essence, is the pleasure, or relief from pain.—*Mill*, '*Analysis*,' ii. 262.

This theory leaves no room for the operation of conscience, and the idea of duty considered as a motive—at any rate when the discharge of duty is painful. And as a matter of fact it is evident on reflection that

Happiness is not man's only motive.

The proposition that happiness is the sole aim of all human conduct, is nothing if not universal; it must cover all the actions of all human beings, at every moment of their lives and throughout their whole range of conscious motive; it must be equally true of our sensual appetites, our purest emotions, and our intellectual activities. Happiness guides us when we are eating our dinners, or studying metaphysics, or feeding the hungry; when we sacrifice all prospects of future happiness to the loftiest or the most grovelling motives; when we destroy our health and ruin our families for a glass of gin, or walk up to a battery to buy one more chance of victory for a good cause. The love of happiness must express the sole possible motive of Judas Iscariot and his Master; it must explain the conduct of Stylites on his column, of Tiberius at Capreæ, of à Kempis in his cell, and of Nelson in the cockpit of the *Victory*. It must be equally good for saints, martyrs, heroes, cowards, debauchees, ascetics, mystics, cynics, misers, prodigals, men, women, and babes in arms. Truly it must be an elastic principle.—*Stephen*, '*Science of Ethics*,' p. 44.

The name of *Motive* is applied to other things besides Pleasures and Pains, as, for instance, Knowledge and Virtue.—*Ryland*, '*Handbook, &c.*,' p. 112.

Classification of Motives.

It would serve many important ends to have a classification of motives, that is, of the springs of human will and action. To endeavour to give a complete and exhaustive list of them, that is, of the categories of man's moral nature, would, I am aware, be quite as bold an effort as that so often made to determine the categories of the understanding. Such a classification would at the best be very imperfect in the first instance. But, even though only provisionally correct, it might accomplish some useful purposes. In the absence of any arrangement sanctioned by metaphysicians generally, it must suffice to mention here some of the principal motives which very obviously sway the will and impel to action.

The action of our internal powers.

1. As the lambs frisk, and the colt gambols, and as the child is in perpetual rotation, so man's internal powers are for ever impelling him to exertion, independent altogether of any external object, or even of any further internal ends to be gained.

2. Whatever is contemplated as capable of securing pleasure is felt to be desirable, and whatever is apprehended as likely to inflict pain is avoided. This is so very obvious a swaying power with human beings, that it has been noticed, and commonly greatly exaggerated, in every account which has been given of man's active and moral nature. The mistake of the vulgar, and especially of the sensational systems,

is that they have represented pleasure and pain as the sole contemplated ends by which man is or can be swayed. It is our object in these paragraphs to show that man can be influenced by other motives, better and worse.

3. There are certain appetencies in man, bodily and mental, which crave for gratification, and this independent of the pleasure to be secured by their indulgence. Of this description are the appetites of hunger, thirst, and sex, and the mental tendencies to seek for knowledge, esteem, society, power, property. These appetencies may connect themselves with the other two classes already specified, but still they are different. They will tend to act as natural inclinations, but still they look towards particular external objects. We may come to gratify them for the sake of the pleasure, but in the first instance we seek the objects for their own sakes, and it is in seeking the objects we obtain gratification. They operate to some extent in the breasts of all, and they come to exercise a fearfully controlling and grasping power over the minds of multitudes.

4. Man is impelled by an inward principle, more or less powerful in the case of different individuals, and varying widely in the objects desired, to seek for the beautiful in inanimate or in animate objects, in grand or lovely scenes in nature, in statues, paintings, buildings, fine composition in prose or poetry, and in the countenances or forms of man or woman.

5. It is not to be omitted that the moral power in man is not only (as I hope to show) a knowing and judging faculty; it has a prompting energy, and leads us, when a corrupt will does not interfere, to such acts as the worship of God and beneficence to man.

In whatever way we may classify them, these, or such as these, are the motives by which man is naturally swayed. Upon these native and primary principles of actions, others, acquired and secondary, come to be grafted. Thus money, not originally desired for its own sake, may come to be coveted as fitted to gratify the love of power, or the love of pleasure. Or, a particular fellow-man, at first indifferent, comes to be avoided, because he seems inclined to thwart us in some of our favourite ends, such as the acquisition of wealth or of fame. It is a peculiarity of our nature that these secondary principles may become primary ones, and prompt us to seek, for their own sakes, objects which were at first coveted solely because they tended to promote further ends.—*M'Cosh*, '*Intuitions, &c.*,' pp. 246–8.

A classification of motives, or natural impulses which urge to action, has been given, under which they have been presented in three groups,—Desires, Affections, and Judgments. Between the two first and the last a clear line of separation runs, warranting their classification as Dispositions and Judgments. The distinction of these two is broadly marked. The one class includes forces which impel, only by their own inherent strength as feelings; and are non-rational. The other class includes only forces which are rational as well as impelling, and which impel by reason of their rational character, thereby constituting a specific kind of motive. The difference between these two is so great that the impelling power of the latter can be experienced only in a rational nature, whereas impulses of the former class may belong to natures of a lower type, and may be experienced by them in a large degree, though not always to the full measure of human nature. The one is recognition of a rule of life, as a rational motive; the other is experience of disposition as motive-force. Upham, in a very interesting passage, proposes a classification of motives into personal and moral ('Treatise on the Will,' ii. sec. 133, p. 207). The distinction is important, but the designations are unfortunate, as moral motives are pre-eminently personal.—*Calderwood*, '*Moral Philosophy*,' p. 178.

It has been common to distinguish motives as *external* or *objective*, and as *internal* or *subjective*. Regarded objectively, motives are those external objects or circumstances, which, when contemplated, give rise to views or feelings which prompt or influence the will. Regarded subjectively, motives are those internal views or feelings which arise on the contemplation of external objects or circumstances. It is only in a secondary or remote sense, however, that external objects or circumstances can be called motives, or be said to move the will. Motives are, strictly speaking, subjective—as they are internal states or affections of mind in the agent.—*Fleming*, '*Vocab. of Phil.*,' pp. 329, 331.

The final classification of Motives is the classification of pleasurable and painful feelings. [But see above.]—*Bain*, '*Mental Science*,' p. 347.

The Relation of Motives to Volitions.

All Volitions depend upon Motives.

An exercise of pure will is unknown in consciousness. We may will to think, or to sympathise with one in suffering, or to restrain our fears, but we cannot will to will. This is a simple interpretation of the nature of Will. 'A mere will without any motive is chimerical and contradictory' (Leibnitz, 'Fourth Paper, Letters of Leibnitz and Clarke,' p. 93). Reid states it thus,—'Every act of will must have an object. He that wills must will something' ('Active Powers,' Essay ii. 1.; Hamilton, 531). 'Volitions never exist independently of motives' (Upham, 'The Will,' sec. 136, p. 213).—*Calderwood*, '*Moral Philosophy*,' p. 169.

But all Motives do not produce Volition.

The first requisite here is a satisfactory explanation of the nature of Motives, by which they may be sharply and unmistakably distinguished from Volitions. Edwards gives the definition thus,—'By *motive* I mean the whole of that which moves, excites, or invites the mind to volition, whether that be one thing singly, or many things conjunctly' ('Freedom of the Will,' pt. i. sec. ii.) This is objectionable on many accounts. We are dealing with the comparative force of *mental powers*, but this applies as well to things or external objects. And since it is admitted that external objects awaken in us such impulses as desire and affection, there is no need for the wide popular use of the term, which would reckon money and place as motives to action. More serious, however, is the objection that the definition begs the question in dispute. If the law of mental activity be that motives excite to volition, further philosophic investigation is useless. The matter is settled on the necessitarian side. The will is not free. The object awakens the motive, the motive excites the volition, and the action is the result. The object, together with sensibility of nature, which makes me liable to its influence, is the cause of my action. Such a theory might have some fair claim to acceptance if it applied to an irrational nature, but is quite inadequate where motives must be classified as rational and irrational. Motives so different in nature must be regulated in their exercise by different laws.—*Calderwood*, '*Moral Philosophy*,' p. 176.

The will can select among motives.

The will can select, among the motives which present themselves, those which the Moral Sense approves as the most worthy, and can *intensify the force* of these by *fixing the attention* upon them; whilst it can, in like manner, keep to a great extent out of sight, those which it feels ought not to be admitted, and can thus *diminish their force*. And thus at last, while the decision is really formed by the "preponderance of motives," it is the action of the will in modifying the force of these motives, that really determines *which* shall preponderate.—*Carpenter*, '*Mental Physiology*,' p. 420.

The Moral Character of Motives.

Without motive man is not a reasonable or a responsible being.

Suppose the will to act without any motive or reason whatever, by a blind caprice, an impulse without an aim, and responsibility would cease. Such an agent would be like the fictitious atoms of Epicurns, that turn aside a little from the right line, without any reason why they deviate one way more than another. But he must cease thereby to be a reasonable being. He becomes an embodied chance, a capricious and senseless atom. For surely to act even on a mistaken motive, and from an insufficient reason, is at least one step higher than to act with no motive or reason whatever.—*Birks, 'Moral Science,'* p. 79.

The merit of an action depends on the quality of the motive.

Let us start from a particular case. I sign what I know to be a malicious libel. I am then a malevolent liar. My conduct proves that I am neither benevolent nor truthful. I deserve blame, and my conduct is demeritorious. But it is proved that my hand was held by overpowering force. My action then was not wrong, or rather it was not my action. My body was employed by somebody else, as my pen was employed. My character then had no influence upon the result. I may have been the most truthful and benevolent of men. Suppose it now proved that a pistol was held to my head, or a bribe offered to me. How am I now to be judged? From the whole operative motive, and the total implication as to character. The criterion is, what was the quality of the motive indicated, and how far is it indicative of a certain constitution of my character in respect of morality?—*Stephen, 'Science of Ethics,'* p. 279.

There is no action so slight, nor so mean, but it may be done to a great purpose, and ennobled therefore; nor is any purpose so great but that slight actions may help it, and may be so done as to help it much, most especially that chief of all purposes, the pleasing of God. Hence George Herbert—

> 'A servant with this clause
> Makes drudgery divine:
> Who sweeps a room, as for thy laws,
> Makes that and the action fine.'

—*Ruskin, 'Seven Lamps of Architecture,'* p. 4.

The Power of Motive.

It varies according to the differing sensibility of men.

The same objects and circumstances may have different effects, not only upon different individuals, but even upon the same individuals at different times. A man of slow or narrow intellect is unable to perceive the value or importance of an object when presented to him, or the propriety or advantage of a course of conduct that may be pointed out to him, so clearly or so quickly as a man of large and vigorous intellect. The consequence will be, that with the same motives (objectively considered) presented to them, the one may remain indifferent and indolent in reference to the advantage held out, while the other will at once apprehend and pursue it. A man of dull or cold affections will contemplate a spectacle of pain or want, without feeling any desire or making any exertion to relieve it; while he whose sensibilities are more acute and lively, will instantly be moved to the most active and generous efforts. An action which will be contemplated with horror by a man of tender conscience, will be done without compunction by him whose moral sense has not been sufficiently exercised to discern between good and evil.—*Fleming, 'Vocab. of Phil.,'* p. 331.

The efficacy of motives is determined by the individuality, as a motive can only obtain influence over me because I am what I am.—*Martensen, 'Christian Ethics,'* i. 119.

Its influence is weakened by physical exhaustion.

Exhaustion, and natural inaction of the powers, are a bar to the influence of motives. When the system is exhausted or physically indisposed, a more than ordinary motive is required to bring on exertion. The exhausted mountain guide can be got to proceed only by the promise of an extra fee. Napoleon took his men across the Alps by plying them with the rattle of the drums, when everything else failed.—*Bain, 'Mental Science,'* p. 355.

III. ACTION.

Two Kinds of Bodily Actions—Volitional and Automatic.

The former are those which are called forth by a distinct effort of the will, and are directed to the execution of a definite *purpose;* whilst the latter are performed in respondence to an internal prompting of which we may or may not be conscious, and are not dependent on any preformed intention,—being executed, to use a common expression, 'mechanically.'—*Carpenter*, '*Mental Physiology*,' p. 16.

The man in full possession of his volitional power can use it (1) in giving bodily effect to his mental decision, by either putting in action the muscles which will execute the movement he has determined on, or by restraining them from the action to which they are prompted by some other impulse; and (2) in controlling and directing that succession of mental operations by which the determination is arrived at. —*Carpenter*, '*Mental Physiology*,' p. 378.

The process involved in the simplest type of voluntary action may be described as follows:—The initial stage is the rise of some desire in the mind. This desire is accompanied by the representation of some movement (motor representation) which is recognised as subserving the realisation of the object. The recognition of the causal relation of the action to the result involves a germ of belief in the attainability of the object of desire or in the efficacy of the action. Finally, we have the carrying out of the action thus represented. This may be described as the direction of the active impulse involved in the state of desire into the definite channel of action suggested. This last stage of the process of volition is known as the act. The desire which precedes and determines this is called its moving force, stimulus, or *motive.* Since this motive involves the anticipation of the final realisation, this consummation is spoken of as the object, purpose, or *end* of the action, and correlatively, the action as the *means* of gaining or realising the object of desire. — *Sully*, '*Psychology*,' p. 588.

IV. HABIT.

Its Nature.

Habit Defined.

Habit is that facility which the mind acquires in all its exertions, both animal and intellectual, in consequence of practice. —*Stewart*, '*Works*,' ii. 258.

The Moral Habits are the acquirements relating to Feelings and Volitions. Besides the intellectual acquirements properly so called, as Language, Science, &c., we have a series of growths, consisting in the increase or diminution of the feelings, and in modifications of the strength of the will, whereby some motives gain and others lose in practical efficacy. We speak of habits of Courage, Fortitude, Command of Temper, meaning that those qualities have attained, through education, a degree not attaching to them naturally.—*Bain*, '*Mental Science*,' p. 385.

Distinguished from Instinct.

Habit differs from instinct, not in its nature, but in its origin; the last being natural, the first acquired. Both operate without will or intention, without thought, and therefore may be called mechanical principles.—*Reid*, '*Works*,' p. 550.

Classification of Habits.

Habits may be divided into active and passive; those things which we do by an act of the will, and those things which we suffer by the agency of some external power.—*Smith*, '*Moral Philosophy*,' p. 383.

There are habits of perception and habits of action. An instance of the former is our constant and even involuntary readiness in correcting the impressions of our sight, concerning magnitudes and distances, so as to substitute judgment in the room of sensation, imperceptibly to ourselves. And it seems as if all other associations of ideas not naturally connected might be called *passive habits*, as properly as our readiness in understanding languages upon sight, or hearing of words And our readiness in speaking and writing them is an instance of the latter, of active habits. For distinctness we may consider habits as belonging to the body or the mind.—*Butler*, '*Analogy*,' pt. i chap. v. § ii.

Formation of Habit.

The principal means is repeated action.

The wonderful effect of practice in the formation of habits has been often and justly taken notice of as one of the most curious circumstances in the human constitution. A mechanical operation, for example, which we at first performed with the utmost difficulty, comes in time to be so familiar to us that we are able to perform it without the smallest danger of mistake; even while the attention appears to be completely engaged with other subjects. In consequence of the association of ideas, the different steps of the process present themselves successively to the thoughts, without any recollection on our part, and with a degree of rapidity proportioned to the length of our experience. — *Stewart*, '*Works*,' ii. 124.

Habits belonging to the body seem produced by repeated acts. In like manner habits of the mind are produced by the exertion of inward practical principles, *i.e.*, by carrying them into act, or acting upon them; the principles of obedience, of veracity, justice, and charity. Nor can these habits be formed by any external course of action, otherwise than as it proceeds from these principles; because it is only these inward principles exerted, which are strictly acts of obedience, of veracity, of justice, and of charity. So likewise habits of attention, industry, self-government, are in the same manner acquired by exercise; and habits of envy and revenge by indulgence, whether in outward act, or in thought and intention, *i.e.*, inward act; for such intention is an act. Resolutions also to do well are properly acts. And endeavouring to enforce upon our minds a practical sense of virtue, or to beget in others that practical sense of it which a man really has himself, is a virtuous act All these, therefore, may and will contribute towards forming good habits But going over the theory of virtue in one's thoughts, talking well and drawing fine pictures of it; this is so far from conducing to form a habit of it in him who thus employs himself, that it may harden the mind in a contrary course —*Butler*, '*Analogy*,' pt i, ch. v. sec ii.

In the first place, a certain *repetition* is necessary, greater or less according to the change that has to be effected, and to the absence of other favouring circumstances. In the second place, the mind may be more or less *concentrated* on the acquisition Moral progress depends greatly on the bent of the learner towards the special acquisition —*Bain*, '*Mental Science*,' p. 385.

Effect of Habit

It gives facility of action.

We are capable, not only of acting, and of having different momentary impressions made upon us, but of getting a new facility in any kind of action, and of settled alterations in our temper or character. The power of the last two is the power of habits. —*Butler*, '*Analogy*,' pt i. ch. v sec ii.

It diminishes sensibility.

It appears to be a general law that habit diminishes physical sensibility, whatever affects any organ of the body, affects it less by repetition Brandy is begun in teaspoons; but the effect is so soon lost, that a more generous and expanded vehicle is very soon had recourse to; the same heat to the stomach, and the same intoxication to the head, cannot be produced by the same quantity of liquor So with perfumes; wear scented powder, and in a month you will cease to perceive it. Habituate yourself to cold or to heat, and they cease to affect you. Eat Cayenne pepper, and you will find it perpetually necessary to increase the quantity in order to produce the effect

'My perfumed doublet,' says Montaigne, 'gratifies my own smelling at first, as well as that of others; but after I have worn it three or four days together, I no more perceive it; but it is yet more strange that custom, notwithstanding the long intermissions and intervals, should yet have the power to unite and establish the effect of its impressions upon our senses, as is manifest in those who live near to steeples and the frequent noise of bells. I myself lie at home in a tower, where every morning and evening, a very great bell rings out the *Ave Maria*, the noise of which shakes my very tower, and at first seemed insupportable to me; but having now a good while kept that lodging, I am so used to it, that I hear it without any manner of offence, and often without awaking at it. Plato reprehends a boy for playing at some childish game. "Thou reprovest me," says the boy, "for a very little thing." "Custom," replied Plato, "is *no* little thing." And he was in the right; for I find that our greatest vices derive their first propensity from our most tender infancy, and that our principal education depends upon the nurse.'

In all these cases, the sensibility of the different parts of the body is diminished by repetition, and the same substances applied to them cannot produce the same effects. The habit, it should be observed, does not act by individual substances, but often by classes; if you have accustomed yourself to opium, all soporific drugs have less effect upon you; if to one species of wine, you are capable of bearing a greater quantity of any other, the sensibility of the body is not only diminished towards that object, but towards many others similar to it; chiefly, however, towards the object upon which the habit was founded.—*Smith*, '*Moral Philosophy*,' p. 386.

Its influence on human happiness.

Everyone must be familiar with the effects of habit. A walk upon the quarter-deck, though intolerably confined, becomes so agreeable by custom, that a sailor in his walk on shore, very often confines himself within the same bounds. 'I knew a man,' says Lord Kaimes, 'who had relinquished the sea for a country life: in the corner of his garden he reared an artificial mount, with a level summit, resembling most accurately a quarter-deck, not only in shape but in size; and here he generally walked.'—*Smith*, '*Moral Philosophy*,' p. 381.

It is impossible not to perceive that powerful effect which habit must exercise upon human happiness, by connecting the future with the present, and exposing us to do again that which we have already done. If we wish to know who is the most degraded and the most wretched of human beings; if it be any object of curiosity in moral science, to gauge the dimensions of wretchedness, and to see how deep the miseries of man can reach;—if this be any object of curiosity, look for the man who has practised a vice so long, that he curses it and clings to it, that he pursues it, because he feels a great law of his nature driving him on towards it, but, reaching it, knows that it will gnaw his heart, and tear his vitals, and make him roll himself in the dust with anguish. Say everything for vice which you can say,—magnify any pleasure as much as you please, but don't believe you can keep it; don't believe you have any secret for sending on quicker the sluggish blood, and for refreshing the faded nerve. Nero and Caligula, and all those who have had the vices and the riches of the world at their command, have never been able to do this. Yet you will not quit what you do not love; and you will linger on over the putrid fragments, and the nauseous carrion, after the blood, and the taste, and the sweetness are vanished away. But the wise toil, and the true glory of life, is to turn all these provisions of nature—all these great laws of the mind—to good; and to seize hold of the power of habit, for fixing and securing virtue: for if the difficulties with which we begin were always to continue, we might all cry out with Brutus—'I have followed thee, O

Virtue! as a real thing, and thou art but a name!' But the state which repays us, is that habitual virtue, which makes it as natural to a man to act right, as to breathe; which so incorporates goodness with the system, that pure thoughts are conceived without study, and just actions performed without effort: as it is the perfection of health, when every bodily organ acts without exciting attention; when the heart beats and the lungs play, and the pulses flow, without reminding us that the mechanism of life is at work. So it is with the beauty of moral life! when man is just, and generous, and good, without knowing that he is practising any virtue, or overcoming any difficulty: and the truly happy man is he who, at the close of a long life, has so changed his original nature, that he feels it an effort to do wrong, and a mere compliance with habit to perform every great and sacred duty of life.—*Smith*, '*Moral Philosophy*,' p. 396.

Its power in the religious life.

The long practised Christian, who, through God's mercy, has brought God's presence near to him, is moved by God dwelling in him, and needs not but act on instinct. He does his duty unconsciously. It is natural to him to obey. This excellent obedience is obedience *on habit*.—*Newman*, '*Sermons*,' i. 75.

Influence on Conduct.

Previously acquired habits automatically incite us to do as we have been before accustomed to do under the like circumstances, without the idea of prospective pleasure or pain, or of right or wrong, being at all present to our minds. Where the habits have been judiciously formed in the first instance, this tendency is an extremely useful one, prompting us to do that spontaneously which might otherwise require a powerful effort of the will; but if, on the other hand, a bad set of habits have grown up with the growth of the individual, or if a single bad tendency be allowed to become an habitual spring of action, a far stronger effort of volition will be required to determine the conduct in opposition to them. This is especially the case when the habitual idea possesses an emotional character, and thus becomes the source of *desires*; for the more frequently these are yielded to, the more powerful is the solicitation they exert.—*Carpenter*, '*Mental Physiology*,' pp. 414, 415.

XVIII.

LIBERTY, NECESSITY, DETERMINISM.

Various Explanations of Terms.

Liberty or Freedom.

The idea of liberty is the idea of a power in any agent to do or forbear any particular action, according to the determination or thought of the mind, whereby either of them is preferred to the other; where either of them is not in the power of the agent to be produced by him according to his volition, there he is not at liberty; that agent is under necessity.—*Locke*, '*Human Understanding*,' II. xxi. 8.

By the liberty of a Moral Agent, I understand a power over the determinations of his own Will. If, in any action, he had power to will what he did, or not to will it, in that action he is free.—*Reid*, '*Works*,' p. 599.

On this Sir W. Hamilton remarks in a note to his edition of Reid: 'That is to say, Moral Liberty does not merely consist in the power of *doing what we will*, but in the power of *willing what we will*. For a power over the determinations of our Will supposes an act of Will that our Will should determine so and so; for we can only freely exert power through a rational determination or Volition. This definition of Liberty is right.'

The power of will consists only in this, that we are able to do or not to do the same thing, or rather in this alone, that in pursuing or shunning what is proposed to us by the understanding, we so act that we are not conscious of being determined to a particular action by any external force.—*Descartes*, '*Meditations*,' iv.

Moral freedom is the power of choice, which belongs to the very essence of happiness. It is a luxury which intelligent beings hold to be beyond all price. The inward exercise of this liberty is a privilege of which the rational soul cannot be deprived. Liberty, however, is also employed to denote freedom of action.—*Murphy*, '*Human Mind*,' p. 185.

Freedom is power to choose. It is therefore involved in will. Hence it can only be destroyed by the destruction of the will. It is the indispensable condition of accountability, as conscience is its foundation. Freedom, however, is also used to denote the power to act according to choice. In this sense it is the measure of responsibility. Hence it appears that reason, which includes conscience, yields the foundation; will, which confers freedom, the condition; and power, the measure of moral responsibility.—*Murphy*, '*Human Mind*,' p. 192.

It is carefully to be remembered, that freedom consists in the dependence of the existence or not existence of any action, upon our volition of it; and not in the dependence of any action, or its contrary, on our preference. A man standing on a cliff is at liberty to leap twenty yards downwards into the sea, not because he has a power to do the contrary action, which is to leap twenty yards upwards, for that he cannot do; but he is therefore free because he has a power to leap or not to leap. But if a greater force than his either holds him fast or tumbles him down, he is no longer free in that case; because the doing or forbearance of that particular action is no longer in his power. In this, then, consists our freedom, viz., in our being able to act or not to act, according as we shall choose or will.—*Locke*, '*Human Understanding*,' II. xxi. 27.

This is a clear approach to the Necessitarian idea of Freedom, which may be gathered from the following extract:—

The Necessitarian doctrine, in denying freedom of will, does not altogether refuse a place to freedom. But the only liberty which it acknowledges is liberty of acting as we will, denominated freedom from constraint or coercion. 'I say that a thing is *free* which exists and acts by the sole necessity of its nature' (Spinoza, Letter 62, 'Life, Corresp. and Ethics,' by R. Willis, M.D., p. 393). 'By liberty we can only mean a power of acting or not acting, according to the determinations of the Will' (Hume, 'Essays,' ii. 110). By freedom or liberty in an agent is meant, 'being free from hindrance or impediment in the way of doing or conducting, in any respect, as he wills' (Edwards, 'The Will,' pt. i. sec. 5).—*Calderwood*, '*Moral Philosophy*,' p. 194.

Necessity.

Besides the use of the term to imply what we cannot avoid thinking or judging, the word Necessity is often applied to the doctrine which denies the freedom of the human will, and even to that form of the doctrine which confines itself to asserting that volitions have invariable antecedents which would enable any person who knew *all* the antecedents to predict the volitions with perfect accuracy.—*Monck*, '*Sir W. Hamilton*,' p. 184.

A necessary action is one the contrary of which is impossible.—*Fleming*, '*Vocab. of Phil.*,' p. 343.

There are two schemes of necessity,—the necessitation by *efficient*—the necessitation by *final* causes. The former is brute or blind fate; the latter rational determinism. Though their practical results be the same, they ought to be carefully distinguished in theory.—*Hamilton*, '*Reid's Works*,' p. 87.

The terms used in this controversy are said to be inappropriate.

The capital objection to Free-will is the unsuitability, irrelevance, or impropriety of the metaphor 'freedom' in the question of the sequence of motive and act in volition. The proper meaning of 'free' is the absence of external compulsion; every sentient being, under a motive to act, and not interfered with by any other being, is to all intents free; the fox impelled by hunger, and proceeding unmolested to a poultry-yard, is a free agent. Free trade, free soil, free press, have all intelligible significations; but the question whether, without any reference to outward compulsion, a man in following the bent of his own motives, is free or is necessitated by his motives, has no relevance.—*Bain*, '*Mental and Moral Science*,' p. 398.

The upholders of the scheme have a double objection to the name Necessitarianism, as descriptive of their theory, *first*, because it seems to convey that they have no place for liberty, and, *secondly*, because it seems to imply that they really hold that men are constrained in their actions; both of which they deny. Thus Mr Mill, as an upholder of the theory, speaks of it as 'the falsely-called Doctrine of Necessity,'—preferring 'the fairer name of Determinism,' and says, that the word Necessity 'in this application, signifies only invariability' ('Exam.,' p. 552). Determinism is an unsuitable word, because on both sides a doctrine of determination of will is held, the dispute being between self-determination, and motive-determination.—*Calderwood*, '*Moral Philosophy*,' p. 194.

Exposition of the Rival Doctrines.

Liberty.

The will is free. In saying so, I mean to assert not merely that it is free to act as it pleases—indeed this maxim is not universally true, for the will may often be hindered from action, as when I will to move my arm, and it refuses to obey because of paralysis. I claim for it an anterior and a higher power, a power in the mind to choose, and, when it chooses, a consciousness that it might choose otherwise.—*M'Cosh*, '*Intuitions of the Mind*,' p. 270.

Properly speaking, the will does not furnish incitements, inducements, or motives; these come from the appetencies. It is the province of the *Will*, seated above them, to sanction or restrain them when they present themselves, and to decide among them when they are competing with each other for the mastery. The characteristic property of emotion is attachment or repugnance, with associated excitement. The distinguishing quality of will is choice or rejection. Inducements being held out, the mind, in the exercise of will, sanctions or refuses. It assumes a number of forms, in all of which there is the element of choice. If the object is present, we positively choose it or adopt it; if the object is absent, we wish for it; if it is to be obtained by some exertion on our part, we form a resolution to take the steps necessary to procure it.—*M'Cosh*, '*Intuitions of the Mind*,' p. 250.

In every act of volition I am fully conscious that I can at this moment act in either of two ways, and that, all the antecedent phenomena being precisely the same, I may determine one way to day and another way to-morrow.—*Mansel*, '*Prolegomena Logica*,' p. 152.

Human actions done consciously and with choice do not, like the operations of material nature, present a distinct order of occurrence, and so admit of generalisation and prediction. That is to say, actions resulting from choice cannot be classified with the ordinary phenomena of causation in respect to their invariable order and conditional certainty.—*Sully*, '*Sensation, &c.*,' p. 118.

We float down the stream of life as

nature and fate impel us; we cannot pass the bounds within which the ship of our life restrains us; but upon this ship our movements are free. We experience influences and impressions of various kinds, but we possess freedom of choice. We are placed in manifold connections, but we have the power of the initiative; we are able to begin what is new, though in connection with what is old. Our actions are occasioned by external or internal causes, but in every action we are conscious that we could have acted differently. This ability to act differently, this power of the initiative, of deciding for ourselves, is freedom.—*Luthardt*, '*Moral Truths*,' p. 50.

Kant's Categories of Freedom.

Table of the Categories of Freedom relatively to the Notions of Good and Evil.

I. QUANTITY.

Subjective, according to maxims (*practical opinions* of the individual).

Objective, according to principles (*precepts*).

A priori, both objective and subjective principles of freedom (*laws*).

II. QUALITY.

Practical rules of *action* (*præceptivæ*).
Practical rules of *omission* (*prohibitivæ*).
Practical rules of *exceptions* (*exceptivæ*).

III. RELATION.

To *personality*.
To the *condition* of the person.
Reciprocal, of one person to the condition of the others.

IV. MODALITY.

The *Permitted* and the *Forbidden.*
Duty and the *contrary to duty.*
Perfect and *imperfect duty.*

It will at once be observed that in this table freedom is considered as a sort of causality not subject to empirical principles of determination, in regard to actions possible by it, which are phenomena in the world of sense; and that, consequently, it is referred to the categories which concern its physical possibility, whilst yet each category is taken so universally that the determining principle of that causality can be placed outside the world of sense in freedom as a property of a being in the world of intelligence; and, finally, the categories of modality introduce the transition from practical principles generally to those of morality, but only *problematically*. These can be established *dogmatically* only by the moral law.—*Kant*, '*Theory of Ethics*,' p. 158.

Necessity.

Correctly conceived, the doctrine called Philosophical Necessity is simply this: that, given the motives which are present to an individual's mind and given likewise the character and disposition of the individual, the manner in which he will act may be unerringly inferred; that if we knew the person thoroughly, and knew all the inducements which are acting upon him, we could foretell his conduct with as much certainty as we can predict any physical event.—*Mill*, '*Logic*,' ii. 416.

Necessitarians affirm, as a truth of experience, that volitions do, in point of fact, follow determinate moral antecedents with the same uniformity, and (when we have sufficient knowledge of the circumstances) with the same certainty, as physical effects follow their physical causes. These moral antecedents are desires, aversions, habits, and dispositions, combined with outward circumstances suited to call those internal incentives into action. All these again are effects of causes, those of them which are mental being consequences of education, and of other mental and physical influences.—*Mill*, '*Examination of Hamilton*,' p. 560.

The same motive, in the same circumstances, will be followed by the same action. The uniformity of sequence, admitted to prevail in the physical world, is held to exist in the mental world, although the terms of the sequence are of a different character, as involving states of the subjective consciousness.—*Bain, 'Mental and Moral Science,'* p. 396.

The doctrine of Necessity is clearly distinguishable from Fatalism. Pure fatalism holds that our actions do not depend on our desires. A superior power overrides our wishes and bends us according to its will. Modified fatalism proceeds upon the determination of our will by motives, but holds that our character is made *for* us and not by us, so that we are not responsible for our actions, and should in vain attempt to alter them. The true doctrine of Causation holds that in so far as our character is amenable to moral discipline, we can improve it if we desire. The volitions tending to improve our character are as capable of being predicted as any voluntary actions. And necessity means only this possibility of being foreseen, so that we are no more free in the formation of our character, than in our subsequent volitions. —*Bain, 'Mental and Moral Science,'* p. 428.

The distinctive features of Necessitarianism or Determinism are, *negatively*, the denial of freedom in willing to act; and *positively*, the presentation of a theory of Will, professedly adequate to account for all the facts of consciousness which bear upon the direction of human conduct.

The Necessitarian theory, on its negative or critical side, rests upon an application of the law of causality. It urges that every event follows a cause; that this holds true in the sphere of mind as well as of matter; and so applies to volitions as well as sensations. At this point there is no divergence of opinion. Indeed, most libertarians go further than necessitarians here, and do not halt, like Mr Mill, at the statement that the effect 'certainly and invariably' *does* follow its cause, but advance to the position that it *must* do so. Liberty of indifference and liberty of caprice are repudiated, and are not to be set to the account of libertarianism, any more than a doctrine of constraint is to be charged against necessitarianism. These are the extremes, taken in the heat of conflict, to be abandoned in calmer mood. That every volition must have a cause, is a necessity freely admitted.

The Necessitarian theory not only insists upon the application of the law of causality within the region of mind, as to which all are agreed, but further insists upon an *interpretation* of the law in accordance with the analogy of the physical world. Looking from the effect backwards to the cause, it maintains that the law of causality warrants the affirmation, not only that an adequate cause has acted, but also *how* it has acted. Looking from the cause forward to the effect, it maintains on warrant of the law of causality, not only that the cause has produced the effect, but that it was *necessitated* to produce that effect. But this is something more than an application of the law of causality. With the law, it carries an interpretation founded on knowledge gathered in a particular sphere. It is an argument from matter to mind, and as such needs to be vindicated on the basis of facts, not merely proclaimed on the authority of a general law.—*Calderwood, 'Moral Philosophy,'* p. 196.

The Free Will Controversy.

Arguments in favour of Freedom.

It is attested by Consciousness.

The fact of liberty may be proved from the direct consciousness of liberty.—*Hamilton, 'Reid's Works.'*

This truth is revealed to us by immediate consciousness, and is not to be set aside by any other truth whatever. It is a first truth equal to the highest, to no one of which will it ever yield. It cannot be set aside by any other truth, not even by any other first truth, and certainly by no derived truth. Whatever other proposition is true, this is true also, that man's will is free.—*M'Cosh, 'Intuitions, &c.,'* p. 270.

Of legitimate hypotheses there are three available forms,—(1) constrained action, under dominion of some controlling power, distinct from the Will itself; (2) spontaneous action, according to an inherent and invariable law of energy operating within the Will itself; or (3) free action, admitting of variation within a sphere where alternative courses are equally possible.

The hypothesis of *constrained action* of Will is invalidated on the ground of inconsistency with the recognised facts of consciousness. Of these facts, the following are the most important, that Intelligence and Disposition are controlled,—that we are conscious of personal control over these powers, so that their exercise is in the direction of our volitions,—and that we praise or blame ourselves as the authors of the subsequent actions. To prove that these are only suppositions and not facts, has been found too hard a task for the supporters of the hypothesis of constrained action. If we cannot plead the testimony of consciousness as to the manner in which Will is brought into exercise, we have its clear testimony as to the fact of the Will's control over the other powers of mind. Whatever be the law of its own exercise, Will is free from the dominion of intellect and disposition. It is not controlled by them, but controls both. The strongest motive does not determine the Will, but the Will determines what motives shall be allowed to gain strength.

The hypothesis of *spontaneous action*, according to an invariable law operating within the Will itself, is invalidated by the facts of consciousness. The facts indicated in the previous paragraph are inexplicable on this supposition. While the fact of control over intellect and disposition is obvious, it is equally clear that the control is not so uniform as to favour belief in a law of spontaneity as characteristic of Will. So far from every disposition being uniformly gratified or checked as it arises, there are great variations in the measure of control maintained. Inasmuch as intellect is brought into use, sometimes as guide and encourager of dispositions, sometimes as their restrainer, there is no such uniformity in the manner of control, as to harmonise with a law of spontaneity in Will, similar to that which applies to the dispositions themselves when uncontrolled.

The hypothesis of *free action* as the law of exercise for the Will itself, is the only one which harmonises with the facts of consciousness. Relative freedom, in the sense of freedom from control of intellect and disposition on the part of the Will, being established by simple analysis of the facts of consciousness, controlling power on the part of the Will over both intellect and disposition being recognised in exercise within consciousness, a theory of the Will is completed only by maintaining that this power is distinct in nature from any other known to us, and that freedom of action in adopting available alternatives, is the law of its exercise.—*Calderwood*, '*Moral Philosophy*,' p. 189.

The fact that we are free is given us in the consciousness of an uncompromising law of Duty, in the consciousness of our moral accountability.—*Hamilton*, '*Metaphysics*,' ii. 413.

The principal argument in favour of Freedom may be very briefly stated; it is simply the testimony of consciousness. We *know*, for it is a fact attested alike by conscience and consciousness, that when two courses of action are presented to us, we are free to choose between them, and therefore have only ourselves to approve or blame for the consequences of that choice. Hence, after the consequences of our conduct have become manifest, we all feel self-reproach or self-gratulation, because we know that we might have willed differently.—*Bowen*, '*Modern Philosophy*,' p. 296.

Attested also by the fact of accountability and man's power to design.

The arguments to prove that man is endowed with moral liberty, which have the greatest weight with me, are three: *first*, Because he has a natural conviction or belief that in many cases he acts freely;

secondly, Because he is accountable; and, *thirdly*, Because he is able to prosecute an end by a long series of means adapted to it. —*Reid*, '*Works*,' p. 616.

Necessity begs the question.

The Necessitarian really begs the question by taking for granted the doctrine of the Materialist. He assumes that mind is not distinct from Matter, or in other words, that there is no such separate and peculiar existence as mind; that man is only a machine, which is but apparently animate, and therefore that he falls entirely under the domain of the *causa fiendi*, and moves only as he is moved by Physical Causes, strictly so called. If this Materialist theory were true, I admit that the doctrine of the Necessitarian would thereby be demonstrated; for I cannot even imagine any change taking place in Matter, except through the operation of some efficient Cause, whereby it is necessarily determined to be what it is, and I cannot see how a Necessitarian can logically avoid being also a Materialist.—*Bowen*, '*Modern Philosophy*,' p. 298.

Confession of a Fatalist.

I myself believe that I have a feeling of Liberty even at the very moment when I am writing against Liberty, upon grounds which I regard as incontrovertible. Zeno was a fatalist only in theory; in practice, he did not act in conformity with that conviction.—*Hommel*.

Difficulties of Necessity.

Necessitarianism encounters difficulties, arising from its own nature, in attempting to construct a harmonious theory of moral government, and to interpret the moral sentiments common to men.

(1.) Necessitarianism has difficulty in accounting for the consciousness of Moral Responsibility, and for the justice of personal liability to punishment.

(2.) A philosophy of the moral sentiments, including self-approbation and self-condemnation, shame and remorse, is peculiarly difficult under the necessitarian hypothesis. Remorse may be taken as the example. Priestley treats of it thus,—'A man, when he reproaches himself for any particular action in his past conduct, may fancy that if he was in the same situation again, he would have acted differently. But this is a mere deception, and if he examines himself strictly, and takes in all the circumstances, he may be satisfied that, with the same inward disposition of mind, and with precisely the same views of things as he had then, and exclusive of all others which he has acquired by reflection since, he could not have acted otherwise than he did' ('Illust. of Phil Necessity,' p 99; see also Belsham's 'Elements,' p. 406). It is at least an awkward escape from a theoretic difficulty to maintain that the whole human race is deceived. The philosophic question is this,—What power belongs to us as intellectual beings? Have we such power, that a man can attain to accurate views of the moral quality of an action before he perform it, as well as after the action is done? The negative cannot be maintained on a Utilitarian theory of morals, any more than on an Intuitional theory.—*Calderwood*, '*Moral Philosophy*,' p. 200.

Arguments for Necessity.

Self-determination not in the power of the Will.

If the will, which we find governs the members of the body, and determines and commands their motions and actions, does also govern itself, and determine its own motions and acts, it doubtless determines them the same way, even by antecedent volitions. The will determines which way the hands and feet shall move, by an act of volition or choice; and there is no other way of the will's determining, directing or commanding anything at all. Whatsoever the will commands, it commands by an act of the will; and if it has itself under its command, and determines itself in its own acts, it doubtless does it the same way that it determines other things which are under its command. So that if the freedom of the will consists in this, that it has itself and its own acts under its command and direction, and its own volitions are determined by itself, it will follow, that every free volition arises from another antecedent volition, directing and commanding that; and if that directing volition be also free, in that also the will is determined—that is to say, that directing volition is determined by another going before that, and so on, until we come to the first volition in the whole series, and if that first volition be free, and the will self-determined in it, then that is determined by another volition preceding that, which is a contradiction; because, by the supposition, it can have none before it to direct or determine it, being the first in the train. But if that first volition is not determined by any preceding act of the will, then that act is not determined by the will, and so is not free, in the Arminian notion of freedom, which consists in the will's self-determination.—*Edwards, 'Freedom of the Will,'* pt. ii sec. I.

The Necessitarian alleges that we could not have willed differently (than we did), because no particular volition would be possible, if it were not determined by some antecedent motive or cause to be what it is. If all the antecedent circumstances, the agent's character and this motive included, should remain unchanged, the volition must be repeated; otherwise, a given cause would not produce any effect, which is a contradiction, or there would be a change without a cause, which is impossible. —*Bowen, 'Modern Philosophy,'* p. 297.

The interpretation of the testimony of consciousness is not reliable.

As to the appeal which has been made to consciousness, as testifying in an indisputable manner to our freedom of will, we must think of that as follows:—Consciousness has been said to be our ultimate and infallible criterion of truth; to affirm that it deceives itself is to destroy the mere possibility of every certain science. In the first place, let us remark that consciousness is to internal phenomena what observation is to external facts. The generality of people know what they think and feel, without exactly knowing the laws of thought, of mental co-existences and sequences, in the same way as their senses reveal rivers, mountains, cities, &c., to them, but without giving them an exact and precise knowledge of these things. Nothing is more common than disagreement in human appreciations of size, forces, weights, forms, colours, &c. If this be so in the case of the objects of our external senses, what reason have we for believing that the internal sense is more exact? Are not metaphysical disputes in themselves a proof of the contrary? Besides if we grant to consciousness the privilege of infallibility, it can last for only a short moment; and that does not constitute a science. Consciousness being strictly applicable to any individual person, and for one instant only, it contains the minimum of information. This is the atom of knowledge. If we wish to go beyond this short moment, we must have recourse to memory, and we know that memory is fallible. Thus, while the infallibility lasts, there is no science, and when the science begins, there is no infallibility.—*Ribot, 'English Psychology,'* p. 251.

To be conscious of free-will must mean to be conscious, before I have decided, that I am able to decide either way. Exception may be taken *in limine* to the use of the word consciousness in such an application. Consciousness tells me what I do or feel. But what I am *able* to do is not a subject of consciousness. Consciousness is not prophetic; we are conscious of what is, not of what will or can be. We never know that we are able to do a thing except from having done it, or something equal or similar to it.—*Mill, 'Examination of Hamilton,'* p. 564.

Minor arguments.

In favour of Necessity it has been said:—

(1) That human Liberty respects only the actions that are subsequent to Volition; and that power over the determinations of

the Will is inconceivable and involves a contradiction. (2.) That Liberty is inconsistent with the influence of Motives, that it would make human actions capricious, and man governable by God or man.— —*Reid, 'Works,'* p. 624.

Hume held that the whole dispute is merely verbal

It will not require many words to prove that all mankind have ever agreed in the doctrine of liberty as well as in that of necessity, and that the whole dispute, in this respect also, has been hitherto merely verbal. For what is meant by liberty when applied to voluntary actions? We cannot surely mean that actions have so little connexion with motives, inclinations, and circumstances, that one does not follow with a certain degree of uniformity from the other, and that one affords no inference by which we can conclude the existence of the other For these are plain and acknowledged matters of fact. By liberty, then, we can only mean *a power of acting or not acting, according to the determinations of the will*; that is, if we chuse to remain at rest we may; if we chuse to move we also may Now this hypothetical liberty is universally allowed to belong to every one who is not a prisoner and in chains Here, then, is no subject of dispute —*Hume, 'Philosophical Works,'* iv. 77, 78

The Exercise of Freedom

Is attainable through attention

As freedom of action is attainable through rational control of the whole nature, the key to the exercise of such freedom is found in the power of ATTENTION. This is the key to possible superiority over circumstances and dispositions, and also to the possibility of uniform guidance by the reason The ruling type of human freedom, as recognised in consciousness, is discovered in the control exercised over attention. Intellect exerts its governing power only as we put it to use for this end, and that means attention Objects, when contemplated by us, touch our sensibility, and awaken dispositions which have the force of motives. This being the law of our experience, we weaken or strengthen these lower motives according as we direct our attention Our experience under contemplation of objects is the product of natural constitution, and is not subject of volition; but the continuance and increase of such sensibility, with attendant dispositions, are elements of experience constantly under our own control, according as attention is bestowed upon the object, or withdrawn from the object, and concentrated upon another. —*Calderwood, 'Moral Philosophy,'* p. 187.

Is not interfered with by the play of motives

Both rational motives, and lower motives, including desires and affections, have some influence in determining the exercise of Will Both Intelligence and Disposition are capable of spontaneous action, and in accordance with this law of their activity, both afford *occasion* for the exercise of Will. An exercise of pure Will is impossible. The Will is thus dependent upon the other energies of our nature for the primary condition of its exercise. Motives do so far determine the Will, as to fix the direction and form of the volitions. This, however, establishes nothing as to power or force to control the Will; though it does discover a measure of exercise on their part independently of Will.—*Calderwood, 'Moral Philosophy,'* p 179.

An advocate of Freewill must admit that a volition is determined without a *Cause*, but he does not need to assert that it is determined without a *Reason*. Now *Motives* are Reasons, and the relation between a Reason and its Consequent is often entirely distinct from that between a Cause and its Effect.—*Bowen, 'Modern Philosophy,'* p 298.

Is irreconcilable with Pantheism

All forms of pantheism which do not ascribe a separate will to God, are liable to the objection that they suppose God to produce in man a free will not possessed by Himself from eternity. If the other alternative be taken, and will be ascribed to Deity, then have we two wills in the universe, the will of God and the will of man, and it follows that all is not one in any intelligible sense, for we have now two distinct wills, which may run counter to each other. Whatever be the philosophic system adopted, we have, as matter of fact, the hundred of millions of distinct wills possessed by human beings. These separate wills show by one process that God must have a distinct will, and by another process that there must be more than one will in the universe, and both conclusions are inconsistent with a system which says—all is one.—*M'Cosh*, '*Intuitions, &c.*,' p. 403.

Free Will is held to be Essential to

Personal Existence.

There are two conditions which I conceive as essential to my personal existence in every possible mode, and such as could not be removed without the destruction of myself as a conscious being. These two conditions are *time* and *free agency*.—*Mansel*, '*Metaphysics*,' p. 360.

Morality.

Man is a moral agent only as he is accountable for his actions,—in other words, as he is the object of praise or blame; and this he is, only inasmuch as he has prescribed to him a rule of duty, and as he is able to act, or not to act, in conformity with its precepts. The possibility of morality thus depends on the possibility of liberty; for if man be not a free agent, he is not the author of his actions, and has therefore no responsibility,—no moral personality at all.—*Hamilton*, '*Metaphysics*,' i. 33.

DETERMINISM.

Another Name for Necessity.

Both Sir W. Hamilton and Mr. Mansel sometimes call (the Doctrine of Necessity) by the fairer name of Determinism. But both of them, when they come to close quarters with the doctrine, in general call it either Necessity, or, less excusably, Fatalism. The truth is, that the assailants of the doctrine cannot do without the associations engendered by the double meaning of the word Necessity, which, in this application, signifies only invariability, but in its common employment, compulsion.—*Mill*, '*Examination of Hamilton*,' p. 492.

As stated by J. S. Mill.

Correctly conceived, the doctrine called Philosophical Necessity is simply this: that, given the motives which are present to an individual's mind, and given likewise the character and disposition of the individual, the manner in which he will act might be unerringly inferred: that if we knew the person thoroughly, and knew all the inducements which are acting upon him, we could foretell his conduct with as much certainty as we can predict any physical event.—'*System of Logic*,' ii. 422.

As stated by J. Muller.

Determinism supports itself on the principle that man when he decides is already decided, and does not act from a spontaneous freedom of choice, but according to his own distinctive individuality—which includes also his moral character, and the particular bias of his will. According to this, his conduct proceeds from himself, in virtue of that self-dependence which belongs to him as an individual; yet at the same time it springs, by strict necessity, from causes which at the moment of choice are beyond his control. Viewed apart from the ever present but ever subordinate influence of outward circumstances, his behaviour is the never-failing product of the collective character of his inner life. If at the moment when he is called to any decision of the will, his whole inner life, in its minutest outlines, were as in a picture unveiled to our view,—his notions of right and wrong, his principles and thoughts, the strength and idiosyncrasy of his affections and desires, his inclinations and prejudices, even those most secret and hardly known even to himself,—we should be able, provided of course that we possessed the requisite judging faculty, to predict with unerring certainty how in any case he would decide.—'*Christian Doctrine of Sin,*' ii. 43, 44.

Partial Determinism, as held by J. Müller.

The view obtained from the standing-point that we have established (is that) the determination of the present by means of the past is not denied, but is partly limited and partly traced back to a former self-determining. If this complex and modified doctrine of freedom can be maintained, freedom can assert its validity against its opponents. At the same time, determinism is not absolutely excluded, but some truth is recognised therein, and Freedom attains its own full recognition and definiteness by blending Determinism with it.—'*Christian Doctrine of Sin,*' ii. 63.

Determinism of Schopenhauer.

Only that which I actually did, could I do, must I do. Schopenhauer, who strenuously maintains determinism, seeks to illustrate the subject by the following example:—'Let us suppose a man standing on the street and saying to himself, It is now six o'clock in the evening, the day's work is done, I may then take a walk, or I may go to the club, or I may ascend the tower and see the setting of the sun, or I may go to the theatre, or I may go and visit this friend or that one, or I may run out at the city gate into the wide world, and never come home again. All these things are in my own power, I have perfect freedom to do any of them. Yet now I will do none of them, but equally of my own free-will I will go home again to my wife.' 'This,' continues Schopenhauer, 'is exactly the same as if the water should say: I can heave huge billows (yes, doubtless, in the open sea in a storm); I can rush furiously along (yes, in the bed of a river); I can leap down bubbling and foaming (yes, in a waterfall); I can mount like a sunbeam in the air (yes, in a fountain); finally, I can boil, and, boiling, disappear (yes, at 80° of heat on Réaumur's thermometer): however, I will do none of these things, but remain of my own accord in my tranquil dam, smooth as a river.' As the water can only do any of these things when the exciting causes of one or the other of them are present, so can the man only do what he imagines he is able of himself to determine under the same conditions. So long as the cause is not present, it is impossible to him; but when this enters, he, like the water, *must* do it if presented under corresponding circumstances. The man must thus go home to his wife.—*Martensen,* '*Christian Ethics,*' i. 116, 117.

Determinism and Moral Responsibility.

The Determinist can give to the fundamental terms of Ethics perfectly clear and definite meanings. The distinctions thus obtained give us a practically sufficient basis for criminal law; while the normal sentiments actually existing are seen to be appropriate and useful, as a part of the natural adaptation of social man to his conditions of life. The Determinist allows that, in a sense, 'ought' implies 'can;' that a man is only morally bound to do what is 'in his power;' and that only acts from which a man 'could have abstained' are proper subjects of punishment or moral condemnation. But he explains 'can' and 'in his power' to imply only the absence of all insuperable obstacles *except* want of sufficient motive.—*Sidgwick,* '*Methods of Ethics,*' p. 63.

Determinism and Punishment.

There are two ends which, on the Necessitarian theory, are sufficient to justify punishment,—the benefit of the offender himself, and the protection of others. The first justifies it, because to benefit a person cannot be to do him an injury. To punish him for his own good, provided the inflictor has any proper title to constitute himself a judge, is no more unjust than to administer medicine. As far, indeed, as respects the criminal himself, the theory of punishment is that, by counterbalancing the influence of present temptations or acquired bad habits, it restores the mind to that normal preponderance of the love of right which many moralists and theologians consider to constitute the true definition of freedom. In its other aspect, punishment is a precaution taken by society in self-defence. To make this just, the only condition required is, that the end which society is attempting to enforce by punishment should be a just one. Used as a means of aggression by society on the just rights of the individual, punishment is unjust. Used to protect the just rights of others against unjust aggression by the offender, it is just. —*Mill, 'Examination of Hamilton,'* p. 510.

Criticism of Determinism.

It is based on a wrong idea of Moral development.

Determinism has often made use of the conception of development to aid its argument, and it may, therefore, seem strange that this conception should be used as a weapon against it. But if we examine this doctrine more closely we find that it is based upon quite a mistaken conception of development. If each moment be only the necessary consequence of the preceding, in which therefore it must always have been contained, how could it ever come to be something more—to be an advance on the preceding? Each successive step would be only a repetition of the preceding, indeed it could not be called a step in advance, for it would have no distinctive features marking it as different from the preceding; it would be the same step occurring at a different time, modified, perhaps, by the coincidence of other circumstances. Now it is clear that on such a theory the words 'step' and 'development' lose all their meaning. The successive stages of true development are never linked together according to the law of analysis, but they are united by the most living synthesis. It is not from the outset a perfected plan which has only to be carried out in various external conditions; but this distinctive and perfected plan is produced by means of the development itself, which springs from an indwelling active and determining principle.—*Muller, 'Doctrine of Sin,'* ii. 55, 56.

The decision of the will cannot be calculated.

As moral development proceeds only by means of a progressive self-determining, which cannot be regarded as a mere product of determinations to which the will has already surrendered both itself and its moral life, we must maintain, in opposition to the Deterministic view, that the decisions of a man's will must ever be beforehand unknown and unknowable to his fellow-men, however exact their knowledge and correct their judgment. Therefore, the very best adapted influences brought to bear upon a man which have in view these decisions, or the results of which are dependent upon them, can never secure a certain given result.—*Muller, 'Doctrine of Sin,'* ii. 64.

See further under "NECESSITY."

D.—MORAL PHILOSOPHY, OR ETHICS.

XIX.

DEFINITIONS AND SCOPE.

It is not easy to define in a single phrase the subject commonly called Ethics in such a manner as to meet with general acceptance, as its boundaries and relations to cognate subjects are variously conceived by writers of different schools, and rather indefinitely by mankind in general. Nor does the derivation of the term help us much. Ethics (ἠθικά) originally meant that which relates to ἦθος ('character'); the treatise of Aristotle's, however, to which the term was first applied, is not concerned with character considered simply as character, but with its good and bad qualities. Indeed, the antithesis of 'good' and 'bad' in some form is involved in all ethical affirmation; and its presence constitutes a fundamental distinction between the science or study of ethics and any department of physical inquiry.—*Sidgwick*, '*Encyc. Brit.*,' viii. 574.

Kant.

When the Law of Freedom is applied to human conduct, and is itself the ground determining an action, so as to ascertain and fix its inward, and therefore also its outward conformity to the law, then the knowledge *à priori* resulting from this formal determination of the maxims of the will is the science of Ethics.—'*Metaphysic of Ethics*,' p. 161.

Ueberweg.

Ethics is the doctrine of the Normative laws of human volition and action which rest on the idea (*i.e.*, on the type-notion) of the *Good*. The place which Ethics occupies in the system of Philosophy is a position after Psychology, on a line with Logic and Æsthetics, and before Pædagogic and the Philosophies of Religion and History.—*Appendix D to Ueberweg's 'Logic.'*

Herbert Spencer.

Ethics has for its subject-matter the most highly-evolved conduct as displayed by the most highly-evolved being, Man—is a specification of those traits which his conduct assumes on reaching its limit of evolution. Conceived thus as comprehending the laws of right living at large, Ethics has a wider field than is commonly assigned to it. Beyond the conduct commonly approved or reprobated as right or wrong, it includes all conduct which furthers or hinders, in either direct or indirect ways, the welfare of self or others.—'*Data of Ethics*,' p. 281.

Dr. Martineau.

Ethics may be briefly defined as the doctrine of human character. They assume as their basis the fact that men are prone to criticise themselves and others, and cannot help admiring in various degrees some expressions of affection and will, condemning others.—'*Types of Ethical Theory*,' i. 1.

John Grote.

Moral Philosophy is the Art of Life in its highest sense. If we understand by *life* what the Greeks meant by βίος as different from ζωή, and by *living* the putting forth the powers and faculties for use and enjoyment, moral philosophy is the general and summary, or architectonic, art of this. That is, it deals with the relation to each other of the powers, faculties, and other portions of man which are concerned with this activity and with their harmony as a whole.

Moral philosophy, however, is more than simply an art or practical science, it is an art which sets before it an *ideal*.—'*Moral Ideals*,' p. 12.

XX.

CONSCIENCE.

Its Nature.

The popular name for the Moral Faculty applies to a cognitive power Conscience. *Conscience* and *Consciousness* are similarly compounded, and are in fact originally the same word—conscientia Conscience is immediate knowledge of moral law, as clear and indubitable as a simple fact of consciousness. Conscience is, however, popularly applied to the whole moral nature of man. This free use of the name makes it often synonymous with consciousness, or the knowledge of the harmony of personal conduct with moral law.—*Calderwood*, '*Handbook of Moral Philosophy*,' p 78.

As *Science* means *Knowledge*, *Conscience* etymologically means self-knowledge; and such is the meaning of the word in Latin and French, and of the corresponding word in Greek (*conscientia*, *conscience*, *συνείδησις*). But the English word implies a moral standard of action in the mind, as well as a consciousness of our own actions. It may be convenient to us to mark this distinction of an internal Moral Standard, as one part of Conscience, and Self-Knowledge, or Consciousness, as another part The one is the Internal Law; the other, the Internal Accuser, Witness, and Judge. —*Whewell*, '*Elements of Morality*,' p 148.

The name of Conscience has always been, and will always continue to be, popularly used in a much wider sense than that in which the designation can be employed under strict philosophic warrant. It is thus commonly made to embrace all that is connected with our moral decisions, within the sphere of personal consciousness Thus our moral judgments are attributed directly to conscience itself, and that even when they are discredited as erroneous. So in like manner all experience of moral sentiment is referred directly to Conscience. With this wide popular use of the term Conscience, a variety of phrases descriptive of the condition of the faculty has found currency in popular discourse. Of these, the following may be taken as examples. An unenlightened Conscience, a scrupulous Conscience, a tender Conscience, a hardened Conscience, an upbraiding Conscience.—*Calderwood*, '*Handbook of Moral Philosophy*,' p. 83.

Stoical Origin of the Term.

The most important of moral terms, the crowning triumph of ethical nomenclature, *συνείδησις*, conscientia, the internal, absolute, supreme judge of individual action, if not struck in the mint of the Stoics, at all events became current coin through their influence.—*Lightfoot*, '*Philippians*,' p. 301.

Definitions and Descriptions.

Conscience was described by Cicero as the God ruling within us, by the Stoics as the sovereignty of reason.—*Lecky*, '*Hist. Eur. Morals*,' i. 83.

Conscience I define to be a Faculty or Habit of the Practical Understanding, which enables the mind of man, by the use of Reason and Argument, to apply the light which it has to particular moral actions.—*Sanderson*, '*Lectures on Conscience*, *&c*.,' p. 2.

'The Conscience is that in me which says, I ought or I ought not' 'The act of Conscience is an act in me. I may pass judgment on other men's acts, but that is another process; I am abusing terms, and what the terms represent if I identify it with the Conscience.' 'The ought does not belong to things—it does not suggest some vague possibility for *their* improvement—it is linked inseparably to me.'—*Maurice*, '*The Conscience*,' pp. 31, 34, 52.

The mind can take a view of what passes within itself, its propensions, aversions, passions, affections, and of the several actions consequent thereupon. In this survey it approves of one, disapproves of another, and towards a third is affected in neither of these ways, but is quite indifferent. This principle in man, by which he approves or disapproves his heart, temper, and actions, is conscience; for this is the strict sense of the word, though sometimes it is used so as to take in more.—*Butler*, '*Sermons*,' i.

Conscience is that power of mind by which moral law is discovered to each individual for the guidance of his conduct. It is the Reason, as it discovers to us absolute moral truth—having the authority of sovereign moral law. It is an essential requisite for the direction of an intelligent free-will agent, and affords the basis for moral obligation and responsibility in human life.—*Calderwood*, '*Moral Philosophy*,' p. 77.

Our consciousness reveals to us not only our most secret acts, but our desires, affections, and intentions. These are the especial subjects of morality, and we cannot think of them without considering them as right or wrong. We approve or disapprove of what we have done, or tried to do. We consider our acts, external and internal, with reference to a moral standard of right and wrong. We recognise them as virtuous or vicious. The Faculty or Habit of doing this is Conscience.—*Whewell*, '*Elements of Morality*,' p. 148.

Conscience is that in a man which points to what is above him, which declares the supremacy of a right that he did not mould and cannot alter.—*Maurice*, '*The Conscience*,' p. 161.

Conscience is not mere impulse, the impulse of obedience and subordination, the aim of which is God and God's kingdom; it is not mere instinct which makes known to man what in an ethical respect is serviceable to him, and what he must avoid for the preservation of his soul, just as the instinct of animals makes known to them what is serviceable to their self-preservation, and incites them to avoid the opposite. It is consciousness, knowledge, man's joint acquaintance with himself and with God, the consciousness direct, essential, differing from all consciousness of reflection and idea of our dependence not merely on the law, but on the binding and determining *authority*, which speaks to us through the law. —*Martensen*, '*Christian Ethics*,' i. 356.

The peculiar character of the moral sentiments consists in their *exclusive reference to states of will*; and every feeling which has that quality, when it is purified from all admixture with different objects, becomes capable of being absorbed into Conscience, and of being assimilated to it, so as to become part of it.—*Mackintosh*, *Dissertation II.*, '*Encyclop. Brit.*,' ed. viii.

Conscience is the brightness and splendour of the eternal light, a spotless mirror of the Divine Majesty, and the image of the goodness of God.—*St. Bernard.*

Conscience is not an echo or an abode of an immediate divine self-attestation, but an active consciousness of a divine law established in man's heart; for all self-consciousness of created natures capable of self-consciousness is naturally at once a consciousness of their dependence on God and a consciousness of their duty to allow themselves to be determined by the will of God, and consciousness of the general purport of that will. That which is said by ancients and moderns of the conscience, as God's voice in us, has in it this truth, that the testimony of conscience certainly rests on a divine foundation, woven in our natural condition, *scil.* on a divine law in man, ordained with his created constitution, the existence of which, its claims and judgments, are removed from his subjective control.—*Delitzsch*, '*Biblical Psychology*,' p. 165.

It is a Distinguishing Feature in Man.

Whatever foreshadowings of this sense may be discerned, as is sometimes alleged, in the higher animals, there is at least one thing of which there is no trace among them, and that is, a feeling of continuous responsibility for the whole of life and for its successive actions. But each man feels that all his acts constitute an abiding element of his personal and individual being, and that he has a living and abiding responsibility for them.—*Wace, 'Christianity and Morality,'* p. 200.

Conscience is peculiar to man. We see not a vestige of it in brute animals. A man who seriously charged a brute with a crime would be laughed at. They may do actions hurtful to themselves or to man. They may have qualities or acquire habits that lead to such actions; and that is all we mean when we call them vicious. But they cannot be immoral; nor can they be virtuous. They are not capable of self-government. They cannot lay down a rule to themselves which they are not to transgress, though prompted by appetite or ruffled by passion.—*Reid, 'Works,'* p. 596.

Conscience, in discovering to us first principles for the guidance of conduct and formation of moral character, constitutes a leading distinction of human nature. The basis of personal life is thereby laid in self-evident absolute truth.—*Calderwood, 'Moral Philosophy,'* p. 82.

Proof of its Existence.

From moral judgments and distinctions.

That we have this moral approving and disapproving faculty, is certain from our experiencing it in ourselves and recognising it in each other. It appears from our exercising it unavoidably in the approbation and disapprobation even of feigned characters: from the words, *right* and *wrong*, *odious* and *amiable*, *base* and *worthy*, with many others of like signification in all languages, applied to actions and characters; from our natural sense of gratitude, which implies a distinction between merely being the instrument of good, and intending it: from the like distinction, every one makes, between injury and mere harm, which, Hobbes says, is peculiar to mankind; and between injury and just punishment, a distinction plainly natural, prior to the consideration of human laws. It is manifest great part of common language, and of common behaviour over the world, is formed upon supposition of such a moral faculty.—*Butler, 'Dissertations,'* ii.

It cannot possibly be denied that there is this principle of reflection or conscience in human nature. Suppose a man to relieve an innocent person in great distress; suppose the same man afterwards, in the fury of anger, to do the greatest mischief to a person who had given no just cause of offence; to aggravate the injury, add the circumstance of former friendship and obligation from the injured person; let the man who is supposed to have done these two different actions, coolly reflect upon them afterwards, without regard to their consequences to himself: to assert that any common man would be affected in the same way towards these different actions, that he would make no distinction between them, but approve or disapprove them equally, is too glaring a falsity to need being confuted. There is, therefore, this principle of reflection or conscience in mankind.—*Butler, 'Sermons,'* i.

From its action.

There is nothing we feel more certain of than conscience. To deny it is to overthrow the foundation of all certainty, and to annihilate therewith the whole moral constitution of the world, which rests upon it. No man can deny conscience with a good conscience. Even while we are trying to deny it, it makes itself felt by its inward reproofs; and we cannot deny it without belying ourselves. Conscience is assuredly a fact.—*Luthardt, 'Fundamental Truths,'* p. 58.

Conscience is the last thing left to man, after he has squandered and lost all else that God has given him. It is the last tie by which God retains a hold upon the man who has erred and strayed from Him, and by which He reminds him of the home he has forsaken. Even in the most degraded ages of heathenism it was still a power, and the times of deepest decay have been just those which have yielded the most touching evidence of its activity.—*Luthardt*, '*Moral Truths*,' p. 53

Theories of Conscience.

Simple and Original.

Conscience is original, and no additamentum to our person; and there can be no duty to procure one; but every man has, as a moral being, a conscience.—*Kant*, '*Metaphysic of Ethics*,' p. 217.

Some philosophers, with whom I agree, ascribe the power of determining what is morally good, and what is morally ill, to an original power or faculty in man, which they call the Moral Sense, the Moral Faculty, Conscience. This opinion seems to me to be the truth, to wit, that, by an original power of the mind, when we come to years of understanding and reflection, we not only have the notions of right and wrong in conduct, but perceive certain things to be right, and others to be wrong. —*Reid*, '*Works*,' p. 589

We must hold conscience to be simple and unresolvable, till we fall in with a successful decomposition of it into its elements. In the absence of any such decomposition, we hold that there are no simpler elements in the human mind which will yield us the ideas of the morally good and evil, of moral obligation and guilt, of merit and demerit.—*M'Cosh*, '*Method of the Divine Government*,' p 305.

We have just as much reason for trusting the sense of Right with the postulate of objective authority which it carries, as for believing in the components of the rainbow or the infinitude of space. These ideas are all acquisitions, in the sense that there was a time when they were not to be found in the creatures from which we descend They are all evolved, in the sense that, gradually and one by one, they cropped up into consciousness amid the crowd of feelings which they entered as strangers They are all original, or *sui generis*, in the sense that they are intrinsically dissimilar to the predecessors with which they mingle, so that by no rational scrutiny could you, out of the contents of these predecessors, invent and preconceive them, any more than you can predict the psychology of a million years hence. Whence then the strange anxiety to get rid of this originality, and assimilate again what you had registered as a differentiation? You say that, when you undress the 'moral intuition' and lay aside fold after fold of its disguise, you find nothing at last but naked pleasure and utility: then how is it that no foresight, with largest command of psychologic clothes, would enable you to invert the experiment and dress up these nudities into the august form of Duty? To say that the conscience is but the compressed contents of an inherited calculus of the agreeable and the serviceable, is no better than for one who had been colour-blind to insist, that the red which he has gained is nothing but his familiar green with some queer mask. It cannot be denied that the sense of right has earned its separate name, by appearing to those who have it and speak of it to one another essentially different from the desire of pleasure, from the perception of related means and ends, and from coercive fear.—*Martineau*, '*Types of Ethical Theory*,' ii 362, 363.

The position of conscience in our nature is wholly unique While each of our senses or appetites has a restricted sphere of operation, it is the function of conscience to survey the whole constitution of our being, and assign limits to the gratification of all our various passions and desires Differing not in degree, but in kind, from the other principles of our nature, we feel that a course of conduct which is opposed to it may be intelligibly described as unnatural, even when in accordance with our most natural appetites, for to conscience is assigned the prerogative of both judging and restraining them all.—*Lecky*, '*Hist European Morals*,' i. 83.

Conscience in me says 'I ought' and 'I ought not.' There is no difference about the question whether these words 'ought' and 'ought not' do exist in our language, whether there are not equivalent words in the language of every civilised nation. There is no difference about the question whether they are deeply fixed in human speech; no one seriously dreams of extracting them out of it. Nor, I believe, if we understand one another, will there be much hesitation in admitting the maxim for which I have been contending, that none of the things I see or handle suggest the word, that the moment I speak of myself, it starts forth full armed.—*Maurice*, '*The Conscience*,' p. 51.

Equivalent to Moral Reason

Richard Cumberland

The (Moral) Faculty is the Reason, apprehending the exact Nature of Things, and determining accordingly the modes of action that are best suited to promote the happiness of rational agents.

Of the Faculty under the name of *Conscience* he gives this description: 'The mind is conscious to itself of all its own actions, and both can and often does observe what counsels produced them; it naturally sits a judge upon its own actions, and thence procures to itself either tranquillity and joy or anxiety and sorrow.' The principal design of his whole book is to show 'how this power of the mind, either by itself, or excited by external objects, forms certain universal practical propositions, which give us a more distinct idea of the happiness of mankind, and pronounces by what actions of ours, in all variety of circumstances, that happiness may most effectually be obtained' (Conscience is thus only Reason, or the knowing faculty in general, as specially concerned about actions in their effect upon happiness; it rarely takes the place of the more general term.)—*Bain*, '*Moral Science*,' p. 557.

Kant.

Conscience is man's practical Reason, which does, in all circumstances, hold before him his law of duty, in order to absolve or to condemn him. It has accordingly no objective import, and refers only to the subject, affecting his moral sense by its own intrinsic action.—'*Metaphysic of Ethics*,' p. 217.

Complex and Derived.

The Moral Faculty is not simple, but complex and derived. It is practicable to analyse or resolve the Moral Faculty; and in doing so, to explain both its peculiar property and the similarity of moral judgments so far as existing among men. We begin by estimating the operation of—(1.) Prudence or Self-interest, which obviously has much to do with moral conduct. If we set an example of injustice, it may be taken up and repeated to such a degree that we can count upon nothing: social security comes to an end. (2.) Sympathy or Fellow-Feeling, the source of our disinterested actions. It is a consequence of our sympathetic endowment that we revolt from inflicting pain on another, and even forego a certain satisfaction to self rather than be the occasion of suffering to a fellow-creature. (3.) The Emotions generally, which may co-operate with Prudence and with Sympathy in a way to make both the one and the other more efficacious.—*Bain*, '*Mental and Moral Science*,' pp. 453, 454.

That the moral sentiment is in part instinctive may be allowed. It is probable that, as the result of long ages of social experience, a habit of feeling and judging in a moral way has been formed, which transmits itself to each new child as an instinctive disposition to fall in with and conform to the moral law. Yet supposing this to be so, it remains indisputable that the moral faculty is to a large extent built up in the course of the individual life.—*Sully*, '*Psychology*,' p. 559.

Theory of Hobbes.

It is either science or opinion which we commonly mean by the word conscience; for men say that such and such a thing is true in or upon their conscience; which they never do when they think it doubtful, and therefore they know, or think they know it to be true. But men, when they say things upon their conscience, are not, therefore, presumed certainly to know the truth of what they say; it remaineth then that that word is used by them that have an opinion, not only of the truth of the thing, but also of their knowledge of it, to which the truth of the opinion is consequent. Conscience I therefore define to be *opinion of evidence.*—'*Human Nature,*' ch. v sec. 8.

Bain.

Conscience is an imitation within ourselves of the government without us; and even when differing in what it prescribes from the current morality, the mode of its action is still parallel to the archetype.—'*Emotions, &c.,*' p. 285

Leslie Stephen

The moral sense is, according to me, a product of the social factor. It is the sum of certain instincts which have come to be imperfectly organised in the race, and which are vigorous in proportion as the society is healthy and vigorous.—'*Science of Ethics,*' p. 372.

Schopenhauer

The Elements of Conscience may be computed thus: 'One fifth, fear of man; one fifth, superstition; one fifth, prejudice; one fifth, vanity, one fifth, custom.'—*Schopenhauer, in Professor Calderwood's* '*Moral Philosophy,*' p 140.

Evolutional Theory.

Increased sympathy, as well as an increased recognition by each unit of the 'social organism' of what he might do for the gratification of his own wants or desires, without bringing pain upon himself through the anger of his fellows, would gradually teach him the necessity of subordinating within certain limits his realisation of egoistic impulses, and the need, even for the sake of his own happiness, of continually bearing in mind the wants and wishes of his fellow-men.

Equally important among savage races, are those limitations which 'expediency' compels the individual to recognise, as imposed by his fellow-men upon the freedom of his own actions. Such considerations, in concert with a strengthening sympathy, gradually tend to build up within him an inward monitor, or 'Conscience,' at the same time that there arise embryo notions of Right and Duty, constituting the foundations of a dawning 'Moral Sense.'—*Bastian,* '*The Brain, &c.,*' p 416.

Equivalent to Moral Sense.

On account of the view taken of the functions of Conscience, it is commonly named by Utilitarians, 'The Moral Sense.'

Conscience is represented as a form of Feeling, involving reverence for moral distinctions, and impelling to their observance. Sometimes conscience has been regarded rather as a restraining force, involving 'a pain more or less intense, attendant on violation of duty.'—*Calderwood,* '*Moral Philosophy,*' p 139.

Can Conscience be Educated?

Most answer, Yes.

Like all our other powers, conscience comes to maturity by insensible degrees, and may be much aided in its strength and vigour by proper culture. In the first period of life, children are not capable of distinguishing right from wrong in human conduct. The seeds, as it were, of moral discernment are planted in the mind by Him that made us. They grow up in their proper season, and are at first tender and delicate and easily warped. Their progress depends very much upon their being duly cultivated and properly exercised. We must not therefore think, because man has the natural power of discerning what is right and what is wrong, that he has no need of instruction; that this power has no need of cultivation and improvement; that he may safely rely upon the suggestions of his mind, or upon opinions he has got, he knows not how.—*Reid*, '*Works*,' p. 595.

The development of Conscience is especially conditional on the development of knowledge. It is also conditional on the *will*, which, unlike, nay contrary to knowledge, throughout the whole history has exerted a restraining, obstructive influence on the cultivation of the conscience. Therefore the conscience on its human side often requires to be corrected and enlightened, and is always to be cultivated. The conscience may be blunt and require to be sharpened; it may be lethargic and require to be roused.—*Martensen*, '*Christian Ethics*,' i. 365.

It is the duty of man constantly to prosecute his moral and intellectual culture. We must labour to *enlighten* and *instruct* our conscience. This task can never be ended. So long as life and powers of thought remain to us, we may always be able to acquire a still clearer and higher view than we yet possess, of the supreme law of our being. We never can have done all that is in our power, in this respect. Conscience is never fully formed, but always in the course of formation. — *Whewell*, '*Elements of Morality*,' p. 150.

A few say, No.

Conscience is a faculty which from its very nature cannot be educated. Education, either in the sense of instruction or training, is impossible. As well propose to teach the eye how and what to see, and the ear how and what to hear, as to teach Reason how to perceive the self-evident, and what truths are of this nature. All these have been provided for in the human constitution.—*Calderwood*, '*Moral Philosophy*,' p. 81.

An erring conscience is a chimera; for although in the objective judgment, whether or not anything be a duty, mankind may very easily go wrong—yet subjectively, whether I have compared an action with my practical (here judiciary) reason for the behoof of such objective judgment, does not admit of any mistake; and if there were any, then would no practical judgment have been pronounced,—a case excluding alike the possibility of error or of truth.—*Kant*, '*Metaphysic of Ethics*,' p. 217.

Conscience may be corrupted and deadened.

It is a common way of accounting for the anomalies in man's moral state to say, in a loose and general way, that the conscience has lost its control over the other faculties of the human mind. Now, it is quite true that the conscience has lost its proper control, but it has not lost all power. On the contrary, it is in some respects as active and energetic as ever. It works not the less powerfully because it works destructively. A court of justice perverted into a court of injustice may be as active in its latter as in its former capacity. The Court of Inquisition in Spain, the Star-Chamber and the Court of High Commission in the reign of the Stuarts in our own country, and the Tribunals in Paris in the Reign of Terror, were as busily employed and as powerful as the most righteous courts of justice that ever sat in the same kingdoms. It is not conceivable that the conscience should ever cease to exist in the breast of any responsible agent; certain it is that in man's present nature it often wields a tremendous energy. Misery never reaches its utmost intensity till it comes to be inflicted by the scourges of an accusing conscience. Wickedness never becomes so unrelenting as when it seems to have received the sanction of the moral law. What might otherwise have been a mere impulse of blind passion, becomes now persevering and systematic villainy or cruelty. Not unfrequently it assumes the shape of cool-blooded persecution, committed without reluctance and without remorse. The conscience now shows what had been its power for good if properly exercised, and how it can bear down and subordinate all the other and mere sympathetic feelings of the mind.—*M'Cosh, 'Method of the Divine Government'* (1850).

It is true that the conscience itself has not remained unaffected by the universal corruption wherewith sin has overspread our whole being. Both its truth and its power have been weakened. In the heathen nations, conscience has gone astray and does not rightly understand its office. And how often does the power of sin get the upper hand and so paralyse the operation of conscience that its authority is slighted! Yet, in the midst of all this corruption and perversion of conscience, the fact is not abolished.—*Luthardt, 'Moral Truths,'* p. 53.

Functions of Conscience.

Generally.

Conscience, whether we regard it as an original faculty or as a product of the association of ideas, exercises two distinct functions. It points out a difference between right and wrong, and, when its commands are violated, it inflicts a certain measure of suffering and disturbance. The first function it exercises persistently through life; the second it only exercises under certain special circumstances. It is scarcely conceivable that a man in possession of his faculties should pass a life of gross depravity and crime without being conscious that he was doing wrong; but it is extremely possible for him to do so without this 'consciousness having any appreciable influence on his tranquillity.'—*Lecky, 'Hist. European Morals,'* i. 62.

What is the operation of its voice? Is it content with proclaiming to you the general supremacy of a righteous law? Does it not, on the contrary, search your hearts and try your thoughts, and see if there be any wicked way in you? Does it not with a mysterious justice deal with your personal character, your private, individual, and peculiar responsibilities, making allowance for your weaknesses, condemning you in proportion to the wilfulness of your sin; but above all things meeting you at every turn and in every instant of your lives with the particular warning and guidance you need?—*Wace, 'Christianity and Morality,'* p. 198.

Particularly.

It testifies to

Right and Wrong.

The truths immediately testified by our moral faculty are the first principles of all moral reasoning, from which all our knowledge of duty must be deduced. By moral reasoning I understand all reasoning that is brought to prove that such conduct is right, and deserving of moral approbation; or that it is wrong; or that it is indifferent, and in itself neither morally good nor ill.—*Reid, 'Works,'* p. 590.

The Conscience in man bears its own clear testimony. This faculty of our nature, or representative of the Judge in our personality, is simply, in relation to sin, the registrar of its guilt. It is the moral consciousness, rather of instinct than of reflection, though also of both, faithfully assuming the personal responsibility of the sin and anticipating its consequences.—*Pope, 'Christian Theology,'* ii. 34.

Conscience bears witness to our actions: so St. Paul, 'Their conscience bearing witness;' and in this sense conscience is a practical memory.—*Jeremy Taylor, 'Works,'* ix. 17.

The Moral Faculty stamps our actions as right or wrong. This faculty, which we cannot help regarding as the authoritative voice of Him who made us, corresponds exactly, in its functions and its judgments, to the moral law delivered on Mount Sinai. The one is the objective, the other the subjective law, whose authority we recognise as different but parallel revelations of the one true God.—*Crawford, 'The Atonement,'* p. 523.

Conscience speaks to man most clearly when the voices of the world are mute; and often must it say to man in dreams what it cannot succeed in telling him in his waking moments.—*Martensen*, '*Christian Ethics*,' i 360

Conscience is the looking-glass of the soul. And a man looking into his conscience, instructed with the Word of God, its proper rule, is by St James compared to 'a man beholding his natural face in a glass'—*Jeremy Taylor*, '*Works*,' ix 19

A God

Those clear, precise, categorical orders, which are imposed (by conscience) in varying degrees of urgency upon all human wills, point to a really living Ruler of men, in whom man cannot disbelieve without doing violence to himself.—*Liddon*, '*Elements of Religion*,' 1881.

Men's consciences are truer than their intellects. However they may employ the subtlety of their intellects to dull their conscience, they feel in their heart of hearts that there is a Judge, that guilt is punished, that they are guilty. Intellect carries the question out of itself into the region of surmising and disputings. Conscience is compelled to receive it back into its own court, and to give the sentence, which it would withhold. Like the god of the heathen fable, who changed himself into all sorts of forms, but when he was held fast gave at the last the true answer, conscience shrinks back, twists, writhes, evades, turns away, but in the end it will answer truly when it must.—*Pusey*, '*Minor Prophets*,' p. 198

Conscience is unsatisfied, according to Kant, unless there exists some Being above the world, who can hereafter reconcile the discrepancies which exist between virtue and fortune in this present life, in His quality as an arbiter of human conduct.—*Liddon*, '*Elements of Religion*,' 1881.

It guides.

The Moral Faculty determines itself to be the guide of action and of life, in contradistinction from all other faculties or natural principles of action: in the very same manner as speculative reason directly and naturally judges of speculative truth and falsehood; and at the same time is attended with a consciousness upon *reflection* that the natural right to judge of them belongs to it.—*Butler*, '*Dissertations*,' ii. (note).

Conscience is evidently intended by nature to be the immediate guide and director of our conduct after we arrive at the years of understanding. Like the bodily eye, it naturally looks forward, though its attention may be turned back to the past. To conceive, as some seem to have done, that its office is only to reflect on past actions, and to approve or disapprove, is as if a man should conceive that the office of his eyes is only to look back upon the road he has travelled, and to see whether it be clean or dirty,—a mistake which no man can make who has made the proper use of his eyes.—*Reid*, '*Works*,' p. 597

It speaks for God.

This originally intellectual and ethical (for it refers to duty) disposition of our nature, called conscience, has this peculiarity, that although this whole matter is an affair of man with himself, he notwithstanding finds his reason constrained to carry on the suit, as if it were at the instigation of another person; for the procedure is the conduct of a cause before a court. Now, that he who is the accused by his conscience should be figured to be just the same person as his judge, is an absurd representation of a tribunal; since in such event the accuser would always lose his suit. Conscience must therefore represent to itself always some other than itself as Judge, unless it is to arrive at a contradiction with itself. This other may be either a real—or an ideal person,—the product of reason.—*Kant*, '*Metaphysic of Ethics*,' p. 255

It is not merely the authority of a moral law which conscience brings to bear upon man, but it accredits itself to him as an expression of the Divine will against which there is no appeal. For though it is saying too much to call conscience the voice of God Himself, it yet bears testimony in the soul to that will of God, which we bear within us as the law of our being, and summons both our wills and deeds before its judgment-seat, to receive therefrom the moral law which is to guide, or the moral sentence which is to condemn them. —*Luthardt*, '*Moral Truths*,' p 54

God hath given us conscience to be in His stead to us, to give us laws, and to exact obedience to those laws, to punish them that prevaricate, and to reward the obedient. And therefore conscience is called 'the household guardian,' 'the domestic god,' 'the spirit or angel of the place'—*Taylor*, '*Works*,' ix. 4.

Conscience is the voice of God in the soul, which witnesses to our sinfulness and ill-desert, and to His essential justice. . Every man feels that his moral relations to God are never settled in this life, and hence the characteristic testimony of the conscience, in spite of great individual differences as to light, sensibility, &c, has always been coincident with the word of God, that 'after death' comes the judgment —*Hodge*, 1869

It records, and its records are permanent

Conscience is the *record* of offences committed.—*Wheuell*, '*Elements, &c*,' p. 149.

The records of Conscience are permanent. Acts that to others are dead still live for the doer of them. Coleridge tells the story of an ignorant servant girl who, in the delirium of a fever, repeated sentences of Greek and Hebrew, which she had heard her master repeat years before whilst she was sweeping his study. He deduces this lesson from the tale 'It may be more possible for heaven and earth to pass away, than that a single act, a single thought, should be loosened or lost from that living chain of causes, with all the links of which the freewill, our only absolute self, is co-extensive and co-present. And this perchance is that dread book of judgment in the mysterious hieroglyphics of which every idle word is recorded.—*Maurice*, '*The Conscience*,' p 49 *seq*.

It judges

Every man is a little world within himself, and in this little world there is a court of judicature erected, wherein, next under God, the conscience sits as the supreme judge, from whom there is no appeal; that passeth sentence upon us, upon all our actions, upon all our intentions, for our persons, absolving one, condemning another; for our actions, allowing one, forbidding another. If that condemn us, in vain shall all the world beside acquit us; and, if that clear us, the doom which the world passeth upon us is frivolous and ineffectual —*Hall*, '*Works*,' vi. 375

It is the special function of conscience to say when a particular appetency should be allowed and when it should be restrained, in doing so it addresses itself to the will. The conscience thus claims to be above, not only our natural appetencies, but above the will, which ought to yield as soon as the decision of conscience is given, not that it can set itself altogether above nature, not that it should set itself above nature; it is its office to sit in judgment on appetencies which are natural or may be acquired, and it works through freewill as an essential element of our nature —*M'Cosh*, '*Intuitions of the Mind*,' p. 285.

Conscience, the Judge, must pronounce its decision according to Conscience, the Law. If we have not transgressed the Law of Conscience, Conscience acquits us. If we have violated the Law of Conscience, Conscience condemns us.—*Wheivell*, '*Elements of Morality*,' p 149.

Laws of the working of the conscience as Judge.—

First. It is of mental, and of mental acts exclusively, that the conscience judges. It has no judgment whatever to pronounce on a mere bodily act. We look out at the window and we see two individuals in different places chastising two different children The conscience pronounces no judgment in the one case or the other, whatever the feelings may do, until we have learned the motives which have led to the performance of the acts.

Secondly It is of acts of the will, and of acts of the will exclusively, that the conscience judges. In saying so, we use *will* in a large sense, as large as that department which has been allotted to it, we believe, by God in the human mind. We use it as including all wishes, desires, intentions, and resolutions, all that is properly active and personal in man

Thirdly The conscience approves and disapproves, not of isolated acts merely, but also of the mind or agent manifested in these acts The conscience judges according to truth, and regards all mental acts as the mind acting, and pronounces its verdict, not so much on the abstract act as on the mind voluntarily acting in them

Fourthly The conscience pronounces its decision on the state of mind of the responsible agent, as the same is presented to it The conscience is in the position of a barrister whose opinion is asked in matters of legal difficulty In both cases the judgment given proceeds on the supposed accuracy of a representation submitted, but which may be very partial or very perverted

It follows—*Fifthly That there may be much uncertainty, or confusion, or positive error in the judgments of the conscience, because given upon false representations.* It follows that the conscience of two different individuals, or of the same individual at different times, may *seem* to pronounce two different judgments on the same deed. We say *seem*, for in reality the two deeds are different and the judgments differ, because the deeds as presented to the conscience are not the same

Sixthly. The decisions of the conscience are of various kinds. They may be classified as follows —First, the conscience approves of the morally right. Secondly, it condemns what is evil Thirdly, it declares when evil has been committed that punishment is due.—*M'Cosh*, '*Method of the Divine Government*' (1850).

If we analyse the feeling which the conscience gives us concerning wrong-doing, it is this —(1) Conscience demands reparation to the injured party, (2) punishment as a satisfaction to the law, and this to be regarded as just by the guilty party; (3) alienation or separation between the guilty and the innocent The inward voice of Conscience is always saying that God ought not to forgive us without some reparation made for the injury done to Himself, to the universe, and to ourselves.—*Clarke*, '*Orthodoxy*,' pp 246, 248

Dugald Stewart has observed, that in the most rapid reading of a book to one's self, there is a distinct volition for every word, every syllable, though it may seem sometimes that the mind gathers up the page almost with a single glance of the eye Thus the play of the will is habitual, imperceptible, yet none the less actual, and made up of distinct intervals. So it must be with the conscience There is a judgment of the conscience upon everything. It may be so rapid, so transitory, swifter than the lightning, so brief as the most evanescent, imperceptible shade of thought, that it is not distinctly noticed, and cannot be, except by some supernatural arrest of the being fixing it on the last momentary act or interval; but it exists, as truly as the will exists, although its separate movements may not be noticed —*Cheever*, '*Bibliotheca Sacra*,' p. 476 (1851).

History presents many examples of a mixture of motives Lilienhorn had been raised from obscurity and wretchedness by Gustavus, King of Sweden, promoted to the rank of commandant of the guard, and had the complete confidence of his sovereign. But when a conspiracy was formed against his master, he joined it, instigated by the hope held out to him of commanding the national guard, and holding in his hand the destinies of the kingdom Meanwhile he endeavoured, by a kind of compromise, to keep his allegiance to the king his benefactor. He wrote him an anonymous letter, informing him of particulars, which must have convinced the king of the veracity of the statement, of an unsuccessful attempt that had been made to take his life some time before, describing the plan which the conspirators had now formed, and warning him against going to a particular ball, where the assassination was to be committed. In this way he sought to satisfy his conscience, when it threw out doubts as to the propriety of the course which he was pursuing. He spent the evening on which the conspiracy was to take effect in the king's apartment, saw him read the anonymous letter sent him, and upon the generous and headstrong king's despising the warning, followed him to the ball, and was present when he was shot. Now, take us to the closet of this man, and let us see him writing the letter which was fitted to save his sovereign—show us this, and no more, and we say, How becoming! how generous! but let us follow him through the whole scenes, and we change our tone, and arraign him of treachery, and we do so at the very instant when he writes the letter, and seems most magnanimous.—*M'Cosh, 'Method of Divine Government'* (1850).

It warns.

Our moral nature seems to carry a more special message to every man,—that he must submit to the Judge. This is a feeling which may lie very much dormant in many states of the existence of man; as when he is engrossed in business, or absorbed in schemes of earthly ambition, but it seizes many a quiet moment to insinuate the truth committed to it; it awakes with terrible power in the state of relaxation which succeeds the fever heat of the evil propensities; it issues its lightning flashes in the dark hour of disappointment; it raises its sharp voice in the stillness of the sick chamber; and gives forth foreboding utterances, which few dare despise when they realise the thought that the time of their departure is at hand. The conscience in this life is the anticipation of the archangel's trumpet summoning all men to the judgment, and in the other world may become the worm that never dies, and the fire that is not quenched.—*M'Cosh, 'Intuitions of the Mind,'* p. 444.

How deeply seated the conscience is in the human soul, is seen in the effect which sudden calamities produce in guilty men, even when unaided by any determinate notion or fears of punishment after death; as if the vast pyre of the last judgment were already kindled in an unknown distance, and some flashes of it, darting forth at intervals beyond the rest, were flying and lighting upon the face of his soul.—*Coleridge.*

It punishes.

The binding to punishment is an act of conscience as it is a judge, and is intended to affright a sinner and to punish him; but it is such a punishment as is the beginning of hell torments, and unless the wound be cured, will never end till eternity itself shall go into a grave.—*Jeremy Taylor, 'Works,'* ix. 21.

In the evil conscience there is an inward disquietude and dispeace, distress and wretchedness in the present. The violated demands of the law weigh on the evil consciousness as an oppressive burden, which literally makes the mind heavy. And not only is it felt as a burden, but also as an inward scourge, which chases the transgressor like a wild beast, as we see in the case of Orestes, who was pursued by recollections; and in the case of Cain, who, a fugitive and a vagabond on the earth, in vain endeavours to flee from himself and from the accusation which sounds from the depth of his being. The criminal trembles in solitude; is terrified by the rustling of a leaf, imagines that avenging spirits will suddenly rush in upon him and hurl him into woe.—*Martensen, 'Christian Ethics,'* i. 361–2.

An evil conscience makes man a coward, timorous as a child in a church porch at midnight. It makes the strongest men to tremble like the keepers of the house of an old man's tabernacle.—*Jeremy Taylor*, '*Works*,' ix. 25.

Not with a feeling of repentance, which ever includes a hope, however anxious, and a longing, but in boundless despair, in *horror of himself*, Judas declares, 'I have betrayed innocent blood,' and casts from him the thirty pieces of silver. In despair, King Richard III. speaks, while his fate is overtaking him, and after he had dreamed his darker dreams of conscience, which have made his heart despondent:—

> 'My conscience hath a thousand several tongues;
> And every tongue brings in a several tale,
> And every tale condemns me for a villain.'

—*Martensen*, '*Christian Ethics*,' ii. 137.

It imparts pleasure.

The moral faculty can never be employed without emotion. The feelings, which are its necessary train or accompaniment in all its exercises, impart to them all their liveliness and fervour. They communicate to the soul that noble elevation which it feels on the contemplation of benevolence, of devotedness in a good cause, and patriotism and piety under all their forms.—*M'Cosh*, '*Method of the Divine Government*,' p. 307.

The design of the moral sentiment is to render sensible to the soul the connexion of virtue and happiness.—*Cousin.*

A good conscience has not merely present inward peace, but is always accompanied by a blessed anticipation of the future, even if present circumstances are dark enough.—*Martensen*, '*Christian Ethics*,' i. 361.

It reveals the moral harmony of our nature.

Conscience, in subjecting our other powers to its authority, reveals the moral harmony of our natural powers, and provides what is essential for moral training of our whole being. All subject powers are powers naturally under regulation for their exercise, and all regulated powers are capable of training. In this way, our dispositions, affections, and desires are placed under guidance in accordance with the demands of moral law.—*Calderwood*, '*Moral Philosophy*,' p. 82.

The Government of Conscience.

The Right of Conscience.

This faculty was placed within to be our proper governor; to direct and regulate all under principles, passions, and motives of action. This is its right and office. How often soever men violate and rebelliously refuse to submit to it, for supposed interest which they cannot otherwise obtain, or for the sake of passion which they cannot gratify, this makes no alteration as to the natural right and office of conscience.—*Butler*, '*Sermons*,' ii.

We are not over conscience, but under it. It is not under our power, but has power over us. We do not correct and direct it, but it corrects and chastises us.—*Luthardt*, '*Fundamental Truths*,' p. 59.

Authority of Conscience.

Conscience, in discovering to us moral law for the guidance of our actions, has authority over all other springs of activity within us. We may with clear philosophic warrant attribute to the power discovering to us all moral law the authority which belongs to each of the laws thereby made known. 'The authority of Conscience' is an abbreviated form for expressing the authority which is common to all the laws of morality.—*Calderwood*, '*Moral Philosophy*,' p. 78.

Other principles of action may have more strength, but this only has authority. From its nature, it has an authority to direct and determine with regard to our conduct; to judge, to acquit, to condemn, and even to punish; an authority which belongs to no other principle of the human mind. It is the candle of the Lord set up within us, to guide our steps. Other principles may urge and impel, but this only authorises. Other principles ought to be controlled by this; this may be, but never ought to be controlled by any other, and never can be with innocence.—*Reid*, '*Works*,' p. 597.

The authority of conscience is not found in any predominating force belonging to it as a faculty, but altogether in the character of the truth which it discovers. The authority is not found in the nature of the faculty itself. The faculty is a power of sight, such as makes a perception of self evident truth possible to man, and contributes nothing to the truth which is perceived. To the truth itself belongs inherent authority, by which is meant, absolute right of command, not force to constrain.—*Calderwood*, '*Moral Philosophy*,' p. 80.

Conscience is an authority. All bow before its power. We may disregard its behests, but we are obliged to listen to its reproving voice. We may harden ourselves against its reproofs, but we cannot succeed in annihilating them. Conscience is independent of the will. We do not command it, but it commands us.—*Luthardt*, '*Fundamental Truths*,' p. 59.

This authority is not ultimate.

We cannot properly refer to our Conscience as an Ultimate Authority. It has only a subordinate and intermediate authority; standing between the Supreme Law, to which it is bound to conform, and our own actions, which must conform to it, in order to be moral. Conscience is not a standard, but its object is to determine what is right.—*Whewell*, '*Elements of Morality*,' p. 151.

But is derived from God.

Strong as conscience is to elevate, control, and command, a personal God is needed by man to give to his conscience energy and life. Personality without is required to reinforce the personality within. Conscience itself is but another name for the moral person within, when exalted to its most energetic self-assertion and having to do with the individual self in its most characteristic manifestation, as it determines the character by its individual will. The other self within us is often powerless to enforce obedience. Much as we may respect its commands when forced to hear them, we can, alas, too easily shut our ears to its voice. But when this better self represents the living God, who, though greater than conscience, speaks through conscience, then conscience takes the throne of the universe, and her voice is that of the Eternal King to which all loyal subjects respond with rejoicing assent, and with the exalting hope that the right will triumph, they rejoice that God reigns in righteousness.—*Porter*, '*Agnosticism*,' pp. 11, 12.

Supremacy of Conscience.

The 'Supremacy of Conscience' is an abbreviated expression for the sovereignty of moral laws over the forms of activity to which their authority applies. In its reference to motives, acts, and ends, moral law has an unquestionable and unchangeable authority.—*Calderwood*, '*Moral Philosophy*,' p. 80.

That principle by which we survey, and either approve or disapprove of our own heart, temper, and actions, is not only to be considered as what in its turn is to have some influence, which may be said of every passion, of the lowest appetite; but as from its very nature manifestly claiming superiority over all others, insomuch that you cannot form a notion of this faculty, conscience, without taking in judgment, direction, superintendency. This is a constituent part of the idea, that is, of the faculty itself; and to preside and govern, from the very economy and constitution of man, belongs to it. Had it strength, as it has right—had it power, as it has manifest authority—it would absolutely govern the world.—*Butler*, '*Sermons*,' ii.

Controlling Power of Conscience needed

When the calculating, expediential Understanding has superseded the Conscience and the Reason, the Senses soon rush out from their dens, and sweep away everything before them. If there be nothing brighter than the reflected light of the moon, the wild beasts will not keep in their lair. And when that moon, after having reached a moment of apparent glory, by looking full at the sun, fancies it may turn away from the sun and still have light in itself, it straightway begins to wane, and ere long goes out altogether, leaving its worshippers in the darkness which they had vainly dreamt it would enlighten. This was seen in the Roman Empire. It was seen in the last century all over Europe, above all in France.—'*Guesses at Truth*,' p. 80.

Manifestations of Conscience.

In Legislation.

The conscience of the heathen world was deposited in its legislation. Divine authority was on all hands sought and invented for these laws. The law of Israel was the revelation of the Divine will. It thus became the objective conscience of the nation, the former and purifier of its moral knowledge and notions. Simple as the Ten Commandments may sound, there is nothing in the whole literature of the nations that can be compared with them for the purity, earnestness, and universality of the moral consciousness therein deposited.—*Luthardt*, '*Moral Truths*,' p. 55.

In Society.

Conscience does not express itself merely in the individual, but also in society. That there is not merely an individual, but also a social conscience, rests on this, that human individuals are not personal atoms, which have only their own individual duties, but that they are *organically* combined into a social whole, where in regard to *social* duties they are solidarically bound (one for all, and all for one), and thus have a common responsibility, and with each other fall under the same doom. Where the social conscience is vigorous and lively, it will also bear testimony to itself through public opinion. — *Martensen*, '*Christian Ethics*,' i. 366.

In the Nation.

Most heartily do I accept a phrase which you will often hear from the wisest men, and find in the best books,—'The conscience of a nation.' I should regard the loss of it as an unspeakable calamity. The nation, for which men are content to live and die, must have a Conscience, a Conscience to which each of its citizens feel that an appeal can be made; a Conscience which makes it capable of evil acts; a Conscience which gives it a permanence from age to age.—*Maurice*, '*The Conscience*,' p. 163.

States and Kinds of Conscience.

Conscience, by its several habitudes and relations, or tendencies toward its proper object, is divided into several kinds. These are :—

1. *A right or sure conscience.* A right conscience is that which guides our actions by right and proportioned means to a right end; *i.e.*, God's glory, or any honest purpose of justice or religion, charity or civil conversation. For a right conscience is nothing but right reason reduced to practice, and conducting moral actions.

2. *A confident or erroneous conscience*; that is, such which indeed is misinformed, but yet assents to its object with the same confidence as does the right and sure. For our conscience is not a good guide unless we be truly informed and know it. If we be confident and yet deceived, we are like an erring traveller who, being out of the way and thinking himself right, spurs his horse and runs full speed.

3. *A probable or thinking conscience,*

which is an imperfect assent to an uncertain proposition, in which one part is indeed clearly and fully chosen, but with an explicit or implicit notice that the contrary is also fairly eligible. A probable conscience dwells so between the sure and the doubtful that it partakes something of both.

4. *A doubtful conscience.* This considers the probabilities on each side, and dares not choose, and cannot. The will cannot interpose by reason of fear and an uncertain spirit. The conscience assents to neither side of the question, and brings no direct obligation.

5. *A scrupulous conscience.* A scruple is a great trouble of mind proceeding from a little motive, and a great indisposition, by which the conscience, though sufficiently determined by proper arguments, dares not proceed to action, or if it do, it cannot rest. Some persons dare not eat for fear of gluttony; they fear that they shall sleep too much, and that keeps them waking.—*Taylor*, '*Works*,' vol. ix. bk. i. (condensed).

When a man is uncertain what is right and what is wrong, his conscience is *doubtful*. When the doubts turn rather upon special points than upon the general course of action, they are *scruples of conscience*. What a person can do without offending against his conscience, when the question has been deliberately propounded and solved in his own mind, he does with a *safe conscience*, or with a *good conscience*.—*Whewell*, '*Elements of Morality*,' p. 153.

We find the conscience operating in a number of perverted ways in the human breast.

FIRST, THERE IS AN UNENLIGHTENED CONSCIENCE. The mind makes no inquiry into the objects presented to it; but taking them as they come, the conscience decides upon them as they cast up.

SECONDLY, THERE IS A PERVERTED CONSCIENCE. This form differs from the other only in degree. It is a farther stage of the same malady. There is not only ignorance, there is positive mistake.

THIRDLY, THERE IS AN UNFAITHFUL CONSCIENCE, or a conscience which does not inform man of his sins, arising from an unwillingness to look seriously at the evil committed, and an attempt to keep it out of sight.

FOURTHLY, THERE IS A TROUBLED CONSCIENCE. Southey, in one of his poems, tells us of a bell—which had been suspended on a rock, difficult in navigation, that the sound given as the waves beat upon it might warn the mariner of the propinquity to danger—having had its rope cut by pirates, because of the warning which it uttered. It so happened, however, that at a future period these very pirates struck upon that rock which they had stripped of its means of admonishing them. Which things may be unto us for an allegory. Mankind take pains to stifle the voice that would admonish them, and they partially succeed, but it is only to find themselves sinking at last in more fearful misery.—*M'Cosh*, '*Method of the Divine Government*' (1850).

Rules of Conscience.

Are they needed? On this question contrary opinions are given.

I think no rules can be of use to the Conscience. Even when they are recommended by such eloquence as Jeremy Taylor's, they do not settle the cases of Conscience which they undertake to settle; they leave those cases more unsettled than ever. The Conscience asks for Laws [general principles], not rules; for freedom, not chains; for education, not suppression.—*Maurice*, '*The Conscience*,' p. 190.

Rules of the Conscience, even when they are unfolded with the greatest ability by a thoroughly good, earnest, practical man, are unfavourable to goodness and earnestness, and are not helpful in practice. Rules of conscience were drawn up expressly because guides of souls had 'made the cases of conscience and the actions of men's lives as unstable as the water and immeasurable as the dimensions of the moon.' Yet the ultimate resource is to fall back upon these guides of souls, to confess that the rules are impotent without them, and that the final appeal must be to their wisdom. Men will always prefer a man to a rule — *Maurice, 'The Conscience,'* pp. 109, 113

Conscience can never execute her office as she ought, unless some rules are established by which she is to be obliged; for wherever there is an active virtue wholly undetermined in its own nature, and able to act well or ill, it is necessary there should be some law or rule to govern and direct its actions. Lest the conscience should commit mistakes in examining, judging, and directing, it is fit there should be a fixed rule as a standard by which the Conscience herself should be tried.—*Sanderson, 'Lectures on Conscience, &c,'* p. 88.

The Supreme Rule of Conscience.

The proper rule of the Conscience is that which God the Supreme Lawgiver has prescribed to it, i e, the Holy Scripture, or the Word of God written, is not the adequate rule of conscience, but the proper and adequate rule of conscience is the Will of God,—in what manner soever it may be revealed to mankind. There is a conscience in all men, even in the heathens who never heard of Moses or of Christ.—*Sanderson, 'Lectures on Conscience, &c,'* Lect. IV.

If we now inquire what is the supreme rule of Conscience, the answer can only be, that it is the Will of God, so far as it is made known to man. Both the Morality of Reason and Christian Morality give us a knowledge of the Will of God; and these are the two main portions of the supreme rule of conscience.—*Whewell, 'Elements of Morality,'* p. 288.

Moral discernment implies, in the notion of it, a rule of action, and a rule of a very peculiar kind, for it carries in it authority and a right of direction; authority in such a sense as that we cannot depart from it without being self-condemned. The dictates of this moral faculty, which are by nature a rule to us, are the laws of God —*Butler, 'Analogy,'* pt. i. chap. vi.

Conscience must be subordinate to the revealed Word as its fixed rule and guiding-star —*Christlieb, 'Modern Doubt, &c.,'* p. 132.

Cases of Conscience.

How they arise.

A man is *bound in conscience* to do what he thinks right; but he is also bound to employ his faculties diligently in ascertaining what is right. In most cases the rule of Duty is so plain and obvious that no doubt arises as to the course of action, and thus no internal inquiry brings the conscience into notice. In cases in which there appear to be conflicting duties, or reasons for opposite courses of action, we must endeavour to decide between them, by enlightening and instructing the conscience; and these are specially termed Cases of Conscience.

The question, in every case of conscience, really is, not, How may Duty be evaded; but, *What is Duty?*—not, How may I avoid doing what I ought to do? but, What ought I to do?—*Whewell, 'Elements of Morality,'* pp. 153, 154.

A number of these cases of conscience with which the Casuist professes to deal, and which, whether he deals with them or not, perplex our conduct and distract our thoughts, takes their rise in the demands: Ought I, or ought I not, to obey the commands of this Pleasure or this Pain, or of this Nature which appears to be their mistress? Ought I, or ought I not, to obey the commands of this Society, this Majority, which is able to enforce its decrees by terrible penalties, and which has various bribes for bringing me into sympathy with it? Ought I, or ought I not, to perform certain services, to offer certain sacrifices, at the bidding of some *invisible* divinity?—*Maurice, 'The Conscience,'* p. 75 *seq.*

A great number, perhaps the greatest number of men, hover between Nature and Conscience. They cannot silence the 'ought not.' But they ask themselves *why* they should pay heed to it, *why* they should not take this or that pleasure which it seems to prohibit, undergo this or that painful effort which it seems to enjoin? 'What is this restraining, tormenting voice? From what cavern does it issue? Do I clearly catch its messages? Are they indeed saying, Avoid this and this? Do this and this?' Hence begin cases of Conscience. Such cases are not imaginary, but enter into the transactions of every day, and are mingled with the threads of each man's existence.—*Maurice, 'The Conscience,'* p. 81.

The demands of Pleasure or of Nature upon me, the demands of Society upon me, both suggest cases of their own. But *the* case is that which the Roman poet [Lucretius] has raised. These are powers which demand *evil* things of me. Ought I to acknowledge their demand? Very numerous are the cases which fall under this head.—*Maurice, 'The Conscience,'* p. 97.

Before all the Cynic's ruling faculty (the Cynic is in Epictetus the minister of religion) must be purer than the sun; and if it is not, he must necessarily be a cunning knave and a fellow of no principle, since, while he himself is entangled in some vice, he will reprove others. For see how the matter stands,—to these kings and tyrants their guards and arms give the power of reproving some persons, and of being able even to punish those who do wrong, though they are themselves bad; but to a Cynic, instead of arms and guards, it is conscience which gives this power. When he knows that he has watched and laboured for mankind, and has slept pure, and sleep has left him still purer, and that he thought whatever he has thought as a friend of the gods, as a minister, as a participator of the power of Zeus, and that on all occasions he is ready to say, 'Lead me, O Zeus; and thou, O Destiny,' and also, 'If so it pleases the gods, so let it be;' why should he not have confidence to speak freely to his own brothers, to his children,—in a word, to his kinsmen?—*Epictetus, 'Discourses,'* p. 262.

Liberty of Conscience.

Mistaken notions of it.

Liberty of Conscience cannot bear some senses which loose thinkers attach to it. (1.) Liberty of Conscience cannot mean liberty to *do* what I like. That, in the judgment of the wisest men, of those who speak most from experience, is bondage. It is from my likings that I must be emancipated, if I would be a free man. (2.) It cannot mean liberty to *think* what I like. The thoughts of men must be brought under government, lest they should become their oppressors. The scientific man tells us that we are always in danger of putting our thoughts and conceptions of the thing between us and that which is. He bids us seek the thing as it is. We must not pervert the facts which we are examining. All our determinations must fall before the truth when that is discovered to us. (3.) It cannot be a gift which men are to ask of senates, or sanhedrims, or assemblies of the people. They have it not to bestow; if they had, no one could receive it of them. They who groan because any of these bodies withhold it from them, have not yet learnt what it is. — *Maurice, 'The Conscience,'* 136 *seq.*

Danger of interfering with it.

In every instance to which we can point, a Society which has succeeded in choking or weakening the Conscience of any of its members, has undermined its own existence, and the defeat of such experiments has been the preservation and security of the Society that has attempted them. The banishment of the Moors from Spain helped to turn a chivalrous and Christian nation into an ambitious, gold-worshipping, tyrannical nation. The Stuarts sought to extinguish the Puritans and Covenanters in England and Scotland; we owe any vigour which there is in Great Britain to their failure.—*Maurice, 'The Conscience,'* p. 138 *seq.*

It is a fruit of Christianity.

The first defenders of Christianity were also the first proclaimers of liberty of conscience; and how much soever this principle may at times have been sinned against by the advocates of the Church, yet liberty of conscience, the necessity of which has now become a matter of universal conviction and admission, was itself a fruit of Christianity.—*Luthardt*, '*Fundamental Truths*,' p. 278.

God alone can bind the conscience.—*Martensen*, '*Christian Ethics*,' i. 365.

Peace of Conscience.

Signs of true peace.

1. Peace of conscience is a rest after a severe inquiry. When Hezekiah was upon his deathbed, as he supposed, he examined his state of life, and found it had been innocent in the great lines and periods of it; and he was justly confident. Peace of conscience is a fruit of holiness, and therefore can never be in wicked persons, of notorious evil lives.

2. That rest, which is only in the days of prosperity, is not a just and a holy peace, but that which is in the days of sorrow and affliction. If in the days of sorrow a man's heart condemns him not, it is great odds, but it is a holy peace.

3. Peace of conscience is a blessing that is given to all holy penitents more or less, at some time or other, according as their repentance proceeds, and their hope is exercised.

4. True peace of conscience is always joined with a holy fear; a fear to offend and a fear of the divine displeasure for what we have offended. it is rational, and holy, and humble; neither carelessness nor presumption is in it.

5. True peace of conscience is not a sleep procured by the tongues of flatterers, or opinions of men, but is a peace from within, relying upon God and its own just measures. — *Taylor*, '*Works*,' ix. 32–34 (condensed).

It is the great support of society.

The great prop of society (which upholdeth the safety, peace, and welfare thereof, in observing laws, dispensing justice, discharging trusts, keeping contracts) is conscience, or a sense of duty towards God, obliging us to perform that which is just and equal, quickened by hope of rewards and fear of punishments from Him; excluding which principle no worldly consideration is strong enough to hold men fast; or can farther dispose many to do right, or observe faith, or hold peace, than appetite or interest, or humour (things very slippery and uncertain) do hold them.—*Barrow.*

Laws have awakened the Conscience, and the Conscience being awakened owns the majesty of Laws. The command 'Thou shalt not' would have been uttered in vain if there had not been called forth an 'I ought not' in the hearer. The Conscience having a profound reverence for Law as Law, turning to it for a protection against mere opinion, will rather incur any punishment than trifle with its authority. On the other hand, reverence for law is the only protection of reverence for Conscience.—*Maurice*, '*The Conscience*,' pp. 154, 157, 158.

XXI.

THE MORAL STANDARD

THE GENERAL IDEA

The Good and the Right.

In ancient Ethics—the good.

The object of the Ethical Science is the Supreme Good of the individual citizen—the end of all ends, with reference to his desires, his actions, and his feelings—the end which he seeks for itself and without any ulterior aim—the end which comprehends all his other ends as merely partial or instrumental, and determines their comparative value in his estimation.—*Grote, 'Aristotle,'* p. 500.

We may consider the action to which we are morally prompted as 'good' in itself—not merely as a means to some ulterior Good, but as a part of what is conceived as the agent's Ultimate Good. This was the fundamental ethical conception in the Greek schools of Moral Philosophy generally; including even the Stoics, though their system is in this respect a transitional link between ancient and modern ethics.—*Sidgwick, 'Method of Ethics,'* p. 101.

In the sphere of the known *the idea of the good* is ultimate, and needs an effort to be seen, but, once seen, compels the conclusion that here is the cause, for all things else, of whatever is beautiful and right: in the visible world, parent of light and of its lord; in the intellectual world, bearing itself the lordship, and from itself supplying truth and reason. And thus it is which must fix the eye of one who is to act with wisdom in private or in public life.—*Plato, 'Republic,'* bk. vii.

The Categorical Imperative.

There is an imperative which commands a certain conduct immediately, without having as its condition any other purpose to be attained by it. This imperative is Categorical. It concerns not the matter of the action, or its intended result, but its form and the principle of which it is itself a result; and what is essentially good in it consists in the mental disposition, let the consequences be what they may. This imperative may be called that of morality.

There is but one categorical imperative, namely this: *Act only on that maxim whereby thou canst at the same time will that it should become a universal law.*—*Abbott, 'Kant's Theory of Ethics,'* pp. 33, 38.

Rendered possible by Freedom.

What makes the categorical imperative possible is this, that the idea of freedom makes me a member of an intelligible world, in consequence of which, if I were nothing else, all my actions *would* always conform to the autonomy of the will; but as I at the same time intuite myself as a member of the world of sense, they *ought* so to conform, and this *categorical* 'ought' implies a synthetic *à priori* proposition, inasmuch as besides my will as affected by sensible desires, there is added further the idea of the same will but as belonging to the world of the understanding, pure and practical of itself, which contains the supreme condition according to Reason of the former will; precisely as to the intuitions of sense there are added concepts of the understanding which of themselves signify nothing but regular form in general, and in this way synthetic *à priori* propositions become possible, on which all knowledge of physical nature rests.—*Kant, 'Theory of Ethics,'* pp. 74, 75.

Absolute Good.

The conception of an ideal—that is to say, of something infinitely superior to anything which exists—is essential to moral science. Moral science assumes that in each particular case, above the action to which nature inclines us, there is another possible and better one, more conformable to the essence of man, and which reason commands us to perform. True human science is not, then, the simple reflex of human nature. The true man is not the same as the actual man. For example, the latter loves life, and will sacrifice anything to preserve it; the former, on the contrary, will sacrifice everything, even his life, for something other than himself; and it is he who is in the right.—*Janet, 'The Theory of Morals,'* p. 129.

Self-devoted activity to the perfection of Man.

Professor Green's Ideal of Virtue.

The development of morality is founded on the action in man of an idea of true and absolute good, consisting in the full realisation of the capabilities of the human soul. This idea, however, according to our view, acts in man, to begin with, only as a demand unconscious of the full nature of its object. The demand is, indeed, from the outset quite different from a desire for pleasure. It is at its lowest a demand for some well-being which shall be common to the individual desiring it with others; and only as such does it yield those institutions of the family, the tribe, and the state, which further determine the morality of the individual. The formation of more adequate conceptions to the end to which the demand is directed, we have traced to two influences, separable for purposes of abstract thought, but not in fact,—one, the natural development, under favouring conditions, of the institutions just mentioned, to which the demand gives rise; the other, reflection alike upon these institutions and upon those well-reputed habits of action which have been formed in their maintenance and as their effect. Under these influences there has arisen, through a process of which we have endeavoured to trace the outline, on the one hand an ever-widening conception of the range of persons between whom the common good is common, on the other a conception of the nature of the common good itself, consistent with its being the object of a universal society co-extensive with mankind. The good has come to be conceived with increasing clearness, not as anything which one man or set of men can gain or enjoy to the exclusion of others, but as a spiritual activity in which all may partake, and in which all must partake, if it is to amount to a full realisation of the faculties of the human soul. Thus the ideal of virtue which our consciences acknowledge has come to be the devotion of character and life, in whatever channel the idiosyncrasy and circumstances of the individual may determine, to a perfecting of man, which is itself conceived not as an external end to be attained by goodness, but as consisting in such a life of self-devoted activity on the part of all persons.—*Green, 'Prolegomena to Ethics,'* pp. 308, 309.

ETHICAL THEORIES.

I. SELFISHNESS, OR EGOISM.

Its Nature as a Moral Principle.

'Egoism' denotes a system which prescribes actions as means to the end of the individual's happiness or pleasure. The ruling motive in such a system is commonly said to be 'self-love.' The ambiguous meaning of 'egoism' and 'self-love' has been a frequent source of confusion in ethical discussion. In order to fit these terms for the purpose of scientific discussion, we must, while retaining the main part of their signification, endeavour to make it more precise. Accordingly, we must explain that by Egoism we mean Egoistic Hedonism, a system that fixes as the reasonable ultimate end of each individual's action his own greatest possible Happiness: and by 'greatest Happiness' we must definitely understand the greatest possible amount of pleasure, or, more strictly, as pains have to be balanced against pleasures, the greatest possible surplus of pleasure over pain. — *Sidgwick, 'Methods of Ethics,'* pp. 83, 116.

The principle is quaintly expressed in part of the epitaph on the gravestone of Robert Cycroft in the churchyard of Homersfield, Suffolk:—

> 'As I walked by myself, I talked to myself,
> And thus myself said to me,
> Look to thyself, and take care of thyself,
> For nobody cares for thee'

Egoism wraps us up in our own interests. —*Martensen*

Theory of Helvetius

Helvetius finds in self-love, which prompts us to seek pleasure and ward off pain, the only proper motive of human conduct, holding that the right guidance of self-love by education and legislation is all that is necessary to bring it into harmony with the common good. Complete suppression of the passions leads to stupidity; passion fructifies the mind, but needs to be regulated. He who secures his own interests in such a manner as not to prejudice, but rather to further the interests of others, is the good man.—*Ueberweg, 'Hist of Phil,'* ii 129

In France, the name of Helvetius (author of *De l'esprit, De l'homme,* &c, 1715–1771) is identified with a serious, and perfectly consistent, attempt to reduce all morality to direct Self-interest. Though he adopted this ultimate interpretation of the facts, Helvetius was by no means the 'low and loose moralist' that he has been described to be; and, in particular, his own practice displayed a rare benevolence.—*Bain, 'Moral Science,'* p. 598.

Illustrations of his teaching.

The desire of greatness is always produced by the fear of pain or love of sensual pleasure, to which all the other pleasures must necessarily be reduced.

Friendship

Love implies want, without which there is no friendship; for this would be an effect without a cause. Not all men have the same wants, and, therefore, the friendship which subsists between them is founded on different motives: some want pleasure or money, others credit; these conversation, those a confidant to whom they may disburthen their hearts There are, consequently, friends of money, of intrigue, of wit, and of misfortune

The power of friendship is in proportion, not to the honesty of two friends, but to the interest by which they are united.

Justice

Our love of equity is always subordinate to our love of power: Man, solely anxious for himself, seeks nothing but his own happiness; if he respects equity, it is want that compels him to it.

Whatever disinterested love we may affect to have, *without interest to love virtue, there is no virtue.—'De l'Esprit,'* essay ii, *quoted by Martineau, 'Types, &c.,'* ii. 292, 293.

Objections to this Principle

There is no sure rule for carrying it out.

There is no scientific short-cut to the ascertainment of the right means to the individual's happiness; every attempt to find a 'high priori road' to this goal, brings us back inevitably to the empirical method For, instead of a clear principle universally valid, we only get at best a vague and general rule based on considerations which it is important not to overlook, but the relative value of which we can only estimate by careful observation and comparison of individual experiences.—*Sidgwick, 'Methods of Ethics,'* p 194.

It is fatal to self-sacrifice

The egoist has an easy explanation of self-sacrificing actions. The charitable man, who gives money to the poor which he might have spent in luxury, is repaid by a glow of self complacency; the missionary, who leaves house and home to convert savages, hopes for a reward in heaven; the physician, who sacrifices health to comfort prisoners or sufferers in a plague-stricken city, is eager for praise and shrinks from general contempt. In all cases, and however skilfully disguised, some personal gratification supplies the cogent motive. A man may conceivably be unselfish, but, so far as really unselfish, he is a fool for his pains. He will only do good to others, if a wise or a thoroughly enlightened man, so far as he expects to derive some benefit for himself. No man, it is argued, can sacrifice himself knowingly and intentionally. — *Stephen*, '*Science of Ethics*,' p. 220

It is often at variance with Virtue and Duty.

The coincidence between Virtue and Happiness is not complete and universal. We may conceive the coincidence becoming perfect in a Utopia where men were as much in accord on Moral as they are now on Mathematical questions, where Law was in perfect harmony with Moral Opinion, and all offences were discovered and duly punished. But just in proportion as existing societies and existing men fall short of this ideal, rules of conduct based on the principles of Egoism must diverge from those which most men are accustomed to recognise as prescribed by Duty and Virtue. —*Stephen*, '*Science of Ethics*,' p. 174.

It does violence to the better side of human nature.

Man has a native affection which leads him to feel an interest in his fellow-men, and is capable of being moved by whatever affects them. These affections have been called ALTRUISTIC. We are naturally inclined to wish that others may possess whatever we regard as appetible, and that they may be preserved from all that we regard as evil. This is the kindliness towards a brother man which will flow out like a fountain unless it is restrained by selfishness, and which we should seek to have so elevated and sanctified that it may become the grace of benevolence leading us to do unto others even as we would that they should do unto us.—*M'Cosh*, '*The Emotions*,' p. 112.

It degrades benevolent action.

The egoist denies that conferring pleasure upon others can ever be an ultimate motive. The desire to give happiness is always capable of a further analysis, which shows it to include a desire of happiness for ourselves. So I may be kind to you in order that you may hereafter be kind to me, and at a given instant of kindness I may not be distinctly conscious of the ultimate end. But, according to the egoist, such an end must always exist. The goal of every conceivable desire is some state of agreeable consciousness of my own. I may not look to the end of the vista of intended consequences, but, if I look, I shall always see my own reflection.—*Stephen*, '*Science of Ethics*,' p. 224.

It is the Principle of Sin.

As sin had its origin in the desire of man to be his own master, without at the same time being willing to be God's servant, and thus arose in disobedience of God; and as sin in the human race is the continuance of this disobedience; so egoism must be adjudged, as the subjective moment, of worldliness, to be the prime mover in the kingdom of sin, because it is the selfishness in itself reflected, which in reference to the love of the world has the higher spirituality. It was self, his own will, which man wished to enjoy in the forbidden fruit.—*Martensen*, '*Christian Ethics*,' i. 101.

II. LAW OF THE STATE OR HUMAN SOCIETY.

Foundation of Early Social Life.

The Patriarchal Theory.

The effect of the evidence derived from comparative jurisprudence is to establish that view of the primeval condition of the human race which is known as the Patriarchal Theory. There is no doubt that this theory was originally based on the Scriptural history of the Hebrew Patriarchs in Lower Asia The points which lie on the surface of the history are these —The eldest male parent—the eldest ascendant—is absolutely supreme in his household His dominion extends to life and death, and is as unqualified over his children and their houses as over his slaves; indeed, the relations of sonship and serfdom appear to differ in little beyond the higher capacity which the child in blood possesses of becoming one day the head of a family himself The flocks and herds of the children are the flocks and herds of the father; and the possessions of the parent, which he holds in a representative rather than in a proprietary character, are equally divided at his death among his descendants in the first degree, the eldest son sometimes receiving a double share under the name of a birthright, but more generally endowed with no hereditary advantage beyond an honorary precedence. —*Maine, 'Ancient Law,'* pp. 122, 123.

Moral Responsibility in Ancient Society

The moral elevation and moral debasement of the individual appear to be confounded with, or postponed to, the merits and offences of the group to which the individual belongs If the community sins, its guilt is much more than the sum of the offences committed by its members; the crime is a corporate act, and extends in its consequences to many more persons than have shared in its actual perpetration. If, on the other hand, the individual is conspicuously guilty, it is his children, his kinsfolk, his tribesmen, or his fellow-citizens, who suffer with him, and sometimes for him It thus happens that the ideas of moral responsibility and retribution often seem to be more clearly realised at very ancient than at more advanced periods, for, as the family group is immortal, and its liability to punishment indefinite, the primitive mind is not perplexed by the questions which become troublesome as soon as the individual is conceived as altogether separate from the group.—*Maine, 'Ancient Law,'* p. 127.

Civil Law the foundation of Morality Hobbes

The desires and other passions of men are in themselves no sin. No more are the actions that proceed from those passions, till they know a law that forbids them; which, till laws be made, they cannot know, nor can any law be made till they have agreed upon the person that shall make it.

Where there is no common power, there is no law: where no law, no injustice. Force and fraud are in war the two cardinal virtues. Justice and injustice are none of the faculties neither of the body nor mind If they were, they might be in a man that were alone in the world, as well as his senses and passions They are qualities that relate to men in society, not in solitude.—*'Leviathan,'* ch. xiii.

Moral Philosophy is nothing else but the science of what is 'good' and 'evil,' in the conversation and society of mankind. 'Good' and 'evil' are names that signify our appetites and aversions, which in different tempers, customs, and doctrines of men, are different: and divers men differ not only in their judgment on the senses of what is pleasant and unpleasant to the taste, smell, hearing, touch, and sight; but also of what is conformable or disagreeable to reason, in the actions of common life.—*'Leviathan,'* ch. xv.

Where no covenant hath preceded, there hath no right been transferred, and every man has right to everything; and consequently no action can be unjust But when a covenant is made, then to break it is 'unjust': and the definition of 'injustice,' is no other than 'the not performance of covenant.' And whatsoever is not unjust is 'just.'

But because covenants of mutual trust, where there is a fear of not performance on either part, are invalid; though the original of justice be the making of covenants, yet injustice actually there can be none, till the cause of such fear be taken away; which while men are in the natural condition of war cannot be done Therefore before the names of just and unjust can have place, there must be some coercive power, to compel men equally to the performance of their covenants by the terror of some punishment, greater than the benefit they expect by the breach of their covenant; and such power there is none before the erection of a commonwealth — '*Leviathan*,' ch xv

Professor Bain.

The Ethical End is a certain portion of the welfare of human beings living together in society, realised through rules of conduct duly enforced

The obvious intention of morality is the good of mankind. The precepts—do not steal, do not kill, fulfil agreements, speak truth—whatever other reasons may be assigned for them, have a direct tendency to prevent great evils that might otherwise arise in the intercourse of human beings.— '*Moral Science*,' p 434

Morality analogous to Civil Government.

Moral duties are a set of rules, precepts, or prescriptions for the direction of human conduct in a certain sphere or province. These rules are enforced by two kinds of motives, requiring to be kept distinct

One class of rules are made compulsory by the infliction of pain, in the case of violation or neglect The pain so inflicted is termed a Penalty or Punishment; it is one of the most familiar experiences of all human beings living in society

The institution that issues Rules of this class, and inflicts punishment when they are not complied with, is termed Government, or authority, all its rules are authoritative, or obligatory, they are Laws strictly so-called, Laws proper Punishment, Government, Authority, Superiority, Obligation, Law, Duty,—define each other; they are all different modes of regarding the same fact

Morality is thus in every respect analogous to Civil Government, or the Law of the Land Nay, farther, it squares, to a very great extent, with Political Authority. The points where the two coincide, and those where they do not coincide, may be briefly stated —

1 All the most essential parts of Morality are adopted and carried out by the Law of the Land The rules for protecting person and property, for fulfilling contracts, for performing reciprocal duties, are rules or laws of the State, and are enforced by the State, through its own machinery. The penalties inflicted by public authority constitute what is called the Political Sanction; they are the most severe, and the most strictly and dispassionately administered, of all penalties.

2. There are certain Moral duties enforced, not by public and official authority, but by the members of the community in the private capacity. These are sometimes called the Laws of Honour, because they are punished by withdrawing from the violator the honour or esteem of his fellow-citizens Courage, Prudence as regards self, Chastity, Orthodoxy of opinion, a certain conformity in Tastes and Usages, —are all prescribed by the mass of each community, to a greater or less extent, and are insisted on under penalty of social disgrace and excommunication This is the Social or the Popular Sanction

Public opinion also chimes in with the Law, and adds its own sanction to the legal penalties for offences: unless the law happens to be in conflict with the popular sentiment Criminals condemned by the law are additionally punished by social disgrace.

3 The Law of the Land contains many enactments, besides the Moral Code and the machinery for executing it The Province of Government passes beyond the properly protective function, and includes many institutions of public convenience, which are not identified with right and wrong —'*Moral Science*,' pp 435, 436.

Moral rules supported by Rewards.

The second class of Rules (see previous quotation) are supported, not by penalties, but by Rewards Society, instead of punishing men for not being charitable or benevolent, praises and otherwise rewards them, when they are so. Hence, although Morality inculcates benevolence, this is not a Law proper; it is not obligatory, authoritative, or binding; it is purely voluntary, and is termed merit, virtuous and noble conduct.

The conduct rewarded by Society is chiefly resolvable into Beneficence. Whoever is moved to incur sacrifices, or to go through labours, for the good of others, is the object, not merely of gratitude from the persons benefited, but of approbation from society at large.

Any remarkable strictness or fidelity in the discharge of duties properly so called, receives general esteem.—'*Moral Science*,' pp. 426, 427 (*see also Professor Bain's 'Theory of Conscience*,' sect. xix.).

Criticism of Professor Bain's State Conscience Theory.

As applied to education.

The external authority of the parent or teacher, I maintain, is useless unless he appeals to that which is within the child, is mischievous unless it is exerted to call that forth. The external authority must become an internal authority, not co-operating with the forces which are seeking to crush the 'I' in the child, but working against those forces to deliver the child from their dominion. The teacher will endeavour so to contrive his punishment that 'the sentiment of the forbidden' may always be accompanied with the sentiment of trust in the person who has forbidden. If the child is taught to have a dread of him as one who is an inflicter of pain, not to have a reverence for him as one who cares for it and is seeking to save it from its own folly—if the child is instructed carefully to separate the pain which rises out of its own acts from the pain which he inflicts, so that it may associate the pain with him rather than with them—then all has been done which human art can do to make it grow up a contemptible coward, crouching to every majority which threatens it with the punishments that it has learnt to regard as the greatest and only evils; one who may at last, 'in the maturity of a well-disposed mind,' become the spontaneous agent of a majority in trampling out in others the freedom which has been so assiduously trampled out in him. A parent or a teacher who pursues this object is of all the ministers of a community the one whom it should regard with the greatest abhorrence, seeing that he is bringing up for it, not citizens, but slaves.—*Maurice*, '*The Conscience*,' pp. 67, 68.

Is destructive of nobility of character.

There has been a disposition in many to say that our soldiers and sailors must be drilled according to the maxims of Mr. Bain's education, that they may have a merely public Conscience. 'What would become of us,' it has been asked, 'if each of them felt himself to be an *I*, said for himself, "*I* ought and *I* ought not?"' My answer is this, I know not what would have become of us in any great crisis if this personal feeling had *not* been awakened; if every man had not felt that *he* was expected to do his duty; if duty *had* been understood by each sailor or soldier in Mr. Bain's sense as the dread of punishment; if the captain who asked for obedience had been just the person towards whom that slavish dread was most directed. Unless the obedience of our sailors and soldiers had been diametrically the reverse of that sentiment which Mr. Bain describes, I believe there is not a regiment which would not have turned its back in the day of battle, not a ship which would not have struck its flag. The charm of the captain's eye and voice, of his example and his sympathy, this, as all witnesses whose testimony is worth anything have declared, has had an electrical influence upon hosts which could enable them to face punishments from enemies considerably more terrible than any which the most savage vengeance could devise for desertion. It is not the thought of what a majority will say or do, that can stir any individual man to stand where he is put to die. It is that he has been aroused to the conviction, 'I am here, and here I ought to be'—*Maurice*, '*The Conscience*,' pp. 68, 69.

Society the most frightful of bugbears.

No power that I ever heard of is so 'abstract, unseen, unproducible,' as the Society which is put forth to terrify and crush each man who dares to claim a distinct existence. Where is it, what is it, who brought it forth? Parents, Schoolmasters, Legislators, are its agents. It remains full of ghostly dread, gathering into itself all that is most tremendous in the phantoms which we boast that modern enlightenment has driven from our nurseries.—*Maurice*, '*The Conscience*,' p. 72.

III. ASCETICISM

Described.

Asceticism, from Greek ἄσκησις, meaning the exercise or training to which the athletes subjected themselves when preparing for the games or contests, is used metaphorically to denote the habitual practice of exercising restraint over, or subduing, the bodily desires and affections which tend to lower objects, in order thereby to advance in the higher life of purity and virtue. It is the means by which the mind withdraws itself from the hindrances and temptations of the world, and clears its vision for what is spiritual and true. In its lowest stage it consists in the mortification of the flesh by fasting, penance, and the like; but in a higher sense it involves the uprooting of all worldly or temporal desires, and withdrawal from the natural relations of life.—'*Encyclop. Brit.*,' ii. 676.

The name may be applied to every system which teaches man, not to govern his wants by subordinating them to reason and the law of duty, but to stifle them entirely, or at least to resist them as much as we can; and these are not only the wants of the body, but still more those of the heart, the imagination, and the mind; for society, the family, most of the sciences and arts of civilisation, are proscribed sometimes as rigorously as physical pleasures. The care of the Soul and the contemplation of the Deity are the only employments.—'*Dict. des Sciences Phil.*'

As a striking instance of the unfairness which prejudice can produce in a mind usually most clear and just, the description of Bentham may be quoted. He says:—

By the principle of asceticism I mean that principle, which, like the principle of utility, approves or disapproves of any action, according to the tendency which it appears to have to augment or diminish the happiness of the party whose interest is in question; but in an inverse manner: approving of actions in as far as they tend to diminish his happiness; disapproving of them in as far as they tend to augment it.—'*Principles of Morals and Legislation*,' p. 9.

Its Origin and Growth.

Amongst men generally.

The origin of this aspect of thought or mode of action is to be found in the widespread idea, not wholly Oriental, that in Unity or Identity alone is true goodness and happiness, while in Multiplicity or Difference is evil and misery. Unity is but the abstract expression for God, the Absolute, or Spirit, and Multiplicity for Matter, in which both Orientals and Greeks thought to find the origin of evil. Now in man exist both spirit, which is the shadow of or emanation from the divine, and body, with its various desires and passions, which is of the nature of matter, and therefore in itself evil. True happiness—nay, true life for man—consists in contemplation of God, absorption into the divine unity and essence; and this ecstatic vision can only be attained by the cultivation of the spirit, and the mortification of the body. The desires and passions must be subdued, rooted up, and the means recommended are solitude, poverty, celibacy, fasting, and penance. We find, accordingly, that in all nations, those who seek divine illumination prepare themselves by these means. In this respect the Hindoo fakirs, jogis, dervishes, gymnosophists, and the numerous sect of the Buddhists, are at one with the Hebrew Nazarites, and Chasidim, and with the priests of the Grecian mysteries.—'*Encyclop. Brit.*,' ii. 676, 677.

Amongst the Brahmans.

The practice of austerities is so interwoven with Brahmanism, under all the phases it has assumed, that we cannot realise its existence apart from the principles of the ascetic.

The practice of asceticism is supposed by the Brahmans to have commenced at a very early period, and it leads to the possession of an energy the most mighty. The Hindu ascetics of more recent times are in many instances those who have fulfilled their supposed destiny as men, and then retire into the wilderness, that, instead of assuming another form at their death, they may be prepared for reabsorption in the supreme essence. In abstaining from animal food the Brahmans are stricter than the Buddhists; but the followers of Gótama never knowingly take life, and, therefore, regard the pasuyajna or aswamédha, a sacrifice supposed by the Brahmans to be highly efficacious, with great abhorrence. —*Hardy*, '*Eastern Monachism*,' pp. 348, 351.

In Christianity.

Whence derived.

The principle of asceticism—and this is allowed on all sides—was in force before Christianity. The Essenes, for instance, among the Jews, owed their existence as a sect to this principle. It was dominant in the oriental systems of antagonism between mind and matter. It asserted itself even among the more sensuous philosophers of Greece, with their larger sympathy for the pleasurable development of man's physical energies. But the fuller and more systematic development of the ascetic life among Christians is contemporaneous with Christianity coming into contact with the Alexandrine school of thought, and exhibits itself first in a country subject to the combined influences of Judaism and of the Platonic philosophy. Indeed, the great and fundamental principle on which asceticism, in its narrower meaning, rests—of a two fold morality, one expressed in 'Precepts' of universal obligation for the multitude, and one expressed in 'Counsels of Perfection,' intended only for those more advanced in holiness, with its doctrine that the passions are to be extirpated rather than controlled—is very closely akin to the Platonic or Pythagorean distinction between the life according to nature and the life above nature.—*Smith*, '*Dict. of Christian Antiq.*,' i. 147.

Amongst the heathen, those who led lives consecrated to meditation were usually termed ascetics. Now, it sometimes happened that heathen ascetics were led by their earnest pursuit of moral perfection to embrace Christianity; and having become Christians, they still adhered to their former habits of life, which in themselves contained nothing repugnant to Christianity. Others, again, in whom Christianity first produced a more serious turn of life, adopted these habits as a token of the change that had been wrought in them. In the warmth of their first love, upon their baptism, they immediately gave to the church-fund or to the poor a large portion of their earthly property, or all that they had. Within the bosom of the church they led a quiet, retired life, supporting themselves by the labour of their hands, remaining unmarried, and devoting to objects of Christian charity all that remained over and above their earnings, after barely satisfying the most necessary wants of life. Such Christians were called the Abstinent Ascetics.—*Neander*, '*Church History*,' i. 380, 381 (abridged).

Stages of development.

During the first century and a half of Christianity there are no indications of ascetics as a distinct class. While the first fervour of conversion lasted, and while the church, as a small and compact community, was struggling for existence against opposing forces on every side, the profession of Christianity was itself a profession of the ascetic spirit, in other words, of endurance, of hardihood, of constant self-denial.

For about a century subsequent to 150 A.D. there begin to be traces of an asceticism more sharply defined and occupying a more distinct position; but not as yet requiring its votaries to separate themselves entirely from the rest of their community. Athenagoras speaks of persons habitually abstaining from matrimony. Eusebius mentions devout persons, ascetics, who ministered to the poor.

The middle of the third century marks an era in the development of Christian asceticism. Antony, Paul, Ammon, and other Egyptian Christians, not content, as the ascetics before them, to lead a life of extraordinary strictness and severity in towns and villages, aspired to a more thorough estrangement of themselves from all earthly ties; and by their teaching and example led very many to the wilderness, there to live and die in almost utter seclusion from their fellows.

About the middle of the fourth century Christian asceticism begins to assume a corporate character. The term ascetic begins now to be nearly equivalent to monastic. The history of asceticism, after the institution of monastic societies, belongs to the history of monasticism.—*Smith*, '*Dict. of Christian Antiq.*,' i. 148.

A one-sided ascetical tendency easily introduced itself into the earliest stages of the development of the Christian life, and more particularly in the case of those who embraced Christianity with their whole soul. Wherever religion awakened in the first place a feeling of disgust at all worldly pursuits, and enkindled in the mind the holy flame of love for the divine, this first movement would readily assume an ascetical shape. There arose an undue estimation of the ascetical contemplative life and of celibacy, which was carried to the extreme of promising to such a life a more exalted state of future blessedness.—*Neander*, '*Church History*,' i. 383.

The Spirit of Judaism contrary to asceticism.

If any religion appeared opposed to asceticism, it was Judaism, which, resting on the doctrine of creation, had always expressed spiritual promises in the language of temporal blessing. Neither its priesthood nor its prophets were placed outside common life. To fear God, to keep His commandments, to rejoice with the wife of his youth, to see his house filled with children like a quiver full of arrows, to meditate on the sacred books under his vine and his fig tree, whilst blessing God for what the clouds distil upon man abundantly—this was the ideal set before a child of Israel.—*Pressensé*, '*La Vie Ecclés.*,' p. 524.

Primitive Christianity not ascetic.

Primitive Christianity engaged in conflict with that sensuality which ruins the soul by withering it. But it did not yield to the temptation of asceticism. It did not desire to destroy the body but to subdue it; it not only accepted the family but it founded it afresh as we see it to-day. Its greatest apostle was in his moral temperament an ascetic, and he has expressed his preferences in his usual free and energetic language, but this makes all the more remarkable his lofty conception of the Christian life, which is entirely opposed to asceticism, since on the one hand he carefully guards himself from identifying evil with the corporal element in man, and on the other he desires that the disciple of Christ, whether he eat or drink, should do all for God through Jesus Christ.—*Pressensé*, '*La Vie Ecclés.*,' p. 525.

Distinction between Christian and Gnostic asceticism.

In this whole matter we must carefully distinguish two forms of asceticism, antagonistic and irreconcilable in spirit and principle, though similar in form; the Gnostic dualistic, and the Catholic. The former of these did certainly come from heathenism, but the latter sprang independently from the Christian spirit of self-denial and longing for moral perfection, and in spite of all its excrescences, has performed an important mission in the history of the church —*Schaff, 'History of the Christian Church,'* ii 153

Its Perversion and Use

The mistake of asceticism.

Christianity was designed to be the principle that should rule the world It was to take into itself and appropriate to its own ends all that belongs to man and the world But to effect this it was necessary that it should first enter into a conflict with what had hitherto been the ruling principle of the world—a conflict with sin and the principle of heathenism The purification of all this must be the first aim of Christianity. In the temporary development, this negative aggressive tendency must necessarily appear first; and it might easily gain an undue predominance, so as to repress for a while the positive element of appropriation, by which alone the problem of Christianity could ever attain to its solution Hence a one-sided ascetical tendency easily introduced itself —*Neander, 'Church History,'* i 382

With the cessation of persecution, the opportunities of displaying heroism in confession and martyrdom had ceased Hence many persons, seeing the corruption which was now too manifest in the nominally Christian society, and not understanding that the truer and more courageous course was to work in the midst of the world and against its evil, thought to attain a more elevated spirituality by withdrawing from mankind, and devoting themselves to austerity of life and to endeavours after undisturbed communion with heaven —*Robertson, 'Church History'*

It is a negative and false morality which, in the spirit of asceticism and with the idea of perfection, would weaken and crush every impulse in man not directly religious or moral. For rather would we call that a healthy condition of life, wherein those highest impulses in their full import go hand in hand with the other instincts which bring life into conformity with nature, the demands of both being harmoniously fulfilled In order to this harmony it is of course necessary that the latter instincts, and endeavours connected with them, be unconditionally subordinated to those which spring from conscience and the consciousness of God Thus in progressive development they may be elevated into close and positive union with those all embracing and all-sanctifying energies —a goal which St. Paul set before us in 1 Cor. x 31, and other passages.—*Muller, 'Christian Doctrine of Sin,'* i 154

Asceticism is not a victory but a defeat; it retires from the conflict, it despairs of subduing the corporal element, it knows no method except to annihilate —*Pressensé, 'La Vie Ecclés.,'* p 525

Asceticism as such is only an exercise of virtue, in which the virtue has no other substance than the mere exercise itself Asceticism allows society to lie entirely beyond it, undertakes no duty for its benefit, but is only occupied with its own blessedness, and with purely formal actions, which are merely preparatory, and which have found graphic expression in the task which is often imposed on young monks: to spend the day in planting sticks in the sand, in order that by this useless, aimless labour, they may be exercised in self-denial, in obedience, and in patience, but from which they can never succeed in producing any result —*Martensen, 'Christian Ethics,'* i 297

Ascetic life, monastic life, pietism, afford examples of one-sidedness The Christian duty of life is here placed exclusively in cleansing from sin, in the mortification of the flesh, in dying to the world, but concerning the development of human talents and powers by Christ's Spirit, of creative, life-giving effects, there is no mention There is only the suggestion of a blessed death; but of a blessed life already in the present time there is no hint.—*Martensen, 'Christian Ethics,'* i 317.

What may be called ascetical theories of Perfection are to be traced in every age. In their general tendency they have declined from the spirit of the New Testament, and that in two ways:—

1. They have laid too much stress on the human effort, thereby dishonouring the supremacy of the Holy Ghost, who carries on His work without the instrumentality too often adopted by asceticism, and is, after all, the sole Agent in the spirit's sanctification.

2. They have too carefully distinguished between common and elect Christians, by adopting the Saviour's so-called *Counsels of Perfection* as the guide to a higher life, interdicted to those who do not receive the counsels. But our Lord did not summon some men to a perfection denied to others, though He did summon some men to duties not required in all cases of others.—*Pope, 'Christian Theology,'* iii. 66.

The True Asceticism.

Asceticism is a development of the religious tendency in man that has been almost universal, and has the highest sanction. Its definition is given by St. Paul in words which at once recommend it and guard it, and promise its genuine fruit. *Exercise thyself rather unto godliness.* The rules of the religious life must be such as tend to godliness, which includes, and indeed is, the total suppression of pride, vainglory, personal sense of meritoriousness, exultation in external religion, and morbid self-anatomy. Godliness is the reward of this discipline, even as it must be its end. St. Paul said of himself, *I exercise myself to have always a conscience void of offence toward God and toward men.* In both passages a pure asceticism is recommended.—*Pope, 'Christian Theology,'* iii 65.

Above all, exercise thy abstinence in this—in refraining both from speaking and listening to evil, and cleanse thy heart from all pollution, from all revengeful feelings, and from all covetousness; and on the day that thou fastest content thyself with bread, vegetables, and water, and thank God for these. But reckon up on this day what thy meal would otherwise have cost thee, and give the amount that it comes to to some widow, or orphan, or to the poor.—*'Shepherd of Hermas.'*

St. Paul declares that the kingdom of Heaven consists not 'in meat and drink,' neither, therefore, in abstaining from wine and flesh, but 'in righteousness, and peace, and joy in the Holy Ghost.' Abstinence is a virtue of the soul, consisting not in that which is without, but in that which is within the man. Abstinence has reference not to some one thing alone, not merely to pleasure, but abstinence consists also in disposing money, in taming the tongue, and in obtaining by reason the mastery over sin.—*Clement of Alexandria.*

The external practices of a godly asceticism are both the expression and the instrumental aids of internal discipline. First, and as mediating between inward and outward discipline, comes *Abstinence*, which is either a grace or a duty. This means in general the non-indulgence of appetite as towards things, and of affections as towards persons; and may be either internal or external also. *Fasting* is the more express and formal act, brought from the Old Testament by our Lord, who indirectly enjoined it both by His example and by His precept. But whatever ascetic practices are adopted must be under the restraint and regulation of one law. *Exercise thyself rather unto godliness.*—*Pope, 'Christian Theology'* iii. 210.

Romanist and Protestant contrasted.

According to Romish doctrine, ascetic practices are in themselves holy, meritorious, and expiatory; according to Protestant teaching, asceticism is only a means in the warfare with the flesh, and its practice only justified so far as it is required therein. The Romish Church requires abstinence and various ascetic exercises, as proofs of piety. Our Church rejects this doctrine; for such exercises are not proofs of piety, but only means of attaining it. In this latter aspect they are both lawful and necessary.—*Luthardt, 'Moral Truths,'* pp. 295, 82.

Value of Asceticism to great men.

An Ascetic, to all intents and purposes, every man must be who has a work to do, and who determines that it shall be done, let the inducements to abandon it or neglect it be what they may. Because Napoleon the First chose what was painful in preference to what was pleasant, he was able to trample upon those peoples and monarchs who accounted pleasure the end of life, whose greatest desire was to avoid pain. No Alpine snows, no armed men could withstand him. Only when he encountered men who had learnt, as he had learnt, to claim dominion over circumstances, to endure suffering for the sake of a higher end, could that strength, which he had won through his Asceticism, be broken.—*Maurice, 'The Conscience,'* p. 78.

For instances of Asceticism see the Church Histories of Robertson, Neander, and others.

IV. MORAL SENSE THEORY.

Shaftesbury.

Shaftesbury's doctrine on this head may, perhaps, briefly be summed up as follows: Each man has from the first a natural sense of right and wrong, a 'Moral Sense' or 'Conscience' (all of which expressions he employs as synonymous). This sense is, in its natural condition, wholly or mainly, emotional, but, as it admits of constant education and improvement, the rational or reflective element in it gradually becomes more prominent. Its decisions are generally described as if they were immediate, and, beyond the occasional recognition of a rational as well as an emotional element, little or no attempt is made to analyse it. In all these respects, Shaftesbury's 'Moral Sense' differs little from the 'Conscience' subsequently described by Butler, the main distinctions being that with Butler the rational or reflective element assumes greater prominence than with Shaftesbury, while, on the other hand, the 'Conscience' of the one writer is invested with a more absolute and uniform character than is the 'Moral Sense' of the other.—*Fowler, 'Shaftesbury and Hutcheson,'* p. 82.

Doctrine of Francis Hutcheson.

There is, as each one by close attention and reflection may convince himself, a natural and immediate determination to approve certain affections, and actions consequent upon them, not referred to any other quality perceivable by our other senses or by reasoning. When we call this determination a *sense* or *instinct*, we are not supposing it of that low kind dependent on bodily organs, such as even the brutes have. It may be a constant settled determination in the soul itself, as much as our powers of judging and reasoning. And it is pretty plain that *reason* is only a subservient power to our ultimate determinations either of perception or will. The ultimate end is settled by some sense, and some determination of will: by some sense we enjoy happiness, and self-love determines to it without reasoning. Reason can only direct to the means; or compare two ends previously constituted by some other immediate powers.—*'System of Moral Philosophy,'* bk. i. ch. iv. sec. iv.

The Moral Sense in Relation to Virtue and Benevolence.

By Hutcheson the general view of Shaftesbury is more fully developed, with several new psychological distinctions; including the separation of calm benevolence, as well as, after Butler, calm self-love, from the turbulent passions, selfish or social. Hutcheson also follows Butler in laying stress on the regulating and controlling function of the Moral Sense; but he still regards kind affections as the principal objects of moral approbation,—the calm and extensive affections being preferred to the turbulent and narrow. The most excellent disposition, he holds, which naturally gains the highest approbation is either the calm, stable, universal good-will to all, by which a man is determined to desire the highest happiness of the greatest possible system of sensitive beings, or the desire and love of moral excellence, which in man is inseparable from the universal good will that it chiefly approves. These two principles cannot conflict, and therefore there is no practical need of determining which is highest: Hutcheson is disposed to treat them as co-ordinate. Only in a secondary sense is approval due to certain abilities and dispositions immediately connected with virtuous affections, as candour, veracity, fortitude, sense of honour; while in a lower grade still are placed sciences and arts, along with even bodily skills and gifts; indeed the approbation we give to these is not strictly moral, but is referred to the sense of decency or dignity, which, as well as the sense of honour, is to be distinguished from the moral sense. Calm self-love Hutcheson regards as not in itself an object either of moral approbation or disapprobation; the actions which flow solely from self-love and yet evidence no want of benevolence, having no hurtful effect upon others, seem perfectly indifferent in a moral sense: at the same time he enters into a careful analysis of the elements of happiness, in order to show that a true regard for private interest always coincides with the moral sense and with benevolence. While thus maintaining Shaftesbury's harmony between public and private good, Hutcheson is still more careful to establish the strict disinterestedness of benevolent affections.—*Sidgwick*, '*Outlines of the History of Ethics*,' pp. 197–199.

V. ETHICS OF SYMPATHY.

Adam Smith.

Were it possible that a human creature could grow up to manhood in some solitary place, without any communication with his own species, he could no more think of his own character, of the propriety or demerit of his own sentiments and conduct, of the beauty or deformity of his own mind, than of the beauty or deformity of his own face. All these are objects which he cannot easily see, which naturally he does not look at, and with regard to which he is provided with no mirror which can present them to his view. Bring him into society, and he is immediately provided with the mirror which he wanted before. It is placed in the countenance and behaviour of those he lives with, which always mark when they enter into, and when they disapprove of his sentiments; and it is here that he first views the propriety and impropriety of his own passions, the beauty and deformity of his own mind. To a man who from his birth was a stranger to society, the objects of his passions, the external bodies which either pleased or hurt him, would occupy his whole attention. The passion themselves, the desires or aversions, the joys or sorrows, which those objects excited, though of all things the most immediately present to him, could scarce ever be the objects of his thoughts. The idea of them could never interest him so much as to call upon his attentive consideration. The consideration of his joy could excite in him no new joy, nor that of his sorrow any new sorrow, though the consideration of the causes of those passions might often excite both. Bring him into society, and all his own passions will immediately become the causes of new passions. He will observe that mankind approve of some of them, and are disgusted by others. He will be elevated in the one case, and cast down in the other; his desires and aversions, his joys and sorrows, will now often become the causes of new desires and new aversions, new joys and new sorrows: they will now, therefore, interest him deeply, and often call upon his most attentive consideration.—'*Theory of Moral Sentiments*,' pt. iii. ch. i.

Adam Smith does not deny the actuality or importance of that sympathetic pleasure in the perceived or inferred effects of virtues and vices on which Hume laid stress. He does not, however, think that the essential part of common moral sentiment is constituted by this, but rather by a more direct sympathy with the impulses that prompt to action or expression. The spontaneous play of this sympathy he treats as an original and inexplicable fact of human nature; but he considers that its action is powerfully sustained by the pleasure that each man finds in the accord of his feeling with another's. By means of this primary element, compounded in various ways, Adam Smith explains all the different phenomena of the moral consciousness. He takes, first, the semi-moral notion of 'propriety' or 'decorum,' and endeavours to show inductively that our application of this notion to the social behaviour of another is determined by our degree of sympathy with the feeling expressed in such behaviour. 'To approve of the passions of another as suitable to their objects, is the same thing as to sympathise with them.' Similarly, we disapprove of passion exhibited in a degree to which our sympathy cannot reach; and even, too, when it falls short; since, as he acutely points out, we often sympathise with the merely imagined feeling of others, and are thus disappointed when we find the reality absent. Thus the prescriptions of good taste in the expression of feeling may be summed up in the principle, 'Reduce or raise the expression to that with which spectators will sympathise.' When the effort to restrain feeling is exhibited in a degree which surprises as well as pleases, it excites admiration as a virtue or excellence; such excellences Smith quaintly calls the 'awful and respectable,' contrasting them with the 'amiable virtues' which we attribute to persons by whom the opposite effort to sympathise is exhibited in a remarkable degree. From the sentiments of propriety and admiration we proceed to the sense of merit and demerit. Here a more complex phenomenon presents itself for analysis. We have to distinguish in the sense of merit (1) a direct sympathy with the sentiments of the agent, and (2) an indirect sympathy with the gratitude of those who receive the benefit of his actions. In the case of demerit, a direct antipathy to the feelings of the misdoer takes the place of sympathy; but the chief part of the sentiment excited is sympathy with the resentment of those injured by the misdeed. The object of this sympathetic indignation, impelling us to punish, is what we call injustice; and thus the remarkable stringency of the obligation to act justly is explained, since the recognition of any action as unjust implies that we approve of its being forcibly obstructed or punished.—*Sidgwick*, '*Outlines of the History of Ethics*' pp. 205, 206.

VI. UTILITARIANISM OR UNIVERSALISTIC HEDONISM.

Its Main Position.

By Utilitarianism is meant the ethical theory that the conduct which, under any given circumstance, is objectively right, is that which will produce the greatest amount of happiness on the whole; that is, taking into account all whose happiness is affected by the conduct. It would tend to clearness if we might call this principle, and the method based upon it, by some such name as 'Universalistic Hedonism.'—*Sidgwick*, '*Methods of Ethics*,' p. 407.

The Utilitarian maintains that we have by nature absolutely no knowledge of merit or demerit, of the comparative excellence of our feelings and actions, and that we derive these notions solely from an observation of the course of life which is conducive to human happiness. That which makes actions good is, that they increase the happiness or diminish the pains of mankind. That which constitutes their demerit is their opposite tendency. To procure 'the greatest happiness for the greatest number' is therefore the highest aim of the moralist, the supreme type and expression of virtue. All that is meant by saying we ought to do an action is, that if we do not do it, we shall suffer. A desire to obtain happiness and to avoid pain, is the only possible motive to action.—*Lecky*, '*European Morals*,' i. 3, 5.

Utilitarianism is the system which endeavours to construct the moral rule exclusively from the principle of happiness The general assumption upon which it proceeds may be easily laid down. Happiness is the sole end of conduct; the 'utility' of an action is its tendency to produce happiness; its morality is measured by its utility; that conduct is right which produces most happiness, and by this we must be understood to mean which produces most happiness on the average, for since we can seldom calculate more than a small part of the consequences of any action, we are forced to act upon rules corresponding to the general limits of observation.—*Stephen*, '*Science of Ethics*,' p. 355.

Forms of Utilitarianism.

Four main forms

The doctrine which makes utility the exclusive test of right and wrong, and decides on the moral character of actions by their supposed or expected consequences alone, may assume very different forms The first is the theological, in which it borrows, but in borrowing distorts and partially degrades, some great truths of the Christian revelation. God wills the happiness of mankind. He commands us to practise universal beneficence. His will is sanctioned by promises and threatenings, that are to be fulfilled in a future life. Therefore self-love requires us to obey His command, and to practise works of social kindness, in hope of gaining the promised reward. But in applying the principle we are left to our own judgment; and the known tendencies of actions, deduced from experience, are said to be our chief guide.

The second form of the doctrine is the philanthropic or benevolent. All the motives of religious faith are either formally set aside, or silently disappear from view. In their place there is borrowed from the rival doctrine of intuitive morality a vast *à priori* maxim, the supreme, the essential obligation, needing no proof, and assumed to be self-evident, of universal philanthropy or benevolence. But this great principle, whether borrowed from Christianity, or from philosophic idealism, is no sooner assumed, than it is disguised, concealed, and consubstantiated, under the form and accidents of a complex process of experiment and calculation. The whole business of morals is to calculate results, and work out problems of maxima from imperfect premises; while the one element which alone has a truly ethical character, the deliberate, earnest, conscientious aim to do good to our fellows, and in so doing to please and serve the common Creator and Preserver of mankind, is left habitually out of sight, lest it should embarrass and disturb that process of arithmetic on which the whole science is made to depend.

The third form is the philosophically selfish, or that of Epicurus and his later disciples. It recognises no religious faith in its scheme of morals, nor any need for motives drawn from the Christian message of a life to come. Neither does it purloin from the Scriptures the second great commandment and then conceal the precious treasure, as Achan hid the talent of gold in the soil of his tent, burying it in the heart of a system of pleasure-seeking arithmetic, with which it has no natural connection. It lays down the principle, based on certain animal instincts, that the attainment of personal pleasure is the main end and business of life. And then it proceeds to mitigate the harshness and prune away the grossness of the naked theory, by insisting on the need of a wise and thoughtful prudence, grounded on the lessons of experience, to free men from the pursuit of vicious indulgence and to prove the superior gain of temperance, kindness, the restraint of passion, and the cultivation of private friendship And there can be no doubt that the laws of prudence, when really studied and observed, may form the first steps in an upward progress, from which the mind must, soon or late, gain clear glimpses of higher and holier laws of action than the pursuit of selfish and personal pleasure alone.

The fourth and last form is that of political selfishness. Virtue, on this view, consists in a habit of submission to outward laws, created and sustained by the fear of human punishment. Instead of rising above the love of fame,

'That last infirmity of noble minds,'

it consists rather in one of the worst infirmities of minds both feeble and ignoble; that is, in the animal fear of physical suffering, engrained and engrafted in the heart by cultivating the habits and instincts of a slave.—*Birks*, '*Moral Science*,' pp. 266–68.

Ancient Forms

Aristippus and the Cyrenaic School.

Aristippus defines Pleasure as the sensation of gentle motion, the end of life. The sage aims to enjoy pleasure without being controlled by it. Intellectual culture alone fits one for true enjoyment. No one kind of pleasure is superior to another, only the degree and duration of pleasure determines its worth. No pleasure is, as such, bad, though it may often arise from bad causes. To enjoy the present is the true business of man.—*Ueberweg*, '*Hist. of Phil.*,' i. 95.

The Epicurean School.

See under "ANCIENT SCHOOLS OF PHILOSOPHY," "EPICUREAN," Section XI.

Modern Forms.

Hobbes.

Hobbes (1588–1679), in making happiness the standard, applies the term to personal happiness. 'Whatsoever is the object of *any man's appetite* or desire, that is it which he for his part calleth good; and the object of his hate and aversion, evil; and of his contempt, vile and inconsiderable. For these words of good, evil, and contemptible are ever used with relation to the person that useth them; there being nothing simply and absolutely so; nor any common rule of good and evil to be taken from the nature of the objects themselves; but from the person of the man, where there is no commonwealth; or in a commonwealth, from the person of him that representeth it, or from an arbitrator or judge whom men disagreeing shall by consent set up and make his sentence the rule thereof. . . Of good there be three kinds: good in the promise, that is, *pulchrum*, good in effect, as the end desired, which is called *jucundum*, delightful; and good as the means, which is called *utile*, profitable; and as many of evil; for evil in promise is that they call *turpe*, evil in effect and end is *molestum*, unpleasant, troublesome; and evil in means, *inutile*, unprofitable, hurtful' ('Leviathan,' 1651, part i. chap. vi., Molesworth's ed., vol. iii. p. 41). With Hobbes, personal appetite is a sufficient guide; anything is good as it happens to be desired. 'There is no such *finis ultimus*, utmost aim, nor *summum bonum*, greatest good, as is spoken of in the books of the old moral philosophers' (Ib., chap. xi. vol. iii. p. 85).—*Calderwood*, '*Moral Philosophy*,' p. 128.

Bentham.

Nature has placed mankind under the governance of two sovereign masters, pain and pleasure. It is for them alone to point out what we ought to do, as well as to determine what we shall do. On the one hand the standard of right and wrong, on the other the chain of causes and effects, are fastened to their throne. They govern us in all we do, in all we say, in all we think: every effort we can make to throw off our subjection will serve but to demonstrate and confirm it. The principle of utility recognises this subjection, and assumes it for the foundation of that system the object of which is to rear the fabric of felicity by the hands of reason and of law. By the principle of utility is meant that principle which approves or disapproves of every action whatsoever, according to the tendency which it appears to have to augment or diminish the happiness of the party whose interest is in question.—*Bentham*, '*Introduction, &c.*,' '*Principles of Morals, &c.*,' p. 1.

The logic of utility consists in setting out, in all the operations of the judgment, from the calculation or comparison of pains and pleasures, and in not allowing the interference of any other idea.

I am a partisan of the principle of utility, when I measure my approbation or disapprobation of a public or private act by its tendency to produce pleasure or pain; when I employ the words *just*, *unjust*, *moral*, *immoral*, *good*, *bad*, simply as collective terms, including the ideas of certain pains or pleasures; it being always understood that I use the words *pain* and *pleasure* in their ordinary signification, without inventing any arbitrary definition for the sake of excluding certain pleasures, or denying the existence of certain pains. In this matter we want no refinement, no metaphysics. It is not necessary to consult Plato or Aristotle. Pain and pleasure are what every one feels to be such, the peasant and the prince, the unlearned and the philosopher.

He who adopts the principle of utility esteems virtue to be a good, only on account of the pleasures which result from it; he regards vice as an evil, only because of the pains which it produces. Moral good is *good* only by its tendency to produce physical good. Moral evil is *evil* only by its tendency to produce physical evil.—'*Theory of Legislation*.'

John Stuart Mill.

According to the Greatest Happiness Principle, the ultimate end, with reference to and for the sake of which all other things are desirable (whether we are considering our own good or that of other people), is an existence exempt as far as possible from pain, and as rich as possible in enjoyments, both in point of quantity and quality; the test of quality, and the rule for measuring it against quantity, being the preference felt by those who, in their opportunities of experience, to which must be added their habits of self-consciousness and self-observation, are best furnished with the means of comparison. This being, according to the utilitarian opinion, the end of human action, is necessarily also the standard of morality, which may accordingly be defined the rules and precepts for human conduct, by the observance of which an existence such as has been described might be, to the greatest extent possible, secured to all mankind; and not to them only, but, so far as the nature of things admits, to the whole sentient creation.—'*Utilitarianism*,' p. 17.

It is quite compatible with the principle of utility to recognise the fact that some *kinds* of pleasure are more desirable and more valuable than others. It would be absurd that while, in estimating all other things, quality is considered as well as quantity, the estimation of pleasures should be supposed to depend on quantity alone.—'*Utilitarianism*,' p. 11.

The creed which accepts as the foundation of morals, Utility, or the greatest Happiness Principle, holds that actions are right in proportion as they tend to promote happiness, wrong as they tend to produce the reverse of happiness. By happiness is intended pleasure, and the absence of pain; by unhappiness, pain and the privation of pleasure. To give a clear view of the moral standard set up by the theory, much more requires to be said; in particular what things it includes in the ideas of pain and pleasure; and to what extent this is left an open question. But these supplementary explanations do not affect the theory of life on which this theory of morality is grounded—namely, that pleasure, and freedom from pain, are the only things desirable as ends; and that all desirable things (which are as numerous in the utilitarian as in any other scheme) are desirable either for the pleasure inherent in themselves, or as means to the promotion of pleasure and the prevention of pain.—'*Utilitarianism*,' pp. 9, 10.

The standard not the agent's own pleasure.

The happiness which forms the utilitarian standard of what is right in conduct, is not the agent's own happiness, but that of all concerned. As between his own happiness and that of others, utilitarianism requires him to be as strictly impartial as a disinterested and benevolent spectator. In the golden rule of Jesus of Nazareth, we read the complete spirit of the ethics of utility.

To do as one would be done by, and to love one's neighbour as oneself, constitute the ideal perfection of utilitarian morality — '*Utilitarianism*,' p 24

H. Spencer. Rational Utilitarianism.

Empirical Utilitarianism a transitional form.

The view which I contend for is, that Morality properly so called—the science of right conduct—has for its object to determine *how* and *why* certain modes of conduct are detrimental, and certain other modes beneficial. These good and bad results cannot be accidental, but must be necessary consequences of the constitution of things; and I conceive it to be the business of Moral Science to deduce, from the laws of life and the conditions of existence, what kinds of action necessarily tend to produce happiness, and what kinds to produce unhappiness. Having done this, its deductions are to be recognised as laws of conduct, and are to be conformed to irrespective of a direct estimation of happiness or misery.

Perhaps an analogy will most clearly show my meaning. During its early stages, planetary Astronomy consisted of nothing more than accumulated observations respecting the positions and motions of the sun and planets, from which accumulated observations it came by and by to be empirically predicted, with an approach to truth, that certain of the heavenly bodies would have certain positions at certain times. But the modern science of planetary Astronomy consists of deductions from the law of gravitation—deductions showing why the celestial bodies *necessarily* occupy certain places at certain times. Now, the kind of relation which thus exists between ancient and modern Astronomy is analogous to the kind of relation which, I conceive, exists between the Expediency-Morality and Moral Science properly so called. And the objection which I have to the current Utilitarianism is, that it recognises no more developed form of Morality—does not see that it has reached but the initial stage of Moral Science.—*Letter to Mr. J. S. Mill, quoted in* '*Data of Ethics*,' p. 57, 58.

Method of Rational Utilitarianism.

All the current methods of ethics have one general defect—they neglect ultimate causal connections. Of course I do not mean that they wholly ignore the natural consequences of actions; but I mean that they recognise them only incidentally. They do not erect into a method the ascertaining of necessary relations between causes and effects, and deducing rules of conduct from formulated statements of them.

Every science begins by accumulating observations, and presently generalises these empirically; but only when it reaches the stage at which its empirical generalisations are included in a rational generalisation, does it become developed science. Ethics, which is a science dealing with the conduct of associated human beings, regarded under one of its aspects, has to undergo a like transformation; and, at present undeveloped, can be considered a developed science only when it has undergone this transformation. — '*Data of Ethics*,' pp 61, 62.

Utility as the foundation of Law.

God designs the happiness of all His sentient creatures. Some human actions forward that benevolent purpose, or their tendencies are beneficent or useful. Other human actions are adverse to that purpose, or their tendencies are mischievous or pernicious. The former, as promoting his purpose, God has enjoined. The latter, as opposed to his purpose, God has forbidden.

Inasmuch as the goodness of God is boundless and impartial, He designs the greatest happiness of all His sentient creatures: He wills that the aggregate of their enjoyments shall find no nearer limit than that which is inevitably set to it by their finite and imperfect nature. From the probable effects of our actions on the greatest happiness of all, or from the tendencies of human actions to increase or diminish that aggregate, we may infer the laws which he has given, but has not expressed or revealed.—*Austin*, '*Jurisprudence*,' Lect. ii., p. 109.

If our conduct were truly adjusted to the principle of general utility, our conduct would conform, for the most part, to *rules*: rules which emanate from the Deity, and to which the tendencies of human actions are the guide or index.—*Austin*, '*Jurisprudence*,' p. 117.

Christian Utilitarianism.

God, when He created the human species, wished their happiness, and made for them the provision which He has made, with that view and for that purpose.

God wills and wishes the happiness of His creatures. And this conclusion being once established, we are at liberty to go on with the rule built upon it, namely, 'that the method of coming at the will of God, concerning any action, by the light of nature, is to inquire into the tendency of that action to promote or diminish the general happiness.'

So, then, actions are to be estimated by their tendency. Whatever is expedient is right. It is the utility of any moral rule alone, which constitutes the obligation of it.—*Paley*, '*Moral Philosophy*,' bk. ii. chaps. v. and vi.

There is prevalent, among many professed Christians, a view of the Divine government which may be called 'Christian Utilitarianism.' It is not uncommon for religious persons to write and to speak as though the one great end sought by the Divine Ruler were the enjoyment of His creatures. It is urged that benevolence is one of the most glorious attributes of the Divine nature, that, being infinitely benevolent, God must desire to see all His creatures happy, that revealed religion has the happiness of men for its one great end, and that, sooner or later, pain and sorrow must be banished from the universe, and the reign of perfect, unbroken, and eternal happiness must be established. Paley has even defined virtue as 'the doing good to mankind, in obedience to the will of God, and *for the sake of everlasting happiness*.' He teaches that the will of God is indeed the rule, but that everlasting happiness is the motive to virtuous conduct.—*Thomson*, '*Utilitarianism*,' pp. 43, 44.

Criticism of Utilitarianism.

As a Theory of Life.

Of the 'faculties more elevated' which belong to man, each must serve a higher end, according to its own nature. The end of intelligence is knowledge; of memory, recollection; of will, self-direction; of affection, such as love or sympathy, the good of another. If the end of each power is in harmony with its own nature, Intelligence, Memory, Will, and Affection, being entirely different in nature from Sensibility, cannot all have the same end. To say, for example, that sensibility and intellect have the same end, is to contradict the only rule by which the natural end of a power can be decided. It is to say that Passivity has the same end as Activity, which is practically to enunciate the contradiction that Passivity and Activity are the same.

While each power has its own end determined by its own nature, it is possible for an intelligent being to use any one of his powers, merely for the sake of the pleasure attending on its use, and not for its natural end. The possibility of this is restricted to an intelligent being capable of forming a conception of happiness, and contemplating the voluntary use of means for a selected end. The lower animals experience pleasure in accordance with laws of their nature, which operate irrespective of any control from the animals themselves. So it is with the laws of our sentient nature. But an entire revolution of being occurs where intelligent self-direction is possible. In a being thus endowed, powers are capable of being used according to the conceptions and purposes of the being himself. It thus becomes possible to use a power, not only for its natural end, but for other and subordinate ends, and even, in some measure, for ends contrary to its nature. Thus forming a conception of pleasure as an end, we may seek this end in the use of any one of our powers. Each one of them has a distinct form of pleasure associated with its exercise; ascertaining this, and being able to determine the use of our powers, we can bring them into exercise for the sake of the pleasure attending upon their use. But when such a thing happens, it is not under the law determining the natural use of the power, but by special determination of our own. We cannot change the nature of the power, or alter the end which it naturally serves, but we often voluntarily employ a power for the sake of the attendant pleasure, and not for its own natural end. This is done when we employ the intellect, not for the discovery of truth, but for the pleasure which attends on the search for truth; or, when we cherish sympathy, not for the sake of relieving the sufferer, but for the luxury of feeling which we experience.

If a general conception can be formed of the end or final object of our being, it must be by reference to the higher or governing powers of our nature, and as these are intellectual or rational, the end of our being is not pleasure, but the full and harmonious use of all our powers for the accomplishment of their own natural ends. These natural ends admit of a threefold classification. As concerned with our own being, it is the end of life to secure the development and forthputting of all its energies; with other beings, their development and performance of their life-work; and finally and transcendently, with the Absolute Being Himself, devotion to Him as the source of our being and the ruler of our destiny.—*Calderwood*, '*Moral Philosophy*,' p. 132.

Insufficiency of the Utilitarian Standard.

It appears to me that the utilitarian formula (namely, that action is right or good in proportion as it tends to promote happiness), if meant not only to describe a fact, but to express also the meaning of rightness or goodness, or tell us what it is that constitutes the rightness or goodness of an action, is insufficient, whatever modification he may give to the idea of happiness, or in whatever way he may determine that. Right action may be conducive to happiness, as it may be to various other things, and this may be one character to know it by; but if it is intended to express that it is this conduciveness which, in our world of men, makes the rightness or goodness, the formula, as I have said, is insufficient. For that there is and must be recognised by men a goodness or valuableness quite different from conduciveness to happiness cannot, I think, be doubted. There is nothing which need surprise us in there being more than one sort of moral value attaching to actions; and it is far better to submit to whatever philosophical disappointments we may feel in having to acknowledge such a plurality, than to outrage at once the well observed sentiment of men and the inward language of our own heart and reason. If we listen to the voice of human nature, we must put by the side of the utilitarian formula, as a sister, one of this kind. 'Actions are right and good in proportion as they rise above the *merely* natural or animal conditions of human nature (as self-care or self-preservation), and the obedience to immediate impulse, more especially to the impulses of bodily passion and excitement.—*Grote*, '*Exam. of Utilitarian Phil.*,' pp. 119, 120.

As a Theory of Morals.

Agreeableness and utility are not moral conceptions, nor have they any connection with morality. What a man does, merely because it is agreeable, is not virtue. Therefore the Epicurean system was justly thought by Cicero and the best moralists among the ancients to subvert morality, and to substitute another principle in its room; and this system is liable to the same censure.—*Reid*, '*Active Powers*,' v. 5.

In some respects society, whether moral or political, may be considered an aggregation of similar units, but in far more important respects it is an organisation of dissimilar members The general happiness, as a fact, is the sum of the happiness of the individuals; but as an object to be aimed at it is not this, but it is to be attained by the acting of each according to the relations in which he is placed in society It is these different relations, rendering as they do the individuals *dissimilar* in circumstances, which more truly convert mere juxtaposition into society than anything of similarity does. This latter is needed in certain most important respects, not, indeed, in any form of equality, but in the form of common understanding and sympathy; but the various need and the power of mutual benefit which *dissimilarity* of circumstances produces are as vital to the society as the other points, and do more to make it necessary and fruitful. By moral relations and moral society, as distinguished from political, I understand men as stronger and weaker, benefactors and benefited, trusters and trusted, or linked together in other moral relations similar to these, besides the natural relations, as of family, which partially coincide with these; lastly, supposing there is no other relation, as linked together in any case by the general relation of human brotherhood And if we are to answer the question, *Whose* happiness are we to promote? we must answer it by saying, Not the happiness of all alike, ourselves taking share with the rest, but the happiness (if we are so to describe it) of each one with whom we have to do, according to the moral relation in which we stand to him The happiness which we are to promote is that of those who are benefitable by us, who want something of us, or have claim upon us, according to their wants and claims —*Grote*, '*Exam of Utilitarian Phil.*,' pp 95, 96.

It cannot furnish a sure basis of morals.

The situation of the theory is briefly this,—Utility is the basis of moral distinctions; but some limit must be assigned to the principle, for we do not make everything a moral rule that we consider useful Utility made compulsory is the standard of morality; Morality is thus an institution of society; Conscience is an imitation of the government of society; Conscience is first fear of authority, and then respect for it; but, 'even in the most unanimous notions of mankind, there can be no such thing as a standard overriding the judgment of every separate intelligence;' the individual must therefore emancipate himself from authority, in order to be 'a law to himself;' to this end he must recognise the intent and meaning of the law; for this purpose he must fall back on Utility. It is not, however, all Utility, but only Utility made compulsory, which affords the basis of morals, and it is Society which determines what shall be made compulsory. How can every separate intelligence emancipate itself? How can it find to its own satisfaction a rule of life so essentially superior to the authority of Society, as to warrant independent action in opposition to the teaching of Society?—*Calderwood*, '*Moral Philosophy*,' p. 143.

The theory which makes 'the greatest happiness of the greatest number' the test of moral action, loses all its value, if it be without a scientific basis for moral obligation If there be one thing which specially commends the theory to our admiration, it is the aspect of universal benevolence which it wears. But, in order to be accepted as a sound theory of Benevolence, it must establish on a philosophic basis a doctrine of unvarying obligation to act benevolently. Mr. Mill puts the question thus,—'Why am I bound to promote the general happiness? If my own happiness lies in something else, why may I not give that the preference?' Mr Mill answers, 'If the view adopted by the utilitarian philosophy of the nature of the moral sense be correct, this difficulty will always present itself, until the influences which form moral character have taken the same hold of the principle which they have taken of some of the consequences — until, by the improvement of education, the feeling of unity with our fellow-creatures shall be (what it cannot be doubted that Christ intended it to be) as deeply rooted in our character, and to our consciousness as completely a part of our nature, as the horror of crime is in an ordinarily well-brought-up young person,' p. 40. This is an admirable passage. But it fails to meet the scientific demands upon an Ethical Theory. It concerns obedience, not obligation; and vividly portrays the need for renovation of nature before the law of benevolence can become the general rule of life among us. But the difficulty of attaining uniform consistent benevolence in practice is not the subject engaging attention. The philosophic difficulty of constructing a theory of morals is one thing; the practical difficulty of rendering uniform obedience to the requirements of morality is quite another thing. Doubtless, it is beyond the power of Moral Philosophy to make men obey the law; but it is the part of Moral Philosophy to show that there is a moral law to be obeyed. Mr. Mill's answer is insufficient because of the wide separation between theory and practice. That the practical difficulty of personal conformity with the law of benevolence 'will always be felt until the influences which form moral character have taken hold of the principle,' is certain. But the question is, what obligation rests on the person who would form his character aright, to accept this principle of benevolence as the rule of conduct? It is certain that Christ intended the feeling of unity with our fellow-creatures to be deeply rooted in our character; but it is no less certain that in order to secure the fulfilment of His intention, Christ proclaimed the principle of benevolence as a law for Humanity. And, in order to establish a philosophy of benevolence, Moral Philosophy must show that the principle of benevolence is a law of natural obligation. If we are to escape the admission that Selfishness is dutiful, we must pass Mr. Darwin's view, that persistent desire is the ground of obligation. If we are to maintain that morality requires a man to keep his promise, even though he is not forced to do so, we must pass Professor Bain's view, that external authority is the source of duty. And now, if we are to avoid the position, that a man is freed from obligation by simply disowning it, we must pass Mr. Mill's view, that personal feeling is the source of obligation. Has, then, Utilitarianism no answer to the question, What is the source of Obligation? 'Why am I bound to promote the general happiness?' Must Philosophy, before attempting an answer, wait until the improvement of education has rooted in the character of all men a feeling of unity with their fellow-creatures? If so, on what ground must education proceed? On Prudence, which means only Self-interest? or on Natural Law? The Intuitional Theory gives its answer thus,—The standard of morals has in itself the authority of law, binding on every intelligence capable of understanding and applying it. A man cannot live and escape obligation, however much he violate it. But, the standard of Happiness cannot be the standard of morals, because the agreeable, or desirable, does not in itself possess 'binding force' to determine the action of moral beings.—*Calderwood, 'Moral Philosophy,'* 151, 152.

The utilitarian theory, though undoubtedly held by many men of the purest, and by some men of the most heroic virtue, would if carried to its logical conclusions prove subversive of Morality, and especially, and in the very highest degree, unfavourable to self-denial and to heroism. Even if it explains these, it fails to justify them, and conscience being traced to a mere confusion of the means of happiness with its end, would be wholly unable to resist the solvent of criticism.—*Lecky, 'European Morals,'* i 68.

Pleasure and Pain are not identical with right and wrong.

Though men seek pleasure for its own sake, they cannot seek pain for its own sake. The law of our nature which makes pleasure-seeking possible, makes pain-seeking impossible There are no actions which have pain as their end If, therefore, pleasure be the end of life, it is impossible to go against it, and the classification of certain actions as morally wrong altogether disappears —*Calderwood*, '*Moral Philosophy*,' p. 134.

When Moralists assert, that what we call virtue derives its reputation solely from its utility, and that the interest of the agent is the one motive to practise it, our first question is naturally how far this theory agrees with the feelings and with the language of mankind. But if tested by this criterion, there never was a doctrine more emphatically condemned than utilitarianism. In all its stages and all its assertions, it is in direct opposition to common language and to common sentiments In all nations and in all ages, the ideas of interest and utility on the one hand and virtue on the other, have been regarded by the multitude as perfectly distinct, and all languages recognise the distinction. The terms, honour, justice, rectitude or virtue, and their equivalents in every language, present to the mind ideas essentially and broadly differing from the terms prudence, sagacity, or interest. The two lines of conduct may coincide, but they are never confused, and we have not the slightest difficulty in imagining them antagonistic.—*Lecky*, '*European Morals*,' i 34

The very ingenuity of the various attempts that have been made to identify the conception of *right* with that of *expedient* or *agreeable*, or any other quality, is itself a witness against them; for no such elaborate reasoning would be required, were it not necessary to silence or pervert the instinctive testimony of a too stubborn consciousness —*Mansel*, '*Metaphysics*,' p. 159

The good is such, independent of pleasurable consequences.

The good is good, altogether independent of the pleasure it may bring. There is a good which does not immediately contemplate the production of happiness. Such, for example, are love to God, the glorifying of God, and the hallowing of His name: these have no respect, in our entertaining and cherishing them, to an augmentation of the Divine felicity No doubt such an act or spirit may, by reflexion of light, tend to brighten our own felicity; but this is an indirect effect, which follows only where we cherish the temper and perform the corresponding work in the idea that it is right. We do deeds of justice to the distant, to the departed, and the dead, who never may be conscious of what we have performed. Even in regard to services performed with the view of promoting the happiness of the individual, or of the community, we are made to feel that, if happiness be good, the benevolence which leads us to seek the happiness of others is still better, is alone morally good. In all cases the conscience constrains us to decide that virtue is good, whether it does or does not contemplate the production of pleasure.—*M'Cosh*, '*Intuitions of the Mind*,' p. 265.

Virtue will not bring pleasure, if pleasure be its sole aim.

The pleasure of virtue is one which can only be obtained on the express condition of its not being the object sought. Thus, for example, it has often been observed that prayer, by a law of our nature, and apart from all supernatural intervention, exercises a reflex influence of a very beneficial character upon the minds of the worshippers. The man who offers up his petitions with passionate earnestness, with unfaltering faith, and with a vivid realisation of the presence of an Unseen Being, has risen to a condition of mind which is itself eminently favourable both to his own happiness and to the expansion of his moral qualities. But he who expects nothing more will never attain this. To him who neither believes nor hopes that his petitions will receive a response, such a mental state is impossible. — *Lecky*, '*European Morals*,' i. 36.

The happy man is not he whose happiness is his only care.—*Reid.*

If what is painful is wrong, moral evil is a means to moral good.

Pain may be endured as a means to an end, even as a means for securing happiness. The pain of a surgical operation for the sake of health, the pain of self-denial for the sake of moral training, are examples. This fact makes a further inroad upon the theory. Moral evil cannot be used as a means of moral good. In making the production of happiness the test of right actions, and the production of pain the test of wrong actions, moral distinctions are hopelessly confused, and even immoral men may gain a reputation for goodness (see Plato's 'Gorgias,' 499). That the painful may lead to the pleasurable, is proof that pleasure and pain are not by their own nature ends in themselves, but simply attendants on personal action. Of contraries, the one cannot produce the other.—*Calderwood, 'Moral Philosophy,'* p. 135.

Utilitarianism cannot furnish a law of Duty.

Our moral constitution declares that we ought to promote the happiness of all who are susceptible of happiness. The only plausible form of the utilitarian theory of morals is that elaborated by Bentham, who says that we ought to promote the greatest happiness of the greatest number. But why *ought* we to do so? Whence get we the *should*, the *obligation*, the *duty?* Why should I seek the happiness of any other being than myself? why the happiness of a great number, or of the greatest number? why the happiness even of any one individual beyond the unit of self? If the advocates of the 'greatest happiness' principle will only answer this question thoroughly, they must call in a moral principle, or take refuge in a system against which our own nature rebels, in a theory which says that we are not required to do more than look after our own gratifications. The very advocates of the greatest happiness theory are thus constrained, in consistency with their view, to call in an ethical principle, and this will be found, if they examine it, to require more from man than that he should further the felicity of others. But while it covers vastly more ground, it certainly includes this, that we are bound, as much as in us lies, to promote the welfare of all who are capable of having their misery alleviated or their felicity enhanced.—*M'Cosh, 'Intuitions, &c.,'* p. 265.

A man is prudent when he consults his real interest; but he cannot be virtuous, if he has no regard to duty.—*Reid.*

On a Utilitarian Theory, the problem concerning moral obligation wears this form.—If tendency to produce happiness determine the rightness of an action, how can we rise above the agreeable and desirable, to find philosophic warrant for a doctrine of personal obligation? Utilitarianism meets its last and severest test in the attempt to distinguish between the desirable, which is the optional; and the dutiful, which is the imperative.

That happiness is by our nature desirable, is a fact which neither constitutes a law of personal obligation, nor obviates the necessity for having one. It cannot constitute a law of action, for the desirable has power only to attract, not to command. Besides, the desirable may often be the unattainable. The dutiful is not only the possible, but the binding. Neither can the desirability of happiness obviate the necessity for a law of obligation in the guidance of life. All pleasures are desirable, but all cannot be enjoyed at once; of pleasures, some are higher in quality, some lower, but the higher cannot always be preferred to the lower, therefore the quality of pleasure does not of itself afford a sufficient rule for selection. If man must sometimes surrender a higher enjoyment for a lower, and yet rigidly restrict lower pleasures for the sake of higher attainment and action, we need to discover the ground of these necessities. Analysis discovers a *physical necessity,* since man must eat, as well as think;

rest, as well as work; and an *intellectual necessity*, since man must concentrate his attention in order to successfully guide his efforts, and must therefore do some things, and leave others unattempted; but, within the possibilities of human effort, there is still another necessity, since of the things which a man can do, he recognises some as binding upon him in a sense in which others are not, and this is *moral necessity*.—*Calderwood*, '*Moral Philosophy*,' p. 145.

Duty and Happiness are sometimes opposed.

I am, for my part, convinced that there are occasions upon which we have to choose between two masters. This way is the path of duty; that is the path of happiness. We shall at times have to choose, and to choose with our eyes open. Let us take as illustration any of the famous cases of Moralists. Regulus preferred death by torture to dishonour. Was he acting for his own happiness? Would a man in the position of Regulus have greater chance of happiness, for possessing such a sense of honour as would determine him to martyrdom? I think that it is impossible to answer in the affirmative. Many men live 'infamous and contented' after saving life at the expense of honour.—*Stephen*, '*Science of Ethics*,' p. 427.

There is no absolute coincidence between virtue and happiness. I cannot prove that it is always prudent to act rightly, or that it is always happiest to be virtuous.—*Stephen*, '*Science of Ethics*,' p. 434.

The highest nature is rarely the happiest. The mind of Petronius Arbiter was probably more unclouded than that of Marcus Aurelius. For eighteen centuries the religious instinct of Christendom has recognised its ideal in the form of a 'Man of Sorrows.'—*Lecky*, '*European Morals*,' i. 70.

Hence on this theory virtue is an uncertain quantity.

Pleasures are of many kinds. They may either be pure and healthy, or vicious and diseased. And hence, if moral duty depends on a mere summation of pleasures, and an attempted calculation of their total amount, irrespective of any higher standard, it must be as mutable as those pleasures themselves, which form its component elements. No chain can be stronger than its weakest link. In the view of pure utilitarianism, when the doctrine abides in its native simplicity, and is neither infected nor improved by an attempt to ally it with Stoic or Christian elements, moral right must be as mutable as the capricious likings and dislikings of the most fretful, the most childish, or the most vicious among those who are included in the wide universe of moral agents. It may be inferred logically, from the principle thus laid down, that it is as much one part of moral duty to gratify the lusts of the impure, or the malice of the devilish, as to please the pure and the benevolent, and win the approval of the best and wisest of mankind.—*Birks*, '*Moral Science*,' p. 232.

It is said that since morality depends upon the calculus of happiness, since men's conceptions of happiness vary within almost indefinite limits, and since the tendency of actions to produce particular kinds of happiness is only to be discovered by examining a vast variety of complex phenomena which elude all scientific inquiry, the rules which result must necessarily be arbitrary or indefinitely fluctuating. If at one moment they take one shape, there is no assignable reason why they should not take another at any other time or place. Since, again, we start from individual conceptions of happiness, and we have no more reason for assigning special importance to the judgment of one man than to that of any other, or of preferring the estimate of the saint to the estimate of the sinner, the standard which results from the average judgment must be an inferior or debasing standard.—*Stephen*, '*Science of Ethics*,' p. 358.

Temperance will, as a rule, procure a man most pleasure, because it will make him healthy; but if he were certain to die to-morrow, he might get most pleasure by being drunk to-night. It will make him fitter for work, and, therefore, as a rule, secure him a more comfortable position; but in particular cases, it might lose him the favour of some immoral person who could do him a service.—*Stephen*, '*Science of Ethics*,' p 432.

The moral character of motive is destroyed.

The search after motive is one of the prominent causes of men's bewilderment in the investigation of questions of morals. This is a pursuit in which every moment employed is a moment wasted. All motives are abstractedly good. No man has ever had, can, or could have a motive different from the pursuit of pleasure or the shunning of pain.—*Bentham*, '*Deontology*,' i. 126.

The motive has nothing to do with the morality of the action, though much with the worth of the agent.—*Mill*, '*Utilitarianism*,' p. 26.

According to Bentham, there is but one motive possible, the pursuit of our own enjoyment. The most virtuous, the most vicious, and the most indifferent of actions, if measured by this test, would be exactly the same, and an investigation of motives should therefore be altogether excluded from our moral judgments.—*Lecky*, '*European Morals*,' i. 39.

Utilitarianism cannot attain to a theory of benevolence.

A theory of benevolence is logically unattainable under a utilitarian system. Since Bentham's time, Utilitarianism has given prominence to benevolence, making 'The greatest happiness of the greatest number' its standard of rectitude. But in this it has amended its ethical form only by the sacrifice of logical consistency. If happiness is the sole end of life, it must be the happiness of that life to which it is the end. To make the happiness of others the end of individual life, is to leave the utilitarian basis, by deserting the theory of life on which it rests. Utilitarianism is in the very singular position of professing itself a theory of universal benevolence, and yet laying its foundations on the ground that personal happiness is the sole end of life. As long as it maintains that 'pleasure and freedom from pain are the only things desirable as ends,' the maxim must mean that these are the only things desirable as ends for each individual, and here its Moral Philosophy must end. To do good to others for the sake of our own happiness, is, however, compatible with the theory; but this is not benevolence, and whatever honour belongs to the propounder of such a theory may be fairly claimed for Hobbes.—*Calderwood*, '*Moral Philosophy*,' p. 136.

As a theory it is essentially selfish.

This theory, refined and imposing as it may appear, is still essentially a selfish one. Even when sacrificing all earthly objects through love of virtue, the good man is simply seeking his greatest enjoyment, indulging a kind of mental luxury, which gives him more pleasure than what he foregoes, just as the miser finds more pleasure in accumulation than in any form of expenditure.—*Lecky*, '*European Morals*,' i. 31.

It implies a calculation immoral in its nature.

The doctrine which assumes that pleasures are to be courted simply because they please, and suffering to be avoided simply because it is painful, turns a mere animal instinct into a fundamental rule of moral arithmetic. On what warrant is this rule assumed? First principles, we are told, must be clear and evident, like the axioms of mathematics. And then it is assumed, in the next paragraph, that pleasures of disease, of vice, and malevolence, are to enter into our calculation side by side with the pleasures of Christian piety or social kindness, and must weigh equally in the scale if their amount or quantity be the same. But a calculation of results, based on such a confusion of moral opposites, is immoral in its own nature. Instead of founding a system of genuine ethics, it may be said to involve a guilty and fatal apotheosis of vice, disease, and folly. All reckoning of moral consequences is the use of a high and noble faculty of man's being. It is not a lawless process, to be conducted by the capricious decisions of an erring philosophy, when it confounds or denies distinctions on which the foundations of morality depend. It is subject to laws of moral duty. The pleasures to be compared must be tried by a higher standard than of their seeming intensity alone. Factors introduced by human vice and folly must be thrown aside, since they only tend to lower the tone of thought, and to prevent any true solution of a hard problem. For surely it is no less immoral to accept the diseased pleasures of others, their corrupt and malevolent passions, or their gross and sensual practices, for positive elements to guide my actions by an attempt to increase and enlarge them, than to indulge the like pleasures in my own person.—*Birks*, '*Moral Science*,' p. 274.

It implies an impossible calculation.

Notwithstanding the claim of great precision which utilitarian writers so boastfully make, the standard by which they profess to measure morals is itself absolutely incapable of definition or accurate explanation. Happiness is one of the most indeterminate and undefinable words in the language, and what are the conditions of 'the greatest possible happiness,' no one can precisely say. No two nations, perhaps no two individuals, would find them the same.—*Lecky*, '*European Morals*,' i. 40.

Pleasure is essentially subjective and individual, and hence incapable of measurement. This is shown by the doubts and difficulties which accompany all attempts to construct a 'scientific' Hedonism. Our estimates of our own past experience of pleasure and pain are neither definite nor consistent; still less can we appropriate the past experience of others.—*Ryland*, '*Handbook of Moral Philosophy*,' p. 127.

The calculation, viewed on the side of science, is impossible. It requires the summation of an infinite series. And the series is one of which the laws, as borrowed from experience only, are so immensely complex, that we cannot be sure even of a rude approach to its total value, by attempting to add together a few of its nearest terms. We cannot tell by such means whether it may not prove divergent, so that negative terms of greater amount may render futile our poor attempts to find its approximate value. And the infinity is not of a single, but of a double and triple kind. We have to trace out the results of the proposed action, not for a few hours or days only, but through a whole lifetime, or to distant generations, and throughout the life to come. We have to sum them up by the theory, not with regard to ourselves alone, but to the whole family of mankind, and even to the countless numbers of generations still unborn. We must further trace them in connection with the immense variety of possible pains and pleasures, and their degrees of intensity. Each of the fifteen classes which Bentham has enumerated admits clearly of an almost countless diversity, not only in the strength of each conceivable form of pain and pleasure, but in the elements out of which they arise, and which must vary, more or less, with the moral antecedent which the problem requires us to determine.

The summation required is not only of an infinite series, with a threefold infinity of time, of persons, and of elements. It is also one of quantities wholly incommensurable. In geometry we may form a sum of numbers, or of lines, or of surfaces, or of cubical space. But we cannot form a sum of numbers with lines, or of lines with surfaces, or of surfaces with solid space of three dimensions. In each case a wide chasm of unlikeness or infinitude separates the proposed elements from each other. And in the moral problem, as proposed by utilitarian theories, the difficulty is just the same. It is owned by one of the latest advocates and revisers of the system that pleasures may differ in quality as well as quantity, and the admission is said to be quite consistent with the maintenance of the general system. The concession is candid and just But the apology which attends it, for a master and teacher of logic, is most illogical The essence and foundation of the theory is, that the rightness or wrongness of actions must be determined by a summation of all the pains and pleasure which they generate, or to which they lead. But if these pleasures are owned to differ in quality as well as mere amount, the problem is either owned to be impracticable, or else completely changes its form —*Birks*, '*Moral Science*,' pp 276–8

Practical Objections

It furnishes no sufficient test of virtue

Does utilitarianism furnish a sufficient test of virtuous acts and of virtuous motives? It tells us that a good deed is one tending to promote the greatest happiness of the greatest number But in the complicated affairs of this world the most far-sighted cannot know for certain what may be the total consequences of any one act; and the great body of mankind feel as if they were looking out on a tangled forest, and need a guide to direct them. Utilitarian moralists, like Bentham, may draw out schemes of tendencies for us; but the specific rules have no obliging authority, and, even when understood and appreciated, are difficult of application, and are ever bringing us into cross avenues into which we may be led by self-deceit.—*M'Cosh*, '*Examination of Mill*,' p 373

If the excellence of virtue consists solely in its utility or tendency to promote the happiness of men, a machine, a fertile field, or a navigable river would all possess in a very high degree the element of virtue. If we restrict the term to human actions which are useful to society, we should still be compelled to canonise a crowd of acts which are utterly remote from all our ordinary notions of Morality. — *Lecky*, '*European Morals*,' i. 38.

Nor any sufficient test of sin.

What is sin, according to utilitarianism? It is acknowledged not to be the mere omission to look to the general good What then does it consist in? Mr. Mill speaks of 'reproach' being one of the checks on evil; but when is reproach justifiable? Not knowing what to make of sin, the system provides no place for repentance The boundary line between moral good and evil is drawn so uncertainly, that persons will ever be tempted to cross it without allowing that they have done so,—the more so that they are not told what they should do when they have crossed it.—*M'Cosh*, '*Examination of Mill*,' p 377

It degrades friendship

Where can there be a place for friendship, or who can be a friend to any one, whom he does not love 'ipsum propter ipsum,' himself for his own sake? What is it to love, but to wish any one to be enriched with the greatest benefits, even though there should be no return from those benefits to him who desires them? But it benefits me, you may say, to be of that disposition. Nay, perhaps, to *seem* to have it For you cannot *be* such, unless you *are* such And how can you be such unless that love itself has possession of you? And this comes to pass, not by introducing the conception of its usefulness, but it is born of itself, and springs up of its own accord But you say, I follow utility. Thy friendship then will last, so long as some gain shall follow it, and if utility makes a friendship, the same will unmake and destroy it.—*Cicero*, '*De Fin.*,' ii 24.

Criticisms of Hedonism, from the British Hegelian standpoint.

Hedonism, opposed to moral consciousness.

When moral persons without a theory on the matter are told that the moral end for the individual and the race is the getting a maximum surplusage of pleasurable feeling, and that there is nothing in the world which has the smallest moral value except this end and the means to it, there is no gainsaying that they repudiate such a result. They feel that there are things 'we should choose even if no pleasure come from them;' and then, if we choose these things, being good, for ourselves, then we must choose them also for the race, if we care for the race as we do for ourselves. We may be told, indeed, that a vulgar objection of this sort is founded on a misunderstanding; but we believe that never, except on a misunderstanding, has the moral consciousness in any case acquiesced in Hedonism. And we must say, I think, that, supposing it possible that Hedonism could be worked, yet common moral opinion is decided against its being what it professes to be, a sufficient account of morals.—*Bradley, 'Ethical Studies,'* p. 81.

Illusory nature of the Hedonistic end.

Pleasures are a perishing series. This one comes, and the intense self-feeling proclaims satisfaction. It is gone, and *we* are not satisfied. It was not that one, then, but this one now; and this one now is gone. It was not that one, then, but another and another; but another and another do not give us what we want: we are still left eager and confident, till the flush of feeling dies down, and when it is gone there is nothing left. We are where we began, so far as the getting happiness goes; and we have not found ourselves, and we are not satisfied.

This is common experience, and it is the practical refutation of Hedonism, or of the seeking happiness in pleasure. Happiness for the ordinary man means neither a pleasure nor a number of pleasures. It means in general the finding of himself, or the satisfaction of himself as a whole; and in particular it means the realisation of his concrete ideal of life. '*This* is happiness,' he says, not identifying happiness with one pleasure or a number of them, but understanding by it, '*in* this is become fact what I have at heart.' But the Hedonist has said, Happiness is pleasure, and the Hedonist knows that happiness is a whole. How, then, if pleasures make no system, if they are a number of perishing particulars, can the whole that is sought in them be found? It is the old question, how find the universal in mere particulars? And the answer is the old answer, In their sum. The self is to be found, happiness is to be realised, in the sum of the moments of the feeling self. The practical direction is, get *all* pleasures, and you will have got happiness; and we saw above its well-known practical issue in weariness and dissatisfaction.—*Bradley, 'Ethical Studies,'* pp. 87, 88.

Summary of Objections against Utilitarianism.

1. The radical doctrine of Utilitarianism, viz., that Pleasure is the '*summum bonum*,' is erroneous. For—

(1.) Pleasure is not the natural, universal, and supreme end of the actions of a moral being.

(2.) If Pleasure is not the proper end of individual life, it cannot be that of the life of society.

(3.) Pleasure cannot be deemed the highest end contemplated by the government of God.

2. The Utilitarian test is one impossible to apply.

(1.) What pleasures are to be calculated?

(2.) Whose pleasures are to be taken into account?

(3.) Are the pleasures of men to be regarded without reference to their character?

(4.) How are we to estimate the pleasures of people in different stages of moral development?

(5.) How are pleasures to be weighed against pleasures, and how are pleasures and pains to be compared?

(6.) How far is it justifiable to inflict pain, if there is a prospect that an excess of pleasure may ensue?

(7.) It is often impossible so to calculate the consequences of actions as to foretell what pleasures and what pains will follow.

(8.) Who shall be intrusted with the responsible offices of estimating and foretelling consequences, and so of deciding what conduct is virtuous and praiseworthy, and what is not?

(9.) There is an obvious ambiguity in the expression, 'The greatest happiness of the greatest number.'

3. Utilitarianism misapprehends the relations between Virtue and Pleasure

(1.) There is no logical pathway from pure Hedonism to the Utilitarian doctrine.

(2.) It is not a fact that all virtuous action tends to promote immediate happiness, *i. e.*, in this world

(3.) Utilitarianism bases Morality far too much upon the passive nature of man—upon his sentiency and capacity for enjoyment.

(4.) In this life pleasures and pains are not apportioned in consonance with the character and deserts of men

4. Utilitarianism gives no explanation of the Moral Imperative, the 'ought.'—*Thomson*, '*Utilitarianism*,' pp 23–42 (condensed).

VII. ALTRUISM.

What it is.

Definition.

We define Altruism as being all action, which, in the normal course of things, benefits others, instead of benefiting self.—*Spencer*, '*Data of Ethics*,' p. 201.

A man is altruistic who loves his neighbour as himself, who gives money to the poor which he might have spent in luxury; who leaves house and home to convert savages, who sacrifices health to comfort prisoners, or suffers in a plague-stricken city. Sir Philip Sidney was altruistic when he gave the cup of water to the wounded soldier, instead of slaking his own dying thirst. Such deeds make our nerves tingle at the hearing, and ennoble the dreary wastes of folly and selfishness recorded in history.—*Stephen*, '*Science of Ethics*,' p. 220.

Comte identifies altruism with morality

The state of altruism is what Comte means by '*Morality*.' Any being, actuated by benevolent instincts, is *ipso facto* a *moral* being. And if to this condition he adds the imaginative contemplation of a perfect social future, in which the same disposition shall nowhere fail, he is thereby constituted a *religious* being.—*Martineau*, '*Types of Ethical Theory*,' i 425

Altruistic sentiments.

Intelligent creatures that live in presence of one another, and are exposed to like causes of pleasure and pain, acquire capacities for participating in one another's pleasures and pains. As a society advances in organisation, the inter-dependence of its parts increases, and the well-being of each is more bound up with the well-being of all, there results the growth of feelings which find satisfaction in the well-being of all. The feelings thus described are the altruistic sentiments, they are the unselfish emotions.—*Spencer*, '*Psychology*,' ii. 609, 610.

Leading forms of altruistic sentiment.

The simpler forms are. (1.) Unmixed generosity—the sentiment of generosity proper, where there is no contemplation of a reward to be reaped from the benefaction. (2.) The sentiment of pity—the feeling which prompts endeavours to mitigate pain, being itself a pain constituted by representation of pain in another. This sympathy with pain puts a check on the intentional infliction of pain, it prompts efforts to assuage pain that is already being borne.

The more complex forms are:—(1.) The sentiment of justice. This sentiment consists of representations of those emotions which others feel, when actually or prospectively forbidden the activities by which pleasures are to be gained or pains escaped. (2.) The sentiment of mercy—the state of consciousness in which the execution of an act prompted by the sentiment of justice is prevented by an out-balancing pity—by a representation of the suffering to be inflicted.—*Spencer*, '*Psychology*,' ii. 613–23 (condensed).

To the Positivist the object of morals is to make our sympathetic instincts preponderate as far as possible over the selfish instincts, social feelings over personal feelings. This way of viewing the subject is peculiar to the new philosophy, for no other system has included the more recent additions to the theory of human nature, of which Catholicism gave so imperfect a representation.—*Comte*, '*Positive Polity*,' i. 73.

Based upon sympathy.

Sympathy is not identical with altruism, but it is the essential condition of altruism. I cannot be truly altruistic, that is, until the knowledge of another man's pain is painful to me. That is the groundwork of the more complex sentiments which are involved in all truly moral conduct, morality implying the existence of certain desires which have for their immediate object the happiness of others.—*Stephen*, '*Science of Ethics*,' p. 239.

Its Development.

A gradual advance.

In the parental instinct, with the actions it prompts, we have the primordial altruism; while in sympathy, with the actions it prompts, we have the developed altruism.

As there has been an advance by degrees from unconscious parental altruism [as in reproduction by fission or gemmation] to conscious parental altruism [as in material sacrifices of parents for children] of the highest kind, so there has been an advance by degrees from the altruism of the family to social altruism. Only where family altruism has been most fostered, has social altruism become conspicuous. In the Aryan family we see that family feeling, first extending itself to the gens and the tribe, and afterwards to the society formed of related tribes, prepared the way for fellow-feeling among citizens not of the same stock.—*Spencer*, '*Psychology*,' ii. 626; '*Data of Ethics*,' 204, 205.

By the growth of imagination.

A sympathetic consciousness of human welfare at large is furthered by making altruistic actions habitual. Both this special and the general sympathetic consciousness become stronger and wider in proportion as the power of mental representation increases, and the imagination of consequences, immediate and remote, grows more vivid and comprehensive.—*Spencer*, '*Psychology*,' ii. 621.

Altruistic sentiments tend to become more complicated.

A reciprocal excitement between sympathy and the tender emotion must be recognised as habitually complicating altruistic sentiments of all kinds. Wherever there exists the tender emotion, the sympathies are more easily excited, and wherever sympathy, pleasurable or painful, has been aroused, more or less of the tender emotion is awakened along with them. This communion arises inevitably. The primordial altruism and the developed altruism naturally become connected. Remote as are their roots, they grow inextricably entangled, because the circumstances which arouse them have in common the relation of benefactor to beneficiary.—*Spencer*, '*Psychology*,' ii. 626.

Its Relation to Egoism.

Egoism precedes altruism.

A creature must live before it can act. From this it is a corollary that the acts by which each maintains his own life must, speaking generally, precede in imperativeness all other acts of which he is capable. That is to say, Ethics has to recognise the truth, that egoism comes before altruism. Unless each duly cares for himself, his care for all others is ended by death; and if each thus dies, there remain no others to be cared for. Little account as our ethical reasonings take of it, yet is the fact obvious that since happiness and misery are infectious, such regard for self as conduces to health and high spirits is a benefaction to others, and such disregard of self as brings on suffering, bodily or mental, is a malefaction to others. The individual who is inadequately egoistic loses more or less of his ability to be altruistic. And from self-abnegation in excess there results, not only an inability to help others, but the infliction of positive burdens on them.—*Spencer*, '*Data of Ethics*,' pp. 187, 194, 198.

The egoistic aspect of altruistic pleasure.

Whether knowingly or unknowingly gained, the state of mind accompanying altruistic action, being a pleasurable state, is to be counted in the sum of pleasures which the individual can receive; and in this sense cannot be other than egoistic. As every other agreeable emotion raises the tide of life, so does the agreeable emotion which accompanies a benevolent deed. The joy felt in witnessing others' joy exalts the vital functions, and so gives a greater capacity for pleasures in general.—*Spencer*, '*Data of Ethics*,' 214.

Personal welfare depends on the growth of altruistic sentiments.

Personal welfare depends on due regard for the welfare of others. The man who, expending his energies wholly on private affairs refuses to take trouble about public affairs, is blind to the fact that his own business is made possible only by the maintenance of a healthy social state, and that he loses all round by defective governmental arrangements. Where there are many like-minded with himself—where, as a consequence, office comes to be filled by political adventurers and opinion is swayed by demagogues—where bribery vitiates the administration of law and makes fraudulent State-transactions habitual; heavy penalties fall on the community at large, and, among others, on those who have thus done everything for self and nothing for society. Their investments are insecure; recovery of their debts is difficult; and even their lives are less safe than they would otherwise have been.

In the same way, each has a private interest in public morals, and profits by improving them. Indeed the improvement of others, physically, intellectually, and morally, personally concerns each; since their imperfections tell in raising the cost of all the commodities he buys, in increasing the taxes and rates he pays, and in the losses of time, trouble, and money, daily brought on him by others' carelessness, stupidity, and unconscientiousness.—*Spencer*, '*Data of Ethics*,' 205, 208, 211.

Whether one member suffer, all the members suffer with it; or one member be honoured, all the members rejoice with it.—*St. Paul*, 1 *Cor.* xii. 26.

Wherefore lift up the hands that hang down, and the palsied knees; and make straight paths for your feet, that that which is lame be not turned out of the way, but rather be healed. Looking carefully lest there be any man that falleth short of the grace of God; lest any root of bitterness springing up trouble you, and thereby the many be defiled.—*Heb.* xii. 12, 13, 15.

VIII. SOCIALISM.

Definition.

The word Socialism, which originated among the English Communists, and was assumed by them as a name to designate their own doctrine, is now, on the Continent, employed in a larger sense; not necessarily implying Communism, or the entire abolition of private property, but applied to any system which requires that the land and the instruments of production should be the property, not of individuals, but of communities or associations, or of the government.—*Mill*, '*Political Economy*,' bk. ii. ch. i. sec. 2.

The Problem of Socialism.

The foundation of all socialistic claims is the assertion that the effect of the present social system is to increase inequality, the condition of the labourers becoming daily worse, while the wealth of the capitalists and landowners is always augmenting.—*Laveleye*, '*Socialism of To-day*,' p. xxxvii.

There are deep wrongs in the present constitution of society, but they are not wrongs inherent in the constitution of man, nor in those social laws which are as truly the laws of the Creator as are the laws of the physical universe. They are wrongs resulting from bad adjustments which it is within our power to amend. The ideal social state is not that in which each gets an equal amount of wealth, but in which each gets in proportion to his contribution to the general stock. And in such a social state there would not be less incentive than now; there would be far more incentive. Men will be more industrious and more moral, better workmen and better citizens, if each takes his earnings and carries them home to his family, than when they put their earnings in a pot, and gamble for them until some have far more than they have earned, and others have little or nothing.—*George*, '*Social Problems*,' p. 77.

Socialists maintain that the means of production are already great enough to furnish all men with a sufficient competency, if only the produce were more evenly divided; and indeed, if the number of things are reckoned up which are either useless or superfluous, or even harmful, but which monopolise so large a portion of the working hours, it may well be thought that were those hours exclusively employed in the creation of useful things, there would be enough to satisfy largely the needs of all. Inequality gives rise to superfluity and luxury, which divert capital and labour from the production of necessaries; hence the destitution of the masses. 'Were there no luxury,' said Rousseau, 'there would be no poor.' 'The fact that many men are occupied in making clothes for one individual, is the cause of there being many people without clothes' (Montesquieu).—*Laveleye*, '*Socialism of To-day*,' Introd., xl.

France the Birthplace of Modern Socialism.

It was from France that came the first ideas of social transformation and revolution. This was recognised by Karl Marx, the most learned of German socialists. 'The emancipation of Germany will be that of all humanity,' he wrote in a review, some numbers of which appeared in Paris in 1844, 'but when all is ready in Germany, the insurrection will only wake at the crowing of the Gallic cock.'—*Laveleye*, '*Socialism of To-day*,' p. 7.

Socialism of Fourier (b. 1772 in Besançon).

The central idea of Fourier's social scheme is association. The all-pervading attraction which he discovered draws man to man and reveals the will of God. It is passionate attraction—*attraction passionée*. It urges men to union. This law of attraction is universal and eternal, but men have thrown obstacles in its way so that it has not had free course. Consequently, we have been driven into wrong and abnormal paths. When we return to right ways—when we follow the directions given us by attraction, as indicated in our twelve passions or desires—universal harmony will again reign, economic goods—an indispensable condition of human development—will be obtained in abundance. Products will be increased many fold, owing, first, to the operation of the passion to labour and to benefit society; secondly, to the economy of associated effort.—*Ely*, '*French and German Socialism*,' p. 91.

His classification of the passions.

Since happiness and misery depend upon the latitude allowed our passions—our propensities—it is necessary to enumerate these. They are divided into three classes—the one class tending to *luxe*, *luxisme*, luxury; the second tending to groups; the third to series. By *luxe* is meant the gratification of the desires of the five senses—hearing, seeing, feeling, tasting, smelling—each one constituting a passion. These are sensual in the original sense of the word, or sensitive. Four passions tend to groups—namely, amity or friendship, love, paternity or the family feeling (familism), and ambition. These are effective. The three remaining passions are distributive, and belong to the series. They are the passions called *cabaliste*, *papillonne*, and *composite*. The passion *cabaliste* is the desire for intrigue, for planning and contriving. It is strong in women and the ambitious. In itself it would tend to destroy the unity of social life, as would also the passion of *papillonne*, or *alternate* (the love of change). These are, however, harmonised by the passion *composite* (the desire of union). All twelve passions unite together into the one mighty, all-controlling impulse called *unitéisme*, which is the love felt for others united in society, and is a passion unknown save in civilisation.—*Ely*, '*French and German Socialism*,' pp. 91, 92.

St. Simonism.

The St. Simonism scheme does not contemplate an equal, but an unequal division of the produce; it does not propose that all should be occupied alike, but differently, according to their vocation or capacity; the function of each being assigned, like grades in a regiment, by the choice of the directing authority, and the remuneration being by salary, proportioned to the importance, in the eyes of that authority, of the function itself, and the merits of the person who fulfils it. For the constitution of the ruling body, different plans might be adopted, consistently with the essentials of the system. It might be appointed by popular suffrage. In the idea of the original authors, the rulers were supposed to be persons of genius and virtue, who obtained the voluntary adhesion of the rest by the force of mental superiority.—*Mill*, '*Political Economy*,' bk. ii. chap. i. sec. 4.

Socialism in Germany.

Fichte.

To find the first manifestations of modern socialism in Germany, we must refer back to Kant's most famous disciple Fichte, who was inspired by the idea of the French Revolution, as he himself declares. In his 'Materials for the Justification of the French Revolution,' he writes: 'Property can have no other origin than labour. Whoever does not work has no right to obtain the means of existence from society.' In 1796, he proclaimed 'the right to property.' He says, in his 'Principles of Natural Right': 'Whosoever has not the means of living is not bound to recognise or respect the property of others, seeing that, as regards him, the principles of the social contract have been violated. Every one should have some property; society owes to all the means of work, and all should work in order to live.'—*Laveleye*, '*Socialism of To-day*,' p. 7.

Ferdinand Lasalle.

German socialism is, it is hardly too much to say, the creation of Ferdinand Lasalle. Of course there were socialists in Germany before Lasalle. Fichte, to go no further back, had taught it from the standpoint of the speculative philosopher and philanthropist. Schleiermacher, it may be remembered, was brought up in a religious community that practised it. Weitling, with some allies, preached it in a pithless and hazy way as a gospel to the poor, and, finding little encouragement, went to America to work it out experimentally there. The young Hegelians made it part of their philosophic creed. The Silesian weavers, superseded by machinery and perishing for want of work, raised it as a wild inarticulate cry for bread, and dignified it with the sanction of tears and blood. And Karl Marx and Friedrich Engels, in 1848, summoned the proletariate of the whole world to make it the aim and instrument of a universal revolution. But it was Lasalle who first really brought it from the clouds, and made it a living historical force in the common politics of the day.—*Rae*, '*Contemporary Socialism*,' pp. 64, 65.

Private Ownership of Land affirmed to be Unjust.

If we are all here by the equal permission of the Creator, we are all here with an equal title to the enjoyment of His bounty—with an equal right to the use of all that nature so impartially offers. This is a right which is natural and inalienable; it is a right which rests in every human being as he enters the world, and which, during his continuance in the world, can be limited only by the equal rights of others There is in Nature no such thing as a fee simple in land. There is on earth no power which can rightfully make a grant of exclusive ownership in land. If all existing men were to unite to grant away their equal rights, they could not grant away the right of those who follow them. For what are we but tenants of a day? Have we made the earth, that we should determine the rights of those who after us shall tenant it in their turn? The Almighty, who created the earth for man and man for the earth, has entailed it upon all the generations of the children of men by a decree written upon the constitution of all things,—a decree which no human action can bar and no prescription determine.—*George, 'Progress and Poverty,'* p 262.

Land Nationalisation asserted to be the only Remedy

There is but one way to remove an evil, and that is, to remove its cause Poverty deepens as wealth increases, and wages are forced down while productive power grows, because land, which is the source of all wealth and the field of all labour, is monopolised To extirpate property, to make wages what justice commands they should be, the full earnings of the labourer, we must, therefore, substitute for the individual ownership of land a common ownership. Nothing else will go to the cause of the evil, in nothing else is there the slightest hope

This, then, is the remedy for the unjust and unequal distribution of wealth apparent in modern civilisation, and for all the evils which flow from it—*we must make land common property*.—*George, 'Progress and Poverty,'* p. 52.

Socialism and Christianity.

Communism of the Early Christians affirmed

Modern Communists, with their sympathisers, affirm that Communism was the natural outcome of the Law of Equality implied in Christ's teaching That the principle did not hold its ground is ascribed by them to the ambition and worldliness of the Church as she increased in power, especially after her official recognition as the state religion of the Roman Empire. After this alliance with wealth and grandeur, they say the Church rapidly departed from the simplicity of the gospel, and consoled herself by the acquisition of temporal aggrandisement for her disappointment in not attaining to the long-deferred hope of a final 'restitution of all things.'—*Kaufmann, 'Socialism and Communism,'* p 11.

Jesus Christ Himself not only proclaimed, preached, and prescribed Communism as a consequence of fraternity, but practised it with His apostles.—*Cabet, quoted by Kaufmann*

Denied

On the other hand, the defenders of the principle of individual property as opposed to Communism (which in their opinion is 'a mutiny against society'), deny that the Church ever sanctioned officially, or that her Founder ever recommended, such a custom as that of 'having all things in common.'—*Kaufmann, 'Socialism and Communism,'* p. 11

Irreligious character of modern socialism.

Most contemporary socialists have turned their backs on religion They sometimes speak of it with a kind of suppressed and settled bitterness, as of a friend that has proved faithless: 'We are not atheists, we have simply done with God.' They seem to feel that, if there be a God, He is at any rate no God for them, that He is the God of the rich, and cares nothing for the poor, and there is a vein of most touching though most illogical reproach in their hostility towards a Deity whom they yet declare to have no existence They say in their hearts, There is no God, or only one whom they decline to serve, for He is no friend to the labouring man, and has never all these centuries done anything for him This atheism seems as much matter of class antipathy as of free-thought; and the semi-political element in it lends a peculiar bitterness to the socialistic attacks on religion and the Church, which are regarded as main pillars of the established order of things, and irreconcilable obstructives to all socialistic dreams —*Rae*, '*Contemporary Socialism*,' p 239.

God not the author of social distress.

Though it may take the language of prayer, it is blasphemy that attributes to the inscrutable decrees of Providence the suffering and brutishness that come of poverty; that turns with folded hands to the All-Father, and lays on Him the responsibility for the want and crime of our great cities. We degrade the Everlasting We slander the Just One A merciful man would have better ordered the world, a just man would crush with his foot such an ulcerous ant-hill! It is not the Almighty, but we who are responsible for the vice and misery that fester amid our civilisation. The Creator showers upon us His gifts—more than enough for all. But like swine scrambling for food, we tread them in the mire—tread them in the mire, while we tear and rend each other. — *George*, '*Progress and Poverty*,' p. 424.

Christian Socialism

F. D. Maurice.

His great wish was to Christianise Socialism, not to Christian-Socialise the universe. He believed that there were great truths involved in the principle of co-operation which were essentially Christian truths; and that as these had acquired a bad name because of the falsehoods that were mixed up with them, it was pre-eminently the business of a man who was set to preach truth to face the personal obloquy that would attend the task of separating the true from the false, and defending the true.—'*Life of F. D. Maurice*,' ii 41

God's order seems to me more than ever the antagonist of man's systems; Christian Socialism is in my mind the assertion of God's order Every attempt, however small and feeble, to bring it forth, I honour and desire to assist Every attempt to hide it under a great machinery, I must protest against, as hindering the gradual development of what I regard as a divine purpose, as an attempt to create a new constitution of society, when what we want is that the old constitution should exhibit its true functions and energies.—*Maurice*, *Letter to Mr. Ludlow*, '*Life, &c.*,' ii 44

C. Kingsley.

The true 'Reformer's Guide,' the true poor man's book, the true 'Voice of God against tyrants, idlers, and humbugs, is the Bible.' The Bible demands for the poor as much, and more, than they demand for themselves; it expresses the deepest yearnings of the poor man's heart far more nobly, more searchingly, more daringly, more eloquently than any modern orator has done I say, it gives a ray of hope, say rather a certain dawn of a glorious future, such as no universal suffrage, free trade, communism, organisation of labour. or any other Morrison's-pill-measure can give; and yet of a future which will embrace all that is good in these,—a future of conscience, of justice, of freedom, when idlers and oppressors shall no more dare to plead parchment and Acts of Parliament for their iniquities. I say, the Bible promises this, not in a few places only, but throughout; it is the thought which runs through the whole Bible—justice from God to those whom men oppress, glory from God to those whom men despise Does that look like the invention of tyrants and prelates? The Bible is the poor man's comfort and the rich man's warning —*Parson Lot*, '*Letters to the Chartists*,' Letter II

George.

"The poor ye have always with you" If ever a scripture has been wrested to the devil's service, this is that scripture How often have these words been distorted from their obvious meaning to soothe conscience into acquiescence in human misery and degradation—to bolster that blasphemy, the very negation and denial of Christ's teachings, that the All Wise and Most Merciful, the Infinite Father, has decreed that so many of His creatures must be poor, in order that others of His creatures to whom He wills the good things of life should enjoy the pleasure and virtue of doling out alms! "The poor ye have always with you," said Christ, but all His teachings supply the limitation, 'until the coming of the Kingdom' In that Kingdom of God *on earth*, that Kingdom of justice and love for which He taught His followers to strive and pray, there will be no poor But though the faith and the hope and the striving for this Kingdom are of the very essence of Christ's teaching, the staunchest disbelievers and revilers of its possibility are found among those who call themselves Christians —'*Social Problems*,' p. 104

The Millennium of Christian Socialism

With want destroyed; with greed changed to noble passions, with the fraternity that is born of equality taking the place of the jealousy and fear that now array men against each other, with mental power loosed by conditions that give to the humblest comfort and leisure; and who shall measure the heights to which our civilisation may soar? Words fail the thought! It is the Golden Age, of which poets have sung and high-raised seers have told in metaphor! It is the glorious vision which has always haunted man with gleams of fitful splendour. It is what he saw whose eyes at Patmos were closed in a trance It is the culmination of Christianity—the City of God on earth, with its walls of jasper and its gates of pearl! It is the reign of the Prince of Peace!—*George*, '*Progress and Poverty*,' p. 426.

Errors of Socialism

As to value of individual interest.

The fundamental error of most Socialists is not taking sufficient account of the fact that individual interest is the indispensable incentive to labour and economy It is true that minds purified by the elevated principles of religion or philosophy act upon sentiments of charity, devotion, and honour; but for the regular production of wealth the stimulus of personal interest and responsibility is needed —*Laveleye*, '*Socialism*,' p. 43.

As to social value of private property

Socialists ignore the civilising value of private property and inheritance, because they think of property only as a means of immediate enjoyment, and not as a means of progress and moral development They would allow private property only in what is termed consumers' wealth You might still own your clothes, or even purchase your house and garden But producers' wealth, they hold, should be common property, and neither be owned nor inherited by individuals If this theory were to be enforced, it would be fatal to progress Private property has all along been a great factor in civilisation, but the private property that has been so has been much more producers' than consumers'. Consumers' wealth is a limited instrument of enjoyment, producers' is a power of immense capability in the hands of the competent. Socialists are really more individualistic than their opponents, in the view they take of the function of property. They look upon it purely as a means for gratifying the desires of individuals, and ignore the immense social value it possesses as a nurse of the industrial virtues, and an agency in the progressive development of society from generation to generation —*Rae*, '*Contemporary Socialism*,' p 387

Socialism would destroy freedom

Under a *régime* of Socialism freedom would be choked. Take, for example, a point of great importance both for personal and for social development, the choice of occupations Socialism promises a free choice of occupations; but that is vain, for the relative numbers that are now required in any particular occupation are necessarily determined by the demands of the consumers for the particular commodity the occupation in question sets itself to supply. Freedom of choice is, therefore, limited at present by natural conditions, which cause no murmuring; but these natural conditions would still exist under the socialist *régime*, and yet they would perforce appear in the guise of legal and artificial restrictions. It would be the choice of the State that would determine who should enter the more desirable occupations, and not the choice of the individuals themselves. The same difficulties would attend the distribution of the fertile and the poor soils. Even consumption would not escape State inquisition and guidance, for an economy that pretended to do away with commercial vicissitudes must take care that a change of fashion does not extinguish a particular industry by superseding the articles it produces.—*Rae*, '*Contemporary Socialism*,' pp. 388, 389.

IX. INTUITIONISM.

(See under INTUITION, INTUITIONS.)

The Intuitional Theory of Morals.

'The fundamental assumption of this theory is that we have the power of seeing clearly, within a certain range, what actions are right and reasonable in themselves, apart from their consequences (except such consequences as are included in the notion of the acts). This power is commonly called the faculty of Moral Intuition.

'The term "Intuitional" is used to denote the method which recognises rightness as a quality belonging to actions independently of their conduciveness to any ulterior end. The term implies that the presence of the quality is ascertained by simply "looking at" the actions themselves, without considering their consequences.'—*Sidgwick*, '*Methods of Ethics*' (second edition), pp. 176, 185.

When we speak of an Intuitional Theory of Moral Distinctions, we mean that the Law which decides what is right is so connected with the nature of the Person, that the recognition of it is involved in intelligent self-direction. The knowledge is immediate, and its *source* is found within the mind itself. When we say of moral truth that it is self-evidencing, we mean that the Law carries in itself the evidence of its own truth. Taking Mr. Herbert Spencer's form, we may say it is 'indisputable.' Indisputability, however, may apply in two directions—to facts and to principles. The Moral Law affords an example of the latter. As to the *Validity* of the principle, the evidence of that lies in its own nature as a proposition or formulated truth. When we say that moral truth is its own warrant, we mean that it is by its nature an authoritative principle of conduct. Its credentials belong to its nature. Such laws of human conduct are 'the unwritten laws,' which Socrates says cannot be violated without punishment ('Mem.,' iv. 4, 13).—*Calderwood*, '*Moral Philosophy*,' p. 36.

'The moralists of the intuitive school, to state their opinions in the broadest form, believe that we have a natural power of perceiving that some qualities, such as benevolence, chastity, or veracity, are better than others, and that we ought to cultivate them, and to repress their opposites. In other words, they contend, that by the constitution of our nature, the notion of right carries with it a feeling of obligation; that is, to say, a course of conduct is our duty, is in itself, and apart from all consequences, an intelligible and sufficient reason for practising it; and that we derive the first principles of our duties from intuition.'

'They acknowledge indeed that the effect of actions upon the happiness of mankind forms a most important element in determining their moral quality, but they maintain that without natural moral perceptions we never should have known that it was our duty to seek the happiness of mankind when it diverged from our own, and they deny that virtue was either originally evolved from, or is necessarily proportioned to utility. Virtue, they believe, is something more than a calculation or a habit. It is impossible to conceive its fundamental principles reversed. Our judgments of it are not the results of elaborate or difficult deductions, but are simple, intuitive, and decisive.'—*Lecky, 'European Morals,'* i. 3, 71.

The Object of Moral Intuition

Individual actions, according to some.

Is it individual action that is in the first place apprehended to be right, and are all valid propositions in Ethics obtained by generalisation from such particular judgments? This was the 'induction' which Socrates used, his plan was to work towards the true definition of each ethical term by examining and comparing different instances of its application. The popular view of conscience seems to point to such a method, since the dictates of conscience are commonly thought to relate to particular actions. This inductive method may be called Instinctive Intuitionism.—*Ryland, 'Handbook, &c.,'* p. 120.

Our intuitions are perceptions of individual objects or individual truths; and in order to reach an axiom or 'principle of morals,' there is need of a discursive principle of generalisation. The proper account is that the law is generalised out of our direct perceptions. On the bare contemplation of an ungrateful spirit, the conscience at once declares it to be evil, apart from the conscious apprehension or application of any general principle. Our moral intuitions are not *à priori* forms, which the mind imposes on objects, but immediate perceptions of qualities in certain objects, that is, in the voluntary dispositions and actions of intelligent beings.—*M'Cosh, 'Examination of Mill,'* p. 365.

The cognitions which this method attempts to systematise are primarily direct intuitions of the moral qualities of particular kinds of actions, regarded for the most part in their external relations.—*Sidgwick, 'Methods of Ethics'* (second edition), p. 183.

Moral rules, according to others.

Another logical method followed by the typical Christian Moralists (Butler, &c.), assumes that we can discern general moral rules with clear and finally valid intuition. Such rules are sometimes called moral axioms, and compared with the axioms of geometry, in respect of definiteness, certainty, and self-evidence. Hence the method is deductive, a given action is brought under one of these rules, and then pronounced right or wrong. Mr. Sidgwick calls this Dogmatic Intuitionism.—*Ryland, 'Handbook, &c.,'* p. 121.

Moral principles, according to a third school.

Philosophic Intuitionism attempts to find some one or two principles from which these current moral rules may themselves be deduced, and thus reduced to a more systematic form. Such attempts have been made by Clarke, Kant, &c.—*Ryland, 'Handbook, &c.,'* p. 121.

What is Intuitively Apprehended?

Intuitional Moralists differ on this question. The following views have been held:—(1) The quality perceived is the rightness of actions, and the moral obligation to perform them (Butler); (2) Their goodness, or desirability; (3) Their moral beauty.—*Ryland, 'Handbook, &c.,'* p. 121.

The Ultimate Reason.

There are further differences as to the ultimate reason for doing what is intuitively ascertained to be right, *e.g.* (1) The reason for obeying it is contained in the intuition itself (Kant); (2) Conformity to the Divine Will (ordinary Christian Moralists); (3) Conformity to Nature (Shaftesbury). A word or two may be said of the first of these. The mere recognition that '*I ought* to do this' is the only adequate reason why I should do it, says Kant; if I do the action for any other reason, the act is not truly moral; it is only when we do what we ought *because* we ought, that we are truly moral. This bindingness of duty for its own sake alone, is what Kant calls the *Categorical* (as opposed to a hypothetical) *Imperative.*—*Ryland,* '*Handbook, &c.*,' p 122.

This Theory is in Harmony with Scripture.

The principle is also clearly recognised, that moral truths, apprehended by a moral faculty, are one main and essential part of the evidence of a Divine revelation. By this means alone can its reception be fully distinguished from mere credulity and blind superstition. There is an abundant appeal, it is true, to evidence of a lower and more sensible kind But even here the presence of a moral element is implied The miracles of Christ were themselves works of mercy, and parables of Divine grace; and the prophecies, to which appeal is made, are described with emphasis as the words of holy men, who spake under the impulse of the Holy Spirit of God. But in other cases this moral element in the testimony stands alone, and appears in fuller relief. 'Which of you convinceth Me of sin? and if I say the truth, why do ye not believe Me?' And the Apostle, treading in the steps of his Divine Master, describes the main object of his own preaching in those impressive words,—'By manifestation of the truth commending ourselves to every man's conscience in the sight of God.'—*Birks,* '*Moral Science,*' p. 190.

Some Objections answered.

Intuitionalists make happiness an end.

It is often said that intuitive moralists in their reasonings are guilty of continually abandoning their principles, by themselves appealing to the tendency of certain acts to promote human happiness as a justification, and the charge is usually accompanied by a challenge to show any confessed virtue that has not that tendency. To the first objection it may be shortly answered that no intuitive moralist ever dreamed of doubting that benevolence or charity, or, in other words, the promotion of the happiness of man, is a duty But, while he cordially recognises this branch of virtue, and while he has therefore a perfect right to allege the beneficial effects of a virtue in its defence, he refuses to admit that all virtue can be reduced to this single principle. He believes that chastity and truth have an independent value, distinct from their influence on happiness. [See also above.] —*Lecky,* '*European Morals,*' i 40

The Standards of excellence vary.

From the time of Locke, objections have been continually brought against the theory of natural moral perceptions, upon the ground that some actions which were admitted as lawful in one age have been regarded as immoral in another. All these become absolutely worthless, when it is perceived that in every age virtue has consisted in the cultivation of the same feelings, though the standards of excellence attained have been different.—*Lecky,* '*European Morals,*' p 113.

X. THE WILL OF GOD—THE MORAL LAW

The Laws of God

The Divine laws, or the laws of God, are laws set by God to His human creatures. They are laws or rules, *properly* so called.

As distinguished from duties imposed by human laws, duties imposed by the Divine laws may be called *religious duties*

As distinguished from violations of duties imposed by human laws, violations of religious duties are styled *sins*.

As distinguished from sanctions annexed to human laws, the sanctions annexed to the Divine laws may be called *religious sanctions.* They consist of the evils, or pains, which we may suffer here or hereafter, by the immediate appointment of God, and as *consequences* of breaking His commandments.—*Austin,* '*Jurisprudence,*' Lecture II., p. 106.

Revealed and Unrevealed Laws of God.

Of the Divine laws, or the laws of God, some are *revealed* or promulgated, and others are *unrevealed.* Such of the laws of

God as are unrevealed are not unfrequently denoted by the following names or phrases: 'the law of nature,' 'natural law,' 'the law manifested to man by the light of nature or reason,' 'the laws, precepts, or dictates of natural religion.'

With regard to the laws which God is pleased to *reveal*, the way wherein they are manifested is easily conceived They are *express* commands, portions of the *word* of God, commands signified to men through the medium of human language, and uttered by God directly or by servants whom He sends to announce them

Such of the Divine laws as are *unrevealed*, are laws set by God to His human creatures, but not through the medium of human language, or not expressly.—*Austin*, '*Jurisprudence*,' Lecture II, p. 107.

THE MORAL LAW

Its Nature.

Essential Characteristics.

Moral law is law given by an intelligent being to an intelligent being, to specify and determine his proper relations, first, to other intelligent beings, secondly, to non-intelligent creatures, thirdly, to unconscious things, and finally, to specify and determine his relations to the Lawgiver, in case of obedience on the one hand and of disobedience on the other Such law goes into force by virtue of the mere authority of the Lawgiver. Authority means the recognised right of one intelligent being to command another. Seeing that authority by itself moves only mental and moral forces, and not physical ones, the law assumes, on the part of those subjected to it, capacity, on the one hand, for comprehending its practical intent, and on the other, for complying with it, or refusing compliance It assumes, moreover, the existence in them of a conscience of right and wrong, and of the love of good and the dread of evil, and appeals to these as moving powers,—to the conscience by simple manifestation of the right and wrong, and to the hope and fear by the promise of good in the case of obedience, and the threat of evil in case of disobedience. The feeling of the superiority of right to wrong, awakened by simple presentation of the two in contrast, and the hope and fear awakened by the promise and the threat, constitute the working forces of the law, whereby to impel to obedience and draw off from disobedience.—*Arthur*, '*Physical and Moral Law*,' p. 115.

Moral laws are derived from the nature and will of God and the character and condition of man, and may be understood and adopted by man, as a being endowed with intelligence and will, to be the rules by which to regulate his actions. It is right to speak the truth Gratitude should be cherished. These things are in accordance with the nature and condition of man, and with the will of God—that is, they are in accordance with the moral law of conscience and of revelation.—*Fleming*, '*Vocab. of Phil.*,' p. 287.

Universality and necessity are provisions which are inseparable from the law of the good in our inner being, and without which it would not have the character of law. It manifests itself as *universally* binding; for whilst it addresses itself with its demands to the individual, it embraces at the same time the whole world of personality as binding upon all.—*Martensen*, '*Christian Ethics*,' i. 345.

The first way in which man becomes conscious of a higher union between morality and religion, is by recognising God as the author of the Moral Law and the Surety of its validity, and by acknowledging the moral law to be the rule according to which the divine will guides his life Leibnitz says, 'God is the only immediate and outward (*i.e.*, distinct from the subject) object of the soul—external objects of sense are but mediately and indirectly known.' This thought of Leibnitz is clearly in keeping with his system of fore-ordained harmony, but, as genius has often discovered truth when the premises from which it thought to arrive at it were false, this remark still contains a deep truth though its subjective presuppositions have long since been overthrown. If Leibnitz is right, God is also the only immediate object of our moral obligation, the foundation of all other obligations, every moral duty is a duty towards God, and whatever truly binds us in our conscience is the will of God; obedience to the law is obedience rendered to the living God, 'of whom, in whom, and to whom' we are. The relation in which the rational creature stands to God his Creator, when it is true and normal, is the first and closest; from Him all moral law of life springs, on Him it depends at every point of its development, and to Him it ever returns from its manifold determinations as to a fixed centre,—'from Him, in Him, and to Him.'—*Muller*, '*Christian Doctrine of Sin*,' i. 80, 81.

'All men must do so and so,' not all lawyers, or soldiers, or sailors must do. Of course, each man has special duties corresponding to his particular position in life. But this means simply that the same general principle is applicable in an indefinite variety of relations.—*Stephen*, '*Science of Ethics*,' p. 147.

The moral law is no hypothetical imperative that issues only prescripts of profit for empirical ends, it is a *categorical imperative*, a law, universal and binding, on every rational will.—(*Kant*) *Schwegler*, '*Hist. of Phil.*,' p. 233.

The general truths involved in moral judgments are not generalised truths, dependent for their validity on an induction of particulars, but self-evident truths, known independently of induction. They are as clearly recognised when a single testing case is presented for adjudication as when a thousand such cases have been decided. In this relation the Inductive Method guides merely to the fact that such truths are discovered in consciousness. But Induction as little explains the intellectual and ethical authority of these truths, as it settles the nature of the facts pertaining to physical science. The rightness of Honesty is not proved by an induction of particulars. But the conclusion that 'Honesty is the best policy' is essentially a generalisation from experience.—*Calderwood*, '*Moral Phil.*,' p. 31.

Its precepts generally admitted.

It is worth noticing that, amidst much diversity of opinion as to minor points, the great principles of Morals are generally admitted and acquiesced in. It is agreed—

1. That men, in all ages and in all nations of the world, have acknowledged a distinction between *some* actions as *right* and *others* as *wrong*.

2. That this distinction is recognised by means of a separate power or peculiar faculty of the mind, or by Reason, evolving peculiar ideas and operating under peculiar sanctions.

3. That the existence of a separate power or faculty, or this peculiarity in the exercise of Reason, implies some correspondent nature, or character, or relation, predicable of human actions, of which Conscience is the arbiter or judge.

Lastly. That the connection between the Moral Faculty and that in human actions to which it has reference, is a connection that is permanent and unalterable; for they who call Conscience a sense admit that its decisions are not arbitrary, but determined by the nature of its objects; and they who call virtue a relation admit that it is a relation which, while the nature of God and the nature of man remain the same, cannot be changed. The constitution of things and the course of Providence, or, in one word, the will of God, is the high and clear point to which all moral discussions tend, and in which all moral actions terminate. And should we, at any time, be ungrateful enough to forget this, or impious enough to doubt it, by feigning that morality is a thing of man's making, the first violence or insult which we offer to our moral nature is vindicated in a way that is sufficient to enlighten if not to reclaim us. Conscience claims her high prerogative. Virtue asserts her heavenly origin, and we are made to see and feel that the ties by which we are drawn into conformity with the will of God are indeed the cords of love and the bands of a man—the means and measures of infinite goodness, fitted to a rational but imperfect nature; for they bind us to happiness by binding us to duty, and lead us to seek God's glory, because in doing so we accomplish our own perfection and blessedness.

Moral and Physical Law.

The difference between them

What is called law in physics is not really law in any scientific or philosophical sense, but, whether viewed scientifically or philosophically, is nothing more or less than Rule, and can be called law only in a metaphorical sense. In the realm of morals we find law in the proper sense, in the sense that is clear to the philosopher, that is inevitable to the jurist, that is 'understanded of the people,' that is wrought into all the act and thought of humanity ever since the first of its steps that have left any print on the sands of time Now law, in this proper and familiar sense, is found in the realm of morals to be the instrument of preserving order between man and man, and thus to be, in effect, the instrument of preserving society itself—*Arthur, 'Physical and Moral Law,'* p. 15

A physical law is invariable and inviolable; a moral law is invariable but not inviolable An invariable law means one that cannot be altered, and an inviolable law means one that cannot be broken—*Arthur, 'Physical and Moral Law,'* p. 15

The difference between the law of nature and the law of morality is this, that only the latter expresses a 'must' which at the same time is an 'ought.'—*Martensen, 'Christian Ethics,'* i. 346.

They are not antagonistic.

Whilst we maintain the essential difference between the law of nature and the law of morality, we by no means teach an indissoluble dualism, and cannot with Kant, whose theory forms a contrast with that of Schleiermacher, acknowledge an irreconcilable antagonism between the law of morality and the law of nature,—a dualism in consequence of which there must be in man an incessant struggle between reason and natural impulse, virtue and the exercise of the senses, duty and inclination Such an irreconcilable dualism between the law of morality and the law of nature would not merely place an unsolved dualism in the being of God, since it is the same God who reveals Himself in both worlds, but would also destroy the unity of human nature; whereas it is the same man, whose brain, nervous system, circulation of the blood, and instinctive desires are determined by the law of nature, but whose will must determine itself according to the law of morality, and under the postulate of an absolute dualism would be doomed to an incessant and resultless contest.—*Martensen, 'Christian Ethics,'* p. 347.

The Object of Moral Law

The first object of moral law is to elevate the doer of it; the second, to make him happy in his relations with his fellows, and to make them happy in their relations with him. Were the moral law, as found in Holy Scripture, fulfilled in every person, no one in the world would be a despicable man. No one in the world would make himself miserable in his relations with his family, the public, or the nation No one would make others miserable in their relations with him Every man would be noble, happy, a centre of happy influences. —*Arthur, 'Physical and Moral Law,'* p. 201.

The Application of Moral Law

A principal end of morality

To lay down, in their universal form, the laws according to which the conduct of a free agent ought to be regulated, and to apply them to the different situations of human life, is the end of morality.—*Whewell, 'Systematic Morality,'* Lecture I.

In relation to action;

It does not make an action good

An action is not right merely in consequence of a law declaring it to be so. But the declaration of the law proceeds upon the antecedent rightness of the action — *Fleming, 'Vocab. of Phil.,'* p 288

Nor does a good intention

The goodness of intention is not sufficient to constitute an action morally good, that is, a good intention cannot alone, and of itself, procure that any human act should be morally good; or which is the same, in the words of the Apostle, Evil ought not to be done, that good may come.—*Sanderson, 'Lectures on Conscience, &c,'* p 33

Example does not constitute moral law

Neither the judgment nor the example of any man ought to be of such authority with us, that our conscience may securely rest in either of them Nor are we to conclude that what any person of learning or sanctity has formerly done was done justly, or may hereafter be done lawfully

The insufficiency of example as the rule of our own conduct appears.—first, from the fact that *all* the actions of good men are not objects of imitation, and it is not easy to distinguish which of them we may propose for exemplars, and which not. The most pious persons have their failings, and so far are evil examples. Secondly, actions expressly commended in the Word of God are not offered to us in all their *circumstances* as objects of our imitation: the Hebrew midwives, in preserving the Hebrew infants, excused their contempt of the king's commands by a lie Thirdly, the moral quality of an action frequently depends upon the circumstances amid which it is performed, and circumstances never remain exactly the same in any two cases The truth is, examples are designed rather as helps and supports to inspire us with vigour and alacrity, rather than as a rule of life.—*Sanderson, 'Lectures on Conscience, &c.,'* Lect III (condensed)

When an action is good.

No action can justly be said to be morally good unless the *matter* be lawful, the *intention* right, and the *circumstances* proper; consequently no act can be done with a safe conscience, whatsoever the intention be, that is either unlawful in the *object* or defective in the *circumstances*.—*Sanderson, 'Lectures on Conscience, &c,'* p 39

Moral Law must descend to common life.

In order to serve the ends intended by it, ethics must settle what are the duties of different classes of persons, according to the relation in which they stand to each other, such as rulers and subjects, parents and children, masters and servants, and what the path which individuals should follow in certain circumstances,—it may be, very difficult and perplexing In consequence of the affairs of human life being very complicated, demonstration can be carried but a very little way in ethics In order to be able to enunciate general principles for our guidance, or to promulgate useful precepts, the ethical inquirer must condescend to come down from his *à priori* heights to the level in which mankind live and walk and work.—*M'Cosh, 'Intuitions of the Mind,'* p 362.

Moral Law in Relation to Man

It is a mark at once of freedom and dependence.

The law of morality frees man so far from the law of necessity, as it imprints on him the mark of freedom, stamps him as a citizen in a kingdom which is higher than the necessity of nature, and where everything is weighed and measured by a different standard from that of nature. But it also impresses on him a higher mark of dependence In virtue of this law, which embraces the whole world of humanity, this is determined as at once the world of *liberty* and of *authority*, whilst nature is only that of necessity and of power Authority and liberty, or free-will—around these two poles revolves the moral world.—*Martensen, 'Christian Ethics,'* p. 348.

It should ever be an object of reverence

Two things there are which, the oftener and the more steadfastly we consider, fill the mind with an ever new, an ever rising admiration and reverence—*the Starry Heaven above, the Moral Law within.* Both I contemplate lying clear before me, and I connect both immediately with the consciousness of my being. The one departs from the place I occupy in the outer world of sense; expands beyond the limits of imagination that connection of my being with worlds rising above worlds, and systems blending into systems; and protends it also to the illimitable times of their periodic movement—to its commencement and continuance. The other departs from my invisible self, from my personality; and represents me in a world, truly infinite indeed, but whose infinity is to be fathomed only by the intellect. The aspect of it elevates my worth as *an intelligence* even to infinitude; and this through my personality, in which the moral law reveals a faculty of life independent of my animal nature, nay, of the whole material world. It proposes my moral worth for the absolute end of my activity, conceding no compromise of its imperative to a necessitation of nature, and spurning in its infinity the limits and conditions of my present transitory life.—*Kant, 'Pure Practical Reason'* (conclusion).

On the evolution theory moral law is not immutable.

The actual moral law develops, and therefore changes, whatever may be said of the ideal law. We must regard the moral instincts as dependent upon human nature or human society, and therefore liable to vary in so far as their subject is liable to vary. We cannot mean by eternity or immutability, that the moral law will remain unaltered even if the conditions upon which it depends be altered. With different conditions the morality would be different. At present any change is small. The variation, whatever it is, must correspond to a process of evolution, not to what would be called arbitrary modification.—*Stephen, 'Science of Ethics,'* pp. 153, 154 (condensed).

Moral good is moral good to all intelligences so high in the scale of being as to be able to discern it. I lay down this position in order to guard against the idea that moral excellence is something depending on the peculiar nature of man, and that it is allowable to suppose that there may be intelligent beings in other worlds to whom virtue does not appear as virtue. Such a view seems altogether inconsistent with our intuitive convictions, and would effectually undermine the foundations of morality. It is allowable to suppose that there may be beings in other worlds who see no beauty in the colours or in the shapes and proportions which we so much admire; but I cannot admit that there are any intelligent and responsible beings who look on malevolence as a virtue or justice as a sin.—*M'Cosh, 'Intuitions, &c.,'* p. 255.

Will of God not available as the rule of Right.

Whoever affirms the will of God to be the rule of right means that, to ascertain our duty, we must consult the will of God; which, therefore, we must have some prior and independent resource for knowing. Originally, no doubt, that resource was assumed to be the Scriptures, regarded as 'the oracles of God;' which could be studied to find the heads and contents of duty, just as a code is searched to determine the problems of civil law. Increasing knowledge of the Scriptures rendering it evident that they contain a good deal that is not the will of God, and pay slight heed to a good deal that is, the moralist of this school was driven to seek another test as supplement or substitute; naming now one thing, now another, but, with most acceptance, the conduciveness of acts to the happiness of men.—*Martineau, 'Types of Ethical Theory,'* ii. 217, 218.

MYSTICISM IN MORALS

Philosophical Basis of Mysticism

Mysticism rests on two facts of human nature. On the one hand, human life can, at the best, afford but very imperfect good; and, on the other, no human being can acquire even this good, without an effort which is not natural, and which is followed by a fatigue that can be relieved only by allowing the bent spring to be relaxed, and our faculties to return to their natural and primitive mode of action.

From these two facts spring mysticism. If the only means of obtaining any good in this life is an effort which is against nature, —and if, even then, a man, the most favoured by circumstances, only secures the shadow of good, is it not plain that the pursuit and acquisition of good is not the end of the present life, and that to hope or search for it implies an equal delusion? Man has truly an end and destiny to attain; but to seek it here is folly, for our lot in life is disappointment. To resign ourselves to our weakness,—to renounce all effort and action,—to await death, that it may break our fetters, and place us in an order of things where the accomplishment of our end will be possible,—this is our only reasonable course, our only true vocation. —*Jouffroy*, '*Introduction to Ethics*,' pp. 123, 124 (abridged).

The Doctrine of the Christian Mystics

Self is the centre and essence of all Sin, and the *surrender of self* the one simple condition of union with God. Among other things the doctrine has this meaning: that the will, whenever it goes astray, follows the direction of *individual* tendency and wish,—the forces of the Ego unrestrained by reverence for a good that is not ours, and that, only when all regard to those personal interests is merged in devotion to that heirarchy of affections which, in being universal, is Divine, is the mood begun which sets man and God at one. To have *no wish, no claim, no reluctance* to be taken hither or thither, but to yield one's self up as the organ of a higher spirit, which disposes of us as may be fit, constitutes the mystic ideal of perfect life. —*Martineau*, '*Types of Ethical Theory*,' i 73 (abridged).

The Desire for Rest.

A place of rest! Yes, in that one word, *Rest*, lies all the longing of the mystic. Every creature in heaven above, and in the earth beneath, saith Master Eckart, all things in the height and all things in the depth, have one yearning, one ceaseless, unfathomable desire, one voice of aspiration: it is for rest; and again, for rest; and even, till the end of time, for rest! The mystics have constituted themselves the interpreters of these sighs and groans of the travailing creation; they are the hierophants to gather, and express, and offer them to heaven; they are the teachers to weary, weeping men of the way whereby they may attain, even on this side the grave, a serenity like that of heaven —*Vaughan*, '*Hours with the Mystics*,' i. 263.

Mysticism in the Greek Church

Dionysius the Areopagite.

Dionysius is the mythical hero of mysticism. You find traces of him everywhere. Go almost where you will through the writings of the mediæval mystics, into their depth of nihilism, up their heights of rapture or of speculation, through their overgrowth of fancy, you find his authority cited, his words employed, his opinions more or less fully transmitted. Passages from the Areopagite were culled, as their warrant and their insignia, by the priestly ambassadors of mysticism, with as much care and reverence as the sacred verbenæ that grew within the enclosure of the Capitoline by the Fetiales of Rome —*Vaughan*, '*Hours with the Mystics*,' i. 119.

His doctrine of emanation.

All things have emanated from God, and the end of all is to return to God. Such return—deification, he calls it—is the consummation of the creature, that God may finally be all in all. A process of evolution, a centrifugal movement in the Divine Nature, is substituted in reality for creation. The antithesis of this is the centripetal process, or movement of involution, which draws all existence towards the point of the Divine centre. The degree of real existence possessed by any being, is the amount of God in that being—for God is the existence in all things. Yet He Himself cannot be said to exist, for He is above existence. The more or less of God, which the various creatures possess, is determined by the proximity of their order to the centre.—*Vaughan*, '*Hours with the Mystics*,' i. 113, 114.

Of the work of Christ.

The work of Christ is thrown into the background to make room for the Church. The Saviour answers, with Dionysius, rather to the Logos of the Platonist than to the Son of God revealed in Scripture. He is allowed to be, as incarnate, the founder of the Ecclesiastical Hierarchy; but, as such, he is removed from men by the long chain of priestly orders, and is less the Redeemer, than remotely the illuminator of the species.

Purification, illumination, perfection,—the three great stages of ascent to God (which plays so important a part in almost every succeeding attempt to systematise mysticism), are mystically represented by the three sacraments,—Baptism, the Eucharist, and Unction. The Church is the great Mystagogue: its liturgy and offices a profound and elaborate system of symbolism.—*Vaughan*, '*Hours with the Mystics*,' i. 115.

Mysticism in Germany

The general character and result of German mysticism is that it transplants Christianity from the intellect into the heart, from speculation into sentiment, from the school into life,—that apprehending its substance more simply, morally, and energetically, and presenting it in a German dress, it converts it into a popular cause,—that waging direct or indirect warfare with the Romish ecclesiastical and scholastic system, it restores a spiritual and free Christianity, more congenial with the German taste and mind, and by this means, on a large and general scale, paves the way for the emancipation, both of faith, and in matters of faith, of the nation, from the tyranny of Romanism.—*Ullmann*, '*Reformers before the Reformation*,' ii. 186.

Its principal tendencies.

Of these we distinguish four, though we are sensible that the one often overflows into the other. The four are the poetical, the sentimental, the speculative, and the practical mysticism of Germany. Each of them is represented by a distinguished personage or production, the first by *Suso*, the second by *Tauler*, the third by the author of the '*German Theology*,' the fourth by Staupitz.—*Ullmann*, '*Reformers before the Reformation*,' ii. 186.

German and French Mysticism contrasted.

Speaking generally, it may be said that France exhibits the mysticism of sentiment, Germany the mysticism of thought. Almost every later German mystic has been a secluded student—almost every mystic of modern France has been a brilliant controversialist. If Jacob Behmen had appeared in France, he must have counted disciples by units, where in Germany he reckoned them by hundreds. If Madame Guyon had been born in Germany, rigid Lutheranism might have given her some annoyance; but her earnestness would have redeemed her enthusiasm from ridicule, and she would have lived and died the honoured precursor of modern German Pietism. The simplicity and strength of purpose which characterise so many of the German mystics, appear to much advantage beside the vanity and affectation which have so frequently attended the manifestations of mysticism in France.—*Vaughan*, '*Hours with the Mystics*,' ii. 275, 276. (See 'MYSTICISM,' in Philosophy, sect. xiii.)

XI. PESSIMISM

Its Oriental Origin.

In orthodox Brahmanism, as in Buddhism, a keen sense of human misery forms the starting-point. Yet the solution of the dark mystery is widely different in the two cases. According to the Brahmanic philosophy, though the created world is a regrettable accident, its effects can be neutralised. And this is effected by the absorption of the human soul in the Universal Spirit or Brahma, the true source of being, thought, and happiness. Thus a mode of a permanent and satisfying existence is secured, and an optimistic *Weltanschauung* finally substituted for a pessimistic.

In Buddhism, on the contrary, as Mr Max Muller has well pointed out, the pessimistic view of life receives no such happy solution; and this philosophy is to be regarded as pessimism pure and simple, and as the direct progenitor of the modern German systems. Buddha (or his followers) denies the existence not only of a Creator, but of an Absolute Being. There is no reality anywhere, neither in the past nor in the future. True wisdom consists in a perception of the nothingness of all things, and in a desire to become nothing, to be blown out, to enter into Nirvâna, that is to say, extinction. The perfect attainment of this condition would be reached only at death. Yet even during life a partial anticipation of it might be secured, namely, in a condition of mind freed from all desire and feeling.—*Sully*, '*Pessimism*,' pp. 37, 38.

Metaphysical Basis.

The World as Idea.

'The world is my idea':—this is a truth which holds good for everything that lives and knows, though man alone can bring it into reflective and abstract consciousness. If he really does this, he has attained to philosophical wisdom. No truth is more certain, more independent of all others, and less in need of proof than this, that all that exists for knowledge, and therefore this whole world, is only object in relation to subject, perception of a perceiver, in a word, idea.—*Schopenhauer*, '*The World as Will and Idea*,' i. 3.

The World as Will.

In every emergence of an act of will from the obscure depths of our inner being into the knowing consciousness, a direct transition occurs of the 'thing in itself,' which lies outside time, into the phenomenal world. Accordingly the act of will is indeed only the closest and most distinct *manifestation* of the 'thing in itself;' yet it follows from this that if all other manifestations or phenomena could be known by us as directly and inwardly, we would be obliged to assert them to be that which the will is in us. Thus in this sense I teach that the inner nature of everything is *will*, and I call will the 'thing in itself.'—*Schopenhauer*, '*The World as Will, &c.*,' ii. 407.

The universal will is *a will to live.* Amid its manifold appearances we discern its unity. The rush of this vast Force into activity accounts for all the phenomena of the universe. Hence the endless and irreconcilable strife which the world presents to the observer, and which indeed he feels in his own nature. The impulses come into conflict with one another, so that none can be realised, can find satisfaction. Life, Consciousness, *Suffering*,—these are the results of 'the will to live,' which realises itself in individual experience, and in the history of the human race.—*Thomson*, '*Modern Pessimism*,' p. 26.

Will not defined by Schopenhauer.

Schopenhauer nowhere defines what he means by will, except by telling us that it contains the various manifestations of impulse and feeling, and by marking it off from intellect. He is very particular on this last point, affirming in one place that 'we must think away the co-operation of the intellect, if we would comprehend the nature of will in itself, and thereby penetrate as far as possible into the inner parts of nature.' According to modern psychology, mind consists of three essentially different activities—feeling, intellect, and volition. Schopenhauer distinguishes the third of these from the second, but not from the first.—*Sully, 'Pessimism,'* p. 85.

Hartmann's Philosophy of the Unconscious.

Failure of the Philosophy of Consciousness

The more Philosophy has abandoned the dogmatic assumption of immediate cognition through sense or understanding, and the more it has perceived the highly indirect cognisability of everything previously regarded as immediate content of consciousness, the higher naturally has risen the value of indirect proofs of existence. Accordingly, reflective minds have from time to time appeared who have felt constrained to fall back upon the existence of unconscious ideas as the cause of certain mental phenomena otherwise totally inexplicable. To collect these phenomena, to render probable the existence of unconscious ideas and unconscious will, from the evidence of the particular cases, and through their combination to raise this probability to a degree bordering on certainty, is the object of the first two sections of the present work.—*'Philosophy of the Unconscious,'* i 2.

Principle of the Unconscious the only explanation of Phenomena.

By means of the principle of the Unconscious, the phenomena in question receive their only possible explanation, an explanation which either has not been expressly stated before, or could not obtain recognition, for the simple reason that the principle itself can only be established through a comparison of *all* the relevant phenomena. Moreover, by the application of this as yet undeveloped principle, a prospect opens up of quite novel modes of treating matters hitherto supposed to be perfectly well known. A number of the contrarieties and antinomies of earlier creeds and systems are reconciled by the adoption of a higher point of view, embracing within its scope opposed aspects as incomplete truths. In a word, the principle is shown to be in the highest degree fruitful for special questions. Far more important than this, however, is the way in which the principle of the Unconscious is imperceptibly extended beyond the physical and psychical domains, to achieve the solution of problems which, to adopt the common language, would be said to belong to the province of *metaphysics.*—*'Philosophy of the Unconscious,'* i. 3.

Unconsciousness of the Will.

The will itself can *never* become conscious, because it can never contradict itself. There may very well be several desires at variance with one another, but volition at any moment is in truth only the resultant of *all* the simultaneous desires; consequently, can always be only conformable to itself. If, now, consciousness is an accident which the will bestows upon that of which it is compelled to recognise, not itself, but something foreign as its cause, in short, what enters into opposition with it, the will can never impart consciousness to itself, because here the thing to be compared and the standard of comparison are one and the same; they can never be different or at all at variance with one another. The will also never gets so far as to recognise something else as its cause; rather the appearance of its spontaneity is indestructible, since it is the primal actuality, and all that lies behind is potential, that is, unreal. Whilst displeasure, then, *must always* become conscious, and pleasure *can* become so under certain circumstances, the will is said *never* to be able to become conscious. This latter result perhaps appears unexpected, yet experience fully confirms it.—*'Philosophy of the Unconscious,'* ii 96, 97.

Schopenhauer maintains that this is the worst of all possible worlds.

This world is so arranged as to be able

to maintain itself with great difficulty; but if it were a little worse, it could no longer maintain itself. Consequently a worse world, since it could not continue to exist, is absolutely impossible: thus this world itself is the worst of all possible worlds. For not only if the planets were to run their heads together, but even if any one of the actually appearing perturbations of their course, instead of being gradually balanced by others, continued to increase, the world would soon reach its end. The earthquake of Lisbon, the earthquake of Haiti, the destruction of Pompeii, are only small, playful hints of what is possible. A small alteration of the atmosphere, which cannot even be chemically proved, causes cholera, yellow fever, black death, &c., which carry off millions of men; a somewhat greater alteration would extinguish all life. A very moderate increase of heat would dry up all the rivers and springs. The brutes have received just barely so much in the way of organs and powers as enables them to procure with the greatest exertion sustenance for their own lives and food for their offspring; therefore if a brute loses a limb, or even the full use of one, it must generally perish. Even of the human race, powerful as are the weapons it possesses in understanding and reason, nine-tenths live in constant conflict and want, always balancing themselves with difficulty and effort upon the brink of destruction. Thus throughout, as for the continuance of the whole, so also for that of each individual being, the conditions are barely and scantily given, but nothing over. The individual life is a ceaseless battle for existence itself; while at every step destruction threatens it. Just because this threat is so often fulfilled, provision had to be made, by means of the enormous excess of the germs, that the destruction of the individuals should not involve that of the species, for which alone nature really cares. The world is therefore as bad as it possibly can be if it is to continue to be at all.—*Schopenhauer*, '*The World as Will and Idea*,' iii. 395, 396.

The misery of human life.

The life of the great majority is only a constant struggle for existence itself, with the certainty of losing it at last. But what enables them to endure this wearisome battle, is not so much the love of life as the fear of death, which yet stands in the background as inevitable, and may come upon them at any moment. Life itself is a sea, full of rocks and whirlpools, which man avoids with the greatest care and solicitude, although he knows that even if he succeeds in getting through with all his efforts and skill, he yet by doing so comes nearer at every step to the greatest, the total, inevitable, and irremediable shipwreck, death; nay, even steers right upon it: this is the final goal of the laborious voyage, and worse for him than all the rocks from which he has escaped.

Now it is well worth observing that, on the other hand, the suffering and misery of life may easily increase to such an extent that death itself, in the flight from which the whole of life consists, becomes desirable, and we hasten towards it voluntarily; and again, on the other hand, that as soon as want and suffering permit rest to a man, ennui is at once so near that he necessarily requires diversion. The striving after existence is what occupies all living things and maintains them in motion. But when existence is assured, then they know not what to do with it; and thus the second thing that sets them in motion is the effort to get free from the burden of existence, to make it cease to be felt, 'to kill time,' *i.e.*, to escape from ennui.—*Schopenhauer*, '*The World as Will and Idea*,' i. 403, 404.

The attempted proof that this world is the worst of all possible ones, is a manifest sophism; everywhere else Schopenhauer himself tries to maintain and prove nothing further than that the existence of this world is worse than its non-existence, and this assertion I hold to be correct.—*Hartmann*, '*Philosophy of the Unconscious*,' iii. 12.

Virtue consists in sympathy with the suffering.

If that veil of Mâyâ, the *principium individuationis*, is lifted from the eyes of a man, to such an extent that he no longer makes the egoistical distinction between his person and that of others, but takes as much interest in the sufferings of other individuals as in his own, and therefore is not only benevolent in the highest degree, but even ready to sacrifice his own individuality whenever such a sacrifice will save a number of other persons, then it clearly follows that such a man, who recognises in all beings his own inmost and true self, must also regard the infinite suffering of all suffering beings as his own, and take on himself the pain of the whole world.—*Schopenhauer*, '*The World as Will, &c.*,' i. 489.

And leads to asceticism.

Whoever, by renouncing every accidental advantage, desires for himself no other lot than that of humanity in general, cannot desire even this long. The clinging to life and its pleasures must now soon yield, and give place to a universal renunciation; consequently the denial of the will will take place. Since now, in accordance with this, poverty, privation, and special sufferings of many kinds are introduced simply by the perfect exercise of the moral virtues, asceticism in the narrowest sense,—thus the surrender of all possessions, the intentional seeking out of what is disagreeable and repulsive, self-mortification, fasts, the hair shirt, and the scourge—all this is rejected by many, and perhaps rightly, as superfluous. Justice itself is the hair shirt that constantly harasses its owner, and the charity that gives away what is needed, provides constant fasts.—*Schopenhauer*, '*The World as Will, &c.*,' iii. 425.

Pessimistic view of annihilation.

There is upon this point a difference, almost amusing to consider, between the two German champions of the doctrine. The elder — Schopenhauer — would have each man act for himself, and negative that 'will to live' which involves men in misery so great. The younger — Hartmann — thinks that each man should for the present affirm the 'will to live,' and that efforts should be made to promote amongst men a knowledge of the cause and of the cure of life's wretchedness, so that a general determination may in due time be arrived at by all the members of the race, who may by one great and combined effort achieve the wished-for and happy result, the extinction of human life and consciousness, and the relapse into universal oblivion and repose!—*Thomson*, '*Modern Pessimism*,' p. 37.

Meliorism, as a Reconciler of Optimism and Pessimism.

By (Meliorism) I would understand the faith which affirms not merely our power of lessening evil—this nobody questions—but also our ability to increase the amount of positive good. It is, indeed, only this latter idea which can really stimulate and sustain human endeavour. It might be possible, if life were not to be got rid of, to bring ourselves to labour in order to reduce to a minimum an inevitable excess of misery. But pessimism would seem to dictate to wise men the most speedy conclusion of life, both their own and that of all for whom they care. Meliorism, on the other hand, escapes this final contradictory outcome of a life-theory. By recognising the possibility of happiness, and the ability of each individual consciously to do something to increase the sum total of human welfare, present and future, meliorism gives us a practical creed sufficient to inspire ardent and prolonged endeavour. Lives nourished and invigorated by this ideal have been and still may be seen among us, and the appearance of but a single example proves the adequacy of the belief.—*Sully*, '*Pessimism*,' pp. 399, 400.

XXII.

MORAL OBLIGATION

I. MORAL SANCTIONS

Necessity for these

'A law, as jurists tells us, is the command of a sovereign enforced by a sanction; and the essence of law, therefore, depends upon the ultimate appeal to coercion; or, in other words, upon the circumstance that, if you do not obey the law, you may be made to obey it.'

'The "sanction" must supply the motive-power by which individuals are to be made virtuous. It is for the practical moralist the culminating point of all ethical theory.'—*Stephen*, '*Science of Ethics*,' pp. 140, 397.

The Nature of Moral Sanction

Sanction is a confirmation of the moral character of an action, which follows it in experience.—*Calderwood*, '*Moral Philosophy*,' p. 148.

'The pain or pleasure which is attached to a law forms what is called its sanction' (Bentham). On the other hand, Austin restricts the term to mean the 'evil (*i.e.*, pain) which will probably be incurred in case a demand be disobeyed.'—*Ryland*, '*Handbook, &c.*,' p. 147.

Why should a man be virtuous? The answer depends upon the answer to the previous question, What is it to be virtuous? If, for example, virtue means all such conduct as promotes happiness, the motives to virtuous conduct must be all such motives as impel a man to aim at increasing the sum of happiness. These motives constitute the sanction, and the sanction may be defined either as an intrinsic or an extrinsic sanction; it may, that is, be argued either that virtuous conduct invariably leads to consequences which are desirable to every man, whether he be or be not virtuous; or, on the other hand, that virtuous conduct as such, and irrespectively of any future consequences, makes the agent happier. Some moralists say that a good man will go to heaven, and a bad man to hell. Others, that virtue is itself heaven, and vice hell.—*Stephen*, '*Science of Ethics*,' p. 396.

Moral law being imposed only by authority, and not by resistless force, admits of being broken, and even contemplates the occurrence of that case. But though broken, so far is it from being annulled, that thereupon the authority which gave the law calls up force to vindicate it, though force had not been employed to impose compliance with it. Force does vindicate it by inflicting the penalty. The threat of penalty is the sanction of the law. Corresponding with this, and co-operating with it, is the prospect of reward for obedience. Even when no specific reward is set forth, every law implies the most comprehensive of all forms of reward, that is, the upholding of the doer of it in all the rights and privileges of the innocent.—*Arthur*, '*Physical and Moral Law*,' p. 116.

The Different Kinds of Sanctions.

1. *Classified.*

Bentham distinguishes four kinds of Sanctions:—

(*a*) *Physical*—due to nature, acting without human intervention.

(*b*) *Moral*—or social—due to the spontaneous disposition of our fellow-men, their friendship, hatred, esteem, &c.

(*c*) *Political*—or legal—due to the action of the magistrate in virtue of the laws.

(*d*) *Religious*.—*Ryland*, '*Handbook, &c.*,' p. 147.

2. *Stated.*

According to Christian Ethics.

Sanction is the guard thrown around a command or duty, to enforce its performance: the sanction of a duty not done is the punishment of the person who fails. The only sanction of [moral] law is the displeasure of God: but that displeasure in its fullest expression is postponed to the Great Day. The preliminary tokens of it in this world are but the beginnings of wrath; the judgment is indeed begun, and the word Eternal has entered into time; but Christianity makes the future world, with its judgment at the threshold, the issue of all its moral teaching.—*Pope*, '*Christian Theology*,' iii. 159.

The sanctions of rewards and punishments which God has annexed to His laws have not, in any proper sense, the nature of obligation. They are only motives to virtue, adapted to the state and condition, the weakness and insensibility of man. They do not make or constitute duty, but presuppose it.—*Adams*, '*Sermon on Nature and Obligation of Virtue.*'

The consequences which naturally attend virtue and vice are the sanction of duty, or of doing what is right, as they are intended to encourage us to the discharge of it, and to deter us from the breach or neglect of it. And these natural consequences of virtue and vice are also a declaration, on the part of God, that He is in favour of the one and against the other, and are intimations that His love of the one and His hatred of the other may be more fully manifested hereafter. By Locke, Paley, and Bentham the term sanction, or enforcement of obedience, is applied to reward as well as to punishment. But Mr. Austin ('Province of Jurisprudence Determined,' p. 10) confines it to the latter; perhaps because human laws only punish, and do not reward.—*Fleming*, '*Vocab. of Phil.*,' p. 448.

According to Shaftesbury.

As to the *sanctions* of morality, that is to say, the considerations or influences which impel men to right-doing or deter them from wrong-doing, Shaftesbury's answer is perfectly clear. The principal sanction with him is the approbation or disapprobation of the Moral Sense. As nothing can be more delightful than the witness of a good conscience, so nothing can be more painful than the remorse which follows on a bad action. 'To a rational creature it must be horribly offensive and grievous to have the reflection in his mind of any unjust action or behaviour which he knows to be naturally odious and ill-deserving.' With this sanction is combined, in the case of those who have any true sense of religion, the love and reverence of a beneficent, just, and wise God, whose example serves 'to raise and increase the affection towards Virtue, and to submit and subdue all other affections to that alone.'—*Fowler*, '*Shaftesbury and Hutcheson*,' p. 83.

According to Utilitarianism.

The sanctions we may classify as External and Internal. The former class will include both 'Legal Sanctions,' or penalties inflicted by the authority, direct or indirect, of the sovereign; and 'Social Sanctions,' which are either the pleasures that may be expected from the approval and good-will of our fellow-men generally, and the services that they will be prompted to render both by this good-will and by their appreciation of the usefulness of good conduct, or the annoyances and losses that are to be feared from their distrust and dislike. In so far as the happiness earned by virtue comes from internal sources, it will lie in the pleasurable emotion attending virtuous action, or in the absence of remorse, or in some effect on the mental constitution of the agent produced by the maintenance of virtuous habits.—*Sidgwick*, '*Methods of Ethics*' (second edition), p. 148.

The majority of disciples assure us that the secular sanctions of utilitarianism are sufficient to establish their theory, or in other words, that our duty coincides so strictly with our interest, when rightly understood, that a perfectly prudent man would necessarily become a perfectly virtuous man. Bodily vice, they tell us, ultimately brings bodily weakness and suffering. Extravagance is followed by ruin, unbridled passions by the loss of domestic peace; disregard for the interests of others by social or legal penalties; while on the other hand, the most moral is also the most tranquil disposition; benevolence is one of the truest of our pleasures, and virtue may become by habit an essential of enjoyment.

This theory of the perfect coincidence of virtue and interest rightly understood, contains no doubt a certain amount of truth, but only of the most general kind. The virtue which is most conducive to happiness is plainly that which can be realised without much suffering, and sustained without much effort. The selfish theory of morals applies only to the virtues that harmonise with the individual's temperament, and not to that much higher form of virtue which is sustained in defiance of temperament. There are men whose whole lives are spent in willing one thing and desiring the opposite. In such cases as these, virtue clearly involves a sacrifice of happiness, for the suffering caused by resisting natural tendencies is much greater than would ensue from their moderate gratification. The plain truth is that no proposition can be more palpably and egregiously false than the assertion that, as far as this world is concerned, it is invariably conducive to the happiness of a man to pursue the most virtuous career. Circumstances and dispositions will make one man find his highest happiness in the happiness, and another man in the misery, of his kind; and if the second man acts according to his interest, the utilitarian, however much he may deplore the result, has no right to blame or condemn the agent. — *Lecky*, '*European Morals*,' i. 59–63 (abridged).

The Moral Law is Independent of its Sanctions.

It is undeniably true, that moral obligations would remain certain, though it were not certain what would, upon the whole, be the consequences of observing or violating them. For, these obligations arise immediately and necessarily from the judgment of our own mind, unless perverted, which we cannot violate without being self-condemned. And they would be certain too, from considerations of interest. For though it were doubtful what will be the future consequences of virtue and vice, yet it is, however, credible, that they may have those consequences which religion teaches us they will: and this credibility is a certain obligation in point of prudence, to abstain from all wickedness, and to live in the conscientious practice of all that is good.—*Butler*, '*Analogy*,' pt. i. ch. vii.

II. DUTY

The Conception of Duty.

Duty defined.

Duty is that action to which a person is bound. Duty is hence the matter of obligation; and there may be one duty, in so far as the act is concerned, although different modes in which the obligation may be constituted, *i.e.*, juridical or ethical. —*Kant*, '*Metaphysic of Ethics*,' p. 171.

Duty is the necessity of an act, out of reverence felt for law.—*Kant*, '*Metaphysic of Ethics*,' p. 11.

Duty is that which we *ought* to do—that which we are under *obligation* to do. In seeing a thing to be right, we see at the same time that it is our duty to do it. There is a complete synthesis between rectitude and obligation.—*Fleming*, '*Vocab. of Phil.*,' p. 148.

Duty is that which is due from one to another. My duty is that which I owe to another, according to the means I have in my power. Here the measure of my duty is my power; and the special ground of duty lies in the exact relation in which I stand to the other party.—*Murphy*, '*Human Mind*,' p. 193.

Duty, according to Paley, implies in all

cases a command issuing from a superior, who has attached to obedience or disobedience pleasure or pain, and the supreme law-giver, whose commands are the basis of duty, is God.—*Ueberweg, 'Hist of Phil,'* ii 91

The notions of Duty and Right Conduct, as commonly employed, do not coincide altogether. There is certainly some right conduct, and that very necessary and important, to which we do not generally apply the notion of duty. For example, it is right that we should eat and drink enough; but we do not commonly speak of this as a duty. It would appear that those actions to which we are sufficiently impelled by natural desire are not called duties, because no moral impulse is needed for doing them. In the last century, when our country was thought to require more population, it was often seriously said to be a man's duty to society to take a wife: but now that the opposite view prevails, and the 'surplus population' presents itself as a difficulty to be met, no one would call this action a duty, except in jest or as a relic of an old manner of speech. We shall therefore keep most close to usage if we define Duties as 'those Right actions or abstinences, for the adequate accomplishment of which a moral impulse is at least occasionally necessary.'—*Sidgwick, 'Methods of Ethics,'* p. 190.

The Conception elevated by Christ.

Christ hath shown man what is good. Duty is transfigured by its connection with redemption: 'Ye are not your own.' It finds its standard in Jesus; its sphere in His kingdom; and its one object in the Redeeming Triune God.—*Pope, 'Christian Theology,'* iii. 166.

Sublimity of the idea of Duty.

Duty! thou great, thou exalted name! Wondrous thought, that workest neither by fond insinuation, flattery, nor by any threat, but merely by holding up thy naked law in the soul, and so extorting for thyself always reverence, if not always obedience,—before whom all appetites are dumb, however secretly they rebel,—whence thy original? And where find we the root of thy august descent, thus loftily disclaiming all kindred with appetite and want? to be in like manner descended from which root is the unchanging condition of that worth which mankind can alone impart to themselves?—*Kant, 'Metaphysic of Ethics,'* p. 127.

Kant extols duty as a sublime and great name, that covers nothing which savours of favouritism or insinuation, but demands submission, threatening nothing which is calculated to excite a natural aversion in the mind, or designed to move by fear, but merely preventing a law which of itself finds universal entrance into the mind of man, and which even against the will of man wins his reverence, if not always his obedience—a law before which all inclinations grow dumb, even though they secretly work against it.—*Ueberweg, 'Hist. of Phil.,'* ii. 184.

Stern Lawgiver! yet thou dost wear
The Godhead's most benignant grace:
Nor know we anything so fair
As is the smile upon thy face:
Flowers laugh before thee on their beds;
And fragrance in thy footing treads;
Thou dost preserve the stars from wrong;
And the most ancient heavens, thro' thee, are fresh and strong.
—*Wordsworth, 'Ode to Duty.'*

Duty and Virtue distinguished from each other.

Duties are *actions*, or courses of action, considered as being right. Virtues are the *habits* of the soul, by which we perform duties. We approve duty, but we esteem and admire and love virtue. Virtue and duty differ, as the habit and act; as the internal disposition, and the outward manifestation.—*Whewell, 'Elements of Morality,'* pp. 56, 97.

Virtue is a species of excellence: and we do not regard behaviour as excellent when it is such as the majority of mankind would exhibit, and such as a man would be severely blamed for not exhibiting. Between the actions for which a person is praised and those for which he is blamed, there seems to be an intermediate region, where the notion of duty applies, but not that of virtue. We should scarcely say that it was virtuous to pay one's debts, or keep one's aged parents from starving: because these are duties which most men perform, and only bad men neglect. Again, there are excellent actions which we do not commonly call duties, though we praise men for doing them: as for a rich man to live very plainly and devote his income to works of public beneficence. At the same time the lines of distinction are very doubtfully drawn on either side: for we certainly call men virtuous for doing what is strictly their duty.—*Sidgwick*, '*Methods of Ethics*,' p. 191.

Duty is also used as necessarily implying that view of morality which may conveniently be called *jural*, the looking at ethics as a system of rules or laws. In this sense duty may be regarded as an idealisation of law. We note the following characteristics of duty when used in this way as distinguished from virtue. (1.) It is conceived as distinct and explicit. (2.) It takes cognisance, not of any risings above, but only of fallings below the standard—'We may fail in our duty, but we cannot do more than our duty. Thus while virtue is a scale rising indefinitely upwards, duty is a scale descending downwards.' And (3.) unlike virtue, it is conceived as involving a second party to whom we owe something, and a third party with an enforcing power.—*Grote*, '*Moral Ideals*,' ch. vii. (abridged).

Duty as distinguished from Prudence and Interest.

Prudence is self-surrender to the strongest impulse; Duty is self-surrender to the highest.

Prudence, in a world morally constituted, where sin has to be visited, and a scale of authority to be felt, will be different from what it else would be, and have new elements of pain to deal with, Duty will modify Prudence by adding fresh terms to her problem; not that Prudence, out of its own essence, can ever constitute Duty.—*Martineau*, '*Types of Ethical Theory*,' ii. 69, 71.

The Classification of Duties.

Duties, according to the Stoics, are respectively duties to self and duties to others. The former concern the preservation of self. The latter concern the relations of individuals socially.—*Schwegler*, '*Hist. of Phil.*,' p. 129.

The ordinary common-sense view divides duties into duties towards God, towards one's neighbour, and towards one's self. But this classification is not altogether satisfactory, because all duties are in a sense duties towards God. If we leave out this as a separate head, excellences of conduct may be brought under two classes, extra-regarding and self-regarding. But the lines of demarcation are not, it must be confessed, very clear. Even drunkenness and suicide are considered to be offences against the family of the man who commits them, as well as against himself. Perhaps, however, this is the best available classification. Under the head of *extra-regarding* Duties we should bring Benevolence, Justice, and Truth: under the head of self-regarding we should bring Temperance, Purity, Courage, and Prudence.—*Ryland*, '*Handbook, &c.*,' p. 150.

Duties depend upon the social position of men, and other like conditions. There are duties of parents and children, of husbands and wives, of friends, of neighbours, of magistrates, of members of various bodies and professions. There belong to each man the duties of his station. Our duties, so far as they regard our special relations to particular persons, may be termed our *relative* duties.—*Whewell*, '*Elements of Morality*,' p. 99.

The Fulfilment of Duty.

Is best guaranteed by love.

The best guarantee for a faithful pursuit of virtue is an intense love of it.—*Sully*, '*Sensations, &c.*,' p. 150

Is above all consequences.

So far is the calculation of consequences from being an infallible, universal criterion of Duty, that it never can be so in any instance. Only when the voice of Duty is silent, or when it has already spoken, may we allowably think of the consequences of a particular action, and calculate how far it is likely to fulfil what Duty has enjoined, either by its general laws or by a specific edict on this occasion. But Duty is above all consequences, and often, at a crisis of difficulty, commands us to throw them overboard. *Fiat Justitia; pereat Mundus.* It commands us to look neither to the right nor to the left, but straight onward. Hence every signal act of Duty is altogether an act of Faith. It is performed in the assurance that God will take care of the consequences, and will so order the course of the world that, whatever the immediate results may be, His word shall not return to Him empty.—'*Guesses at Truth*,' p. 508.

Motive and Intention

Bentham's distinction between them

Bentham draws a distinction, which it is of prime importance to note, between the *Motive* and the *Intention* of a voluntary act. The *Intention* comprises the whole contemplated operations of the act, both those for the sake of which, and those in spite of which, we do it. The *Motive* comprises only the former. Now, as these can be nothing but some pleasures or advantages intrinsically worth having, and allowable where there is no set-off on the other side, there can be no such thing as *a bad motive*, the thief and the honest trader both have the same spring to their industry, the love of gain, and if that were all, both would be equally respectable. The difference lies in the residuary part of the intention, viz., the privation and injury to others, which fails to restrain the thief and does restrain the merchant. To judge, therefore, of the morality of an act, we must look, Bentham insists, not at the motive in particular, but at its *whole intention*, and we must pronounce every act right (relatively to the agent) which is performed with intention of consequences predominantly pleasurable. —*Martineau*, '*Types of Ethical Theory*,' ii 252, 253.

If the merit of an action depends on no other circumstance than the quantity of good intended by the agent, then the rectitude of an action can in no case be influenced by the mutual relations of the parties,—a conclusion contradicted by the universal judgment of mankind in favour of the paramount obligations of various other duties. It is sufficient to mention the obligations of gratitude, of veracity, and of justice. Unless we admit these duties to be *immediately* obligatory, we must admit the maxim, that a good end may sanctify any means necessary for its attainment; or, in other words, that it would be lawful for us to dispense with the obligations of veracity and justice whenever by doing so we had a prospect of promoting any of the essential interests of society.—*Stewart*, '*Philosophy of Moral Powers*,' '*Works*,' vii. 231.

Rewards and Punishments.

Represented by Paley as the basis of moral obligation.

Let it be asked, Why am I obliged to keep my word? and the answer will be, Because I am 'urged to do so by a violent motive (namely, the expectation of being, after this life, rewarded if I do, and punished for it if I do not), resulting from the command of another' (namely, of God). *Paley*, '*Moral Philosophy*,' bk. ii. ch. iii.

Virtue is the doing good to mankind, in obedience to the will of God, and for the sake of everlasting happiness.—*Paley*, '*Moral Philosophy*,' bk. i. ch. vii.

Rewards are not sanctions

Rewards are indisputably *motives* to comply with the wishes of others. But to talk of commands and duties as *sanctioned* or *enforced* by rewards, or to talk of rewards as *obliging* or *constraining* to obedience, is surely a wide departure from the established meaning of the term . . . If a law holds out a *reward* as an inducement to do some act, an eventual *right* is conferred, and not an *obligation* imposed, upon those who shall act accordingly,—the imperative part of the law being addressed or directed to the party whom it requires to *render* the reward.—*Austin*, '*Jurisprudence*,' Lecture I.

Punishment, according to Bain, the commencement of moral obligation.

Authority, or punishment, is the commencement of the state of mind recognised under the various names—Conscience, the Moral Sense, the Sentiment of Obligation. The major part of every community adopt certain rules of conduct necessary for the common preservation, or ministering to the common well-being. They find it not merely their interest, but the very condition of their existence, to observe a number of maxims of individual restraint, and of respect to one another's feelings in regard to person, property, and good name. Obedience must be spontaneous on the part of the larger number, or on those whose influence preponderates in the society; as regards the rest, compulsion may be brought to bear. Every one, not of himself disposed to follow the rules prescribed by the community, is subjected to some infliction of pain, to supply the absence of other motives, the infliction increasing in severity until obedience is attained. It is familiarity with this *régime* of compulsion, and of suffering constantly increasing until resistance is overborne, that plants in the infant and youthful mind the first germ of the sense of obligation.—*Bain*, '*Emotions and the Will*,' p. 467.

Satisfaction and Remorse.

Darwin's theory of the evolution of conscience.

At the moment of action, man will no doubt be apt to follow the stronger impulse; and though this may occasionally prompt him to the noblest deeds, it will more commonly lead him to gratify his own desires at the expense of other men. But after their gratification, when past and weaker impressions are judged by the ever-enduring social instinct, and by his deep regard for the good opinion of his fellows, retribution will surely come. He will then feel remorse, repentance, regret, or shame; this latter feeling, however, relates almost exclusively to the judgment of others. He will consequently resolve more or less firmly to act differently for the future; and this is conscience; for conscience looks backwards, and serves as a guide for the future.

The nature and strength of the feelings which we call regret, shame, repentance, or remorse, depend apparently not only on the strength of the violated instinct, but partly on the strength of the temptation, and often still more on the judgment of our fellows. How far each man values the appreciation of others, depends on the strength of his innate or acquired feeling of sympathy, and on his own capacity for reasoning out the remote consequences of his acts. Another element is most important, although not necessary, the reverence or fear of the Gods, or spirits, believed in by each man: and this applies especially in cases of remorse.—'*Descent of Man*,' p. 114.

Dr Martineau's criticism of it.

I am far from denying that the process here described really takes place: the question is, whether the feeling in which it issues is identical with the moral sentiment of which it professes to give an account. The whole stress of the explanation is thrown upon a *time-measure*: a short want is gratified; a long one is disappointed: so, the disappointment survives, and that is all. But, surely these conditions may occur, without a trace of the phenomenon which is the object of our quest. The incidents of outward nature may realise them without any human will at all. Do you say, 'Of course it is understood that, in order to give rise to the feeling in question, the agent must himself be the cause of the evil deplored?' Very well: then that feeling must be something more than '*regret*,' and be directed upon something more special than the difference between a brief enjoyment and a long suffering; and, instead of using indifferently the words 'remorse' and 'regret,' we must investigate their specific difference. Let, then, the action proceed, not from the external elements, but from myself: and suppose that I regard myself as strictly a part of the organism of nature, a wheel of given function in its mechanism, with movement determined by its contiguous part, and transmitting the permeating energy to the ulterior, only with consciousness of the successive pulses of change as they occupy and use me. If this conscious intelligence of what goes on within me be *all* that differences me from the outward world, will it supply what is wanting to turn regret into remorse? Surely not: if there is no help for me but to go with the short instinct because it is stronger, and then be disappointed with the long one because it has been weaker, my regret will be just as much a *necessitated pain*, as if not one of the causal links had passed my inner consciousness. I am simply a *victim* of the major *vis*, to which my *conscience* has nothing to say.—'*Types of Ethical Theory*,' ii. 389, 390.

XXIII.

THE VIRTUES.

I. INTELLECTUAL VIRTUES.

Wisdom.

Its place among the virtues.

Wisdom was always placed by the Greek philosophers first in the list of virtues, and regarded as in a manner comprehending all the others: in fact, in the post-Aristotelian schools the notion of the Sage or ideally Wise man (σοφὸς) was regularly employed to exhibit in a concrete form the rules of life laid down by each system.—*Sidgwick*, '*Methods of Ethics*,' p. 229.

Only Practical Wisdom can be classed as a Virtue.

In common Greek usage the term (σοφὸς) would signify excellence in purely speculative science, no less than practical wisdom, and the English term Wisdom has, to some extent, the same ambiguity. It is, however, chiefly used in reference to practice; and even when applied to the region of pure speculation, suggests especially such intellectual gifts and habits as lead to sound practical conclusions: namely, comprehensiveness of view, the habit of attending impartially to a number of diverse considerations difficult to estimate exactly, and skill in determining the relative importance of each. At any rate, it is only Practical Wisdom which we commonly class among Virtues, as distinguished from purely intellectual excellences.—*Sidgwick*, '*Methods of Ethics*,' p. 229.

Aristotle's two kinds of wisdom.

'Wisdom' we, in the case of the arts, ascribe to those whose knowledge of their specific art is most absolutely exact; as, for example, when we call Phidias a 'wise' sculptor, and Polyclitus a 'wise' statuary, meaning by this use of the word 'wisdom' nothing more than the highest perfection of which art is capable; while in some cases again we say that a man is 'wise' in a general sense, and without reference to any such specific knowledge as is implied in the phrase 'wise in nought else,' used by Homer in the Margites—

'Him neither ditcher made the gods nor plough man,
Nor wise in aught besides'

And hence it is clear that 'wisdom,' used as the equivalent of philosophy, will signify the most absolutely exact scientific knowledge, so that the philosopher must not only be assured of the truth of his conclusions, as being deducible from such or such principles, but must further be assured that his principles are absolutely true —'*Ethics*,' bk. vi chap. vii (Williams's translation).

Prudence

Objects of its preference

The objects of prudential preference are the *effects of action upon us* Shall we smart for what we do? or shall we gain by it? shall we suffer loss, shall we profit more, by *this* cause, or by *that?* These are the questions, and the only ones, that are asked in the counsels of prudence Happiness, security, content, so far as they are under human command, are there the grand ends in view, decisive of every alternative. We ask not about the affection it is good *to start from*, but about the result it is pleasant to *tend to*, and choose accordingly —*Martineau*, '*Types of Ethical Theory*,' ii. 65

Distinguished from moral judgment.

Prudence is an affair of *foresight* moral judgment of *insight* The one appreciates what *will be*, the other, what immediately *is*. the one decides between future desirable conditions; the other, between present inward solicitations —*Martineau*, '*Types of Ethical Theory*,' ii. 66

Prudence cannot constitute duty

Prudence, out of its own essence, can never constitute Duty. Mere sentient susceptibility, filtered however fine, gives no moral consciousness; but a moral consciousness, like every other, cannot fail to be attended by joys and sorrows of its own Where the susceptibility of conscience is already acute, its sufferings or satisfactions will be considerable enough for prudence to consult; and the good man would be a fool were he other than good But in proportion as the moral consciousness is obtuse, its pain and pleasure, being fainter, may be neglected with greater impunity; Prudence may make up her accounts, throwing away such inappreciable fractions, and a bad man, without conscience, you cannot call a fool for not acting as if he had one He neglects no elements of happiness about which he cares, and a career which would make better men miserable brings him no distress Compunction he escapes by his insensibility; the sentiments of others are indifferent to him, so long as he holds his place among companions on his own level; and, short of the physiological penalties of nature and the direct punishments of human law, there is nothing to restrain him, on prudential grounds, from following the bent of his predominant inclinations Nothing therefore seems vainer than the attempt to work moral appeals by force of self-interest, and to induce a trial of virtue as a discreet investment To good men your argument is convincing, but superfluous; to the bad, who need it, it is unavailing, because false If you cannot speak home to the conscience at once, condescend to no lower plea. to reach the throne-room of the soul, Divine and holy things must pass by her grand and royal entry, and will refuse to creep up the backstairs of greediness and gain —*Martineau*, '*Types of Ethical Theory*,' ii 71

Paley's distinction between prudence and duty

There is always understood to be a difference between an act of *prudence* and an act of *duty*. Thus, if I distrusted a man who owed me a sum of money, I should reckon it an act of prudence to get another person bound with him; but I should hardly call it an act of duty. On the other hand, it would be thought a very unusual and loose kind of language, to say that, as I had made such a promise, it was *prudent* to perform it, or that, as my friend, when he went abroad, placed a box of jewels in my hands, it would be *prudent* in me to preserve it for him till he returned

Now, in what, you will ask, does the difference consist? inasmuch as, according to our account of the matter, both in the one case and the other, in acts of duty as well as acts of prudence, we consider solely what we ourselves shall gain or lose by the act.

The difference, and the only difference is this, that, in the one case, we consider what we shall gain or lose in the present world; in the other case, we consider also what we shall gain or lose in the world to come.—'*Moral and Political Philosophy*,' bk. ii. ch iii.

Prudence as the Will in its search for happiness.

Recognising evil and good in the distance, we work for remote ends, no less than for present sensations and emotions We have before us the catalogue of possible evils, on one hand, and of possible pleasures on the other, and we know, at the same time, which of the two we are more likely to find on our path We are aware, too, of certain objects that will afflict and pain us in an extraordinary degree, and of certain other objects that will give us an intense flow of pleasure All these different sources and varieties of the two great opposing inspirations play alternately upon our voluntary mechanism, and give the direction to our labours and pursuits. We are constantly avoiding physical injuries, organic disease, cold, hunger, exhaustion, fatigue, and the list of painful sensations and feelings; we are seeking after the opposite of all these generally, while we are devoted with express assiduity to something that has a distinguishing charm to our minds These are the motives personal to each individual, suggested by the contact of each one's susceptibilities with surrounding things. The upshot of the whole, the balance struck in the midst of conflict, is the course of prudence and the search for happiness, that we should severally steer by, if left entirely to ourselves. The stronger impulses of our nature would have their ascendency increased by repetition, and our character would be made up from those two great sources—the original promptings and the habits —*Bain*, '*Emotions and the Will*,' pp. 460, 461.

II THE MORAL VIRTUES—ANCIENT.

JUSTICE.

The Aristotelian Theory

Justice and Injustice are used in two senses,—a larger sense and a narrower sense

In the larger sense, *just behaviour* is equivalent to the observance of law generally; unjust behaviour is equivalent to the violation of law generally. But the law either actually does command, or may be understood to command, that we should perform towards others the acts belonging to each separate head of virtue: it either actually prohibits, or may be understood to prohibit, us from performing towards others any of the acts belonging to each separate head of vice.

Justice, in this sense, is the very fulness of virtue, because it denotes the actual exercise of virtuous behaviour towards others: 'There are many who behave virtuously in regard to their own personal affairs, but who are incapable of doing so in what regards others' *Justice* in the narrower sense is that mode of behaviour whereby a man, in his dealings with others, aims at taking to himself his fair share and no more of the common objects of desire, and willingly consents to endure his fair share of the common hardships.

Justice in this narrower sense is divided into two branches —1. Distributive Justice. 2. Corrective Justice.—*'Grote's Aristotle,'* p. 532.

The Utilitarian.

Justice, in the only sense in which it has a meaning, is an imaginary personage, feigned for the convenience of discourse, whose dictates are the dictates of utility, applied to certain particular cases. Justice, then, is nothing more than an imaginary instrument employed to forward on certain occasions and by certain means the purposes of benevolence. The dictates of justice are nothing more than a part of the dictates of benevolence, which, on certain occasions, are applied to certain subjects, to wit, to certain actions.—*Bentham, 'Introduction, &c.,'* p. 126.

Justice is a name for certain classes of moral rules which concern the essentials of human well-being more nearly, and are therefore of more absolute obligation than any other rules for the guidance of life; and the notion which we have found to be of the essence of the idea of justice, that of a right residing in an individual, implies and testifies to this more binding obligation.—*Mill, 'Utilitarianism,'* p. 88.

The Evolutional.

What is meant by justice? The special case in regard to which the virtue first emerges is that of a partial judge, and the same principle will apply of course to all other persons intrusted with power by the organisation of the community. The judge, again, is unjust so far as he acts from any other considerations than those which are recognised as legitimate by the legal constitution. He has to declare the law, and to apply it to particular cases without fear or favour. He must, therefore, give the same decision whether the persons interested be friends or foes, relations or strangers, rich or poor. And so extending the principle we say that a minister is unjust who distributes offices from other considerations than the fitness of the applicants. A parent is unjust who does not distribute his property to his children equally. The essence of justice, therefore, seems to be the uniform application of rules according to relevant circumstances; or, as we may put it, it is an application to conduct of the principle of sufficient reason. Every difference in my treatment of others must be determined by some principle which is in that case appropriate and sufficient. In this sense, therefore, justice means reasonableness.—*Stephen, 'Science of Ethics,'* p. 212.

The Intuitional.

Justice consists in according to every one his right. The word righteousness is used in our translation of the Scripture in a like extensive signification. As opposed to equity, justice means doing merely what positive law requires, while equity means doing what is fair and right in the circumstances of every particular case.—*Fleming, 'Vocab. of Phil.,'* p. 279.

Analysis of Justice.

Aristotle recognises two kinds of Justice proper—Distributive and Corrective. The former aims at 'equality,' or what is right and fair, in distributing property, privileges, and so on; the latter restores equality by reparation, when the other kind of justice has been violated.

Our common notion of justice includes the following elements:—(1) Mere Impartiality in carrying out distribution; (2) Reparation for injury; (3) Conservative Justice, or observance of those relations, determined by law and custom, which regulate the greater part of our conduct towards others; (4) Ideal Justice. If we look at these closely, we shall see that (1) is simply an exclusion of irrational arbitrariness, partiality, and is so obvious as to be unimportant; while we may refer (2) to Benevolence, rather than Justice. There remain two more important elements. By Conservative Justice is meant the observance of law and contracts, and definite understandings, and also the fulfilment of natural and normal expectations. By Ideal Justice is meant that kind of Justice which is exhibited in right distribution; the Standard, or Ideal, of just distribution being sometimes Individualistic realisation of Freedom ('just value' made equivalent to market value determined by free competition); sometimes Socialistic, the principle of rewarding Desert ('just value' cannot be determined by mere competition of buyers, on this view).

To tabulate the results, the common idea of Justice includes —

1. Impartiality

2 Reparation for injuries (= Benevolence

3 Conservative Justice.
- i In observance of laws and contracts, and definite understandings,
- ii. In fulfilment of natural and normal expectations.

4. Ideal Justice, of which there appear to be two distinct conceptions
- (a.) The Individualistic.
- (b.) The Socialistic.

—*Ryland*, '*Handbook, &c.*,' p. 151

Justice may be distinguished as ethical, economical, and political. The first consists in doing justice between man and man, as men, the second, in doing justice between the members of a family or household; and the third, in doing justice between the members of a community or commonwealth.—*Fleming*, '*Vocab. of Phil.*,' p. 279

The idea of justice supposes two things; a rule of conduct, and a sentiment which sanctions the rule. The first must be supposed common to all mankind, and intended for their good. The other (the sentiment) is a desire that punishment may be suffered by those who infringe the rule. Justice implies something which it is not only right to do, and wrong not to do, but which some individual person can claim from us as his moral right. And the sentiment of justice appears to me to be, the animal desire to repel or retaliate a hurt or damage to oneself, or to those with whom one sympathises.—*Mill*, '*Utilitarianism*,' pp 75, 79

[Revenge is usually said to be 'a perversion of the desire for justice; but Mill reverses this order, and explains Justice by Revenge.']

Mistakes in Regard to Justice

Justice is not identical with law.

Justice is not founded in law, as Hobbes and others hold, but in our idea of what is right. And laws are just or unjust in so far as they do or do not conform to that idea.—*Fleming*, '*Vocab. of Phil.*,' p. 279.

To say there is nothing just or unjust but what is commanded or prohibited by positive laws, is like saying that the radii of a circle were not equal till you had drawn the circumference.—*Montesquieu*, '*Spirit of Laws*,' bk. i. ch. i.

We do not mean by Justice merely conformity to Law. For, first, we do not always call the violators of law unjust, but only of some laws: not, for example, duellers or gamblers. And secondly, we often judge that Law does not completely realise Justice. our notion of Justice furnishes a standard with which we compare actual laws, and pronounce them just or unjust. And, thirdly, there is a part of just conduct which lies outside the sphere of Law: for example, we think that a father may be just or unjust to his children in matters where the law leaves (and ought to leave) him free.—*Sidgwick*, '*Methods of Ethics*,' p. 263.

Hume affirms that the rules of justice vary with men's state and condition.

The rules of equity or justice depend entirely on the particular state and condition in which men are placed, and owe their origin and existence to that UTILITY which results to the public from their strict and regular observance. Reverse, in any considerable circumstance, the condition of men: Produce extreme abundance or extreme necessity: Implant in the human breast perfect moderation and humanity, or perfect rapaciousness and malice: By rendering justice totally *useless*, you thereby totally destroy its essence, and suspend its obligation upon mankind.—*Hume*, '*Philosophical Works*,' iv. 183.

Hume's statement is sufficiently outrageous to answer itself. After judgment pronounced, justice becomes a passion

We are accustomed to represent justice as neutral and impartial, holding the scales. It is so in the department of evidence, because a criminal is not a criminal till he is proved to be one. But guilt once proved, and standing in its own colours before us, justice takes a *side*; she is a partisan and a foe; she becomes retributive justice, and *desires* the punishment of guilt. Justice then becomes an appetite and a passion, and not a discriminating principle only. We see this in the natural and eager interest which the crowd takes in the solemn proceedings of our courts,—in the relish with which they contemplate the judge in his chair of state; confiding in him as the guardian of innocence and avenger of guilt; and the satisfaction with which the final sentence upon crime is received, resembles the satisfaction of some bodily want—hunger or thirst or desire for repose.—*Mozley*, '*Old Test. Lectures*,' p. 90.

Courage, Fortitude.

Aristotle's Definition of Courage

The courageous man is afraid of things such as it befits a man to fear, but of no others; and even these he will make head against on proper occasions, when reason commands, and for the sake of *honour*, which is the end of virtue. To fear nothing, or too little, is rashness or insanity; to fear too much, is timidity: the courageous man is the mean between the two, who fears what he ought, when he ought, as he ought, and with the right views and purposes.—*Grote's* '*Aristotle*,' p. 530.

Sources of Courage

These are:—(1.) Physical vigour of constitution, which resists the withdrawal of the blood from the organic functions. (2.) The Active or Energetic Temperament, or the presence in large quantity of what the shock of fear tends to destroy. (3.) The Sanguine Temperament, which, being a copious fund of emotional vigour, shown in natural buoyancy, fulness of animal spirits, manifestations of warm sociability, and the like, is also the antithesis of depressing agencies—whether mere pain or the aggravations of fear. (4.) Force of Will, arising from the power of the motives to equanimity. (5.) Intellectual Force, which refuses to be overpowered by the fixed idea of an object of fright, and so serves to counterbalance the state of dread. (6.) Knowledge. The victories gained over superstition in the later ages have been due to the more exact acquaintance with nature. Pericles, instructed in astronomy under Anaxagoras, rescued his army from the panic of an eclipse, by a familiar illustration of its true cause.—*Bain*, '*Mental and Moral Science*,' p. 238.

Two Aspects of Courage

A clear line should be drawn between two aspects of courage. The one is the resistance to Fear properly so-called; that is, to the perturbation that exaggerates coming evil—a courageous man, in this sense, is one that possesses the true measure of impending danger, and acts according to that and not according to an excessive measure. The other aspect of courage is that which gives it all its nobleness as a virtue, namely, *Self-sacrifice*, or the deliberate encountering of evil for some honourable or virtuous cause. When a man knowingly risks his life in battle for his country, he may be called courageous, but he is still better described as a heroic and devoted man.—*Bain*, '*Mental and Moral Science*,' p. 489.

Temperance

Aristotle's Definition of Temperance

Temperance is the observance of a rational medium with respect to the pleasure of eating, drinking, and sex. Aristotle seems to be inconsistent when he makes it to belong to those pleasures in which animals generally partake, for other animals do not relish intoxicating liquors, unless, indeed, these are considered as ranking under *drink* generally The temperate man desires these pleasures as he ought, when he ought, within the limits of what is honourable, and, having a proper reference to the amount of his own pecuniary means, just as right reason prescribes. To pursue them more is excess; to pursue them less is defect. There is, however, in estimating excess and defect, a certain tacit reference to the average dispositions of the many

'Wherefore the desires of the temperate man ought to harmonise with reason, for the aim of both is the honourable. And the temperate man desires what he ought, and as he ought, and when: and this, too, is the order of reason'—*Grote's 'Aristotle,'* p 531

Nature and Sphere of Temperance.

The gratification of the Appetites or Bodily Desires, to a certain extent, and under certain conditions, is requisite for the continuance of the individual and of the species, and therefore is not vicious These desires, being mere attributes of the body, cannot have of themselves a moral character They are to be controlled by moral rules, and made subservient to moral affections, and thus are the materials of virtues The habits of thus controlling the bodily desires constitute the virtues of Temperance and Chastity —*Whewell, 'Elements of Morality,'* p 86

Temperance is moderation as to pleasure Aristotle confined it chiefly to pleasures of touch, and of taste in a slight degree Hence, perhaps, Popish writers, in treating of the vices of intemperance or luxury, dwell much on those connected with the senses of touch and taste By Cicero, the Latin word *temperantia* was used to denote the duty of self-government in general.

Temperance was enumerated as one of the four cardinal virtues. It may be manifested in the government and regulation of all our natural appetites, desires, passions, and affections, and may thus give birth to many virtues and restrain from many vices. As distinguished from fortitude, it may be said to consist in guarding against the temptations to pleasure and self-indulgence; while fortitude consists in bearing up against the evils and dangers of life —*Fleming, 'Vocab of Phil.,'* p. 512.

It is Necessary to Health

It is prudent to be temperate, because temperance is necessary to health The primary objection to drunkenness is that it injures the constitution; and if I prove from purely medical considerations that certain drinks are injurious and others innocuous, the rule deduced is a law of prudence, and consequently a part of morality. *Stephen, 'Science of Ethics,'* p 190

Its Connection with Courage and Energy.

Courage and Energy generally are, of course, clearly connected with temperance; and so far as courage is regarded as a virtue, the slothfulness and indifference which spring from all forms of intemperance incur a share of the contempt bestowed upon the quality which is their natural fruit —*Stephen, 'Science of Ethics,'* p 192

Intemperance—its Social Evils

It damages affection

Sensuality implies selfishness A man's love of his bottle is so much deducted from his love of his wife and children. So far as he is taken up with the gratification of his appetites, there is less room for the development of his affections A coward and a sluggard may be affectionate, though his affection will be comparatively useless to its objects; but in a sensual character the affections are killed at the root He is incapable of really loving, as well as of being useful to those whom he loves —*Stephen, 'Science of Ethics,'* p 193.

If I try to sum up the consequences of gluttony, I shall probably think first of the evils to health, of the consequences in the shape of gout, indigestion, and so forth.

But this gives a very imperfect measure of the social evils of gluttony. The difference between the glutton and the temperate man is not that one is more exposed than the other to certain diseases, or that in consequence of the diseases he is less capable of strenuous activity. It is also that the man who is a slave of his belly is less capable of all the higher affections, of intellectual pleasures, or æsthetic and refined enjoyments, and presumably selfish and incapable of extensive sympathies.—*Stephen*, '*Science of Ethics*,' p. 200.

It renders men useless

The intemperate man, according to the common phrase, is an enemy to no one but himself. We have, as we fancy, no right to object to him so long as he only makes a beast of himself in private. But both the spendthrift and the drunkard are really mischievous. A man whose vice injures only himself in the first place becomes also, by a necessary consequence, incapable of benefiting others. If he is an enemy to himself alone, he is also a friend to himself alone. The opium-eater, for example, paralyses his will; so far as he becomes incapable of energetic action he is unfitted for every social duty, and so far as he becomes the slave of his appetite becomes also unfitted for the social sentiments.—*Stephen*, '*Science of Ethics*,' p. 194.

III. MORAL VIRTUES—EXPANDED IN CHRISTIAN TEACHING.

REVERENCE.

Definition.

Reverence we may define as the feeling which accompanies the recognition of Superiority or Worth in others. It does not seem to be necessarily in itself benevolent, though often accompanied by some degree of love. But its ethical characteristics seem analogous to those of benevolent affection, in so far as, while it is not a feeling directly under the control of the will, we yet expect it under certain circumstances, and morally dislike its absence, and perhaps commonly consider the expression of it to be sometimes a duty, even when the feeling itself is absent.—*Sidgwick*, '*Methods of Ethics*,' p. 252.

Reverence is a name for high admiration and deferential regard, without implying authority. We may express reverence and feel deference to a politician, a philanthropist, or a man of learning or science.—*Bain*, '*Mental and Moral Science*,' p. 249.

How it is Developed

The feeling seems to be naturally excited by all kinds of superiority, not merely moral and intellectual excellences, but also superiorities of rank and position; and indeed in the common behaviour of men it is to the latter that it is more regularly and formally rendered.—*Sidgwick*, '*Methods of Ethics*,' p. 252.

Reverence grows out of a sense of constant dependence. It is fostered by that condition of religious thought in which men believe that each incident that befalls them is directly and specially ordained, and when every event is therefore fraught with a moral import. It is fostered by that condition of scientific knowledge in which every portentous natural phenomenon is supposed to be the result of a direct divine interposition, and awakens in consequence emotions of humility and awe. It is fostered in that stage of political life when loyalty or reverence for the sovereign is the dominating passion, when an aristocracy, branching forth from the throne, spreads habits of deference and subordination through every village, when a revolutionary, a democratic, and a sceptical spirit are alike unknown.—*Lecky*, '*European Morals*,' i. 148.

It is a Necessary Element in Great Excellence

There are few persons who are not conscious that no character can attain a supreme degree of excellence, in which a reverential spirit is wanting. Of all the forms of moral goodness it is that to which the epithet beautiful may be most emphatically applied Yet the habits of advancing civilisation are, if I mistake not, on the whole inimical to its growth.—*Lecky*, '*European Morals*,' i 148

Reverence for Sacred Things and for God

There are some things in which we may well envy the members of the Church of Rome,—in nothing more than in the reverence which they feel for whatever has been consecrated to the service of their religion It may be, that they often confound the sign with the thing signified, and merge the truth in the symbol. We, on the other hand, in our eagerness to get rid of the signs, have not been careful enough to preserve the things signified We have sometimes hurt the truth, in stripping off the symbols it was clothed in —'*Guesses at Truth*,' p. 510.

Truth is the basis, as it is the object of reverence, not less than it is of every other virtue. Reverence prostrates herself before a greatness, the reality of which is obvious to her; but she would cease to be reverence if she could exaggerate the greatness which provokes her homage, not less surely than if she could depreciate or deny it. The sentiment which, in contemplating its object, abandons the guidance of fact for that of imagination, is disloyal to that honesty of purpose, which is of the essence of reverence; and it is certain at last to subserve the purposes of the scorner and the spoiler. Even a slight swerving from truth must be painful to genuine reverence.—*Liddon*, '*Bampton Lectures*,' p. 268.

Let knowledge grow from more to more,
But more of reverence in us dwell;
That mind and soul, according well,
May make one music as before.
—*Tennyson*, '*In Memoriam*.'

BENEVOLENCE.

Its Nature

Explained.

There is a natural principle of benevolence in man, which is in some degree to society what self-love is to the individual. And if there be in mankind any disposition to friendship; if there be any such thing as compassion, for compassion is momentary love; if there be any such thing as the paternal or filial affections; if there be any affection in human nature, the object and end of which is the good of another; this is itself benevolence or the love of another. —*Butler*, '*Sermons*,' i.

Benevolence, which is an object of moral approbation, is a fixed and settled disposition to promote the happiness of our fellow-creatures. It is peculiar to a rational nature, and is not to be confounded with those kind affections which are common to us with the brutes. These are subsidiary, in fact, to the principle of Benevolence; and they are always amiable qualities in a character: but so far as they are constitutional, they are certainly in no respect meritorious.

Where a rational and settled Benevolence forms a part of a character, it will render the conduct perfectly uniform, and will exclude the possibility of those inconsistencies that are frequently observable in individuals who give themselves up to the guidance of particular affections, either private or public In truth, all those offices, whether apparently trifling or important, by which the happiness of other men is affected,—Civility, Gentleness, Kindness, Humanity, Patriotism, Universal Benevolence,—are only diversified expressions of the same disposition, according to the circumstances in which it operates, and the relations which the agent bears to others. —*Stewart*, '*Outlines of Moral Philosophy*,' '*Works*,' vi. 79.

Two kinds.

Benevolence naturally divides into two kinds, the *general* and the *particular*. The first is, where we have no friendship, or connection, or esteem for the person, but feel only a general sympathy with him, or a compassion for his pains, and a congratulation with his pleasures The other species of benevolence is founded on an opinion of virtue, on services done us, or on some particular connexions.—*Hume*, '*Philosophical Works*,' iv. 268.

Its main constituent.

In Benevolence, the main constituent is Sympathy, which is not to be confounded with Tenderness. Sympathy prompts us to take on the pleasures and pains of other beings, and act on them as if they were our own.—*Bain*, '*Mental and Moral Science*,' p. 244.

It is not the whole of virtue.

Benevolence, and the want of it, singly considered, are in no sort the whole of virtue and vice. For if this were the case, in the review of one's own character or that of others, our moral understanding and moral sense would be indifferent to everything but the degrees in which benevolence prevailed, and the degrees in which it was wanting. That is, we should neither approve of benevolence to some persons rather than to others, nor disapprove injustice and falsehood upon any other account, than merely as an overbalance of happiness was foreseen likely to be produced by the first and of misery by the second.—*Butler*, '*Dissertation*,' i.

The doctrine of virtue, as consisting in benevolence, false as it is when maintained as universal and exclusive, is yet, when considered as having the sanction of so many enlightened men, a proof at least of the very extensive diffusion of benevolence in the modes of conduct which are denominated virtuous. It may not, indeed, comprehend all the aspects under which man is regarded by us as worthy of our moral approbation, but it comprehends by far the greater number of them,—his relations to his fellow-men, and to all the creatures that live around him, though not the moral relations which bind him to the Greatest of all beings, nor those which are directly worthy of our approbation, as confined to the perfection of his own internal character.—*Brown*, '*Lectures on Ethics*,' p. 253, Lecture 86.

Regarded by some as a supreme virtue.

In modern times, since the revival of independent ethical speculation, there have always been thinkers who have maintained, in some form, the view that Benevolence is a supreme and architectonic virtue, comprehending and summing up all the others, and fitted to regulate them and determine their proper limits and mutual relations. The phase of this view most current at present would seem to be Utilitarianism.—*Sidgwick*, '*The Methods of Ethics*,' p. 236.

It does not exclude self love.

That any affection tends to the happiness of another, does not hinder its tending to one's own happiness too. That others enjoy the benefit of the air and the light of the sun, does not hinder but that these are as much one's own private advantage now, as they would be if we had the property of them exclusive of all others. So a pursuit which tends to promote the good of another, yet may have as great tendency to promote private interest, as a pursuit which does not tend to the good of another at all, or which is mischievous to him. All particular affections whatever equally lead to a course of action for their own gratification, *i.e.*, the gratification of ourselves; and the gratification of each gives delight.—*Butler*, '*Sermons*,' xi.

Benevolent Affections.

Enumerated.

(1.) Compassion or Pity: this means sympathy with distress, and usually supposes an infusion of tender feeling. (2.) Gratitude: this is inspired by the receipt of favours. Its foundation is sympathy; and its ruling principle, the complex idea of justice.—*Bain*, '*Mental and Moral Science*,' p. 245.

The object of benevolence.

As man is so much limited in his capacity, as so small a part of the creation comes under his notice and influence, and as we are not used to consider things in so general a way, it is not to be thought of that the universe should be the object of benevolence to such creatures as we are. The object is too vast. For this reason moral writers also have substituted a less general object for our benevolence, mankind. But this likewise is an object too general, and very much out of our view. Therefore persons more practical have, instead of mankind, put our country; and made the principle of human virtue to consist in the entire uniform love for our country But this is speaking to the upper part of the world. Kingdoms and governments are large; and the sphere of action of far the greatest part of mankind is much narrower than the governments they live under. There plainly is wanting a less general and nearer object of benevolence for the bulk of men. Therefore the Scripture, not being a book of theory and speculation, but a plain rule of life for mankind, has with the utmost possible propriety put the principle of virtue upon the love of our neighbour.—*Butler*, '*Sermons*,' xii.

The duty of cultivating Benevolence.

The general maxim of Benevolence would be commonly said to be, 'that we ought to love all our fellow-men,' or, 'all our fellow-creatures:' but there is some doubt among moralists as to the precise meaning of the term 'love' in this connection: since, according to Kant and others, what is morally prescribed as the Duty of Benevolence is not strictly the affection of love or kindness, so far as this contains an emotional element, but only the determination of the will to seek the good or happiness of others. And I agree that it cannot be a strict duty to feel an emotion, so far as it is not directly within the power of the will to produce it at any given time. Still it seems to me paradoxical to deny that this emotional element is included in our common notion of Charity or Philanthropy, regarded as a Virtue: or that it adds a higher excellence to the mere beneficent disposition of the will, as resulting in more excellent actions. If this be so, it will be a duty to cultivate the affections so far as it is possible to do so: and indeed this would seem (no less than the permanent disposition to do good) to be a normal effect of repeated beneficent resolves and actions Even the poets and popular moralisers have observed that a benefit tends to excite love in the agent towards the person benefited, no less than in the latter towards the agent. It must be admitted, however, that this effect is less certain than the production of the disposition; and that some men are naturally so unattractive to others that these can feel no affection towards them, though they may entertain benevolent dispositions of will. At any rate, it would seem to be a duty generally, and till we find the effort fruitless, to cultivate kind affections towards those whom we ought to benefit; not only by doing kind actions (which are immediately a duty, and therefore need not be prescribed as a means to an end), but by placing ourselves under any natural influences which experience shows to have a tendency to produce affection.—*Sidgwick*, '*Methods of Ethics*,' pp. 236, 237.

Utilitarianism cannot formulate a logical theory of Benevolence.

A theory of Benevolence is logically unattainable under a utilitarian system. Since Bentham's time, Utilitarianism has given prominence to benevolence, making 'the greatest happiness of the greatest number' its standard of rectitude. But in this it has amended its ethical form only by the sacrifice of logical consistency. If happiness is the sole end of life, it must be the happiness of that life to which it is the end. To make the happiness of others the end of individual life, is to leave the utilitarian basis by deserting the theory of life on which it rests. Utilitarianism is in the very singular position of professing itself a theory of universal benevolence, and yet laying its foundations on the ground that personal happiness is the sole end of life. To do good to others for the sake of our own happiness, is, however, compatible with the theory; but this is not benevolence.—*Calderwood*, '*Moral Philosophy*,' p. 136.

GRATITUDE.

Gratitude is a Benevolent Affection

It implies a sense of kindness done or intended, and a desire to return it. It is sometimes also characterised as a moral affection, because the party cherishing it has the idea that he who did or intended kindness to him has done right and deserves a return.—*Fleming*, '*Vocab. of Phil.*,' p. 212.

Gratitude seems generally to combine kindly feeling with some sort of emotional recognition of superiority, as the giver of benefits is in a position of superiority to the receiver.—*Sidgwick*, '*Methods of Ethics*,' p. 258.

The receipt of favour inspires Gratitude; of which the foundation is sympathy, and the ruling principle the complex idea of Justice. Pleasure conferred upon us by another human being, immediately prompts the tender response. With whatever power of sympathy we possess, we enter into the pleasures and pains of the person that has engaged our regards. The highest form of gratitude, which leads us to reciprocate benefits and make acknowledgments, in some proportion to the benefits conferred, is an application of the principle of Justice. *Bain*, '*Mental Science*,' p. 245.

It is a variety of generosity.

Gratitude is a variety of *generosity*, with its indefinite profusion, however, brought to some approximate measure by the extent of the favour conferred, for, though it repudiates all nice calculations and insists on an *ad libitum* range, yet it spends itself and rests in natural equilibrium, when the requital seems in correspondence with the gift. How this correspondence is to be reached, it may be difficult to decide; whether by estimating the effort of the giver, or the service to the receiver, or by framing a compound ratio of the two; or by leaving the whole adjustment to the invisible intensity of the affection. But, in any case, the affection, however expressed, will be owned as a debt on the one side, without being held as a claim on the other. As it lies in the very essence of the affection to accept this paradox of love, it is defective in any one who cannot rest in so generous a relation, but is uneasy till he rids himself of the debt, and obtains his discharge.—*Martineau*, '*Types of Ethical Theory*,' ii. 229, 230.

The duty of gratitude.

It is universally recognised.

The duty of requiting benefits seems to be recognised wherever morality extends: and Intuitionists have justly pointed to this recognition as an instance of a truly universal intuition.—*Sidgwick*, '*Methods of Ethics*,' p. 258.

It is in some cases hard to perform.

To persons of a certain temperament this feeling is often peculiarly hard to attain; owing to their dislike of the position of inferiority: and this again we consider a right feeling to a certain extent, and call it 'independence' or 'proper pride': but this feeling and the effusion of gratitude do not easily mix.—*Sidgwick*, '*Methods of Ethics*,' p. 258.

Gratitude is the rarest of all the virtues. —*Lange*.

The penalty of disregarding it.

Sorrow, care, and discontent with life have very often their foundation in unthankfulness, in a state of mind that will only make claims, but not give thanks. Many men would have been preserved from the abyss of melancholy into which they sunk, could they only have taken heart to thank God.

Not to recognise and value what is truly valuable, not to admire it, not to wish to thank for it, is a sentiment that leads to inward desolation and unfruitfulness.—*Martensen*, '*Christian Ethics*,' pp. 385, 247.

The pleasure of cherishing it.

There is not a more pleasing exercise of mind than Gratitude. It is accompanied with such an inward satisfaction that the duty is sufficiently rewarded by the performance. It is not like the practice of many other virtues, difficult and painful, but attended with so much pleasure, that, were there no positive command which enjoined it, nor any recompense laid up for it hereafter, a generous mind would indulge in it, for the natural gratification which accompanies it.—*Addison*, '*Spectator*,' No 453.

The debt of gratitude can be paid only to the living.

Let us not forget, that if honour be for the dead, gratitude can only be for the living. He who has once stood beside the grave, to look back upon the companionship which has been for ever closed, feeling how impotent *there*, are the wild love and the keen sorrow, to give one instant's pleasure to the pulseless heart, or atone in the lowest measure to the departed spirit for the hour of unkindness, will scarcely for the future incur that debt to the heart, which can only be discharged to the dust. But the lessons which men learn as individuals, they do not learn as nations. Again and again they have seen their noblest descend into the grave, and have thought it enough to garland the tombstone when they had not crowned the brow, and to pay honour to the ashes which they had denied to the spirit.—*Ruskin*, '*Modern Painters*,' sec. i chap. i. § 5.

PITY, OR COMPASSION.

Definitions.

Compassion is a call, a demand of nature, to relieve the unhappy; as hunger is a natural call for food.—*Butler*, '*Upon Compassion*,' Serm. II.

Pity is the *imagination* or *fiction* of future calamity to ourselves, proceeding from the sense of *another* man's calamity.—*Hobbes*, '*Human Nature*,' chap ix sec. 10.

Office of compassion.

Since in many cases it is very much in our power to alleviate the miseries of each other; and benevolence, though natural in man to man, yet is in a very low degree kept down by interest and competitions; and men, for the most part, are so engaged in the business and pleasures of the world, as to overlook and turn away from objects of misery; which are plainly considered as interruptions to them in their way, as intruders upon their business, their gaiety and mirth; compassion is an advocate within us in their behalf, to gain the unhappy admittance and access, to make their case attended to.—*Butler*, '*Upon Compassion*,' Serm. II.

How selfish soever man may be supposed, there are evidently some principles in his nature, which interest him in the fortunes of others, and render their happiness necessary to him, though he derives nothing from it, except the pleasure of seeing it. Of this kind is pity or compassion, the emotion which we feel for the misery of others, when we either see it, or are made to conceive it in a very lively manner. That we often derive sorrow from the sorrow of others, is a matter of fact too obvious to require any instances to prove it; for this sentiment, like all the other original passions of human nature, is by no means confined to the virtuous and humane, though they perhaps may feel it with the most exquisite sensibility. The greatest ruffian, the most hardened violator of the laws of society, is not altogether without it.—*Smith*, '*Theory of Moral Sentiments*,' pt. i. sec. i. chap. i.

It impels us to relieve distress; it serves as a check on resentment and selfishness, and the other principles which lead us to injure the interests of others; but it does not prompt us to the communication of positive happiness. Its object is to *relieve*, and sometimes to *prevent*, suffering, but not to augment the enjoyment of those who are already easy and comfortable. We are disposed to do this by the general spirit of benevolence, but not by the particular affection of pity.—*Stewart, 'Philosophy of the Active Powers,' 'Works,'* vii. 188.

SYMPATHY.

Its Nature is Power to enter into the Feelings of Others.

Sympathy is to enter into the feelings of another, and to act them out as if they were our own It is a species of involuntary imitation, or assumption of the displays of feeling enacted in our presence, which is followed by the rise of the feelings themselves.—*Bain, 'Mental and Moral Science,'* p. 276.

Sympathy is implied in all our thoughts about others. We think about other men by becoming other men. We appropriate provisionally their circumstances and emotions. So far as I sympathise with you, I annex your consciousness — *Stephen, 'Science of Ethics,'* p. 237.

Evolutional Theory of Sympathy

Sympathy is begotten in the breasts of many dumb animals, when they have learned to recognise in their fellows the outward signs of that which they remember as a condition of past distress for themselves. The ideal recurrence of such a state, coupled with a perception implying the similar present suffering of another, prompts to actions for its relief. In such exercise of mere brute sympathy we have one of the most important germs of those altruistic feelings which attain so much breadth and power in higher races of man. —*Bastian, 'Brain, &c.,'* p. 416.

Its Development.

Through Affection

Sympathy with *Joys* or *Sorrows* is a fine element of human character. It originates in the affection which we naturally have towards others All this, however, may be a mere surface sensibility, as fleeting as the play of features on the countenance, or as the chasing of sunshine and shadow on the mountain sides, very pleasant, but evanescent,—as one observed of a sensitive person, ever in smiles and tears, that he was a man of tenderness of nerve rather than of heart. Such persons feel for us, but they do not stand by us, they do not help us. In genuine feeling, sympathy is rooted and grounded in love, and is a branch of love, and a grace of a high order. We are commanded to 'rejoice with them that do rejoice, and weep with them that weep.'

In it our heart beats responsive to the hearts of others. We enter into their feelings; we identify ourselves with them. Our very countenance is apt to take the expression of the feeling into which we enter. When we see others laugh, we are apt to laugh also. We weep with those that weep. We are disposed to run with those that run. We flee with those that flee. When others are striking a blow, we are inclined to lift our arm as if to do the same. It is usually said that all this arises from the principle of imitation. The correct account rather is, that we place ourselves in the position of others, and are thus led to act as they act —*M'Cosh, 'The Emotions,'* p. 133

Through the pleasure it yields.

If beings around him habitually manifest pleasure and but rarely pain, sympathy yields to its possessor a surplus of pleasure; while, contrariwise, if little pleasure is ordinarily witnessed and much pain, sympathy yields a surplus of pain to its possessor. The average development of sympathy must, therefore, be regulated by the average manifestations of pleasure and pain in others. If the social state is such that manifestations of pleasure predominate, sympathy will increase, since sympathetic pleasures, adding to the totality of pleasures enhancing vitality, conduce to the physical prosperity of the most sympathetic, and since the pleasures of sympathy, exceeding its pains in all, lead to an exercise of it which strengthens it —*Spencer, 'Data of Ethics,'* p 244.

General conditions of development

Sympathy supposes (1) one's own remembered experience of pleasure and pain, and (2) a connexion in the mind between the outward signs or expressions of the various feelings and the feelings themselves. We cannot sympathise beyond our experience, nor up to that experience, without some power of recalling it to mind. The child is unable to enter into the joys and griefs of the grown up person; the humble day-labourer can have no fellow-feeling with the cares of the rich, the great, the idle. But sympathy is something more than a mere scientific inference that another person has come under a state of tenderness, of fear, or of rage; it is the being forcibly possessed for the time by the very same feeling.—*Bain*, '*Mental Sciences*,' p 277

Favouring circumstances

The following are the chief circumstances favourable to sympathy (1) Our being disengaged at the time, or free from any intense occupation or prepossession. (2) Our familiarity with the mode of feeling represented to us. The mother easily feels for a mother The timid man cannot enter into the composure of the resolute man. (3) Our relation to the person determines our sympathy, affection, esteem, reverence, attract our attention and make us succumb to the influence of the manifested feeling: hatred or dislike removes us almost from the possibility of fellow-feeling. (4) The energy or intensity of the language, tones, and gestures necessarily determines the strength of the impression and the prompting to sympathy. (5.) The clearness or distinctness of the expression is of great importance in inducing the state on the beholder. This is the talent of the actor and elocutionist (6) A susceptibility to the displays of other men's feelings.—*Bain*, '*Mental Science*,' p 278.

Relation of Sympathy to Imagination.

Its intensity is largely dependent on imaginative power.

What we commonly call sensibility depends in a great measure on the power of imagination. Point out to two men a man reduced by misfortune from easy circumstances to indigence. The one feels merely in proportion to what he perceives by his senses. The other follows in imagination the unfortunate man to his dwelling, and partakes with him and his family in their domestic distress. He pictures the circle of friends they had been forced to leave, the flattering prospects they once indulged, and all the various resources which delicacy and pride suggest to conceal poverty from the world. As he proceeds, he weeps, not for what he sees, but for what he imagines.—*Stewart*, '*Works*,' ii. 452.

There is no doubt in some persons a very wonderful apprehension and divination of that which others are thinking, imagining, purposing. Those who really have that gift we call men and women of genius. Sympathy has much to do with genius, perhaps is the essence of it.—*Maurice*, '*The Conscience*,' p. 33.

In sympathetic persons, representation of the annoyance to be given is so vivid that it often prevents them from doing or saying unpleasant things which they see ought to be done or said; the sentiment of pity checks the infliction of pain, even unduly. In another class of cases, if an individual is not highly imaginative, he may, and often does, rid himself of the disagreeable consciousness by getting out of sight or hearing. But if his imagination is vivid, and if he also sees that the suffering can be diminished by his aid, then he cannot escape from his disagreeable consciousness by going away; since the represented pain continues with him, impelling him to return and assist.—*Spencer*, '*Principles of Psychology*,' ii. 615.

In this way is explained the excitation of sympathy by imitation, and of imitation by sympathy.

'I have often remarked,' says Burke, 'that on mimicking the looks and gestures of angry or placid, or frightened or daring men, I have involuntarily found my mind turned to that passion whose appearance I endeavoured to imitate.' Here is an important fact, but it is not correctly stated; that which comes first is put last. The only effective way of mimicking a passion is to call up by the fancy an object or scene fitted to awaken the feeling.

I rather think that sympathetic action is to be accounted for very much in this way: we put ourselves in the position of others, by calling up by the idea the same feelings, which go out in the same manifestations. Tears shed are apt to call forth tears in the beholder, or quite as readily in the listener to the tale told which makes us realise the position. It is the same with laughter, which is apt to be echoed back till the noise rings throughout a large assembly. When a company as a whole is moved, it is difficult for any person to keep his composure. An alarm of fire will spread through a vast congregation, the greater number of whom are actually cognisant of no cause of fear. A panic started by a few soldiers, who believe that they see danger, will often seize a whole army, the great body of whom know no ground for the terror. It is easier for an orator, say a preacher, if only he can get up feeling, to move a large audience than a thin one. There is a reflection of emotion from every person upon every other. We call this contagion, but it is contagion produced by people's being led to cherish the same feelings producing the same outward manifestation. The very contagion of disease is made more powerful by persons being afraid of, and so dwelling much on, the infection.—*M'Cosh, 'The Emotions,'* p. 102.

The very aspect of happiness, joy, prosperity, gives pleasure; that of suffering, pain, sorrow, communicates uneasiness. The human countenance, says Horace, borrows smiles or tears from the human countenance. Reduce a person to solitude, and he loses all enjoyment, except either of the sensual or speculative kind; and that because the movements of his heart are not forwarded by correspondent movements in his fellow creatures. The signs of sorrow and mourning, though arbitrary, affect us with melancholy; but the natural symptoms, tears, and cries, and groans never fail to infuse compassion and uneasiness.—*Hume, 'Philosophical Works,'* iv. 208.

If we have a feeling of trust in certain persons, say our neighbours, or our friends, or our party, or our associates, or our special companions, then we are inclined to act as they act, but by our coming to share their feelings, their affections, and antipathies. When we have a great admiration towards any one for his courage, or his magnanimity, we are especially led to copy him. A brave commander, by going before, may be able to lead his troops into certain death. We have all seen a noble gift, on the part of an individual, calling forth the plaudits and the liberality of many others.—*M'Cosh, 'The Emotions,'* p. 103.

Imagination must be aided, however, by experience.

Higher representative power does not involve greater commiseration, unless there have been received painful experiences like, or akin to, those which are witnessed. For this reason strong persons, though they may be essentially sympathetic in their natures, cannot adequately enter into the feelings of the weak. Never having been nervous or sensitive, they are unable to conceive the sufferings which chronic invalids experience from small perturbing causes.—*Spencer, 'Principles of Psychology,'* ii. 616.

Imagination determines the range of sympathy.

The degree and range of sympathy depend on the clearness and extent of representation. A sympathetic feeling is one not immediately excited by the natural cause of such a feeling, but one that is mediately excited by the presentation of signs habitually associated with such a feeling. Consequently, it presupposes ability to perceive and combine these signs, as well as ability to represent their implications, external or internal, or both. So that there can be sympathy only in proportion as there is power of representation.—*Spencer*, '*Principles of Psychology*,' ii. p. 565.

The limitation of sympathy.

The mere fact that any one is in pain awakens our sympathy; but, unless the causes and attendant circumstances come home to us, the sympathy is neither persistent nor deep. Pains that have never afflicted us, that we know nothing of, that are, in our opinion, justly or needlessly incurred, are dismissed from our thoughts as soon as we are informed of the facts. The tears shed by Alexander, at the end of his conquests, probably failed to stimulate one responsive drop in the most sensitive mind that ever heard his story.—*Bain*, '*Mental Science*,' p. 280.

The Attractive Power of Sympathy.

With the sympathetic being every one feels more sympathy than with others. All conduct themselves with more than usual amiability to a person who hourly discloses a lovable nature. Such a one is practically surrounded by a world of better people than one who is less attractive. If we contrast the state of a man possessing all the material means to happiness, but isolated by his absolute egoism, with the state of an altruistic man, relatively poor in means, but rich in friends, we may see that various gratifications, not to be purchased by money, come in abundance to the last and are inaccessible to the first.—*Spencer*, '*Data of Ethics*,' p. 212.

The craving for sympathy is the common boundary-line between joy and sorrow.—'*Guesses at Truth*,' p. 530.

Pleasure of sympathy.

Whatever may be the cause of sympathy, or however it may be excited, nothing pleases us more than to observe in other men a fellow-feeling with all the emotions of our own breast; nor are we ever so much shocked as by the appearance of the contrary. Those who are fond of deducing all our sentiments from certain refinements of self-love think themselves at no loss to account, according to their own principles, both for this pleasure and this pain. Man, say they, conscious of his own weakness and of the need which he has for the assistance of others, rejoices whenever he observes that they adopt his own passions, because he is then assured of that assistance; and grieves whenever he observes the contrary, because he is then assured of their opposition. But both the pleasure and the pain are always felt so instantaneously, and often upon such frivolous occasions, that it seems evident that neither of them can be derived from any such self-interested consideration. A man is mortified when, after having endeavoured to divert the company, he looks round and sees that nobody laughs at his jests but himself. On the contrary, the mirth of the company is highly agreeable to him, and he regards this correspondence of their sentiments with his own as the greatest applause.—*Smith*, '*Theory of Moral Sentiments*,' pt. i., sec. i., chap. ii.

Purity.

This Virtue is nearly Identical with Chastity.

The notion of Chastity is nearly equivalent to that of Purity, only somewhat more external and superficial.—*Sidgwick*, '*Methods of Ethics*,' p. 330.

The Law of Purity.

It is the same for both sexes.

As society is founded biologically, or as matter of life, on the union of the sexes; so is it founded ethically, or as matter of rational combination, on the common application of the same moral law to both sexes. The obligation to physical, intellectual, and moral purity is exactly the same for both, and, being placed under common law, each of the sexes is constituted the guardian of purity in the other.—*Calderwood*, '*Moral Philosophy*,' p. 265.

Minute rules on this subject are to be deprecated.

Any attempt to lay down minute and detailed rules on this subject seems to be condemned by common sense, as tending to defeat the end of purity: as such minuteness of moral legislation invites men in general to exercise their thoughts on this subject to an extent which is practically dangerous. It was partly owing to the serious oversight of not perceiving that Purity itself forbids too minute a system of rules for the observance of purity, that the mediæval casuistry fell into extreme, and on the whole undeserved disrepute.—*Sidgwick*, '*Methods of Ethics*,' p. 331.

The Standard of Purity is independent of law.

Chastity and fidelity are not to be made by any law. No state can force men and women to marry, or really put down licentious habits, even if it makes the attempt; and, on the other hand, the marriage tie might be equally respected in fact, even if there were no law in regard to it. The law, in fact, recognises one kind of association of the sexes, and bestows certain privileges upon those who are so associated, but it would be a hopeless inversion of consequent and antecedent to suppose that it can really originate it.—*Stephen*, '*Science of Ethics*,' p. 133.

Our common notion of purity implies a standard independent of law: for conformity to this does not necessarily secure purity.—*Sidgwick*, '*Methods of Ethics*,' p. 331.

The Christian law of purity.

Our body was not given us to be the instrument of our own pleasure. It is a noble gift of God, and must fulfil its office, according to the appointment of the Divine Will. It is not a matter that we may deal with at our own discretion; it is the instrument of our personality, and not our absolute property. It is the image of our Creator; it is the temple in which the Holy Ghost carries on His work; it is destined for immortality. Our treatment of our body is not a matter of indifference. No one has a right selfishly to misuse and corrupt beforehand what is not his own, but is to be another's. We ought not to enter upon marriage merely to preserve our purity; we ought also to maintain our purity that we may marry with a good conscience.—*Luthardt*, '*Moral Truths*,' p. 120.

The man who would sin if he could, is as objectionable as the man who sins because he can.—*Stephen*, '*Science of Ethics*,' p. 192.

Its close connection with true manliness and womanliness.

The man who uses his strength to defend the purity of woman, performs the moral part assigned to him in life, and he only is manly in the true ethical sense. The man who uses his power to corrupt woman, is self-degraded, cruel, and cowardly. The woman who, in receiving the protection which is her birthright, uses her influence to refine and elevate, performs her moral part in life. She who uses her influence to corrupt others, debases herself, and makes her life a moral anomaly, specially glaring and offensive because of the refining influence intrusted to her keeping.—*Calderwood*, '*Moral Philosophy*,' p. 266.

The Utilitarian Theory is not Favourable to Purity.

I will simply ask the reader to conceive a mind from which all notion of the intrinsic excellence and nobility of purity was banished, and to suppose such a mind comparing, by a utilitarian standard, a period in which sensuality was almost unbridled, such as the age of Athenian glory, or the English restoration, with a period of austere virtue. The question, which of these societies was morally the best, would thus resolve itself simply into the question, in which there was the greatest amount of enjoyment and the smallest amount of suffering. The pleasures of domestic life, the pleasures resulting from a freer social intercourse, the different degrees of suffering inflicted on those who violated the law of chastity, the ulterior consequences of each mode of life upon population, would be the chief elements of the comparison. Can any one believe that the balance of enjoyment would be so unquestionably and so largely on the side of the more austere society, as to justify the degree of superiority which is assigned to it?—*Lecky, 'European Morals,'* i. 51.

The Perception of Beauty Depends on Purity of Mind.

It is necessary to the existence of an idea of beauty, that the sensual pleasure which may be its basis should be accompanied first with joy, then with love of the object, then with the perception of kindness in a superior intelligence, finally, with thankfulness and veneration towards that intelligence itself; and as no idea can be at all considered as in any way an idea of beauty, until it be made up of these emotions, any more than we can be said to have an idea of a letter of which we perceive the perfume and the fair writing, without understanding the contents of it, or intent of it; and as these emotions are in no way resultant from, nor obtainable by, any operation of the Intellect; it is evident that the sensation of beauty is not sensual on the one hand, nor is it intellectual on the other, but is dependent on a pure, right, and open state of the heart, both for its truth and for its intensity, insomuch that even the right after-action of the Intellect upon facts of beauty so apprehended, is dependent on the acuteness of the heart-feeling about them. We see constantly that men having naturally acute perceptions of the beautiful, yet not receiving it with a pure heart, nor into their hearts at all, never comprehend it, nor receive good from it, but make it a mere minister to their desires, and accompaniment and seasoning of lower sensual pleasures, until all their emotions take the same earthly stamp, and the sense of beauty sinks into the servant of lust.—*Ruskin, 'Modern Painters,'* II. pt. iii. chap. ii. § 8.

TRUTHFULNESS.

Statement of the Duty.

The duty of Truth is not to utter words which *might*, according to common usage, produce in other minds beliefs corresponding to our own, but words which we believe will have this result on the persons whom we address.—*Sidgwick, 'Methods of Ethics,'* p. 315.

Veracity is a term which must be regarded as including something more than the simple avoidance of direct falsehood. In the ordinary intercourse of life it is readily understood that a man is offending against truth, not only when he utters a deliberate falsehood, but also when in his statement of a case he suppresses or endeavours to conceal essential facts, or makes positive assertions without having conscientiously verified their grounds.—*Lecky, 'European Morals,'* i. 143.

Truthfulness a wide principle.

Not only lying, but every mode of conveying a false belief, is prohibited by the principle of truth. This especially applies when we convey a belief of our own intention in a matter affecting him whom we address; that is, when we make a promise. We are bound by the duty of truth to promise only what we intend to perform. All deceit, fraud, duplicity, imposition, is excluded by the duty of truth.—*Whewell, 'Elements of Morality,'* p. 121.

Necessity of this Virtue.

In social life.

It needs no demonstration that some regard for truth is implied in the simplest social state. Language is at once the product of society, and essential to anything that can be called a society. No mutual understanding can exist without a communication of thought, of which language is the most perfect and the indispensable instrument. To say that language is necessary, is to say that truth is necessary, for otherwise we should speak of signs which have no signification. Lying itself is only possible when some degree of mutual understanding has been reached, and truthfulness is therefore an essential condition of all social development — *Stephen*, '*Science of Ethics*,' p. 202.

All men have a right to our fidelity to Truth. Society is based on this principle. —*Pope*, '*Christian Theology*,' iii. 236.

In reasoning.

A conception of truth is implied in all reasoning, for reasoning is nothing but a perception of truth and error.—*Stephen*, '*Science of Ethics*,' p. 206.

In literature.

How many faithful sentences are written now? that is, sentences dictated by a pure love of truth, without any wish, save that of expressing the truth fully and clearly,—sentences in which there is neither a spark of light too much, nor a shade of darkness. —'*Guesses at Truth*,' p. 370.

In secret.

'To thine own self be true,
And it must follow, as the day the night,
Thou canst not then be false to any man.'
Shakespeare, '*Hamlet*,' act i. sc. 3.

Is the Law of Truth absolute?

Recent Moralists answer, Yes.

Kant regards it as a duty owed to oneself to speak the truth, because 'a lie is an abandonment, or, as it were, annihilation of the dignity of man.'—*Sidgwick*, '*Methods of Ethics*,' p. 316.

The obligation of truthfulness is generally stated as absolute. Philosophers have deduced all virtues from truth, and this absoluteness of statement is favourable to the method; for, though purity and courage give rise to rules which are almost invariable, such as fidelity in marriage or to military obedience, still they seem to include an empirical element. The particular marriage law, for example, may vary, and it is conceivable at least that polygamy may be the rule in one period and monogamy in another, whilst the decision as to the superiority of either rule would depend upon variable conditions of human life. The rule of truthfulness, on the other hand, seems to possess the *à priori* quality of a mathematical axiom. It seems possible to say that it is always right to speak the truth, as it is always true that two and two make four. Truth, in short, being always the same, truthfulness must be unvarying. Thus, 'Be truthful' means, 'Speak the truth whatever the consequences, whether the teller or the hearer receives benefit or injury.'—*Stephen*, '*Science of Ethics*,' p. 205.

St. Augustine is the doctor of the great and common view that all untruths are lies, and that there can be *no* just cause of untruth.—*Newman*, '*Apologia*,' p. 349.

Great Moralists, however, have affirmed the contrary.

To tell a lie for charity, to save a man's life, the life of a friend, of a husband, of a prince, of a useful and a public person, hath not only been done at all times, but commended by great, and wise, and good men. Who would not save his father's life at the charge of a harmless lie, from persecutors and tyrants?—*Taylor*.

There are falsehoods which are not lies, that is, which are not criminal.—*Paley*.

The general rule is, that truth should never be violated: there must, however, be some exceptions. If, for instance, a murderer should ask you which way a man is gone.—*Johnson*.

It seems to me very dangerous, be it ever allowable or not, to lie or equivocate in order to preserve some great temporal or spiritual benefit. As to Johnson's case of a murderer asking you which way a man had gone, I should have anticipated that, had such a difficulty happened to him, his first act would have been to knock the man down, and to call out for the police; and next, if he was worsted in the conflict, he would not have given the ruffian the information he asked at whatever risk to himself. I think he would have let himself be killed first. I do not think that he would have told a lie.—*Newman*, '*Apologia*,' p. 361

Better die than lie.—*Tennyson*, '*Queen Mary*.'

Truth.

Is universally admired.

Veracity becomes the first virtue in the moral type, and no character is regarded with any kind of approbation in which it is wanting. It is made, more than any other, the test distinguishing a good from a bad man. We accordingly find that, even where the impositions of trade are very numerous, the supreme excellence of veracity is cordially admitted in theory, and it is one of the first virtues that every man aspiring to moral excellence endeavours to cultivate.—*Lecky*, '*European Morals*,' i. 144

There is nobody in the commonwealth of learning who does not profess himself a lover of truth; and there is not a rational creature that would not take it amiss to be thought otherwise of. And yet, for all this, one may truly say that there are very few lovers of truth for truth's sake, even among those who persuade themselves that they are so.—*Locke*, '*Human Understanding*,' bk. iv chap. xix 1.

Is strengthened by practice

Speaking truth is like writing fair, and comes only by practice; it is less a matter of will than of habit, and I doubt if any occasion can be trivial which permits the practice and formation of such a habit.—*Ruskin*, '*Seven Lamps, &c.*,' ch. ii. sect. i.

Friendship.

Aristotle.

Friendship, if not in itself a virtue, at least involves and implies virtue: and it is, moreover, an absolute essential for a happy life, since without friends no man would choose to live, although possessed of every other good thing. And, indeed, it is when men are rich, or possessed of high office, or of great hereditary power, that they seem most especially to stand in need of friends. For wherein does such prosperity profit us, if we are deprived of the power of doing good to others, of which power friends are the special object, and which is most praiseworthy when exercised in their behalf, or how can such prosperity be guarded and preserved without the aid of friends? For the greater it is, the more precarious will it be. In poverty, moreover, and in all other forms of evil fortune, friends are held to be our only refuge. And to the young, friendship is of aid in that it keeps them clear of faults, and to the old, in that it gives kindly attention, and supplies those deficiencies in action which are always the result of infirmity; and to those who are in their full prime, in that it makes noble achievements easier.

The two together stepping are the better able both to think and to act.—'*Ethics*,' bk. viii. ch. i. (Williams' translation).

Perfect friendship is based on goodness.

That friendship which obtains between those who are good, and who resemble one another in that they are similarly and equally virtuous, is complete and perfect in itself. For men of this sort will, each of them equally with the other, feel a mutual and reciprocal wish that that may be their lot which is, from the point of view of their virtue, their highest good; and it must be remembered that their virtue is an essential element in their character, and not an indirect result of it.—'*Ethics*,' bk. viii. ch. iii.

And is disinterested.

It is those who wish well to their friend for his own sake who have the highest claim to the title of friend, inasmuch as the friendship of such exists and is felt by them for the sake of their friends alone, and not as an indirect result of any form of self-seeking —'*Ethics*,' bk. viii. ch. iii.

SELF-DENIAL

The virtue of Self-denial is one that receives the commendation of society, and stands high in the morality of reward. Still it is a means to an end. The operation of the associating principle tends to raise it above this point to the rank of a final end. And there is an ascetic scheme of life that proceeds upon this supposition; but the generality of mankind, in practice, if not always in theory, disavow it.—*Bain*, '*Mental and Moral Science*,' p. 445.

The Christian Self-denial

Self-denial and self-control are not the same. The latter is only an element of the former, and is only the right self-control when it is the handmaid of self-denial. Self-denial, in its deepest root, is obedience, is the practical strengthening (exertion) of humility, and the actual death of pride, which is by no means implied in self-control, which can fitly co-exist with pride and disobedience. It is only self-denial that leads not only to outward, bodily, but also to inward *chastity*, understanding by chastity, in the widest sense, the subordination of the sensuous, the natural, under the spirit or the divine, so that the natural attains in us to no unsuitable self-dependence. It is self-denial that also leads to true *poverty*, that is, the internal independence of worldly things, of earthly possession and honour, of all desire of the phenomenal. For he that denies himself, and is thereby confirmed in the One unchangeable thing, is not taken possession of by the worldly things, but possesses them as if he possessed them not. On the other hand, it may also indeed be said that, without self-control, self-denial and obedience cannot be carried out. We can only be God's servants when we are masters in the bodily and spiritual organism entrusted to us.—*Martensen*, '*Christian Ethics*,' ii. 411, 412.

XXIV.

THE IMMORTALITY OF MAN

What is meant by 'Natural Immortality.'

It must not be supposed that they who assert the natural immortality of the soul are of opinion that it is absolutely incapable of annihilation even by the infinite power of the Creator who first gave it being, but only that it is not liable to be broken or dissolved by the ordinary laws of nature or motion. The soul is indivisible, incorporeal, unextended, and is consequently incorruptible. Nothing can be plainer than that the motions, changes, decays, and dissolutions which are hourly seen to befall natural bodies, cannot possibly affect an active, simple, uncompounded substance: such a being therefore is indissoluble by the force of nature; that is to say—the soul of man is *naturally* immortal.—*Berkeley*, '*Philosophical Works*,' i. 229.

The Doctrine of Immortality.

The Christian Doctrine.

The Gospel does not say to us, 'Create an immortality for yourselves by "living conformably to moral order," or by "thinking on the Eternal and the Absolute."' It says rather, 'You are already, whether you know it or not, whether you will it or not, immortal beings. You cannot now be other than immortal, for the simple reason that God has gifted you with an indestructible principle of life.' This immortality of the soul is personal, and must admit the persistence of memory, affection, and character, as tests of continued personal life. The Christian Faith also bids us look forward to a resurrection of that very body which has been throughout our earthly life the instrument, the dwelling-house, perchance the faithful transcript of the personal soul within it And the risen body, transfigured, translucent with spiritual glory, will still assert in the courts of heaven the deathless endurance of our personality in its unimpaired completeness. — *Liddon*, '*University Sermons*,' pp. 128, 134.

The Positivist Doctrine.

Our conception is as real and human on the one side, as it is boundless and inspiring on the other. It is a conception of kindred aspects—the first is the indefinite persistence throughout human life of all thoughts, acts and feelings, however remote in time; the second is the mysterious and boundless extent to which all human actions and ideas affect the living, transfuse and colour the present, until they are absorbed in the ocean of the past, and thus join in the end to mould the future The dead are living, around us and in us, active and revered as they never were in life We hear their voices, not in the hollow echoes of the tomb, but at our firesides, and in the good and pure words of every worthy man around us, in the swelling record of science art, poetry, philosophy, and morals; in all that forms our mental and moral food. Their ceasing to breathe, and meet us, and talk with us in the flesh, has not destroyed the reality of their social and human influence. We live by one another,—and therefore we live again in one another, and quite as much after death as before it, and often very much more after it — *Harrison*, '*Address to Positivist Society*,' Dec. 31, 1883.

Positivists say, 'We believe in immortality—the immortality of thought and character. Our bodies may decay, but our souls will exist in the ideas which they have originated or transmitted. Conspicuous moral effort, an example of courage, of disinterestedness, of toil under discouragements and in the face of difficulties, is a thing which lives. We may ourselves succumb to the law of annihilation, but at least we may enrich the race with a legacy of moral force, or of moral beauty.'—*Liddon*, '*University Sermons*,' p 123

Materialism denies immortality.

The soul is the product of the brain's development, just as muscular action is produced by development of the muscles, and secretion by that of the glands. To assume the existence of a soul, which uses the brain as an instrument with which to work as it pleases, is utter nonsense Physiology distinctly and categorically pronounces against any individual immortality, and against all ideas which are connected with the figment of a separate existence of the soul.—*Vogt*, '*Physiologische Briefe*.'

Arguments in Favour of Immortality.

Plato's reasoning

The doctrine of the immortality of the soul is founded by Plato, in the 'Phædrus,' on the nature of the soul, as the self-moving principle of all motion, in the 'Republic,' on the fact that the life of the soul is not destroyed by moral badness, which yet, as the natural evil and enemy of the soul, ought, if anything could effect this, to effect its destruction; in the 'Timæus,' on the goodness of God, who, notwithstanding that the nature of the soul as a generated essence subjects it to the possibility of destruction, cannot will that what has been put together in so beautiful a manner should again be dissolved; in the 'Phædo,' finally, this doctrine is supported, partly by an argument drawn from the nature of the subjective activity of the philosopher, whose striving after knowledge involves the desire for incorporeal existence, *i.e.*, the desire to die, and partly on a series of objective arguments.—*Ueberweg*, '*Hist of Phil.*,' i. 127.

Arguments of Christian writers.

No evidence that death is the destruction of the soul.

There is the intuition of self as a being, a substance, a spiritual substance. Every one is immediately conscious of a self, different from the material objects which press themselves on his notice, and of the action of mental attributes in no way resembling the properties of matter, of lofty thoughts and far-ranging imaginations and high moral sentiments, of lively and fervent emotions, and of a power of choice and fixed resolution. The circumstance that the bodily organism is dissolved at death, is no proof that these qualities or the existence in which they inhere shall perish. We see the body die, but we never see the spirit die. We know that the soul has existed; we have no evidence that it ceases to exist. The burden of proof may legitimately be laid on those who maintain that it does. The soul exists as a substance, and will continue to exist, unless destroyed by a power from without capable of producing this special effect.—*M'Cosh, 'Intuitions, &c.,'* p. 392.

The facts which point towards the termination of our present state of existence, are connected with our physical nature, not with our mental. In physical life there is a progression of bodily development until maturity is reached, after which there is gradual decay. But in mind there is the law of progress, without evidence of the same law of decay. That our nature is one, and that weakness of body can entail restraint upon mental action, are admitted facts, but the latter places the source of restraint in the body, not in the mind. Besides, the body may be dismembered, and the mind continue active as before. The phenomena of consciousness connected with amputation are of interest here. But chief importance attaches to the contrast between the facts of physical and mental life during the infirmities of age. At such a time, when the recollection of the occurrences of the day is difficult, recollections of events which happened threescore years before are vivid and exact. Such facts point towards the possibility of continued existence of the spirit, apart from the body. See Taylor's 'Physical Theory of Another Life.'—*Calderwood, 'Moral Philosophy,'* p. 259.

The facts of our present moral life.

The facts of our moral life seem to warrant a conclusion to the certainty of a future state. If there be moral obligation and responsibility, their full significance can be realised only in another state of being, where account of moral actions can be rendered. On this line of reflection, it is legitimate to conclude that the future state must be one of rewards and punishments.—*Calderwood, 'Moral Philosophy,'* p. 260.

There is the conviction of moral obligation and responsibility, pointing to a judgment day and a state of righteous retribution. The argument built on this ground is felt by many strong minds to be the strongest of all. Kant, so severe in his criticism of the physical argument, yields to the moral one. Chalmers fondly dwells on it as the one which actually carries weight with mankind. It proceeds on the existence of a moral faculty; but its validity does not depend on any peculiar view which may be taken by us of the moral powers in man. It is enough that man is acknowledged to be under moral obligation—under moral law: that law is imperative—it commands and it forbids; that it is a supreme law—claiming authority over all faculties and affections, over, in particular, all voluntary desires and acts. This law in the heart points to a Lawgiver who hath planted it in our constitution, and who sanctions and upholds it. Upon our recognising God as Lawgiver, the conscience announces that we are accountable to Him; 'so then every one of us shall give account of himself to God.' But if we are to give account to God, there must be a day of reckoning to arrive—in this life, or, if not in this life, in the life to come. He who hath appointed the law must needs be judge, He who hath appointed it so authoritatively, and proclaimed it so publicly, must needs inquire whether it has or has not been obeyed. But this judicial work is not fully discharged in this present state of things, and therefore we look for another —*M'Cosh, 'Intuitions of the Mind,'* p. 393

The arguments for the soul's immortality are very various in their degree of abstruseness or popularity. Thus our immortality has been deduced by some thinkers, as by Leibnitz, from an analysis of the nature of the soul. By others it has been argued that the mere idea of an Infinite God and of an endless life implies that the thinking being who has conceived it must be immortal. The universal desire for a deeper and more lasting happiness than can be found on earth, has always appeared to Christian philosophers, eminently to the great Augustine, to point to that future of which the Psalmist sings. But the consideration by which this truth is most frequently fortified, expanded, propagated in the heart and mind of the people, is that man suffers, and is also a moral agent, and that between his moral action and his suffering there is no regular correspondence, nay, rather, there is a perpetual jar and disproportion. From age to age a Tiberius wears the purple, while the pride and flower of human virtue is being crucified between two thieves. In endeavouring to counterbalance the force of this perpetual and universal fact, the secret thoughts, and the accustomed sayings, and the irrepressible emotions of men, mount with the strong certainty of a moral intuition towards an eternal world —*Liddon, 'University Sermons,'* p. 116.

The universality of the belief.

It is as universal as belief in God. It has prevailed among all nations of high mental attainments, while others have had at least a notion of it. It was this belief that the deceased were not the dead but the living, which in Egypt built the pyramids, and which yet bears testimony to its own existence in the mummies, it was this which bestowed upon the Germanic nations the joyful courage with which they met death in the field of battle, it was this which gathered the noblest of the Greeks about those secret doctrines of the Eleusinian Mysteries, which would give them that consolation in death which their religion did not give them. It is true that it was Christianity which first raised this belief to a certainty; yet still it is as universal as belief in God, and is the inheritance of every nation. This universality proves it to be a *necessary* idea of the human mind; necessary not only for the reason, but for the life.—*Luthardt, 'Saving Truths,'* p. 250

Subsidiary arguments.

Upon these arguments others grow which have more or less of force. There is, for example, the shrinking from annihilation, the longing for immortality, — a feeling which seems to guarantee the veracity of the expectation cherished. Then there are affections, pure and holy, springing up on earth, but not allowed to be gratified on earth, but which we may hope to have satisfied to the full in heaven. There are attachments and profitable friendships firmly clenched only to be violently snapped asunder by the stroke of death, but which we expect to have renewed in a place where there are no breaches. Do not these swelling feelings which agitate the bosoms of friends, when one of them is summoned away, seem to show that the divided waters are yet to meet? Then we see from time to time intellectual powers cultivated to the utmost, but blasted in the flower when they seemed to promise a large fruit. May we not believe that in a universe in which nothing is made in vain, and nothing of God's workmanship lost, these powers have been nurtured to serve some great and good end in a future state of existence? These facts combined seem to show that there are means instituted in this world which have their full consummation in the world to come.—*M'Cosh, 'Intuitions of the Mind,'* p. 396.

The doctrine is not to be established by rigid demonstration.

While the most prominent facts of our life thus combine to support the belief that there is for man a great Future, there is nothing which logically warrants an inference to Immortality of existence. Such a conclusion can be sustained neither from the immateriality of the soul, the favourite logical basis (see Dr S Clarke's 'Answer to Dodwell,' with Defences); nor from the ceaseless motion of the soul, as with Plato in the 'Phædrus;' nor from the ideas of abstract beauty, goodness, and magnitude, as in the 'Phædo,' nor from the nature of the soul as a simple being, as argued by Moses Mendelssohn (1729–1786) in his 'Phädon.' The finite, since it is not the self-sufficient, cannot afford an argument towards immortality. The nature which is dependent upon the Absolute Being for its origin must be dependent on His will for its continuance. While, therefore, Futurity of Existence is clearly involved in the facts of the present life, Eternity of existence must depend upon the Divine Will, and can be known only as matter of distinct revelation, not as matter of metaphysical deduction. All that is greatest in us points to an unmeasurable future. Thither we must look for the solution of many of our dark problems, and for that purity and grandeur of personal life unknown in the present state. But Immortality, if it be ours, must be the gift of God. Over the best intellect, if it be restricted to pure speculation, must hang the great uncertainty which found utterance in the closing words of the 'Apology' of Socrates: 'The hour to depart has come,—for me to die, for you to live; but which of us is going to a better state is unknown to every one except to God.'—*Calderwood, 'Moral Philosophy,'* p. 261.

The doctrine of the soul's immortality cannot be established by rigid demonstration, any more than that of the Divine existence. But in the one, as in the other, there are necessary principles involved which look to obvious facts, and issue in a conviction which may be described as natural. The expounded argument is the expression of processes which are spontaneous. It draws materials from a variety of quarters and admits of accumulation. No one of the elements is in itself conclusive, but in the whole there is a high probability quite entitled to demand belief and practical action.—*M'Cosh, 'Intuitions of the Mind,'* p. 292.

But it is a doctrine due to Revelation.

In reality it is the gospel and the gospel alone, that has brought life and immortality to light. Nothing could set in a fuller light the infinite obligations which mankind have to Divine revelation; since we find that no other medium could ascertain this great and important truth.—*Hume, 'Philosophical Works,'* iv. 399, 406.

Life and immortality were brought to light by the gospel. The gospel has opened 'a new and living way' to heaven. It has converted the better guesses and speculations of philosophy into certainties. The authority of the Lord Jesus Christ, Divine and Infallible, is the true and sufficient basis of this doctrine in the Christian soul. He sanctions the anticipatory statements of the Old Testament, and the dogmatic enunciations of the Apostles whom He sent. His own utterances cover the whole area of what is revealed upon the subject.—*Liddon, 'University Sermons,'* pp. 112, 116.

Conditional Immortality.

Professor Challis's 'Scriptural Doctrine of Immortality.'

Although Adam was created in the image of his Maker in respect to being endowed with powers of understanding and reasoning, and although he was made capable of learning and doing righteousness, he was not originally *made righteous*, forasmuch as he sinned; but those whom God makes righteous sin no more, because all the works of God are perfect. He par took of natural life, but not of spiritual life. He was, as St. Paul says, 'of the earth, earthy' (p. 13).

St. Paul in Rom. viii. 2 speaks of 'the law of sin and death,' meaning that sin and death are invariably related to each other as antecedent and consequent. By an irrevocable law death is ordained to be 'the wages of sin.' Of ourselves we can judge that it does not consist with the power and wisdom of an omnipotent and omniscient Creator that the sinful should live for ever. But if this be so, it must evidently be true also that immortality, being exemption from death, is the *consequence* of freedom from sin, that is, of perfect righteousness. This is as necessary a law as the other. Hence the inquiry respecting the means by which man is made immortal resolves itself into inquiring by what means he is made righteous (pp. 8, 9).

Since we have admitted, as a necessary and self-evident principle, that righteousness is the foundation of immortality, and Scripture presents to us in Abel an instance of the attainment of righteousness by faith, it follows that *faith is a means of partaking of immortality* (p. 25).

I have maintained that on the day that Adam fell into disobedience by the wiles of Satan, his Creator made a promise by covenant that he and his offspring should in the end be freed from the power of Satan and evil, and partake of immortality. The terms of the covenant were that man must pass through toil, and pain, and death, that thereby his spirit might be formed for receiving the gift of an immortal life. Evidence of an intelligent belief in the efficacy of these conditions was given by the faithful of old by their sacrificing clean animals. In process of time the only begotten Son of God satisfied in His own person the very same conditions. At the same time He made sure the grounds for belief of the fulfilment of the covenanted promise, first by marvellous works before He suffered, and after His death by resurrection from the grave the third day, which gave proof of the reality of a power that could overcome death. Out of love to those whom He vouchsafes to call His brethren, He showed how they must undergo physical suffering and the pains of death, in order that their spirits might be formed for an endless life. It was with understanding and belief that the way to life was made sure by fellowship with Christ in suffering, that some of the most favoured of His faithful followers, apostles and apostolic men, willingly suffered after His example.

But pain and death are not in this way efficacious for salvation, unless they be accompanied by a faith which lays hold of the covenant and promise of life made and ratified from the beginning by God. Those who, having this faith, do good works are God's elect, who live again at the first resurrection, to die no more. The rest of mankind, although they go through suffering and death, and although their sufferings are not without effect in forming their spirits for immortality (such is the virtue of the sacrifice of the Son of God), rise to be judged for their unbelief and unrighteousness, and to be condemned to undergo a second death. Yet several portions of Scripture necessitate the conclusion that the consecration of the way to life through death by the death of the Son of God, which applies to the death of believers, applies also to the second death of unbelievers; so that this death also is followed by life (pp. 110–12).

When the final judgment has had complete effect, there will no longer be objective existence of any whose names are not in the book of life, because all will have been made meet for the inheritance of life.—*Challis, 'Scriptural Doctrine of Immortality.'*

Edward White—'Life in Christ.'

From the simple account furnished in Genesis, we are to understand that Adam was not created in the possession of immortality either in his body or soul; yet, also, that he was not created under a definite sentence of death, as was the rest of the creation around him, since the prospect of 'living for ever' by the help of the 'tree of life' was open to him upon the condition of obedience during his trial;—in other words, the first man was not created immortal, but was placed on probation in order to become so. Viewed as he was in himself, there was a noble creature,—the offspring of God,—endowed with capacities for ruling over the world, and for holding communion with Heaven; but as to his origin, his foundation was in the dust, and the image of the Creator was impressed upon a nature, if a 'little lower than the angels,' still also no higher than the animals as to unconditional immortality. His upright form and 'human face divine,' gave token of a spirit formed for intercourse with the Eternal; yet his feet rested on the same earth which gave support to all the 'creeping things' which it brought forth, and, like the subjects of his dominion, 'his breath was in his nostrils.'—'*Life in Christ*,' p. 100.

The original threatening, 'In the day that thou eatest thereof thou shalt surely die,' was intended to signify a literal, immediate, and final dissolution of the nature of Adam as a man; his death, in the ordinary sense of the word, without any reference whatever to the state, or even to the survival of the spirit beyond.—'*Life in Christ*,' p. 108.

The bestowment of Immortal Life in the restored divine Image is believed by us to be the very object of the Incarnation of the Deity.

This mighty change in human nature and destiny, involved in the bestowment of everlasting life, is conveyed to mankind through the channel of the Incarnation, the Incarnation of 'the Life,' of the 'Logos,' or Word of God; who being before all worlds, and creating all things as the Word of the Father, 'became flesh,' took on Himself our mortal nature, 'yet without sin,' and as the Christ, or Anointed One, died on the Cross, as a Divine, self-sacrificing Mediator between God and man, so reconciling in the Divine Mind the act of grace with the equilibrium of government.

God still further unites the Divine Essence with man's mortal nature in the Regeneration of the Individual, by the indwelling of the Holy Spirit, 'the Lord and Giver of Life,' whose gracious inhabitation applies the remedy of redemption by communicating to good men of every age and generation God-likeness and immortality, to the soul by spiritual regeneration, and to the body by resurrection.—'*Life in Christ*,' p. 117.

Man's Moral Nature a Witness for God.

We are led from the very existence of our moral feelings, to the conception of the existence of attributes, the same in kind, however exalted in degree, in the Divine Being. The sense of Truth implies its actual existence in a being who is Himself its source and centre; and the longing for a yet higher measure of it, which is experienced in the greatest force by those who have already attained the truest and widest view, is the testimony of our own souls to the Truth of the Divine Nature. The perception of Right, in like manner, leads us to the Absolute lawgiver who implanted it in our constitution; and, as has been well remarked, 'all the appeals of innocence against unrighteous force are appeals to eternal justice, and all the visions of moral purity are glimpses of the infinite excellence.' The aspirations of the more exalted moral natures after a yet higher state of holiness and purity, can only be satisfied by the contemplation of such perfection as no merely Human being has ever attained; and it is only in the contemplation of the Divine Ideal that they meet their appropriate object. And the sentiment of Beauty, especially as it rises from the *material* to the *spiritual*, passes beyond the noblest creations of Art, and the most perfect realisation of it in the outward life, and soars into the region of the Unseen, where alone the Imagination can freely expand itself in the contemplation of such beauty as no objective representation can embody. And it is by combining, so far as our capacity will admit, the ideas which we thus derive from reflection upon the facts of our own consciousness, with those which we draw from the contemplation of the Universe around us, that we form the justest conception of the Divine Being of which our finite minds are capable. We are led to conceive of Him as the absolute, unchangeable, self-existent,—infinite in duration,—illimitable in space,—the highest ideal of Truth, Right, and Beauty,—the all-Powerful source of that agency which we recognise in the phenomena of Nature,—the all-Wise designer of that wondrous plan, whose original perfection is the real source of the uniformity and harmony which we recognise in its operation,—the all-Benevolent contriver of the happiness of His sentient creatures,—the all-Just disposer of events in the Moral world, for the evolution of the ultimate ends for which Man was called into existence.—*Carpenter*, '*Mental Physiology*,' pp. 246, 247.

There is in man a littleness which dwarfs and cramps all that is strong and noble in him; but there is also a grandeur hard to understand except as the image in a warped and tiny mirror of a grandeur elsewhere existing, over which such limits have no sway. Man has a WILL so weak as to be drawn aside from right by the most unworthy allurements, daunted by the most despicable difficulties, palsied with ignoble sloth; yet capable also of holding its own purpose and choice against the world. He has an INTELLECT, weak enough to be befooled by transparent fallacies and led astray at every step by prejudice and passion; yet powerful enough to measure the distances and motions of the stars, to track the invisible sound-waves and light-waves in their courses, and to win from Nature the key of empire. He has LOVE, which wastes itself among the dregs of life, or suffers selfishness to wither it at the root; but also which is able to lift him to the sublime height of self-sacrifice, and is the inexhaustible fount of the deepest and purest happiness he knows or can imagine. He has CONSCIENCE—the sense of right and wrong—easily perverted, and which has by turns justified every crime and condemned every virtue; yet which nevertheless proclaims that right, not wrong—everlasting righteousness, not self-willed injustice—is the imperial law of the universe. I ask, Is the scale in which these attributes are seen in man their true scale? Is it reasonable to think so? Or is there anything irrational in the belief, nay, the certainty that they demand, in order to realise the ideas which human nature perpetually suggests and continually disappoints, a scale of grandeur and perfection no less than infinite? Do they not assure us, as with a voice from the very depths of our being, that there must be a SUPREME WILL, irresistible, unswerving, pervading and controlling the universe, the source of all law, but a law to itself, guided unchangeably by infinite knowledge, absolute righteousness, perfect love?—*Conder*, '*Basis of Faith*,' pp. 70, 71.

From the enjoyment of virtue springs the idea of a virtuous; from the enjoyment of freedom, the idea of a free; from the enjoyment of life, the idea of a living; from the enjoyment of the divine, the idea of a godlike, and of a God.—*Jacobi*, *quoted by Hamilton*, '*Discussions*,' p. 19, note.

God is a necessity of man's nature.

God made man to seek Him. The search after God is a thing of nature. In other words, religion is so natural to man that it is simplest truth to say, he is by nature religious. It is not a discovery or invention due to an art or artifice, but a holy necessity of nature made by its Maker. No one ever discovered sight or invented hearing. Man saw because he had eyes, heard because he had ears; the sense created the sensations. Speech was no invention or discovery; it grew, and man was hardly conscious of its growth, out of the marvellous alliance in him of the physical ability to utter sounds, and the rational ability to think thoughts, until it stood without and lived around him like a subtle, articulated, universalised reason. And religion is as natural as sight, or hearing, or speech—as natural, because as native and as essential to his nature Hence, man gets into religion as into other natural things—his mother-tongue, his home or filial affections—spontaneously, without conscious effort, but to get out of it he has to reason himself into a new and strange position, force his mind to live in a state of watchful antagonism towards its own deepest tendencies. No man is an atheist by nature, only by art and an art that has to offer to nature ceaseless resistance—*Fairbairn*, '*City of God*,' pp. 79, 80.

And also of the race

In seeking for peoples that know no God, who live without faith or worship, where do our philosophers go? Do they select for their inquiries peoples that have stood on the highest pinnacle of civilisation, and do they, while the peoples stand there, point with proud and disdainful finger to the men in whom their culture blossomed into its most splendid flower? No, not they. But they go to some cannibal South Sea island, scarce touched by the foot or known to the science of the white man, or to some degraded and wretched African tribe, and then, with these specimens, dug from the very heart of the most dismal barbarism, they come forward and cry, 'Behold, peoples who acknowledge no God!' Well, then, let us accept the specimen, and only answer, 'Compare that atheistic race of yours with our theistic races, and let the distance between cannibalism and Christian culture measure the space that divides peoples who believe in no God, and peoples who believe in Him, and have laboured to follow His Spirit and fulfil His ends'—*Fairbairn*, '*City of God*,' pp 87, 88.

The study of Philosophy should lead to clearer knowledge of God.

Our most pressing need is a deeper and more living study of the Science of Mind or Spirit. That science ought no longer to remain disconnected from man's actual life, but to be brought into more intimate conjunction with it. The human mind aspiring after knowledge ought not to be directed to mathematical studies, and told to limit itself to them; by far the most important matter for it is to bring it into a closer contact with present, and a more fruitful study of past, human realities. The only objects of our direct knowledge are Man and Humanity, and in contemplating these we soon arrive at the perception that they both have their first Cause, neither in physical Nature, nor in themselves, but in an Eternal Thought and Will, which Humanity, in its collective development, represents without exhausting. Now, more than ever before, are we called to make an earnest use of the knowledge thus earned by such strenuous and toilsome effort, and through the contemplation of God, Man, and Humanity,—constituting as they do the eternal and only Substantial Being,—to build up our own religious consciousness, and through that, our whole spiritual life, to the end that we may emerge from the chaotic confusion of prior ages into the clear light of divine knowledge, and rise out of the slavery beneath absolute rulers into the freedom of the kingdom of God.—*Bunsen*, '*God in History*,' iii. 340.

Man is the microcosm of existence; consciousness, within a narrow focus, concentrates a knowledge of the universe and of God; psychology is thus the abstract of all science, human and divine. As in the external world, all phænomena may be reduced to the two great laws of Action and Reaction; so, in the internal, all the facts of consciousness may be reduced to one fundamental fact, comprising in like manner two principles and their correlation, and these principles are again the *One* or the *Infinite*, the *Many* or the *Finite*, and the *Connection of the infinite and finite*.—*Hamilton*, '*Discussions*,' p. 9.

Though man be not identical with the Deity, still is he 'created in the image of God.' It is indeed only through an analogy of the human with the Divine nature, that we are percipient and recipient of Divinity.—*Hamilton*, '*Discussions*,' p. 19.

Man the interpretation of Nature.

Can man be explained, can his history be written in 'the terms of matter, motion, and force?' Whatever interprets him must interpret the institutions he has formed, the religions he has developed, the societies and states he has founded, the literatures he has created, the systems he has built, the arts he has discovered and perfected, the good he has achieved, the evil he has done, the progress he has made. Have these terms, 'institutions,' 'religions,' 'societies,' 'states,' 'literatures,' 'arts,' 'evil,' 'good,' 'progress,' 'achieved,' 'made,' 'done,' any physical equivalents? Could they be translated into the speech of physics, and it remain an intelligible and veracious speech? If such speech be applicable to man, then his history may know motion, but not progress; may suffer or escape a breakdown, but not endure or cause evil. If the speech be inapplicable, how did evolution accomplish so extraordinary a revolution, as by mechanical laws to change the primordial atoms with which it started, into a being whose nature was at once moral and rational, whose conduct was regulated freely from within, whose acts had an ethical quality, and were all liable to praise or blame? Can the terms good, righteous, wise, benevolent be applied to men and nations, and be denied to the Power that has directed the ways of man and reigned over the nations? or, to vary the terms without changing the sense, can man be in any sense a moral being without having his development governed by moral laws? These are questions that go to the root of the matter, that must be settled before we can determine the nature of that cause which is at once primal and ultimate —*Fairbairn*, '*City of God*,' pp. 71, 72.

Christianity satisfies man's moral nature.

Man alone, of the inhabitants of the earth, has the power to apprehend and to hope for a deathless life. Men are not to be persuaded that this bodily and earthly life comprises the whole of their being; they have good reasons for believing otherwise. The expectation of an endless hereafter is not merely a conclusion derived from argument; it springs from a natural tendency, a *spiritual aspiration*, strengthened by moral discipline We refuse to believe that we were made with deathless hopes, destined to be quenched in the cold waters of annihilation and oblivion. Yet reason is insufficient to transform this longing into a definite belief We can, whilst taught by reason alone, go no further than hope will lead us:

> 'The hope that, of the living whole,
> No part shall fail beyond the grave,
> Derives it not from what we have
> The likest God within the soul?'
> —*In Memoriam.*

A religion which shall command the acceptance of man's nature, must satisfy man's loftiest yearnings and anticipations with regard to the future, and must reveal a prospect worthy of man's power and capacities

The teaching of Christianity is definite upon these points. It encourages the hope that in a higher condition of existence our best aspirations shall be allowed a wider scope There will be provision for increase of knowledge; for here 'we know in part,' but there shall 'we know even as we are known' There will be assimilation of character to Him who is supremely good; for 'the pure in heart shall see God.' There will be limitless accessions to happiness; 'blessed are the dead that die in the Lord.' There will be abundant room for the exercise of our social sympathies, in 'the general assembly and church of the first-born, which are written in heaven.' There will be, what is pre-eminently congenial to the Christian heart, intimate fellowship with Christ Himself for 'there shall we ever be with the Lord' There will be eternal security and felicity: for 'they go no more out.'—*Thomson*, '*Witness of Man's Moral Nature to Christianity*,' pp. 51–53.

INDEX OF NAMES.

INDEX OF SUBJECTS.

PRINTED BY BALLANTYNE, HANSON AND CO., EDINBURGH AND LONDON.

Milton Keynes UK
Ingram Content Group UK Ltd.
UKHW050650181123
432521UK00012B/14